UTAH BUSINESS LAW

FOR ENTREPRENEURS AND MANAGERS

Edited by:

David W. Read, *Weber State University*

Ezekiel R. Dumke IV, *Dumke Law, LLP*

Aaron S. Bartholomew, *Utah Valley University*

Brent J. Clayton, *Hirschi Steele & Baer PLLC*

Printed in the United States of America

First Printing, 2016

ISBN 978-0-692-59240-3

The Utah State Bar Association
Business Law Section
645 South 200 East
Salt Lake City, Utah 84111

http://businesslaw.utahbar.org

EDITORIAL BOARD

Cody Winchester, *Phillips, Ryther & Winchester*
Andrew Wright, *Strong and Hanni*
Lon Jenkins, *Dorsey and Whitney*
Andrew L. Howell, *York Howell*
Brent Hawkins, B*ennett Tueller Johnson & Deere*
Robert Wilkinson, *Anderson Call & Wilkinson*
Paul Durham, *Durham Jones & Pinegar*
Pamela Larsen, *Deseret Mutual Benefit Administrators*
Lincoln Harris, *Richards Brandt Miller Nelson*
Keith A. Call, *Snow Christensen & Martineau*
Andrew Deis, *Deiss Law*
David P. Hirschi, *Hirschi Steele & Baer, PLLC*
Justin Atwater, *Wright Development Group*
Kenneth Ashton, *Snell & Wilmer, LLP*
Brian Johnson, *Strong and Hanni*
Matthew Wadsworth, *Arnold Wadsworth & Coggins*
Steven Clayton, *Cottonwood Residential*
R. Roman Groesbeck, *Wadsworth Development Group*
Victor A. Pollak, *Fabian VanCott*
Wm. Shane Topham, *Callister Nebeker & McCullough*
Denver C. Snuffer, Jr., *Nelson, Snuffer, Dahle & Poulsen, P.C.*

CONTENTS

Contracts

Real Estate

Potential Sources of Business Liability

Business Insurance

Creditor's Rights

Bankruptcy

Intellectual Property

Chapter 1

Editors' Introduction

David W. Read[1]
Ezekiel R. Dumke, IV[2]
Aaron S. Bartholomew[3]
Brent J. Clayton[4]

Utah Business Law for Entrepreneurs and Managers is written by lawyers, but is not necessarily for lawyers.

The Business Law Section of the Utah State Bar conceived of this project as a way to make business law more easily accessible to non-lawyer innovators, managers, students, and start-ups.

Not only does the Business Law Section recognize the Great State of Utah as a major hub of business and entrepreneurship, so have a number of national publications. The *New Yorker* recently published an article on "How Utah Became the Next Silicon Valley," citing Utah—the

[1]David Read is an assistant professor of business law and business ethics in the Goddard School of Business & Economics at Weber State University. He earned a MSc in Political Theory at the London School of Economics and Political Science and a JD at the University of Houston Law Center. His research interests are in business law, business ethics, and employment law. David co-founded the Utah Journal of Family Law, a publication of the Family Law Section of the Utah State Bar Association. He currently serves as an editor of the Utah Journal of Family Law. David lives in Salt Lake City and maintains a divorce litigation practice along the Wasatch front.

[2]Ezekiel R. Dumke, IV - Recently relocated to Austin, Texas, Ezekiel "Zeke" R. Dumke IV maintains a practice based in Salt Lake City, Utah focusing on forward thinking business related matters including intellectual property litigation and strategy, venture capital structuring, and complex corporate transactions. Zeke has both professional and personal knowledge of the needs of complex business clients and actively advises clients, as well as his family's four-generation office, on portfolio managers, direct investments, and actively managed opportunities. Zeke is an active local and national angel investor, as well as advising companies on early stage development throughout the West. Personally, Zeke with his wife and three beautiful children enjoy exploring the outdoors, experiencing new cultures, and actively trying to better the community through their family foundation.

[3]Aaron S. Bartholomew has taught business law at Utah Valley University since 2007, where he is tenured associate professor in the Woodbury School of Business. Aaron has practiced law privately since 2004, worked as a juvenile court public defender, and currently is in-house counsel for a conglomeration of businesses operating in the Intermountain West.

[4]Brent is a partner at the law firm Hirschi Steele & Baer, PLLC, a practice division of Davis Miles McGuire Gardner. He specializes in business and real estate transactional law and graduated in 2009 from the University of Utah S.J. Quinney College of Law, cum laude. He served on the executive committee of the Utah State Bar's Business Law Section from 2011-2015, including serving as its Chair from 2014-2015.

metropolitan areas of Salt Lake City, Ogden, and Provo, in particular—as one of the top places to do business in the U.S.[5] Additional evidence of Utah's thriving business activity can be seen by the more than 30,000 Limited Liability Companies (LLCs) formed in 2014 alone, to say nothing of other type of business structures formed.[6]

Like it or not, business owners and managers today have to deal with more legal issues than ever before. While some prefer to ignore this reality, this volume aims to help those who would rather have their eyes wide open and make informed decisions when confronted with legal problems.

Every lawyer-author in this book works with business owners and managers who face major legal problems—a lawsuit, harassment accusation in the workplace, and similar crises. They understand how intimidating and distracting these events are and this book aspires to take away some of the fear and unease about the law and how the judicial system works.

This book covers questions most every business manager does and will encounter, covering questions of entity formation at the beginning of a business's life, to ongoing concerns about human resources, collection on past-due accounts, licensing, and many other topics.

This project would not be possible without the contributions of the excellent lawyers who are the principal authors of this book. They are each known for the depth of knowledge on the subjects they have written, and have generously volunteered to support this project.

On a final critical note, this book is not legal advice and does not suggest or create an attorney-client relationship between this book's contributors and any reader. This book is intended to provide a general knowledge of the law, and its readers should consult a licensed attorney for legal advice.

[5]Vara, Vauhini, *How Utah Became the Next Silicon Valley*, February 3, 2015, (last visited on October 22, 2015) http://www.newyorker.com/business/currency/utah-became-next-silicon-valley.

[6]*See* http://corporations.utah.gov/services/statistics.html (last visited on October 22, 2015).

CHAPTER 2

PRAGMATIC THOUGHTS ON LITIGATION AND YOUR BUSINESS

CHAD S. PEHRSON, ESQ.[1]

Introduction

Litigation can wreck your business. It can ruin your sleep and rip apart what you built through years or even decades of hard work. It is expensive, exhausting, distracting, and emotionally damaging. But with the right approach, litigation can be managed and overcome just like all of the other obstacles that confronted your business to this point. This chapter presents a quick overview of litigation, with emphasis on pragmatic considerations.

What litigation will come your way? That may be tough to predict in advance, and it certainly depends on your type of business. You might affirmatively sue a supplier for failure to deliver products as ordered. The supplier may sue you for failing to pay on time. An employee may sue you for discrimination. You may sue a co-founder of your venture (or she may sue you). A customer could suffer a personal injury on your property. A larger competitor may be worried by your success, and will sue you in hopes of crushing you, under guise of having interfered with their customers or employees, or somehow stolen their trade secrets.

While the specific type of litigation may be uncertain, a dispute will eventually pay an unwelcome visit to your growing business.[2] In all likelihood, the litigation will be costly, emotional, and damaging. Keep

[1]Mr. Pehrson is a shareholder at Parr Brown Gee & Loveless; his practice focuses on complex commercial litigation involving intellectual property and securities.

[2]On a yearly basis from 2003 to 2012, state trial-level courts reported total incoming non-traffic civil cases of approximately 20 million each year. *See* National Center for State Courts, *Examining the Work of State Courts*, available through courtstatistics.org.

in mind that not only will you have to bear the costs of the litigation and the risks of an adverse verdict, the existence of litigation itself may dry up interest in your business from private or venture funding.

So You've Been Sued (Or, You Want to Sue Someone)

You have not formally been sued until "service" is effectuated. Service occurs when a copy of the complaint and summons is delivered to you or to an authorized representative of your business. Sometimes service occurs through "personal service," meaning an individual hired by your adversary will personally deliver documents to you. In other situations, service may occur via mail.

Once you have been served, it is not time to call up the other side to complain, negotiate, or yell. None of that will help, and will likely hurt. Rather, court deadlines are fast approaching, and it is time to lawyer up.[3]

If you have not been sued, but are convinced that you need to take affirmative action against another person or entity, do not delay the process. Seek out legal counsel promptly to advise you on the situation. The law dictates that if you do not bring your suit within a specified period of time (which differ depending on the type of suit), that you may lose your right to bring the suit at all.

Selecting Litigation Counsel[4]

Choosing the right lawyer matters. As you begin looking for the right litigation counsel, you will want to consider the following:

- **Litigation expertise, including expertise in the specific type of lawsuit that you are facing:** Understand first that litigation is a specialty among lawyers. And within litigation, attorneys often further specialize, focusing their time on certain types of litigation. Whether you are facing an employment, contract,

[3]It is of course possible to represent yourself if the legal proceedings involve only you; however, if the legal proceedings involve your business and your business is an entity such as a corporation or an LLC, then the entity must have licensed legal counsel.

[4]While this chapter is about litigation, long before your business is mature enough to have been sued or be suing, you surely must have hired a good business attorney. The right business attorney is as important to your venture as having an accountant and bookkeeper. That attorney's job, in part, is to give you advice that will help you avoid litigation. The tips in this chapter for hiring a litigation attorney also largely apply to the process for hiring a business attorney.

intellectual property or other type of dispute, you want an attorney with expertise in that particular type of suit.

- **Knowledge about your business (or willingness to learn):** You want an attorney who either knows about your type of business, or cares enough to learn about your business.
- **Experience:** more so than other professions, the legal profession (and the judge who will decide important aspects of your case) respects seniority and experience—be extremely careful when hiring an attorney without any gray hairs;
- **Size of law firm:** Three general categories of options here: a lawyer who works at large firm, a small firm, or is a solo practitioner. Advantages of a large firm include reliability, accountability, access to numerous specialists, easy collaboration with other successful attorneys, and access to a large amount of internal knowledge. Meanwhile, some small firms are also sophisticated, may be more flexible in how they work with you, and also may be more excited about your business. As to the solo practitioner category, a wider range of competence exists, as you might expect. Such lawyers have the most flexibility in setting costs of representation.
- **Price/Billable rate:** Generally speaking, attorneys in greater demand and with more experience and expertise are able to charge more per hour. However, it is not accurate to conflate an attorney's offered billable rate with overall cost or efficiency. In short, the attorney with the higher billable rate may have the right expertise for your case, and ultimately cost less than an alternative option advertising a lower rate.
- **Integrity:** You of course need to trust that your attorney will competently represent your interests in the litigation. But you also need to trust that your attorney will bill you fairly,[5] tell you the truth about your case,[6] represent you diligently

[5]Rule 1.5 of the Utah Rules of Professional Conduct states that "[a] lawyer shall not make an agreement for, charge or collect an unreasonable fee or an unreasonable amount for expenses."

[6]Rule 1.4(b) of the Utah Rules of Professional Conduct states that "[a] lawyer shall explain a matter to the extent reasonably necessary to permit the client to make informed decisions regarding the representation."

and promptly,[7] preserve your confidences,[8] avoid conflicts of interest,[9] and maintain professional integrity.

- **Reputation:** An attorney's reputation is her stock-in-trade, with both the courts and fellow practitioners. In short, that reputation is important to the prospects of your case.

Once you have considered the above factors, begin the process of selecting your attorney. Do not select your attorney via vague word-of-mouth from friends or family. The following are steps to consider in the process:

- **Inquire with your business attorney:** You should ask your business attorney for advice and recommendations as to whom to select as your litigation counsel. Where the prospective litigation counsel is a colleague of your business attorney, your business attorney will typically be motivated to select a competent colleague and work behind the scenes to help with a smooth relationship. However, it would be a mistake to allow your business attorney to make the selection for you. While your business attorney's input should be considered and valued, her evaluation should not replace your own evaluation.

- **Research and recommendations:** Seek out other recommendations from your business networking circle. Attorneys, especially those unbiased by the prospect of obtaining the work for themselves, are often knowledgeable sources about the right attorney for the job. Furthermore, consider the literature available as to attorney recommendations. As one example, Chambers & Partners conducts systematic interviews and research, and identifies top firms and practitioners within geographic areas.[10] Other companies purport to perform a similar task, although many do not observe any distinction

[7] Rule 1.3 of the Utah Rules of Professional Conduct states that "A lawyer shall act with reasonable diligence and promptness in representing a client."

[8] Rule 1.6 of the Utah Rules of Professional Conduct states that "A lawyer shall not reveal information relating to the representation of a client" except under certain narrowly defined situations, such as when authorized by the client and when necessary to carry out the representation.

[9] Rule 1.7 of the Utah Rules of Professional Conduct addresses conflicts of interest.

[10] *See* Chambers & Partners, Utah Rankings, available at http://www.chambersandpartners.com/13289/228/editorial/5/1.

between objective, researched recommendations and paid advertising. Other possible avenues of research would be to investigate bar complaints against the attorney or firm,[11] whether the prospective attorney and firm has previously been sued by clients,[12] or whether the attorney and firm have sued clients for unpaid fees or sought attorney's liens.[13]

- **Interviews:** Your relationship with your attorney is personal and sometimes intense. You need to get along with the person. In-person interviews are the best way to gauge fit. Even on a relatively small matter, plan on interviewing at least two attorneys. On larger matters, consider three or more interviews. For these interviews, be prepared with a list of questions, including topics such as experience, qualifications, gut reaction to your case, references (specifically ask if you can speak with any former clients who were involved in similar cases). Depending on the size of the litigation, you may not be hiring just one attorney– rather, you will hire a team of attorneys and staff—a junior, a mid-level and a senior attorney as well as paralegals. In a significant case, ask to meet with all the attorneys that might be staffed to your case.
- **Significance of decision.** You are entitled to counsel of your choosing. Mid-litigation, you may fire your attorneys and hire new attorneys. However, numerous transaction costs come along with a change in counsel; therefore, it is far better to make the right decision at the outset.

Once you have made the decision about which attorney and law firm to hire, it is time to negotiate an engagement letter. As a general

[11]The Utah Bar is an organization of Utah's lawyers and judges, and exists to regulate the conduct of lawyers. The bar cannot give you legal advice, but it can answer certain questions about your lawyer as well as the process of obtaining an attorney. http://www.utahbar.org/public-services/public-faq/

[12]The existence of a handful of such suits would likely be of no or little significance; however, the existence of many suits deserves some inquiry.

[13]Pursuant to Utah law, a lawyer automatically receives a lien on any money or property that is the "subject of or connected with the work performed." Utah Code Ann. § 38-2-7(2). To pursue the lien, the attorney must meet notice and other statutory obligations. Attorneys may also sue their clients for unpaid fees. As to any one specific situation, it is difficult to assess the merits in such a dispute. However, the existence of numerous such suits involving the prospective attorney/firm shows an inability to productively manage the client relationship. Furthermore, it shows a propensity and willingness to aggressively turn legal skills against the former client. Generally, the top firms in Utah, as a matter of policy, will neither sue a former client nor seek a lien. Such practices are more common among less-established firms, particularly those managed by young or imprudent attorneys.

practice, Utah attorneys will provide a written explanation of the attorney-client relationship and fee agreement. The lawyer will likely send you a letter and ask you to sign it. In some circumstances, the terms proposed by the lawyer may be adequate and fair. However, these letters and the terms included in them are generally binding on you and the attorney; think of the letters as a contract, and negotiate as appropriate.

The following are typical terms included in an engagement letter:

- **Names of attorneys and paralegals who are likely to work on the case, and their hourly rates:** Consider adding a provision that will require the firm to advise you in writing if additional unnamed attorneys will used on the case.
- **Statement that the hourly rates may increase on an annual basis:** Consider adding a provision that disallows such increases without your authorization, with authorization contemplated only where attorney provides justification for the increase in hourly rate.
- **Retainer amount:** A retainer is a pre-payment for services not yet performed. The retainer is deposited in the law firm's client trust fund, to be dispensed to the firm only upon billing for services actually performed. If the services are never performed, then the law firm is required to return the unused retainer amount to the client. Some retainers are applied to the first billing, although more commonly the retainer amount is held until a final billing. Many clients, especially small businesses, are often overly concerned about the retainer amount, and are resistant to pay. However, paying a large retainer will likely improve the attorney's confidence in you, which may lead to improvement in your service. No attorney enjoys working for a company that is a slow-pay or a no-pay, and resistance to paying a retainer is a sign that the attorney can expect future payment problems and complaints.
- **Jury waiver:** This term may obligate you to waive your typical right to a jury trial in the event you file a malpractice lawsuit against the law firm.

- **Mandatory arbitration:** This term may obligate you to waive your typical right to file a lawsuit against the law firm. Instead you would be obligated to bring your claim in a private arbitration. Such arbitration provisions are popular in business-to-business interactions; however, many attorneys believe that arbitration is often as expensive as litigation, in part because the arbitrator must be paid an hourly fee for adjudicating the matter.
- **Interest on late-paid invoices:** No reason justifies agreeing to pay exorbitant interest on late payments. I have seen engagement letters specifying 24% annual interest. Something around 10-12% is more reasonable, sufficient to motivate you to pay the bill on-time without proving punitive if unforeseen calamity affects your ability to pay.
- **Costs of copies, faxes, etc.:** Consider asking for the amount of these costs to be identified, or in the alternative, insert a term requiring that such costs be passed through to the client at the same cost incurred by the firm. Ask yourself: is there a reason to be paying 25 cents per copy when the law firm likely pays a few cents per copy?
- **Electronic research databases:** In litigation, an attorney's stock-in-trade is the ability to find comparable cases and judicial decisions, as to which arguments of relevance or non-relevance will be presented to the court. To do so effectively, the attorney must scour electronic databases; these databases are expensive. Passing such costs onto clients may be justifiable. However, some clients with sufficient leverage refuse to pay these passed-on research costs. Additionally, free services like Google Scholar are increasingly available that allow attorneys to conduct free searches without incurring database charges.
- **Out-of-pocket costs:** Nearly every litigation matter will incur substantial expenses payable to entities other than the law firm. Such costs include filing fees, process server fees, deposition fees, travel expenses, expert fees. Determine now whether you would like to pay these costs directly, or whether you can ask the firm to pay them for you and then invoice you for the amounts paid.

- **Billing:** By and large, attorneys are old-fashioned. Typically bills are sent out once a month, and often with some lag time tagged onto that schedule. Given this frequency, it is easy to be surprised by bills. Consider asking the attorney to send out twice-monthly invoices, and to do so via email on specified dates (such as the 1st and 15th).

So How Much Will this Cost Me, and Am I Going to Win?

The above two questions require an attorney to be a fortune teller. Attorneys are not fortune tellers; they cannot predict the future.

As to "How much this will cost me?", clients often ask an attorney to prepare a litigation budget that contains some estimates. Such estimates are difficult to provide, as most of how much a litigation will cost depends on unknowns, including the behavior of the opposing side. Litigation takes unforeseen turns. Nonetheless, these estimates provide an accountability framework that can be helpful for guiding attorney and client expectations and communications. You should set expectations for regular consultations with the lawyer about the billings in the case. You will benefit if you can frame these consultations as driven by your business finances and practices, rather than as frustrations about your attorney's practices. Most attorneys do their level best for their clients, and may interpret ongoing and poorly framed questions about billings as an attack upon their character or competence. If predictability is important to your business, you could also ask your attorney for a weekly update on hours spent that week.

As to the second question ("Am I going to win?"), your attorney is obligated to provide you a candid assessment of your prospects of success in the litigation. These predictions will often include an explanation of the law that will apply to your case, and caveats that the application of that law to your case will depend upon the facts that emerge—many of which are not yet known. Generally, any dispute that has risen to the litigation is not a slam dunk case for either side. You may of course feel that the case is a slam dunk for you, but part of your attorney's job in giving you the best candid advice is to help you recognize the risk that the Court may not interpret the facts in the same way that you do. Furthermore, your attorney should help you recognize that even in a very strong case, inherent uncertainty exists in the process of adjudication. You may initially feel that this advice means that your attorney is "not on your side" and "does not believe you." Resist this reaction. Your attorney's job is not to tell you what you want to hear. Her job is to give her best advice in an effort to help you make informed decisions about the case. Rest assured that when it comes time for your attorney to advocate your case in court and to the opposing attorney, she will be your zealous advocate.

Litigation Commences, Law Firm Engaged—Off to the Races

A separate chapter in this book addresses various substantive proceedings in litigation. Suffice to say, litigation can be very complicated.

Part of your attorney's job is to explain the proceedings to you. The following are some general thoughts on the pragmatics of the situations you will confront. Consideration of these topics may help you know what questions to ask your attorney.

- **Motion practice.** A motion is a party's request for the Court to rule on some issue. There are numerous different kinds of motions. Most motions are not "dispositive," a term used to mean that the outcome of a particular motion will determine whether you win or lose your case. In strategizing whether to bring a motion, always ask your attorney the following: the cost of preparing and arguing the motion; the likely effect upon the opposing party; the possible outcomes; and the strategic goals for the motion in view of the overall case.
- **Discovery.** Our judicial system emphasizes the rights of all parties to full information relating to the relevant facts of the case. This means that you need to turn over all your "stuff"—documents, texts, emails, financial information—you name it, you'll likely have to provide it to the other side. This process can be absurdly expensive. Even where your lawyer is supremely cost conscious, discovery costs will always seem excessive. Still, some lawyers unnecessarily expand the scope of discovery to materials that are not truly essential, file too many discovery motions, and fail to develop a working relationship with the opposing attorney that

can reduce costs for all involved. At the outset of the litigation, you may well have been impressed by the "bulldog" attorney.[14] If that bulldog is not able to be pragmatic and negotiate during discovery, those failings will show up in additional zeros on your invoices.

- **Trial.** Modernly, most cases (likely more than 95%) never reach the trial stage. Cases settle. They are dismissed by plaintiffs who run out of zest or funds for a years-long fight. They are resolved by the judge on a dispositive motion. But only rarely are they tried to a jury of your peers. In terms of trial strategy, pay close attention to the instructions of your attorney. The jury will be watching you throughout the trial, and don't think that your persona will not be assessed and weighed. If you are in a large-stakes trial, consider bringing in separate appellate counsel to observe the proceedings and offer occasional tips to trial counsel.
- **Complaining Does Not Help.** During litigation, you can spend your time in a lot of ways. You can focus on your personal health, your business, and on providing specific support to your attorney as asked. Or, as many litigants prefer, you can obsessively complain about the system, the judge, your attorney, the other side's attorney, and myriad other perceived injustices. Rest assured, it is a 100% probability that the judge assigned to your case is not "out to get you." Our judicial system is not perfect, but it dramatically better than the system in any other country in the world. Granted, attorneys and court fees can be expensive, and litigation takes a substantial amount of time. But here in America, you get a fair shot at a remedy for the wrong that harmed your business.
- **(Almost) Always Agree to Early Mediation.** Mediation is a voluntary appearance before an experienced attorney (often a former judge) who will attempt to facilitate a settlement.

[14]If you think you need a mean and ornery attorney to be successful in litigation, you are wrong. Consider the following advice given from Abraham Lincoln: "Discourage litigation. Persuade your neighbors to compromise whenever you can. Point out to them how the nominal winner is often a real loser---in fees, expenses, and waste of time. As a peacemaker the lawyer has a superior opportunity of being a good man. There will still be business enough." *Notes for a Law Lecture*, The Collected Works of Abraham Lincoln edited by Roy P. Basler, Volume II, (July 1, 1850), p. 81.

Relatively speaking, mediation is cheap and it often succeeds where there are any reasonable prospects at a settlement. Carefully and repeatedly inquire with your attorney about the right time to mediate a case. Be skeptical about an attorney's advice to refuse to mediate a case.

- **Do Not Get Confused by Emotion, Justice, Revenge and Other Irrelevant Feelings:** Litigation is (Almost) Always About Money. Consider rationally whether settlement makes fiscal sense. You may feel like you ought to fight the moral fight to prove the other side wrong. The longstanding advice to not litigate out of principle is still true. Do not do it. Litigation should (almost) always be a business decision. As a simple example, consider an offer to settle your case that would require you to pay $50,000. Your attorney informs you that she thinks you have a 75 percent chance of winning the case and paying nothing, but that it will cost $100K in legal fees to get through trial. Furthermore, if you lose at trial, you will lose an additional $100K. If you settle, you will pay $50K. If you proceed, you will surely incur $100,000 in expenses, and you have the statistical probability of incurring an additional $25K (not to mention a risk of incurring an additional $100K). In such a situation, only a fool proceeds where the grounds for doing so are purely emotional. Granted, in some situations, though, legitimate broad business reasons may exist that justify continuing the litigation. Such rationales include establishing a pattern of practice or a market message. Be aware, though, that while such tactics and strategy sound strong and therefore appealing, they are also expensive. They should be considered carefully in light of your entire business strategy and budget.
- **Disputes with Hired Attorney—Before or After Conclusion of Litigation.** Hopefully, the care you exercised in selecting your litigation counsel increased the probability of a favorable experience. However, if during litigation, you become convinced that your attorney is not zealously or competently representing you, you may consider switching counsel. Just

like every other professional (engineers, doctors, accountants), attorneys are responsible to perform their obligations pursuant to an acceptable standard of care. If you feel that your attorney has breached the relevant standard of care, you may bring a lawsuit against your attorney for legal malpractice. In either setting, carefully and objectively evaluate the situation, preferably with the assistance of unbiased separate legal counsel.

As to fees, if you feel that your attorney has overcharged you, you are not alone. Legal services are expensive. Clients often feel that they are too expensive. The legal test for whether charges are appropriate asks whether they were reasonable under the circumstances. To determine that for yourself, first speak candidly with the attorney about the charges. If that discussion does not resolve your concerns, consider retaining a new attorney to ask her thoughts on the matter. Understand that if this counsel is hoping to replace your current litigation counsel, her perspective may not be unbiased. The Utah State bar also has a "fee dispute resolution services" that may prove helpful in achieving a voluntary resolution.[15]

Conclusion

At the end of a litigation, first pay your lawyer,[16] and then take a vacation! After your vacation, it's time for your business to evaluate what was learned from the dispute. Speak with both your litigation counsel and business counsel about possible measures to implement to try to avoid future litigation or reduce future litigation risk.

[15]http://www.utahbar.org/public-services/fee-dispute-resolution-service/ Furthermore, the Utah State Bar also allows you to file complaints against your attorney, and will investigate such complaints. This process functions primarily to regulate the profession, and protect the public from problem attorneys. Therefore, it is certainly not a dispute pathway analogous to filing a malpractice suit.

[16]Despites any reputation to the contrary, the legal profession appreciates humor.

CHAPTER 3

CIVIL TRIAL LITIGATION

THE ANATOMY OF A CIVIL CASE

HONORABLE THOMAS L. KAY[1]

I. INTRODUCTION

This chapter will cover the basic elements of a typical civil case. As a point of departure, it is important to understand that there are two types of legal cases: civil and criminal. Criminal cases involve offenses against the state; i.e., violations of state or federal laws. Criminal cases are always prosecuted by the government and carry the potential of criminal penalties, including jail and criminal fines. For example, the State of Utah might charge the C.E.O. of a start-up company with securities fraud and then, upon conviction, require the C.E.O. to pay a fine and serve time in jail.

Conversely, civil cases involve wrongs by one or more persons or organizations against one or more persons or organizations. For example, a company might sue another company for failing to abide by the terms of their business contract. Notably, even the government could file a civil case against a citizen or organization. But remember, civil cases do not carry criminal penalties. Rather, the goal of a civil case is to determine if any remedy is owed to the party bringing the case. These remedies involve either monetary awards or court orders requiring or forbidding certain behavior by the non-prevailing party. For example, in a law suit for patent infringement, a company might sue a patent violator for the profits the violator acquired from the violation, as well

[1]Judge Thomas L. Kay has been a Utah State District Judge for over 17 years. Prior to becoming a judge, he was a trial attorney with Ray, Quinney & Nebeker and Snell & Wilmer. He received his BA degree in English from the University of Utah and his law degree from BYU. He loves to play tennis, hike, and write poetry.

as a court order forbidding the violator from continuing to engage in its infringing behavior.

A. All civil cases follow the same rules, except for Small Claims cases.

Civil cases are governed by statutes and case law. Statutes are the laws that the legislature has enacted. Statutes can, among other things, create legal duties and limit or preclude the remedies a court can award. Case law refers to the body of previous court cases that either interpret statutes or develop judicial law.

Additionally, the court has adopted rules that govern civil cases procedurally. There are two sets of civil procedural rules: those for small claims and those for all other claims. Small claims courts only hear cases where the amount in controversy in less than a certain dollar amount prescribed by statute, currently set at $10,000. *See* Utah Code § 78A-8-102. Small claims cases follow a simplified set of court rules known as the Utah Rules of Small Claims Procedure. All other civil cases at the trial level follow the Utah Rules of Civil Procedure ("URCP"). Each step of civil case is governed by a corresponding rule in the URCP. This chapter will summarize some of the content of some of the rules, but should not be considered a substitute for referencing the rules themselves or seeking competent legal counsel.

Not all civil cases will have each of the elements we will discuss.

No two civil cases involve the exact same set of facts, and consequently, each case tends to develop uniquely. This chapter focuses on the possible procedural paths a typical, non-small-claims case can take. Although not all civil cases will necessarily have each of the elements described in the balance of this chapter, understanding the overall anatomy of a civil case is critical to making informed decisions about business litigation.

II. THE BEGINNING OF A CIVIL CASE

A. Timing

The URCP sets out deadlines for most actions that a party can take in the course of litigation. Rule 6 clarifies how each time period is to be accounted for and what standard applies to a party that is seeking additional time. The rule is not complicated, though it is detailed, so a careful, informed reading of the rule will likely be the best way to understand it. The important principle to understand is that failure to meet a deadline can have serious, detrimental effects on your case. In most cases, the party seeking to take an action after the prescribed time period will have to show good cause and/or lack of prejudice to the other party in order to have its mistake excused. This is a difficult standard to meet. It is much easier to plan ahead and file/serve documents in a timely matter than to seek for retroactive leniency from the Court that may or may not be granted.

B. The Complaint

A civil case begins in one of two ways: (1) the filing of complaint with the court, or (2) the delivery of copy of a complaint and a summons to the party against whom a claim is being made. URCP 3. The person making the complaint is the "plaintiff." The person against whom the complaint is filed is the "defendant." The complaint sets forth who the parties are, the basis for the claim, and why the court has jurisdiction (i.e., authority to hear the case).

C. Summons and Service

If a complaint has been filed with the court, a copy of it must be delivered to the defendant along with a summons; i.e., a written order from the court requiring the defendant to answer the complaint by a certain date. URCP 4(b)(i), (c)(1). If the complaint was originally delivered to the defendant, then the complaint, the summons, as well as proof of delivery must be filed with the court within ten days of the service.

The method by which the summons and the complaint are delivered to the defendant is referred to as "service," while the actual documents themselves are referred to as "process." URCP 4 dictates how and when service can be accomplished as follows:

- <u>When does service have to be done by?</u> Process must be served on defendant within 120 days of filing the process with the court. Conversely, if the plaintiff elects to serve the defendant before filing with the court, the defendant must file a copy of the process with the court within ten days of serving the defendant. Failure to meet these deadlines results in dismissal of the case. URCP 4(b)(i); URCP 3(a).

- What types of service are allowed? Unless there is special court order, service can only be accomplished by mail or in person. URCP 4(2)(A). Personal service has a few specific rules:
  - *Personal service* can be performed by any person eighteen years of age or older at the time of service who is not a party to the action or a party's attorney. With a few exceptions, service can be made by delivering process to the defendant personally, to some person of suitable age and discretion residing at the defendant's house or usual place of abode, or to the defendant's duly authorized agent. URCP 4(d)(1).

    Notably, special rules govern service of process if the defendant is a corporation, partnership, or unincorporated association which is subject to suit. Generally, service can be performed in such cases by delivering process to "a managing or general agent, or other agent authorized by appointment or law to receive service of process . . . ." URCP 4(d)(1)(E).
  - *Service by mail* can be accomplished in one of two ways: (1) mailing the process and having the defendant sign a document indicating receipt, or (2) requesting the defendant to waive service of the summons. In the later situation, the plaintiff must mail a copy of the complaint to the defendant with a request to waive service of a summons. For domestic mail, the court request must allow the defendant at least twenty days after sending the request to return the waiver. If the waiver is properly returned, the defendant is allowed extra time to respond to the complaint (forty-five days). If the defendant refuses the waiver request, the court will require the defendant to pay the costs subsequently incurred to effectuate personal service. URCP 4(d)(2), (f).

- *Special court orders* can permit service by other means, such as publication, in unique circumstances. URCP 4(d)(4)(B).

D. Default Judgment

1. URCP Rule 55

Once a complaint and summons have been properly served, the party on whom they have been served (i.e., the defendant) must make a proper response in order to avoid default judgment.[2] Default judgment means that the court is awarding the plaintiff the relief she requested in her complaint, even though there has not been a trial. In other words, the plaintiff is deemed to have won the law suit.

2. Motion and order in supplemental proceedings

A motion an order in a supplemental proceeding is a way for a judgment creditor to find out how the defendant will pay the judgment.

3. Order to show cause

If a judgment debtor does not appear for the supplemental proceeding, the plaintiff can as for an order to show cause.

4. Bench warrant

Failure to appear to show cause and/or repeated failure to abide by another court order can result in the judge issuing an arrest warrant for that person. These warrants, known as bench warrants, authorize law enforcement to arrest the person on sight. The person is then brought before the judge—i.e., before the judge's bench—to explain why she is failing to abide by the court's orders.

5. Garnishment

A writ of garnishment is a court order authorizing the seizure of a defendant's property that is in control of someone other than the defendant. Importantly, writs are available when the defendant is

---

[2] These responses are discussed in Part D, *infra*.

indebted to the plaintiff. A court can issue a writ either before or after final judgment has been entered. URCP 64D(a).

E. Possible Responses to the Complaint

In lieu of filing an answer to a complaint, a defendant may file a motion to dismiss or a motion for a more definite statement. A defendant can also file a petition to remove the case to federal court. Each of these options can have a different effect, and each is only appropriate in certain circumstances.

1. The Answer

Although other responses are possible, the most common response to a complaint is an answer. An answer, just as its name implies, responds to the complaint, usually by denying or admitting the allegations in the complaint and raising affirmative defenses. URCP Rule 8. Under most circumstances, the answer must be served within twenty days of the service of the complaint. URCP 12(a). An answer can also include a counterclaim, cross-claim, third-party complaint, or jury demand. URCP 12.

a. Counterclaim

A counterclaim is a claim for relief that the defendant has against the plaintiff. There are two types of counterclaims: compulsory and permissive. Generally, compulsory counterclaims are, as their name implies, claims that must be made when a defendant is answering a plaintiff's complaint. URCP 13(a). Failure to properly raise the claim precludes the party from raising it at a future proceeding.

Conversely, permissive claims can be made in the same proceeding, but are not waived if they are not raised. The difference between the two is that compulsory claims arise out of the same "transaction and occurrence" as the defendant's complaint, all other counterclaims are permissive. URCP 13 (a), (b). For example, in a breach of contract complaint filed by a plaintiff against a defendant, the defendant might answer by including a counterclaim for tortious interference with a business relationship or breach of the covenant of good faith and fair dealing. If the plaintiff's breach of contract claim was based on the same event as the defendant's breach of the covenant of good faith and fair dealing, then the defendant's claim would be compulsory. Conversely, it is likely that the toritous interference with a business relationship claim would be permissive if it referred to plaintiff's unrelated actions.

b. Cross-Claim

Some cases will have multiple defendants or multiple plaintiffs. When this occurs, there is potential for these co-parties to have legal claims against each other. These claims are cross-claims; i.e., a claim by a defendant against another defendant or a plaintiff against another plaintiff. Cross-claims must arise out of either the same transaction or occurrence or relate to property that is the subject-matter of the original complaint. URCP 13 (f).

c. Third-Party Complaint

A third-party complaint is a claim brought against a party that was not initially included in the action. Either party can make a third-party complaint, though plaintiffs can only do so for purposes of a counterclaim. These types of complaints are made when one of the original parties to the action alleges that someone who is not a party to the lawsuit is at least partially responsible for paying the claim (or counterclaim) being brought against them. For example, if a homeowner was suing his general contractor for breach of contract for faulty work, the general contractor could bring in the subcontractor who did the work as a third-party defendant. *See* URCP 14.

d. Jury Demand

With some exceptions, civil cases can either be decided by a jury or judge. Either party may demand a jury trial, but must do so in writing to the court within ten days after service of the last pleading—e.g., the complaint or answer—and must serve this demand on the other party. URCP 38(b). Failure to abide by these conditions waives the right to trial by jury. URCP 38(d). Consequently, it is important to consider the merits of a jury trial before filing a complaint.

2. Motion to Dismiss

A motion[3] to dismiss is a request asking the court to dismiss the case. This request, depending on the claim and the circumstances, can be with or without prejudice. The difference is that dismissing a claim with prejudice will preclude the plaintiff from ever filing a complaint arising from the same transaction/occurrence and involving the same claim and defendant again. Conversely, dismissing a claim without prejudice will dispose of the current action but leave the plaintiff the option of correcting the deficiency in the original complaint and refiling it with the court at a later date. URCP 12(b) covers some of the basic motions to dismiss as set forth below that a defendant might make in response to a defendant's complaint.

a. Lack of subject matter or personal jurisdiction

Courts don't have unlimited authority: they can only decide cases that they are authorized to hear. This authority is referred to as jurisdiction. In order to hear a case the court must have the authority over the people involved in a case (i.e., personal jurisdiction) and authority to hear the subject of the litigation (i.e., subject matter jurisdiction). Subject matter jurisdiction is generally determined by statute or constitution, and is a less common objection in Utah because district courts here have very broad authority to hear different types of cases. However, one example of where this authority has been limited is that small claims courts are not authorized to hear matters involving sums greater than $10,000.

Motions to dismiss for lack of personal jurisdiction generally only arise if the one of the defendants is not a resident of the state. In these cases, the court must look at the defendant's connections to the state to see if they are legally sufficient to justify exercising authority over her.

b. Improper venue

Improper venue motions to dismiss arise when the defendant concedes that a Utah court has subject matter and personal jurisdiction, but argues that the specific Utah court in which the case was filed is not is not the appropriate place to try the case. This claim could be based on a contractual provision between the parties that requires disagreements

[3]All motions, including motions to dismiss, must be formatted and served according to the URCP. *See* URCP 7.

between the parties to be heard by a certain court or on arguments that another court (i.e., another forum) is the more convenient and logical place to have the case heard.

c. Insufficiency of process or service of process

These motions are made when a defendant alleges that the plaintiff has failed to follow the URCP regarding the form of the pleading; i.e., the process. Contrastingly, motions based on insufficiency of service of process allege the URCP were not met in the way the process was delivered—i.e., served. For example, if the plaintiff never served the defendant with the complaint, then a court could dismiss a case for insufficiency of service.

d. Failure to state a claim upon which relief can be granted

The law only recognizes certain types of complaints that a plaintiff can bring against a defendant. Additionally, URCP 8(a) requires that all complaints lay out the basic facts that show they are entitled to relief. Thus, if a complaint fails to set out legally cognizable complaint it can be dismissed.

e. Failure to join an indispensable party

Some claims involve the rights of more than just the parties in the original action; i.e., the party or parties that were included in the original pleading. If a nonparty's rights are implicated to a high enough degree, then the law requires that she be made a party to the action so that her rights aren't affected without her having a chance to be represented. Failure to join such a party can result in dismissal.

3. Motion for more definite statement, URCP Rule 12(e) and Rule 7

The party submitting a pleading to the court has an obligation to communicate clearly. If the pleading is overly vague or ambiguous, the opposing party can move for a definite statement; i.e., ask that the court require the submitting party to clarify what they are stating in their pleading. Once the motion has been granted, the drafting party has ten days to clarify its pleading, otherwise, it may be dismissed.

4. Removal Petition

In the United States there are two general court classifications: federal and state. Federal courts are, of course, run by the federal government, and likewise, state courts are run by their respective state. Whereas state district courts are courts of general jurisdiction,—i.e., they can hear almost all types of cases—federal courts have much more limited jurisdiction—i.e., they only hear cases that involve certain types of claims or certain types of people. Notably, there is some overlap between the jurisdiction of state and federal courts. In these cases, if a defendant timely requests it, federal courts have authority to take a case that was filed in a state court and instead hear it in federal court. The legal term for this is "removal."

a. Rule 81(c), Federal Rules of Civil Procedure.

This rule states that cases that are removed to federal district court are governed by the Federal Rules of Civil Procedure, and that certain timelines apply for responding to pleadings and motions.

b. 28 United States Code § 1446

This is the federal law that governs the procedures that must be followed to have a case removed from state to federal court. In general, only a defendant can remove a state case to federal court and must do so within thirty days after receiving notice that there is a claim filed in state court that is removable to federal court. This is accomplished by filing a notice of removal in the appropriate federal court.

5. Motion for judgment on the pleadings, Rule 12 (c) and Rule 7, URCP

Once all of the pleadings have been completed, a plaintiff may move for judgment on the pleadings. This motion essentially asks the court to look at the pleadings—i.e., the answer and the complaint—, and only the pleadings, and determine if, assuming everything stated therein is true, the plaintiff is entitled to any relief. This type of judgment is typically brought by a plaintiff when a defendant's answer fails to deny the allegations set forth in the plaintiff's complaint. In other words, if the plaintiff has properly plead her complaint, and the defendant admits to everything alleged in the complaint, there is no need for a trial. The judge can look at the pleadings and grant judgment for the plaintiff.

III. DISCOVERY

A. Obtaining information from parties and individuals with knowledge

Once the initial pleading are complete, parties begin the process of obtaining information relevant to the case from the opposing party. This process is referred to as "discovery." There are a number of different ways to request and receive relevant information, many of which have specific deadlines. These are discussed in the following.

B. Interrogatories, Rule 33, URCP

Parties can submit written questions—interrogatories—to any other party to the lawsuit during the discovery period. The number of questions allowed is set by court rule and changes depending on the amount of damages claimed. Once a party has received an interrogatory, it has twenty-eight days to respond to it under oath or affirmation.

C. Request for Production of Documents, Rule 34, URCP

A party may serve written request on another party to the lawsuit to produce documents and other tangible things that are relevant to a lawsuit. The party receiving such a request has twenty-eight days in which to respond to the request. The number of requests allowed is generally determined by the amount of damages claimed.

D. Request for Admissions, Rule 36, URCP

"A party may serve upon any other party a written request to admit the truth of any discoverable matter set forth in the request, including the genuineness of any document." URCP 36(a). The party receiving such a request has twenty-eight days in which to respond to the request.

The number of requests allowed is generally determined by the amount of damages claimed.

E. Physical and mental examinations, Rule 35, URCP

When the mental or physical condition or attribute of a party or someone in the custody or control of a party is relevant and in controversy, the opposing party may ask the court to order that person to submit to a physical or mental examination by a qualified professional.

F. Depositions, Rules 30–32, URCP

Depositions are the process whereby a witness's testimony is taken, under oath, before trial. Typically, and much like traditional questioning at trial, attorneys are present at depositions and ask questions and make objections. The testimony is then recorded and transcribed, and it can, under some circumstances, be used at trial as evidence. The number of depositions allowed is determined by court rule and is a function of the amount of damages sought. There are a number of rules governing the process and scope of depositions. A few of them are summarized below.

1. Reasonable notice

"The party deposing a witness shall give reasonable notice in writing to every other party. The notice shall state the date, time and place of for the deposition and the name and address of each witness." URCP 30(b)(1).

2. Can request that documents be brought to deposition

"The notice to a party witness may be accompanied by a request under Rule 34 for the production of documents and tangible things at the deposition." URCP 30(b)(4).

3. Subpoena, Rule 45, URCP

A person who is a party to the case is required to make herself available for deposition testimony without any order of the court. However, a person who is not a party to a case cannot be compelled to be deposed without being served with a subpoena as set forth in URCP

45. A subpoena is a written order from the court requiring the named individual to appear at a certain time and place to be deposed.

G. Disclosures under Rule 26

The discovery tools discussed above require a party to request information before it is produced. However, under URCP 26, there is a significant amount of information that a party is required to produce without waiting for a request. Specifically, each party must provide, to the other parties to the lawsuit, among other things:

1. "the name and, if known, the address of and telephone number of:"

a. "each individual likely to have discoverable information supporting its claims or defenses . . ." and

b. "each fact witness the party may call in its case-in-chief . . . "; and

2. "a copy of all documents, data compilations, electronically stored information, and tangible things in possession or control of the party that the party may offer in its case-in-chief . . . ."

URCP 26(a)(1)(A)–(B). Plaintiffs must make these required disclosures within "14 days after service of he first answer to the complaint." Defendants must make required disclosures within "28 days after the plaintiff's first disclosure or after that defendant's appearance, whichever is later." URCP 26 (a)(2).

IV. DISCOVERY MOTIONS

A. Rule 37and Rule 7, URCP

When a party fails to follow the discovery rules, there are a number of sanctions a court can impose against it. These are set forth in URCP 37 and include excluding evidence, ordering a party to pay another party's attorney fees, and rendering default judgment in favor of one party. Sanctions are usually preceded by a motion to compel and a motion for sanctions.

B. Motion to Compel

When an opposing party fails follow discovery rules the other party usually makes a motion to compel the party to follow the rules; i.e., they ask the court to order the party to comply with discovery rules.

C. Motion for Sanctions

After a party has failed to comply with discovery order and rule, or in some cases, just a discovery rule, the party alleging noncompliance can make a motion for the court to impose sanctions.

V. PRETRIAL CONFERENCES, SCHEDULING AND MANAGEMENT CONFERENCES AND ORDERS

A. Default Discovery Deadlines and Other Requirements

Rule 26 creates standardized, default deadlines for discovery based on the amount and type of damages sought. The idea behind this is that parties should need to perform less discovery, and therefore need less time to complete discovery, when the amount in controversy is lower. Rule 26 creates three "tiers" of cases, each of which has limitations on how much discovery can be performed and when. Tier 1 covers cases where the amount sought is less than $50,000. Tier 2 covers cases where the amount sought is more than $50,000 but less than $300,000, or non-monetary relief is sought (e.g., a request for an injunction prohibiting a business for infringing on a patent). Finally, Tier 3 covers cases where the amount in controversy is in excess of $300,000. The parties are required to follow the deadlines and requirements of the tier under which their case falls unless they agree to modify them or, in special circumstances, the court grants an exception. *See* URCP 29.

B. Pretrial Conferences

Occasionally, it will be necessary or useful for parties to have a special meeting with the judge before trial in order to expedite the disposition of the case, discourage wasteful activities, extend discovery deadlines, improve the quality of the trial, etc. In such cases, the court can, in its own discretion or on a motion by one of the parties, order the parties to appear before the court to resolve the issue. These are referred to generally as pretrial conferences. URCP Rule 16.

C. Final Pretrial/Settlement Conference

"The court, in its discretion or upon motion, may direct the attorneys and, when appropriate, the parties to appear for such purposes as settlement and trial management. The conference shall be shall be held as close to the time of trial as reasonable under the circumstances." URCP 16(c).

VI. POST-DISCOVERY MATTERS

A. Settlement

Parties often make offers to settle a claim before it goes all the way to trial. Settling a claim means that the plaintiff agrees to dismiss its claim against the defendant, usually in exchange for something of value from the defendant. For example, in a negligence action arising out of car accident, the injured plaintiff might agree to drop its claim against the driver-defendant in exchange for having the defendant agree to pay all of plaintiff's accident-related medical bills.

Settling a case is often in the best interest of both parties because it shortens the length of the litigation and in so doing reduces attorney bills and the time and stress spent waiting for the final resolution of claim. There are a number of tools that parties can use to facilitate a settlement of the issues, including an offer of judgment, mediation, and arbitration.

B. Offer of Judgment, Rule 68, URCP

The URCP has a special provision that encourages parties to settle cases before trial if a reasonable settlement offer is made. Namely, Rule 68 authorizes, under certain circumstances, a party that has had a settlement offer rejected to collect its court costs—though not attorney fees—from the rejecting party. There are, however, some limitations on when and how much of such costs can be recovered. Assuming it otherwise follows the procedures of Rule 68, an offering party can only collect its costs if the amount awarded at trial to the rejecting party is less than the amount offered by the offering party. Furthermore, the party can only collect its costs from the date of the offer through the end of trial. However, as an additional incentive to accept reasonable settlement offers, the offering party is relieved from the obligation to pay the court costs and/or attorney fees—if awarded by the court—of the rejecting party from the offer date as well.

C. Mediation & Arbitration

Mediation and arbitration both involve inviting a neutral third party to help settle a case. Although mediation and arbitration can be required by law, they are usually not mandatory unless provided for by contract. E.g., many business contracts include provisions requiring arbitration or mediation in lieu of litigation or as a prerequisite to litigation. Additionally, some parties in litigation elect to go through mediation or arbitration as a means of expediting settlement of the case.

Mediation. Mediation involves inviting a third-party to listen to both sides of a case, and then facilitate a settlement by building bridges of understanding between the parties. Thus a mediator doesn't actually decide a case. Rather, a mediator tries to help the parties settle the case themselves by clarifying their positions, thinking through alternatives, and discussing possible outcomes if the case goes to trial. Mediation can be, but traditionally is not, binding on the parties. Meaning, the parties are not obligated to follow any advice the mediator gives or reach an agreement after the mediation session. Whether mediation is binding or not is function of the governing law or contract, if either is applicable. The cost of mediator is usually split between the parties.

Arbitration. Arbitration involves inviting one or more third-parties to judge a case. In other words, arbitration is essentially a trial conducted by non-judge. Typically, the arbiter(s) will be agreed on by the parties. Both parties will present their evidence and arguments, and the arbiter(s) will decide the case just as a judge or jury would. Arbitration usually is, but need not be, binding on the parties. Just like mediation, this is a function of what the governing law or contract states, if anything. If arbitration is binding, then the decision of the arbiter(s) will be mandatory, just as if it were issued by a court. The cost of arbitration is usually split between the parties.

D. Motion for Summary Judgment

1. Different from Motions to Dismiss and for Judgment on Pleadings

After discovery, but before trial, either party can file for a motion for summary judgment. In order to understand the role of motion for summary judgment, it is useful to understand the purpose of a trial. The purpose of a trial is to let the fact finder, the jury in a jury trial and the judge in a bench trial, to decide what actually happened as a factual matter. For example, in most cases, the parties disagree about things such as whether money was paid, whether certain representations were made, or who was agreed to in a contract. The parties then present evidence, in the form of exhibits and questions to witnesses to convince the jury (or judge) of their version of what happened. Once the facts are determined, the judge's role in a jury or bench trial is to apply the law to the facts. The judge doesn't need witnesses or other evidence to decide how to apply the law to the facts. Consequently, if the parties can agree as to what happened, then there is no need for trial.

A motion for summary judgment is similar to motions for judgment on the pleadings or motions to dismiss in that it essentially argues that the parties agree to the facts—i.e., what happened—and all that remains is for the judge to apply the law to the uncontroverted facts. It is different in that requires the nonmoving party to present some form of admissible evidence—i.e., affidavits, depositions, answers to interrogatories, etc.—reasonably supporting every element of their claim(s). Consequently, the judge will not weigh the credibility of the submitted evidence. Rather, the judge will review the submitted evidence to see if there is anything to support all of the necessary elements of a party's claims. If a party fails to present evidence on any element of a claim, that claim will be dismissed with prejudice. Conversely, if there is some form of evidence, then the claim(s) can proceed to trial.

Notably, summary judgment can be brought, granted, or denied on multiple claims in a case. It is common for an initial complaint to be very broad: i.e., it will make many claims that may not all be supported by the evidence. Then, as the discovery process proceeds and parties come to understand better what evidence is actually available to support their claims, they will often use motions for summary judgment to pare down the claims before trial.

2. Rule 56 and Rule 7, URCP

Rules 56 and 7 govern the procedures that must be followed when submitting a motion for summary judgment.

A party submitting motion for summary judgment is required to "contain a statement of material facts as to which the moving party contends that no [genuine disagreement between the parties] exists. Each fact [is required to] be separately stated and . . . supported by citation to relevant materials, such as affidavits or discovery materials." URCP 7(c)(3)(A). The opposing party's responsive memorandum must "contain a verbatim restatement of each of the moving party's facts that is controverted, and may contain a separate statement of additional facts in dispute. For each of the . . . facts that is controverted, the opposing party shall provide an explanation of the grounds for any dispute, supported by citation to relevant materials . . . ." URCP 7(c)(3)(B).

There are time limits imposed by the rule. In most cases, a motion for summary judgment cannot be served until twenty days after the commencement of the action. URCP 56(a). Additionally, after a motion has been served, the opposing party has ten days after service to file a memorandum in opposition. The moving party then has five days to file a reply to the memorandum in opposition,

As noted earlier, motions for summary judgment are not typically filed until after discovery has begun to some extent. This allows the parties to better ascertain what kind of evidence exists. Thus, under Rule 56(f) the Court can "refuse the application for summary judgment or may order a continuance to permit" additional evidence to be obtained.

3. Request to Submit

A court will not consider a motion for summary judgment, or any other motion, until one of the parties has notified the Court. The method for notifying the Court is filing a request to submit. A request to submit may not be filed until briefing is completed. Briefing is considered completed when either (1) both parties have prepared and served all of the pertinent memoranda the URCP authorizes for the particular motion, or (2) when the URCP time period for filing the pertinent, authorized memoranda has run out.

VII. FINAL PRETRIAL CONFERENCE

A. Parties and Attorneys present

Although not necessarily required under the URCP, courts often hold a final pretrial conference shortly before a scheduled trial. The general goal of these conferences is to discuss and decide any issues that will help the trial go smoothly and fairly. Although the purpose of this conference can vary, the following topics are often discussed. *See* URCP 16.

1. Settlement

Courts will often encourage the parties to consider settling the matter before trial. Thus, at a final pretrial conference, the Court might inquire as to what settlement efforts the parties have undertaken and if any aspects of the case have been or likely will be settled. Even if a global resolution cannot be reached, it is often advantageous for the parties to narrow the number of issues that are contested at trial. Doing this can avoid trial-related expenses and, in certain circumstances, aid the trier of fact by simplifying the issues to be decided.

2. Jury Instructions or Findings of Fact/Conclusions of Law

The Court will often discuss jury instructions and make evidentiary rulings. Jury instructions are the direction the court gives the jury regarding how jury members must behave during trial, the criteria upon which they must base their decision, and the best way they can reach their verdict. *See* URCP 51. For example, every jury trial has instructions relating to the elements the plaintiff must prove in order to recover.

Evidentiary rulings govern what evidence can be presented to the jury and the manner in which it must be presented. Although a judge can wait until trial to make evidentiary rulings, many judges will try to identify and resolve troublesome issues before hand to ensure a smooth and fair trial. A common pretrial motion is a motion in limine; i.e., a motion that sets restrictions on how and whether a party can reference certain issues or evidence. A party that feels that certain evidence is overly prejudicial will usually make a pretrial motion in limine asking the court to bar the party from mentioning the prejudicial material.

3. Rule 26 Pretrial Disclosures

Each party is required to disclose the name, telephone number, and address of each witness the party may call at trial. Furthermore, each party is required to name the witnesses who are expected to present testimony through deposition and provide a copy of that deposition. Lastly, each party must present a copy of all exhibits—charts, summaries, and other exhibits used for demonstration—and must delineate which exhibits will be used and which exhibits might be used.

VIII. TRIAL

A. Jury Trial

If a case has not been settled and a jury trial has been requested and granted, a jury trial will be held. The number of jurors required depends on the type of case. In civil matters where the amount in controversy is $20,000 or more, eight jurors are required unless the parties agree otherwise.

1. Notice to potential jurors

Potential jurors are selected at random from driver's license and voter registration lists. Notice is sent out to a certain number of potential jurors who are ordered to appear in court on certain day at a certain time.

2. Jury selection, Rule 47, URCP

Not every person who receives notice of selection as a potential juror will actually be selected as a juror. This is because certain people may have prejudices or connections to the case that would prevent them from trying the case fairly and neutrally. Consequently, both parties have an opportunity to inquire into a potential juror's background in order to ascertain if that person will be a fair and just juror. If a juror's answer to a question reveals an unacceptable bias towards or connection to the case, the Court will dismiss the juror. Both parties also have the opportunity to dismiss a limited number of jurors without cause. In this sense, "without cause" means that there is no legally justifiable reason for keeping the person off the trial, but the party feels that the person would otherwise be unlikely to grant a verdict in their favor and thus doesn't want the person to sit on her trial. Once a jury has been selected, the case will proceed, starting with opening statements.

3. Opening statements

Typically, each party's attorney will give an opening statement to the court. This statement will outline what the case is about, the party's theory of the case, and the party's thinks the evidence will show.

4. Presentation of evidence

Evidence is anything that tends to prove or disprove the existence of a disputed fact. It can be testimony, or documents, or objects, or photographs, or stipulations, or certain qualified opinions, or any combination of these things. Of course, if a judge orders that something not be received as evidence, a jury will not be able to consider it in reaching its verdict.

The plaintiff will offer its evidence first followed by the defendant. Each side may also offer rebuttal evidence after hearing the witnesses and seeing the exhibits offered by the other side. Some times the lawyers may agree that certain facts exist in trial or before, perhaps at the pretrial conference. A jury must accept any agreed or stipulated facts as having been proved. In limited instances, a judge may also take "judicial notice" of a well-known fact. In civil cases, a jury must accept judicially noticed facts as being true.

5. Motion for a directed verdict, Rule 50, URCP

In civil cases, the person bringing suit—i.e., the plaintiff—has the burden of presenting evidence in furtherance of her claim. In other words, the plaintiff has the obligation to prove her claim rather than the defendant having the obligation to disprove her claim. In civil cases, the standard of proof is a preponderance of the evidence. This means that, after considering and comparing all the evidence presented in court, the convincing weight thereof must be in favor of the party making the claim. If the evidence is evenly balanced or if the balance is not in favor of the claimant, then the claimant has not met its burden as to that claim.

A plaintiff might move for a directed verdict if, after the plaintiff has presented all of her evidence, no reasonable juror could reach a verdict in the plaintiff's favor. A directed verdict is where the court directs the jury to find in favor of the moving party, thus preventing the jury from deliberating and deciding the case. A directed verdict is usually granted only if the plaintiff has failed to present any evidence is in support of an element of their claim. For example, in order for a plaintiff to prevail in a negligence claim, she must prove that the defendant owed her a duty, that the defendant breached that duty, that the breach caused her harm, and that the harm resulted in damages. Thus, if a plaintiff failed to present any evidence that the alleged breach caused damages, the defendant would likely have a motion for directed verdict granted.

6. Jury instructions and objections

Before, after, and occasionally during the presentation of evidence, the court will give the jury instructions. As noted earlier, these instructions tell a jury concerning their duties and conduct, the elements and burden of proof for the claim, and the procedure the trial will follow. Attorneys can object to the form of a written instruction if they do so before it is given to the jury. *See* URCP 51.

7. Closing arguments

After all of the evidence has been presented the attorneys for the parties will have an opportunity to make closing arguments to the jury. Typically, lawyers use closing arguments to summarize and argue the case. They share their respective views of the evidence, how it relates to the law and how they think the jury should decide the case.

8. Jury Verdict

In order for a jury to reach a verdict in a civil case, only three-fourths of the jurors (or more) need to be in agreement. This is different than a verdict in a criminal trial, which requires a unanimous decision.

B. Bench Trial

In some cases the right to a jury trial is not available or has been waived by the parties. When this happens, the judge will hear the case in a bench trial. In a bench trial, the judge assumes the jury's role as a fact finder; i.e., the judge evaluates the evidence and issues a verdict. The procedure that is followed in a bench trial is much the same as in a jury trial. The attorneys will have an opportunity to give opening and closing statements and evidence will be presented.

There are, however, two differences of particular note. If, after a plaintiff has presented her evidence, the defendant feels that there has not been evidence presented as to a particular element of the claim, the defendant may make a motion to dismiss the claim. *See* URCP 41(b). This motion takes the place of motion for directed verdict, which is only applicable in jury trials. The second difference is that in a bench trial a judge is required to make findings of fact and conclusions of law when issuing her ruling. URCP 52. A finding of fact is a statement of what the evidence has shown. A conclusion of law is a statement of how the law applies to the facts.

IX. POST-TRIAL MOTIONS

Parties often feel that the judge or jury reached an incorrect verdict. Assuming that there is proper basis and it is timely made, a party can always appeal the verdict to the appellate court. However, there are also a number of post-trial motions a party can make in the court that tried the case (i.e., the trial court).

A. Motion for a new trial, Rule 59, URCP

Either party may make motion for a new trial, and the court may also order a new trial on its own initiative. However, in either case, the action must be taken within ten days after entry of judgment. A new trial can be granted for number of reasons, including:

- Irregularity of an element of the trial;
- Abuse of discretion;
- Accident or surprise;
- Jury Misconduct;
- Newly discovered evidence;
- Excessive or inadequate damages;
- Insufficiency of the evidence; and
- Error in law

B. Motion for judgment notwithstanding the verdict, Rule 50, URCP

A motion for judgment notwithstanding the verdict, as its name implies, asks the judge to enter a judgment in favor of the moving party despite an adverse jury verdict. The basis for this motion is the same as that for a directed verdict: the moving party is arguing that there was not sufficient evidence presented at trial regarding one of the elements of the cause of action. Motions for judgment notwithstanding the verdict must be brought within ten days after entry of judgment and can only be brought if the party also made a motion for a directed verdict during the trial.

C. Motion for relief from judgment, Rule 60, URCP

A motion for relief from judgment asks the court to relieve a party from an adverse judgment. There are number of bases under which a court can grant such a motion, including:

- Mistake, inadvertence, surprise, or excusable neglect;
- Newly discovered evidence;
- Fraud, misrepresentation, or other misconduct of an adverse party;

- Clerical mistake;
- The judgment has been satisfied, released, or discharged;
- A prior judgment on which the present judgment is based has been reversed;
- It is no longer equitable that the judgment should have prospective application; and
- Any other reason justifying relief from the operation of the judgment.

All motions must be made within a reasonable amount of time, and for motions made for any of the first three bulleted reasons, that amount of time cannot be greater than after the judgment, order, or proceeding was entered or taken.

X. POST-JUDGMENT MATTERS

When a party receives a favorable pecuniary judgment, there are a number of ways the party can collect on that judgment. The process for collecting the judgment after trial is much the same as that discussed under default judgments supra II.D.

A. Motion and order in supplemental proceedings

A court can order a party with an outstanding judgment to appear in a supplemental proceeding. The purpose of the proceeding is for the party to provide information that will aid in the collection of the judgment; e.g., the name of their employer, the nature and location of property they own, etc. An order to show cause, bench warrant, and garnishment can be ordered as set forth in supra II.D.

B. Execution and sale of defendant's assets, Rule 64E, URCP

After a final judgment has been entered in a matter, the prevailing party can, with permission of the court, seize and sell the property of the non-prevailing party in order to satisfy the judgment. The procedural path for accomplishing this is a writ of execution and is governed by Rule 64E.

XI. SPECIAL PROCEEDINGS

A. Prejudgment Writs in General, Rule 64A, URCP

There are a number of prejudgment orders—i.e., orders a court can make before issuing its final ruling and order in a matter—, often called "writs," that a court can issue. In general, all writs requires a showing that the property sought is not exempt from execution, that the writ is not being sought to hinder, delay, or defraud any of defendant's creditors, and that there is a substantial likelihood that the person seeking the writ will prevail on the merits of the underlying claim. In addition to these general requirements, certain writs have certain requirements.

B. Writs of replevin, Rule 64B, URCP

A writ of replevin is a court order that requires a defendant to deliver specific personal property she is holding to the plaintiff. In order for the court to issue such an order, the plaintiff must show that she is entitled to possession of the property in question and that the defendant is wrongfully detaining the property. URCP 64A.

C. Attachment, Rule 64C, URCP

A prejudgment writ of attachment allows the plaintiff to seize the defendant's property. A writ of attachment can be granted if the plaintiff shows: (1) that the defendant is indebted to the plaintiff; (2) that the action is based on a contract, or that the defendant is a foreign corporation or not a resident of Utah, or the writ of attachment is based on statute; and (3) that the payment of the claim has not been secured by a property lien in Utah.

D. Temporary Restraining Order (TRO), Rule 65A, URCP

A TRO is a temporary court order that, if granted, would compel a party to do or refrain from doing certain acts. A TRO or preliminary injunction can be obtained if the applicant shows: (1) that the applicant would suffer irreparable harm without the order; (2) the threatened injury to the applicant would outweigh the damage caused by the proposed order; (3) the order would not be against public policy; and

(4) there is a substantial likelihood that the applicant will prevail on the merits of the underlying claim. URCP 65(A)(e).

E. Preliminary injunctions, Rule 65A, URCP

When a TRO is obtained a preliminary injunction hearing must be set within 10 days in order to continue the injunction.

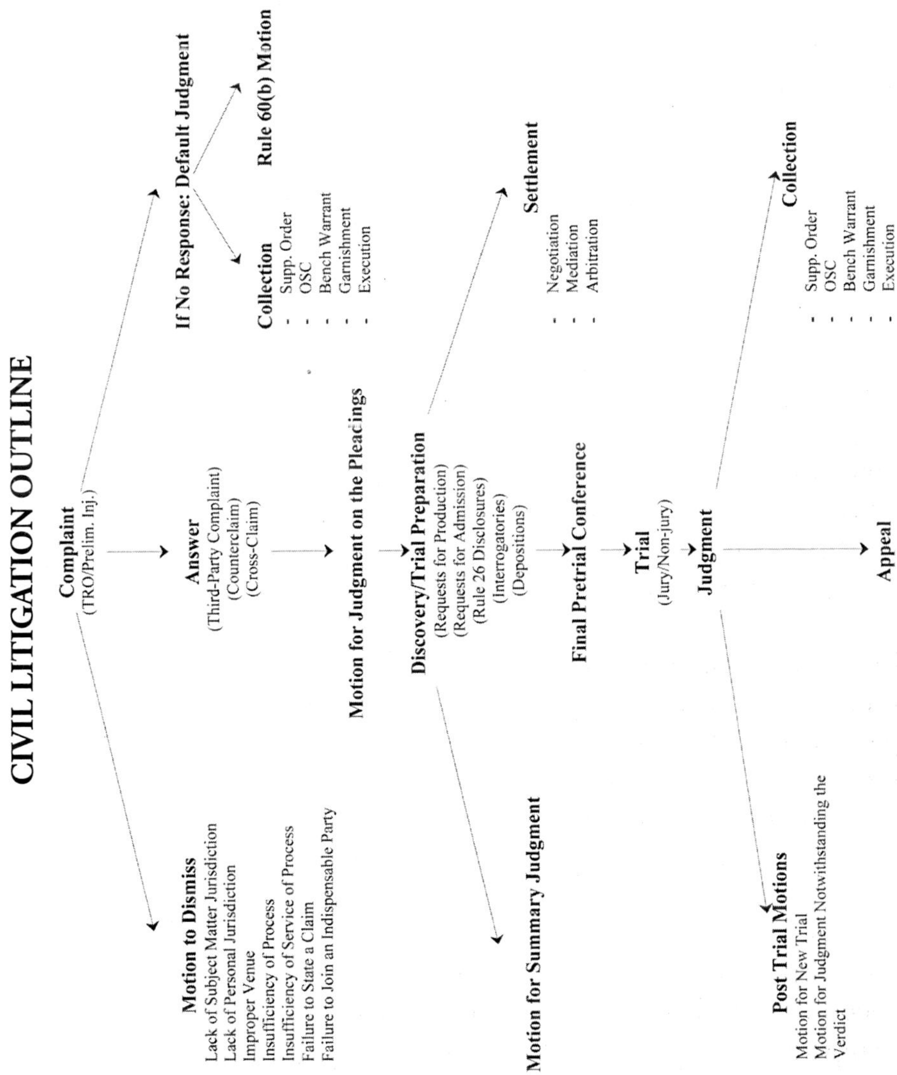
CIVIL LITIGATION OUTLINE
Complaint
(TRO/Prelim. Inj.)
Motion to Dismiss
- Lack of Subject Matter Jurisdiction
- Lack of Personal Jurisdiction
- Improper Venue
- Insufficiency of Process
- Insufficiency of Service of Process
- Failure to State a Claim
- Failure to Join an Indispensable Party
Answer
(Third-Party Complaint)
(Counterclaim)
(Cross-Claim)
If No Response: Default Judgment
Collection
- Supp. Order
- OSC
- Bench Warrant
- Garnishment
- Execution
Rule 60(b) Motion
Motion for Judgment on the Pleadings
Motion for Summary Judgment
Discovery/Trial Preparation
(Requests for Production)
(Requests for Admission)
(Rule 26 Disclosures)
(Interrogatories)
(Depositions)
Settlement
- Negotiation
- Mediation
- Arbitration
Final Pretrial Conference
Trial
(Jury/Non-jury)
Judgment
Post Trial Motions
- Motion for New Trial
- Motion for Judgment Notwithstanding the Verdict
Appeal
Collection
- Supp. Order
- OSC
- Bench Warrant
- Garnishment
- Execution

CHAPTER 4

CHOOSING A BUSINESS ENTITY

ANDREW L. HOWELL[1]
STEPHEN J. MAYFIELD[2]

Business Entities. In the world of business there are numerous entities or business structures which can be used to form and administer a business or commercial enterprise. While there are aspects of business which are common to all commercial enterprises, there is not one entity or structure that is appropriate for all. Each business will have its own set of priorities, capitalization and expense issues, owners and investors, and even differing personalities between members and management that must be considered. All of those factors are relevant in considering which business entity to use.

For some, the need for a simple structure is a priority, in which case a sole proprietorship or a single member LLC can be effective. For other, more sophisticated businesses, the need to structure a business based on tax planning can be of primary importance. Partnerships, limited liability companies and small business corporation (or S Corps) give business owners a variety of options for tax planning. For large operations, despite apparent negative tax implications, sometimes the

[1]**Andrew L. Howell** is the co-founding and Managing Partner at York Howell & Guymon, practicing exclusively in the areas of tax and estate planning and business and corporate structuring. Andrew is an undergraduate of the University of Utah and holds his legal degree from the S.J. Quinney School of Law at the University of Utah. Andrew has been nominated as Utah Legal Elite many times and currently serves the section chairman of the estate planning section of the Utah State Bar, having served on the executive committee for the last 4 years. An avid fly fisherman and outdoor enthusiast, he loves spending time with his wife and three children pursuing these passions.

[2]**Stephen J. Mayfield** is an attorney at York Howell & Guymon, practicing in the areas of corporate law, tax and estate planning. Stephen is a graduate of the University of Utah, and holds a J.D. from the Chicago-Kent College of Law (Illinois Institute of Technology) and a LL.M. in Taxation from Denver University. He is a Salt Lake City native who enjoys spending time in the outdoors with his family, skiing, cycling and playing guitar.

good old fashioned corporation (also known as a C Corp) is the best option. Often more than one type of entity will be appropriate for a given business. In order to determine which entity is best it is necessary to undergo a detailed analysis of numerous applicable factors and weighing of priorities.

Many professionals feel that tax benefits and liability protections are the primary forces to consider when determining what form of business structure is appropriate for the particular business needs. While the authors agree that these are two very important considerations, there are at least twenty (20) other factors that should reviewed as well. Many of these factors are beyond the scope of this chapter, but you are encouraged to consider such things as, marketing, branding, business succession and exit strategies, compartmentalization of risk, future financing and investment criteria, to name just a few.

This article is written to briefly outline the various business entities that are available to business owners and to provide details regarding the factors that weigh for or against use of each. It is not meant to be an exhaustive list of the entity types that are available and certainly not a complete dialogue of all factors to consider. Additionally, most of the focus of this chapter will be regarding entity structures appropriate for "for profit" entities. Non-profit or low profit enity planning is an animal all to it's own.

While tax issues are not always the guiding factor, proper tax structure for a business can often have a significant impact on the profitability of a business or on the attractiveness of a business to potential investors. Therefore in addition to exploration of the fundamentals regarding various business options, substantial reference is included to tax structuring and tax based operations.

Sole Proprietorship. A sole proprietorship ("SP") is not a formal business entity. It is the oldest form of doing business and has existed since long before state recognized entities. Simply stated, a SP is fancy way of saying "doing business on your own." It is owned by an individual and is the simplest form of business entity, though again it is not technically an entity. All of the income of the SP is taxable to the proprietor and all assets are likewise owned by the proprietor.

The owner of a SP can operate the business that is the subject of the SP in his or her own name or the SP can use a formal business name registration commonly referred to as Doing Business As or "DBA." A SP can obtain a DBA typically by registering with the county or counties where doing business. The SP then has a formal business name registration, which is protectable intellectual property, but that is the extent of any protections afforded to the owner of the SP. Although a SP can own property and assets, as well as enter into contracts and conduct business, the SP has no separation from the owner, and therefore the owner has no liability protection from the creditors and liabilities of the SP.

The only real advantage to operating a SP as opposed to any other business structure is the simplicity with which the SP can be organized and can conduct business. Unlike a corporation or limited liability company, there are no annual filings to be completed with the state where doing business, and tax reporting for the SP is done simply by reporting business income on Schedule C of the SP owner's personal income tax return.

In addition to concern for no limited liability protection, the SP has the other disadvantages of income still being subject to self-employment tax and fringe benefits are generally not deductible. The owner of the SP is not eligible for any fringe benefit that an employee may enjoy in other business structures.

General Partnership. It is common under the laws of the various states of the United States for a partnership to exist anytime there are two or more individuals who join or work together in a common commercial enterprise. If there is no formal written partnership agreement then state law regarding partnerships will govern the rules of administration and the duties of the partners involved.

A partnership exists as a separate entity from its partners. This means that the assets and property used in the partnership is deemed to be the property of the partnership rather than of the individual partners. Typically, partners will contribute cash, tangible property and even securities to the partnership as initial and ongoing capitalization. The individual partners' percentage of ownership in the partnership is determined by the amount of capital and property contributed in relation to the other partners.

In a general partnership all of the partners are deemed to be general partners, and as such they are jointly and severally liable for all of the liabilities of the partnership. Also, each partner of a general partnership has the authority to bind the partnership when the partner acts in the normal course of business. Common law rules and various state laws, including the Uniform Partnership Act (UPA) in states where it has been adopted govern the administration of partnerships.

Partnerships are also commonly referred to as a type of pass-through entity because all of the income and losses flow through from the partnership level to the individual partners. Upon formation each partner will have a capital account that is a reflection of the amount of capital or the value of any assets contributed to the partnership. A partner's capital account increases whenever the partner is allocated a portion of profits or revenue and the capital account decreases when a distribution is made to the partner. Taxation of a partnership is governed by subchapter K of the Internal Revenue Code, which is one of the more complex sections of the U.S tax code.

Limited Partnership. Limited partnerships are statutorily created entities. A limited partnership is typically formed by filing with the state a certificate of limited partnership. A limited partnership can also be formed by filing articles of conversion to convert an existing entity into a limited partnership. Similar to a general partnership there must be at least two partners, but in the limited partnership one or more partners may be the general partner with the remaining partners known as limited partners. The general partners have unlimited liability and typically manage or actively participate in the business of the limited partnership as well have full authority over all of the assets of the partnership. Because a general partner is subject to unlimited liability a general partner is often organized as a corporation or limited liability company in order to shield liability away from the individual general partner. However, it is this characteristic of the general partner being personally subject to the liabilities and debts of the general partnership which makes this entity choice less popular. This is especially true with the advent of the limited liability company as an entity option.

General partners typically have a small percentage of ownership anywhere from 1-10% of ownership. The general partnership interest is also often granted by the partnership in exchange for a promise to provide services to the partnership rather than in exchange for a capital contribution of assets or cash.

Limited partners do not actively participate in the general partnership and have no management control. Rather their involvement is intended and even required to be limited, essentially leaving the limited partner as only a passive investor. Because of this lack of management and active participation in the business of the partnership the limited partner has the protections of limited liability. This means that in the event of a lawsuit or other liability against the limited partnership, the limited partner's loss potential is limited only to the limited partner's contribution to the partnership.

The tax laws and regulations for partnerships under Subchapter K of the Internal Revenue Code apply equally to general and limited partnerships. Subchapter K provides the benefit of the partnership not being subject to double taxation because all income flows through to the partners in proportion to their respective percentage of ownership. The partnership also enjoys tax-free status on formation, meaning that all contributions to the partnership by the forming or later contributing partners are deemed tax free to the partner.

One characteristic that is unique to the partnership is the ability of partners to take tax-free distributions of property or assets from the partnership. There is no such thing as a tax-free distribution of property in a corporation. All distributions of property, including any property which has been originally contributed by a shareholder to a corporation, is deemed to be a dividend and is therefore subject to tax as such. Whereas with a partnership, partners have the flexibility to contribute to and receive liquidating distributions from a partnership without being taxed.

One of the primary tax benefits of a partnership is the ability to enter into qualified non-recourse finance to acquire assets such as real estate. When a partner contributes capital or assets to a partnership the partner receives a tax basis for the partnership interest. For tax purposes basis is an important tool because in a partnership a partner can deduct losses of the partnership up to the amount of the partner's basis in the partnership. Qualified non-recourse financing is a loan taken to acquire real property and there is no personal liability to the partners for repayment of the loan. A loan taken by the partnership that is qualified non-recourse is allocated to all of the partners, which results in an increase in the individual partners' basis in the partnership. Thus giving the partners greater basis from which losses of the partnership can be deducted.

Partnerships are notorious for one characteristic which can be financially burdensome, especially to limited partners. A partnership is generally not required to issue a distribution of profit to the partners. However, because the partnership is a flow-through entity with all partnership income being allocated or attributable to the individual partners on a pro-rata basis (unless a special allocation of income or loss is made – see below) each partner must pay tax on his or her share of partnership income regardless of whether a distribution of profit is distributed to the partners. This scenario is referred to as "Phantom Income." If a partnership is profitable then at the end of the year, the general or managing partner is required to issue a K-1 to each partner, which shows the partner's share of partnership income. A K-1is also provided to the IRS similar to how a W-2 is issued by employers. Upon receipt of the K-1 each partner is required to report his or her share of the partnership income with the partner's annual 1040 tax return. If the partnership does not distribute the revenue from the partnership and if the partner does not have sufficient outside revenue or capital sources available to pay the tax on the partner's share of partnership income it can leave the partner in a difficult situation with the IRS. This problem can be avoided by proper drafting of the partnership agreement.

Another special tax rule that exists in the partnership world is the ability of partners to make special allocations of income and loss. In general the partnership agreement governs how items of income, gain, loss or deduction will be allocated among the partners. If there is no partnership agreement or if the agreement does not provide guidance as to how those items are to be allocated then each partner's share of income, gain, loss or deduction will be determined according to the partner's percentage of ownership in the partnership. However, tax law governing partnerships gives flexibility for a partnership to allocate income or loss disproportionately as long as the allocation has what is referred as "substantial economic effect."[7] This ability to make special allocations gives the partnership the ability to return cash or assets to a partner before distributing income or other items of loss to other partners. This can allow the partnership to allocate income to partners in a lower income tax bracket or may allow the partnership to pass on losses of the partnership to partners with higher outside income.

The general partner manages the business of the partnership. As a result of that active participation in the business the general partner's income or share of the profits of the partnership is subject to self-employment tax.[8] Active participation is key concept in partnership law. If a limited partner participates in the operation of the partnership up to 500 or more hours per year then the limited partner will be deemed to have actively participated and his income or share of income from the partnership will be subject to self-employment tax.

General partners have a responsibility to the limited partners. General partners have sole control of the business of the partnership and have the ability to act for and contractually bind the partnership. The general partner is therefore accountable to the limited partners as a fiduciary. A general partner may breach such fiduciary duties by failing to notify the limited partners of the sale of a partnership asset. As a general rule a general partner may not take a business opportunity which should be shared with the partnership away from the partnership. Although a general partner does have the right to participate in similar business ventures to the extent that there is no conflict of interest, there is tension there between the general partners' duty to the partnership and the limited partnership and the general partners' freedom to pursue his or her own interest. One of the general partners' primary duties is disclosure of all information that is pertinent to the interests of the limited partners.

General partners may not exceed the authority granted to them in the partnership agreement to use partnership funds and assets for

---

[7]IRC Section 704 (b) and (e)

[8]If income arises from passive investments such as dividends, interest, capital gains, and rent it will not be subject to self-employment tax for the general partner.

anything other than the business and pursuits of the partnership. For example, if a general partner obtains a loan on behalf of the partnership from a creditor or lender who has knowledge that the loan will render the partnership insolvent or which is contrary to the terms of the partnership agreement, the lender may not then rely on the authority of the general partner to pursue a claim of default against the partnership.

Corporations. Corporations have long been used by business owners and investors as one of the most common business structures. A corporation is a separate business person with a separate identity from its shareholders. A corporation is formed by filing with the state articles of incorporation. Once articles are filed and accepted, the state will typically issue a corporate charter declaring the existence of the corporation and authorizing it to do business in that state.

Corporations have several important characteristics which are attractive to business owners and investors. First shareholders of a corporation enjoy limited liability, which means the shareholders are not personally subject to the debts and liabilities of the corporation and are not personally responsible for the corporation's activities. A corporation has centralized management where ownership through shareholders is distinct from the management operations provided by the management team or group customarily referred to as the board of directors. A corporation will typically also have officers who conduct the day to day operations of the corporation.

Shareholders of a corporation are its owners. They have the collective financial interest in the corporation and the power to elect the management of the corporation. The shareholders have borne the financial risk associated with forming and operating the corporation and are therefore granted power to dictate the terms by which the corporation will operate. Subject to federal and state securities laws, shareholders can freely sell or transfer their interests or shares in the corporation. It is often the ease with which one can acquire shares or stock in a company that makes investing in a corporation so attractive to investors. This is particularly true with regard to investing in large corporations whose shares are openly traded on one or more of the formal stock exchanges.

Corporations also enjoy indefinite existence, subject to state law. Typically the state statute governing formation and operation of a corporation provides that corporation duly formed in the state will exist for an indefinite period of time. Of course a corporation can cease operations and the shareholders elect to have the corporation dissolved with the assets distributed to the shareholders on pro rata basis.

In addition to the state law which governs corporate operations, a corporation is generally governed by bylaws of operations commonly known simply as the bylaws. The bylaws are typically written by an attorney or a qualified business advisor of the corporation and are accepted by resolution of the shareholders. The bylaws outline the rules of operation for the corporation as previously determined by the shareholders or as recommended by legal counsel. Once the bylaws are in place the shareholders, directors and officers are bound to act according to its terms. Of course bylaws can be modified but a majority or sometimes even a unanimous vote of the shareholders is required to do so.

The management structure of a corporation is one of its primary characteristics which makes the corporation unique and in many cases complex. As mentioned above, shareholders assumed the financial risk to form and capitalize the corporation. As a result the board of directors and officers owe the shareholders certain duties, such as the duty of care and the duty of loyalty. These duties are akin to fiduciary duties and the members of the board in particular are expected to act in the best interest of the shareholders.

It is important to understand the relationship between ownership of a corporation through its shareholders and the management conducted through its board of directors and officers. The shareholders are the owners, but at least in the case of large corporations with numerous shareholders, the shareholders are not able or inclined to manage the business of the corporation. The shareholders elect a board of directors, which generally consists of an odd number of directors somewhere between three and nine members. The board of directors often is made up of various individuals with specific knowledge and experience regarding the operations of the corporation and its business, or the board will include individuals with specialized training, such as business lawyers or CPAs, whose experience and expertise is useful in determining what is best for the corporation.

The procedure and timing for election of the members of the board of directors is usually outlined in the corporation bylaws. Board of directors elections generally occur every year or every other year and will often include staggered director elections, meaning that only a certain number of directors will stand for reelection each year. The practice of staggered elections is seen as beneficial to a corporation as a way to maintain continuity among the board. Staggered board elections ensures that every time there is an election at least some number of directors will remain, and therefore the process of overseeing the business of the corporation will always include at least some directors who have been involved from the prior year.

The board of directors will typically meet at least once per year but in many cases the board will meet on a bi-annual, quarterly or even monthly basis depending upon the frequency with which the board is directed to meet pursuant to the bylaws of the corporation. Typically the bylaws of the corporation will enable the board to meet as often as the members board, or some minimum required number, may feel is necessary.

The day to day operations of a corporation are conducted by the officers of the corporation. The officers are generally the president, vice-president, treasurer and secretary. Other titles of corporate officers are chief executive officer, chief operating officer, chief financial officer and even chief legal counsel. These terms are often used interchangeably with the positions of president, vice-president, treasurer and secretary. The duties and titles of such officers are generally outlined in the bylaws.

One of the benefits to operating a corporation is that corporations have been used in business for many years. Most states have a long legal history of corporate operations, which includes statutes and existing case law that in some states goes back literally hundreds of years. The existence of long-standing statutes and case law makes operations of a corporation predictable. Delaware is a state that is often recognized as having very good corporate statutes and case law. Many other states have enacted statutes governing corporate operations that are either modeled on or largely influenced by Delaware's corporate statutes.

State laws governing corporate operations often require various formalities. As noted, formation requires the filing of articles of incorporation. Typically a corporation is also required to file with the state an annual list of officers and to renew its charter. This is usually to be accompanied by a filing fee seen by the state as a reasonable fee paid in exchange for state recognition of the corporation and for privilege of operating under the laws and protections of that state. Additional formalities that are generally required include annual shareholder meetings, annual directors meetings, annual accounting and report to shareholder, annual shareholder election of directors and probably most important maintaining proper separation between the shareholders and the company. Small corporations sometimes run into trouble when shareholders also occupy positions on the board and as officers, and in doing so comingle the assets or funds of the corporation with their own funds and assets. Such a breakdown can often lead to what is referred to as "piercing the corporate veil" by creditors of the shareholders of the corporation. When the corporate veil is pierced the corporation is disregarded, the limited liability protection for with the corporation exists is set aside and the shareholders can be personally liable for the debts and liabilities of the corporation. In order to maintain the integrity of the corporation, proper working and economic formalities must be maintained.

A corporation can be taxed either as a C Corporation or as an S Corporation or sub-chapter S small business corporation (also colloquially referred to as an S Corp). It is not uncommon for the shareholder of a corporation taxed as an S Corp to state he or she owns an S Corp. The reality is there is no such thing as an S Corp for formation purposes. Rather corporations exist due to formation at the state level due to filing of articles of incorporation. How the corporation will be taxed is function of what type of tax structure the shareholders elect for the corporation. The default tax structure of a corporation upon formation is for it to be taxed as C Corporation. If the shareholders or management team of the corporation elect for the corporation to be taxed as an S Corporation they will file a Form 2553 with the IRS thereby informing the IRS that the corporation has elected to be taxed accordingly.

To further complicate the issue; it is important to note that when an entity is formed, it is formed at the given state level. If a Utah corporation is formed, the state of Utah does not care what type of corporation you are (i.e. "C" corp or "S" corp), it is the IRS that is concerned with the form of taxation. This is an important distinction as other entity types, LLCs for example, can also "elect" to be treated as S Corporations with the IRS while maintaining their status as an LLC with the given state of their formation. This can result in confusion and should be done carefully as when an LLC elects to be treated as an S Corporation, the specific rules to be qualified as an S Corporation must now be met by the LLC. For example; the LLC will now have to make sure there are less than 100 owners (or owner groups) of the LLC, all members of the LLC are qualified shareholders of an S Corporation and the LLC can have only one class of ownership. Preferred and common interests in the LLC will no longer be allowed. These are all issues that are not present with an LLC that does not make an S Election as the IRS will assume the LLC is to be taxed as a partnership. The authors advise caution in proceeding this way in creating an LLC that will be taxed in a different manner.

The benefits of existing as a C Corporation include the ability to take large deductions for providing numerous fringe benefits for employees. However, the downside of operating as a C Corporation is that the corporation is subject to double taxation. This means that the corporation will pay tax on its revenue as earned, and the shareholders will be taxed on their individual share of profits distributed as dividends. In order to ameliorate the effect of double taxation large corporations often seek to pay as much in fringe benefits and executive compensation as possible to mitigate the corporate level tax. If a corporation requires numerous employees to maintain the operations of the corporation then a C Corporation structure may be the best structure in order to provide fringe benefits which are attractive to potential employees.

When a corporation elects to be taxed as an S Corp it will then become a flow-through entity somewhat similar to a partnership, but an S Corp is much more than an incorporated partnership and there are key differences between the two. Under the current Internal Revenue Code an S Corp has no more than 100 shareholders. Shareholders may only be taxpaying U.S. resident individuals and there can only be one class of stock. This means that shareholders of an S Corp must receive distributions based upon percentage of ownership, and there cannot be any preferred class of shareholders.

Non-Profit Corporations. As previously mentioned, only a brief discussion will take place regarding Non-Profit Corporations. Non-profit planning, including not just Non-Profit Corporations, but private foundations, trusts and low profit corporations and LLCs all have very strict rules and guidelines that should be fully investigated.

A non-profit organization is typically a non-profit corporation and is organized at the state level similar to any other corporation. Its existence is generally for the purpose of benefit some specific social cause, such as a charity, school, sporting event or other enterprise which exists to benefit a cause rather than to generate a profit. A non-profit organization is formed at the state level but only obtains federal tax benefits (for itself and contributors) after it applies to the Internal Revenue Service to be recognized as a tax-exempt organization such as a 501(c)(3) organization. The Internal Revenue Code allows for certain entities to be tax-exempt for certain social purposes, these include organizing to be a private foundation with a charitable purpose or to be a charitable supporting organization. The moniker of 501(c)(3) refers to the Internal Revenue Tax Code Section 501(c)(3). There are numerous other Tax Code Sections under which a non-profit organization can seek tax exempt status.

Limited Liability Company. For many years the partnership structure was the fundamental business entity for start-up enterprises. However, due to the susceptibility of personal liability by the general partners, and even limited partners who were deemed to actively participate in the business, as well as due to strict partnership rules regarding administration and taxation, business owners began to seek other options with which to operate small businesses. Prior to the advent of the limited liability company the only option available to business owners for limited liability protection was to form a corporation. However, due to the formalities required in maintaining a corporation coupled often with disadvantageous corporate tax laws, business owners sought for another entity type to run small businesses. The answer came when Wyoming enacted the first limited liability company statute in 1977, interestingly created similarly in some respects to the 1892 German GmbH Code and the Panamanian LLC.

A limited liability company, or LLC, is formed by an organizer who files articles of organization, or in some states by filing a certificate of organization. LLCs have numerous characteristics which make them attractive to small business owners and investors. The first of which is limited liability for all members. In a corporation the investors are referred to as shareholders who receive shares for their respective investment. In the LLC a contributing person becomes a member and typically receives units and/or a percentage of ownership in the LLC. The limited liability protection provided to LLC members allows both the passive investment members and those members taking an active role in the administration and management of the business to enjoy limited liability protection. The LLC member's liability is limited to his or her interest or investment in the company. Although a member can be found personally liable in the event of any personal guarantee made by the member or in the event of actions that allow for claims against the member on the grounds of laws governing tort, fraud or illegal actions.

The LLC provides great flexibility for its members. State laws governing LLCs generally provide wide latitude for members of an LLC to dictate the terms of operation and to reduce those terms to an operating agreement. Of course in the absence of an operating agreement state laws generally provide default rules for administration, but the members can often contract around or out of those default rules. This makes for large opportunity for various types of investors, whether passive, active, preferred or a combination of investment options.

An LLC is a pass-through entity just like a partnership, and the default tax structure is for the LLC to be taxed as a partnership subject to Subchapter K of the Internal Revenue Code. However, as previously mentioned, an LLC can also be taxed as an S Corp which is preferable for LLCs that provide professional services or that are in the business of selling goods. An LLC can even be a C Corp if so desired by the members. Many states allow for single member LLCs, in which case the LLC will be taxed as a sole proprietorship in the absence of any other tax structure designation by the single member.

One disadvantage to operating an LLC is lack of uniformity between the states. Therefore when a business is operating in more than one state it may face unexpected rules or consequences by doing business in a particular state. Various states treat LLC activities and taxation differently, such as differences with minimum capital taxes, fees issued on the number of K-1s issued to members and potential taxes when assets are transferred to the LLC. Some states require a franchise tax or a minimum fee payable to the state for the benefit of operating as an LLC in that state. Some states such as Illinois, New Hampshire, Tennessee and Wisconsin subject LLCs to an income tax based on percentages. Other states impose taxes based on capital accounts or the number of members. California is well known as one of the most aggressively taxing states of LLCs with its annual fee and additional tax based on profitability.

The LLC is managed either by members or by managers elected by the members. A person does not typically have to be a member to be a manager, unless required by the members in the operating agreement. The LLC management structure can be simple with as little as one manager, or it can be as complex as a corporation with a board of managers (or board of directors) with company officers such as president, secretary and treasurer. Again the flexibility allowed by most LLC statutes gives the members the ability to determine rules of administration and management that meet the needs and circumstances of the LLC as they arise. It is not uncommon for the members of an LLC to amend the terms of the company operating agreement multiple times as circumstances change and as the number of members and investors increase.

The use of an LLC is excellent for holding passive investments, such as rental real estate, investment in stock portfolios and other interest or passive income generating investments. The LLC is attractive in this scenario because of the ease by which the members can place property and investments in and take out of the LLC. Also, because of the limited liability protection afforded to members of the LLC, the LLC is an effective device for asset protection by the member from his or her personal creditors. In many states the sole remedy for the creditor of a member of an LLC is for the creditor to obtain a "charging order" against the member's interest in the LLC. This means that if a creditor obtains a personal judgment against the member, rather than being able to get the member's interest in the company, or worse attach the company's assets, the creditor only obtains the charging order which is essentially a lien against the member's share of LLC distributions. The assets of the company remain protected and the distributions remain protected as well because generally the management of the company will have discretion whether to make a distribution. Some states allow for foreclosure of a charging order, but only after another lengthy legal proceeding by which the creditor must show by a stringent legal standard that a distribution is unlikely. Regardless, the structure provides the member substantial asset protection and at worst will typically provide the member with leverage in reaching a settlement that is favorable to the member.

As with all entity types, LLCs are not without limitations. As mentioned above the default tax structure of the LLC is for it to be taxed as a partnership. This means that the same tax issues that exist with a partnership, such as potential for phantom income, exist with LLCs as well. Also, due to the ease at which an LLC can be formed and operated often business partners and co-investors will form an LLC without taking the time to fully understand the default state law governing the LLC or to obtain a comprehensive operating agreement. In the absence of such an agreement that clearly defines the intent of the parties, state law will govern which can often lead to unintended consequences, particularly with regard to determination of ownership percentages, distributions of profits, taxation, succession of ownership, management power and dispute resolution among members or managers.

Many state LLC statues include nuances which allow for the creation of different types of LLCs such as a Series LLC, PLLC, L3C and the Restricted LLC. The Series LLC allows for the creation of one LLC but allows that each asset of the LLC will be treated separately for liability protection purposes. In the authors' opinion, series LLCs are not as protective of a structure as another structure in which there is a parent LLC or "holding company" that then owns 100% interest in separate single member LLCs to compartmentalize risk. This is due to numerous court cases that have attacked the efficacy of the series LLC and the non-uniformity of series LLC statutes throughout the Country. Not all states allow for series LLCs and although they had been popular a few years ago, many planners are simply choosing not to use them anymore due to these issues. Although the series LLC may contain numerous rental properties, in theory if there is a liability attributable to one of the properties, the other properties are deemed to be held in a separate LLC, thereby making the non-liability related properties unavailable to the creditor of the LLC. In order to maintain the limited liability between the assets it is generally recommended that each separate income-producing asset be administered separately from an accounting perspective. In essence, each series under the series LLC must be run with it's own books and accounting and therefore results in similar complexities to just having the parent holding company with single member LLCs underneath.

The PLLC or Professional Limited Liability Company is useful to professional service providers such as physicians, attorneys, accountant and architects. While no type of entity will protect a professional service provider from personal liability attributable to the professional services provided, it does create a formal structure from which the professional can conduct business and any contractual or other business related liabilities not attributable directly to the providing of professional services will be subject to the limited liability structure available to all LLCs.

The L3C or low-profit LLC provides the financial benefits of the LLC for business administration but also gives social benefits enjoyed by the non-profit corporation. The L3C is a for-profit company and is generally engaged in a commercial enterprise, but the purpose of the commercial enterprise is typically to benefit some social cause or purpose. The L3C is also organized in conjunction with a non-profit organization to provide a profit-generating format that will benefit the non-profit but not subject the non-profit to taxation and cause the non-profit to lose its tax exempt status. This is especially attractive for private foundations. Each year private foundations are required to donate 5% of average net assets for charitable purposes. This 5% can be contributed to a L3C, which company can take higher risks and attract private sector investment which might not ordinarily support a charity or socially conscious enterprise.

To the author's knowledge only Nevada allows for a Restricted LLC. This rare entity was established in Nevada for advanced estate planning purposes to enable strategic gift giving that will allow for a potentially higher discount on the value of a gift due to lack of marketability and lack of control by the member. The Nevada law allows for a restriction on distributions up to ten years which is designed to deflate the value of partial ownership interests.

CHAPTER 5

SOLE PROPRIETORSHIPS

LANGDON T. OWEN[1]

A sole proprietorship is one human being doing business without a formal organization, that is, without a wholly owned corporation or a single member limited liability company. Thus, all business is done in the individual's name or in an assumed business name held by the individual. The individual would be fully responsible for all debts and liabilities of his or her business, and would be sued personally and could have all non-exempt assets, including personal assets or investments having nothing to do with the proprietorship business, seized by reason of such business debts and liabilities.

Start-up expenses for doing business without any form of organization certainly would not include any organization expenses. The start-up process would be very simple: get any necessary licenses and zoning approvals, file an assumed name application if such a name is desired, and go at it. If any employees will be hired, a separate tax identification number would be needed, otherwise, the individual may use his or her Social Security number.

All income from the business would be reported on the individual's form 1040 tax return, likely using Schedule C. Individuals do not need to qualify to do business in other states, but may need to register any

[1]Langdon T. Owen, Jr. is a member of the law firm of Cohne Kinghorn, p.c. in Salt Lake City, Utah. Mr. Owen is a transactional lawyer who practices in such areas as estate and tax planning, business and commercial transactions, health care law, nonprofit organizations, probate, and real estate. He has practiced law since 1977. He holds a Juris Doctor degree from the University of Utah (1977) and a Bachelor of Arts degree from the University of California, Berkeley (1973, with great distinction).

assumed name. To the extent business is done in more than one state, income tax returns would need to be filed in each state with an income tax, and normal sales tax and other tax and regulatory requirements would need to be met in each such state.

If the proprietor has employees or other agents, all employment laws, tax withholding rules, and other laws relating to employees or agents will apply. Among these applicable rules, the rule of respondeat superior and other agency rules will make the employing sole proprietor personally liable for any actions done in the scope of the employment or agency by the employee or agent.

The simplicity of a sole proprietorship may be attractive to people doing modest, relatively risk free businesses. Business insurance should be obtained; an individual's homeowner's policy will very likely exclude any coverage for business operations. Insurance will be the only real protection the sole proprietor will have against liabilities.

Although some business people think that because banks and some vendors or customers will require personal guarantees of the individual, a single owner organization will have little value. This view can be mistaken, because there are a number of areas of risk for which an organization providing limited liability can add a level of protection, including limiting and isolating liabilities arising from uninsured tortious acts of employees or from non-guaranteed contacts with vendors, customers, and others. As will be pointed out in this work, no form of organization provides protection from all risk, but a form of organization providing limited liability should be at least seriously considered for almost every business larger than a child's lemonade stand.

CHAPTER 6

GENERAL PARTNERSHIPS, JOINT VENTURES, AND LIMITED LIABILITY PARTNERSHIPS

LANGDON T. OWEN[1]

Let's spend some time going into moderate detail about general partnerships. This attention is justifiable because the general partnership is the oldest form of business organization involving more than one person, and, as such, sets the stage for later forms of organization which distinguish themselves from partnerships either by a little (such as limited partnerships or limited liability companies) or by a lot (such as corporations). Thus, a number of key features of partnerships are either removed or carried over (perhaps in a modified form) in other types of organizations. Understanding such matters as to partnerships will help greatly in the understanding of the other types of organization.

This attention is also justified because partnerships and the types of organizations closely related to them (i.e., the unincorporated partnership derived forms of business organization known as limited partnerships and limited liability companies) have undergone the greatest changes under recent Utah legislation. The corporate form has been much less changed. Partnerships have had the most profound changes; the 100 year old act governing general partnerships was totally replaced with a brand new act based on an entirely new separate entity paradigm. Thus

---

[1]Langdon T. Owen, Jr. is a member of the law firm of Cohne Kinghorn, p.c. in Salt Lake City, Utah. Mr. Owen is a transactional lawyer who practices in such areas as estate and tax planning, business and commercial transactions, health care law, nonprofit organizations, probate, and real estate. He has practiced law since 1977. He holds a Juris Doctor degree from the University of Utah (1977) and a Bachelor of Arts degree from the University of California, Berkeley (1973, with great distinction).

much of what you think you know about general partnerships may no longer be so.

1. What Are They? General partnerships are a form of enterprise involving more than one person carrying on a business for profit. Joint ventures are a form of general partnership directed at a limited project. Sometimes the term "joint venture" is loosely used to describe a contractual relationship, usually rather close, between two or more parties but which is not actually a partnership (usually because losses and expenses or gain and income are not shared). If the definition of a partnership is met, a relationship will be a partnership even if the parties call it something else, thus distinguishing a mere contractual or ownership arrangement from a partnership can be critical.

It is very important to understand partnerships because it is the fallback form of organization that will apply where two or more persons (which may include organizations) do business in a common enterprise, and because where there is a partnership, each partner, without fault or other involvement, may become personally liable based on the acts of another partner in the scope of the business.

a. **Source of Rules.** At one time every state except Louisiana had adopted a version of the Uniform Partnership Act (1914). Utah's law was still based on this act until the Utah Uniform Partnership Act became effective January 1, 2014. UCA § 48-1d-101 *et seq*. We will focus on the new Utah law, which became effective in 2014. However, we will sometimes mention the prior partnership act for comparison and because the prior act is still effective until January 1, 2016, for partnerships existing before 2014, unless the partnership elects to be governed by the new Act. Unless otherwise specified, a reference to the Act is to the new 2014 Act; we will call the old act the "old act." The old act is found at UCA §§ 48-1-1through 48-1-48.

b. **Partnership Definitions.** General partnerships formed in 2014 and later are governed by the Act, UCA §§ 48-1d-101 *et seq.*, which defines general partnerships. The Act also defines a variation on general partnerships, called limited liability partnerships (discussed below in this general partnership section), which should not be confused with limited partnerships or limited liability companies. The limited liability partnership provisions, in addition to dealing with domestic (i.e., Utah) and foreign (i.e., other states) entities also include provisions dealing with professional services limited liability partnerships. See UCA §§ 48-1d-1101 *et seq.* for limited liability partnerships generally, 48-1d-1201 *et seq.* for foreign limited liability partnerships, and 48-1d-1301 for professional services limited liability partnerships.

i. Partnership. A partnership is an association of two or more persons (a term including organizations) to carry on as co-owners a business for profit, formed under the Act or becoming subject to the Act by a merger, interest exchange, conversion, domestication, or the coming of January 1, 2016. UCA § 48-1d-102(12). It includes limited liability partnerships. If a partnership is not a limited liability partnership (or a limited partnership (under a separate statute)) the partnership is usually called a general partnership due to the general liability of the partners. Partners are liable, jointly and severally for all partnership debts, obligations, and liabilities. UCA § 48-1d-306(1). (However, as discussed below, there is an exception for limited liability partnerships.)

ii. Joint Venture. A joint venture is not defined in the New Act and does not need to be. Under the old act it was an association of two or more persons to carry on as co-owners a single business enterprise. UCA § 48-1-3.1. "The parties must combine their property, money, effects, skill, labor and knowledge. As a general rule, there must be (1) a community of interest in the performance of the common purpose, (2) a joint proprietary interest in the subject matter, (3) a mutual right to control, (4) a right to share in the profits, and (5) unless there is an agreement to the contrary, a duty to share in any losses which may be sustained." *Bassett v. Baker*, 530 P.2d 1, 2 (Utah 1974). Although the *Bassett* court originally established these elements for the purpose of determining the existence of a joint venture, they have since been used to determine the existence of partnerships as well. See *Mardanlou v. Ghaffarian*, 135 P.3d 904 (Ut. App. 2006) (applying the *Bassett* elements to a partnership). The *Bassett* description is still useful. The definition of "partnership" under the New Act is certainly broad enough to cover a joint venture as a partnership, but one with a more limited scope of operations.

iii. Limited Liability Partnership. A limited liability partnership (abbreviated as "LLP") is a partnership that has filed a statement of qualification under the provisions of UCA § 48-1d-1101, *et seq*. A limited liability partnership is not the same thing as a limited partnership; limited partnerships have their own governing statute as a separate form of organization (discussed later in this work). A limited liability partnership is a variation of a general partnership, but without general liability.

The statement of qualification for a limited liability partnership needs to be approved by the vote or consent necessary to amend the partnership agreement, or, if there are specific provisions in the agreement relating to contributions to the partnership, the vote or consent necessary to amend those specific provisions. UCA § 48-1d-1101(2). For example, if the generally required vote to amend the agreement were a simple majority but it would require a 75% majority to amend the provisions on obligations to contribute to the partnership, a 75% majority vote would be needed to authorize filing a statement of qualification.

The difference between a normal general partnership and a limited liability partnership is that no partner of a limited liability partnership is personally liable, directly or indirectly, by way of contribution or otherwise, for the debts, obligations, or other liabilities of the partnership. UCA § 48-1d-306(3). Naturally, everyone is liable for their own negligence or misconduct because the liability limitation is limited to being or acting as a partner. Also, professionals are expressly made liable for their acts or omissions. UCA § 48-1d-306(6). Further, any limitation of liability is subject to rules allowing the piercing of the veil between the organization and its owners so that in cases of abuse creditors of one can reach assets of the other; this issue has mostly arisen with corporations and limited liability companies in the past, but the rules have more general applicability. It is always wise to look to good insurance coverage as the first line of defense, and entity limits on liability as the second line of defense. Partnerships qualifying as LLPs will want to amend inconsistent partnership agreements with provisions which assumed full general liability because such provisions would otherwise confuse the liability issue. However, the liability protection applies despite contrary provisions in the partnership agreement as it existed immediately before the vote or consent to qualify. UCA § 48-1d-306(3)(a).

All forms of organization providing for limited liability require a filing with the state; in Utah the filing is made with the Utah Department of Commerce, Division of Corporations and Commercial Code ("Division"). This is true of corporations, limited liability companies, and limited partnerships, and it is true of LLPs as well. UCA § 48-1d-1101 (for LLP). The failure to maintain the filing by a simple annual report filed with the Division, or otherwise losing the effect of the filing (e.g., it can be revoked by the state in certain cases), will result in the organization's either being wound up (if the partners so choose) or continuing but as a general partnership with general liability. UCA §§ 48-1d-1102 (administrative revocation).

iv. Determining Partnership Status. The statute provides some additional rules to determine if an association is a partnership or if a person is a partner or liable as a partner. These rules apply both to general partnerships and to LLPs. They are important in determining whether a partnership exists and whether a person is liable as a general partner to third parties. From these provisions, we learn:

- Receipt of a share of profits creates a presumption that the person is a partner, but no such inference is drawn where the profits are paid in these ways: as a debt by installments or otherwise, as wages for compensation to an employee or independent contractor for services, as rent to a landlord, as an annuity or retirement or health benefit as to a deceased or retired partner, as interest on a loan though the amounts vary with profits, or as consideration for the sale of the good will of a business by installments or otherwise. UCA § 48-1d-202(3)(c).
- Mere co-ownership (joint tenancy, tenancy-in-common, etc.) does not alone establish a partnership, whether or not the co-owners share profits made by the use of the property. UCA § 48-1d-202(3)(a).
- Mere sharing of gross returns alone (i.e., instead of bottom line profits after expenses) does not establish a partnership, whether or not the sharers have a common right or interest in the property from which the returns are derived. UCA § 48-1d-202(3)(b).
- A person claiming (orally, in writing, or by action) to be a

partner in an actual or nonexistent partnership who really is not one, becomes liable to third persons who give credit either acting in reliance on the representation as to an actual or apparent partnership, or acting even without knowing of the representation where the person has made the representation in a public manner. If partnership liability results, the person is liable as if a partner. Otherwise, the representing person and all persons (partners or not) who consent to the contract or representation are jointly and severally liable. This is partnership by estoppel, or liability as a purported partner, as to obligations to third persons. UCA § 48-d1-308. It does not create any actual partnership rights.

c. **Formation and State Qualification.** No written agreement is needed to form a general partnership, and no central filing is needed (other than for limited liability partnerships). Utah allows a "statement of partnership authority" to be filed. UCA § 48-1d-303. The statement of authority may be relied on by third persons in determining who has authority to bind the partnership to third persons, where the third person gives value in reliance on the grant of authority unless the third person has knowledge to the contrary or the statement of authority has been cancelled, modified, or superseded. UCA § 48-1d-303(5).

i. Law Governing. In Utah, general partnerships formed after 2013 are governed by UCA § 48-1d-101, *et seq.* Under general conflicts of laws principles, a partnership without an express choice of law provision would be governed by the law of the state where the contract is made or the state with the most significant contacts. This may not be clear where parties are from different states. States, like Utah, with a version of the Revised Uniform Partnership Act follow a different rule and provide that the internal affairs of a general partnership are governed by the law of the state in which the partnership has its principal office. This, too, may not always be clear with partners spread among a number of states. Also, if the partnership is a Utah limited liability partnership having filed and qualified in Utah for that status, Utah law governs. UCA § 48-1d-104.

ii. Use of Assumed Name. An assumed name filing and the appointment of a registered agent are needed if the partnership does business under a name different from the names of its partners. UCA §§ 42-2-5 and 42-2-11. The penalties for not doing so are that access to the courts to pursue a claim, counterclaim, etc., is denied until the filing requirements are met, and a late filing fee penalty may be charged. UCA § 42-2-10. Filings of assumed names are only effective for three years and need to be re-filed to remain effective. UCA § 42-2-8.

ii. Qualification in Other States. General partnerships with only individuals as partners generally don't need to become qualified to do business in other states. However, they will need to comply with the other state's assumed name requirements and if claiming limited liability partnership status, will need to comply with the other state's registration requirements. Partnerships with corporate or other organizations as partners may need to qualify to do business in other jurisdictions. Business licensing laws will apply wherever a partnership operates. Partnerships which are limited liability partnerships will need to register in other states. See UCA § 48-1d-1202 requiring foreign limited liability partnerships to register in Utah.

2. Certain Features. A number of noteworthy features relate to general partnerships. Except as to general liability, these features also apply to LLPs.

a. **Owners.** There is no such thing as a single-owner partnership. Any form of organization or individuals can be partners without any upward limitation in number, but there must be at least two. The partner's rights are its rights to a transferrable interest (UCA § 48-1d-602) and an equal right to participate in management (UCA § 48-1d-402(1). As we will see later, these two aspects of a partnership interest are separable. Differences arising in the ordinary course of partnership activities are decided by a majority of the partners. UCA § 48-1d-402(4). The partner's transferrable interest in the partnership is the right as initially owned by a person (although it could later be transferred to someone else) as a partner, to receive distributions. UCA § 48-1d-102(25). This transferrable interest is personal property. UCA § 48-1d-602. A person may become a partner without either acquiring a transferable interest or making or being obligated to make a contribution to the partnership. UCA § 48-1d-401. A partner is not a co-owner of partnership property and thus has no separate right to transfer partnership property voluntarily or involuntarily. UCA § 48-1d-601. A partner is not entitled to remuneration for services for the partnership except reasonable compensation for winding-up UCA § 48-1d-402(3).

b. **Entity Theory**. Under earlier law, the owners of a general partnership were, for most purposes, treated in the aggregate, with the partnership being a relationship among them, not an entity. This is no longer the case for Utah general partnerships. Under the new paradigm of the Act, partnerships are now treated as entities separate from their partners. UCA § 48-1d-201. This is a very profound change. Partnerships could and still will hold title to property in the partnership name (UCA § 48-1d-203) but it is no longer a "tenancy in partnership" among the partners. Partnerships could and still can sue and be sued in the partnership name. Ut. Rul. of Civ. Proc. ("URCP") 17(d). A partner can only use or possess partnership property on behalf of the partnership. UCA § 48-1d-402(2). This was true under the old act as well. Now, however, the organization itself is the focus not the partners.

The partnership is no longer dissolved on a change in the relationship caused by a partner ceasing to be involved in the carrying on of the business. Under the old act dissolution was a change in who was in the relationship and did not generally lead to winding up. (See old act at former UCA § 48-1-26.) Rather, as we will see below, under the new Act certain events are required to trigger dissolution and wind-up, and a dissolution will lead to wind-up and will not be treated as only a separate change in relationship (even without wind-up) as under former law. Basically, under the old act an addition or subtraction of a partner created a new relationship, thus, in effect, a new partnership. No longer.

c. **Business**. Partnerships are business organizations only; there are no not-for-profit partnerships. UCA § 48-1d-102(12). Just about any business can be in partnership form. (Some financial institutions and certain other businesses are required to be corporations.)

d. **Flexible**. There are minimal statutory requirements for general partnerships. They are mostly creatures of contract. Thus, they can be very flexible for determining how profits, losses, particular items of income or expense, or distributions are to be shared among the partners at various times and under various circumstances. The complexity often comes in determining the tax effects of such arrangements.

c. **Tax**. Let's review in very broad strokes some key tax features of partnerships. These features can be critical in choosing a form of organization. Partnership tax rules are very different from corporate tax rules.

i. Partnership Tax Status. The federal income tax rules for partnerships have their own methods for determining which organizations are subject to the partnership tax rules. These methods overlap with, but are not identical with, state law methods for determining partnership existence. See Internal Revenue Code ("IRC") § 7701(a)(2).

ii. Pass Through and Allocations. In general, partnership tax rules provide for a pass through of income and deductions, etc. to the partners without the entity level tax typical of the corporate tax regime (at least without a special S-corporation election). Partnership tax rules allow for great flexibility including the special allocation of tax items among the partners impossible for any corporation with or without the special S-corporation election. With a special allocation, for example, one partner may receive all profits and another all losses for a period of time, if the arrangement has substantial economic effect. The complexity of partnership taxation derives from the need to have some limits to such great flexibility. IRC Subchapter K, § 701, *et seq*. These rules can lead to some timing surprises where a tax benefit today can lead to tax liability tomorrow, but without a cash distribution to help pay the tax (sometimes termed "phantom income"). Tax effects pass through to partners whether or not there are any distributions. This can mean that if the partnership has profits, but the partnership does not make a distribution, the partners must pay their taxes on their shares of profits from some other source of funds. This can be ameliorated by agreement. Distributions have their own tax effect designed to allow but one level of taxation, at the partner level.

iii. Step Up Basis. Partnership taxed organizations are the only ones in which it is possible to obtain on death (and certain other events) not only a step up in income tax basis for a partnership interest (outside basis), but also, and importantly, obtain a similar step up in basis for the partner's share of the assets held by the partnership itself (inside basis). IRC §§ 754 and 743. This is a highly desirable feature because it can truly eliminate built in gains at death for a partner's family.

iv. Self-Employment Tax. Partners who provide services are not employees. IRC § 707(a) and (c); Rev.Rul. 69-194, 1969-1 C.B. 256. They are not subject to wage withholding for federal income tax or Social Security (FICA, Federal Insurance Contributions Act) or Medicare taxes. Rather they pay income tax through the filing of quarterly estimated tax reports, and pay self-employment tax (OASDI, Old Age Survivor and Disability Insurance) at the same rates with the same limits as the FICA and Medicare tax, except that what would be the employee's half of these taxes in the corporate tax regime are deductible by the partner. IRC § 164(f). A partner's tax base for these purposes is not W-2 income, because they are not employees, but is their full distributive share less certain take-away items such as rents, royalties, and capital gain, designed to reduce the share to approximately the amount attributable to personal service income. See IRC §§ 1401 and 1402.

v. Benefits. Many compensation-type programs are available to partners as well as employees. For example, although the contributions are determined by a different formula (based on distributive shares with adjustments (i.e., take-aways) instead of on W-2 income (with some possible adjustments as with corporations), partnerships may have, and partners may benefit under, tax qualified retirement plans such as profit sharing and 401K type plans – a very important benefit. Health insurance is available; the premiums are not deductible by the partnership, but are deductible above the line (i.e., in determining adjust gross income) on the partner's personal tax returns. IRC § 162(1)(1)(B). However, other benefits are more restricted; for example, group term life insurance, cafeteria plans, meals and lodging at the employer's premises, etc., are not available for partners as self-employed persons.

f. **Tax Audit Authority**. Federal income tax issues relating to partnership operations are audited and determined at the partnership level unless a special exception applies for small partnerships (10 or fewer partners, none of whom are nonresident aliens or any kind of tax flow-through or tax-disregarded entity; a typical revocable trust is a grantor trust and thus a disregarded entity which would prevent application of the exception). IRC §§ 6621, 6231(a)(1)(B). Where the exception does not apply, a tax matters partner will be named either by the partnership, or if this is not done, by a fallback rule appointing the partner with the largest profits interest. All partners may participate in proceedings, but the tax matters partner decides whether to litigate and in what forum and is required to keep partners informed. See IRC §§ 6223(g), 6226(a) and (b).

g. **State Taxes**. Partners are generally required to file nonresident tax returns in all states in which the partnership does business. This is true in Utah, too. Some states require or allow combined reporting by the partnership in lieu of individual filings, but Utah does not. Some states require the withholding of taxes on a nonresident partner's distributive shares of income from that state, but Utah does not. See UCA § 59-10-301, *et seq*.

h. **Fallback Form**. A general partnership is the form of organization a business with more than one co-owner will be, unless the owners organize the business as some other form of organization and also properly maintain that other organization so that it is not involuntarily dissolved by the state and is not disregarded by courts and creditors. If for any of these reasons a business of two or more persons fails to be another form of organization by inadvertence or otherwise, it will be a general partnership with general liability for its partners because it will not have qualified for, or will have lost its qualification for, treatment as an LLP.

i. **Risk**. General partnerships leave the partners more at risk for loss of their assets outside the business by reason of a partnership liability because (as we will discuss further below) each partner is an agent for, and can bind, the partnership (UCA § 48-1d-301) and because each partner has general liability, jointly and severally, for the obligations of the business (other than for the special exception for qualified limited liability partnerships). UCA § 48-1d-306. Such liability includes the obligation to make contributions in winding up to pay obligations where the partnership assets are insufficient to pay claims from periods when the partnership was not a LLP. UCA § 48-1d-906(3). This general liability is no longer based on the former cross agency theory under the old act which old act employed an aggregate concept where every partner was the agent of every other partner since no separate entity existed; rather the liability is now based on the New Act provisions specifying such liability for what is now a separate entity.

The liability of a general partner may be released on dissociation either by agreement of the creditor and of the partnership or else by a material change in the nature or time of payment of the obligation where the change is made by the creditor with knowledge or notice of the dissociation but without the consent of the dissociated person. UCA § 48-1d-803(3) and (4). The need for partnership consent is to help protect other partners because they may be called on to pay a greater share of the obligation if one former partner is released.

j. **How Bound to Third Parties.** Generally, as we have seen, each partner can bind the partnership, and each can bind the other partners as well, because each is an agent for the partnership, and general partners are liable for partnership obligations. Thus, for a general partner who is liable for partnership obligations, how the partnership becomes bound is very important. It is, of course, also important for others dealing with the partnership.

i. Binding the Business. A partner binds the partnership and other partners in apparently carrying on the business in the ordinary course, except where the other party knows the partner has no actual authority, or, outside the ordinary course, where actually authorized by the other partners. UCA § 48-1d-301. Authority is determined under the partnership agreement (see UCA § 48-1d-106) and under the rule that all partners have equal right to bind the partnership. UCA § 48-1d-402(1). An act in contravention of any restrictions on a partner's authority will still bind the partnership, unless the other person knew or had notice of the restriction. UCA § 48-1d-301(1).

A partnership may, if it wants, but need not, file a statement of authority with the Division describing who can bind the partnership or any limits the ability of a person to bind it. UCA § 48-1d-303. Third parties may rely on such a statement in most circumstances. A person does not become liable as a partner merely because someone else has named that person in a statement of partnership authority (UCA §48-1d-308(3)) and does not continue to be liable after otherwise ceasing to be liable, merely because of a failure to file a statement of dissociation or an amendment to a statement of authority to reflect dissociation. UCA § 48-1d-308(4).

ii. Dissociated Partner. A person who is a dissociated (we will deal with dissociation later) former partner may still bind the partnership for two years after dissociation if the act would have bound the partnership before dissociation, and the other party does not know or have notice of the dissociation and reasonably believes the person is a partner. Naturally, the dissociated person will be liable for any damage to the partnership and the partners. UCA § 48-1d-802(1) and (2). Further, the dissociation does not itself discharge the dissociated former partner for any obligation incurred earlier. After dissociation the dissociated former partner generally is not liable to third persons for later obligations, but nevertheless will be liable if the later obligation (even if not incurred through his or her own act) arises within 2 years after dissociation and is of the sort the dissociated person would have been liable for before dissociation, and if the third party does not have knowledge or notice of the dissociation. UCA § 45-1d-803. A notice of dissociation, however, must be filed with the Division.

iii. Bad Conduct. Wrongful acts of a partner in the ordinary course of business or with authority of the other partners creates partnership liability, and the misapplication of third-party funds or property by a partner in the scope of apparent authority or while in the custody of the partnership will create partnership liability. UCA §§ 48-1d-305.

iv. Estoppel. Also, if all the partners consent to a nonpartner representing himself or herself as a partner, the partnership becomes liable. UCA § 48-1d-308.

v. Dissolution. The power to bind the partnership changes in the event of dissolution (subject to the rights of third parties without actual or constructive notice of dissolution or of the lack of authority) and becomes limited to actions to wind up the business. UCA § 48-1d-904(1). A partner who acts outside of what is appropriate to winding up with knowledge of the dissolution and the termination of authority will be liable to the partnership and other partners for damage caused. UCA § 48-1d-905 (c)(1). Also, by an act after dissolution a person who is a dissociated former partner may cause the partnership to be bound to third persons who don't have notice of the dissociation and who believe the person is a partner, where the act occurs within two years of the dissociation, and the act is appropriate for winding up. UCA § 48-1d-904(2). Naturally, the dissociated person will be liable to the partnership and its partners for any damage caused. UCA § 48-1d-905(2).

k. **Separable Interests**. A partner's interest under the Act is in two parts: first, a transferable interest (defined at UCA § 48-1d-102(25)) to receive distributions in accordance with the partnership agreement, which interest in distributions is originally associated with a person's partnership interest but continues whether or not the person continues as a partner or owns the interest; and, second, all other rights and duties. A transfer of the transferable interest is generally permissible but is not effective where a transferee has notice that the transfer is in violation of a restriction on transfer contained in the partnership agreement. UCA § 48-1d-603(5). The other rights of a partner, such as management rights and access to partnership information, are not transferable and do not transfer to a transferee. UCA § 48-1d-603(1)(c).

Transferees, including transferees through sale or gift or disassociated partners (we will return to this concept) who are always treated as transferees upon disassociation, receive (or if a disassociated partner, retain) distributions to which the transferor would otherwise be entitled and also receive a right to seek a judicial equitable winding up. UCA § 48-1d-603(2). A distribution means a transfer "on account of a transferable interest or in the person's capacity as a partner." UCA § 48-1d-102(4). A distribution, by definition, does not include reasonable compensation or benefits for services. UCA § 48-1d-102(4)(b). However, other issues with respect to compensatory payments remain. The Act provides that "a partner is not entitled to remuneration for services performed for the partnership, except for reasonable compensation for services rendered in winding up..." UCA § 48-1d-402(3). Presumably, this apparent inconsistency between the definition of distribution and the statutory rights of a partner may be affected by the economic terms of the partnership agreement which may allow what would otherwise not exist. UCA § 48-1d-106.

l. **Charging Order**. One way a transferable interest may be transferred is by a creditor of a member, including a creditor on matters wholly unrelated to the business (e.g., through a divorce, judgment in a personal injury case, etc.), obtaining a judgment against the partner and then obtaining a charging order against the partner's transferable interest. To obtain a charging order, a judgment creditor applies to a court which may enter such an order against the transferable interest of a judgment debtor who is a partner or transferee. The order, when granted, is a lien on the transferable interest. The partnership is then served with the order and from then on pays to the holder of the order any distributions that would otherwise be paid to the judgment debtor. UCA § 48-1d-604(1).

i. Exclusive Remedy. The charging order remedy is the exclusive remedy of a judgment creditor against a partner or against a transferee. UCA § 48-1d-604(7). Thus, if a transferee of a transferable interest (which eventually may include a creditor foreclosing a charging order lien) suffers a judgment, the stream of distributions is not seized or garnished in the usual way but would need to be made subject to a further charging order. The exclusive remedy provision does not, however, apply to security interests under Article 9 of the Uniform Commercial Code which are subject to their own remedies. Compensatory payments may need to be garnished in the usual way since they are excluded from the definition of a distribution.

ii. Foreclosure. The creditor holding the charging order may then request the court to foreclose the lien of the charging order. The creditor must show, however, that distributions will not pay the judgment within a reasonable time. On the sale, the purchaser at the sale receives only the transferable interest in distributions and becomes a mere transferee. UCA § 48-1d-604(3). To stop the foreclosure, the charged partner, the partnership, or any other partner, may pay the judgment in full before the court's order of foreclosure. UCA § 48-1d-604(4) and (5).

iii. Purpose. The general purpose of the charging order is not so much to help protect the partner who is the debtor, but to protect the other partners who could suffer if they were to be reduced to receiving a share of the proceeds of a nail by nail, board by board liquidation instead of retaining a share in a going concern as they intended.

m. **Dissociation**. Dissociation is the separation of the partner's partnership interest into the transferable interest and the other rights (e.g., management rights, etc.) where the management rights terminate. Transfers of transferable interests do not alone cause disassociation as a partner (UCA § 48-1d-603(1)(b)), so it is possible for a partner to have no right to distributions yet maintain management rights, at least until the other partners dissociate that partner. Several things can cause dissociation. The dissociation may be rightful or wrongful (potentially giving rise to damages), but any partner can dissociate at any time. UCA § 48-1d-701(1). In addition, some other events will cause dissociation, such as, among others: (i) events stated in the partnership agreement; (ii) expulsion under the partnership agreement; (iii) expulsion by unanimous consent of other partners when it is unlawful to carry on activities with the person, when the person's entire transferable interest is transferred (including, e.g., on foreclosure, but not before, of a charging order) or when a corporation, a partnership, or a limited liability company member is dissolved (corporations losing their charter get a 90-day period to cure (UCA § 48-1d-701(4)(c)(ii)), but, partnerships or limited liability companies administratively dissolved do not receive such grace); (iv) expulsion by court order; (v) death of the partner; or (vi) distribution of the entire transferable interest by a trust or estate which is a partner. Also, dissociation of a partner occurs on a partner's bankruptcy or other insolvency process (e.g., receiver, assignment for creditors, etc.) or on appointment of a guardian or other incapacity finding by a court. UCA § 48-1d-701. The idea is that management rights do not fall into the hands of others where the remaining partners have not agreed to this.

n. **Buy-Out on Dissociation**. Where dissociation occurs without a resulting winding up, the dissociated person must be bought out under UCA § 48-1d-801 absent some other agreement. The buyout price under that section is determined by a pro-forma liquidation: the amount that would have been distributable under UCA § 48-1d-906(2) (return of contributions, and distributive share of any excess) as if the assets of the partnership were sold for the greater of liquidation value or the value as a going concern of the entire business without that dissociated person, with interest accruing on the price from dissociation, but subject to offsets for amounts owing by the person to the partnership whether or not currently due. UCA § 48-1d-801(1) and (2).

The partnership either may tender payment, or else may tender a proposal for deferred payments when the partner has wrongfully dissociated; in either case the tender must be accompanied by financial information, an explanation of how the price was calculated, and a notice that the payment is in full satisfaction of the purchase obligation unless the dissociated person brings an action within 120 days to determine price, offsets, or other terms of the purchase obligation. UCA § 48-1d-801(5) through (9). Any such action needs to be brought within 120 days of the notice or, if there is no notice, one year from demand for payment. UCA § 48-1d-801(9).

The wrongful dissociation by a partner before the end of the definite term or completion of the particular undertaking, where these apply, prevents the person from being entitled to payment before the term ends or the undertaking is completed, unless a court determines earlier payment will not create an undue hardship to the business. For example, if the partnership has a 50 year term, would it be reasonable to make the dissociated former partner wait this long? Any deferred obligation must bear interest and be adequately secured. UCA § 48-1d-801(8).

o. **Contributions**. A partner need not make or agree to make a contribution to be a partner. UCA § 48-1d-401(3). Any contribution made can be of property or services provided or to be provided or of some other benefit to the partnership. UCA § 48-1d-501. The liability to make an agreed contribution continues and is not excused by death, disability, dissolution (e.g., of an organization that is a partner), or other inability to perform personally (e.g., services), rather the partnership may require an equal value in money if the agreed contribution of something other than money is not made. UCA § 48-1d-502(1) and (2). The obligation to make a contribution may be compromised only with unanimous consent of the partners, and a third party extending credit or otherwise acting in reliance on the obligation to make the contribution can enforce the obligation. UCA § 48-1d-502(3). Contributions do not determine allocations of profits and losses or interim (i.e., pre-liquidation) distributions unless the partnership agreement says they do. See UCA

§ 48-1d-503(1) (distributions are in equal shares). Contributions are a factor, however, in liquidating distributions on winding up because, as we will see, un-returned contributions are returned first out of any surplus left after creditors have been paid, before final distributions are made based on distribution shares. UCA § 48-1d-906(2).

p. **Distribution Rights**. Generally partners receive equal distributions, subject to the rights of proper transferees or under charging orders. UCA § 48-1d-503(1). This means that if this is not the deal among the partners a specific provision in the partnership agreement will be necessary. For example, it is often part of a deal that sharing will be in proportion to capital accounts; any such deal will require an agreement requiring capital accounts and stating the sharing provisions.

i. Timing and Type of Distributions. No distributions before winding up are required under the Act, but the partners may agree to interim distributions. UCA § 48-1d-503(2). This agreement may be ad hoc or may be in the partnership agreement. Only money is required to be distributed, but distributions in kind are possible if the property is fungible and distributions are proportionate to rights to distributions. UCA § 48-1d-503(3). Again, this can be restructured by express agreement. When a partner or transferee becomes entitled to a distribution, the partner or transferee becomes a creditor of the partnership, subject, however, to any offsets the partnership may have against the distributee. UCA § 48-1d-503(4).

ii. Improper Distributions. Distributions by a limited liability partnership are not proper, however, where the distribution would leave the LLP unable to pay its debts as they come due, or would leave the total assets at less than the amount needed to pay liabilities plus, unless the agreement provides otherwise, the amount need to pay those with a higher priority right to distributions, including on liquidation. UCA § 48-1d-504(1). This restriction does not apply where the partnership is not an LLP, presumably because the creditors have access to the assets of all the general partners. Any partner who consents to an improper distribution by an LLP is personally liable to the LLP for the excess amount distributed. UCA § 48-1d-505(1). Also, any person receiving the improper distribution knowing it to be improper is personally liable to the LLP to the extent of the excess distribution received. UCA § 48-1d-505(2). There is a two year statute of limitations for such claims of the LLP to recover excess distributions from consenting partners or knowing recipients. UCA § 48-1d-505(4).

q. **Term and Dissolution.** A partnership is a sometime thing. It can be dissolved on a number of triggering events. Dissolution leads to winding up the partnership affairs. Understanding dissolution is important to understanding the investor's exit options, and the ability of creditors of the owners to reach the business assets sooner rather than later.

i. Trigger Events. Under the new Act, a partnership dissolves and its affairs are wound up only in certain events, but the partnership is not expected to last indefinitely. In a partnership at will, any notice of the express will to withdraw by a partner (this is not the same as dissociation by other events) will cause dissolution. UCA § 48-1d-901(1).

On the other hand, if the partnership is not a partnership at will but is a partnership for a particular term (say a term of years such as 10 years) or a particular undertaking (such as constructing and selling a building), dissolution occurs in one of three ways: (1) on dissociation of a partner by death, incapacity, bankruptcy or insolvency event, complete distribution of the transferrable interest of a trust or estate, or the termination of an entity (e.g., another business organization) that is a partner, if within 90 days of the event at least half the partners vote or consent (a rightful dissociation is treated as such a consent by the dissociated partner) to wind-up the partnership (without such a vote – the partnership continues); (2) on the express consent of all partners to wind-up, or (3) the expiration of the partnership term or the completion of its undertaking. UCA § 48-1d-901(2).

Other triggers for dissolution which apply regardless of whether the partnership is at will or for a term or undertaking, are events or circumstances specified in the partnership agreement, a court order, or the passage of 90 days during which there are not at least two partners (i.e., not just transferees). UCA § 48-1d-901(3) through (6).

ii. Court Ordered Dissolution. The kinds of court orders that cause dissolution arise in two circumstances, on request by a partner, and on request by a transferee, and these two circumstances require different grounds before the court will order the dissolution. If a partner asks for the court order, the grounds the partner needs to demonstrate are that, substantially all the affairs of the partnership are unlawful to conduct, the economic purpose of the partnership is likely to be unreasonably frustrated, a partner has engaged in conduct relating to the partnership's affairs making it not reasonably practical to carry on the business in partnership with that partner, or it is not reasonably practical to carry on the partnership's affairs in conformity with the partnership agreement. UCA § 48-1d-901(4).

Where the request for the court ordered dissolution is from a transferee, the grounds are different from those needed where a partner makes the request. The transferee needs to show the court that it is equitable to wind up the partnership either at the end of the partnership term or conclusion of the particular partnership's undertaking where there was a term or particular undertaking at the time of the transfer or entry of the charging order giving rise to the transfer, or else at any time where the partnership was a partnership at will at the time of transfer or entry of the charging order giving rise to the transfer.

iii. Existence During Dissolution Process. A dissolved partnership continues for purposes of winding up; thus dissolution does not completely terminate the partnership until winding-up is completed. UCA § 48-1d-902. Business as usual ceases, however, the partnership may preserve its activities, affairs, and property as a going concern for a reasonable time. UCA § 48-1d-902(2)(b)(ii). A termination statement may be filed with the Division, typically on completion of the winding up. UCA § 48-1d-902(2)(b)(vi).

iv. Control of Winding Up. The winding up is controlled by the partners including a partner whose dissociation caused the dissolution (unless the dissociation by that partner was wrongful), or, if there are no partners, by the personal or legal representative of the last person who was a partner. UCA § 48-1d-902(3) and (4). If that personal or legal representative fails to exercise the right to control winding up, transferees by majority of rights to distributions can appoint a person to act. That person has the powers but not the general liability of a general partner for acting to wind up the partnership affairs. UCA § 48-1d-902(4). If there is no such person appointed within a reasonable time, or for other good cause, a court can be asked to supervise the winding up. This request may come from a partner or any one entitled to participate in winding up which apparently could include, as applicable, the personal or legal representative of the last partner, or transferees. UCA § 48-1d-902(5).

r. **Rescission of Dissolution**. If the partnership is dissolved, the partnership cannot nevertheless continue, rather it must wind up its affairs (i.e., liquidate). However, the dissolution may be rescinded unless a termination statement (which is a statement filed with the Division to the effect that the partnership is terminated) is effective or a court order of dissolution has been entered. The rescission requires the vote or consent of every partner and the rescinding of any filed statement of dissolution. If the partnership rescinds dissolution, it continues as if no dissolution occurred. UCA § 48-1d-903. The concept of administrative dissolution (usually with some right to obtain reinstatement) which applies to other types of business organizations does not apply to general partnerships which may not need to make any filing with the Division. If a limited liability partnership election is filed and not maintained, the result is general liability, not entity dissolution unless the partners choose to dissolve.

s. **Liquidating Distributions**. On wind up, creditors are paid first, including partners who are creditors. UCA § 48-1d-906(1). Then any surplus goes to return contributions not earlier returned in proportion to the value of unreturned contributions, and anything left is distributed amount partners and transferees in proportion to their rights to distributions. These distributions must be paid in money. UCA § 48-1d-906(2), (4), and (5). If assets are insufficient to satisfy the partnership obligations incurred while the partnership was not a limited liability partnership, then each person who is unreleased (by the creditor and the partnership or by a material change in the obligation by a creditor knowing of the dissociation but without the dissociated former general partner's consent) and who was a general partner at the time the obligation was incurred (such a person need not be a partner at time of dissolution and winding up, but may be a dissociated former partner) must contribute to pay such obligations in proportion to each such person's right to receive distributions in effect when the obligation was incurred. UCA § 48-1d-906(3). The persons liable and the proportions of liability can change over time. If one such person fails to contribute a full share, the others must contribute more. There is a right to obtain contributions from those failing to contribute a full share if a person is required to pay more than that person's own share. UCA § 48-1d-906(3)(b) to (d).

A dissolved limited liability partnership may give notice to known creditors with non-contingent pre-dissolution claims to file their claims within not fewer than 120 days or be barred. If a claim is made and rejected, the creditor must bring an action no later than 90 days after receiving notice of rejection. UCA § 48-1d-907. Other pre-dissolution claims not earlier barred may be barred in three years if a notice to creditors is published by the dissolved limited liability partnership. Creditors with unbarred claims can enforce them against the undistributed assets or against those receiving a distribution to the extent of the distributee's proportionate share of the claim or of the assets distributed, whichever is less, but the total for all claims can't exceed the assets distributed to the distributee. UCA § 48-1d-908. This process does not apply to general partners where the partnership has never been a limited liability partnership, but if it is a limited liability partnership at dissolution the notice to known creditors can also bar claims against a general partner or dissociated former general partner otherwise without a liability limitation. UCA § 48-1d-907(2)(e).

t. **Formality.** General partnerships are generally operated without a great deal of formality, but are flexible enough to allow greater formality under a partnership agreement if the partners desire it.

u. **Fair Treatment.** Partners have the right to a certain level of fair treatment from the partnership and partners, including rights to business information, some protection by fiduciary duties, and indemnity.

i. Rights to Information. Partners can have access to business information. Such rights cannot be unreasonably restricted, but reasonable restrictions on use and remedies for abuse may be agreed. UCA § 48-1d-106(3)(d). Under the Act, the information rights include, at a minimum:

– Partners are entitled to have partnership books kept at the principal place of business with reasonable access to inspect and copy them to the extent material to his or her rights and duties as a general partner. (UCA § 48-1d-403(1) and (2).

- Partners are entitled to receive without demand information concerning the partnership's affairs which is material to the exercise of a partner's rights and duties (UCA § 48-1d-403(3)(a)), and to receive on demand and subject to paying the cost to produce it, other information concerning the partnership unless the demand is unreasonable or improper. (UCA § 48-1d-403(3)(b) and (7).
- Dissociated partners, however, can only obtain the material information in good faith and for the period they were a partner. (UCA § 48-1d-403(5).

ii. Fiduciary and Related Duties. The general fiduciary and related duties which protect partners are described in the Act. They are modifiable within rather broad limits, and it is possible that additional duties may be found by courts based on the actual confidential relationship of the partners. The duties described in the Act are:

- The general covenant of commercial good faith and fair dealing, which is implied in all contracts, will apply to the discharge of duties and obligations under the partnership agreement (UCA § 48-1d-405(4)). It may not be waived, but standards may be agreed upon if not unconscionable or against public policy. UCA § 48-1d-106(3)(f).
- The duty of care of a partner in the conduct or winding up of the partnership is only to refrain from engaging in grossly negligent or reckless conduct or a knowing violation of law. UCA § 48-1d-405(3). This is a considerably lower standard than applied before the New Act. Also, this lower duty may be further altered under the partnership agreement except to authorize intentional misconduct or a knowing violation of law. UCA § 48-1d-106(4)(b)(iii). If a higher standard than gross negligence is desired it must be stated in the partnership agreement. The definition in the Act or the agreement of the duty of care is very important because there can be no remedy (in damages or in equity) where

there is no duty to be breached. Although the Act could have provided a higher standard of due care combined with a damage limitation where gross negligence (or worse) is not involved (as was the case with the old limited liability company act), thus leaving open the possibility of an equitable remedy for breach of the duty of due care, this Act has not done so; absent a contrary agreement, remedies appear to be all or nothing based on the defined duty.

- A partner's duty of loyalty includes (there could be more): first the duty to account to the partnership and hold as trustee for it, property, profits, or benefits from the conduct or winding up of the partnership affairs, from the personal use by the partner of partnership property, or from the appropriation of partnership opportunities; second, the duty to refrain from dealing with the partnership on behalf of a person with an interest adverse to the partnership, but it is a defense that any such transaction is fair to the partnership; and, third, the duty to refrain from competing with the partnership before its dissolution. UCA § 48-1d-405. On the other hand, these aspects of the duty of loyalty may be altered or eliminated under the partnership agreement if the alteration or elimination is not unconscionable or against public policy. UCA § 48-1d-106(4)(6). The agreement may also specify how things otherwise violative of the duty of loyalty may be authorized or ratified by independent persons (UCA § 48-1d-106(4)(a), and even without such a procedural provision, all partners may authorize or ratify a specific act or transaction which otherwise violates the duty of loyalty (UCA § 48-1d-405(6)).

iii. Indemnity. Partners are entitled to expense reimbursement (UCA § 48-1d-404(1)) and to indemnity against claims, liabilities, and obligations incurred in the capacity as a partner which do not arise from breach of the management rights of partners (see UCA § 48-1d-402), the standards of conduct of partners (see UCA § 48-1d-405 on care and loyalty), or of the restrictions on distributions (see UCA § 48-1d-504). UCA § 48-1d-404(2). Also, an operating agreement may not relieve or exonerate a person from liability for conduct involving bad faith, willful misconduct, or recklessness. UCA § 48-1d-206(3)(g). Partners may receive advances of defense expenses on a promise to repay the advances if the partner is not ultimately determined not to be entitled to indemnity. UCA § 48-1d-404(3). There is no special authorization procedure required for any of these payments, which is quite unlike the rules for corporations where there are much more detailed limits on indemnity and special procedures required to authorize payments.

v. **Partnership Agreement**. Partnerships are largely matters of agreement. The agreement should be, but need not be, in writing. UCA § 48-1d-102(13). The partnership agreement governs relations among the partnership and the partners as such. UCA §§ 48-1d-106(1)(a) and 107. The partnership agreement is originally made among all the partners. UCA § 48-1d-102(13). It can, however, specify how it is to be amended. UCA § 48-1d-106(1)(c). Thus amendment need not be unanimous if the agreement provides otherwise. Also, the agreement may require the consent of a third party (for example, a creditor or a transferee) to any amendment. UCA § 48-1d-108(1).

i. Effect on Former Partners of Amendments. An amendment can affect the rights relating to obligations of the partnership or partners to transferees or persons dissociated, except where restricted under a court order to effectuate a charging order, or where the change would impose a new obligation on the transferee or dissociated person, or where the change would prejudice the rights arising before the amendment under the Act (at UCA § 48-1d-801) of a dissociated person to be bought out. UCA § 48-1d-108(2).

ii. Restrictions on Agreements. Not many matters are restricted from being changed by agreement. UCA § 48-1d-106. Among the most important items restricted are that: the contractual obligation of good faith cannot be eliminated (although standards for its application may be provided if not unconscionable or against public policy), a person may not be exonerated or relieved of liability for conduct involving bad faith, willful misconduct, or willfulness, information rights cannot be varied except for reasonable restrictions on information availability or use or for providing appropriate remedies for misuse, the power of a partner to dissociate cannot be varied except to require written notice (i.e., in a record), causes of judicial dissolution or dissolution after 90 days without at least two members can't be varied, and certain requirements relating to winding up cannot be varied.

3. Why Are General Partnerships Used? For most businesses most of the time, some other form of organization will be more appropriate than a general partnership; an LLP would usually be better, and other forms of organization may be better still. If the business is a general partnership, it is mostly by accident or error. However, there are special circumstances when general partnerships can be a desirable form of organization.

a. **Desirable Uses.** The general liability feature is often a negative, but in the right circumstances such liability sometimes can be a positive or at least a neutral feature, and these circumstances are generally the conditions for general partnerships being desirable.

i. Other Liability Limits. General partnerships are sometimes used as joint venture vehicles between companies that otherwise have limited liability. Thus, the flexibility of the general partnership and its automatic imposition of shared liability for the venture may be attractive to corporations or limited liability companies (sometimes through special purpose subsidiaries) which want to share control of an enterprise, be able to withdraw cash from it without leaving much of a reserve behind, yet have assurance that each partner is required to fund obligations and liabilities as they arise. Special allocations and basis determinations, etc., for tax purposes are easier to accomplish where all partners have general liability. Although other forms of organization such as a limited liability partnership, a limited partnership, or a limited liability company, could be used to accomplish similar results by agreement, the relative simplicity of a general partnership may tip the scale toward its use for some ventures.

ii. Carefully Selected Partners. Some individuals (or organizations without limited liability) may choose the general partnership form of organization for similar reasons of simplicity of sharing and funding as with the corporate joint venture. However, they should do so only when the partners are very carefully chosen for integrity and responsibility, are of similarly solid financial standing, and the business is not excessively risky and can be adequately insured.

iii. Professionals. Some professional practices (lawyers, accountants, etc.) have been partnerships for generations before the advent of more recent forms of organization such as limited liability companies, and have long-established compensation and buy-out arrangements based on the partnership form of organization which the partners desire to continue. These groups were the lobbying force for the limited liability partnership which limits a partner's risk, particularly the risk of the malpractice of the professional in the next office; such liabilities can cause enormous damages either in areas not covered by insurance or in amounts in excess of insurance coverage. Also, on a partner's buy out, at retirement for example, the partnership and remaining partners might benefit from special tax rules relating to certain assets, notably unrealized receivables and goodwill, applicable to "general partners" in a service partnership. See IRC § 736(b)(2) and (c).

b. **Areas Where Not Desirable.** Business owners seeking liability protection generally have shunned general partnerships, and rightly so, at least prior to the advent of limited liability partnerships with relatively broad protection. However, there can be other reasons, often tax driven, to avoid them, as well. Some examples are:

i. Like-kind Exchanges. Persons desiring to use the IRC § 1031 like-kind exchange to defer income on the transfer of property (usually real estate) and to reinvest in some other similar property, will actively avoid partnership treatment for tax purposes. Where real estate is involved, real estate interests can be exchanged and then only for other real estate interests. Partnership interests, even interests in general partnerships holding nothing but the real property, do not qualify. The problem often comes up in tenancy-in-common arrangements where a person desires to exchange out of, say, a modest apartment building presently owned, for a tenancy-in-common interest in a professionally-run tenancy-in-common program involving, say, a very large office building. There it is important that the arrangement taken as a whole, including powers of attorney or management agreements, does not amount to a partnership.

ii. Oil and Gas. Oil and gas development transactions are regularly established, at least on their face, as state law tenancies-in-common. However, these arrangements could also potentially be treated as partnerships for state law or federal tax purposes. The owners can sometimes elect out of partnership taxation where that type of taxation is not desired. The owners will also generally take steps to prevent state law general partnership treatment where general liability is not desirable.

CHAPTER 7

LIMITED PARTNERSHIP AND LIMITED LIABILITY LIMITED PARTNERSHIP

LANGDON T. OWEN[1]

Limited partnerships are rather analogous to general partnerships in many ways, so you may want to review the discussion of general partnerships earlier in this work if you have not already done so. In our discussion of limited partnerships, we will refer regularly to the general partnership treatment of an issue and will focus here mostly on areas where there are significant substantive differences.

1. **What Are They?** As with general partnerships, limited partnerships are a type of business organization by which two or more persons carry on a business for profit, but limited partnerships may also carry on non-profit affairs. The key difference between general and limited partnerships, however, is that with limited partnerships there must be at least one general partner with management authority and (except for limited liability limited partnerships) with general liability of the sort applicable to general partners of a general partnership (which has not elected limited liability partnership treatment), and there must be at least one limited partner without the management authority of a general partner and also without general liability. See UCA § 48-2e-201(4). Another important difference is that limited partnerships have long been treated as entities separate from their owners; in Utah such

[1]Langdon T. Owen, Jr. is a member of the law firm of Cohne Kinghorn, p.c. in Salt Lake City, Utah. Mr. Owen is a transactional lawyer who practices in such areas as estate and tax planning, business and commercial transactions, health care law, nonprofit organizations, probate, and real estate. He has practiced law since 1977. He holds a Juris Doctor degree from the University of Utah (1977) and a Bachelor of Arts degree from the University of California, Berkeley (1973, with great distinction).

separate entity treatment did not apply to general partnerships until the new partnership act became effective January 1, 2014.

a. **Source of Rules.** Limited partnerships are governed by the Utah Uniform Limited Partnership Act, UCA § 48-2e-101 et seq. which became effective January 1, 2014 for newly organized limited partnerships (the "Act"). Limited partnerships organized earlier remain subject to prior law (located at UCA § 48-2a-100 et seq.) until January 1, 2016 when the old law is repealed and the new Act applies to all limited partnerships. UCA § 48-2e-1205. A limited partnership governed by the old law could, if it desired, elect to be covered earlier by the new Act. UCA § 48-2e-1205(1)(b). The law of Utah governs the internal affairs of limited partnerships organized in Utah. UCA §§ 48-2e-106, 48-2e-102(13). This is consistent with the choice of law rules in the other states relating to business organizations where state organization is required, and is different from the rule applicable to general partnerships.

b. **Limited Liability Limited Partnerships.** The new Act creates a new variation on limited partnerships, called a limited liability limited partnership. This variation is still a limited partnership, but has an election made in its certificate of organization so that the general partners of it will not have general liability for the obligations of the limited partnership. UCA §§ 48-2e-102(11) and 48-2e-404(3). Thus, the general partners of the limited liability limited partnership are treated in much the same way as the general partners of a limited liability partnership – the limited partnership itself is solely liable, and the general partners are not personally liable, directly or indirectly, by way of contribution or otherwise, for a debt, obligation, or other liability of a limited partnership, solely by reason of being or acting as a general partner. UCA § 48-2e-404(3). Other grounds for personal liability, such as personal wrong doing, are not excluded.

c. **Formation and State Qualification.** A limited liability company must file a certificate of limited partnership. UCA § 48-2e-201(1). The certificate is filed with the Utah Department of Commerce, Division of Corporations and Commercial Code (the "Division"). UCA

§§ 48-2e-102(5) and 48-2e-201(1). The certificate must state certain required elements and may contain other statements, but cannot state things that could not be done in a limited partnership agreement. UCA § 48-2e-201(2) and (3). Without an effective filed certificate, there is no limited partnership; rather the business is treated as a general partnership (unless some other form of organization applies). A certificate is just that, a certificate - it is not, as such, a binding document like a partnership agreement. It is possible that a partnership agreement or part of one could be filed as a certificate, in which case the document may serve both functions, but the purpose of the certificate, unlike articles of incorporation, is to declare a claim to limited liability, not to bind the members to specific provisions. The binding provisions are left to the partnership agreement itself. The certificate will usually be bare bones in keeping with its limited function. It may refer to matters in the partnership agreement for which public notice is desired (e.g., transfer restrictions) but other than that will likely keep to the information required under the Act. The minimum requirements are simple: the name of the limited partnership, the address of its principal office, the name and address of its registered agent in Utah, the name and address of each general partner, and whether the organization is a limited liability limited partnership. UCA § 48-2e-201(3).

The limited partnership is not actually formed on the filing of the certificate; there must also be at least two persons (this includes entities) who are partners of whom at least one is a general partner and at least one is a limited partner. UCA § 48-2e-201(4).

d. **Assumed Name.** Like all businesses, a limited partnership may use an assumed name in which to do business. If it does so it needs to make an assumed name filing with the Division every three years. UCA §§ 42-2-5, 42-2-8, and 42-2-11. If it fails to make the filing, the limited partnership may be deprived of the use of the courts for making claims or counterclaims until the filing has been made and may be charged a late fee. UCA § 42-2-10.

e. **Qualification in Other States.** Limited partnerships need to register to do business in other states if under the law of the other state it is doing business in that state. See UCA § 48-2e-902 requiring foreign limited partnerships to register in Utah. The penalty for failure to qualify is usually a ban to the use of the courts of the state to assert claims or counterclaims until the organization has qualified; in some states harsher penalties may also apply. The assumed name requirements and business licensing rules of the other state would need to be met as well.

2. **Certain Features.** Let's look at some key features of limited partnerships.

a. **Owners.** There are two major classes of partners – general and limited. There may be sub-classes created as well under the partnership agreement with different rights, for example, different rights to profits or distributions. Without a limited liability limited partnership election, general partners have general liability, jointly and severally for partnership obligations (UCA § 48-2e-404(1)), but limited partners don't (if, however, they act in a way that otherwise creates personal liability, limited partners will be directly personally liable, but they are not automatically liable for partnership obligations) UCA § 48-2e-302. Any form of limited liability, including a limited partner or a general partner of a limited liability limited partnership, is, however, subject to long standing rules which may allow a piercing of the veil by creditors between the organization and its owners. This allows the creditors of one to reach the assets of the other under conditions found abusive such as gross undercapitalization, commingling of funds, fraud, etc. The general liability of a general partner of a limited liability partnership is the same as that of a general partner of a general partnership (i.e., without a limited liability partnership election), and is described in this work in the portion dealing with general partnerships, so we will not discuss it again here. With the LLLP election, such general liability does not apply even to the general partners and the difference between the two major classes in the limited partnership becomes management rights – general partners are the managerial class, while limited partners have much more restricted rights. UCA §§ 48-2e-402 (general partner is the agent of the partnership) and 48-2e-406 (management rights of general partner); UCA § 48-2e-302 (a limited partner is not an agent of the partnership just by reason of being a limited partner). Each of the classes has a separable transferable interest in distributions. UCA § 48-2e-701; see definition of distribution at UCA § 48-2e-102(4). The transferable interest is personal property. UCA § 48-2e-701. Consistent with the treatment of general partners of a general partnership, general partners of a limited partnership are not entitled to remuneration for services performed for the limited partnership except in winding up. UCA § 48-2e-406. This provision appears to mean that remuneration is not inherent in the position of general partner; a partnership agreement could provide for some form of service compensation.

b. **Management.** As we have seen, general partners manage limited partnerships with equal management powers. The partners holding limited and general partnership interests can overlap so that one person may be both a limited and general partner, perhaps in different proportions as to each class. UCA § 48-2e-116. In performing their general partner management functions, general partners have equal rights and act by majority. UCA § 48-2e-406(1). Each general partner can by his or her act alone bind the limited partnership in the apparent scope of partnership activities, unless the general partner lacked authority on the matter (e.g., under the partnership agreement) and the other person with whom the general partner was dealing knew or had notice that the general partner lacked authority. UCA § 48-2e-402. Outside the apparent scope of partnership activities, the general partner needs actual authority to bind the limited partnership. Further, the general partner can bind the limited partnership by his or her wrongful (i.e., actionable) conduct (UCA § 48-2e-403). The general partner has the power to bind the limited partnership after dissolution in the same way a general partner of a general partnership could bind the partnership: where appropriate for winding up, or even if not, where the action would otherwise have bound the limited partnership before dissolution and the other person does not know of or have notice of the dissolution. UCA § 48-2e-804(1). Also, a dissociated former general partner can bind the limited partnership for up to two years after dissociation where the other person does not know or have notice of the dissociation and the act otherwise is appropriate to winding up or would otherwise have bound the limited partnership. UCA § 48-2e-804(2).

Unlike general partnerships (including limited liability partnerships) and limited liability companies, there is no statutory provision dealing with the filing of a statement of authority for a limited partnership (including for a limited liability limited partnership). The certificate must state who are the general partners and must be amended when the identity of a general partner changes. UCA §§ 48-2e-201(2)(d) (initial certificate) and 48-2e-202(4) (amendment).

c. **Limited Partner Voting and Consent Rights.** Although limited partners do not have the management rights of a general partner, they do have some rights to vote and, under the Act, their consent is necessary for certain major transactions or changes. The affirmative vote or consent of all partners (general and limited) is required to amend the partnership agreement, to amend the certificate of limited partnership to add or remove a limited liability limited partnership election, to sell, lease, exchange, or otherwise dispose of all or substantially all the limited partnership's property, with or without good will, other than in the visual and regular course of business, or to approve a merger, interest exchange, conversion, or domestication transaction (these sorts of entity modification transactions are described at UCA 48-2e-1101 et seq.). UCA 48-2e-406(2). Also, electing a general partner generally takes the affirmative vote of all partners. UCA § 48-2e-402(1)(iv). These statutory voting and consent rights of limited partners may be changed by provisions of the limited partnership agreement, except that the agreement cannot eliminate the need for the consent of all general partners to delete any limited liability limited partnership election (UCA § 48-2e-112(3)(e)) or to change the consent rights of all partners as to mergers and other entity modification transactions (UCA § 48-2e-112(3)(o)).

d. **Business and Non-Profit Flexibility.** Limited partnerships, like general partnerships are generally for business, but unlike general partnerships, limited partnerships may be organized for non-profit purposes. UCA § 48-2e-104(2). Like general partnerships, limited partnerships are quite flexible except for the requirement of a general partner managerial class of interest.

e. **Taxes.** Both general and limited partnerships are subject to the same pass-through tax treatment as general partnerships and other partnership derived forms of organization such as limited liability companies. The availability of tax favored benefit programs, the tax and if rules and the state's tax rules all apply very similarly with respect to limited partnerships as they do with general partnerships (discussed earlier in this work).

General partners in limited partnerships also pay self-employment tax the same as general partners in general partnerships, but limited partners who are passive do not. Prop. Reg. § 1.1402(a)-2(b)(1/13/97) (defining limited partners for these tax purposes as a partner without authority to contract, without personal liability, and who does not participate in the business for more than 500 hours per year). Under these regulations a single person might possibly hold a general interest (with management rights) subject to self-employment tax and also a limited passive investment interest not subject to self-employment tax. This difference in self-employment tax is an important tax difference between general partners (in general or limited partnerships) and limited partners.

f. **Separable Interests.** The interests of general and limited partners in a limited partnership are separable into two pieces: transferable interests and all other rights and duties. UCA § 48-2e-701. This is the same as with general partnerships. Thus, as described more fully earlier in this work with respect to general partnerships, the transferable interest is personal property (UCA § 48-2e-701), is generally transferable except where restricted and where the person receiving the interest has knowledge or notice of the restriction (UCA § 48-2e-702(1)(a) and (6)), does not carry with it on transfer any rights to management, voting, or information which remain with the transferring partner unless otherwise provided (UCA §§ 48-2e-702(1)(c) and 48-2e-702(7)), but only carries with it on transfer rights to distributions (UCA §§ 48-2e-102(4) and 48-2e-702(2)).

g. **Charging Orders.** Also as described earlier in this work with respect to general partnerships, the transferable interest may be made subject to a charging order by a court on application by a creditor with a judgment against the partner (or a transferee) entitling the creditor to receive the distributions otherwise payable to the debtor. UCA § 48-2e-703(1). The charging order is a foreclosable lien against the transferable interest which may be foreclosed by the holder of the order if it is shown that distributions will not pay the judgment in a reasonable time. UCA § 48-2e-703(3). As with general partnerships, there are rights of the debtor, the limited partnership, or the other partners to pay the judgment to prevent foreclosure (UCA § 48-2e-703(4)) and the court can make orders necessary to effectuate the collection of the distributions charged (UCA § 48-2e-703(2)). The charging order is the exclusive remedy for enforcing a judgment against a partner or transferee. UCA § 48-2e-701(7). All this is very parallel to the treatment of charging orders with respect to general partnerships (and, it should be noted, with respect to limited liability companies, as well) and raises the same concerns as those described in the discussion in this work of general partnerships.

h. **Dissociation.** The concept of a severable interest is associated with the concept of the charging order. The concept of a severable interest also gives rise to the concept of dissociation which is where the transferable interest is separated from the other rights of a partner and those other rights terminate, leaving only the transferable interest (i.e., rights to distributions) to be held by the dissociated partner. Dissociation works similarly in limited partnerships as it does in general partnerships. The parallel is very close between the general partner of a general partnership and that of a limited partnership. See UCA § 48-2e-603 (dissociation as a general partner). There is, however, some modest difference between dissociation of a general partner and that of a limited partner. We won't repeat the description of the causes of dissociation of a general partner which is discussed earlier in this work. Rather, we will focus on the specific differences relating to limited partners.

i. Causes of Dissociation. For an individual who is a general partner, among other causes of dissociation, dissociation is caused by the individual's death, the appointment of a guardian or conservator for the individual, or by a court order that the individual has become incapable of performing his or her duties as a general partner. UCA § 48-2e-603(6). For a limited partner, however, death (among other things) will cause dissociation, but, because a limited partner has no management functions, the appointment of a guardian or conservator, or a court order of incapability will not impair obligations or duties. UCA § 48-2e-601(2)(f). Otherwise, the causes of dissociation are virtually identical for general or limited partners.

ii. Right to Dissociate. Another difference between general and limited partners is that limited partners do not have the right to dissociate as a limited partner before completion of winding up (UCA § 48-2e-601(1)) but a general partner may dissociate at will at any time, rightfully or wrongfully (UCA § 48-2e-604).

iii. Effects of Dissociation. There are some differences in the effects of dissociation between dissociations of general and limited partners. Dissociation makes the former partner (whether general or limited) a transferee only, without the voting, management, or similar rights of a partner (whether general or limited, as applicable). UCA §§ 48-2e-602(1)(a) and (c) (limited partner) and 48-2e-605(1)(a) and (d), (general partner). The partners duties also end; thus a dissociated limited partner no longer is subject to the contractual obligation of good faith and fair dealing, and a dissociated general partner no longer is subject to the management standards of conduct of a general partner (see UCA § 48-2e-409) such as the duty to refrain from competing, or to refrain from being grossly negligent, or to meet the contractual obligation of good faith and fair dealing. UCA §§ 48-2e-602(1)(b) (limited partner) and 48-2e-605(1)(b) (general partner).

However, dissociation does not discharge any debt, obligation, or liability incurred while a partner (whether general or limited). UCA §§ 48-2e-602(2) (limited partner), 48-2e-605(2) (general partner). The dissociated general partner can file a statement of dissociation with the Division and request an amendment to the certificate of limited partnership to reflect the dissociation; this helps put the world on notice of the dissociation in order to prevent further liabilities to persons who may erroneously rely on a belief that the dissociated person is still a general partner. UCA § 48-2e-605(1)(c). See UCA §§ 48-2e-606 (power to bind the limited partnership after dissociation and liability for doing so), 48-2e-607 (liability to third persons for up to two years where the third person does not have knowledge or notice of dissociation and reasonably believes the person is a general partner). A dissociated general partner's general liability (i.e., incurred while the limited partnership is not a limited liability limited partnership) is not released except either by the agreement both of the creditor affected and of the partnership as well, or else by a material change in the obligation made by a creditor knowing or on notice of the dissociation but without the consent of the dissociated former general partner. UCA § 48-2e-607(4) and (5).

i. **No Buy-Out on Dissociation.** One effect of dissociation that is quite different between general partnerships and limited partnerships is that while a general partner in a general partnership may be entitled to be bought out where the dissociation does not lead to winding up (see UCA § 48-1d-801), this is not the case for either a general or limited partner of a limited partnership. The limited partnership Act is silent on the point, thus any such buyout, if desired, would need to be provided in the limited partnership agreement. This difference reflects the difference in the life expectancies of the two forms of partnership – a general partnership usually is not expected to last beyond its partners (they are typically for a term, a specific undertaking, or at will), but a limited partnership is expected to be perpetual. See UCA § 48-2e-104(3).

j. **Contributions.** Contributions are treated the same as with general partnerships. None are needed to obtain either a general or limited partnership interest. UCA §§ 48-2e-401(2) (general partner), 48-2e-301(2) (limited partner). Contributions may be in any form, may be required by the limited partnership to be paid in money if not provided in the agreed form, are not excused by death, disability, dissolution, or other inability to perform, may only be compromised by unanimous partner consent, and may be enforced by a relying creditor. UCA §§ 48-2e-502 and 501. Contributions have no necessary effect on distributions (absent an agreement) except on dissolution and winding up. UCA §§ 48-2e-503 and 813(2). All this is the same as with general partnerships and described in more detail in the portion of this work dealing with them.

k. **Distributions.** Also the same as with general partnerships is the treatment of distributions prior to winding up. They are made equally and are discretionary, for example. UCA § 48-2e-503. One difference between general and limited partnerships is that the same restrictions on distributions applicable to limited liability partnerships (but not to general partnerships where the partners still have general liability) will apply to all limited partnerships, even those that have general partners with general liability (i.e., those without the limited liability limited partnership election). UCA § 48-2e-504(1). The reason for this difference seems to be that with a general partnership with general liability, all partners are at risk of personal liability to creditors; with a limited partnership, at least the limited partners will not be at such risk.

l. **Term and Dissolution.** While limited partnerships are expected to be perpetual, they will often end earlier than expected because things can happen to dissociate partners (general or limited) and thus may cause, early dissolution and winding up.

i. Trigger Events for Dissolution. If any general partner is dissociated, the partners by majority (based on shares of distributions) vote either to dissolve (if there is at least one other general partner) or else not to dissolve (if there is no other general partner) but to name at least one general partner within 90 days of the dissociation. UCA § 48-2e-801(c). Also, if the last limited partner is dissociated the partnership dissolves unless within 90 days of the dissociation another limited partner is admitted. UCA § 48-2e-801(d). The same is true if there is only one partner left, another partner (general or limited as needed) needs to be admitted within 90 days. UCA § 48-2e-801(e).

Dissolution may also be caused by an event or circumstance that the limited partnership agreement says will cause dissolution (UCA § 48-2e-801(a)), the vote or consent of all general partners and of a majority of the rights to distributions of limited partners to dissolve (UCA § 48-2e-801(b)), or the entry of a court order of dissolution on application of a partner (of either class) on grounds that substantially all of the conduct of the limited partnership's activities and affairs is unlawful, or it is not reasonably practical to carry on the activities or affairs in accordance with the limited partnership agreement. UCA § 48-2e-801(f). Unlike the case with general partnerships, there is no provision for transferees to request a court ordered dissolution. Also, the Division could administratively dissolve the limited partnership for failure timely (i.e., within 60 days) to pay fees or taxes, file an annual report, or have a registered agent. UCA §§ 48-2e-801(g) and 810.

ii. Winding Up. Once dissolution has been triggered, it leads to winding up. The limited partnership continues for this purpose of winding up. UCA § 48-2e-802(1). In winding up debts are paid, claims resolved, property is liquidated or transferred, and final distributions made. Generally, the limited partnership can only act toward liquidation and winding up, not maintain business as usual (UCA § 48-2e-802(1) and (2), but it may preserve its activities, affairs, and property as a going concern for a reasonable time. UCA § 48-2e-802(2)(b)(ii). The winding up is done by the remaining general partner or general partners, but if there are none, by a person appointed by a majority of the rights to distributions of the limited partners, and such appointed person (who need not be a partner) has the powers but not the general liability of a general partner so long as the person exercises the powers solely for winding up. UCA § 48-2e-802(3). An amended certificate must be filed to identify the person and show that the appointed person has this authority to wind up the limited partnership. UCA § 48-2e-802(3)(b). If no such person can be found and appointed, or if other good cause exists, any partner may request judicial supervision of the winding up. UCA § 48-2e-802(4). There is no similar provision for a transferee to request judicial supervision; this is different from the situation for general partnerships where transferees under some circumstances could make such a request.

m. **Rescission of Dissolution.** A limited partnership may rescind its dissolution unless a statement of termination has been filed with the Division, or the dissolution is an order of the court or is an administrative dissolution by the Division. UCA § 48-2e-803. In order to rescind a dissolution, all partners must vote or consent to the rescission, and a corrective amendment to the certificate must be filed with the Division if an amendment had earlier been filed stating that the limited partnership is dissolved. UCA § 48-2e-803(2). Once properly rescinded, the business can resume like the limited partnership had never dissolved. UCA § 48-2e-803(3).

n. **Liquidating Distributions.** Liquidating distributions are made in a way quite like the way they are made by general partnerships. In winding up, creditors are paid first, including partners who are creditors. UCA § 48-2e-813(1). Any surplus is distributed, subject to any charging order, first to the holder of a transferable interest to return the value of contributions made but not yet returned, then to partners in proportion to their rights to distributions just before dissolution (except as necessary to reflect transfers of transferable interests). UCA § 48-2e-813(2). If assets are insufficient to pay all creditors, each person who has not been released after dissociation as a general partner (i.e., by reason of an agreement by the creditor and the partnership, or by a material change in the obligation made by a creditor knowing of the dissociation but without the former general partner's consent; UCA § 48-2e-607(4) and (5) must contribute to pay the obligations incurred while he or she was a general partner with general liability, in an amount to cover his or her own share, determined by rights to distributions, and also to cover the share of any other such general partner who fails to contribute a full share. The contributing person has a right to contribution against those failing to pay their full shares. UCA § 48-2e-813(3).

A dissolved limited partnership may give notice to known creditors to file non-contingent pre-dissolution clams not fewer than 120 days and bring action with 90 days of rejection or the claim will be barred, including as to any general partners or dissociated general partners who otherwise would have general liability. UCA § 48-2e-806. Also, by publishing a notice to other creditors the limited partnership can cause their claims not earlier barred to be barred within three years. UCA § 48-2e-807. An unbarred claim can be enforced against undistributed assets, or after distribution, against distributees to the extent of their proportionate share of the claim or of the assets distributed, whichever is less, but in no event over the total amount distributed to the distributee after dissolution. UCA § 48-2e-807(b). This is the same procedure applicable to limited liability partnerships.

o. **Formality.** The division of interests into a general managerial class, and a limited, investment class with some limited consent and voting rights adds a level of formality to a limited partnership beyond what one usually finds in a general partnership. However, the general partners of a limited partnership may still act with relative informality compared with corporations or with many limited liability companies. Mere failure to follow formalities is not fatal to limited liability for the partners who are otherwise entitled to it. UCA § 48-2-303(2). Naturally, the limited partnership agreement can add more formality if the parties desire this.

p. **Fair Treatment.** General and limited partners in a limited partnership receive some protections from having access to books and records, from benefitting from some level of fiduciary duty owed by those in management, and from indemnity.

i. Rights to Information. A general partner, being in the management class, has broad rights to access the books and records of the limited partnership; a limited partner has narrower rights to access.

Certain information is required to be kept at the principal office of the limited partnership. UCA § 48-2e-115. A general partner can inspect and copy such required information at any time with no particular purpose. UCA § 48-2e-407(1). A limited partner can inspect and copy it without a particular purpose as well, but may be required to make a demand 10 days before access is permitted. UCA § 48-2e-304(1).

On reasonable notice a general partner can inspect and copy any record regarding the activities, affairs, financial condition, and other circumstances of the limited partnership to the extent material to the general partner's rights and duties. UCA § 48-2e-407(2). For a limited partner, this same information is available to the extent just and reasonable and if sought for a purpose reasonably related to his or her interest as a limited partner, he or she pays costs and makes a written (i.e., by a record) demand describing with reasonable particularity the information sought and the purpose for seeking it, and the information sought is directly related to his or her purpose. UCA § 48-2e-304(2) and (7).

A general partner is to be provided without demand information the limited partnership knows is material to the proper exercise of the general partner's rights and duties, and on demand (subject to paying costs) any other information concerning the limited partnership except to the extent the demand is unreasonable or improper under the circumstances. UCA § 48-2e-407(3) and (7). A limited partner, on the other hand only is provided without demand information material to any matter on which the limited partner has a right to vote or consent; there is no demand right for other information beyond that described above. UCA § 48-2e-304(4).

A legal representative of a general partner or a limited partner dissociated by reason of death has the information rights of a current limited partner just described. UCA §§ 48-2e-704(2), 48-2e-304(10), 48-2e-407(9)(a). On a transfer, the transferee does not succeed to information rights, because the transferor retains all rights other than the transferable interest in distributions. UCA § 48-2e-702(1)(c)(ii) and (7). On dissociation, the partner (general or limited) becomes a mere transferee (subject to some special rules relating to mergers and similar entity change transactions), and thus the former partner has no rights to information except for an account of transactions after dissolution of the limited partnership. UCA §§ 48-2e-701(3) (transferee), 48-2e-605(1)(d) (general), 48-2e-6-2(1)(c) (limited). However, a dissociated limited or general partner may on 10 days demand made in good faith receive information relating to the time he or she was a general or limited partner (as the case may be) and he or she meets the same requirements a limited partner would generally need to meet to obtain information, such as making a written demand stating the information desired and its purpose, the purpose is reasonably related to the partner's interest, and the information directly relates to that purpose. UCA §§ 48-2e-407(5) (general), 48-2e-304(5) (limited).

ii. Fiduciary and Related Duties. The fiduciary duties of care and loyalty a general partner owes the limited partnership and its other partners (general or limited) are the same as those owed by a general partner of a general partnership and are subject to the same sorts of modification by agreement as with general partnerships. (These matters are described above in this work). UCA §§ 48-2e-409, 48-2e-112(3)(f) and (4). Limited partners, however, owe no such fiduciary duties. UCA § 48-2e-305(2). Both general and limited partners owe a non-waivable contractual duty of good faith and fair dealing. UCA §§ 48-2e-305(1) (limited), 48-2e-409(4) (general), 48-2e-112(3)(g) (duty of good faith may not be eliminated, but may be defined if not unconscionable or against public policy).

iii. Indemnity. General partners in a limited partnership are entitled to expense reimbursement, indemnity against liabilities, and advancement of defense expenses, and subject to the same limitations, as are general partners in a general partnership (as described above in this work). UCA §§ 48-2e-408 (indemnity), 48-2e-112(3)(h) (no exoneration for bad faith, willful misconduct, or recklessness). Limited partners, who are without a management role, have no such indemnity rights under the Act. Subject to the limits against exoneration for bad faith, willful misconduct, and recklessness, a limited partnership agreement could provide some protection if a limited partner were to be sued in that capacity. If a person has a dual capacity as a general and as a limited partner, the Act's indemnity provision would apply to the general partner capacity only, but it would apply.

3. **Why Are Limited Partnerships Used?** Limited partnerships have traditionally been used mostly for relatively passive investments like rental real estate. The real estate industry has been a rather large scale user of limited partnerships; some transactions have been huge. However, their use is not limited to managing these sorts of investments.

a. **Typical Uses.** Real estate holding businesses are likely to continue to be significant users of limited partnerships, but operating businesses can find them attractive as well. There are some publicly traded operating businesses organized as limited partnerships, generally to obtain pass-through tax treatment for the business. As we have seen already, a limited partnership could even be used for non-profit operations; this use is very rare, and most charities are organized as non-profit corporations or trusts. The flexibility of a limited partnership, its centralized management structure, and particularly its favorable tax treatment, have been its strongest draws for entrepreneurs. Except for certain financial institutions required to operate as corporations, just about any industry could use the limited partnership format.

Limited partnerships, and limited liability companies as well, are often used in family estate planning. They are often better than corporations for holding appreciating assets, making gifts of interests in a limited partnership (or LLC) is easier than transfers of numerous underlying assets held in the organization, and the lack-of-control and lack-of-marketability discounts in value for gift, estate, and generation skipping tax purposes (in appropriate cases), along with inside as well as outside income tax basis step up at death, and charging order protection from creditors, makes them attractive to estate planners.

Where Not Typically Used. Traditionally, professionals have not used limited partnerships because any material participation in operations could have destroyed their limited liability. Under the new Act, this will not be so – a limited partner may retain limited liability despite performing services for the limited partnership or participating in management or control. UCA § 48-2e-303(1). However, the centralized management structure may not be attractive for some professionals. Unlike limited liability companies and corporations, there are no special professional provisions in the limited partnership Act. For professionals, either the regular limited liability company or corporation, or the professional limited liability company or corporation, may well continue to be the more attractive choice, but the choice is not as clear as before now that the features of LLCs and limited partnerships are more like each other.

CHAPTER 8

CORPORATIONS

LANGDON T. OWEN[1]

Corporations have long been a form of organization favored by entrepreneurs. Although in recent years, the use of limited liability companies have been growing very quickly, and they have become the entity of choice for holding capital assets likely to increase in value (such as real estate and certain kinds of intellectual property), corporations still remain quite popular for operating businesses. In particular, small businesses often choose a corporation with an election under subchapter S of the Internal Revenue Code (known as the S-election) to have income and loss pass through to the shareholders without a corporate level tax. For many small businesses, the choice may boil down to an LLC or a corporation with the S-election (sometimes referred to as S-corporations). S-corporations are not a special form of corporation but a normal state law corporation with a simple capital structure (one class of stock) qualifying for (fewer than 100 stockholders, stockholders are only individuals, certain trusts, etc.) and making the special S-election for tax purposes. Large businesses are almost always corporations; for example, there are very few publicly traded LLCs or limited partnerships.

1. **What are They?** Corporations are creatures of state statute. All states have corporation statutes. The state grants a charter on filing articles

[1]Langdon T. Owen, Jr. is a member of the law firm of Cohne Kinghorn, p.c. in Salt Lake City, Utah. Mr. Owen is a transactional lawyer who practices in such areas as estate and tax planning, business and commercial transactions, health care law, nonprofit organizations, probate, and real estate. He has practiced law since 1977. He holds a Juris Doctor degree from the University of Utah (1977) and a Bachelor of Arts degree from the University of California, Berkeley (1973, with great distinction).

of incorporation. UCA § 16-10a-203. This creates the corporation which is treated as a legal person separate from its stockholders. With such state recognition, the organization is a corporation, without such recognition, it is not. (There have been some cases where a de-facto corporation has been found by the courts in order to provide some equitable relief in certain circumstances, but such cases were rare exceptions and the doctrine has been abolished in Utah. American Vending Services, Inc. v. Morse, 881 P.2d 917 (Ut. 1994).) The sort of analysis of the relationship used to determine partnership status is unnecessary for corporations.

The rights and obligations of the stockholders (see UCA §§ 16-10a-701 to 740), and of the directors and officers (see UCA §§ 16-10a-801 to 853) are heavily governed by statute and there is less flexibility for variation than with partnerships and limited liability companies. Some range of choices is available on some matters, and other matters can be modified by agreement (see UCA §§ 16-10a-730 (voting trusts), 731 (voting agreements), 732 (shareholder agreements), but a corporation is still by and large a creature of statute rather than of contract, unlike various kinds of partnership or limited liability companies. For some businesses relative statutory rigidity may not be a good thing, but for others, such as large publicly traded businesses, a well-defined and understood organizational form is highly desirable to investors. They can have a pretty good idea of what they are getting into without having to analyze the structure from the ground up.

a. **Source of Rules.** Utah corporations are generally governed by UCA §§ 16-10a-101 et seq.; however there are special rules, which we will ignore, for insurance companies and financial institutions. Also, corporations may be not for profit, and there is a separate non-profit corporation act with which we will not deal. The state law to apply to the internal affairs of the corporation is generally the law of its state of incorporation, regardless of where it does business, or where its shareholders, directors, or officers reside. See Restatement 2d conflicts of Laws (1971) §§ 303-309.

b. **Formation and State Qualification.** A Utah corporation is formed when articles of incorporation are filed with the Utah

Department of Commerce, Division of Corporations and Commercial Code (the "Division") by one or more incorporators at least 18 years old. UCA §§ 16-10a-201 (incorporators), 202 (articles), 203 (incorporation). The articles are binding on the corporation and those with an interest in the corporation. The articles are thus not like a mere certificate as with limited liability companies or limited partnerships or limited liability partnerships. The articles need to do more than provide a notice of a claim of limited liability and thus are required to contain certain things, and may contain other things as well if desired. The content of the articles is specified at UCA § 16-10a-202 and includes: the purpose of the corporation (which can be broad such as "any lawful business" or narrow), the name of the corporation (satisfying the naming rules of UCA § 16-10a-401), the number of authorized shares, a designation of the classes of shares (such as common, non-cumulative, non-voting, preferred, etc.), for any class of shares a designation of the preferences, limitations, and relative rights of that class (UCA § 16-10a-601(1); provided in the articles at least prior to the issuance of a class), information about the registered agent and registered office of the corporation (as required under UCA § 16-17-203(1)), the name and address of each incorporation. The incorporators must sign the articles. UCA § 16-10a-202(5). Such signatures are an affirmation under penalty of perjury that the document is the act or deed of the person or entity on behalf of which it is signed and that the facts stated in the document are true. UCA § 16-10a-120(9). The incorporators need not be or become officers, directors, or shareholders. Articles often contain the names of the initial board of directors; if not, the incorporators later name the directors. UCA § 16-10a-205(1)(b).

After the articles are filed, and the initial board has been named, the board holds an organizational meeting to get the corporation functioning by electing officers, adopting bylaws, and taking other actions. The other actions may, and commonly do, include receiving the acceptance of the members of the board to serve, adopting a form of stock certificate and stock records, authorizing the receipt of the consideration for shares and the issuance of shares to the initial stockholders (corporate seals are no longer needed, so a seal need not be authorized), adopting a fiscal year, adopting various agreements such as bank account agreements and bank signature authorizations, shareholder agreements, and employment agreements, and authorizing the making of the S-election (if this is desired).

The bylaws are typically adopted by the board (UCA § 16-10a-206) although without a board yet acting incorporators may do so and if they don't, the shareholders may do so. The Bylaws will contain the organization's governance provisions. Typically, the bylaws will set the rules for calling and giving notices of meetings of shareholders and the board setting record dates for shareholders entitled to vote at a meeting, allowing or disallowing informal action (i.e., without formal meetings), designating the offices of the corporation (e.g., president, vice presidents, secretary, treasurer, etc.) and their duties, specifying how shares are transferred, providing indemnity of officers and directors and others. All these provisions of the bylaws must meet the requirements of the Corporate Act, which sets some minimum standards.

Other organizational actions typical for any form of business, may be needed as well, such as obtaining a tax identification number from the IRS, a sales tax license from the state, a business license from the local city or county, and any required zoning or regulatory approvals which may be required.

If the business will operate outside of Utah, it will need to register to do business as a foreign corporation in each state in which it will do business. The definition of "doing business" varies from state to state. See UCA § 10-10a-1501 et seq. for Utah's rules.

Annual reports are required to be filed by the corporation with the Division in order to avoid administrative dissolution. See UCA § 16-10a-1420.

2. **Certain Features.** Corporations are rather distinct from the various forms of partnership and from partnership derived limited liability companies. The following is a review of some key features of corporations. The partnership derived forms of organization, which in Utah are general partnerships and limited liability partnerships, limited partnerships and limited liability limited partnerships, and limited liability companies, all are descendants of the older form of general partnership, and thus bear a strong family resemblance to each other. Corporations are quite distinct from these partnership derived forms of organization.

a. **Limited Liability.** Corporations were the first form of organization to offer limited liability to all investors, whether passive or active in the business. Thus shareholders are not responsible for corporate obligations. UCA § 16-10a-622(1). However, the articles could provide otherwise. UCA § 16-10a-622(2). Also, the statute specifies that shareholders, acting as such, have no fiduciary duties to other shareholders or the corporation. UCA § 16-10a-622(3).

i. Piercing the Veil. The corporate veil of limited liability for shareholders may be "pierced" (i.e., made ineffective) so that shareholder assets can be subjected to corporate debts in a number of circumstances where the corporate form is being abused. The classic cases are where the corporation is being used to perpetrate a fraud, or where the corporation is insufficiently capitalized so that normally expected uninsured obligations are unlikely to be paid (e.g., on dissolution), or where the corporate form is not honored by the shareholders who comingle corporate funds and assets with their own or use corporate assets to pay personal obligations; the failure to follow corporate formalities (e.g., not holding annual meetings) is some evidence of not respecting the corporate form but is generally not itself determinative. See UCA § 16-10a-701(3) (failure to hold annual meeting does not work a forfeiture of the charter or cause dissolution); *Baldwin v. Matthew R. White Investments, Inc.*, 669 F. Supp. 1054 (D.Ut.1987).

ii. Reverse Veil Piercing. The issue of veil piercing can work in the other direction as well, in that a creditor may be able to gain access to corporate assets for a shareholder's obligation, where the corporate form is abused so that the shareholder and the corporation are essentially alter egos. As with veil piercing generally, this remedy usually would apply where there are one or a few, usually closely related, shareholders.

iii. Liability Concerns. In addition to veil piercing, there are other areas where the corporate veil will not help a shareholder. For example, if the shareholder is acting as an officer, director, employee, or agent, and personally does something wrongful, such as to have personally been negligent or participated in a fraud, or to have been involved in violating a statute, that shareholder can be held responsible for his or her own fault. The corporation also will be responsible. Persons responsible to collect, report, and pay over taxes, such as withheld payroll taxes and sales taxes will be personally responsible for taxes not paid over. See IRC § 6672. There are other state and federal laws imposing personal liability for which the corporation's general limitations on liability will not provide protection. A business owner is well advised to protect the corporate shield, to obtain good insurance coverage, and to maintain a legal compliance and risk reduction plan.

b. **Management Structure.** The basic management structure of a corporation is not overly complex. Stockholders hold shares, which can be of various classes, such as preferred (as to dividends, liquidating distributions, etc.) or nonvoting classes (see UCA § 16-10a-601(3)), but at least one class will have general voting rights (UCA § 16-10a-601(2)). These voting stockholders elect and may remove the members of the board of directors (see UCA §§ 16-10a-804 and 808) who provide policy guidance and direction for the business (UCA § 16-10a-801). The corporation is required to have an annual meeting of shareholders each year to take action on various matters including electing directors. UCA § 16-10a-701. The directors generally elect or appoint officers who carry out the board's policies and the business operations of the corporation under the supervision of the board of directors. UCA §§ 16-10a-830 and 831. This management structure may be varied in Utah and in some other states by agreement so that, for example, the shareholders could directly control operations. UCA § 16-10a-732(1)(2).

c. **Transferability.** The shares of stock are generally freely transferable (assuming the seller can find a buyer, and assuming all applicable state and federal securities laws have been complied with or exemptions from such laws have been obtained) and the shares carry with them all rights of the stockholder, such as rights to dividends, to liquidating distributions, and to voting rights. This is in sharp contrast to the various types of partnerships and to limited liability companies where the partners or members interests are divided between distribution rights which may be transferable and voting and management rights which are not absent consents from the other partners or members. Among other things, this means that if a creditor of a stockholder seizes the shares of stock, the creditor can vote them and if there are sufficient votes, can liquidate the business despite the harm this could cause to the other stockholders. No charging order concept applies to help protect the other stockholders.

However, voting and control aspects of corporations can be made subject to irrevocable proxies (coupled with an interest), voting trusts, voting agreements, and shareholder agreements. See UCA §§ 16-10a-722(4) (proxies coupled with an interest), 730 (voting trusts), 731 (voting agreements), and 732 (shareholder agreements). To be binding on transferees, shareholder agreements need to be conspicuously noted on the front or back of share certificates or information statement for uncertificated shares. UCA § 16-10a-732(3).

Corporate shares may be evidenced by certificates, but need not be. Article 8 of the Uniform Commercial Code applies to the endorsement and other transfer of certificated and uncertificated securities. See UCA § 70A-8-100 et seq. particularly part 3 (§§ 70A-8-301 -307 on transfer) and part 4 (§§ 70A-8-401 – 409.1 on registration).

State and federal securities laws apply to the purchase or sale of securities, and corporate stock is always a security. See 15 USC § 77b(a)(1) (also known as § 2(a)(1) of the Securities Act of 1933), *Landreth Timber Co. v. Landreth*, 471 U.S. 681 (1985), UCA § 61-1-13(1)(ee)(i)(B). As a consequence, exceptions to securities registration requirements need to apply or the stock will need to be registered (see 15 UCA § 77e(a) and UCA § 61-1-7) under state and federal law, and whether or not registered, the various anti-fraud provisions of state and federal law will apply. (See, e.g., Securities Act of 1933 § 17a, Securities and Exchange Act of 1934 § 10(b), UCA § 61-1-1). With respect to the partnership derived forms of organization, whether or not an interest is a security requires an in-depth analysis; the answer is simple for corporate stock.

d. **Fiduciary Duties of Management.** The fiduciary duties owed by the directors and officers to the corporation are relatively more robust than for partnership derived forms of organization and are less likely to be modified to reduce them to the detriment of the investors to the same depths available for partnership derived organizations. Duty modifications which can substantially reduce the fiduciary duties owed to investors are expressly provided for as to the Utah forms of partnership and limited liability companies, which are creatures of contract; if pushed to their limits the duties of those managing such partnership derived organizations can be reduced to only avoiding intentional misconduct or a knowing violation of law. See, e.g., UCA §§ 48-3a-112(4)(c) and 48-1d-106(4)(b)(iii).

Directors and officers of corporations need to discharge their duties in good faith, with the care and prudence of an ordinary person in a like position, and in a manner they reasonably believe to be in the best interests of the corporation. UCA § 16-10a-840(1). Liability to the corporation and its shareholders is limited, however, to where the director or officer has breached or failed to perform his or her duties as described above, and the breach or failure constitutes gross negligence, willful misconduct, or intentional infliction of harm on the corporation or shareholders. UCA § 16-10a-840(4). Further, under UCA § 16-10a-841 a corporation can, in its articles or bylaws, eliminate or limit liability of a director to the corporation or shareholders except for: financial benefits to which the director is not entitled, intentional infliction of harm to the corporation or its shareholders, making unlawful distributions, or an intentional violation of criminal law. UCA § 16-10a-841(1). Thus, although damage liability can be limited, the basic duty remains due care (i.e., a negligence standard) so that other remedies, such as equitable remedies like injunctions, may be available. This is in contrast to the partnership derived forms of organization where the very duty itself is to refrain from gross negligence or is some lower modified standard, thus apparently removing any equitable or other remedy for breach of due care since there is simply no duty of due care.

e. **Indemnity.** In a good many situations a corporation may be able to indemnify its officers, directors, employees, and agents in the event they should be held liable for actions in such capacities or by reason of holding such capacities. Directors have a somewhat preferred position as to indemnity. Directors may be entitled to mandatory indemnification for defense expenses, except to the extent limited by the articles, when the director succeeds in defense of a claim arising because he or she was a director. UCA § 16-10a-903. Also, a court can order indemnity of directors in some circumstances. UCA § 16-10a-905. Officers, employees, and agents are not so entitled to mandatory indemnification but the corporation is authorized to indemnify them (UCA § 16-10a-907) and is also authorized to indemnify directors beyond the mandatory indemnity. See UCA §§ 16-10a-902 and 904 through 907. There are rules however, requiring the approval by independent persons in a particular case of such indemnity payments or of the advancement of defense costs. UCA §§ 16-10a-904 and 906. For example, advances of expenses can only be made if there is a written affirmation by the director that he or she has met the applicable standard of conduct, the director agrees to repay the advances if it is ultimately determined that he or she is not entitled to indemnity under the Act, and determination is made by the corporation through independent persons that the facts then known would not preclude indemnification. UCA § 16-10a-904(1). Also, there are some types of obligations which are not indemnifiable, at all, such as those not in good faith and not believed to be in the interests of the corporation or in a criminal proceeding where the person had reasonable cause to believe his or her conduct was unlawful. UCA § 16-10a-901-909. These provisions applicable to corporations are more complex, and generally are more protective of the organization, than are the analogous provisions applicable to partnership derived organizations. Indemnity provisions meeting the statutory requirements could be contained in the bylaws or a separate agreement.

f. **Tax.** Generally corporations are taxed on their income at the corporate level and any dividends or other distributions are taxed at the stockholder level. The following is a very simplified example. Tax issues are dealt with elsewhere in this work, but a little tax talk is needed here to understand the nature of corporations as a separate person. Assume the corporation earns a dollar of net income after all expenses. This dollar is taxed at, say, 35% by the federal government and 5% by a state government. Thus 40¢ of the dollar has been used to pay taxes. Assume next that the 60¢ left is paid as a dividend to the stockholders. It may be taxed at say 15% by the federal government and 5% by a state government. Thus, an additional 12¢ is paid in tax. The result is that, in our example, 52¢ of the dollar of net income, or majority of it, has gone to pay taxes. This is how big corporations are taxed.

This result is not what small businesses want, so the Internal Revenue Code ("IRC") provides for a special election, known as the S-election, for small businesses to eliminate the corporate level tax and have all the income or loss pass through to the stockholders to be taxed at their personal tax rates, whatever they happen to be. IRC § 1361. Let's apply such an election to our example of the $1.00 of net income. This $1.00 passes through to the stockholders and may be taxed at say 30% by the federal government (the top bracket is 39.6% in 2014) and 5% by some states. This means 35¢ is paid in taxes and 65¢ is left for the stockholders. The S-election brings small business corporation taxation closer to the pass through tax treatment of the partnership taxed forms of organization, which are partnerships of various types and limited liability companies.

g. **Stockholder Status.** Stockholders stay stockholders as long as they own shares and (absent an agreement otherwise) do not lose the votes tied to the shares of stock; they do not get dissociated or lose votes on death, incapacity, bankruptcy, transfer to third persons, and so on. This is quite unlike the effect of such events on partners or LLC members. The shares may pass to others on such events, but the votes go with them. There is no statutory assumption for corporations that a shareholder has the sort of personal arrangement as is typical with the partnership derived organizations, such that management and voting should cease when the particular person is no longer involved. If shareholders want such treatment they must specifically agree to it; the owners of partnership derived organizations get such treatment unless they specifically agree otherwise. For similar reasons, shareholders do not get expelled from corporations where investors in the partnership derived organizations might be expelled. Rather to remove a shareholder from the organization, a buy-out agreement of some kind would be necessary. Although shareholders acting as directors could be voted out of office, and shareholders acting as officers or employees could be fired, they remain shareholders with votes until bought out.

h. **Term and Dissolution.** Corporations are forever, which is to say perpetual, unless the articles specifically provide otherwise. They are required to be dissolved and liquidated only on a vote of the shareholders, or a revocation of their charters by the state, or a court's order. If dissolved, the corporation continues to exist in order to wind-up its affairs. This winding up process can deal with creditors and can be an effective alternative to bankruptcy for a financially troubled corporation, but may also apply for a fully solvent corporation.

i. Voluntary Dissolution. Dissolution may be accomplished by the corporation itself deciding to dissolve. Before shares are issued, this is done by the board of directors. UCA § 16-10a-1401. After shares are issued, this is done in two steps, first by the board recommending dissolution (and the board can condition the effectiveness of the dissolution on any basis), or by the board communicating a determination not to make a recommendation, to the shareholders; and second, by the shareholders authorizing the dissolution by majority vote of each voting group (unless a greater number is required by the articles or bylaws). UCA § 16-10a-1402. The corporation then files with the Division articles of dissolution describing the authorization for the dissolution. UCA § 16-10a-1403. The corporation can still revoke the dissolution within 120 days of its authorization by following the same process as for authorizing the dissolution, and the corporation then files articles of revocation describing the authorization for the revocation. UCA § 16-10a-1404.

ii. Administrative Dissolution. Dissolution can also be accomplished by action of the Division where the corporation does not pay taxes, fees, or penalties imposed by law, does not timely file an annual report with the Division, does not maintain a registered agent in Utah for 30 days or more, does not give notice of a change in or resignation of its registered agent within 30 days, or where any period of duration stated in the articles expires. UCA § 16-10a-1421. The corporation can correct matters within 60 days of notice from the Division. UCA § 16-10a-1421. If administrative dissolution becomes effective, the corporation may apply for reinstatement within two years. UCA § 16-10a-1422. If reinstated, the reinstatement relates back to the date of the administrative dissolution, and all corporate acts in the meantime are effective and enforceable as if dissolution had not occurred. UCA § 16-10a-1422.

iii. Court-Ordered Dissolution. Dissolution can also be required by court order. There are three potential plaintiffs: the state, a shareholder, or a creditor. The state acts through the attorney general or the director of the Division and can have the court cause dissolution if it establishes that the articles were obtained by fraud or the corporation has continued to exceed or abuse the authority conferred by law. UCA § 16-10a-1430(1).

A shareholder may have the court cause dissolution if it establishes that there is a deadlock on the board that the shareholders can't break, and the deadlock has or will cause irreparable injury or prevent the corporation's affairs being conducted to the advantage of the shareholders, that the directors or those in control have acted, are acting, or will act in a manner that is illegal, oppressive, or fraudulent, that the shareholders are deadlocked in voting power and unable for two consecutive annual meetings to elect successors to directors whose terms have expired or would expire with the election of successors, or that the corporate assets are being misapplied or wasted. UCA § 16-10a-1430(2). However, in order to prevent a dissolution by a shareholder of a corporation that is not publicly traded, the corporation or if the corporation does not, the other shareholders, can elect to purchase the shares of the petitioning disgruntled shareholder at fair value. The procedure for this election and valuation is specified in the Act. UCA § 16-10a-1434.

Creditors may have the court cause dissolution if the creditor can establish that the creditor has a judgment, execution on it has been returned unsatisfied, and the corporation is insolvent, or can establish that the corporation is insolvent and the corporation has admitted in writing that the creditor's claim is due and owing. UCA § 16-10a-1430.

In addition, a corporation can ask the court to continue a voluntary dissolution under court supervision. UCA § 10-10a-1430(4). In any judicial dissolution the court has authority to appoint receivers or custodians of corporate property. UCA § 16-10a-1432.

iv. <u>Liquidation and Claims Process.</u> The corporation, on dissolution, must cease business as usual and can only take actions to wind up and liquidate. The corporation continues to exist for this purpose of winding up, holding its property under the control of its board elected in the same way and under the same standards of conduct as before. UCA § 16-10a-1405. The corporation can give notice to known claimants to raise claims in not fewer than 120 days or be barred from later raising the claim. The corporation then can reject a claim in 90 days (or it is deemed accepted), and the claimant must bring a proceeding to enforce the claim within 90 days of its rejection or be barred from enforcing the claim later. UCA § 16-10a-1406.

If notice is published, unknown claims (not otherwise barred) can be barred if not brought within five years of publication. UCA § 16-10a-1407(3). Without such a published notice, the previously unbarred claims are barred after seven years. UCA § 16-10a-1407(5). The claims are made against the undistributed assets of the corporation, or if distributed, against the shareholders who received them up to the value at the time of distribution, and on returning the asset value, the shareholder may seek contribution from the other shareholders. UCA § 16-10a-1408.

i. <u>**Formality.**</u> Formality is required in corporate governance, absent some specific agreement otherwise, and a failure to follow corporate formalities can be a factor in determining that limited liability protection should not apply if those running the business do not honor the entity. Other factors would apply as well in determining whether to pierce the corporate veil, but for corporations, formalities are more of a factor than for partnership derived organizations.

3. <u>**Why Are Corporations Used?**</u> About any business could be incorporated. However, in some states, but not Utah (see UCA § 58-67-

802), there is a corporate practice of medicine doctrine which forbids physicians from practicing in the corporate form.

Corporations are used for most publicly traded companies. Naturally these larger public corporations do not qualify for the S-election. It is relatively easy to switch into corporate form. A company could start as, say, a limited liability company, and then later change into a corporation for going public, or for other purposes, and if qualifying could make an S-election. This sort of change from a partnership taxed organization into a corporation usually can be done without tax cost, but the converse is not true: a corporation, with or without the S-election, cannot be changed into a limited liability company or other partnership taxed organization without a taxable event occurring. It is not unusual for a company to start as an LLC in order to provide tax benefits to investors during a development stage, then switch to corporate form when going public.

Corporations are also used for closely held businesses, often with the S-election in order to eliminate one (the corporate) layer of taxation. Corporations involving closely held businesses should not be used to hold appreciating assets such as real property; this is true whether or not the S-election is made. The tax cost of holding appreciating assets in corporate form is generally too great. For example, if the real estate is distributed in kind proportionately to the shareholders, this is treated as a sale, potentially triggering tax on the gain in two levels for C-corporations (those without the S-election) or in one level for S-corporations (with the S-election); if a partnership taxed organization made the same distribution, it would generally be a non-taxable event.

The S-election also makes estate planning more difficult due to restrictions on classes of stock and restrictions on the kinds of trusts which may hold shares without disqualifying the S-election. This is another good reason to keep highly valuable appreciating assets out of corporate form.

Corporations are sometimes used in closely held businesses without the S-election in two situations. The first is where the corporation is in a service business (e.g., like law) so that all (or substantially all) of the net income of the company is paid to the service providers (e.g., like the lawyers) as reasonable compensation by the end of the year. The corporate level of tax is removed in such a situation by the deduction to the corporation for the payment of reasonable compensation.

The second situation is where no non-liquidating distributions (i.e., dividends) are expected; the corporation intends to finance itself by retaining all its earnings. It pays tax at say 35¢ on the dollar to the federal government and 5¢ on the dollar to various states. This combined rate may be equal to or lower than the effective tax rate applicable to the shareholders who, if in high brackets could pay 39.6¢ on the dollar in federal tax and say, 5¢ on the dollar in state taxes. Years later the shareholders sell their stock for capital gains rates, typically lower than the rates for ordinary income. The time delay in the second level of tax and the potentially lower brackets may make this strategy attractive.

Corporations, with or without the S-election can use certain forms of tax deferred reorganization where there is a substantial continuity of equity interests maintained in the transactions. These can be useful and include mergers, stock for stock acquisitions, stock for asset acquisitions, certain split up and spin off transactions, and a few other types of transactions. IRC § 368 and related sections. Thus, in an acquisitive reorganization all or most of the shareholders of a target in an acquisition would obtain stock of the acquirer as the consideration for the transaction. The key is that the business stays in corporate form and all or substantially all the shares of the target remain shareholders of the acquirer; this distinguishes these transactions from taxable sales. These reorganization rules make possible, albeit with a certain level of complexity, doing some sorts of transactions which would otherwise trigger the immediate recognition of gain (like a sale). For partnership-taxed organizations, similar results are achieved with different mechanisms such as certain mergers and certain liquidations (which could be deemed liquidations for tax purposes, but perhaps not an actual liquidation for state law purposes) which liquidations are generally tax free except as to "hot assets" like ordinary income items like inventory, accounts receivable, and depreciation recapture.

Corporations with the S-election are sometimes used to keep the Social Security tax on shareholder-employees lower than the self-employment tax would be on partner or member service providers of a partnership taxed organization. The difference is that the S-corporation shareholders can set their W-2 compensation (i.e., salaries) at the lower end of market rates, and the Social Security tax applies to this W-2 compensation as its tax base. Partners (including LLC members) are not employees and have no such W-2 income; their tax base is set by a formula starting with their full distributive shares, less some take-away items (e.g., rents, royalties, capital gain) designed to get close to an amount based on hands-on services (like what employees are paid for). These take-away items do not always result in an amount of tax base equal to or lower than the low-end market compensation of the S-corp shareholder-employee. To the extent the base for the self-employment tax on partnership members is a little higher, more self-employment tax would be payable than would be payable for the S-corp shareholder-employee. However, particularly when the personal deduction at the partner level for half the self-employment tax and other factors are considered, the difference may not be great. Where the reasonable compensation is almost always going to exceed the Social Security wage base limit for a year ($117,000 for 2014), such as for physicians who seldom make less, the only tax saved would be on the potentially 3.8% Medicare tax and additional Medicare tax which have no caps on the earnings base for the tax. It may take a sharp pencil and good profit projections to figure out if the potential savings is worth the other costs of operating as an S-corp, such as one class of stock, limited trusts, lack of an inside step-up basis at death among other considerations.

It is an illegitimate use of a corporation with the S-election to set shareholder compensation at below the range of a fair market levels. This is simply wrongful tax evasion and is, of course, subject to various tax penalties.

CHAPTER 9

LIMITED LIABILITY COMPANY

LEAH BENNION[1]

You may have heard this before, but LLCs are creatures of contract. It is critical for LLCs to understand the statutory defaults and protections (or lack thereof) so members and managers may comport themselves in a way that protects themselves, and the company, and in a way that is consistent with their desires for the operation of the entity.

So what statute are we dealing with?

While there are a few exceptions, after January 1, 2016, the 2014 Utah Revised Uniform Limited Liability Company Act, Utah Code Ann. § 48-3a-101, et seq., (the "2014 LLC Act") will govern all Utah LLCs as well as all foreign LLCs qualified to do business in Utah, replacing the Utah Revised Limited Liability Company Act (the "Old LLC Act"). Prior to January 1st, 2016, the 2014 LLC Act will govern those LLCs organized after January 1, 2014 and those that have elected to be governed under the act that was organized prior to January 1, 2014. So while there are two LLC acts that are effective currently, that will end in a few short months.

The verbiage

Just as a matter of house-cleaning, let's get some of the verbiage out of the way that commonly trips up young companies. Many people are familiar with the common terms in corporations, so I will use these terms

[1]Leah has focused her practice at the Clearwater Law and Governance Group, LLC in corporate/securities and employment law practice areas, including entity formation, corporate tax, sales and acquisitions and intellectual property dispute resolution. She has also assisted clients with wrongful termination, ERISA and ADA claims. Leah graduated from the University of Denver, Sturm College of Law in 2009.

as a comparison. In corporations the equity holders of the Company are called shareholders and the securities they possess are called shares or stock. Corporations are governed by management: a CEO, a president, a vice president, etc. Additionally, corporations are required to have a board of directors. The board of directors allocates capital, and selects and oversees management, while the management team, well, they "manage" the everyday business affairs of the corporation. There are some actions upon which management must receive approval from the board of directors, and some things on which the corporation must receive shareholder approval. On a very high-level, this is how a corporation functions.

By contrast, in an LLC the equity holders are called unitholders or members and the equity they possess may be called an interest which is represented in percentages or may be referred to as a unit. The governance of LLCs is only generally specified by the statute and is more fully described in the Operating Agreement. LLCs do not typically have the management and board dynamic, although it is possible to set up a similar structure. All LLCs have members and by default an LLC is member-managed, unless the Operating Agreement expressly provides otherwise. This is an important default rule to note.

Member-Managed LLCs

Under the 2014 LLC Act, all LLCs are member-managed by default.[2] But what does member-managed mean? Does it mean that each member can bind the Company in a transaction? Does it mean that a majority vote must be taken? Let's look at the statute to let our confusion set in a little bit more.

The 2014 LLC Act specifically states that in a member-managed LLC "each member has equal rights in the management and conduct of the limited liability company's activities and affairs." However, the 2014 LLC Act also states that "A member is not an agent of a limited liability company solely by reason of being a member." And finally the 2014 LLC Act states that: "[a] difference arising among members as to a matter in the ordinary course of the activities of the limited liability company

[2]LLCs must affirmatively elect the manager-managed status in their operating agreement to overcome this default.

shall be decided by a majority of the members;" and "[a]n act outside the ordinary course of the activities and affairs of the limited liability company may be undertaken with the affirmative vote or consent of all members." Ok, well at least we know that unusual activities require a unanimous vote of members, but what about activities in the ordinary course of business? The 2014 LLC Act seems to say that all members have equal authority, but no members have authority just by being members. Hmm. There's a bit of space for conjecture in there. I'll talk about the filing of a statement of authority in a section below, but barring the filing of this document, can one member of a member-managed LLC just enter into a contract that binds the company? Most likely the answer is no, but you can see how there is some confusion in this area. The filing of the statement of authority, as discussed below would help this tremendously, but for even greater clarity, even a member-managed LLC should spell out who has authority to do what, and how in the operating agreement. And be prepared for persons dealing with your LLC to ask for proof of your authority to act.

Manager-Managed LLCs

Complexities arise as the number of members increase, and complexities or conflicts may by virtue of the fact that some members may be more involved in the Company than others. Therefore, LLCs may want to consider whether the structure of a manager-managed LLC would more appropriately suit their potential for growth. In manager-managed LLCs the managers typically act like management of a corporation. The Manager is exclusively in charge of the activities and affairs of the LLC, or if there is more than one Manager, the activities are typically handled by a majority vote of Managers. Just as in member-managed LLCs, in manager-managed LLCs members are still required to approved mergers or other activities outside the ordinary course of business. Additionally, the Operating Agreement may not be amended without the approval of the members.

Nothing is certain except death and taxes

One of the reason founders choose the LLC format is for tax purposes. People often refer to corporations as having "double taxation."

That term means that corporate income is taxed twice: once to the corporation itself, and again to shareholders when earnings are paid-out as dividends. However, this is only true for earnings that are paid. In closely held corporations a difference between earnings and distributions rarely occurs because these small corporations rarely pay out dividends. Rather, corporations usually choose to pay salaries to employees or wages to consultants, which are deductible as ordinary business expenses, and therefore avoid corporate taxation.

Aside from the double-taxation concern, there are still good tax reasons to adopt the form of an LLC. LLCs are pass-through entities, meaning that losses too are passed on to individual members in their personal capacity. Early stage founders may know that the first year or two may produce losses and may wish to be able to deduct those losses on their personal taxes.

S corporations are also pass-through entities and may be more favorable then an LLC, but there are many limitations on S corporations including the number and type of shareholders and the unavailability of preferred interests, which we won't get into, as that entity choice is beyond the scope of this article. LLCs may have as many members as they would like and can also have preferred interests and participating debt.

Profits and losses can be both allocated and distributed. These are different concepts and taxable income without cash to pay tax is never pleasant. The important thing is that with proper planning, alternatives are possible that would not be self-evident to the lay person.

Taxation of LLCs and Corporations are complex enough, and founders' personal estates may be complex enough that advice from a tax professional may be warranted.

Governing Documents

In a limited liability company, the entity must only file with the State a short certificate of organization. What's interesting is that, under the 2014 LLC Act this certificate no longer specifies the management structure of the LLC, as was done under the Old LLC Act. This is an interesting wrinkle because third-parties and banks may not know if they are dealing with an authorized party or not when entering into transactions with an LLC (see the complexity mentioned previously in the member-managed section). The 2014 LLC Act attempts to resolve this dilemma by allowing for a Statement of Authority to be filed with the Division of Corporations that identifies the managers or members with authority to act on behalf of the LLC (including any limitations on authority, such as the ability to transfer real property). This Statement of Authority may also be filed with the County Recorder in which the LLC owns real property and this certified copy is conclusive. Therefore, any third-parties may want to search for a Statement of Authority at both the Division of Corporations and the County Recorder's office to ensure they are conducting business with an authorized representative of the LLC. Kind of a mess.

Beyond the required Certificate of Organization and the optional Statement of Authority, there are no requirements for documentation for an LLC. While corporations must file Articles of Incorporation and internal By-Laws, each of which can be lengthy and complex, the lack of required documentation for LLCs is a draw for many young companies. However, the reference that LLCs are "creatures of contract" refers to one specific document—the Operating Agreement—and remarkably, this is not filed with the State but is internal to the Company and its members and managers. This is the contact to rule them all. Anything and everything related to the structure and management of the LLC can be and should be in this document. Under both the Old LLC Act and the 2014 LLC Act the Operating Agreement addresses everything from tax structure, to management to the winding up to allocation of profits and losses. Some of these items have default rules under both the Old LLC Act and the 2014 LLC Act, but making sure you are choosing and documenting the right rules for your LLC is critically important.

Oral Operating Agreement

One interesting development in the 2014 LLC Act is the recognition of "oral operating agreements." While oral operating agreements and amendments are authorized, you can see that these types of agreements are much harder to enforce than a signed document.

The Utah evidentiary rule is by a "preponderance of evidence"—which means that more than 50% of the evidence points one way or another. If you have a two member LLC and both members agree that the members should waive fiduciary duties to the highest extent of the law, would you be comfortable knowing that without documentation it may be your word versus the other member's word? So while the prospect of oral operating agreements may have the potential to protect those that haven't gotten around to documenting their decisions, it is much safer and more advisable to have a written and adopted operating agreement.

Fiduciary duties

Fiduciary duties are legal obligations imposed on those who manage a business to act in the interest of the entity or the interest of the owners of the entity. The scope of these duties changes from state to state and between different entities. However, fiduciary duties usually include the "duty of care" and the "duty of loyalty." A third duty of good faith and fair dealing is also described by writers and court cases.

The Old LLC Act adopted these two basic fiduciary duties for persons who manage or control LLC's—the duty of care and the duty of loyalty. The duty of care under the old LLC act requires members and managers to expressly refrain from gross negligence and willful misconduct; additionally, higher standards could be enumerated in the operating agreement or articles of organization. The Old LLC Act also defines the duty of loyalty as refraining from any self-dealing. These duties cannot be reduced or eliminated under any governing documents of the LLC; however the obligation of good faith and fair dealing may be redefined by members in a written agreement if the standard is not unreasonable.

Under the 2014 LLC Act, managers and members owe a duty of care which is defined as refraining from grossly negligent or reckless conduct, intentional misconduct or knowing violation of the law. The 2014 LLC Act also imposes on managers and members the duty of loyalty which includes 1) accounting to the LLC for any benefit received by a member or manager in the winding up of the LLC's affairs, from using the LLC's property, or from usurping business opportunities that should go to the LLC; 2) refraining from working with persons whose interests are adverse to the LLC in dealings with the LLC; and 3) refraining from competition with the LLC prior to dissolution. What is interesting and complex about the 2014 LLC Act is that these duties may be altered or eliminated in an operating agreement so long as such alterations or eliminations are not unconscionable or against public policy and assuming the operating agreement does not authorize intentional misconduct or knowing violations of the law. Additionally, the operating agreement may not waive liability for conduct involving bad faith, willful misconduct or recklessness. Many commentators have noted that this portion of the 2014 LLC Act seems unclear and may allow for an uncomfortable amount of leeway on behalf of judges to hold management liable for misconduct that the LLC had intended to eliminate. Here, again, advice of a legal advisor may be desirable before adopting or changing rules of conduct.

Conclusion

This article barely scratches the surface of important things to know about LLCs. The intent is to give you enough information to help you understand that this area of law is complex and engaging counsel who is intimately familiar with this area of law is well worth your time and money. It is much easier to build a sturdy foundation at the start of an LLC than to clean-up the ill-begotten LLC. But don't let that stop you from cleaning up your LLC either!

Chapter 10

Important Tax Considerations in Starting a Business

Brenda L. Taylor[1]

Major tax considerations in forming a business primarily surround whether or not the business owner wants items of income, loss, credit and deduction ("tax items") taxed at the entity level or at the owner level. An entrepreneur should also be concerned about how to insulate the business from incurring back taxes, interest and penalties as a result of an Internal Revenue Service ("IRS" or "Service") examination, which can be accomplished implementing proper record keeping upon formation. The discussion in this section will be limited to five major types of business entities: partnerships, C corporations, S corporations, and disregarded entities.

Obtaining an EIN: Upon formation, a partnership or corporation should obtain an Employer Identification Number ("EIN"). An EIN can most often be obtained online by going to the IRS website (www.irs.gov). In order to obtain an EIN, a Form SS-4 must be completed. The SS-4 is generally retained by the taxpayer, but in some cases, the IRS will require the taxpayer to submit the form by fax or mail to the IRS. Those circumstances are beyond the discussion in this section. A disregarded entity does not need to obtain an EIN, unless a bank account in the name of the business is needed. An EIN is required in order to file tax

[1]Brenda L. Taylor is a corporate and securities attorney at Greenberg Traurig focusing her practice on corporate transactions and governance. Brenda is experienced in mergers and acquisitions of partnerships and corporations both domestic and foreign, often involving complex tiered structures. Brenda holds a J.D. from the University of Arizona and LL.M. in Taxation from Chapman University.

returns and make certain elections with the IRS, such as a disregarded entity election and S corporation election.

Partnerships: Partnerships are commonly referred to as "pass through" entities because items of income, loss, credit, and deduction flow through the entity to the partner and are taxed at the partner level. Partnerships include such entities as a limited liability company ("LLC"), general partnership, and limited partnership. It should be noted that if a partnership has one partner, the IRS will by default categorize it as a "disregarded entity," which will be discussed later. An entity classified as a disregarded entity by default can file an election with the IRS to be treated as a partnership for tax purposes. This election is made by filing Form 8832 (Entity Classification Election). It should also be noted that a limited liability company with one member or multiple members can also elect to be taxed as a C corporation by filing the same Form 8832 and electing to be treated as an "association taxable as a corporation." A limited liability company can also elect to be treated as an S corporation by filing a Form 2553 (Election by a Small Business Corporation).[2] The taxation of C corporations and S corporations will be discussed later in detail.

Partnership tax items are reported on the partner's income tax return. The partnership files an annual Form 1065 (U.S. Return of Partnership Income). Although the partnership files a return, it does not pay tax at the partnership level. The tax is calculated and paid by each respective partner who receives a Schedule K-1 for Form 1065 (Partner's Share of Income, Deductions, Credits, etc.) from the partnership, which allocates each respective partner's portion of income, loss, deduction and credit. This allocation is normally based on each partner's respective percentage member interest in the partnership. Thus, for 50/50 partners, the allocation of tax items would also be 50/50. The Internal Revenue Code ("IRC") permits partners to make allocations not in conformity with the partner's percentage member interests in the form of a "special allocation." However, there are very strict tests in the IRC applicable to special allocations and a tax professional should be consulted.

Disregarded Entities: As mentioned earlier, partnerships that have one member are classified by default as a disregarded entity. In the case

[2] In this case, it is not necessary for the LLC to first file Form 8832 as long as the Form 2553 is timely filed.

of a limited liability company with one member, the LLC is commonly referred to as a "single member limited liability company" or "SMLLC," which is also considered a disregarded entity. Again, a disregarded entity can file a Form 8832 and elect to be classified as a partnership for tax purposes. Unlike a partnership that files a partnership return (Form 1065), a disregarded entity does not have any requirement to file a return. Instead, the tax items are reported and paid by the single owner on his, her, or its tax return.

C Corporations: C corporations pay tax at the entity level and the shareholders receive dividends, which are taxed to them at special dividends rates.[3] Unlike partnerships in which gain recognition occurs at the partner level, C corporations recognize gain at the entity level. This means that items of income, loss, credit and deduction are calculated at the entity level and tax is paid at the entity level by filing a corporation tax return (Generally, Form 1120 – U.S. Corporation Income Tax Return). The corporation pays tax at graduated corporate income tax rates. It is commonly stated that corporations have "double taxation," meaning that income is taxed twice: Once at the corporate level by the filing of the corporate income tax return, and again at the shareholder level when the income is distributed to the shareholder in the form of a dividend.[4]

S Corporations: An entity treated as a C corporation can elect to be treated as a small business corporation (also known as a Subchapter S Corporation) by filing Form 2553 within two months and 15 days of the beginning of the tax year in which the election is to take effect. In the case of a newly formed corporation, the tax year would normally begin on the date of formation. If that deadline has passed, the IRS permits late election relief subject to meeting certain conditions. A tax professional should be consulted before requesting late election relief from the Service. S corporations are also considered pass-through entities, but aspects of this treatment are different from the treatment of

[3]Dividends rates are currently the same as long term capital gains rates of 20%.

[4]It should be noted that for corporations involved in any type of exporting of products, agricultural commodities, construction services, or architectural services, an election to treat the corporation as an Interest Charge Domestic International Sales Corporation ("IC-DISC") may want to be explored as the IC-DISC is a tax-exempt entity that can have substantial tax savings. IC-DISCs are beyond this scope of this section and a tax professional should be consulted.

partnerships. S corporations avoid the "double taxation" inherent in C corporation. Although corporate income, loss, deduction and credit is determined at the entity level, the tax on the corporate income is paid at the shareholder level. Tax items are passed through to the shareholder through the Schedule K-1 for Form 1120-S (Shareholder's Share of Income, Deductions, Credits, etc.).

Other Tax Considerations: Beyond the scope of this section are other tax-related considerations in forming a business, which are quarterly payments of estimated taxes, required withholding related to payroll taxes, choosing a method of accounting, choosing a tax year for the business, self-employment taxes, and the Additional Medicare Tax as added by the Affordable Care Act ("ACA"). A tax professional should be consulted on these areas.

IRS Examinations: An entrepreneur should be meticulous about keeping adequate books and records of expenses incurred during the formation of a business, as well as after formation during operations. If the business is audited, the IRS will request varying levels of "substantiation," which include, but is not limited to, books and records, receipts, invoices, cancelled checks, bank statements, and credit card statements. An entrepreneur may make a significant capital outlay prior to opening a business, and any documents that support the expenses incurred in making the capital outlay should be retained. It is the opinion of the author that records substantiating business expenses should be retained indefinitely in hard copy or electronic form. Take the example of an entrepreneur who pays for substantial tenant improvements to a retail space in Year 1, and in Year 10 the business owner abandons the space and the improvements. If there is an IRS examination for Year 10, the business owner will need to substantiate the actual existence of the improvements and the cost basis of the improvements. If the business owner has discarded the records, it will be difficult to establish that the improvements in fact existed, let alone the cost basis. If an entrepreneur is vigilant about keeping good books, records, and substantiation of expenses at the outset of the business formation and thereafter, the process of an IRS examination will be less painful.

CHAPTER 11

OBTAINING NECESSARY LICENSES AND PERMITS

ANDREW LILLYWHITE[1]

Before beginning business in Utah, the best resource for knowing what licenses and permits may be required is a consultation with a licensed Utah Attorney who specializes in business law. Furthermore, the State of Utah (www.Utah.gov) and the Small Business Administration (www.SBA.gov) have some helpful online resources. Local Chambers of Commerce and county and city Governments similarly provide additional resources on the subjects of licenses and permits.

Before operating a business, an owner or other authorized person of the business must ensure that the business and, in certain instances, each of its operators and employees obtain the required licenses. Failure to do so in advance of beginning operations can subject the owner and perhaps its operators and employees to civil and criminal penalties. Among others, see Utah Code § 76-8-410 ("Every person who commences or carries on any business, trade, profession, or calling, for the transaction or carrying on of which a license is required by any law, or by any county, city, or town ordinance, without taking out the license required by law or ordinance is guilty of a class B misdemeanor.").

Various licenses and permits affect businesses. For the purposes of this chapter, they include (A) Business Licenses, (B) Professional and Trade-Specific Licenses, and (C) Other Licenses and Permits.

[1]Andrew Lillywhite is an attorney licensed in the State of Utah. His practice focuses on business and estate planning, real property law, and business transactions.

A. Business Licenses.

Business licenses are generally governed by city and county ordinances, and procurement of business licenses is generally achieved through the city and county offices. In unincorporated areas within a county, business licenses are governed by the county. Commonly in Utah, cities, and not counties, require business licenses in incorporated areas of a county.[2]

For example, if George were to open a business within the Salt Lake City limits (which lies within Salt Lake County), he would need to apply for and obtain a Salt Lake City Business License. Moreover, since Salt Lake County does not require a county business license except in unincorporated areas of the county, George need not obtain a Salt Lake County Business License. On the other hand, if Suzan were to open a business within an unincorporated area of Salt Lake County, she would need to obtain a business license from Salt Lake County and not from any particular city.

A common standard for who must obtain a business license in a particular city (or county) is anyone who engages in or carries on any business within that city (or county).[3] Below is a representative example of how one of Utah's largest cities, Salt Lake City defines "business" in this context of activities requiring business licenses:

> Means and includes all activities, trades, professions, or callings engaged in within the corporate limits of Salt Lake City carried on for the business of gain or economic benefit, except that the acts of employees rendering service to employers shall not be included in the term "business" unless otherwise specifically prescribed.[4]

Salt Lake City's definition for "engaging in business" is as follows:

---

[2]It is important to note that many cities and counties may require a business to have registered with the Utah Department of Commerce prior to obtaining a business license, Among other things, such registration allows a business to ensure that the name of their business is available (and, thus, that the name legally belongs to the business), to provide the public, through the Department of Commerce website, notice of the business's registered agent for service of legal process, and to obtain a state-issued entity number for the business that is used in connection with various other license, permit, and tax related activities affecting the business. More information on this process can be found at http://www.commerce.utah.gov/.

[3]See Salt Lake City, UT, Code § 5.02.010.

[4]Id. §5.02.005.

> Means and includes, but is not limited to, the sale of tangible personal property at retail or wholesale, the manufacturing of goods or property, and the rendering of personal services for others for a consideration by persons engaged in any profession, trade, craft, business, occupation or other calling, except the rendering of personal services by an employee to his employer under any contract of personal employment.[5]

In essence, if Leonard is engaged in any for-profit activity and is not doing so as an employee under an employer-employee relationship, then Leonard is responsible for obtaining a business license before engaging in those activities. Without the applicable business license, Leonard could be cited with civil fines or charged with Class B Misdemeanor criminal penalties.

Normally, applying for a business license is simple.[6] Increasingly, a business license application can be completed online for many counties and cities, while many counties and cities may still require a physical form, that can be obtained online or from the city or county offices, to be completed. A fee, which will vary from city to city and county to county, will generally be required with the application. A business owner should contact the city and county where business will be conducted.

For the business license approval process, an inspection by the fire marshal and approval by the city inspector may be required for zoning compliance. Once an initial business license is obtained, annual renewal and fees are usually required to be paid by the business for each year the license remains in force. The business owner should independently ensure that the business activities comply with fire code and zoning ordinances.

In general, a business license is issued to the business that applied for the license and cannot be transferred to another business. Furthermore, a business license is normally specific to the line of business listed on the application. Contact the business licensing division of the city or county to learn whether a new or additional business license is required for the new line of business.

---

[5] *Id.*

[6] However, a background check may be required for some businesses.

Even if the same business with a business license is engaged in business under another DBA ("Doing Business As") the name on the business license, a separate business license certificate might be required—even if no fee is charged for the second certificate. Furthermore, a business licensc may be required for each place of business for one business—even if in the same city or county.

A business's license should be visible in the main reception area of the business. The purpose is dual: to ensure that the business's clients know it is properly licensed and to enable the city or county to inspect for proper display and licensure.

B. Professional and Trade-Specific Licenses.

The Utah Division of Professional Licensing (DOPL) is the main agency in Utah that governs professional licensing. Others agencies in Utah include the following:

Utah Insurance Department (Insurance Agents and Agencies)
Utah Department of Commerce Division of Real Estate (Realtors)
Utah Nursing Assistant Registry (CNAs)
Utah State Bar (Lawyers)
Bureau of Emergency Medical Services (EMTs)
County Health Departments (Food Handlers and Establishments)
Motor Vehicle Enforcement Division (MVED) (Motor Vehicle Related Businesses)

It is also worth noting that the United States Government governs the licensing of certain professions, some of which are identified below. Below is a list of professions licensed under the DOPL[7]):

[7]Utah Department of Professional Licensing, Professions Licensed in Utah https://secure.utah.gov/ datarequest/ professionals/ index.html.

Accountancy
Acupuncture
ADRP
Architect
Athlete Agents
Athletic Trainer
Building Inspector
Burglar Alarm
Chiropractic
Clinical Mental Health
Contractor
Controlled Substance Handler
Cosmetology
Court Reporter
CS Precursor
Deception Detection
Dental
Dietitian
Direct-Entry Midwife
Electrician
Engineer/Land Surveyor
Environmental Health Scientist
Factory Built Housing
Funeral Service
Genetic Counselor
Geologist
Health Facility Administrator
Hearing Instrument
Hunting Guides/Outfitters
Landscape Architect
Lien Recovery Fund Member
Marriage & Family Therapy
Massage
Medical Language Interpreter
Medication Aide - Certified
Naturopathic
Nurse
Occupational Therapy
Optometrist
Osteopathic Physician
Pharmacy
Physical Therapist
Physician
Physician Assistant
Plumber
Podiatric Physician
Preneed
Private Probation Provider
Professional Employer Org
Psychologist
Radiology
Recreational Therapy
Respiratory Care
Security Companies & Guards
Social Work
Speech/Audiology
Substance Use Disorder
Veterinarian
Vocational Rehab Counselor

Below are some businesses and trades which are governed in some form by the United States government, together with their applicable governing agencies.[8]

Agricultural: U.S. Department of Agriculture (USDA).

Alcoholic Beverages: U.S. Treasury's Alcohol and Tobacco Tax and Trade Bureau (TTB) in addition to the local alcohol beverage control board.

Aviation: Federal Aviation Administration (FAA).

Firearms, Ammunition and Explosives: Comply with the Gun Control Act's licensing requirements, which is administered by the Bureau of Alcohol, Tobacco, Firearms and Explosives (ATF).

Fish and Wildlife: U.S. Fish and Wildlife Service.

Commercial Fisheries: NOAA Fisheries Service.

Maritime Transportation: Federal Maritime Commission.

Mining and Drilling on Federal Lands: Bureau of Ocean Energy Management, Regulation and Enforcement (formerly the Minerals Management Service).

Nuclear Energy: U.S. Nuclear Regulatory Commission

Radio and Television Broadcasting: The Federal Communications Commission (FCC).

Transportation and Logistics: U.S. Department of Transportation provides maximum weight guidelines. Permits for oversize/overweight vehicles are issued by state governments.

[8]SBA, Federal Licenses & Permits, https://www.sba.gov/content/what-federal-licenses-and-permits-does-your-business-need.

Licensure of attorneys is, in certain respects, different than many business and professions. Attorneys are considered to be part of a self-governing profession. The Utah State Bar is a nonprofit nongovernmental organization; however, its authority derives from the Supreme Court of Utah. The general rule is that "only persons who are active, licensed members of the Bar in good standing may engage in the practice of law in Utah." Utah SCR 14-802. "The 'practice of law' is defined as the representation of the interests of another person by informing, counseling, advising, assisting, advocating for or drafting documents for that person through application of the law and associated legal principles to that person's facts and circumstances." *Id.*

In general, proper professional licensure of any business or profession has important implications from both a legal requirement standpoint and from a liability standpoint. A person engaging in activity that only a licensed professional is legally authorized to perform will be held to the standards of a practitioner of the profession. Thus, for example, if Jan as an Accountant offers legal advice[9] to her client (regardless of whether the advice turns out to be incorrect according to the standards for attorneys), she would be in trouble for not only engaging in the unauthorized practice of law, but also may be liable to her client for the damages caused by the incorrect legal advice.

Requirements and applications for professional licenses are typically available on the website for the applicable licensing agency. After initial licensure, the agency will usually require periodic renewal with the applicable fees.

C. Other Licenses and Permits.

In addition to the previous licenses and permits, it is important that business owners be aware of the numerous other required licenses and permits that may govern or apply their area of business. Below are a few common examples.

---

[9]"Certified Public Accountants, enrolled IRS agents, public accountants, public bookkeepers, and tax preparers may prepare tax returns." Utah SCR 14-802. Accountants may not form business entities for or otherwise provide legal advice to their clients. Other common sources of the unauthorized practice of law include realtors and closing agents at real estate closings who offer legal advice to their clients regarding the real estate transfer.

1. Construction, Renovation, and Demolition Permits.

Obtaining other licenses and permits may be necessary in a variety of circumstances. One example is construction permits. This type of permit may apply if the business determines it will construct or improve the space in which it operates. The following is an example from the Salt Lake City Building Services (BSCE) website[10]:

> No person, firm or corporation shall erect, construct, enlarge, alter, repair, move, improve, remove, convert or demolish any building, structure or premises, or make any installation, alteration or improvement to the electrical, plumbing or mechanical system in a building, structure or premises, or cause the same to be done, without first obtaining the prescribed permits for each such building or structure or premises from the building official.

2. Zoning Compliance.

A business must comply with zoning restrictions. To find out what type of commercial activities are permitted at the potential business location, a business owner would want to contact the city and county offices where their business is physically located. Zoning restrictions are not set in stone: property owners can apply to have them changed. However, neighboring businesses or residences will be notified of proposed zoning changes and may provide some resistance to the changes. A change to a zoning restriction, often called a variance, is generally handled on a one-off basis, but is not guaranteed to be granted.

3. Fire Department Permits.

Some activities require a permit from the local Fire Department, such as using flammable substances. A couple examples might include an auto body shop that paints cars or a gas station.

4. Sign Permits.

Most cities and counties have restrictions on the size and location of business signage. Contact the local city or county offices where the

[10]Salt Lake City BSCE, BSCE - Frequently Asked Questions, http://www.slcgov.com/building/faqs.

business is physically located to learn the scope and applicability of these restrictions.

5. Sales Tax Licenses.

A person starting a new business or buying an existing business that sells tangible personal property or taxable service may need to apply to the State Tax Commission for a State Sales Tax License. A sales tax license is non-transferrable. A business purchaser should ensure that the sales taxes for the business are paid-up prior to purchasing the business or require a credit on the purchase for paying the sales tax. Furthermore, "[a] separate sales and use tax license must be obtained for each place of business." Utah Admin. Code r. 865-19S-7.

6. Health Department Licenses.

If a business plans to sell food directly to consumers or indirectly through retailers, a permit from the local Health Department will likely be required. The details of the regulations can be obtained from the local Health Department.

Conclusion

Obtaining the proper licenses, registrations and permits is a critical component of legally operating any business in Utah. Before starting a business or purchasing or leasing a business location, an entrepreneur should ensure that the zoning allows the anticipated business activity. If it does, the entrepreneur should turn his or her focus towards obtaining each of the necessary licenses, registrations and permits for the business and its employees, many of which are outlined above. Once all of those items have been secured, the entrepreneur can then turn his or her efforts to the actual successful operation of the business.

CHAPTER 12

STRATEGICALLY STRUCTURING OWNERSHIP AND EMPLOYMENT

GREG PERRY[1]

1. Introduction

This chapter offers basic information for small and mid-sized privately held companies[2] about providing equity incentives for employees or other service providers.[3] The intent of this chapter is to enable entrepreneurs to more effectively interact with company counsel in determining whether and how to set up equity (or similar) incentive plans. Topics addressed include basic structuring of equity incentives, tax planning, and limited securities compliance discussion.[4]

2. Why Give Equity Incentives?

Why give equity incentives to employees? One answer is that often cash is hard to come by in the early in the life of a company. Without cash, it can be difficult for a small business to attract and retain talent. Another reason is that it may pay, in terms of productivity enhancement and incentivizing greater effort, to align the interests of the employees

---

[1]Greg Perry is the General Counsel for Shotgun Creek Investments, LLC, a small real-estate focused private equity group with real estate investments and developments throughout the Western United States. Greg earned his J.D. from New York University School of Law, where he also earned an LLM in taxation. A native of Seattle, Washington, Greg has resided in Utah for the last five years.

[2]This chapter is geared primarily towards S corporations, C corporations, as well as limited liability companies.

[3]Equity awards can be granted to independent contractors that are not employees. For the convenience of this discussion, all service providers will be referred to as employees.

[4]Not covered, among other topics, are: Securities beneficial ownership reporting or registration, 401(k) plans, employee stock ownership plans, ERISA compliance, and retirement or health plans.

with those of management, founders and investors by giving employees an equity stake in the success of the business.

On the other hand, each founder should address whether he or she wants to contend with the headaches, cost and complexity that result from granting equity or equity-related incentives to employees and other service providers. After understanding the structuring, tax and securities issues, and the added fiduciary responsibilities that result from giving equity to employees, many founders determine that the risks and complexities outweigh the hoped-for benefits. In fact, once employees themselves are exposed to the difficult decisions relating to equity incentives, even they may prefer simple cash compensation. Also, many founders place a higher value on their equity than would their employees. Thus, founders may give up, directly or indirectly through higher compliance costs, distraction of management attention and other concerns, far more through equity incentives than they would from paying simple tax-deductible cash bonuses.

Nevertheless, you may still desire to grant equity incentives to employees. Equity incentives can motivate employees for long-term performance in ways that cash cannot. You may be forced to pay below market salaries during the startup period, and a good way to retain and motivate key management positions is through equity compensation.

3. Who Should Receive Equity Incentives?

You may have read about people like Bonnie Brown, the masseuse who took a job at some company called "Google" that paid just $450 a week, but included a pile of stock options that she figured would never be worth anything.[5] Deciding which of your employees will receive equity compensation is a decision that can have significant consequences. In the well-known example of Google, the founders may have been more generous than they needed to be. On the other hand, it is also possible for owners to be too stingy and fail to reward important employees with equity compensation, with the result that employees leave the company for better opportunities. Finding the right balance is a challenge.

An important consideration to keep in mind is that employees who receive equity compensation become more than employees; they become

[5] "Google Options Make Masseuse a Multimillionaire," Katie Hafner, New York Times, November 12, 2007.

part owners. This is often the point, to secure loyalty and motivation of such key personnel. As a fellow owner, a key employee can have the sense of control and responsibility that motivates the employee to work hard and stay committed to the company. On the other hand, if your relationship with the employee deteriorates, without a contract spelling out a means for the company to recover the equity from the employee, it can be more difficult to sever ties with an employee who is also an owner. To protect the company against ensuing problems, companies should give advance consideration to requiring vesting and imposing repurchase options, transfer restrictions and voting covenants on any equity to be granted to employees.

3. How Much Equity Should a Company Award to Employees?

How much of an employee's total compensation should be composed of equity awards? This question has two parts: (1) first, how much of the company should the owners set aside to grant to employees, and (2) second, how much of an employee's salary should be composed of equity incentive awards?

The ownership and board of a company must begin the process of choosing an equity incentive plan by deciding how much of the company they are willing to set aside to compensate certain key employees. Often, owners begin by looking at what they need to retain control of the company, and choose a somewhat arbitrary number that can be used as compensation. The first step in this process is often obtaining a valuation of the company. After all, if a board is going to consider setting aside 15% of the shares of the company as equity compensation, it needs to know what 15% of the company is worth. There are also various tax concerns discussed below that may make it advisable to obtain an independent valuation of the company.

The next question pertains to the percentage of an employee's salary that should be composed of equity compensation. Many industries follow a percentage number to use as a guide (for example, 10%), which may be important to key employees or necessary to recruit or retain key people. The answer will depend on a number of factors, which may include industry norms, the company's ability to pay the cash component of the employee's salary, and the need to provide incentives. The less the company has the ability to pay the market level of cash salary, the more the company may have to make up for it in equity compensation.

5. Basic Types of Equity Incentive Awards

Many companies adopt a generalized equity incentive plan that authorizes the board to grant a variety of equity incentive awards. The company may only decide to grant one type of award, but a plan that allows the granting of a variety of types of awards provides flexibility to the company if needs change over time. This section discusses the different types of awards in a typical equity incentive plan.

Introduction to Stock Options

Stock options are a popular equity compensation award in C corporations. Stock options are essentially a contract between the company and the employee that provides the employee the opportunity to purchase a number of shares of the company stock at a set price for a fixed time. Here are some important terms to understand about stock options:

- ***Vesting:*** Usually the options are subject to a period of restriction on either exercisability or ownership of the option (or both) which is known as "vesting." Different companies and industries choose to have different vesting schedules. Vesting of options over time protects the company and incentivizes the employee to remain.
- ***Exercise:*** The employee can "exercise" her stock options, and purchase the stock from the company for the "exercise price" that is determined at the time of the grant of the options.[6] The exercise price is usually equal to the fair market value at the time of the grant of the stock options.
- ***Option Term:*** An employee must exercise her options before they expire at the end of the "option term" (option grants typically have a 10 year term).

[6] The exercise price is sometimes called the "strike price" or "grant price."

- ***Spread:*** When an employee exercises her option, the "spread" is referred to as the increase in fair market value over the exercise price.
- ***Liquidity:*** Liquidity is often referred to as the ability to sell the shares received upon exercise. As discussed below, legal or tax restrictions, or the lack of a market, can affect the liquidity of options and other equity awards.

Companies like the motivational effect of stock options; the options are only worth something if the company increases in value. Below is a discussion of the two main types of stock options: incentive stock options and non-statutory stock options.

Incentive Stock Options (ISOs)

All stock options are meant to "incentivize" employees. However certain stock options qualify for preferential tax treatment under the tax code, and are defined as "incentive stock options" (also called "statutory stock options" or "ISOs").[7] ISOs have two principal tax benefits: (1) they allow the employee to defer the tax on the spread (the difference between the exercise price and the fair market value at the time of exercise) until after the employee sells the underlying shares, and (2) they allow the employee to qualify for the lower capital gains tax rate on the spread instead of the income being taxed at the ordinary income rate. In order to qualify a plan to grant ISOs, the plan and the stock options issued thereunder must be designed and operated in a matter that complies with a list of requirements, including the following:

- ***Corporations Only.*** Only corporations can grant options that qualify as ISOs.[8] S-corporations can issue ISOs, but keep in mind that S-corporations can only issue a single class of stock to all its shareholders.
- ***Employee vs. Independent Contractor.*** Only employees can be granted ISOs. Independent contractors can only be granted nonqualified options.

[7]Internal Revenue Code Section 422(b). ISOs are also referred to as "statutory stock options."

[8]Code Section 422(b).

- ***Holding Period:*** In order to qualify for long-term capital gains taxation, the optionee must hold the stock received from exercise of the option for at least one year following exercise of the option, and two years following the option grant date.[9]
- ***$100,000 Limit:*** An employee can exercise only $100,000 worth of ISOs during any calendar year,[10] as measured by the fair market value on the grant date for the option.[11]
- ***10% Ownership Rule:*** If at the time the option is granted, the employee owns more than 10 percent of the voting power of the stock of the company (or of its parent or a subsidiary corporation), then the exercise price must be 110% of the fair market value on the grant date.[12]
- ***Shareholder Approved Plan:*** The options must be granted pursuant to a plan approved either before the grant or within one year thereafter by the stockholders that, among other things, fixes the aggregate amount of shares to be issued pursuant to the plan.[13]
- ***Exercise Period:*** The option must be granted within 10 years from the date the shareholders adopt the stock option plan,[14] and the option cannot be exercisable after the expiration of 10 years from the date the option is granted.[15]
- ***Exercise Price:*** At the time of grant of the option, the exercise price cannot be less than the fair market value of the stock.[16] This is discussed further below in the section on NSOs.

---

[9]Code Section 422(a)(1); Treas. Reg. §1.422-1(a)(1)(i)(A).

[10]Treas. Reg. §1.422-4(a)(1-2).

[11]Treas. Reg. §1.422-4(b)(2). Tracking the amounts that employees can exercise to stay under this limit can be a difficult task.

[12]Code Section 422(b)(6).

[13]Code Section 422(b)(1). A stock option plan that allows the company to issue unlimited shares, or even a certain percentage of the outstanding shares, will flunk this test. However the plan can state that the company can issue a percentage of the outstanding shares existing at the time of the adoption of the plan. See Treas. Reg. §1.422-4(b)(3).

[14]Code Section 422(b)(2).

[15]Code Section 422(b)(3).

[16]Code Section 422(b)(4).

- ***Option Transfer Restriction:*** The terms of the option cannot allow the employee to transfer the option before exercise, except through a will.[17]
- ***No Company Tax Deduction:*** The company cannot take a tax deduction when an employee complies with the ISO rules.

Many restrictions must be met to qualify options as ISOs. And the tax benefits of ISOs (you can defer the tax normally imposed after exercise until after disposition of the stock, if ever, and the gain is taxed at long-term capital gain instead of ordinary income rates) can be less than imagined because of the alternative minimum tax (AMT).[18] For private companies, where there is no market to sell the shares received upon exercise, an employee could face an income tax liability without any cash to pay the tax.

Non-Qualified Stock Options (NSOs)

Options that do not qualify as incentive stock options under Code Section 422 are referred to as "non-qualified stock options" (NSOs). NSOs do not have to meet any of the requirements listed above for ISOs. However, if the options have an exercise price that is below the fair market value of the stock on the date the options are granted ("discounted options"), there will be significant tax and penalties due under Code Section 409A.[19]

In order to avoid the penalties of Section 409A, the company must provide evidence that the options were not issued at a discount to fair market value. For private companies, this means obtaining a valuation by an independent appraiser at least annually.[20]

NSOs generally do not have any tax consequences when they are granted, if the exercise price is not less than the fair market value. At the time of exercise, the employee will be taxed on the spread between the exercise price and the fair-market value. This income will be taxed at the

---

[17]Code Section 422(b)(5).

[18]This is the case because the spread upon exercise is a preference item under the AMT rules, which may result in income tax liability depending on the employee's overall tax situation. Section 56(b)(3).

[19]In summary, if 409A applies, the deferred tax is due plus a 20% penalty with applicable interest. Code Section 409(a)(1).

[20]Treas. Reg §1.409A-1(b)(5)(iv)(B)(2)(i).

ordinary income rates. Upon disposition of the stock after exercise of the option, any appreciation would be eligible for capital gains treatment. The company is eligible for a tax deduction equal to the amount of income incurred by the employee taxed as ordinary income.

There are many reasons why companies favor NSOs over ISOs. From the company's perspective, there is less compliance and associated paperwork than with ISOs, and the company gets a tax deduction that it wouldn't receive with ISOs. Employees sometimes favor NSOs because the preferential tax treatment afforded to ISOs comes with too many strings attached. And the tax treatment itself may not be good at all if it triggers payment under the alternative minimum tax. For these reasons, the majority of stock options that are issued are NSOs.

Unrestricted Stock

Unrestricted stock refers to the simple practice of granting shares of stock to an employee as compensation for services, without vesting restrictions. The stock can be granted as a normal part of a salary (such as receiving a certain number of shares with each paycheck) or as a reward for achieving certain performance metrics.

Although unrestricted stock has no vesting, the shares can still be subject to certain restrictions on transferability. For example, the company could require that the shares be resold to the company if the employee quits, or at least provide the company with a right of first refusal. Some companies choose to restrict the voting rights by either requiring that the shares be voted as directed by the CEO or by creating a separate class of nonvoting shares to grant to employees.

The tax consequences of unrestricted stock grants are straightforward. The employee recognizes ordinary income in the amount of the value of the stock at the time of grant, except to the extent income is offset by a payment from the employee to the company equal to the value of the stock purchased.[21] The accompanying tax bill is perhaps the biggest disadvantage to unrestricted stock grants. The company can choose to provide an amount of cash to the employee to cover the tax liability (of

[21]Quite commonly, a company will agree to sell stock to an employee in exchange for cash or a secured promissory note secured by a pledge of the stock back to the company having a fairly long term, such as eight or more years, that would become due on termination of employment or on resale of the stock.

course, that cash bonus is also subject to tax). The company must report the stock grant and any cash bonus on the employee's Form W-2. The company can deduct the amount of the stock grant as a business expense.

Companies choose unrestricted stock grants because they are simple for employees to understand, and have the benefit of a resulting in an immediate ownership stake. Although most companies value the incentives that come with the vesting schedule of options or restricted stock, some companies value the simplicity of unrestricted stock.

Restricted Stock

Restricted stock awards (RSAs) are similar to unrestricted stock, but are subject to a vesting period or other milestone achievement. Companies that prefer to impose a vesting requirement appreciate the effect of the vesting schedule to incentivize employees to remain with the company. As discussed above in the section on "Vesting Incentives," the vesting schedule can either be based on time schedule or based on performance metrics, or even a combination of both. Although it is less common, some companies require the employee to purchase the stock, normally at a discount. However, the shares are granted to the employee on a grant date, and subject to a vesting period.

After grant, but before the vesting period lapses, RSAs are often held in escrow, and the employee is usually entitled to receive any applicable dividends and voting rights. Similar to restricted stock awards are restricted stock units (RSUs). When a company grants RSUs, the employee receives a right to receive the shares after the vesting period lapses, so the shares don't actually transfer until after the vesting period ends. Since the employee does not yet own the stock, RSUs don't allow the employee to enjoy any dividends or voting rights.

The tax consequences of restricted stock are fairly straightforward. An employee that receives restricted stock is not taxed at the time of grant, assuming that the stock is still subject to a vesting period, which the IRS calls a "substantial risk of forfeiture."[22] Thankfully, the IRS does not impose a tax on the value of the stock when it could turn out you never meet the vesting requirements and actually gain full ownership of

[22]Code Sec. 83(c)(1).

the stock. After the vesting period ends, the employee is taxed on the value of the stock (at ordinary income tax rates), and the company is eligible for a tax deduction for the same amount.

An employee can make a special election, however, after an RSA is granted to voluntarily accelerate any tax due upon grant of the restricted stock. Named after its place in the tax code, this election is called a "Section 83(b) Election." Why would an employee make an election to accelerate taxes? Although the election accelerates the tax due (usually a bad thing), any appreciation on the stock after the election is eligible for preferential capital gains treatment, which is lower than ordinary income rates. The election must be made within 30 days of grant.[23] There are risks to the employee if the stock declines in value or the employee never fulfills the vesting restrictions. No loss is allowed under Section 83(b) if the stock is forfeited or not received.[24] Employees should weigh carefully the risks and rewards of making the Section 83(b) Election with their tax advisor.

There are several reasons why companies choose restricted stock over stock options. For starters, stock options can easily become worthless if the value of the stock falls below the exercise price, while whole shares that are granted with restricted stock usually retain some value, even if it declines. In addition, because restricted stock retains some value, less shares are required to be granted, as opposed to stock options. A rule of thumb is that each restricted share is worth about three options.[25] As a result of this reality, stock options appear to result in more dilution on a company's earnings per share ratio than restricted stock.

Phantom Stock

Some companies want to tie part of an employee's compensation to stock performance, but don't want to actually transfer shares to employees. With phantom stock, the employee does not actually receive stock, but instead receives a phantom grant of hypothetical shares of the company. After the end of a vesting period or the passing of a certain event (e.g., a performance metric achieved, sale of the company, IPO,

---

[23]Code Sec. 83(b)(2).

[24]Code Sec. 83(b)(1)(B).

[25]Corey Rosen, Pam Chernoff, Elizabeth Dodge, Daniel Janich, Scott Rodrick, and Dan Walter, The Decision-Maker's Guide to Equity Compensation, p. 65 (2007).

etc), the employee receives the value of the shares in cash. Thus, a grant of phantom shares itself has no value until the occurrence of events triggering a payment under the plan.

The tax consequences of phantom stock are similar to receiving a cash bonus. The employee recognizes ordinary income in the amount of the cash received at the time it is received which is reported on the employee's Form W-2, and the IRS will require income and employment tax withholding. The company is allowed a tax deduction for the same amount.

Although it may take some education, employees generally appreciate phantom stock and RSAs because "cash is king," and it can be seen as superior to other stock awards that are not liquid.

Companies that choose phantom stock generally do so because they are reluctant to issue stock of the company to employees. This could be because of concerns about additional dilution, or perhaps staying under the 100-shareholder limit for S-corporations. The downside to the company is that it is obligated to make a big cash payout to the employee if there is a significant appreciation in the company's value.

Direct Stock Purchase Plans

Some businesses want to provide a way for their employees to invest in the company, to raise capital and to allow employees to make a contribution to the future of the company. Smaller, private companies may use direct stock purchase plans to accomplish this goal. In direct stock purchase plans, the shares are normally purchased for their fair market value (without a discount), and thus generally there are no adverse tax consequences (of course, the employee will eventually have tax liability on the gain from her re-sale of the stock). The company is not responsible for any employment taxes. As discussed above with respect to unrestricted stock, some companies can choose to require that the stock be resold to the company or at least a right of first refusal in order to allow the company to keep the stock out of the hands of unwanted outsiders.[26]

---

[26]The direct stock purchase plan discussed above contrasts with the formal employee stock purchase plan as defined under Section 423 of the Code ("ESPP"). These plans are usually used by public companies, and allow the company to sell shares to employees at a discount. Since these plans are mainly used by larger, public companies, they are outside the scope of this chapter.

5. Incentive Awards for Limited Liability Companies

Limited liability companies (LLCs) are the most popular form of business entity for small businesses. This is primarily because LLCs are not taxed separately (at the company level) but instead their income is allocated to the "members" and payable only by them, and thus the "company layer" of taxation is removed. LLCs also enjoy flexibility as to how they share profits of the business among members (who may be capital members and/or only profits interest members). LLCs are advantageous for these reasons, but structurally they are also very different than corporations. Although they do not issue stock, they are able to issue units of LLC member interests or options therefore (or restricted units) and can generally replicate almost any form of equity incentive that is available in a C corporation (other than ISOs).

Capital Interests

The simplest equity compensation award to an employee would be a grant of a capital interest in the LLC, without any restrictions or vesting period. A capital interest is an equity interest in both the profits and the assets of the LLC (very similar to stock in a corporation). Accordingly, LLCs with significant assets or profits will want to think carefully about the value of the interest they intend to grant to employees.

The employee is taxed at the ordinary income rate on the value of the capital interest on the date of grant, and the IRS will require income and employment tax withholding. If the capital interest is subject to restrictions such as a vesting period, the employee will be taxed upon the lapse of the vesting period or other restrictions, unless the employee made a Section 83(b) Election within 30 days of the grant date. The Section 83(b) Election is a trade-off that requires the employee to be taxed on the value of the interest at the time of grant at ordinary income tax rates, but allows any subsequent appreciation to be taxed at capital gains rates (see additional discussion of this election above under the heading "Restricted Stock"). A Section 83(b) Election made at the grant of a capital interest will cause the employee to be treated as a partner for tax purposes, and be allocated a share of the profits or losses of the partnership on a Schedule K-1.

The company is allowed a tax deduction for a corresponding

amount. Before the existing members of an LLC grant a capital interest to an employee, they will want to obtain a valuation of the company to avoid transferring to the employee any pre-grant appreciation in the value of the company.

Profits Interests

Another type of equity compensation award for LLCs is a profits interest. Unlike a capital interest, a profits interest does not give the holder a share of the company's assets (which would be distributed, for example, after a liquidation) or any right to receive income earned by the company before the date of the grant. A profits interest only entitles the employee to a share of the company's future profits earned, or future appreciation in value realized, after the date of grant of the profits interest. The profits interest can be granted without restriction, or subject to vesting requirements.

If the profits interest fits within the safe-harbor criteria outlined by the IRS, there will be no tax upon the grant of the profits interest if under the terms of the profits interest grant, the profits interest has no value at the time of grant.[27] In addition, to meet this safe harbor, the profits interest must (1) be received by the employee in her capacity as a member or in anticipation of becoming a member, (2) the profits interest cannot be related to a substantially certain and predictable stream of income, and (3) the profits interest cannot be taken with an intent to sell it within two years after it is received.[28] The other members of the LLC would not be eligible for any tax deduction if the new member is not taxed after receipt of the profits interest.[29] If the profits interest is vested, or even if it is unvested and the employee has made a Section 83(b) Election, the employee will be treated as a partner and receive tax allocations of profit or loss on a Schedule K-1.

There are administrative burdens to LLCs granting profits interests. Similar to capital interests, the LLC needs to do a valuation of the

[27]Defined under tax law to mean that if the company were hypothetically liquidated immediately after the grant of the profits interest, and all of the company's assets were sold for cash at a price equal to their then fair market value, the plan must in effect provide that nothing at all would be payable to the profits interest holder in respect of such interest.

[28]Rev. Proc. 93-27.

[29]*Id.*

company (usually by a third-party appraiser) at the time of each grant of the profits interest. There will also be a need to adjust the capital accounts of the old members to ensure that the new member does not receive any pre-grant value in the company. The cost and time that it takes to undertake these valuations discourages LLCs from frequent grants of profits interests, but profits interests are becoming increasingly popular because they permit an incentive to be granted without triggering income tax to be paid by the employee or the company as a result of the grant itself.

6. Securities Law Considerations

The securities laws pertaining to the issuance of stock and other securities are extensive, and a detailed discussion is outside the scope of this chapter. However a few issues should be highlighted. Generally, federal securities laws provide that a company cannot offer securities unless a registration statement is filed with the Securities and Exchange Commission (SEC) under the Securities Act of 1934 unless there is an applicable exemption. Because registration with the SEC is very expensive and onerous process, startup companies almost always seek capital in the initial phases through an available exemption.

Rule 701 is a federal exemption from the registration requirements, which allows private companies to offer and grant unregistered securities to employees under non-capital-raising plans. Rule 701 is the most commonly used exemption used in connection with securities offered to employees as equity compensation. Many states have adopted state-law counterpart exemptions for use in situations in which the federal Rule 701 is relied upon. Rule 701 has limitations: The total amount of securities sold under Rule 701 cannot exceed the greater of (1) $1 million, (2) fifteen percent of the total assets of the company, or (3) fifteen percent of the outstanding amount of securities of that class. Alternatively, for grants of incentives that do not comply with Rule 701, compliance with Regulation D, Rule 506, can be used (even along-side one or more Rule 701 grants) to exempt such other incentives from registration requirements under the securities law.

Federal securities laws also require a company to register its shares (i.e., to "go public") when they exceed the 500-person threshold. In summary, when a company has any class of security held by five hundred or more persons, and the Company owns more than $10,000,000 in assets, the company must "go public" and register its shares under the Securities Exchange Act of 1934 and file periodic reports whether it wants to or not.[30] Option holders are not counted toward this number. Certain companies such as Facebook have been forced to go public because of this rule.

7. Conclusion

The decision whether to offer equity incentive awards should be undertaken with a careful consideration of the costs and benefits. Which employees should receive awards, and how much of their compensation should be composed of equity incentive awards, are equally important decisions. There are many different types of equity incentive awards, and it may seem difficult to decide which type of award is right for your company and employees. A competent advisor can assist in these decisions and implement a plan that works for your business.

[30]Securities Exchange Act of 1934, Section 12(g).

CHAPTER 13

BUYING & SELLING A BUSINESS

MAINTAINING AND PIERCING LIMITED LIABILITY: ALTER EGO, SUCCESSOR LIABILITY, AND CONTEMPT

AARON PACINI[1]

One of the most common benefits of organizing or incorporating your business venture into an entity (such as a corporation or a limited liability company) is that the law can limit your personal liability for the business's liabilities to the amount of your investment in that entity.[2] This is called *limited liability*. What this means in practical terms is that, if a creditor successfully sues your entity for an unpaid debt or other liability, that *judgment creditor*[3], while able to lay claim to your business's assets will not be able to obtain your personal assets simply because you are an owner or officer of the entity. Those assets are shielded behind what is often referred to as the *corporate veil*[4] and inaccessible to the judgment creditor—so long as you have not taken steps to reduce or eliminate the effectiveness of the corporate veil.

[1]Aaron Pacini is General Counsel for a renewable energy conglomerate and an alumnus of the University of Virginia School of Law. Previously, Mr. Pacini clerked for the United State District Court for the District of Utah and practiced complex commercial litigation.

[2]While there are advantages to incorporating a business, doing so has its drawbacks as well. For instance, in Utah and many other jurisdictions, entities cannot represent themselves in court as a pro se litigant. Rather, the law requires entities to appoint counsel licensed to practice in that jurisdiction. *See Graham v. Davis Cnty. Solid Waste Mgmt. & Energy Recovery Special Serv. Dist.*, 1999 UT App 136, ¶ 14, 979 P.2d 363 ("[A]n unincorporated association, like a corporate entity, may not be represented by a nonlawyer."); *Rowland v. California Men's Colony*, 506 U.S. 194, 201–02, 113 S.Ct. 716, 121 L.Ed.2d 656 (1993) ("It has been the law for the better part of two centuries ... that a corporation may appear in the federal courts only through licensed counsel."). Failure to do so can result in default judgment against the entity.

[3]A judgment creditor is, "[a] person having a legal right to enforce execution of a judgment for a specific sum of money." JUDGMENT CREDITOR, Black's Law Dictionary (9th ed. 2009), judgment creditor.

[4]The corporate veil is "[t]he legal assumption that the acts of a corporation are not the actions of its shareholders, so that the shareholders are exempt from liability for the corporation's actions." CORPORATE VEIL, Black's Law Dictionary (9th ed. 2009), corporate veil.

Because of this advantage, the corporate form is open to abuse. Some have attempted to use their entity as a shell to stash away their liabilities while draining the assets and profits out of the company for their own personal use. Others have used an entity to hold the business obligations before transferring its business, management, and unencumbered assets to a newly organized entity, free of these obligations. Then, there are others still that may refuse to obey a court's order directing the entity to do something on the belief that the individual is not the entity and, therefore, not liable for the entity's inaction. Are such people still protected by limited liability? Is there ever additional recourse for the creditor? If so, is there a way to decrease your exposure to the risks of operating a legitimate business?

This section discuses three legal theories under which business owners and officers may be held liable for the acts (or inaction) of the business entity notwithstanding the typical protections of the corporate veil: (1) Alter Ego; (2) Successor Liability; and (3) Contempt.

Alter Ego

The first potential exception to limited liability is where the entity is nothing more than the *alter ego* of the owner.[5] If a party successfully obtains a judgment that the entity is the alter ego of the owner, the complaining party will then be permitted to *pierce the corporate veil*[6] and satisfy the judgment against the owner, personally. Under Utah law[7],

---

[5]Alter ego is generally defined as "[a] corporation [or other entity] used by an individual in conducting personal business, the result being that a court may impose liability on the individual by piercing the corporate veil when fraud has been perpetrated on someone dealing with the corporation." ALTER EGO, Black's Law Dictionary (9th ed. 2009)

The alter ego doctrine is applied differently is certain contexts, such as labor law, where the alter ego doctrine is designed to prevent employers from escaping collective bargaining obligations by shifting work to non-union firms that they also own. *UA Local 343 United Ass'n of Journeymen & Apprentices of Plumbing & Pipefitting Indus. of U.S. & Canada, AFL-CIO v. Nor-Cal Plumbing, Inc.*, 48 F.3d 1465, 1475 (9th Cir. 1994).

[6]Piercing the corporate veil is "[t]he judicial act of imposing personal liability on otherwise immune corporate officers, directors, or shareholders for the corporation's wrongful acts." PIERCING THE CORPORATE VEIL, Black's Law Dictionary (9th ed. 2009), piercing the corporate veil

[7]Utah courts have not had great occasion to interpret this doctrine. The Supreme Court of Utah, however, has thus far adopted California's articulation of the law. *See Bushnell v. Barker*, 2012 UT 20, ¶ 13, 274 P.3d 968 (quoting *Shaoxing Cnty. Huayue Imp. & Exp. v. Bhaumik*, 191 Cal.App.4th 1189, 120 Cal.Rptr.3d 303, 310 (2011)); *see also, See d'Elia v. Rice Dev., Inc.*, 2006 UT App 416, ¶ 27, 147 P.3d 515 (stating that "California and Utah differ little in their alter ego doctrines"); *see also, Cascade Energy & Metals Corp. v. Banks*, 896 F.2d 1557, 1575 (10th Cir. 1990) ("California's standard for piercing the corporate veil does not appear to be materially different from Utah's.").

courts evaluate the alter ego theory of liability[8] under the two-pronged *Norman* test:

> (1) there must be such unity of interest and ownership that the separate personalities of the corporation and the individual no longer exist, viz., the corporation is, in fact, the alter ego of one or a few individuals; and (2) the observance of the corporate form would sanction a fraud, promote injustice, or an inequitable result would follow.

Lowry, 2012 UT 39, ¶ 14 (quoting *Norman v. Murray First Thrift & Loan Co.*, 596 P.2d 1028, 1030 (Utah 1979)).

What does this mean? And how do courts evaluate these two prongs? Utah courts look to the following nonexclusive factors in deciding whether the *Norman* test is met:[9]

> (1) undercapitalization of a one-man corporation; (2) failure to observe corporate formalities; (3) nonpayment of dividends; (4) siphoning of corporate funds by the dominant stockholder; (5) nonfunctioning of other officers or directors; (6) absence of corporate records; (7) the use of the corporation as a facade for operations of the dominant stockholder or stockholders; and (8) the use of the corporate entity in promoting injustice or fraud.

Lowry, 2012 UT 39, ¶¶ 16, 20 (quoting *Colman v. Colman*, 743 P.2d 782, 786 (Utah Ct.App.1987)).

---

[8]Unlike a claim for breach of contract or fraud, piercing the corporate veil "is not itself a claim" that can be brought against you or your business, but rather a procedural tool "to disregard the corporate entity and hold the alter ego individual liable for the obligations of the corporation." *Bushnell v. Barker*, 2012 UT 20, ¶ 13, 274 P.3d 968 (quoting *Shaoxing Cnty. Huayue Imp. & Exp. v. Bhaumik*, 191 Cal.App.4th 1189, 120 Cal.Rptr.3d 303, 310 (Cal. App. 2011)). As a result, "an alter ego theory does not need to be alleged in the "underlying lawsuit" or "proved before entry of judgment." *See Misik v. D'Arco*, 197 Cal. App. 4th 1065, 1074-75, 130 Cal. Rptr. 3d 123, 130 (Cal. App. 2011). So long as the alleged alter ego has notice and an opportunity to be heard, a party may pierce the corporate veil "after judgment." *See Misik v. D'Arco*, 197 Cal. App. 4th 1065, 1074-75, 130 Cal. Rptr. 3d 123, 130 (2011).

[9]The focus of the alter ego analysis is on the "entire relationship between various corporate entities and their directors and officers." *Lowry*, 2012 UT 39, ¶ 18. Thus, these factors should be treated as "merely helpful tools and not required elements." *Id.* Evidence of even one factor, in appropriate circumstances, may be enough to meet the requirements of *Norman*. *See Lowry*, 2012 UT 39 at ¶ 22.

Defending against (or proving) that someone has used a business as their alter ego generally requires significant fact discovery and an factually intensive analysis. This can be very expensive. As such, it is important that business owners keep the above *Colman* factors in mind as you run your business.

Successor Liability

As your business develops, your company may acquire assets from another company. But, what about the liabilities of the transferring company? Does acquiring assets from another company put your business at risk for those liabilities? What happens if another entity owes you money and begins transferring its assets to another entity before shuttering its doors along with its unpaid debts?

Generally, where a "company sells or otherwise transfers all its assets to another company, the latter is not responsible for the debts and liabilities of the transferor."[10] As always, however, there are exceptions to this rule. The transferee (purchaser) is liable for the debts and liabilities of the transferor (seller) if:

> (1) the purchaser expressly or impliedly agrees to assume such debts; (2) the transaction amounts to a consolidation or merger of the seller and purchaser; (3) the purchasing corporation is merely a continuation of the selling corporation; or (4) the transaction is entered into fraudulently in order to escape liability for such debts.[11]

Decius v. Action Collection Serv., Inc., 2004 UT App 484, ¶ 8, 105 P.3d 956.

The first exception needs no explanation. The second, or "de facto merger," occurs where the business operation and management continue and require that the purchaser pay for the asset with its own stock. *Id.* In contrast, the third "mere continuation" factor analyzes not whether the business operations continue, but whether the corporate entity

[10] *Decius v. Action Collection Serv., Inc.*, 2004 UT App 484, ¶ 8, 105 P.3d 956.

[11] Although not discussed here, Utah law provides relief for a creditor injured by a debtor's "fraudulent conveyance."

continues; i.e. that there exists a common identity of stock, directors, and stockholders and the existence of only one corporation at the completion of the transfer. *Id.* The fourth factor asks whether or not the asset transfer was colored with fraud to escape the seller's debts.

Similar to alter ego, successor liability is a factually intensive analysis. And, depending on the precise case, the relevant law and its application may not be completely settled.[12] If you find yourself in a situation where you are merging with another company or buying substantial assets of another entity, you will want to consult an attorney.

Contempt

To this point, the discussion has contemplated a dispute between two parties. What happens when the court orders an entity to comply with an order or a rule? Does that obligation fall on the officers of the company, personally? Can the court hold a person in *contempt*[13] because the entity the person works for failed to follow the order?

Some unfortunate parties have incorrectly believed that if a court orders their entity to do something, they, as officers of the company, are not personally at risk if the entity does not comply. This is not the case. In fact, the Supreme Court of the United States has long-held that "[a] command to the corporation is in effect a command to those who are officially responsible for the conduct of its affairs." *Wilson v. United States,* 221 U.S. 361, 376 (1911). Indeed, if those responsible for the entity "prevent compliance or fail to take appropriate action within their power for the performance of the corporate duty, they, no less than the corporation itself, are guilty of disobedience, and may be punished for contempt."[14] *Id.*; *see also, Whole Living, Inc. v. Tolman*, 2:03-CV-272 TS,

---

[12]Various jurisdictions have altered or expanded the four traditional factors. Utah has not yet decided whether to adopt these formulations. *See Decius v. Action Collection Serv., Inc.*, 2004 UT App 484, ¶¶ 9-12, 105 P.3d 956.

[13]Contempt has various definitions and applications. In the legal arena, it can refer to the disturbance or interference with the administration of justice, such as when court is in session. *See* CONTEMPT, Black's Law Dictionary (9th ed. 2009). Contempt can be both civil and criminal, depending on its purpose. A person is in civil contempt when a contempt order is meant to coerce the individual's compliance with an order to compensate an aggrieved party for injuries resulting from another's failure to comply with an order. In contrast, criminal contempt exists to "vindicate a court's authority, as by punishing an individual for disobeying an order, even if the order arises from civil proceedings." *Dickman Family Properties, Inc. v. White*, 2013 UT App 116, ¶ 2, 302 P.3d 833. For this discussion, contempt refers to the general disregard of, or disobedience to, the law. *Id.* The court can impose various sanctions on a party found in contempt, including a fine or incarceration. *Id.*

[14]This law equally applies to "officers of an unincorporated association." *See United States v. Voss*, 82 F.3d 1521, 1525 (10th Cir. 1996) (quoting *United States v. Fleischman*, 339 U.S. 349, 358 (1950)).

2004 WL 2733614 (D. Utah Nov. 29, 2004) (stating that a corporate officer who fails to take appropriate action within his or her power to see that the entity complies with a court's orders "may appropriately be held jointly liable for the contempt") (citations omitted) (attached hereto as Ex. 3). The Tenth Circuit reiterated this statement of the law many times. *See e.g., F.T.C. v. Kuykendall*, 371 F.3d 745, 759 (10th Cir. 2004) (quoting *Wilson* and reemphasizing that "an individual who is responsible for insuring that a corporation complies with a court order cannot escape liability merely by removing himself from the day-to-day operations of the corporation and washing his hands of responsibility"); *see also, United States v. Voss*, 82 F.3d 1521, 1525 (10th Cir. 1996) (with discussion from other jurisdictions).

Utah follows the federal approach. It is now well-established that "[a]n officer or any other agent of a corporation may be personally as responsible as the corporation itself for tortious acts when participating in the wrongdoing . . . ." *d'Elia v. Rice Dev., Inc.*, 2006 UT App 416, ¶¶ 39, 43, 147 P.3d 515 *holding modified on other grounds by Jones & Trevor Mktg., Inc. v. Lowry*, 2012 UT 39, 284 P.3d 630 (further holding that the "imposition of personal liability on corporate officers who participate in a corporation's tortious acts also applies to limited liability members or managers") (citations omitted);[15] *see also, Bennett v. Huish*, 2007 UT App 19, ¶48, 155 P.3d 917 ("[A] corporate officer or director can incur personal liability for his own acts even though the action is done in furtherance of the corporate business.").[16]

The takeaway here is rather straightforward: If the court orders your business entity to do something and it is within your responsibility to comply—do it. Otherwise, the court may hold you personally responsible.

---

[15]Civil contempt is considered a tort. *Coleman v. Espy*, 986 F.2d 1184, 1192 (8th Cir. 1993) (noting that civil contempt is "essentially a tort action").

[16]This rule exists because "to permit an agent of a corporation, in carrying on its business, to inflict wrong and injuries upon others, and then shield himself from liability behind his vicarious character, would both sanction and encourage the perpetration of flagrant and wanton injuries by agents of insolvent and irresponsible corporations." *Mitochon Practice Mgmt., LLC v. Healthcare Tech. Alliance, LLC*, 2:13CV177, 2013 WL 4774705 at*5 (D. Utah Sept. 4, 2013) (quoting *Armed Forces Exchange v. Harrison*, 2003 UT 14, ¶ 20, 70 P.3d 35 (Utah 2003)).

SUMMARY:

The protection of limited liability has its limits. To protect yourself:

- Manage the business as a separate entity from yourself to protect against someone piercing the corporate veil;
- When selling or buying substantial assets from another company, hire an attorney that will ensure that the transaction is appropriately structured to avoid unwanted liability;
- If a court orders your entity to do something and you are in a position of responsibility to comply with that order, do it.

CHAPTER 14

SECURITIES

COMMON STATE AND FEDERAL SECURITIES LAW VIOLATIONS

ERIK A. CHRISTENSEN[1]

Many entrepreneurs learn the hard way that failure to comply with state and federal securities laws in the creation of a business or in connection with entrepreneurial financing can cause crippling regulatory and litigation issues, which later destroy the business. To prevent such risks, entrepreneurs should involve competent securities financing counsel early in all aspects of business organization, financing, and corporate governance. While it might seem like an unnecessary, expensive cost early in the genesis of a business, funds invested in competent securities counsel at the time of business formation will save substantial attorneys' fees, costs, liabilities, regulatory issues, uncertainty and disputes later on in the life of a company. Indeed, it is common for securities lawyers to joke that corporate transactional lawyers are expensive, but securities litigators are much more expensive, which is another way of saying that an ounce of prevention is worth a pound of cure.

Securities Registration or Exemption from Registration

The sale of any ownership interest in a business generally requires that the sale of the ownership interest comply with all applicable state

[1]Erik A. Christiansen is a shareholder at the law firm of Parsons Behle & Latimer, where his practice focuses on commercial litigation and securities litigation. Mr. Christiansen also is the Chair of the Utah Securities Commission, which has certain statutory oversight over the Utah Division of Securities, and which sits as the finders of fact in contested administrative proceedings. Mr. Christiansen also is an adjunct Professor of Law at the S.J. Quinney College of Law at the University of Utah.

and federal securities laws. Typically, for example, the sale of stock or a similar ownership interest in a business must be done so that the sale is exempt from registration with federal and state regulators (for example, in a private offering), or a registration statement must be filed with state and federal regulators (i.e., a public offering).[2] Exemptions from securities registration typically depend on a number of factors, including, for example, the number of persons offered the stock, and the financial net worth, income and sophistication of the purchasers of the stock.[3]

Securities Include Notes, Debentures and Investment Contracts

Many entrepreneurs are surprised to learn that different types of ownership interests are "securities" under state and federal law, regardless of the label used or type of entity involved, and surprised to learn that the sale of ownership interests in or use of certain financing methods requires compliance with state and federal securities laws. For example, in Utah, notes, bonds, debentures, investment contracts, certificates of interest, viatical settlements, certificate of deposits for a security, and interests in a limited liability company, are "securities" subject to regulation under the securities laws. Many entrepreneurs incorrectly believe that raising money by issuing promissory notes, debentures or other debt instruments does not involve the offer and sale of securities, or that selling shares only to friends and family is always legal. Sadly, unprepared and uninformed entrepreneurs later learn the hard way that promissory notes and debentures are, in fact, securities subject to state and federal securities laws, and that if sales are done improperly, even your friends and family can and will sue when life savings are lost in a new business.

Rescission Rights for the Sale of Unregistered Securities

Under state securities laws, if securities, including notes and debentures, are sold to unqualified or unaccredited investors without

---

[2]A registration statement is what is commonly thought of as a public offering or initial public offering. Exempt transactions are generally sold in what are commonly called private offerings.

[3]Crowd funding, however, potentially is available in limited amounts under narrow circumstances carefully prescribed under federal laws and regulations.

a valid exemption from registration or without an effective registration statement, the investors who purchased the notes, securities and/or debentures can and many times do demand rescission of the investment, and can be entitled to a full refund of their investment, along with statutory interest, attorneys' fees and costs, regardless of the success or subsequent failure of the business.[4] In other words, if an entrepreneur does not comply with state and federal securities laws in selling certain ownership interests in a business, the investor can later demand all of their money back, along with statutory interest, attorneys' fees and costs, and the company is obligated to refund the investment, even if the company is losing money and the investment would otherwise have resulted in a net loss. Rescission claims can often later cripple a company if investors panic and demand a refund of their investments and find a securities violation.

General or Limited Solicitations of Investors

Many entrepreneurs also are surprised to learn that there are specific regulations governing the manner and types of solicitations that can be done to obtain investors, including, who can be solicited to invest in a business and under what circumstances. Failure to follow general and limited solicitation regulations can result in an otherwise exempt financing transaction losing its exemption, or even result in the person involved being prosecuted for, among other things, selling unregistered securities without an appropriate securities license. Accordingly, entrepreneurs should always consult competent securities counsel before soliciting investors to purchase interests in or financing a business to make sure that manner and content of any solicitation is legal.

Many entrepreneurs who are short of funds at the inception of a company fail to hire counsel to advise them on the proper way to capitalize a company or to raise money for the business. As a result, many entrepreneurs raise initial capital or subsequent rounds of financing in ways that violate state and federal securities laws, including by raising funds from unqualified investors, raising funds from too many investors so that the offering becomes an unregistered public offering, raising funds

---

[4] The rescission offering then done by the company also must comply with state and federal securities laws.

without appropriate disclosure of risks, raising funds without a properly drafted private placement offering memorandum, raising funds through inappropriate or prohibited advertising of the investment, or diluting earlier investors in ways that violate the rights of earlier investors.

Common Securities Violations

The most common regulatory violations pursued by securities regulators and at issue in private securities litigation involve the sale of unregistered securities by persons who are unlicensed to sell securities, as well as securities fraud violations involving misrepresentations and/or omissions, including those arising out of Ponzi schemes, affinity fraud or other investment schemes.

Misrepresentations

Common securities violations committed by entrepreneurs generally involve intentional and even negligent misrepresentations about the investment and/or company, including, without limitation, misrepresenting the use of investor funds; the safety of the investment; the expected return on the investment; the risks of the investment; the viability or experience of the business; the market opportunities; ownership and status of intellectual property rights; and/or the experience of or liabilities associated with the officers, directors or managing members of the business. For example, it is not unusual for entrepreneurs to induce investors to put money into a company by misrepresenting that a big deal is about to close, and that the investment will dramatically increase in value when the big deal is closed when, in fact, there is no deal pending or the deal is only speculative.

Omissions

Common securities violations also involve actionable omissions, including, without limitation, omissions about the capital structure of the business; the regulatory, criminal, tax lien or bankruptcy history of the officers, directors or managing members; and omissions about known risks to the viability of the business. Indeed, failing to disclose substantial risks to the business, which are known to the insiders, can subject the insiders to liability for securities fraud. For example, raising funds from investors without disclosing an imminent lawsuit, which will put ownership of the company's patent rights at issue, can be an actionable omission. Failing to disclose that the President of the Company filed personal bankruptcy a year earlier, and that there are tax liens on the President's house, also can be an actionable omission. Omissions generally must be material, that is something a reasonable investor would want to know in making an investment decision, and there must be a direct relationship between the parties giving rise to a duty to speak.

Affinity Fraud

In Utah, it is not unusual for dishonest individuals to raise investment funds within their church, neighborhood or community, and to prey on the inherent trust that exists within the community of people that belong to their church, neighborhood or community. Regulators refer to this type of predatory fund raising or investment fraud as "affinity fraud." Examples of affinity fraud include, for example, Bernard Madoff, who preyed on members of the Jewish community in perpetrating his securities fraud, or more locally, Val Southwick, who preyed on members of the LDS church. There was even a Greyhound bus driver in California, for example, who preyed on other Greyhound bus drivers. There are statutory criminal enhancements in Utah law for criminals who exploit members of their own churches or community groups for fraudulent financial gain.

Ponzi Schemes

Much of the affinity fraud that takes place in Utah arises in the context of Ponzi schemes. A Ponzi scheme is generally an investment scheme in which returns to investors are not financed through the success of the underlying business venture, but are taken from principal sums of newly attracted investments. Typically, investors are promised large above-market returns for their investments. Initial investors are actually paid the promised returns, which attract additional investors, but not from the success of the business. Instead, they are paid with funds raised from new investors. In Utah, most Ponzi schemes tend to involve the sale of promissory notes or real property, which provide for a high, and often guaranteed, rate of return. Typically, early investors are paid with investments from new investors, and the illusory high returns paid to early investors help attract additional investors. Ponzi schemes typically thrive in vibrant economies, and collapse when there are difficult economic times and it becomes difficult to find new investors to pay old investors. When a Ponzi scheme can no longer raise sufficient funds from new investors to make payments to old investors, the Ponzi scheme collapses, and investors are left holding the bag.

Often times receivers are appointed to clean up the Ponzi scheme after it collapses, and investors who received more money back than they invested are often surprised to learn that they will be sued by the receiver and required to return the amounts they received in excess of the principal amounts they invested, which interest or false profits are then re-distributed to those investors who lost money in the Ponzi scheme. Professionals who provide services to Ponzi schemes, such as accountants, lawyers, and related investment professionals, also are surprised when the receiver sues them, arguing that they helped perpetuate the fraud, and but for their turning a blind eye, it is alleged that they could have prevented the Ponzi scheme from defrauding additional victims. It also is not uncommon in Utah for there to be a double Ponzi scheme, where the promoter of the Ponzi scheme invests in another Ponzi scheme with the hope of earning his or her way out of the hole in which the initial Ponzi scheme finds itself.

Derivative Liability

Another area that surprises entrepreneurs doing business in Utah is derivative liability for the actions of other officers, directors, managing members or other control persons of a business. Under Utah law, if an officer or director of a company commits securities fraud, the other officers and directors of the company also are liable for securities fraud, unless the innocent officer or director can prove that they did not know of their co-officer's fraud or in the exercise of due diligence, could not have learned of their colleague's fraud.[5] This derivative liability makes it

---

[5]Federal law also imposes similar control person liability on officers, directors and other persons who controlled a corporate wrongdoer, with similar defenses requiring that the officers, directors or other control persons were not aware of the fraud and could not with due diligence have discovered the fraud.

critically important for officers, directors, managing members and other control persons to carefully choose their fellow officers and directors, to make sure that they do not hire dishonest officers or directors, and to make sure that they do not turn a blind eye to any potentially suspect behavior by another officer or director, regardless of the economic benefit to the entity. It also is critically important to design and institute appropriate corporate governance procedures to ferret out and prevent any potential fraudulent conduct by other officers, directors, managing members or other control persons. Indeed, corporate governance is an area where good corporate counsel and careful structuring can guard against derivative liability for the improper actions of another officer or director.

Finders and Unregistered Broker Dealers

Another area where entrepreneurs frequently run into securities law problems involves what are commonly referred to as "finders." Under state and federal securities laws, to be paid a commission or other compensation for arranging for the purchase or sale of a security or other interest in a business, the person receiving the commission or other compensation must have a securities license. Unfortunately, there is a fairly common practice in Utah of people paying "finders" a fee, commission or a percentage of the funds raised for selling stock or raising funds for a company. Indeed, many so-called business brokers who purport to arrange for the purchase or sale of a business are paid a percentage of the sale or purchase price of the business. Business brokers and "finders", however, who do not have a securities license cannot lawfully be paid a commission or other compensation for arranging for the sale or purchase of a business under Utah law. There has been a great deal of litigation in Utah involving the payment of finders' fees and commissions to unlicensed individuals once it is discovered that it is illegal to pay such a fee. Payment of an illegal finders' fee or commission also potentially could subject the person or entity paying such fee or commission to regulatory aiding and abetting liability. Entrepreneurs should not pay finders' fees or commissions to any person or entity that is not properly licensed to engage in the purchase or sale of securities in connection with the purchase or sale of a business. Only licensed broker dealers and registered securities professionals should be paid commissions or other compensation for the purchase or sale of securities. A person also should not accept a commission or other compensation for helping find investors, unless the person has a securities license.

Class Actions, Derivative Actions and Dissenters' Rights

Apart from private and regulatory litigation involving the improper sale of unregistered securities, or investment fraud committed in the sale of securities, entrepreneurs can also face securities litigation in the form of class actions, derivative actions, dissenters' rights actions and dissolution actions.

Securities class actions typically happen in publicly traded companies, and most commonly occur after a significant drop in the trading price of a listed security, or a major corporate change, such as a merger or going private transaction, which impacts the value of the shares of a company. In 2013, according to the Securities Class Action Clearinghouse, there were 166 securities class action lawsuits filed. A total of 97 class actions were filed against firms with stock listed on NASDAQ, and 55 with stocks listed on the NYSE. In 2013, 14.3% of securities class actions were filed against telecommunication services companies, with 8.6% being filed against information technology companies, 8.4% against consumer-oriented companies, and 5.7% against health care companies. Securities class actions are big business. Since the Securities Class Action Clearinghouse started keeping statistics, publicly traded companies have paid in excess of $84 billion in settlements; and there have been 28,024 total defendants, with 1965 settlements. In 2013, there were 375 active securities class action cases, and approximately one in three companies listed on a U.S. exchange was the subject of a class action. The U.S. Chamber Institute for Legal Reform issued a report on February 5, 2014 stating that in 2013 alone, attorneys' fees and expenses in securities class actions totaled $1.1 billion, and that over the past decade, the amount that went to plaintiffs' attorneys from settlements exceeded $10 billion. A recent trend in securities class actions involves public companies with overseas operations. Employees of the overseas operations engage in bribes and/or kickbacks, which are acceptable in the foreign country, but which violate the Foreign Corrupt Practices

Act in the United States. Auditors or whistleblowers discover the bribes and kickbacks, exposing the company to substantial regulatory risk, and the stock market reacts by punishing the stock. A securities class action is a foreseeable and common response to such increasingly common scenarios in the world economy. Needless to say, serving as an officer or director of a publicly traded company comes with substantial risks.

Directors & Officers' Liability Insurance

Typically, officers and directors of public companies are covered by directors and officers' liability insurance, and/or have rights to corporate indemnification by the company in the bylaws, to protect their individual assets in the event of a securities class action lawsuit. Directors and officers' liability policies generally are self-liquidating, so that funds expended on securities class action defense counsel reduce the amount of insurance available under the policy limits. As a result, there is an economic incentive for the plaintiffs, the defendants, and the insurance company to explore settlement of securities class actions in the event that a class action cannot be resolved on a motion to dismiss or summary judgment basis, so that the D&O policy is not exhausted and unavailable for settlement purposes. If an entrepreneur is going to serve as an officer or director of a publicly traded company, it is critical that the person become well informed about the D&O insurance held by the company, the coverage afforded to them under the policy, and the indemnification rights available to the officer or director in the bylaws or articles.

Derivative Actions

In contrast to a securities class action, which seeks to compensate shareholders for the damage done to the value of their shares by some action of the corporation and its officers or directors, shareholder derivative actions, which are closely related and often filed at the same time as securities class actions, seek to compensate the corporation for damages caused to the corporation by actions or inactions by the officers or directors, including, for example, by breach of fiduciary duty, self-dealing and/or corporate waste. For example, objections to excessive compensation paid to officers and directors have recently been the subject of derivative actions filed against officers and directors. Typically, in contrast to securities class actions, officers and directors are not always covered by D&O insurance for purposes of defending a derivative action. Officers and directors should carefully guard against actions which could be considered self-dealing, corporate waste, or otherwise detrimental to the company in ways that go beyond typical business judgment decision making.

Freeze Out Mergers and Dissenters' Rights

In Utah, when a company engages in a merger or other types of change of control transactions that result in a forced sale of an owner's interests in a business entity, the owner who has been forced to sell can challenge the price paid for the forced sale within a very limited period of time, and demand an independent appraisal of the shares if the owner timely objects to the value provided to the seller. Typically, dissenters' rights actions arise in the context of freeze out mergers, where a majority owner merges an entity into another entity for the sole purpose of cashing out one or more minority owners. During the freeze out merger, the majority owner tenders what the majority owner considers to be the fair value for the shares that the minority owner(s) was forced to give up in the merger. The minority owner(s) can then challenge the value paid for the shares, provided that the minority owner(s) acts promptly and files an appropriate appraisal proceeding. Typically, the appraisal proceeding is the exclusive remedy afforded minority owners forced to sell shares in a freeze out merger, and failure to timely challenge the share price in an appraisal proceeding has been held to be a waiver of all other rights to challenge the transaction.

Corporate Opportunity Doctrine

Other potential disputes among shareholders can result in actions for dissolution of the business entity, or allegations of self-dealing, and usurpation of corporate opportunities for personal gain. With respect to the corporate opportunity doctrine, for example, Utah law requires that for an officer, director or control person of a company to pursue an independent corporate opportunity outside of a business which opportunity is in the same business market as their employer, the officer or director must (a) fully and appropriately disclose the opportunity to the company; (b) offer the corporate opportunity to the company; and (c) get permission from the company to pursue the opportunity outside of the company before he or she can pursue the independent corporate opportunity. Many officers and directors have been sued for pursuing a side business without disclosure and permission, which should have been used to benefit their employer, but which they pursued for their own personal gain. An officer or director who has any doubt about whether an outside opportunity is or is not an opportunity that belongs to the company should disclose the opportunity to the board, and seek permission to pursue the opportunity.

Regulatory Actions

Numerous agencies enforce state and federal securities laws, including the United States Securities and Exchange Commission (the "SEC"), the United States Department of Justice ("DOJ"), the Utah Division of Securities, the Financial Industry Regulatory Authority ("FINRA"), district attorneys' ("DAs"), county attorneys, and attorneys generals ("AG") offices, among others. Typically, the SEC investigates matters involving public companies and large fraudulent schemes. The SEC institutes civil proceedings, both in court and in administrative proceedings before administrative law judges. The SEC also works with the DOJ on criminal prosecutions involving federal securities law violations. The Utah Division of Securities, and other state securities agencies, focus on smaller securities violations, including with licensed and unlicensed individuals and companies, and works with DAs, county attorneys, and AGs in state law violations involving criminal conduct. FINRA brings administrative actions against licensed individuals who violate FINRA's rules and regulations, as well as oversees private arbitration proceedings involving brokerage firm customers, and/or disputes between brokerage firms and their registered representatives. Most securities violations are handled in administrative proceedings filed by the SEC, the Utah Division of Securities (or other state agencies), and/or FINRA. Criminal prosecutions by the DOJ, DAs and AGs, however, are common, and typically involve more serious securities violations where an intent to defraud or reckless conduct is present.

It is important to keep in mind that when a person or entity settles or agrees to resolve a state or federal securities violation, even without admitting any liability, in most circumstances, entry of the consented settlement decree will bar the person from ever raising funds for another business under the most common exemptions from securities registration. Federal law precludes a business relying on the most common exemptions from registration of a securities offering if it employs or has any meaningful relationship with a person who has consented to and settled a state or federal securities violation. Accordingly, it is important to hire competent securities regulatory counsel if any action is filed involving alleged violations of state or federal securities laws because even certain cease and desist orders can result in a person's career coming to a sudden end.

Chapter 15

What Is a Security?

Richard W. Sheffield[1]

What is a security? Many entrepreneurs express surprise at the broad scope of the definition as well as the serious implications from failing to abide by securities laws. This section first addresses those implications and then discusses when the securities laws apply by virtue of a security being involved.

The Implications of Selling a Security

When a business offers and sells a security to potential investors, the business must consider the potential application of three primary and separate areas of securities laws:

(a) Registration of the security being sold;

(b) Registration of the business and individuals selling the security; and

(c) Disclosure of adequate information relating to the security (through a private placement memorandum, prospectus or otherwise).

Both Federal and Utah securities laws include all three areas, and if a business receives money or other types of investment without compliance

[1]As chair of the Business, Finance and Real Estate practice at the Utah County law firm of Fillmore Spencer, Richard W. Sheffield counsels clients on a broad range of business, securities, finance, real estate, and other transaction matters. He received his B.A. degree from Brigham Young University, where he was recognized as a summa cum laude graduate, a Hinckley Scholar and the Outstanding Senior in Public Relations, and his law degree from the J. Reuben Clark Law School at BYU, where he served as Note and Comment Editor of the *BYU Law Review*. Among other community roles, Richard has served as President of the Arizona Forum, a member of the national Board of Directors and Executive Committee of the BYU Alumni Association, President of the Timpanogos Legal Center, and a member and President of the Provo School District Board of Education.

or an exemption, it risks being found liable for securities fraud and other civil and even criminal penalties. Moreover, the standard for securities fraud is much lower than for common law fraud, and non-compliance not only puts the business at significant risk, but the business' principals can be held individually liable too.

For example, if a company offers or sells securities without accurate and complete disclosure concerning the nature and risks of the securities and the business, the investors can later sue the company *and* its principals to get their money back, *with interest.* Such a suit can succeed even if the company's floundering did not arise from mismanagement or from any bad faith or wrongdoing. Furthermore, both the U.S. Securities & Exchange Commission and the Utah Securities Division can independently bring actions against non-complying businesses and individuals.

What Constitutes a Security that Makes Securities Laws Applicable?

Stock and Debt. Federal and Utah statutes define the term "security" to include any stock, note, bond, debenture or evidence of indebtedness. 15 U.S.C. §77b(a)(1); Utah Code § 61-1-13(1)(ee)(i). Many properly assume that a security includes any corporate stock, especially if the stock is sold on a stock exchange. However, as noted, a security includes *any* stock, even if in a very small or "Mom and Pop" enterprise. Furthermore, the sale of a business through a stock sale involves the sale of a security. *Landreth Timber Co. v. Landreth*, 471 U.S. 681 (1985).

As noted in the security definitions, promissory notes and other evidences of loan or debt also constitute securities. Consequently, if a company seeks investment by means of stock ownership or by receiving a loan, the transaction involves a security subject to securities laws. A note, evidence of debt or other security can involve a security whether profit or interest accrues at a fixed or a variable rate, and whether the investment is guaranteed or stated as "low-risk." *See, SEC v. Edwards*, 540 U.S. 389, 394 (2004).

Investment Contracts; Profit-Sharing Arrangements. Federal and Utah security definitions expressly list any "investment contract" and any "certificate of interest or participation in a profit-sharing agreement." 15 U.S.C. §77b(a)(1); Utah Code § 61-1-13(1)(ee)(i). These terms address a multitude of other investments that constitute a security by virtue of an enterpise offering an investor a profitable return in one form or another.

In the landmark case of *SEC v. W.J. Howey Co.,* 328 U.S. 293, 66 S.Ct. 1100 (1946), the U.S. Supreme Court found that land sale contracts for Florida citrus groves, combined with a 10-year service contract to manage the groves, were investment contracts – and therefore securities. In now iconic securities language, the Supreme Court held that an investment contract "means a contract, transaction or scheme whereby a person invests his money in a common enterprise and is led to expect profits solely from the efforts of the promoter or a third party." 66 S.Ct. at 1103.

Utah has adopted statutory language that is very similar to the *Howey* decision, stating that an investment contract (therefore, a security) includes "an investment in a common enterprise with the expectation of profit to be derived through the essential managerial efforts of someone other than the investor." Utah Code § 61-1-13(1)(s)(i).

In addition, a second Utah definition of "investment contract" includes an investment by which:

(a) an offeree furnishes initial value;

(b) that is subjected to risks of the enterprise;

(c) with representations that give rise to a reasonable understanding that the offeree will receive a valuable benefit beyond the initial value; and

(d) without the offeree having a right to exercise practical and actual control over the management decisions of the enterprise. Utah Code § 61-1-13(1)(s)(ii).

The *Howey* case and the Utah investment contract definitions clearly show that various transactions and schemes can be found to be securities despite the label given to the transactions by the parties. Countless profit-sharing arrangements have been found to be investment contracts, including sales of franchises and real estate and participatory shares in cemetery lots, mining claims, and fishing boats.

Since the real estate downtown of 2006 to 2012, many more entrepreneurs have offered to assist investors in acquiring homes or other real estate for rental, improvement or sale or in making loans for real estate projects. The entrepreneurs often accompany their offers with various levels of management assistance. These investments should be analyzed to determine whether they constitute securities that require compliance with the securities laws.

If an investor invests value in an enterprise expecting a profitable or valuable return due to efforts of others or without a meaningful management role, that investor can avail himself of the protections and remedies provided under the securities laws. Therefore, a company making an offer or sale to that investor must address each area of securities compliance.

LLC Interests. Across the country, limited liability companies (LLCs) are now formed more frequently than corporations. Utah's security definition expressly includes any "interest in a limited liability company." Utah Code § 61-1-13(1)(ee)(i)(Q). While the Federal Securities laws do not expressly list LLC interests as securities, judicial determinations frequently rule them to be securities, unless a competent and experienced investor has meaningful control over the LLC. *See, Robinson v. Glynn,* 349 F.3d 166 (4th Cir. 2003); *SEC v. Merchant Capital,* 483 F.3d 747 (11th Cir. 2007); and *United States v. Leonard,* 529 F.3d 83 (2d Cir. 2008).

Pre-sale Offers, Certificates and Deposits. Some may assume that the securities laws do not apply until the enterprise actually issues and sells the security. However, Federal and Utah securities statutes also include any:

(a) preorganization certificate or subscription,

(b) certificate of deposit for a security, or

(c) certificate of interest or participation in, temporary or interim certificate for, receipt for, guarantee of, or warrant or right to subscribe to or purchase, a security. 15 U.S.C. §77b(a)(1); Utah Code § 61-1-13(1)(ee)(i).

These terms clearly include any document evidencing an intent or agreement to purchase a security in the future. In fact, besides the inclusiveness of the security definition, the securities laws expressly apply to offers of securities, even if a sale never takes place. Accordingly, wise entrepreneurs consider securities implications prior to even discussing investment with a potential investor.

Other Types of Securities. Federal and Utah securities statutes list many other types of securities that are not specifically addressed here. The statutes also expressly identify other transactions or instruments that are not deemed to be securities. Case law developed through litigation also amplifies and reduces the respective security definitions.

Security Involved Regardless of the Value Given and with Each Investment Decision

As noted in the investment contract definitions, the nature of the investment given for a security is not limited to cash. An investor can give value through exchange of services, goods, future promises, or any other consideration. For example, businesses may give equity ownership or stock options to employees for services rendered without realizing that these are securities transactions.

Some investments require that an investor make an initial payment and then subsequent installments. Other investments may obligate the investor to make an infusion of additional capital under certain circumstances or may make the additional contributions voluntary. Also, sometimes businesses offer to repurchase or redeem stock or other equity interests owned by existing investors.

While the initial investment offering and sale may have been made in full compliance with securities laws, separate analysis and compliance should be made as to the subsequent investment or divestment requirements or possibilities. In these cases a new investment decision faces the investor. He must decide whether to give value in exchange for something in return, even though he may be obligated to do so. Businesses should evaluate and comply with the applicable securities laws at these times too.

If a Security is Involved, What Next?

When a business plans to offer or sell a security, the business should next explore whether an exemption exists that excuses compliance with one or more of the areas of securities regulation. The private placement exemption (under Regulation D or otherwise) often exempts some businesses from securities registration, but qualification for the exemption requires some important analysis and steps that are described in a following section.

However, that exemption does not free a business from compliance with the disclosure or anti-fraud provisions of the securities laws or from evaluating whether the sellers of the securities are required to be registered.

CHAPTER 16

RAISING MONEY AND SECURITIES REGULATION

BRAD JACOBSEN[1]

(a) Issuing a Security.

As described above, whether or not a particular instrument, arrangement or equity interest will be deemed a security or not can be complicated. In short, it is often safe to approach the question with the answer in mind: If you are asking yourself the question "Is it a security?" The answer is likely "yes."

If you are raising money from third parties, you should approach the matter as the issuance of a security. Prior to offering or selling a security in Utah, the security or transaction must either be: (i) registered; (ii) exempt from registration; or (iii) be a federal covered security.

Issuing Securities By Registration: For a company starting a business, it will rarely be recommended that funds be initially raised through the registering of such securities with applicable governmental authorities (i.e., the SEC or a State's Division of Securities). The registration process is complicated, time consuming and expensive. The registration process will require the preparation of a registration statement, review and comment by state and/or federal securities regulators, significant legal and accounting review and assistance and continuing compliance requirements. Registering a security is a book unto itself and will not be discussed herein.

[1]Brad Jacobsen is a partner with Michael Best & Friedrich LLP. He counsels clients on mergers and acquisitions, federal and state securities law compliance, the formation and financing of startup businesses and real estate matters. Mr. Jacobsen has served as an officer and as chairman of the Securities Law Section of the Utah State Bar.

Issuing Securities Pursuant to an Exemption from Registration: The Utah Uniform Securities Act (Section 61-1-14) provides more than 30 exemptions from registration. Most of these exemptions, however, require filings with the state prior to or immediately after the offering. Any person that relies on an exemption has the burden to prove they qualify for the exemption. Most of these exemptions do not apply to a start-up company raising funds to operate a business. It should be noted that there are no exemptions from the anti-fraud provisions of securities laws. An exemption only permits a person to offer or sell a security without registering the security. Accordingly, individuals offering or selling exempt securities may have additional disclosure requirements to satisfy the anti-fraud provisions. The "anti-fraud" provisions of securities laws, in summary, make it illegal to make a misstatement or omission of a material fact in connection with an offering of securities.

The "exempt" offering that most people rely on is the "private offering exemption" specified in Section 4(a)(2) of the Securities Act of 1933 ("the 1933 Act"). In Utah, the applicable provision is Utah Code Section 61-1-14(2)(n) "a transaction not involving a public offering." The "private offering exemption" exempts a transaction by an issuer not involving any public offering from having to register securities with the SEC or state securities divisions. Section 4(a)(2) exempts only an initial sale by an issuer, not resale. Any resale that follows an initial sale must be registered with the SEC or should satisfy an exemption to the 1933 Act.

The SEC defined a private transaction under 4(a)(2) through two cases: *Doran v. Petroleum Management Corp.* and *SEC v. Ralstson Purina.* The two cases defined that a private transaction not involving any public offering involves offerees who do not need the protection of the 1933 Act. Therefore, the offerees must have both information and knowledge to understand the transaction that they are involved in. For an offeree to satisfy the standard, the offeree must possess sophisticated knowledge and either an access to information that a registration statement would normally provide or actual disclosure of the information by the issuer. An issuer has to demonstrate that all offerees meet the test.

An issuer can show that each offeree is qualified to be in a private transaction by a number of different ways. In assessing sophistication of each offeree, the issuer must have pre-existing business relationships with an offeree so that the issuer is familiar with how sophisticated an offeree is, or question an offeree regarding their knowledge and previous business experiences to establish the offeree's sophistication. In connection with access, an offeree is deemed to have access to information if the offeree serves as a director or an executive officer for the issuer or is a family member of an insider. If an offeree has economic bargaining powers big enough to demand access to information, an offeree is also considered as a transactional insider. If the issuer does not wish to provide access, it can always directly disclose relevant information to offerees.

The "private offering exemption" is the *de facto* exemption that most companies use upon formation. The parties organizing a business, contributing capital and being actively involved in the business are issued securities upon formation. Due to such organizers knowledge of the business, activity in the day to day operations and status as "active investors", such individuals generally meet the information and knowledge requirements to satisfy the private offering exemption requirements. A private offering is referred to as a "self-effectuating exemption" in that no filings or information delivery requirements are necessary.

When a company seeks funds from investors that will not be active in the company and were not the "founders" or family members of insiders, then the private offering exemption becomes more difficult to meet. In such cases, a company should consider an exempt offering known as a Regulation D offering (described below).

Issuing Securities Pursuant as a Federal Covered Security: A Federal covered security is a security that is exempt from state registration because either it is registered with the Federal government under the 1933 Act or it is exempt from federal registration under the 1933 Act. Federal covered securities include securities listed or authorized for listing on the NYSE, AMEX, the National Market System of Nasdaq®, registered investment company securities; securities offered or sold to qualified purchasers; securities with respect to certain transactions exempt from Federal registration, including some private placements; and securities that are exempt from Federal registration (Regulation D, Rule 506).

A company raising money through the sale of securities will generally be best advised to issue those securities through a Regulation D ("Reg D"). Reg D is an exemption to the 1933 Act that spells out safe harbors that qualify as a private transaction under Section 4(a)(2) of the 1933 Act (described above). Reg D includes Rules 500 to 508 of the 1933 Act. Reg D exempts only issuers from Section 5 of the Securities Act of 1933, which requires a filing of a registration statement with the SEC and controls use of prospectus and an offer to sell or buy securities before a registration statement is filed. Therefore, issuers who rely on Reg D can issue securities without registering them with the SEC.

Three rules, Rules 504, 505, and 506 of Reg D provide for the bulk of the exemptions under Reg D while other rules deal with general conditions and requirements. Rules 504 and 505 are based on Section 3(b) of the 1933 Act. Section 3(b) grants the SEC the authority to issue rules exempting securities of the dollar amount less than 5 million dollars. Rule 506 arises from section 4(a)(2) of the 1933 Act, which exempts issuers' private placement from registration with the SEC.

Rule 504 applies to issuers who do not have to file reports under the Securities Exchange Act of 1934 ("the Securities Act"). To rely on 504, a company must be a private entity that has not accessed the public capital market and has never been a reporting company under the Securities Act. Rule 504 does not apply to a blank check company, which is defined as a development stage company that either has no specific business plan or purpose or has indicated that its business plan is to engage in a merger or acquisition with an unidentified company or companies, other entity, or person. The 504's aggregate offering price, including offerings made under any 3(b) exemption or in violation of section 5 of the 1933 Act in 12 months preceding the 504 offering, cannot exceed $1 million.

If a company is neither a reporting company under the Securities Act nor a blank check company, it can rely on Rule 504 given that the company satisfies Rule 501 and 502(a), (c), and (d). Rule 502(a) exempts all offers and sales "made more than six months before the start of a Reg D offering or made more than six months after completion of a Reg D offering" from being integrated with or being considered part of the Reg D offering. However, if a company has offered or sold securities that are of "the same or a similar class as those offered or sold under [Reg D], other than those offers or sales of securities under an employee benefit plan," the company can no longer rely on the exemption to integration provided by Rule 502(a). Instead, the company has to consider five factors whether or not offers or sales should be integrated with a Reg D offering. The five factors include, (a) whether the sales are part of a single plan of financing, (b) whether the sales involve issuance of the same class of securities, (c) whether the sales have been made at or about the same time, (d) whether the same type of consideration is being received, and (e) whether the sales are made for the same general purpose. If two offerings are deemed to be integrated, then they have to satisfy a single exemption to the 1933 Act.

Rule 502(c) restricts manner of offering by prohibiting issuers or any person acting on behalf of issuers from using general solicitation or general advertising in selling or offering securities. General solicitation or general advertising is defined to include (1) an advertisement, article, notice or other communication published in any newspaper, magazine, or similar media or broadcast over television or radio; (2) any seminar or meeting with whose attendees have been invited by any general solicitation or general advertising. Giving journalists access to press conferences held abroad, meetings with issuers or selling security holder representatives conducted abroad, or written-press-related materials released abroad, at or in which a present or proposed offering securities is discussed, will not constitute general solicitation or general advertising.

Rule 502(d) imposes limitations on resale. Securities sold under Reg D are treated as restricted securities, equivalent to ones issued in a private transaction under 4(a)(2) of the 1933 Act. When restricted securities are resold, they have to be registered with the SEC or satisfy an exemption to the 1933 Act. Therefore, in order to comply with Rule 504, an issuer has to exercise reasonable care to assure that purchasers of the restricted securities are not underwriters within the meaning of section 2(a)(11) of the 1933 Act. Reasonable care are defined as (1) reasonable inquiry to determine if the purchase is acquiring the securities for himself or for other persons, (2) written disclosure to each purchaser prior to sale that the securities have not been registered under the 1933 Act and, therefore, cannot be resold unless they are registered under the 1933 Act or unless an exemption from registration is available, and (3) placement of a legend on the certificate or other document that evidence the securities stating that the securities have not been registered under the 1933 Act and setting forth or referring to the restrictions on transferability and sale of the securities.

However, Rules 502(c) and 502(d) do not apply if an issuer is one of the followings: (1) the company registers the offering exclusively in one or more states that requires a public filing of a registration statement and a delivery of a substantive disclosure document to investors before sale; (2) the company sells in a state which does not require registration and disclosure delivery when the company has already registered and sold the offering in a state with those requirements; or (3) the company sells exclusively according to state law exemptions that permit general solicitation and advertising, so long as the company sells only to accredited investors. Issuers who satisfy any one of the three conditions can freely conduct general advertising or general solicitation and do not have to place any restriction on the resale of the securities.

Rule 501(a) defines who accredited investors are for purposes of Reg D. The bar to be an accredited investor is not high. For example, if an individual had an individual income in excess of $200,000 in each of the two most recent years or joint income with that person's spouse in excess of $300,000 in each of those years and has a reasonable expectation of reaching the same income level in the current year, according to Rule 501(a), that individual is an accredited investor. Rule 501(a) also provides a set of rules on how to calculate a number of accredited investors.

Rule 505 has a larger price cap of $5 million. Similar to Rule 504, Rule 505 does not apply to issuers that are either blank check companies or companies that are disqualified by Rule 262 of Regulation A. Also, the same aggregate offering rule to that of Rule 504 applies. However, Rule 505 has a stricter set of requirements, forcing issuers to satisfy both Rules 501 and 502. Hence, all the restrictions that applied to Rule 504, including restrictions on resale, manner of offering, and integration as well as 502(b), information requirement, have to be satisfied by issuers who rely on Rule 505. In addition, an issuer can have only up to 35 purchasers. The issuer can exclude accredited investors from the count. If the issuer sells to accredited investors only, it does not have to furnish the investors with the information required under Rule 502(b).

Rule 506 is similar to Rule 505. Issuers under Rule 506 have to satisfy Rules 501 and 502 as well as respecting the 35 purchaser cap. Accredited investors are excluded from the count. However, issuers have to ascertain that each purchaser who is not an accredited investor either alone or with his purchaser representative has such knowledge and experience in financial and business matters that he is capable of evaluating the merits and risks of the prospective investment, or the issuer has to reasonably believe immediately prior to making any sale that such purchaser comes within this description.

There are some advantages to Rule 506. The primary benefit is that a Reg D, Rule 506 offering is deemed to be a "covered security" and is exempt from state filing requirements (other than a simple notice requirements). There is no aggregate offering price limit for securities issued under Rule 506 because the rule stems from section 4(a)(2) of the 1933 Act. Section 4(a)(2) has no limitation on the amount of securities that can be issued under the exemption. The SEC also recently relaxed some requirements of Rule 506 by creating 506(c). Rule 506(c) allows issuers to evade certain requirements of Reg D if they sell only to accredited investors. An offering made under 506(c) has to satisfy Rules 501 and 502(a) and (d) but not (b) or (c). Therefore, issuers can conduct general advertising or general solicitation and offer freely without any restriction on manner of offering. Issuers still have to take reasonable steps to verify that purchasers of securities issued under 506(c) are accredited investors. Furthermore, issuers do not have to register securities but notices with states.

Rule 506 do not allow issuers that are "bad actors" as defined by Rule 506(d). Rule 506(d) disqualifies corporations that have a history of a crime related to the sale or offering of securities. Even a crime by any director or executive officer of a corporation makes the corporation a bad actor, disabling the corporation from relying on Rule 506.

Lastly, Rule 503 requires issuers who issue securities under Reg D to file Form D. However, filing Form D is not a condition to issuing securities under Reg D. Even if an issuer fails to file Form D, the issuer can still rely on Reg D. The failure to file Form D might still cause the SEC to take an action against an issuer. The bottom line is that the issuer should always file Form D with the SEC.

(b) Active Versus Passive Investors.

As described above, the activity of the investors (are they founders, officers, third party passive investors, etc.,) will determine which exempt offering the company should consider as more appropriate. A "private offering" is generally only applicable to founders and active participants in the business with sufficient understanding of the business and financial resources to undertake the risks involved.

Passive investors are generally best suited for a Reg D, Rule 506 offering. In each case, individuals and companies seeking to raise capital should consult with an attorney.

(c) Debt versus equity.

The Division of Securities sums up on its website the securities issues involved in raising capital through debt or equity succinctly as follows:

> Essentially, businesses raise money through equity financing or debt financing. Equity financing is when businesses raise funds by selling an ownership in their business (e.g. stock, partnership interests, limited liability company interests). Debt financing is when businesses raise funds by selling debt in their business (e.g. bonds, notes). Whatever the instrument, if a business raises capital through equity or debt, they are likely issuing a security

In short, whether a company raises funds via debt or equity is a business decision. The issues with respect to compliance with securities laws, however, are the same. Equity and debt are both securities.

(d) Failure to Comply.

Failure to comply with the securities regulations can put both the company and its owners at significant risk of criminal and civil liabilities. Criminal penalties for each violation can be up to 15 years imprisonment. As a matter of practice, jail and criminal fines generally follow some sort of criminal intent – though the line can be very fine on what is deemed to be criminal intent.

One of the greatest, and more likely risks of failure to properly comply with securities laws are the civil liabilities. Intent to not comply is not required to be civilly liable. Under UCA 61-1-22, a person who issues securities in violation of applicable securities laws (both the company and the people in their individual capacities – no corporate veil protection), can be held liable for (1) a full return of all invested funds; (2) an additional 12% annual return on such funds; and (3) the reimbursement of attorneys' fees of the investors who seek rescission. Additionally, if it can be shown that a person's violations were reckless or intentional, triple damages can be imposed. An investor has five years after the act or transaction constituting the violation or the expiration of two years after the discovery by the investor of the facts constituting the violation, whichever expires first, to bring a claim.

(e) Summary

Compliance with securities laws is complicated and the failure to comply can have a material adverse impact on the owners of a company as well as the company itself. Before issuing securities, one should consult with an attorney with experience in securities laws.

CHAPTER 17

CONTRACTS

OVERVIEW OF CONTRACT PRINCIPLES

ANDREW B. SELLERS[1]

You've almost landed your first major customer/supplier after a long road of struggles. It's been tough, maybe the toughest thing you've done. Most don't understand the level of commitment necessary and the true extent of your sacrifice. But wait, you are staring down a 32 page agreement with pen in hand. Half the language makes no sense and the other half doesn't sound nice. Your smaller customers/suppliers haven't demanded a contract. This contract seems like a hurdle, a task, a chore, something in your way that is stopping you from closing the deal. But it's not.

Contracts enhance business. At least they should. And you must learn to utilize them as such.

Hopefully your first brush with contracts comes long before your first major business interaction. Otherwise that interaction will be painful, and at least a few of your non-contract deals will cause a headache or two (and may endanger your entire future business). The importance of contracts really can't be overstated.

As discussed in this chapter, a contract can be simple and easy to understand. You simply need to ensure that you have the proper elements. Contracts establish the rules of the relationship between the parties. In fact, you can view contracts as establishing the law as it pertains to the parties and their defined relationship. As such, contracts are more than a formality. Contracts are necessary, guiding, and protecting tools. Contracts enhance business.

---

[1]Andrew B. Sellers is an associate at Fabian VanCott with a practice emphasizing business and corporate law. He earned his law degree from the Brigham Young University J. Reuben Clark Law School, where he graduated summa cum laude. Andrew obtained his bachelor of arts degree at Brigham Young University, graduating cum laude while majoring in economics.

What is a contract?

A contract is a legally enforceable promise. The law provides a remedy if a party breaks their contractual promise, otherwise known as a breach of contract. Without a contract, you are stuck with a promise, and if that promise is broken, you are left to your devices to make yourself whole. Unless you have some unsavory friends or a vigilante streak, you're left with pestering, moaning, and whining as your remedial tools. And the other side knows it, which is why a contract in effect provides much more than a remedy at law.

The fundamental legal requirements to have a contract are that there is an offer, an acceptance, and consideration. Each of these will be discussed in greater detail later in this chapter. Only some contracts are required to be in writing, which means that a "hand shake" deal may actually be an enforceable contract. Despite this legal reality, common sense dictates having a written contract to avoid unnecessary dispute and costly litigation on whether an oral contract exists and exactly what the oral contract consists of. The prototypical contract is written and consists of recitals (background information), covenants (promises), representations and warranties (disclosures and more promises), and a signature page (acceptance).

What does a contract do (for me)?

Contracts provide an incentive structure. Because there is an underlying enforceable remedy, a contract greatly increases the likelihood that each party will satisfy their obligations. Although 99% of contracts aren't litigated or enforced by a court, contracts provide enormous value by simply providing *potential* legal recourse. You may enjoy this advantage or be influenced yourself by the threat of litigation.

Additionally, a contract is effectively private law among, and established by, the parties. It provides the rules and regulations for private interaction similar to how the Utah Code establishes social rules and regulations. But a contract can be tailored and crafted to a very unique relationship or specific circumstances. A well drafted contract speaks to the parties and its reference provides valuable and current instruction. A contract can guide and answer future questions. Contracts solve problems or establish a mechanism by which problems can be solved.

Contracts can even avoid potential future conflicts.

To illustrate, consider the following example. Two equal business partners have established a successful restaurant chain. After 5 years of grueling but harmonious work including perfecting recipes, leasing prime real estate, and training employees and managers, the business partners have established 3 very successful restaurants. Now, one business partner wants to sit back and enjoy the fairly substantial passive income. The other partner wants to use business profits to move the business forward by franchising. After extensive and often boisterous debate, the partners still can't resolve their fundamentally different goals. Tempers flare and the partnership is crumbling, endangering the business. Without a contract, the partners have no rules to help guide and resolve this conflict. It is like trying to play a game with a friend in which you not only need to play the game (with high stakes), but must first establish the rules! Establishing the rules is so exhausting that actually playing the game may never happen.

Likewise, the business partners, while heated and biased by their respective and adverse goals, without a contract, are forced to try and establish a framework and rules to resolve the dispute. But this is no game: the business and the partners' substantial financial interests are at stake. The conflict may be more than the business can handle. But if the partners had set forth a partnership agreement that established rules on how to resolve partnership disputes, the partners could engage all their efforts on solving the problem. Without a contract, a partnership agreement in this case, to guide and establish a mechanism to resolve this partnership dispute, a possible result is dissolution of the partnership and liquidation of the business—both partners lose and the business is destroyed.

Further, and perhaps more profound, a well drafted contract can avoid conflict altogether by anticipating disputes. The partners in the above example could have established by contract that one of the partners has control or trumps the other if there is a difference on a major business decision. There would have been no resources or energy wasted on a conflict in that situation (of course the trumping partner will "win," but, more importantly, the business wins).

Contracts protect you if things go wrong. But contracts can be much more than that. You can use contracts as a powerful business tool in ways that not only protect your business but also enhances or expands it. Contracts may set out responsibilities or important incentive milestones for employees and officers. Contracts can ensure that a new partner understands her role and duties, while also protecting the business and your interests should that partner fail. Simply, contracts can act to supplement your business plan. They have the power, however, to detract from your business goals as well. To ensure the success of your business, you must become comfortable with contracts. Not only are they an invaluable business tool, but you will often run into customers, suppliers, or circumstances that simply require entering a contract.

In short, your contracts have the ability to enhance your business.

What impact does a "bad" contract have?

The power of a contract goes both ways—a proverbial double edged sword. On the flip-side of enhancing your business, a contract can also severely debilitate you and your business. You may enter into a "bad" contract. The results can be catastrophic. What is a "bad" contract? Here is a quick list.

- An unedited borrowed contract – remember, contracts are private law. They are malleable, flexible, and often highly tailored. Thus, it is an extremely bad idea to "borrow" a contract without extensively reviewing and editing it. If you get an employee contract from your friend's uncle who is a successful business man, it may be catastrophic to use that agreement with your employees (and it may not be). Understand that when you borrow a contract, you are playing with fire. It is most often exhilarating to "resolve" a business problem by using a contract that you spent little time and money crafting, but the fallout could burn your entire business down or the consequences may be totally benign.
- An unfair contract – Contracts are part of business. A contract can set out bad business deals. This isn't so much a legal warning. Be sure you understand the business behind the contract, so you can assess if it is a "bad" contract. Of course, leverage is crucial in determining if a contract is unfair. Unfortunately, if you have no leverage, you may have to either enter a "bad" contract or walk away.

- An unenforceable contract – Contracts have legal requirements, which will be discussed in detail later. If you have an unenforceable contract you are left unprotected and unawares. The repercussions are simply that you no longer have legal recourse. Again, depending on the circumstances, this could be a small problem or a business-debilitating dilemma.
- An incomplete contract – Contracts are meant to govern a private relationship. If the contract fails to provide sufficient coverage, it may become the source of conflict instead of avoiding or solving conflict. There is no magic page number count, as circumstances dictate what is complete and what is not. An absent contract, in a situation where you need a contract, is also a "bad" contract and the most extreme type of incomplete contract.

Avoiding "bad" contracts is essential for your business's survival. Professionals go a long way in pointing out bad contracts, or aspects of a contract that are bad. In many instances, professionals are necessary. Given the discussion above on how pivotal contracts are, every major business transaction should be accompanied by a contract duly reviewed and explained to you by an attorney.

In summary, contracts enhance business. Viewing contracts as a hurdle and then clearing that hurdle will protect your business legally. But adopting this minimalist perspective under-utilizes a powerful business tool that could otherwise enhance and expand your business. Successful entrepreneurs learn this lesson quickly and implement contracts gladly and often.

The remainder of this chapter will cover in more detail fundamental contract law, with an eye toward providing you with tools to identify and assess issues and risks related to contracts.

1. Forming a Contract
2. Defenses to formation
3. Special types of contracts for entrepreneurs

CHAPTER 18

FORMING A CONTRACT

MATTHEW L. ANDERSON[1]

In order to adequately understand how a contract is formed, defining what a contract is will be helpful. There are many definitions of a contract but a simple definition sufficient for this chapter is an enforceable agreement reflecting terms of an exchange of value. Thus, a contract is formed when there is (1) an agreement; (2) for exchange of value; and (3) sufficient terms. It is important to note that a contract doesn't have to be in writing to be enforceable. That said, getting terms in writing is vital to the success of a transaction, and getting the terms in sufficient detail will often save a lot of time and money that would otherwise later be spent in confusion, damaged relationships, and/or litigation. Like a good fence can make good neighbors, a good contract can make or preserve good business relationships. The more clearly the parties can anticipate and define obligations, the less time and money that will be wasted in litigation (and the more time that can be spent making money).

I. Exchange of Value.

The exchange of value in a contract is most often referred to as consideration. An agreement is not enforceable without consideration. In other words, one party is not obligated to give another something if they did not give some value in return. Whether the exchange is a fair exchange is not usually the concern of the courts, unless the disparity in the value exchanged is outrageous or unconscionable, and usually

[1]Matthew L. Anderson is a shareholder at Fabian VanCott, focusing on real property and contract law, for both transaction and litigation matters. He graduated from Columbia Law School in 1996, clerked for the Utah Supreme Court for a year, and has been practicing at Fabian ever since.

only when the disparity is perceived to be a result of one party's limited bargaining power or sophistication. Beyond a minimal level, however, courts will not be concerned about whether it was a fair deal.

The existence of consideration, not the amount, is the focus. Thus, it is important to set forth the consideration in the contract– or at least that there was consideration. For example, it isn't uncommon to see in a deed conveying real property a statement that the property is conveyed for "ten dollars and other valuable consideration." This doesn't mean that the property was actually sold for ten dollars but rather, it is just an indication that there was consideration without going into the specifics. In fact, in the not so distant past, a peppercorn was commonly used to signify consideration.[2] At any rate, courts typically hold that the inadequacy of consideration is not, by itself, a bar to enforcement of a contract.

Practical Tip: In drafting a contract, always set forth the consideration of both parties or recite that adequate consideration was exchanged:

"**WHEREFORE**, in consideration of the mutual covenants and agreements set forth below, and for other good and valuable consideration, the receipt and sufficiency of which are hereby acknowledged, the Parties agree as follows: . . ."

Consideration can come in many forms, including cash, credit, services, a promise to do something, and even a promise not to do something (often referred to as forbearance). Without consideration exchanged by both parties, there is no enforceable contract.[3]

A promise to give a gift is not usually enforceable because gifts are, by definition, generally given without consideration. For example, if a woman promises to give her mother $1 million if she wins the lottery (without receiving anything in return) and then happens to win the lottery, that promise is not enforceable because there was no

[2] Richmond Eng'g & Mfg. Corp. v. Loth, 135 Va. 110, 115 S.E. 774 (1923). Courts have called transactions where parties try to get around the consideration requirement by using something of low value as a "peppercorn transaction." See Kesler, Gilmore & Kronman, The Peppercorn Theory of Consideration, H20, available at (https://h2o.law.harvard.edu/collages/2096)

[3] Cornell Law Definition of Consideration, available at (https://www.law.cornell.edu/wex/consideration

consideration. The mother's attorney might argue that her tireless service and nurturing is more than adequate consideration, but the daughter's attorney might respond that the mother would have given that service (and in fact had already provided that service) with or without the promise of the lottery winnings. If the mother could argue that she did add additional services in exchange for and in reliance on her daughter's promise (thereby adding consideration), the mother would have a better case. Without that additional service, however, the daughter's only obligation to pay lottery winnings to her mother is a moral one.

II. Sufficient Terms.

An enforceable contract also needs terms. If a contract doesn't have enough detail, it cannot be enforced. For example if there was an agreement to sell 10,000 widgets by Friday, but the parties had never settled on a price, a court would have a hard time enforcing that agreement, even if it was clear that both parties agreed to it. It may seem like a silly example, but it has real-world application. If the two parties have had a long-standing relationship in which widgets were bought and sold, and the seller was confident that the price was understood or that it would be agreed upon (because, for example, they had done so in the past), the seller may start production of the widgets. What if in the meantime, however, the price of the raw resources necessary to build your widgets increased suddenly? Could the seller pass the increased costs along to the buyer in the form of a higher price? Conversely, what if the price of the resource dropped? Would the buyer expect a discount? Courts would have a hard time enforcing that agreement.

That said, faced with a contract lacking some terms, a court will try to fill in the gaps left by the parties with terms that are reasonable in the industry or based upon the parties' past relationship. In our example above, if the parties had consistently used the same price and had ignored the cost fluctuations, then a court might feel comfortable inserting a similar set price if one was not specifically agreed to by the parties. Where sufficient evidence is available, courts will try to use terms that can be inferred from the parties' actions. Courts will work to identify the parties' intentions and what they reasonably understood to be the terms of the agreement.[3] However, courts are not comfortable doing this and will, at some point, decide that the contract is not sufficiently formed to be enforceable.

Another example of a missing term might be terms of delivery or payment. Is payment due immediately? Upon invoice? 30 days after invoice? or in installment payments? Failure to agree on terms of payment would not, in itself, defeat an otherwise valid agreement. The Uniform Commercial Code (the "UCC")[5] holds that even if one or more terms are left open, the contract does not fail for indefiniteness if the parties have intended to make a contract and there is a reasonably certain basis for giving an appropriate remedy. In other words, the more that terms are left open, the less likely the court will decide that the parties intended to have a binding agreement.[6]

An enforceable contract must contain sufficiently definite terms and conditions regarding the essential terms of the contract. Courts do not require all of the terms of the contract to be set forth in the agreement, but the major aspects must be addressed. When only incidental details are left out, the contract may still be enforced.[7] For example, in a lease agreement, the essential elements include: the identity of the property, the agreed duration, and the rental amount.[8] Contracts that are found to be too indefinite will be unenforceable. A contract is too indefinite if its terms are so incomplete or uncertain that it is clear that the parties did not regard themselves as having completed the contract.[9]

Disputes often arise because an agreement was not reached in sufficient detail. Often parties agree on central terms, but don't always discuss, much less agree on the details. If sufficient terms are not reached, the court may determine that a legal and binding agreement was never reached. There must be, as it is often put, a meeting of the minds. Courts

---

[4]State v. Terrazas, 2014 UT App 229, ¶ 27, 336 P.3d 594.

[5]The Uniform Commercial Code is a set of laws that generally govern contracts for the sale of personal property (and not real property) that has been adopted, in whole or in part, by all of the states (including Utah, see Utah Code Ann. § 70A-1a-1-1 et seq.).

[6]Sw. Eng'g Co. v. Martin Tractor Co., 205 Kan. 684, 473 P.2d 18 (1970)

[7]UCC § 2-204(3)

[8]Brown's Shoe Fit Co. v. Olch, 955 P.2d 357, 363–64 (Utah Ct. App. 1998).

[9]Steeg v. Scharenberg, 20 Ohio App. 2d 151, 252 N.E.2d 292 (Ohio Ct. App. 1969) (Holding there was not a specific enough description of the property in question to enforce the contract).

have refined that standard to simply require enough evidence that the parties did agree.

There can, of course, be an agreement on some terms but not on others. Whether there was agreement on a sufficient number of terms is the question at the heart of whether a contract has been formed. And, whether a contract has been formed is the threshold question for any attempt to enforce a contract. Whether a contract is enforceable simply refers to whether the court will force the other party to perform the contract, or, more likely, pay damages for its failure to perform the contract.

Courts are much more willing to order a party to pay damages than force it to perform the contract (which is called "specific performance").[10] Specific performance, which is when the court requires the party to perform the contractual obligations that it originally agreed (and then later failed) to perform, is not seen by the courts as an effective and efficient remedy for at least two reasons: (1) the courts do not want to be in the business of monitoring and assessing job performance and completion (nor does it have the physical resources to do so); and (2) it may not be practical to force a party to do something that it was unable or unwilling to do (causing the breach of the contract in the first place). The exception to the doctrine favoring money damages over specific performance is when money damages will not adequately compensate the party. A contract for the sale of real property is one such instance in which the courts often recognize that some parcels of real property are unique and that no remedy other than the conveyance of that real property is adequate. Otherwise, courts are much more inclined to award money damages because getting paid is generally thought of as the ultimate business objective.

III. Agreement.

At the risk of stating the obvious, there must be an agreement before a contract is formed (and is enforceable). An agreement can be reached in writing (like a signed written contract, or an invoice, or even an email exchange), in conversation, in actions or even in acquiescence.

[10] Van Wagner Adver. Corp. v. S & M Enterprises, 67 N.Y.2d 186, 492 N.E.2d 756 (1986) (Illustrating that specific performance will be denied when damages will adequately compensate a breach).

Thus, one must be careful about what is said and done and not just about what is written. While it is certainly easier to enforce a written contract, there are many cases in which a court has enforced a contract that was not in writing. For example, in *Murray v. State*,[11] the Court enforced a settlement despite the fact that there was neither a written agreement nor the parties' signatures. In *Martin v. Scholl*,[12] the Court held that an oral agreement to convey land was enforceable because one party had already partially performed—where the party had changed its position, relying in good faith on the existence of the agreement.

There are even instances in which a party's actions or spoken words have superseded written terms. Such surprises can usually be avoided by specifically prohibiting oral terms and amendments in the contract. These provisions are often referred to as integration clauses.

> *Practical Tip: When drafting a contract, you can avoid surprise terms and amendments by including specific prohibitions of the same in the contract.*

> This Agreement supersedes all prior agreements, understandings, and representations between the Parties with regard to the subject matter hereof and there are no other understandings or agreements between them except as expressly stated herein. This Agreement shall not be modified or amended unless such is in writing and executed by the Parties.

While it seems like a simple analysis to determine whether an agreement has been reached, that is not always the case. Sometimes, there can be a significant dispute as to whether an agreement was reached at all or whether there was an agreement on sufficient detail to constitute a contract (and to be enforceable by the courts).

Just because terms have been negotiated in writing, it isn't necessarily an agreement, and therefore is not enforceable. Letters of Intent (sometimes referred to as an "LOI") can be such a document. A Letter of Intent can be a useful document that facilitates discussion of

---

[11] 737 P.2d 1000 (Utah 1987).

[12] 678 P.2d 274 (Utah 1983).

major terms without getting mired down in the details. Often, parties will memorialize the major terms and leave the details and the actual language of a contract for their attorneys to draft. That being said, LOIs can be a trap for the unwary. The parties to a LOI must be clear as to whether the LOI is binding or whether it is *just* used for discussion. It is even possible to establish that some sections/terms of the LOI that are binding and some that are not. Regardless, it is crucial to clearly define whether the LOI or other term sheet that is negotiated is intended to be binding or not.

> *Practical Tip: Whenever negotiating and drafting a Letter of Intent (or similar document reflecting agreed upon terms), be clear as to whether it is binding, non-binding or which section is binding and which section is not:*
>
> Except where specifically noted otherwise, this is a non-binding letter of intent and does not constitute a binding agreement. Purchaser and Seller shall use diligent efforts to enter into the ______ Agreement within thirty (30) days of execution hereof. If the _________ Agreement is not executed by said date, this letter of intent shall be null and void.
>
> . . .
>
> #. <u>Binding Effect</u>. This letter agreement is not intended to be a binding agreement between the Parties hereto but only as an expression of their mutual intent and understanding, except for Sections ___[for example, confidentiality, non-competition, exclusivity]_____ and this Section, which Sections shall be binding upon and inure to the benefit of the Parties hereto and their respective successors and permitted assigns.

A topic should be covered that is just outside of traditional contract formation. It is the concept of a "quasi-contract." Sometimes these can be referred to as "unjust enrichment" or "*quantum meruit*" claims. The theory behind quasi contract is that the courts will treat a transaction as though it were an enforceable contract even though a contract has not been technically formed. These are contracts that are implied in-fact or implied in-law. Without going into too much detail, a court will order a party to pay damages if (1) a benefit was conferred on it, (2) it was aware of the benefit, and (3) it retained the benefit under circumstances in which it would be unjust if it did not pay for the same (the contract is implied in-law). Similarly, a court will require a party to pay another if (1) the party requested the goods/services, (2) the provider of the services expected compensation for those good/services, and (3) the party knew *or should have known* that the provider was expecting compensation (the contract is implied in-fact). In short, courts will use these theories to treat the parties as if there was a contract when it would be clearly unfair not to do so. Although these quasi-contract claims are quite common, they are often asserted as an alternative to the more straight-forward contract claims, in the event that the court is unable to find the elements of an enforceable contract.

IV. Offer and Acceptance.

The mechanics of contract formation is also important to think through. Simply put, if an offer is made, a contract can be formed upon the acceptance of that offer by its recipient. This, of course, assumes that that the necessary elements discussed above are present.

An offer is valid until it is accepted, expires or is revoked. This is important because an offerer might forget about an earlier offer or casually assume that it is no longer valid (because, for example, of the passage of time or a change in circumstances). For this reason it is prudent to place crucial conditions and a definite expiration date on any offer.

> *Practical Tip: In any offer, always include crucial terms and a deadline. Consider conditioning any deal on the parties agreeing to a fully drafted contract reflecting those terms (and other details). This will give you some control over the formation of the contract, after the offer is accepted.*

Be sure to revoke all outstanding offers that are no longer acceptable.

An offerer can usually revoke an offer at any time *prior* to acceptance. An exception to this rule is when a party may have a contractual right to accept the offer under certain conditions (e.g., price and time-- like an option). Otherwise, until an offer is unconditionally accepted, the offerer controls the validity of the offer. Once the recipient accepts the offer, the offerer is likely contractually bound to the terms of that offer.

If, however, the recipient alters the terms of the offer in any material way, it is not a contract, but a counter offer (whereby the offer/acceptance process repeats). This is true even if the recipient states that the offer is "accepted." In some instances, a recipient may choose to concede on some otherwise objectionable terms in order to lock in other favorable terms by accepting an offer *before* the offer is withdrawn.

Chapter 19

Special Types of Commercial Contracts

Kevin N. Anderson[1]

"Commercial contracts" is a broad term. In this chapter it refers to contracts for the sale[2] of goods.[3] Such contracts typically are governed by Article 2 of the Uniform Commercial Code (UCC). Utah Code Ann. § 70A-2-102. This discussion of commercial contracts is not intended to be a definitive treatise on Article 2 of the UCC, but instead highlight some practical issues that arise in contracts that are subject to the UCC.

I. The Uniform Commercial Code.

A. Scope.

"Goods" must be existing and identified before interest in them may pass.[4] A "contract for sale" can include both a present sale of goods and a contract to sell "future" goods—those to be manufactured or acquired by a seller *after* making a contract of sale and transferred at a *future* time.[5]

Article 2 does not apply, however, to contracts involving the manufacture of something especially for the buyer that is not readily salable to others in manufacturer's regular course of business. In these

---

[1]Mr. Anderson is a partner at Fabian VanCott assisting clients in complex litigation.

[2]A "sale" consists in the passing of title from a seller to a buyer for a price. Utah Code Ann. § 70A-2-106(1).

[3]"Goods" means all things (including specially manufactured goods) that are movable at the time of identification to the contract for sale other than the money in which the price is to be paid, investment securities, and things in action. Utah Code Ann. § 70A-2-105(1). It includes the unborn young of animals, growing crops, and contracts to sell timber, minerals or other identified things attached to realty that may be severed from realty, as described in section 70A-2-107 of the Utah UCC. *Id.* The UCC does not apply to transactions that may look like a sale but are "intended to operate only as a security transaction." Utah Code Ann. § 70A-2-102. Nor does article 2 apply to sales to consumers, farmers or other specified classes of buyers covered by other specific statutes.

[4]Utah Code Ann. § 70A-2-105(2).

[5]Utah Code Ann. § 70A-2-106(1).

cases, the contract would be considered a contract for work, labor, and materials rather than for goods. When a contract's subject matter appears to contain both goods and services—in so called "hybrid transactions"—courts will often look to whether the goods or the services predominate, considering the language of the contract, the nature of the business of the supplier, and the intrinsic worth of the materials.[6] For example, a contract for a turn-key computer system that included custom designed software has been found to be a contract for goods where the hardware and software elements were combined prior to sale.[7]

Goods may be sold as a part interest in identified existing goods.[8] An undivided share in an identified bulk of fungible goods is sufficiently identified to be sold, even if the quantity of the bulk is not determined.[9] Moreover, any agreed proportion of such bulk or any quantity thereof agreed upon by number, weight, or other measure may, to the extent of a seller's interest in the bulk, be sold to a buyer, who becomes an owner in common with the seller.[10] The UCC does not distinguish between new and used goods.

The definition of goods is based on the concept of movability in commerce.[11] Thus, the UCC does not apply to the purchase of a new house, because a new house does not fall within the scope of things that are "goods." Modular homes, however, are "goods" under the UCC until affixed to real property since they are movable at the time of identification to the contract for sale.[12] Similarly, a synthetic stucco product to be applied to an exterior wall was a "good" under the UCC.[13]

B. Creating the Contract.[14]

Under the UCC as adopted in Utah, a contract for the sale of goods may take any form that is sufficient to show an agreement between the

---

[6] *Utah Local Government Trust v. Wheeler Machinery Co.*, 2008 UT 84, ¶¶ 30–32, 199 P.3d 949, 956 (case remanded to apply the predominant purpose test to determine the status of a hybrid transaction under the UCC).

[7] *Id.* at ¶ 31, citing *Neilson Business Equipment Center, Inc. v. Monteleone*, 524 A.2d 1172 (Del. 1987).

[8] Utah Code Ann. § 70A-2-105(3).

[9] Utah Code Ann. § 70A-2-105(4).

[10] *Id.*

[11] § 70A-2-105, cmt. 1.

[12] *State v. Bohne*, 2002 UT 116, 63 P.3d 63.

[13] *Bay Point Condo. Ass'n v. RML Corp.*, 57 Va. Cir. 295, 310–11 (Norfolk 2002).

[14] *See* Chapter 18, *Forming a Contract*, for a general discussion on the formation of contracts.

parties.[15] The contract may be written, oral, or established through conduct that indicates the formation of a contract.[16]

1. <u>Offer</u>.

Article 2 of the UCC follows the general rule that offers are revocable unless the person making the offer (the "offeror") receives consideration for the offer. But there is an additional twist for certain offers made by "merchants."[17] If a merchant signs a written offer and gives assurances that it will be held open for a stated period of time, such as by stating "offer good for the next 30 days," then the merchant may not revoke the offer during the stated period of time. If the merchant does not state a time period, then the time period is a "reasonable time." No consideration from the person receiving the offer (the "offeree") is necessary. The period of irrevocability is—in all cases—limited to three months.[18]

2. <u>Acceptance</u>.

Offers invite acceptance in any reasonable manner.[19] However, an order or offer to buy goods for prompt or current shipment invites acceptance either by a prompt promise to ship the goods or by the prompt or current shipment of goods, even if the goods do not conform to the offer.[20] A prospective buyer's submission of a purchase order to a prospective seller is an offer that may be accepted or rejected by the prospective seller. If an offer encourages acceptance by the offeree's initiating performance, then the performance may be sufficient to accept

---

[15]§ 70A-2-204(1).

[16]However, as discussed in Section § 2-201 of the UCC–and codified by Utah Code Ann. § 70A-2-201—a contract for the sale of goods for a price of more than $500 is not enforceable in court unless it has some written evidence that is sufficient to show an agreement between the parties and is signed by the party against whom enforcement is sought. Exceptions to the statute of frauds apply for contracts between merchants for specifically manufactured goods or where goods or payment have been received and accepted. § 70A-2-201(2)–(3).

[17]A "merchant" is a person who deals in goods of the kind or otherwise by his or her occupation holds himself or herself out as having knowledge or skill particular to the practices or goods involved in the transaction or to whom such knowledge or skill may be attributed by his or her employment of an agent or broker or other intermediary who, by occupation, holds himself or herself out as having such knowledge or skill. Utah Code Ann. § 70A-2-104(1). The term "merchant" can encompass manufacturers, distributors, suppliers of materials, and others in the production and distribution of goods, provided they have the requisite knowledge or skill with respect to the goods.

[18]§ 70A-2-205.

[19]§ 70A-2-206(1)(a).

[20]§ 70A-2-206(1)(b).

the offer if the offeror is notified of the acceptance within a reasonable time.[21]

If the goods shipped in response to an offer to buy are "nonconforming" goods, the shipper creates a bilateral contract but is in breach of the contract from the outset. However, if the shipper timely notifies the buyer that the nonconforming goods are sent as an accommodation to the buyer, the shipment is a counteroffer and not a true acceptance.[22]

3. **Battle of the Forms.**

The UCC deviates from the traditional "mirror image" common-law rule—that an acceptance must "mirror" an offer to create a contract. Instead, any acceptance or written acknowledgment under the UCC given within a reasonable time that indicates the offeree's intent to enter into a contract may be effective as an acceptance.[23] This is true even if the acceptance states additional or different terms than those first proposed by the offeror, unless the offeror specifically states that acceptance is expressly made conditional to the acceptance of the offeror's terms.[24] Without such an express stipulation by the offeror, the inclusion of differing terms of the acceptance in the contract depends on whether both of the parties are merchants.

If at least one of the parties is not a merchant, the contract will only include the terms of the original offer and will not include the additional or altered terms of the acceptance.[25] Instead, the additional or altered terms are construed as proposals for addition to the contract.[26]

If both of the parties are merchants, the additional or altered terms of the acceptance will be included in the contract, unless one of the following is true:

- The offer expressly limits acceptance to the terms of the offer;[27]

---

[21]§ 70A-2-206(2).

[22]§ 70A-2-206 cmt. 4.

[23]§ 70A-2-207(1).

[24]*Id.*

[25]§ 70A-2-207(3).

[26]§ 70A-2-207(2).

[27]§ 70A-2-207(2)(a).

- The additional or altered terms materially alter the contract;[28] or
- The offeror has already objected to the additional or altered terms or objects to them within a reasonable time after receiving notice of them.[29]

4. Unspecified Terms.

Unlike at common-law, unspecified terms do not prevent the formation of a contract if it appears to a court that the parties intended to make a contract and there is a reasonably certain basis for giving an appropriate remedy.[30] The court may simply supply "reasonable" terms to flesh out a binding agreement. However, the parties' words and conduct must indicate their intention to be bound in a contract. Even if parties make a contract leaving material terms open for future determination, there can be no contract if their words and conduct demonstrate a lack of an intention to contract.[31]

a) Price.

Failure to state a price does not prevent the formation of a contract if the parties intended to form a contract without a settled price. If nothing is said as to price, or if the price is left open and the parties fail to agree upon a price, or if a price is to be determined by a third party or external market factor or standard that has not made a determination or been determined, then the price is a "reasonable" price at the time of delivery.[32] If one of the parties is to set the price, the price is to be set in good faith.[33] If an open price term fails to be fixed through the fault of one party, the other party may either cancel the contract or fix a reasonable price.[34] If the parties do not intend to be bound unless the price is fixed or agreed upon, and the price is not fixed or agreed upon, then there is no contract.[35] In such circumstances, the buyer must return

[28] § 70A-2-207(2)(b).

[29] § 70A-2-207(2)(c).

[30] § 70A-2-204(3).

[31] *See generally supra*, n. 14

[32] § 70A-2-305(1).

[33] § 70A-2-305(2). In the case of a merchant, "good faith" means honesty in fact and the observance of reasonable commercial standards of fair dealing in the trade. Utah Code Ann. § 70A-2-103(1)(b).

[34] § 70A-2-305(3).

[35] § 70A-2-305(4).

any goods received or, if unable to do so, pay their reasonable value at the time of delivery, and the seller must return any portion of the price paid on account.

b) Quantity.

Quantity is a necessary term, without which there can be no contract. The quantity must either be stated expressly or be readily determinable. Offers defining the quantity as the buyer's entire requirements or the seller's entire output—so called "requirements contracts"—satisfy this requirement, because the buyer's entire requirements and the seller's entire output are usually readily determinable. In such requirements or output contracts, the quantity must be set in good faith, and the quantity ultimately required or produced must not be unreasonably disproportionate to any stated estimate. In the absence of a stated estimate, any normal or comparable prior requirements or output may be tendered or demanded.[36]

5. The Statute of Frauds.

Parties seeking to enforce a contract should be aware of certain pitfalls in contract formation. Certain defenses exist for those who try to deny the proper formation of a contract for the sale of goods. The most significant of these is the statute of frauds.

In most cases, commercial contracts for the sale of goods for a total price of $500 or more are not enforceable unless there is a commemorative writing signed by the party to be charged or by that party's authorized agent or broker.[37] Virtually any type of writing will suffice, even those incorrectly stating terms, but the contract is not enforceable beyond the quantity of goods shown in the writing.[38] A signature may be any mark or symbol used by a party with the intent to authenticate the writing, and it may appear on any part of the document, even as a party's letterhead.

Whether a contract is for $500 or more after it has been modified depends on its value after modification. If a contract as modified is worth more than $500, the statute of frauds applies. If a contract as modified is

[36] § 70A-2-306(1).

[37] § 70A-2-201(1).

[38] *Id.*

[39] *See* § 70A-2-209(3).

not worth more than $500, the statute of frauds does not apply.[39]

The writing need not conclusively establish the existence of a contract to survive the scrutiny of the statute of frauds. It merely has to provide a basis for believing that the offered oral evidence rests on a real transaction.[40] It may be written in lead pencil on a scratch pad.[41] Quantity is the only essential term necessary for a written memorandum. The quantity need not be accurately stated, but the contract is not enforceable beyond the quantity stated in writing. Thus, the price, terms of delivery, the quality of the goods, and any warranties may all be omitted.[42]

a) Confirmatory Memos Between Merchants.

In contracts between merchants, if, within a reasonable time after their oral agreement, one merchant sends written confirmation of the parties' understanding sufficient to bind the sender, the writing will also bind the receiver if the receiver has reason to know the content of the writing and does not object within 10 days after the writing is received.[43]

b) When No Writing Is Required.

In certain situations, a contract that does not satisfy the statute of frauds but is valid in other respects is still enforceable.

(1) Custom-Made Goods.

When goods are custom made for a buyer or specifically manufactured so that, upon a buyer's default, the seller could not sell them to a third party in the seller's ordinary course of business, the contract for their sale is enforceable without a writing if the seller has, under circumstances that reasonably indicate that the goods are for the buyer, made substantial beginnings in the creation of the goods or made commitments for their acquisition before receiving a notice of repudiation from the buyer.[44]

---

[40] § 70A-2-201 cmt. 1.

[41] *Id.*

[42] *Id.*

[43] § 70A-2-201(2).

[44] § 70A-2-201(3)(a).

(2) **Admission in Pleadings.**

If a party admits in pleadings, testimony, or otherwise in court that a contract of sale was formed, then the contract is enforceable, but only for the quantity of goods so admitted.[45]

(3) **Performance.**

If goods have been paid for and accepted or have been received and accepted, the contract is enforceable without a writing for the quantity of goods actually paid for and accepted or received and accepted.[46]

6. The Parol Evidence Rule.

Terms with respect to which the confirmatory memoranda of the parties agree or that are otherwise set forth in a writing intended by the parties as a final expression of their agreement with respect to such terms as are included therein may not be contradicted by evidence of any prior agreement or of a contemporaneous oral agreement.[47]

a) Explanation or Supplementation of Terms.

Although the parol evidence rule prohibits the contradiction of a written contract, the terms of the contract may be explained or supplemented by (i) a course of performance, a course of dealing, or usage of trade, and (ii) by evidence of consistent additional terms, unless the court finds the writing to have been intended as a complete and exclusive statement of the terms of the agreement.[48] Note that such extrinsic evidence must be consistent with the express terms of the contract, and not contradict the express terms of a contract. A course of performance or course of dealing between the parties or usage of trade in the vocation or trade in which they are engaged or of which they are or should be aware is relevant in ascertaining the meaning of the parties' agreement, may give particular meaning to specific terms of the agreement, and may supplement or qualify the terms of the agreement.[49]

---

[45] § 70A-2-201(3)(b).

[46] § 70A-2-201(3)(c).

[47] § 70A-2-202; *see* § 70A-1a-303(2).

[48] § 70A-2-202(1)–(2); §70A-1a-303.

[49] § 70A-1a-303(d).

A usage of trade applicable in the place in which part of the performance under the agreement is to occur may be so used as to that part of the performance.

(1) Course of Performance.

A "course of performance" is a sequence of conduct between the parties to a particular transaction that exists if (i) the agreement of the parties with respect to the transaction involves repeated occasions for performance by a party and (ii) the other party, with knowledge of the nature of the performance and opportunity for objection to it, accepts the performance or acquiesces in it without objection.[50] Subject to section 2-209 of the UCC (addressing modification, rescission, and waiver), a course of performance is relevant to show a waiver or modification of any term inconsistent with the course of performance.[51]

(2) Course of Dealing.

A "course of dealing" is a sequence of conduct concerning previous transactions between the parties to a particular transaction that is to be fairly regarded as establishing a common basis of understanding for interpreting their expressions and other conduct.[52]

(3) Usage of Trade.

A "usage of trade" is any practice or method of dealing having such regularity of observance in a place, vocation, or trade as to justify an expectation that it will be observed with respect to the transaction in question.[53] The existence and scope of the usage must be proved by facts. If it is established that such a usage is embodied in a trade code or similar record, the interpretation of the record is a question of law. Evidence of a relevant usage of trade offered by one party is not admissible unless that party has given the other party notice that the court finds sufficient to prevent unfair surprise.[54]

---

[50] § 70A-1a-303(1)(a).

[51] § 70A-1a-303(6).

[52] § 70A-1a-303(2).

[53] § 70A-1a-303(3).

[54] § 70A-1a-303(7).

(4) Interpretation and Priority.

Except as otherwise provided in section 1a-303(6),[55] the express terms of an agreement and any applicable course of performance, course of dealing, or usage of trade must be construed whenever reasonable as consistent with each other.[56] If such a construction is unreasonable, then (i) express terms prevail over course of performance, course of dealing, and usage of trade; (ii) course of performance prevails over course of dealing and usage of trade; and (iii) course of dealing prevails over usage of trade.[57]

7. Performance.

a. Seller's Obligation to Deliver.

A seller's obligations to deliver the goods sold to a buyer vary depending on whether the parties intended to have the goods conveyed from the seller and delivered to the buyer by a common carrier.

Noncarrier Cases. In a noncarrier or "direct delivery" case, where the seller is meant to tender the goods directly to the buyer, the seller must put and hold conforming goods at the buyer's disposition and give the buyer any notification reasonably necessary to enable the buyer to take delivery.[58] If the buyer is to take delivery directly from the seller, then the buyer must furnish facilities reasonably suited to the receipt of the goods.[59] The time, place, and manner of delivery may be determined by the contract, but the tender of the goods must be at a reasonable hour.[60] Further, the goods must be kept available for the period reasonably necessary to enable the buyer to take possession of the goods.[61] Unless the parties agree otherwise, the place for delivery of the goods is the seller's place of business, or, if the seller has none, the seller's residence.[62] However, in a contract for the sale of identified goods that

---

[55]§ 70A-1a-303(6) of the UCC provides that "[s]ubject to section 2-209 [addressing waiver and modification], a course of performance is relevant to show a waiver or modification of any term inconsistent with the course of performance."

[56]§ 70A-1a-303(5).

[57]*Id.*

[58]§ 70A-2-503(1).

[59]§ 70A-2-503(1)(b).

[60]§ 70A-2-503(1)(a).

[61]*Id.*

[62]§ 70A-2-308(1).

the parties know at the time of contracting to be in another location, the other location is the place for their delivery.[63]

Carrier Cases. In a carrier or "transportation" case, the parties agree to use a third party, usually a common carrier, to deliver the goods.

– *Shipment Contracts*. In a shipment contract, the seller has not agreed to tender the goods at a particular location. Rather, to satisfy its obligations, the seller need only (i) put the goods in the possession of a carrier and make such contract for their transportation as may be reasonable having regard to the nature of the goods and the circumstances of the case; (ii) obtain and promptly deliver or tender in due form any document necessary to enable the buyer to obtain possession of the goods or otherwise required by the agreement or by usage of trade; and (iii) promptly notify the buyer of the shipment.[64] The seller's failure to notify the buyer of the shipment or to make a proper contract with the carrier is grounds for a rejection only if a material delay or loss ensues.

– *Destination Contracts*. In a contract requiring the seller to tender the goods at a particular destination, the seller must put and hold conforming goods at the buyer's disposition and give the buyer any notification reasonably necessary to enable him or her to take delivery.[65] If the buyer is to take delivery directly from the seller, the buyer must furnish facilities reasonably suited to the receipt of the goods.[66] The time, place, and manner of delivery may be determined by the contract, but the tender of the goods must be at a reasonable hour.[67] Where the goods are in the possession of a bailee and are to be delivered without being moved, then the seller must tender a negotiable document of title covering such goods or procure acknowledgment by the bailee of the buyer's right to the possession of the goods.[68] Tender to the buyer

[63] § 70A-2-308(2).

[64] § 70A-2-504.

[65] § 70A-2-503(3).

[66] *Id.*

[67] *Id.*

[68] § 70A-2-503(4).

of a non-negotiable document of title or a record directing the bailee to deliver the goods to the buyer is sufficient tender unless the buyer seasonably objects.

– *F.O.B. and F.A.S. Contracts*. When a contract specifies that delivery is free on board (F.O.B.) to a particular location, even though used only in connection with the stated price, the seller must, at its own expense and risk, tender the goods in the F.O.B. location.[69] The term may also be used with a vessel, car, or other vehicle, in which case the seller must also, at its own expense and risk, load the goods on the vessel, car, or other vehicle.[70] When a contract is free alongside (F.A.S.) a particular vessel at a named port, the seller's obligation to tender the goods is satisfied by tendering the goods alongside the vessel in the usual manner at that port or at a dock designated and provided by the buyer.[71]

b) Buyer's Obligation to Pay and Right to Inspect.

Unless specified otherwise by the contract, the buyer's tender of payment is a condition of the seller's duty to tender and complete delivery.[72]

Shipment Under Reservation. In a carrier contract, when there is no express payment provision or when the contract specifies cash, the seller may send the goods "under reservation" so that the buyer will be unable to obtain the goods from the carrier until the buyer pays the seller.[73]

Sufficiency of Payment. Tender of payment is sufficient when made by any means or in any manner current in the ordinary course of business unless the seller demands payment in cash and gives the buyer an extension of time reasonably necessary to procure the cash.[74]

---

[69] § 70A-2-319(1)(b).

[70] § 70A-2-319(1)(c).

[71] § 70A-2-319(2)(a).

[72] § 70A-2-511(1).

[73] § 70A-2-505.

[74] § 70A-2-511(2).

Any payment made by check is conditional on the honoring of the check upon presentment by the seller.[75] Accordingly, any payment by check is not a complete tender of payment until the check is paid upon presentment.

Right of Inspection. Unless the contract specifies otherwise, the buyer has a right to inspect the goods before paying for them.[76] The buyer must bear the cost of the inspection, but may recover this cost from the seller if the goods do not conform to the goods ordered and are rejected by the buyer.[77] The buyer's inspection may be at any reasonable time and in any reasonable manner.[78]

c) Buyer's Rejection, Acceptance, and Revocation of Acceptance.

As a general matter, and unless otherwise agreed by contract, the buyer has certain remedies to address the improper performance by the seller.

Complete or Partial Rejection. If the goods or the tender of delivery fail to conform to the contract, the buyer may reject the whole, accept the whole, or accept any commercial unit or units and reject the rest.[79] For any rejection to be effective, the buyer must reject the goods within a reasonable time after their delivery or tender and must seasonably notify the seller of the rejection.[80]

Identifying the Particular Defect. In certain situations, when making a rejection, the buyer must state a particular defect that is ascertainable by reasonable inspection in order to rely on such defect to justify the rejection or establish a breach. First, if the seller could cure the defect with seasonable notice, then the buyer must state the particular defect

[75] § 70A-2-511(3).

[76] § 70A-2-513(1).

[77] § 70A-2-513(2).

[78] § 70A-2-513(1).

[79] § 70A-2-601.

[80] § 70A-2-602(1).

to the seller.[81] Second, between merchants, after rejection the seller may make a written request for a full and final statement from the buyer of all defects on which the buyer bases its rejection.[82]

Buyer's Duties upon Rejection. After rejecting certain goods, the buyer may not exercise any ownership with respect to the rejected goods.[83] If the buyer has possession of the goods before rejection, the buyer has a duty to hold them with reasonable care for a period of time sufficient to permit the seller to remove them; however, the buyer has no further obligations with respect to properly rejected goods.[84]

Merchant Buyer's Duties upon Rejection. When the seller has no agent or place of business in the market of the rejection, a merchant buyer has a duty after the rejection of goods in his or her possession or control to follow any reasonable instructions from the seller with respect to the goods.[85] Instructions are not reasonable if, on the buyer's demand, indemnity for expenses is not provided. In the absence of instructions from the seller, the buyer may make reasonable efforts to sell the goods on behalf of the seller if the goods are perishable or likely to decline in value quickly. The buyer may also store rejected perishable goods on the seller's behalf or reship them to the seller.[86] If the buyer sells any of the goods on the seller's behalf, the buyer is entitled to be reimbursed by the seller or from the sales proceeds for the care and sale of the goods, including sales commissions as are customary in the trade or, if none, to a commission not exceeding 10 percent of the gross proceeds.[87]

Acceptance. The buyer accepts the goods when, after a reasonable opportunity to inspect the goods, the buyer signifies to the seller that either the goods are conforming or that the buyer will take and retain them in spite of their nonconformity.[88] The buyer also accepts the goods

[81] § 70A-2-605(1)(a).

[82] § 70A-2-605(1)(b).

[83] § 70A-2-602(2)(a).

[84] § 70A-2-602(2)(b), (c).

[85] § 70A-2-603(1).

[86] § 70A-2-604.

[87] § 70A-2-603(2).

[88] § 70A-2-606(1)(a).

when, after a reasonable opportunity to inspect the goods, the buyer fails to make an effective rejection of the goods.[89] The buyer also accepts the goods if it performs any act inconsistent with the seller's ownership of the goods.[90] However, if such an act is wrongful as against the seller, it is an acceptance only if ratified by the seller.[91] The buyer's acceptance of a part of a commercial unit is an acceptance of that entire commercial unit.[92]

Effect of Buyer's Acceptance. Once the buyer has accepted the goods, the buyer must pay the contract rate for the goods.[93] The buyer's acceptance precludes the rejection of the accepted goods.[94] If the buyer accepts the goods with the knowledge of a nonconformity, then the acceptance cannot be revoked unless the acceptance was on the reasonable assumption that the seller would seasonably cure the nonconformity.[95] Once the buyer has accepted the goods, the buyer has the burden of establishing any breach with respect to the accepted goods.[96]

Revocation of Acceptance. Even after the buyer has accepted the goods, the buyer may still revoke its acceptance in whole or in part under certain circumstances. As a general rule, the buyer may not revoke its acceptance based on a defect of which it had knowledge at the time of acceptance. If the buyer accepted goods whose nonconformity substantially impairs the value of the goods to the buyer, and if the buyer accepted the goods on the reasonable assumption that the nonconformity would be cured, and if the nonconformity has not been seasonably cured, then the buyer may revoke its acceptance.[97] Also, if the buyer accepted goods whose nonconformity substantially impairs the value of the goods to the buyer, and if the buyer accepted the goods without discovery

[89] § 70A-2-606(1)(b).

[90] § 70A-2-606(1)(c).

[91] *Id.*

[92] § 70A-2-606(2).

[93] § 70A-2-607(1).

[94] § 70A-2-607(2).

[95] *Id.*

[96] § 70A-2-607(4).

[97] § 70A-2-608(1)(a).

of such nonconformity, and if the buyer's acceptance was reasonably induced by either the difficulty of discovering the nonconformity before acceptance or the seller's assurances, then the buyer may revoke its acceptance.[98] The buyer's revocation of acceptance must occur within a reasonable time after the buyer discovers or should have discovered the basis for the revocation and before a substantial change in the condition of the goods that is not caused by its own defects.[99] The buyer's revocation is not effective until the buyer notifies the seller of it.[100] After revocation, a buyer has the same rights and duties with respect to the goods as if the buyer has rejected them.[101] Additionally, section 2-711 of the UCC permits a buyer, upon revocation of acceptance, to recover monetary damages, which may include the purchase price.[102]

d) Impracticability.

Certain events may occur and circumstances may arise that make a seller's bargained-for performance dramatically more difficult, if not impossible. Although at common law, sellers generally assume such risks when they contract, the UCC adds some protections for commercial contracts for the sale of goods. Section 2-615(a) of the UCC provides that any delay in delivery or nondelivery in whole or in part by a seller is not a breach of contract if the seller's performance has been made impracticable either (i) by the occurrence of a contingency, the nonoccurrence of which was a basic assumption on which the contract was made or (ii) by compliance in good faith with any applicable foreign or domestic governmental regulation or order, whether or not it later proves to be invalid.[103]

When such causes affect only part of the seller's capacity to perform, the seller must allocate production and deliveries among its customers but may include regular customers not then under contract and its

---

[98]§ 70A-2-608(1)(b). Note that under both this and the preceding circumstances, the nonconformity must substantially impair the value of the goods to the buyer.

[99]§ 70A-2-608(2).

[100]*Id.*

[101]§ 70A-2-608(3).

[102]U.C.C. § 2-711 (codified at § 70A-2-711).

[103]U.C.C. § 2-615 (codified at § 70A-2-615(1).

own requirements for further manufacture.[104] The seller may allocate by any manner that is fair and reasonable.[105] The seller must also notify the buyer seasonably that there will be delay or nondelivery, and when the seller is making allocations, the seller must notify the buyer of the estimated quota that will be available to the buyer.[106]

This provision does not protect the seller from ordinary increases in cost unless the increase in cost is due to some unforeseen contingency that alters the essential nature of the seller's performance.[107] A severe shortage of raw materials or supplies due to a contingency such as war, embargo, local crop failure, unforeseen shutdown of major sources of supply, or the like, which causes marked increase in cost or altogether prevents a seller from securing supplies necessary for its performance, is within the contemplation of section 2-615 of the UCC.[108] Where a particular source of supply is exclusive under the agreement and fails through casualty, section 2-615 applies.[109]

8. Warranties.

The UCC not only provides for several implied warranties that arise in commercial contracts for the sale of goods but also provides certain guidance as to the creation of express warranties. The UCC dictates that the warranties in commercial contracts for the sale of goods extend not just to the buyers of the goods but to any person whom the manufacturer or seller might reasonably expect to use, consume, or be affected by the goods.[110]

a) Warranty of Title and Warranty Against Infringement.

In all commercial contracts for the sale of goods, there is a warranty by the seller, unless disclaimed as discussed below, that the seller will deliver good title to the goods, that the transfer of the title to the goods

---

[104]§ 70A-2-615(1).

[105]§ 70A-2-615(2).

[106]§ 70A-2-615(3).

[107]§ 70A-2-615 cmt. 4.

[108]*Id.*

[109]§ 70A-2-615 cmt. 5.

[110]§ 70A-2-318

is "rightful," and that the seller will deliver the goods free from any security interest or other lien or encumbrance of which the buyer at the time of contracting has no knowledge.[111] The warranty of title may only be excluded or modified by specific language or by circumstances that give the buyer reason to know that the seller does not claim title in itself or that the seller is purporting to sell only such right or title as it or a third party may have.[112]

Unless otherwise agreed between the parties, a merchant regularly dealing in goods of the kind warrants that the goods will be delivered free of the rightful claim of any third person by way of infringement or the like.[113] However, a buyer who furnishes specifications to a seller must hold the seller harmless against any claim that arises out of compliance with the buyer's specifications.[114]

b) Implied Warranty of Merchantability.

The implied warranty of merchantability arises by operation of law. Unless properly excluded or modified, a warranty that the goods will be merchantable is implied in any contract for their sale where the seller is a merchant with respect to goods of that kind.[115] Selling food and drink for consumption on the premises or elsewhere is subject to the implied warranty of merchantability if the seller is a merchant in food and drink.[116] When a contract is for both goods and services, if the contract is dominated by language designating the sale of goods by a merchant of the same goods, then the implied warranty of merchantability applies.[117] As noted above, determining whether a contract is for goods or for services depends on whether the goods or the services predominates.

---

[111]§ 70A-2-312(1).

[112]§ 70A-2-312(2).

[113]§ 70A-2-312(3).

[114]*Id.*

[115]§ 70A-2-314(1).

[116]*Id.*

[117]*See, e.g.*, *Bonebrake v. Cox*, 499 F.2d 951, 960 (8th Cir. 1974) (cited by *Wirthlin II v. Mameco Int'l, Inc.*, No. 20020977-CA, slip op. at 2 n.1 (Utah Ct. App. Feb. 5, 2004) (unpublished)); *Princess Cruises, Inc. v. Gen. Elec. Co.*, 143 F.3d 828, 833 (4th Cir. 1998).

c) Implied Warranty of Fitness for a Particular Purpose.

The implied warranty of fitness for a particular purpose arises when the seller, at the time of contracting, has reason to know (i) of any particular purpose for which the goods are required and (ii) that the buyer is relying on the seller's skill or judgment to select or furnish suitable goods.[118] Then, unless properly excluded or modified, a warranty is implied that the goods are fit for such purpose.

A "particular purpose" differs from the ordinary purpose for which goods are used. It contemplates a use by the buyer that is specific to the nature of the buyer's business.[119] By contrast, the ordinary purposes for which goods are used are those envisaged in the concept of the implied warranty of merchantability and go to uses that are customarily made of the goods in question. Whether this warranty arises in a particular instance is a question of fact to be determined by the specific circumstances.[120]

To recover for a breach of this warranty, a buyer must prove that (i) the seller had reason to know the particular purpose for which the buyer required the goods; (ii) the seller had reason to know the buyer was relying on the seller's skill or judgment to furnish appropriate goods; and (iii) the buyer in fact relied upon the seller's skill or judgment.[121]

Both the implied warranty of merchantability and the implied warranty of fitness for a particular purpose were excluded by the sales documents signed by the purchasers, where documents conspicuously and expressly excluded the implied warranties of fitness and merchantability, not hidden in fine print, and the sales agreement stated that the vehicle was being purchased "as is."[122]

d) Express Warranties.

Express warranties are created by affirmations, promises, descriptions, or samples provided by the seller to the buyer. The seller

---

[118] § 70A-2-315.

[119] § 70A-2-315 cmt. 2.

[120] § 70A-2-315 cmt. 1.

[121] *Aluminum Co. of America v. Electro Flo Corp.*, 451 F.2d 1115, 1119 (10th Cir. 1971).

[122] *Rawson v. Conover*, 20 P.3d 876, 886 (Utah 2001).

need not use formal words such as "warrant" or "guarantee" or have a specific intent to create a warranty.[123] Sellers create express warranties in three ways.

1. Affirmations or Promises. Any affirmation of fact or promise made by the seller to the buyer that relates to the goods and becomes a part of the basis of the bargain creates an express warranty that the goods will conform to the affirmation or promise.[124]
2. Descriptions. Any description of the goods that is made a part of the basis of the bargain creates an express warranty that the goods will conform to the description.[125]
3. Samples or Models. Any sample or model of the goods that is made a part of the basis of the bargain creates an express warranty that the whole of the goods will conform to the sample or model.[126]

Opinions are not warranties. An affirmation of the value of the goods or a statement purporting to be merely the seller's opinion or commendation of the goods does not create an express warranty.[127] This may be different if the seller has superior knowledge about the goods being sold and does not qualify its statement as being only its opinion. The statement may be treated as a statement of fact and found to be an express warranty with which the goods must comply.[128]

e) Disclaimer of Warranties.

Express Warranties. Express warranties may be negated, at least in part, by words or conduct refuting the words or conduct creating the express warranty. The words or conduct creating an express warranty

---

[123] § 70A-2-313(2).

[124] § 70A-2-313(1)(a).

[125] § 70A-2-313(1)(b).

[126] § 70A-2-313(1)(c).

[127] § 70A-2-313(2).

[128] *See Groen v. Tri-O-Inc.*, 667 P.2d 598, 606, 606 n.10 (Utah 1983).

and the words or conduct negating or limiting the express warranty are construed, wherever reasonable, consistently with each other.[129]

Implied Warranties. The implied warranties of merchantability and fitness for a particular purpose may be disclaimed either by specific disclaimers or by general disclaimers. The UCC provides specific disclaimers for both the implied warranty of merchantability and the implied warranty of fitness for a particular purpose. The UCC states that to exclude or modify the implied warranty of merchantability, the language of the disclaimer must mention merchantability and, in the case of a written disclaimer, must be conspicuous.[130] for the implied warranty of fitness for a particular purpose, the UCC states that the language of the disclaimer must be in writing and must be conspicuous.[131] Language to exclude the implied warranty of fitness for a particular purpose is sufficient if it states, for example, that "[t]here are no warranties which extend beyond the description on the face hereof."[132]

General disclaimers that may serve to disclaim warranties can be created by the language or actions of the parties. The UCC provides for three in particular.

1. General Disclaimer Language. All implied warranties are excluded by expressions like "as is" or "with all faults" or other language that in common understanding call the buyer's attention to the exclusion of warranties and make it plain that there is no implied warranty.[133]
2. Inspection or Refusal to Inspect. When the buyer, before entering into the contract, has examined the goods or the sample or model as fully as desired or has refused to examine the goods, there is no implied warranty with regard to defects

[129] § 70A-2-316(1).

[130] § 70A-2-316(2). The essential purpose of the requirement to use conspicuous language is to protect the buyer from surprise. § 70A-2-316 cmt. 1. Whether a disclaimer provision is conspicuous is a question for the court. 70A-1a-201 (2)(j). The court will consider such factors as the size, type, font, or color used compared to the surrounding text. *Id.*

[131] § 70A-2-316(2).

[132] *Id.*

[133] § 70A-2-316(3)(a).

that an examination should, under the circumstances, have revealed.[134]

3. Course of Dealing. An implied warranty can also be excluded or modified by a course of dealing or course of performance or usage of trade.[135]

The Magnuson-Moss Warranty Act. The Magnuson-Moss Warranty Act of 1975[136] provides additional requirements for written warranties made by manufacturers of consumer products. Under regulations promulgated by the Federal Trade Commission, they must be in writing and fully and conspicuously disclose in simple and readily understandable language the terms and conditions of the warranty.[137] The minimum federal standards for consumer product warranties provide that the warrantor state it will remedy the consumer product within a reasonable time and without charge in the case of a defect, malfunction, or failure to conform with the written warranty,[138] among other things.[139] A warrantor warranting a consumer product must clearly and conspicuously designate the warranty as a "full (statement of duration) warranty" if it meets the federal minimum standards for a full warranty or as a "limited warranty" if it does not meet the federal minimum standards for a full warranty.[140]

f) Limitation of Damages for Breach of Warranty.

Liquidated Damages. Damages for a breach by either party may be liquidated in the agreement, but only to an amount that is reasonable

---

[134] § 70A-2-316(3)(b).

[135] § 70A-2-316(3)(c).

[136] 15 U.S.C. §§ 2301-2312.

[137] 15 U.S.C. § 2302(a). For the Federal Trade Commission's specific regulations on the content of consumer product warranties, see 16 C.F.R. pt. 701 *et seq.*

[138] 15 U.S.C. § 2304(a)(1).

[139] The warrantor may not impose any limitation on the duration of any implied warranty on the product, 15 U.S.C. § 2304(a)(2); exclude or limit consequential damages for the breach of any written or implied warranty, unless the exclusion or limitation appears conspicuously on the face of the warranty, 15 U.S.C. § 2304(a)(3); and must permit the consumer to elect either a refund or a replacement for any product or part of a product that contains a defect or malfunction that the warrantor cannot remedy after a reasonable number of attempts, without charge. 15 U.S.C. § 2304(a)(4).

[140] 15 U.S.C. § 2303(a). The federal minimum standards for a full warranty are described in 15 U.S.C. § 2304.

in the light of the anticipated or actual harm caused by the breach, the difficulties of the proof of loss, and the inconvenience or nonfeasibility of otherwise obtaining an adequate remedy.[141] Unreasonably large liquidated damages are void as a penalty.[142]

Limited Remedies. The parties may also contractually agree to limit the buyer's remedies to the return of the goods and repayment of the price or to the repair and replacement of nonconforming goods or parts.[143]

Consequential Damages. Consequential damages may be limited or excluded unless the limitation or exclusion is unconscionable.[144] Limitation of consequential damages for injury to the person in the case of consumer goods is prima facie unconscionable, but limitation of damages where the loss is commercial is not.[145]

---

[141] § 70A-2-718(1).

[142] § 70A-2-718(1). Utah courts, however, apply an entirely different approach for evaluating the enforceability of liquidated damages clauses contained in contracts not covered by the UCC. Under this common law approach, liquidated damages are not subject to any form of heightened judicial scrutiny and are presumed to be enforceable, unless the court finds the clause unconscionable or unenforceable on other general grounds. *Commercial Real Estate Inv., L.C. v. Comcast of Utah II, Inc.*, 285 P.3d 1193, 1203 (Utah 2012). *See also Brady v. Park*, 302 P.3d 1220, 1226–27 (Utah Ct. App. 2013), *cert. denied*, 308 P.3d 536 (Utah 2013).

[143] § 70A-2-719(1)(a).

[144] § 70A-2-719(3).

[145] *Id.*

CHAPTER 20

DEFENSES TO CONTRACT FORMATION AND ENFORCEMENT

STEVEN A. CLAYTON[1]

The ability of individuals and businesses to build off of each other's strengths through the formation of legally enforceable agreements, contracts, has greatly enhanced the progress, specialization and economic prosperity of our modern age.[2] Contracts, in the entrepreneurial setting, permit an entrepreneur with an improved idea to rapidly "outsource" and build off of the work, experience, specialties and strengths of others and meet the holistic needs of a business operation including suppliers, manufacturers, marketers, retailers, personnel, professional consultants and the like. As these cooperative and specialized efforts swarm around an "improved idea" such ideas are perfected and actualized with increasing precision and success. Not only does the entrepreneur benefit, but its partners as well. As an entrepreneur's specialized partners are permitted to focus on their given expertise, through contracts, their processes are improved. As partners are exposed to an "improved idea," they solve new problems which further enhance their specialty.

Despite the overwhelming benefits provided by contracts in our modern age, contracts have their challenges. Contracts are a static attempt to capture the present cooperative intentions of two or more diverse parties for a shared but unknown future. Cementing diverse intentions for the unknown is what keeps contract lawyers up at night. Recognizing this innate challenge which contracting presents,

---

[1]Steven is an attorney at Cottonwood Residential where he provides transactional and general legal support to multi-family real estate investment, acquisition, management and development company.

[2]Merlin G. Myers, *Kinship, Religion and the Transformation of Society*, Brigham Young University 1975 Speeches, speeches.byu.edu

the law has adopted several rationale for not recognizing or enforcing contracts.

With the intent of providing insight and connection into the sometimes impersonal rationale of contract law (and without reference to family law), I would like to introduce a warm pastel picture of Prince Charming and Princess Bride at their wedding celebration, perched on the palace balcony which overlooks their alpine kingdom on the bay, their subjects and the distant setting sun. Prince Charming and Princess are holding hands having just exchanged wedding bands. What do we expect next? The wedded couple will jump on their stallions and ride side by side into the sunset of bliss, happiness and fulfillment.

What really lies ahead? Complaining subjects, violent invaders, faltering infrastructure, famine, plague and disease, not to mention the interpersonal conflicts that arise in the royal family as a result of these and other life challenges. The Princess feels robbed; her envisioned life of stallions and sunsets has crumbled under the pressures and responsibilities of governing the kingdom. She places increasing blame on the Prince who is always out hunting and gallivanting with royalty while the burdens of ruling rest squarely on the Princess.

The Princess wants out of the marriage contract and a return to her previously simple country life when she sold produce in the town square. She seeks either an annulment (marriage contract was never formed or should never have been recognized by the law) or divorce (marriage contract should no longer be enforced). She has plenty of reasons, including: her own questionable capacity (she was 17 and drunk when she exchanged vows); duress (she was surrounded by armed guards and coerced to say "yes"); misrepresentation (he promised her she would gallivant while he would rule); indefiniteness (she was not informed of the many responsibilities of a princess); writing (the Prince's claim that she had previously agreed to assume leadership responsibilities should have been in writing); mistake (duh…this guy was totally incapable to rule); the circumstances had changed (the Prince had taken a mistress), frustration of purpose (the Prince was sterile and therefore no heir could be produced); public policy (commoners were forbidden to marry royalty by law); good faith (the Prince was dishonest and unfaithful).

Just as the young Princess Bride asks that her marriage contract be invalidated or unenforced, so to do once starry eyed or unwary business partners. As mentioned above, such partners may challenge that a legal contract was ever formed. This can be done by proving that the parties never had a "meeting of the minds" or true understanding of the obligations alleged to have been entered into. This failure may be a result of the agreement never having been memorialized in writing, indefiniteness, the capacity of a party being compromised, fraudulent misrepresentations, mistake, coercion or duress.

A Statute of Frauds defense to contract formation requires that certain contracts must be in writing to be enforceable. These include contracts involving: prenuptial agreements (the Prince should have documented the Princess's willingness to administer the kingdom); contracts that won't be performed within a year of their making; the sale of real property; the guarantee of the debt of another (surety, executor); the sale of goods over $500; the sale of personal property over $5,000, and; the sale of securities.[3] Requiring parties to document their intentions at the time of contracting should minimize dispute over what the terms of an agreement may be thus aiding objective enforcement of a contract should either party contest or breach a contract's provisions. In the case of third parties assuming debt obligations, it protects potential third party guarantors and administrators (persons charged with administering a Will) from assuming unwanted debts (Oh, don't worry, my Dad will guarantee payment of the rent).

One means of proving a contract deficient is to show that such contract is indefinite or uncertain. Our Princess may claim that in no way do the words "do you accept this man to be your lawfully wedded husband" communicate the necessary roles and responsibilities, or "terms of service" that would fall upon her as a princess. In the commercial context, a few of the "essential" elements of a contract may include: the parties, the nature of the goods or services, the price, timing of payment or performance.[4]

---

[3]Restatement (Second) of Contracts § 110 (1981); Utah Code Ann. § 70A-2-201(1) (2015)

[4]Restatement (Second) of Contracts §33 (1981); U.C.C. § 2-204 (2002) A contract does not fail for indefiniteness if "the parties have intended to make a contract and there is a reasonably certain basis for giving an appropriate remedy."

A party may also contest a contract was formed by proving the capacity or authority of that party at the time of contract was deficient or impaired (our young and drunk bride, for example). The understanding of two parties at the time of contracting is often described as a "meeting of the minds". If the ability of one of those minds to comprehend the nature of the commitment being made was compromised at the time of contracting, and the other party knows it, then such contract may be unenforceable.[5] Most states have identified persons over the age of 18 to be sufficiently mature and capable to enter into enforceable agreements.[6] In addition, those who suffer from mental illness or disease or are otherwise impaired in their comprehension because of substance abuse may also be able to void their obligations, especially if the other party new of such mental deficiency and the benefit of the contract has yet to be enjoyed by the incapable party.

Another claim proving that there was no clear understanding is that the contract was fraudulently induced. In our fairy tale, the princess claims she was told by the prince that "she would gallivant while he would rule". When one party misrepresents a fact in order to induce another to enter into a contract, and the other party relies on such representation as rationale to enter into the contract a court may find the contract is void as a result of being "fraudulently induced". Because of the propensity for "he said, she said," reaching back in time through the history of the parties courtship (salesmanship and negotiation), the law has developed several important elements necessary to prove fraud worthy of making a contract void. First, the fraud must concern an important existing fact. In our fairy tale, aspirations about future roles and future commitments may not be specific or concrete enough, such as a representation that "the car is in perfect condition." Second, the false representation must be contrary to current knowledge or recklessly made. Was it clear that our Prince had no intention of ruling when he made the representation? Third, the representation must be made in order to induce a party to enter into the contract. In our case, did the Prince casually mention his propensity for ruling in discussions unassociated with courtship? Fourth, the defrauded party must rely on the representation. Had the Princess

[5] Restatement (Second) of Contracts § 15 (1981); Restatement (Second) of Contracts § 16 (1981)

[6] Restatement (Second) of Contracts § 14 (1981)

purchased party gowns and did she depend on the Prince fulfilling his statement? Fifth, and last, would a party have entered into the contract, regardless of the misrepresentation? Was our Princess so head over heels with the Prince that she would have married him, no matter the personal cost or sacrifice? As you can see, it may be one thing to feel defrauded, but it is quite another to prove that you have been defrauded. Determining the "knowledge" of the fraudulent party and the "reliance" of the defrauded party are difficult propositions to establish.

What about our Princess Bride's claim that she had simply made a mistake? In hindsight it is easy to recognize our mistakes, but should that be grounds for failure to recognize a contract? This idea that enforceable agreements require a "meeting of the minds" or understanding of the parties provides room for the defense of bilateral (both parties) or unilateral (one party) mistakes. A mutual mistake requires both parties to be mistaken about a "basic assumption or important fact upon which they based their bargain."[7] A unilateral mistake requires one party to be mistaken about an "important feature of the contract even though a reasonable effort was made to understand that feature" and, the "mistake was so serious that enforcement would be unconscionable."[8] Our Princess Bride claims that our Prince was incapable of ruling, an important feature of a Prince, which resulted in her having to assume all of the responsibilities of ruling. But shouldn't our Princess have done her "due diligence" and known of the Prince's deficiencies during courtship as she observed his failures and disinterest in passing preparatory lessons in the King's court? Finally, is it unconscionable for a Queen to have to rule? Several Queens before her had been thrust into governing roles upon the death of the King.

One basic tenet of freedom is the "freedom to contract". Therefore a party who is physically forced into, or is a recipient of, an "improper threat" that leaves a party with no alternative but to agree to, a contract should not be held to such a contract (think of our Princess bride surrounded by armed guards at the time of "I do"). Though the idea of physical threat is quickly captured by the mafioso "sign this or else" baseball bat in hand, the concept of improper threat is a little less clear.

---

[7]Model Utah Jury Instructions, Second Edition, CV2129 (2014).

[8]Model Utah Jury Instructions, Second Edition, CV2130 (2014).

A threat is improper if it would result in a crime (I will burn your store down), a criminal prosecution (I'll turn you in for tax fraud), or is the breach of a duty of good faith (I'll quit my five year contract in year four, before the Super Bowl, unless I get another five year extension)[9].

In addition to promoting mutual understanding, the law also works to promote mutual benefit in protecting the weak or unwary from the unscrupulous and advantaged whose contracts may be unconscionable, illegal or lack good faith and fair dealing.

Merriam-Webster defines "unconscionable" to mean: "extremely bad, unfair, or wrong....not guided or controlled by conscience." Unconscionability can be found when "the contract terms are so one-sided as to oppress or surprise an innocent party, or (ii) the contract terms result in an overall imbalance in the parties obligations and rights that is inconsistent with accepted customs and business practices."[10] Unconscionability is more likely to be identified when there is an imbalance in the bargaining power of the two parties as manifest by a "boilerplate" contract which is not the subject of discussion or negotiation.[11] Unconscionable contracts may include a contract for consumer goods disclaiming any and all warranties, or broad activity liability waivers which excuse the negligence of employees serving as guides or instructors. In this same vein, the law does not enforce contracts that are against public policy. Contracting with a hit man, for drugs or with a terrorist organization listed with the State Department creates a voidable contract.[12]

Another rationale for non-enforcement of a contract is that the purpose of the contract has been frustrated, or the purpose of the contract is no longer practical to perform. Frustration of purpose in our fairy tale may include a claim by the Princess that the Prince is sterile and is unable to produce children, one of her primary purposes in marrying. Impracticability of performance in the commercial context may include a "force majeure" or "act of God" such as an earthquake or storm which prevented a party from delivering goods. In both instances

[9]Model Utah Jury Instructions, Second Edition, CV2122 (2014); Restatement (Second) of Contracts § 174-176 (1981).

[10]Model Utah Jury Instructions, Second Edition, CV2127 (2014).

[11]Model Utah Jury Instructions, Second Edition, CV2128 (2014).

[12]Restatement (Second) of Contracts § 178 (1981).

it is important that the claiming party is "without fault" (did not cause the intervening event) and that the non-occurrence of the intervening event was a basic assumption on which the contract was made." [13] The Prince would be hard pressed to prove that the Princess's infertility was not a pre-existing condition and instead resulted from a supervening event.

Partners in business, as partners for life, seek to create a relationship and benefit greater than the sum of their individual parts. The binding and enforceable nature of a contract seeks to honor and sustain the mutual benefit contemplated by these parties, a benefit upon which the parties can rely. Because of this interest in sustaining the intended benefits of contracts, courts are remiss to void or render a contract unenforceable. When they do, a court often finds that the parties failed to come to a clear mutual understanding, or "meeting of the minds", either because of a parties compromised capacity to contract, misrepresentations by one or both parties, mistake, coercion, duress, incomplete terms or terms which should have been in writing. We have also learned that a court may find the terms or purposes of a contract void or unenforceable because they are, so unfair as to be "unconscionable", illegal, useless or excused.

[13]Restatement (Second) of Contracts § 256, 261 (1981); Model Utah Jury Instructions, Second Edition, CV2125 (2014).

CHAPTER 21

THE LAWS OF FRANCHISING

C. JEFFREY THOMPSON[1] WITH CHRISTIAN THOMPSON, BROOKE ASHTON, AND JOSHUA STANLEY

INTRODUCTION

A franchise is a complex business arrangement governed by both federal and state law. It is a concept that is familiar to most people in the retail store context. However, franchising has a broader definition than is commonly understood. Under the Amended FTC Franchise Rule (the "FTC Rule") a franchise is not determined by the business format, or whether the parties call their relationship a "franchise" or a "license," or by a different name, but generally whether or not the following three elements are present in the transaction: 1) the license or grant of a right to use another's (the licensor's) intellectual property; 2) on-going substantial assistance from the person or entity granting the license; and 3) the payment of a fee of more than $500 from the "licensee" to the "licensor" within a certain period of time.[2] If these elements are all present, it is a franchise, no matter the business format. These elements are discussed in more detail below.

Before selling a franchise, the franchisor is required to disclose information about the franchisor and the franchise system. The regulations are similar to the prospectus disclosures in the sale of securities. The purpose is to inform the prospective franchisee about the franchisor and the franchise system and to enable the potential investor/ franchisee to make an informed decision before any binding documents are signed or money is exchanged.

[1]Mr. Thompson is a partner in a Franchise and Business Law Group practicing principally in the areas of franchise, business opportunity, and related fields of product distribution law. He received his Juris Doctor degree from New York University School of Law. Mr. Thompson is recognized by the *US News and World Report* in its *Best Lawyers in America* publication and as a Legal Eagle by the *Franchise Lawyer magazine.*

[2]16 C.F.R. § 436 (1979). The FTC amended the Franchise Rule in 2007. 16 C.F.R. §§ 436, 436.1 (2007).

Drafting the disclosures can be a complex undertaking. The legal practitioner must be well-versed with not only state, federal and international laws relating to franchising and business opportunities, but must also be familiar with laws relating to trademarks, employment, anti-trust, contracts, and industry specific laws and regulations.

There are a number of organizations that are designed to assist an attorney in learning the technicalities of franchise law, and in keeping abreast of changes in the law. Two of the principal organizations are the Forum on Franchising of the Business Section of the American Bar Association and the International Franchise Association. Each of these associations hold an annual legal symposium designed to assist the franchise attorney and franchise professional to learn the most up–to-date information on current franchise issues and changes to the various laws. These symposiums also help franchise attorneys network with other professionals in the franchise industry and obtain other important and pertinent information. Many publications on franchising are also available from the ABA.[3]

WHAT IS A FRANCHISE?

At its most basic level a franchise refers to a business relationship where one business, the "franchisor," allows another business, the "franchisee," the right to conduct a business offering certain designated products and services to others usually associated with a brand name or trademark for a fee. Franchising is also defined by statute in more than a dozen states, and by the Federal Trade Commission ("FTC"). Depending on whether the FTC Rule or state law is being referenced, these elements are often referred to as the: 1) "trademark," or "grant" 2) "marketing plan," "substantial assistance" or "community of interest," and 3) "fee" elements. Each of these defined elements must be satisfied for the business arrangement to be considered a franchise. [4]

---

[3]The beginning franchise attorney may find the ABA's publication titled, *Fundamentals of Franchising* published by the Forum on Franchising, to be particularly helpful. This publication was consulted in preparing this paper *see* FUNDAMENTALS OF FRANCHISING *(Rupert M. Barkoff and Andrew C. Selden ed.,2008).*

[4]The FTC Rule defines a franchise as a "continuing commercial relationship created by any arrangement" where the following elements are included: (1) the franchisee sells goods or services that are substantially associated with the franchisor's trademark, tradename or commercial symbol or must meet the franchisor's quality standards, (2) the franchisor exercises significant control over, or gives the franchisee significant assistance in, the franchisee's method of operation, and (3) the franchisee, as a condition of obtaining or commencing operations, is required to make payment, either directly or indirectly, aggregating more than $500 within six months of commencing such operation. 16 C.F.R. §§ 436.2(a)(1)(i) and 436.2(a)(3)(iii).

While the FTC has defined what a franchise is under the FTC Rule, states that have also enacted franchise laws or regulations that define what constitutes a franchise. These laws may vary from state to state. The following section will examine the elements of this general definition in more detail. It should be noted that the courts often interpret these elements broadly in determining whether or not a specific business relationship constitutes a franchise. Additionally, the definitions below will often refer to "franchisor," "franchisee," and "franchise," but a franchise can still be found regardless of the terms used by the parties.

1. *Trademark or Grant*

The *trademark or grant* element provides the franchisee with the right to use the intellectual property of the franchisor in the franchise business. This use includes such items as trademarks, certain proprietary methods of operations, know how, recipes, etc. The trademark element has been subject to various interpretations. Some courts have found that the distribution of products or services covered by a franchisor's trademark is sufficient to satisfy the substantial association requirement.[6] Under the FTC Rule, it is not just the licensing of the trademark to the franchisee that triggers the trademark element; rather, it is the association of the business with the trademark which creates a franchise relationship, and the express grant of the right to use the franchisor's trademark is not required.[5] If this element is to be avoided, the franchise or license agreement must specifically prohibit the franchise business from using the licensor's trademarks.

2. *Marketing Plan, Community of Interest or Substantial Assistance*

The *marketing plan, community of interest or substantial assistance* element is often difficult to clearly define. Courts look for on-going substantial assistance or control, the sophistication of the assistance

---

[5]*See* Thomas M. Pitegoff & W. Michael Garner, *Franchise Relationship Laws,* in FUNDAMENTALS OF FRANCHISING, 192 (Selden and Barkoff *ed., 2008).*

[6]Master Abrasives Corp. v. Williams, 469 NE 2d 1196 (Indiana APP 1984). Wright-Moore Corp. v. Ricoh Corp., 908 F2d 128 (CA 1990).

and direction from the franchisor, and shared economic interests in the business relationship.[7]

A "marketing plan" has been interpreted as a franchisee being granted the right to engage in the business of offering, selling, or distributing goods or services under a marketing program or system prescribed in substantial part by the franchisor.[8]

Under the FTC Rule, "substantial assistance" can be found where the franchisor exercises significant control over, or gives the franchisee significant assistance in, the franchisee's method of operation.[9] The FTC Interpretive Guide sets forth that the more franchisees reasonably rely upon the franchisor's control or assistance, the more likely the control or assistance will be considered "significant." A franchisee's reliance is likely to be great when they are relatively inexperienced in the business being offered for sale, or when they undertake a large financial risk. Similarly, franchisees are likely to reasonably rely on the franchisor's control or assistance if the control or assistance is unique to that specific franchisor, as opposed to a typical practice employed by all businesses in the same industry.[10] The FTC has also provided specific actions by the supplier, relating to methods of operations, which will automatically trigger the element of "significant control or assistance."[11] The FTC has also given some direction of other actions which may or may not constitute "significant control or assistance" depending on the circumstances and some items that it will not consider when evaluating this element.[12] For

---

[7] *See* Thomas M. Pitegoff & W. Michael Garner, *Franchise Relationship Laws,* in FUNDAMENTALS OF FRANCHISING, 189 (Selden and Barkoff *ed., 2008).*

[8] *See Id.* at 189.

[9] FTC Franchise Rule Compliance Guide, at 2 (2008) https://www.ftc.gov/system/files/documents/plain-language/bus70-franchise-rule-compliance-guide.pdf, (last visited August 5, 2015).

[10] *Id.*

[11] Site approval for unestablished businesses; site design or appearance requirements; hours of operation; production techniques; accounting practices; personnel policies and practices; promotional campaigns requiring franchisee participation or financial contribution; restrictions on customers; location or sales area restrictions; formal sales, repair, or business training programs; establishing accounting systems; furnishing management, marketing, or personnel advice; selecting site locations; furnishing a detailed operations manual. Interpretive Guides to [1979] Franchising and Business Opportunity Ventures Trade Regulation Rule, 44 Federal Register 49966, August 24, 1979.

[12] Trademark controls designed solely to protect the trademark owner's legal ownership rights in the mark; health or safety restrictions required by law or regulation; agreements between a retailer and a trading stamp company providing for the distribution of trading stamps in connection with retail sales of merchandise or service; agreements between a bank credit interchange organization and retailers or member banks for the provision of credit cards and credit services; and assisting distributors in obtaining financing to be able to transact business. FTC Franchise Rule Compliance Guide, at 4 (2008) https://www.ftc.gov/system/files/documents/plain-language/bus70-franchise-rule-compliance-guide.pdf, (last visited August 5, 2015).

instance, the FTC has stated that "assistance with promotional activities is not enough to constitute 'significant' assistance or control and that for control to be considered significant, such control must be for the "entire method of operation."[13] If the product supplied will only be a small portion of the products to be sold by the distributor, then it would not rise to the level of "significant" required under the FTC definition.[14]

Under certain state laws, the marketing plan and community of interest elements (the correlatives of the FTC's significant assistance element) are subject to varying definitions. The marketing plan element generally exists where advice or training is given regarding the operation of the business and the sale of the products or services being offered.[15] In other states, community of interest is generally considered to have broader scope than a marketing plan because as opposed to any intentional marketing activity, a simple continuing financial interest between the parties can trigger this element.[16] Therefore, this applies to almost any commercial contractual relationship, and a distributor must look to the regulations and courts to determine how a particular state defines this element in the community of interest states.[17]

3. *Fee*

The *fee* element relates to separate consideration paid or promised by the franchisee business within a certain time period (usually six months) for the right to enter into the business relationship in combination with the other elements specified above.[18] This fee may either be a direct payment to the franchisor or an affiliate or an indirect payment through

[13]Providing point-of-sale advertising displays, sales kits, product samples and other promotional materials intended to assist the distributor in making sales or assistance in media do not constitute "significant" under the FTC Rule. *Id.*

[14]*Id.*

[15]*See* Thomas M. Pitegoff & W. Michael Garner, *Franchise Relationship Laws,* in FUNDAMENTALS OF FRANCHISING, 189-190 (Selden and Barkoff ed., 2008).

[16]*Id.* at 191.

[17]Wisconsin lists 10 factors to consider in determining whether there is a community of interest: (1) Duration of the parties' relationship; (2) extent and nature of the parties' obligations; (3) the percentage of time or revenue devoted to the grantor's products or services; (4) the percentage of the grantee's gross proceeds or profits derived from the grantor's products or services; (5) the extent and nature of the grantee's territory; (6) the use of the grantor's trademarks or logos; (7) the grantee's financial investment in the inventory, facilities, and goodwill of the alleged dealership; (8) the personnel devoted to the alleged dealership; (9) the amount of money and time spent on advertising and promotions for the supplier's products and services; and (10) the extent of supplemental services provided by the grantee to purchasers of the grantor's products or services. Ziegler Co., Inc. v. Rexnord, Inc., 407 NW2d 873 (ED Wis 1987).

[18]*See* Thomas M. Pitegoff & W. Michael Garner, *Franchise Relationship Laws,* in FUNDAMENTALS OF FRANCHISING, 193-194 (Selden and Barkoff ed., 2008).

the purchase of supplies or equipment at a price above market value.[19]

When evaluating whether a particular fee or cost constitutes a franchise fee, regulators are not limited to initial lump sum payments, but may also consider other payments that occur or are promised within the applicable time period. Any payment that the franchisor/licensee charges to the franchisee/licensee that is not for ordianry business expenses may be considered a franchise fee.

Some examples of fees that may be considered franchise fees are royalty fees, training fees, inventory costs, or any other amount charged by the franchisor that is above market value or not for a business expense. Accordingly, it would appear that the simplest option to avoid being classifed a franchise relationship would be to eliminate any fee that would qualify as a franchise fee. However, due to the very broad interpretation of franchise fees, it can be more difficult to eliminate these types of fees than it would appear at first glance.

For instance, in a supplier distributor relationship, the franchisor/supplier could choose not to charge any fee to the distributor for the right to sell the products, and then the franchisor/supplier could then sell all the products to the distribtor/franchisee for their bona fide wholesale price. However, under this structure, it will be important for the attorney to examine all amounts paid from the franchisee/distributor to the franchisor/supplier to ensure that none of these fees wold qualify as a franchise fee. Additionally, using the fee element to avoid being classified as a franchise relationship can be further complicated by business concerns, which will vary from one business concept to another.

FEDERAL AND STATE REGULATION OF FRANCHISING AND BUSINESS OPPORTUNITIES

As mentioned above, franchising is governed by federal and state law. The franchise and business opportunity laws generally relate to *disclosures* that must be made to the potential franchise buyer, and do not generally regulate the franchise business itself. The federal and state disclosure laws regarding franchising are discussed below.

---

[19] *See Id.*

[20] *See Id.*

1. Federal Franchise Disclosure Requirements

The FTC Rule requires that a franchisor provide a prospective franchisee with a set of 23 disclosures prior to the purchase of a franchise. This disclosure document is referred to as the franchise disclosure document or "FDD." The 23 disclosures or "items" in the FDD include among other things, information regarding the franchisor, its principals, the initial and ongoing fees the franchisee will have to pay, the initial investment required to commence business, initial and ongoing training, the franchisee's territory, and the number of outlets in the franchise system, etc. The franchisee must have these disclosures in hand for a minimum of 14 calendar days before the franchisee can sign an agreement or pay any money to the franchisor.[21]

The FTC does not require that the FDD be registered with the FTC. The FTC Rule only requires that the disclosures be made in compliance with the FTC Rule. The FTC Rule applies in all 50 states, Puerto Rico, Guam, the U.S. Virgin Islands, and other U.S. territories and possessions.[22] Once the FDD has been prepared in accordance with the FTC Rule, the franchisor is free to sell franchises in certain states that do not require a separate state filing. As further discussed below, the states that do not require any additional filings are considered "non-registration states" and the states that do require filings are considered "registration states." However, a number of states with business opportunity laws may also require some form of registration. If a franchisor wishes to sell a franchise in a registration state, or a business opportunity state, the laws of that state must be followed. The additional state requirements must be followed because the relationship between the FTC Rule and state registration laws generally operate in such a way that the more protective of these laws will be enforced.[23] In other words, the FTC Rule will not preempt state laws where the state law requires more detailed or expansive disclosures.

---

[21] *See Id.*

[22] *See also* Rochelle B. Spandorf and Mark B. Forseth, *Franchise Registration* in FUNDAMENTALS OF FRANCHISING, 132 (Selden and Barkoff ed., 2008).

[23] *Id.*

In addition, the FTC Rule specifically provides that it only applies to sales of franchises that are to be located or operated in the United States or its territories and commonwealths, and not whether the prospective franchisee is U.S. resident or U.S citizen.[24] In some states, the law on this issue is unclear, so the statutory provisions must be carefully reviewed if the offer or sale of a franchise to be operated outside of the U.S. is made to a resident of a registration state.

2. State Registration of the Franchise Disclosure Document

Fifteen states have laws and regulations that govern some aspect of selling franchises. Most of these states require that a franchisor register with the state and provide certain disclosures prior to selling franchises in their state. California was the first state to regulate the sale of franchises when it enacted its Franchise Investment Law in 1970.[25] Subsequently, 13 other states enacted laws requiring certain disclosures and some form of registration before a franchisor can offer or sell a franchise.[26] Those states are: Hawaii, Illinois, Indiana, Maryland, Michigan, Minnesota, New York, North Dakota, Rhode Island, South Dakota, Virginia, Washington and Wisconsin.[27]

Each state law is somewhat different, but the states have attempted uniformity through The North American Securities Administrators' Association, Inc. ("NASSA").[28] Most practitioners use the NASAA guidelines in preparing the FDD with state by state requirements made through addenda to the FDD.[29] The above states, together with Oregon, are referred to in this paper as the "Registration States."[30]

Most of the Registration States require registration, including the filing of an application, a required filing fee ranging between $125-$750, consent for service of process, a disclosure document with required exhibits, audited financial statements, and most states review the FDD

[24] *Id.* at 135.

[25] *Id.* at 129.

[26] *Id.*

[27] *Id.*

[28] *Id.*

[29] *Id.*

[30] *Id.*

and provide comments requiring changes to the FDD.[31] Registrations must be renewed or updated annually.

A few Registration States have less onerous registration requirements than others. For example, Michigan has the simplest registration process, requiring only a one-page notice that identifies the franchisor and its agent for service of process in Michigan.[32] The registration is good for one year. Wisconsin and Indiana have a simplified registration process and do not require an examiner's review of the FDD.[33] The registration is complete upon filing an application together with the franchisor's current disclosure document.[34] In Hawaii and South Dakota, the registrations are effective 7 and 10 days respectively, after the application and disclosure document are filed in those states.[35] However, in Hawaii, the applications are subject to review and a stop order may be issued at any time by an examiner.[36]

As with the federal requirements under the FTC Rule, in most instances, the states require that the registered FDD be delivered to the prospective franchisee not less than 14 full calendar days (or 10 business days, depending on the state) before any document can be signed by the prospective franchisee or any consideration can be given to the franchisor.

Additionally, most state franchise laws require the disclosure document to be delivered to prospective franchisees in their state. Depending on the state the prospective franchisee will be considered to be "in the state" where any of the following tests are met:

> 1) meetings between the franchisor and the prospective franchisee take place in the state; 2) the prospect resides in the state; 3) the prospect is domiciled in the state; 4) the acceptance of the offer is directed to the state; 5) the offer originates from the state; 6) the offer is directed to the state (in some states, that the proposed business will be located in the state); or 8) in some states, the

---

[31] *Id.*

[32] *Id.* at 130.

[33] *Id.*

[34] *Id.*

[35] *Id.*

[36] *Id. See also* Haw. Rev. Stat. Ch 482E-I through E-12. S.D. Statement of Policy, July 29, 2001, amended July11, 2002.

proposed franchisees sales territory is located in the state.[37]

Under these scenarios, it is possible that multiple state laws could apply to the sale of single franchise and the franchisor would be required to register in each of the applicable registration states.

Some states, such as California, Hawaii, Illinois, Maryland, Michigan, Minnesota, Rhode Island, Virginia and Wisconsin have an exemption for out of state sales.[38] This means that a franchisor headquartered in one of these states may sell to a prospect that does not reside in the state and whose franchise business will not be located in that state.[39]

Furthermore, in some states, if a franchisor wishes to advertise its franchise to potential franchisees, the franchisor must register its FDD and submit any advertisement for approval before using the advertisement in such state.[40] Exceptions are made for regional and internet advertising, but the state regulations regarding advertising and internet must be followed.[41]

It should be noted, that a franchisor must be also aware that certain state business opportunity laws such as Utah, Texas, Florida, and Connecticut require some type of registration. The registration is generally not complicated, requiring only a short notice, or exemption filing and consent for service of process.

BUSINESS OPPORTUNITY LAWS

When assisting a business in developing a franchise concept, the attorney must understand both franchise and business opportunity laws in order to ensure that the offering complies with applicable laws and regulations. Business opportunity laws are designed to regulate industries that have specified locations and services routes, such as vending machines, electronic amusement machines, rack-jobbers and certain types of dealerships and home manufacturing businesses.[42]

[37] *See also* Rochelle B. Spandorf and Mark B. Forseth, *Franchise Registration* in Fundamentals of franchising 125-157 (Selden and Barkoff ed., 2008).

[38] *Id.* at 164.

[39] *Id.*

[40] *Id.*

[41] *Id.*

[42] *Id.* at 177.

Despite the inherent complexity of franchise laws, there are numerous statutes, regulations, and court opinions providing guidance and clarity. Business opportunity law does not have the same level of clarity. This lack of clarity complicates drafting and often results in increased risk because the various elements of business opportunities are less tested and clear. States have enacted business opportunity laws and regulations, but the definitional elements vary widely from state to state.[43]

A general definition of a "business opportunity" is the sale or lease of any products, equipment, supplies, or services which are sold or leased to a purchaser to enable the purchaser to start a business for which the purchaser is required to pay an initial fee or sum of money which exceeds $500 (or as low as $200 or less in some states) to the seller, and in which the seller represents at least one of the following to the purchaser:

> (1) The purchaser's success with the business opportunity is ensured because the seller or its affiliate will provide, or will assist that purchaser in finding, locations or accounts for the use, operation, or placement of vending machines, racks, display cases, or similar devices, on premises the purchaser does not own or lease;
> (2) The seller or its affiliate or designee will reimburse the purchaser for, or will purchase from the purchaser, goods the purchaser produces, grows, or modifies, or services the purchaser performs, using goods or services supplied by the seller or its affiliate or designee, or resulting from those goods or services;
> (3) The seller guarantees that the purchaser will derive income from the business opportunity which exceeds the price paid or rent charged for the business opportunity or that the seller or its affiliate or designee will refund all or a substantial part of the purchaser's initial payment, or will repurchase any of the products, equipment, supplies, or chattels supplied by the seller, if the purchaser is unsuccessful or dissatisfied with the business opportunity;
> (4) The purchaser's success with the business opportunity is ensured by a marketing plan prescribed in substantial part by the seller or

[43] Alaska, California, Connecticut, Florida, Georgia, Illinois, Indiana, Iowa, Kentucky, Louisiana, Maine, Maryland, Michigan, Nebraska, New Hampshire, North Carolina, Ohio, Oklahoma, South Carolina, South Dakota, Texas, Utah, Virginia, and Washington have business opportunity laws or regulations in various degrees. Alabama, Arkansas, Mississippi, Oregon, and the District of Columbia do not allow deceptive acts, but do not technically have a business opportunity law. *Id.*

its affiliate under which the seller or its affiliate will provide to the purchaser training, or marketing assistance, in the purchaser's method of operation; or
(5) The seller represents that there is a market for the goods or services the purchaser will be selling.[44]

The state definitions for business opportunity also have some exemptions and exceptions, but these exemptions and exceptions may vary widely frome one state to another.[45] Some states exempt franchisors who comply with the FTC Rule or the state franchise laws from their business opportunity definition.[46] Other states have exemptions if the opportunity is sold in conjunction with a registered trademark or the transaction is for a large initial investment or if the seller has a large net worth.[47]

Just as with the franchise definition, these elements are subject to broad interpretation and definitions may vary from one state to another. In order to make a viable national distribution program, each of the elements of the various business opportunity definitions must be addressed. Unfortunately, there is not one exemption that works for all the state business opportunity laws which can be used as a safe harbor when drafting a distribution agreement. State regulators look to the actual course of dealing and not just to the contract terms in determining whether or not the various laws are applicable to a particular distribution agreement.

OTHER LAWS TO CONSIDER

In addition to these franchise/distribution specific statutes and regulations, there are several more general laws and regulations that frequently arise in franchise/distribution relationships. Although this publication does not lend itself for a detailed discussion of these topics, the following will highlight some of these specific statutes and regulations that often impact franchise/license relationships.

---

[44] *See Id.* at 176-179.

[45] *See Id.*

[46] *See Id.*

[47] *See Id.*

Uniform Commercial Code

Some courts will apply the UCC to those provisions of the franchise agreement related to the sale of goods from the franchisor and will apply traditional common law analysis to the other portions of the contract. Article 2 of the UCC contains a number of provisions that potentially affect obligations of "good faith" on "merchants" as those terms are defined including in Section 2-104 of the UCC. These provisions can have an important impact on the relationship between a franchisor/licensor and its franchisee/licensee.

Fair Dealership Laws

Twenty states, Puerto Rico and the U.S. Virgin Islands, have promulgated "relationship" laws concerning elements of the ongoing contractual association and the termination of that associate between manufacturers and dealers or franchisors and franchisees.[48] Any franchise/license relationship that involves manufacture or distribution of goods should take account of these laws and make sure that the agreement and conduct between the parties complies with the requirements of these laws.

Little FTC Acts

Most states have passed "little FTC Acts" which are intended to protect "consumers" from unfair, false, misleading or deceptive trade practices.[49] Franchisors/licensors need to ensure that their practices comply with these acts, and they need to include protective provisions in the agreements should their franchisees/licensees run afoul of these laws.

---

[48]Alaska: Alaska Stat. §§45.45.700 to 45.45.790; Arkansas: Ark. Code Ann. §§4-72-201 to 4-72-210 (Arkansas Franchise Practices Act); California: Cal. Bus. & Prof Code §§20000-20043 (California Franchise Relations Act), Cal. Civ. Code §51.8 (restricts discrimination in franchising), Cal. Civ. Code §§80-86 (California Fair Dealership Law); Connecticut: Conn. Gen. Stat. §§42-133e to 42-133(h); Delaware: Del. Code Ann. tit. 6 §§2551 through 2556 (Delaware Franchise Security Law); Hawaii: Haw. Rev. Stat. §482E-6, Illinois: Ill. Rev. Stat. §§705/18 through 705/20; Indiana: Ind. Code §§23-2-2.7-1 through 23-2-2.7-7, Maryland: Md. Code Ann. Corn. Law §§11-1301 through 11-1307 (Maryland Fair Dealership Act); Michigan: Mich. Comp. Laws §445.1527; Minnesota: Minn. Stat. §80C.14; Mississippi: Miss. Code Ann. §§75-24-51 through 75-24-63; Missouri: Mo. Rev. Stat. §§407.400 through 407.410, 407.413 and 407.420; Nebraska: Neb. Rev. Stat. §§87-401 through 87-410; New Jersey: N.J. Rev. Stat. §§56:10-1 through 56:10-12; North Dakota: N.D. Cent. Code §§51-20.2-01 through 51-20.2-03; Puerto Rico: P.R. Laws Ann. tit. 10 §§278 through 278d; South Dakota: S.D. Codified Laws Ann. §§37-5A-51 through 37-5A-51.1; Virgin Islands: V.I. Code Ann, tit. 12A §§130 through 139; Virginia: Va. Code Ann. §13.1-564; Washington: Wash Rev. Code §§19.100.180 through 19.100.190; and Wisconsin; Wis. Stat. §§135.01 through 135.07.

[49]*See also* Rochelle B. Spandorf and Mark B. Forseth, *Franchise Registration* in FUNDAMENTALS OF FRANCHISING, 132 (Selden and Barkoff ed., 2008).

Price Maintenance

Price maintenance and its effects on brand name and goodwill is an important aspect of any system providing products or services in association with a specific trademark or commercial symbol. Obviously controlling the price of goods has anti-trust implications but recently, the Supreme Court has issued decisions addressing this in the franchise/ license context.

The Supreme Court in the case of *State Oil v. Kahn* [50] held that maximum resale price maintenance is no longer subject to *a per* se rule. And in 2007 the Supreme Court in the case of *Leegin Creative Leather Products, Inc. v. PSKS, Inc.*,[51] held that minimum resale price maintenance is also no longer subject to a *per se* rule. Nevertheless, some states have taken the position that despite the *Leegin* ruling, those states will vigorously enforce their own acts and will criminally prosecute distributors that set minimum prices or otherwise violate the state's little FTC act. A practitioner must be familiary with both federal and state laws in order to protect its client from state antitrust claims.

Other Antitrust Issues

Franchisors may require their distributors to sell products only within a limited geographic area, to a restricted class of customers, for a fixed price (or range of prices), in connection with the sale of other specified products and/or any combination of these and other restrictive practices. Because of the potentially anticompetitive effects of many of these restrictions, the franchisor's/licensor's course of conduct and agreements must comply with these laws, and the franchisor's attorney must continually be updated with knowledge of these laws, their implications, and their potential to impact on the attorney's clients.[52]

NEGOTIABILITY OF THE FRANCHISE AGREEMENT

When representing a franchisee client that is purchasing a franchise, or a franchisor client where a franchisee is requesting an amendment to

---

[50] 522 U.S. 3, 18 (1997).

[51] 127 S.Ct. 2705, 2721 (2007).

[52] *See* Robert T. Joseph & Lee N. Abrams, *Antitrust Law* in FUNDAMENTALS OF FRANCHISING, 229-287 (Selden & Barkoff ed., 2008).

the franchise agreement, the attorney should be aware of the potential for negotiation. It is commonly believed by franchisors, prospective franchisees and franchise attorneys that franchise agreements are not negotiable. Though there are many factors that make a franchisor reluctant to negotiate the terms of its standard franchise agreement, the attorney should assume the franchise agreement is negotiable.[53] A few factors that should be taken into consideration are: the franchisor's need for uniformity among the franchisees in the franchise system; franchisee communication one to another regarding more favorable terms given to a franchisee, and a system that has varying franchise agreements is much more difficult to administer or manage.[54] However, in the right economic situation, it may be to the advantage of the franchisor to negotiate changes to its standard agreement. The willingness of the franchisor to make changes to its franchise agreement usually turns on the bargaining power of the parties.[55]

Some areas of the franchise agreement are easier to negotiate than others. Clearly, it is important to most franchisors to have a uniform system-wide royalty.[56] It is very difficult to negotiate a change in the royalty.[57] However, franchisors are often willing to negotiate a change in the initial fee depending on such factors as the location of the franchise, how many units are proposed to be developed by the franchisee, the reputation of the franchisee, and the business experience of the franchisee, etc.[58] The franchisor may also consider negotiating the territory, the scope of the personal guaranty, and the scope of the covenant not to compete, especially when the potential franchisee or other members of his family are involved in other businesses.[59] Other areas that are often negotiated include, whether or not the franchisee needs to work full time in the business, renewal and renewal fees, default and cure provisions, and the term, etc.[60]

---

[53]See also FUNDAMENTALS OF FRANCHISING, *Supra, note 2*, at 300-303.

[54]*Id.*

[55]*Id.*

[56]*See Id.*

[57]*See Id.*

[58]*See Id.*

[59]*See Id.*

[60]*See Id.*

PRELIMINARY CLIENT DISCUSSIONS

Clients often come to the attorney with a business plan involving a product or service distribution concept ("Marketing Program"), but without having made a decision about whether the concept will be a franchise. It is up to the attorney to guide the client through this process. The role of the attorney in drafting an agreement for a client's Marketing Program is to understand the client's business needs and ensure that the agreement accurately reflects the client's actual distribution program. The attorney also needs to ensure that any required disclosure and the agreement itself is compliant with the varied and complex laws and regulatory schemes that may apply, as discussed above.

In developing a Marketing Program, it is relatively easy for the company or the attorney to trigger application of various laws and regulations that may not have been considered. If the attorney assisting a client in setting up a Marketing Plan does not draft the contract with such laws and regulations in mind, the attorney may be faced with an unhappy client in the future when the client discovers it may have accidentally developed a Marketing Program that is considered a franchise or business opportunity, requiring the company to spend both time and money to comply with the applicable legal framework and any potential penalties and fees.

There are a number of preliminarily issues that should be discussed with a client desiring to establish a nationwide or regional Marketing Program. These issues focus generally on control of marketing, capital and labor available to the supplier, operational controls and legal frameworks. For example, a key factor concerns the product or service to be distributed. What is it about the product that distinguishes it from other products in the broader market place? The client's success in a local market does not assure success in the broader market. The client needs to conceptualize what makes its particular product unique. This analysis will help in developing the Marketing Program.

Secondly, the attorney needs to understand the financial position of the client. The distribution system must satisfy the client's financial needs. Does the client have sufficient capital to introduce a regional or nationwide marketing, sales and distribution program itself or does it need outside capital and labor?

There should also be a discussion as to whether or not product branding and brand identity are important to the client. Branding issues have an impact on both the distribution system and the Marketing Program. Furthermore, the attorney needs to understand the degree of control over operations, training, distribution, marketing and advertising that is important to the client. Such controls will also influence the type of Marketing Program established. In addition, the attorney should understand the network of component suppliers and how that network will interact with the down line distributors. Finally, the attorney should discuss the legal framework of the various methods of distribution available to the client.

Lastly, the attorney should review the following questions with the client to further flush out the Marketing Program:

> 1) Does the business require full time sales persons hired as employees of the Company? 2) Does the business require direct sales such as the internet, social media, catalogue, infomercials, telephone solicitation and, mailers? 3) Does the business require independent contractors such as salesmen and supplier representatives who solicit orders on a commission basis? 4) Does the business require regulated distribution arrangements such as business opportunities, multilevel marketing and franchising? And, 5) Does the business require other methods such as company warehouse centers, joint ventures, license agreements, and wholesale distributor agreements?

CONCLUSION

Practicing franchise law can be interesting, stimulating and far more complex than simply drafting an FDD. Franchising is a relatively new area of the law that is quickly evolving. The attorney practicing franchise law must be well-informed, and have a consistent way of staying abreast to changes in the law.

CHAPTER 22

REAL ESTATE

BUYING AND/OR LEASING

SPENCER TOPHAM[1]

As an entrepreneur, you're probably aware that real property ("real estate" or "property") and its associated legal issues pervade nearly every aspect of business at one time or another: from investing to develop real estate, to leasing office space for your company, real estate issues are inescapable in business. Additionally, in many cases, purchasing real estate or entering into a long term lease for your business will be your largest and most long term investment. Based on the wide body of statutory, regulatory and case law governing real estate in Utah, the space allotted for this chapter will only provide a brief overview of the many areas and their associated legal issues. It may, however, help you to recognize legal issues of which you might not otherwise be aware. As always, the law is complex and it's very important to engage a real estate attorney early in any real estate purchase or leasing process, so you have the benefit of obtaining good legal advice to mitigate potential issues and represent your interests in the transaction.

[1]Wm. Spencer Topham focuses his legal practice on real estate transactions and a wide range of business law issues, including mergers & acquisitions, corporate law, employment compliance, and intellectual property. In his real estate practice, Spencer represents clients in real estate transactions and commercial leasing. He also is experienced in assisting public and private clients in navigating local land use issues and disputes. The business law portion of his practice focuses primarily on representing buyers and sellers of businesses, while also advising existing businesses on their day-to-day legal operations, including corporate, intellectual property and employment law matters. Outside of the office, Spencer maintains an active lifestyle with interests including rock climbing, hiking, snowboarding and weight training.

A. GENERAL REAL ESTATE AND CONTRACT PRINCIPLES

Interests in real estate are merely private contracts, subject to the principles of contract formation, including offer, acceptance and consideration discussed in section A(2) below. Real estate is also governed by federal, state and local laws that may govern the particular interest, such as conveyancing, zoning and environmental laws.

1. The "Bundle of Sticks"

In their first year of law school, law students are generally introduced to property law as a collection of multiple rights, rather than an individual item. In most cases, law professors analogize property rights to a "bundle of sticks," with each stick in the bundle representing a particular right or stream of benefits.[2] The following details some of these rights, using real estate rather than personal property as an example.

(a) *The Right to Control, Use and Possess*. You have the right to use, possess and occupy property you personally own; however, private contracts may also provide the right to use property you don't own, such as in the case of a real estate lease. In either case, there may be public or private restrictions on your right to use and control the property. For example, government regulations may restrict the size and color of a sign you would like to place on a building you own, and a lease agreement may completely restrict signs on real estate you lease. The right of possession also gives you the right to invite others to enter or occupy the real estate.

(b) *The Right to Benefit and Enjoy*. Correspondingly, you also have the right to benefit from anything produced by real estate you own. You also have the right to hold title without any other person (like a former owner), claiming an interest in the real estate. Following

---

[2]*See Provo City Corp. v. Knudsen*, 558 P.2d 1332, 1334 (Utah 1977) ("In that connection it should be borne in mind that in addition to the right of peaceable possession of his property the owner has quite a number of other rights and privileges which he should be able to exercise without limitation or restraint, including in the air above and the earth beneath. They are sometimes referred to as a 'bundle of rights' and compared to a bundle of sticks, each of which may be violated, removed, or dealt with separately.")

the real estate example above, ownership of real estate provides you the right to benefit from rent payments if you decide to lease the real estate. Like the right to use and possess, government regulations (in the form of taxes) may curtail your right to benefit from rents received from the lease. Additionally, private contracts may restrict your ability to lease the building and receive rent.[3]

(c) *The Right to Transfer*. If you decide you want to use your invested capital to purchase new real estate or invest in another venture, you can sell or assign the real estate to another person and receive the benefit or burden of any increase or decrease in value. As with other rights in the bundle, taxes may curtail your potential profits and private contracts (such as recorded covenants, conditions and restrictions) may restrict to whom you may transfer the real estate.

(d) *The Right to Destroy*. It's probably not surprising that you have the right to destroy any real estate you own, again subject to certain restrictions, such as environmental laws.

(e) *The Right to Exclude*. If you own real estate, one of the more significant rights in your "bundle" is the right to exclude other members of society from any occupation, use, benefit, transfer, enjoyment or destruction of the real estate.[4] As in the case of all other rights, even the right to exclude may be curtailed by public or private rights in the form of easements, search warrants, or emergency situations. For example, under Utah law, if a property owner allows a fence line to encroach on his property for a long period of time, the fence line will become the new boundary line.[5]

---

[3]*See* UTAH CODE ANN. § 57-8a-209, setting forth statutes applicable to rental restrictions contained in the governing documents of residential homeowners' associations.

[4]*See Osguthorpe v. Wolf Mountain Resorts, L.C.*, 2010 UT 29, ¶ 25, 232 P.3d 999, 1007 ("[t]he uses a possessor in land may make of the space within his possession are, in general, undefined and are limited only by the rights of others . . . [a] dditionally, one with a possessory interest has the right and intention "to exclude other members of society in general from any present occupation of the land.") (internal quotations and citations omitted).

[5]*See Essential Botanical Farms, LC v. Kay*, 2011 UT 71, ¶ 18, 270 P.3d 430, 435 (discussing the required elements to obtain "boundary by acquiescence" under Utah law).

2. Contract Formation

Although the basics of forming a binding contract were discussed in earlier chapters, it's helpful to quickly review those requirements. A binding contract is formed when (a) one party makes an offer or promises to something, (b) the other party accepts, and (c) there is a valid exchange of value between the parties (known as "consideration").[6] A simple example would be one where I offer to mow your lawn this weekend for $30 and you accept my offer—this example contains offer ("I'll mow your lawn"), acceptance, and consideration (the value received and given, $30 in exchange for the lawn mowing service).

(a) *Offer*. An offer is a "manifestation of willingness to enter into a bargain, so made as to justify another person understanding that his assent to the bargain is invited and will conclude it."[7] For an offer to create a binding contract, the terms of the offer must be definite enough that the contract can be performed, which generally requires the parties to the contract, the length of time for performance (the "term"), the price, and the subject matter or scope of services.[8]

(b) *Acceptance*. An acceptance is "a manifestation of assent to an offer, such that an objective, reasonable person is justified in understanding that a fully enforceable contract has been made."[9] The acceptance must be unconditional and conform to the exact terms of the offer; if the acceptance contains a condition (i.e., "I accept your offer to mow my lawn for $30, *but only if you do it on Saturday*") then a "counteroffer" has been made which rejects the original offer and the original offeror can then either accept or reject the counteroffer (i.e., "I accept your offer to perform the lawn mowing service on Saturday").[10]

---

[6] *See Cea v. Hoffman*, 2012 UT App 101, ¶ 24, 276 P.3d 1178, 1185 ("[g]enerally, formation of a contract requires an offer, an acceptance, and consideration.") (citations omitted).

[7] *Id.*

[8] *Id.* ("[a] lack of definiteness in an agreement may concern the time of performance, the price to be paid, work to be done, property to be transferred, or miscellaneous stipulations to the agreement.") (internal quotations and citations omitted).

[9] *Id.*

[10] *Id.* at ¶ 25, 1185-1186.

(c) Consideration. "Consideration is present when there is an act or promise given in exchange for the other party's promise."[11] The consideration requirement for contract formation simply means that the parties to the contract must exchange something of value. In the lawn mowing example, both parties receive value: you receive the lawn mowing service and I receive $30. Consideration doesn't necessarily need to include money, for instance, if I offer to provide you legal services in exchange for your agreement to wear a shirt with my law firm's logo to a business event, the exchange of value would constitute sufficient consideration to form a contract. Consideration must, however, be mutual: if only one party receives value from the transaction, it will generally be categorized as an offer to make a gift.[12] Although this concept seems simple, even seasoned business people and attorneys can miss this issue in certain contracts.[13]

3. The Statute of Frauds

In addition to the requirements for formation of a valid contract, real estate contracts (such as leases or purchase contracts) are also included as transactions that are covered by the "statute of frauds."[14] The statute of frauds has been enacted throughout the United States (including Utah) and is based on an English statute originally enacted in 1677 and entitled "Act for Prevention of Frauds and Perjuries."[15] Utah's enactment of the statute of frauds requires certain kinds of contracts to be memorialized in writing, including real estate leases longer than one year and sales of real estate or any interest in real estate.[16] Accordingly,

---

[11] *See Cea v. Hoffman*, 2012 UT App 101, ¶ 26, 276 P.3d 1178, 1186.

[12] *See E & H Land, Ltd. v. Farmington City*, 2014 UT App 237, ¶ 29, 336 P.3d 1077, 1086 (discussing the doctrine of promissory estoppel, noting that fact supporting promissory estoppel generally involve ". . . offers to make a gift, where although accepted, no binding contract results because there is no consideration.") (internal quotations and citations omitted).

[13] *See Tomlinson v. Outpost Development, Inc.*, 2011 WL 11048004 (Utah Dist. Ct.), 3 (concluding that certain personal guaranty contracts failed for lack of consideration).

[14] *See* UTAH CODE ANN. § 25-5-3 ("[e]very contract for the leasing for a longer period than one year, or for the sale, of any lands, or any interest in lands, shall be void unless the contract, or some note or memorandum thereof, is in writing subscribed by the party by whom the lease or sale is to be made, or by his lawful agent thereunto authorized in writing.")

[15] George P. Costigan, Jr., THE DATE AND AUTHORSHIP OF THE STATUTE OF FRAUDS, 26 Harv. L. Rev. 329, 332 (1913).

[16] See note 6, *supra*.

unless you're entering into a lease less than one year, make sure the contract is in writing and signed by the parties.

B. INTERESTS IN REAL ESTATE and CONVEYING REAL ESTATE

If you're buying or selling real estate, your interest in the real estate must be conveyed through a deed, which sets forth how the real estate will be owned. A copy of the deed must then be recorded with the county recorder in the county where the real estate is located. A quick note regarding terminology- in this and later sections, the individual (or entity) transferring real estate will be referred to as the "grantor" and the individual receiving the real estate will be referred to as the "grantee."

1. Interests in Real Estate ("Estates")

Before you can convey or purchase real estate, it's helpful to understand some of the specific interests in real estate that can be conveyed, several of which are discussed below.

(a) *Fee Simple*. Fee simple is the most common and complete form of real estate ownership and conveys an interest ". . . clear of all encumbrances or interests of any other person."[17] A fee simple interest is also inheritable.[18] Utah statutes provide that fee simple title to real estate is the presumed interest conveyed, unless the conveyance states that a lesser interest was intended.[19]

(b) *Fee Simple Defeasible*. A fee simple defeasible interest in real estate is conveyed when the extent of fee simple ownership is limited by some condition or covenant, i.e., "[i]f a fee estate can be determined or defeated by an event which is not certain to occur, it is a defeasible fee simple . . . [a] defeasible fee gives a complete set of rights of ownership to

---

[17] *Hall v. Fitzgerald*, 671 P.2d 224, 227 (Utah 1983).

[18] *See* UTAH CODE ANN. § 57-1-2 ("[t]he term "heirs," or other technical words of inheritance or succession, are not requisite to transfer a fee in real estate.").

[19] *See* UTAH CODE ANN. § 57-1-3.

the grantee until the defeating event arises."[20] Defeasible fees are further broken down into two subcategories: fee simple determinable and fee simple subject to condition subsequent.[21]

In the case of fee simple determinable, the defeasible fee terminates automatically once the condition in the conveyance occurs.[22] For example, if I convey real estate to you as long as it is used to operate a zoo, if the land is ever not used for operation of a zoo ownership of the real estate will automatically be transferred to me.

Fee simple subject to a condition subsequent is similar to fee simple determinable because ownership also has a condition attached; however, once the triggering event occurs transfer is not automatic and the original grantor must take steps to reclaim the real estate.[23] If the grantor doesn't take steps to reclaim the real estate, then the real estate does not transfer back to the grantor.[24] In the zoo example, if the land is not used for operation of a zoo, I would be required to "re-enter" the land by taking action to recover it[25] and if I didn't, you would remain the owner.

(c) Life Estate. A life estate conveyance grants a temporary interest to use real estate for the duration of an individual's life (sometimes subject to conditions), and at the end of their life, the real estate will transfer to either the original grantor (reversion) or to a third party (remainder), depending on the language used in the conveyance document. A life estate cannot be inherited, and the holder of a life estate has the right to sell, lease or encumber the real estate, although those interests automatically terminate at the time of the holder's death because the holder cannot transfer a greater interest in the real estate than they possess.[26]

---

[20] *Allen v. Hall*, 2006 UT 70, ¶ 14, 148 P.3d 939, 942 (quoting James H. Backman, *Thomas and Backman on Utah Real Property Law* § 2.02(c), at 43 (1999)).

[21] *See id.*

[22] *Id.*

[23] *Id.* at ¶ 15, 943.

[24] *Id.*

[25] *See* UTAH CODE ANN. § 57-1-5.1 (providing the requirement of an affidavit for termination of a determinable or conditional interest in real estate).

[26] *See* UTAH CODE ANN. § 57-1-4.

2. Types of Real Estate Ownership

Just as there are different interests in real estate that can be conveyed, there are also different forms of real estate ownership, including individual ownership and various forms of co-ownership, the more common forms of which are discussed below.

(a) Individual Ownership. Real estate can be owned by a single individual, but if you're interested in real estate investing, it's generally a better idea to own the real estate through a business entity such as a limited liability company, corporation or partnership. Owning real estate through a business entity helps to mitigate potential individual liability. In most cases, ownership through a business entity is a form of co-ownership between corporate shareholders, limited liability company members, or partners in a partnership.

(b) Joint Tenancy. Joint tenancy is probably the most common form of co-ownership of real estate; it provides joint ownership in the same property with a right of survivorship if one of the tenants dies.[27] For instance, if a husband and wife owned real estate as joint tenants, the wife would own the real estate individually if the husband died (or vice-versa). Similarly, if three individuals owned real estate as joint tenants and one of the individuals died, his or her share would be divided among the remaining individuals. Each individual in a joint tenancy can convey their interest in the real estate; however, the conveyance will sever the joint tenancy and create a tenancy in common (discussed in section B(2)(c)below).[28] A joint tenant's conveyance of their interest in the property does not convey the entire property because a joint tenant can only convey their individual interest in the property.[29]

Under Utah statute, every ownership interest in real estate granted to a husband and wife is presumed to be a joint tenancy with rights of survivorship, unless the conveyance specifically grants another ownership

---

[27] *See Shiba v. Shiba*, 2008 UT 33, ¶ 17, 186 P.3d 329, 333.

[28] *Id.* (citations omitted); *see also* UTAH CODE ANN. § 57-1-5(5)(a) (" . . . [i]f a joint tenant makes a bona fide conveyance of the joint tenant's interest in property held in joint tenancy to himself or herself or another, the joint tenancy is severed and converted into a tenancy in common.").

[29] *See Ashworth v. Bullock*, 2013 UT App 96, ¶ 12, 304 P.3d 74, 78 (internal citations and quotations omitted).

interest.[30] Additionally, a joint tenancy cannot be established between a person and a business entity.[31]

(c) Tenancy in Common. As previously discussed, if a joint tenancy is severed when a joint tenant conveys their interest in real estate, a tenancy in common is created.[32] Tenancy in common differs from joint tenancy because (i) each tenant in common has a full, undivided right of possession of the real estate (regardless of their percentage of ownership),[33] and (ii) there is no right of survivorship.[34] Consequently, tenants in common are free to transfer their individual interests and if a tenant in common dies, his or her share of the real estate passes to his or her heirs under probate law.[35]

3. Deeds

Once you've established the interest in real estate that will be conveyed and how the real estate will be owned, it's necessary to prepare a deed, which is the document that actually conveys the interest in real estate and passes ownership.[36] As previously discussed in section A(3), deeds must be in writing and signed by the grantor to satisfy the requirements of the statute of frauds.[37] Additionally, the deed must be supported by consideration (to create a valid contract) and be delivered to the grantee.[38] Utah statutes provide three main forms of deeds that are differentiated by the particular warranties of title they convey to the grantee.[39]

---

[30] *See* UTAH CODE ANN. § 57-1-5(1)(a)(i).

[31] *See* UTAH CODE ANN. § 57-1-5(1)(a)(ii).

[32] *See* note 28, *supra*.

[33] *See Flying Diamond Corp. v. Rust,* 551 P. 2d 509 (Utah 1976).

[34] See *Ashworth v. Bullock, supra* note 29 at ¶ 11, 78 ("[w]hen a tenant in common dies, that tenant's interest in the property passes to her heirs, rather than to the other tenants in common.") (citations omitted).

[35] *Id.*

[36] *See Wiggill v. Cheney,* 597 P.2d 1351, 1351 (Utah 1979) (citations omitted) (noting that unless a deed is delivered to the grantee, title cannot pass).

[37] *See Julian v. Petersen,* 966 P.2d 878, 881 (Utah Ct. App. 1998) (quotations and citations omitted).

[38] *Id.*

[39] *See* UTAH CODE ANN. § 57-1-12—13.

(a) Warranty Deed. A warranty deed is the most complete transfer of real estate ownership: it transfers fee simple title to real estate and also contains five specific warranties relating to the real estate title.[40] Utah statute contains a specific form for a warranty deed,[41] which describes the five warranties as follows:

i. the grantor lawfully owns fee simple title to the real estate and has the right to immediate possession of the real estate;

ii. the grantor has good right to convey the real estate;

iii. the grantor guarantees the grantee, the grantee's heirs and assigns quiet possession of the real estate;

iv. the real estate is free from all liens and encumbrances; and

v. the grantor, the grantor's heirs and personal representatives will forever warrant and defend title of the real estate in the grantee.[42]

In simple terms, if real estate is conveyed by a warranty deed, the grantee receives the property with warranties that the grantor and all his/her predecessor owners had good title to the real estate, i.e., the real estate is free from all liens and encumbrances. A warranty deed is the strongest deed if you're the grantee/purchaser of real estate, but if you're a seller of real estate you should strongly consider using a special warranty deed (described below) so you aren't assuming liability for the encumbrances of previous owners.

(b) Special Warranty Deed. In contrast to a warranty deed, in a conveyance by a special warranty deed the grantor only warrants title during their period of ownership of the real estate.[43] Utah Statute also provides a form of special warranty deed, which provides warranties that (i) the conveyed real estate is free from all encumbrances made

[40] *See* UTAH CODE ANN. § 57-1-12.

[41] *Id.*

[42] *See* UTAH CODE ANN. § 57-1-12(2)(c).

[43] *See* UTAH CODE ANN. § 57-1-12.5(2)(b).

by the grantor; and (ii) the grantor, the grantor's heirs and personal representatives will forever warrant and defend title of the real estate in the grantee.[44]

Although this distinction may seem minor, it can have major impacts. To illustrate, imagine you purchased a commercial office building in 2014, knowing that the seller purchased the building from the developer in 2012 and the developer had declared bankruptcy in 2013. Then, in January 2015 you then receive a tax notice indicating that the 2011 property tax had not been paid and the county has placed a lien on the building. If the building had been conveyed to you by warranty deed, the seller would have warranted that no encumbrances existed relating to him or the developer, and the seller would be required to pay the tax bill to release the lien. If, however, the building had been conveyed to you by special warranty deed, the seller would not be required to pay the tax bill because the encumbrance related to the developer, not the seller.

(c) Quit Claim Deed. A quit claim deed is the weakest form of deed because it carries no warranties of title and a grantee under a quitclaim deed "acquires only the interest of the grantor."[45] This means that if a grantor conveyed real estate to you by quitclaim deed and it was later discovered that the grantor had no interest in the real estate, then you would have no interest in the real estate. Similar to warranty deeds and special warranty deeds, Utah statute provides a form of quitclaim deed.[46]

4. Recordation

For a deed to be effective, it must be delivered from the grantor to the grantee,[47] but a deed recorded with the county recorder in the county where the property is located creates the presumption of valid delivery.[48]

---

[44] *See* UTAH CODE ANN. § 57-1-12.5.

[45] *See* UTAH CODE ANN. § 57-1-13; *Johnson v. Bell*, 666 P.2d 308, 312 (Utah 1983) (citations omitted).

[46] *See* UTAH CODE ANN. § 57-1-13(1).

[47] *See Jacobs v. Hafen*, 875 P.2d 559, 561 (Utah Ct. App. 1994).

[48] *Id.*; UTAH CODE ANN. § 57-4a-4(1)(d).

In addition to the presumption of valid delivery, recording a document creates other presumptions, including that necessary consideration was given and the person executing the document is the person they claim to be.[49]

C. REAL ESTATE FINANCING: TRUST DEEDS AND LIEN PRIORITY

If you've ever purchased residential or commercial real estate, you're probably aware that (in most cases) the purchase price is financed by the purchaser. The repayment of the resulting loan obligation in this scenario is the most common form of real estate financing or real estate "secured transactions", where the repayment of the loan obligation is "secured" by a lender's lien on the real estate and the lender can foreclose in the event of default on the loan obligation.[50] Because real estate financing and its associated legal issues could fill many books, we'll simply cover some of the basics in this section.

1. Lien Priority

For purposes of real estate financing, the date a document is recorded establishes "**priority**" among lenders, subsequent purchasers and other parties because a recorded document imparts notice to all others of the contents of the document,[51] even if the document contains defects or irregularities.[52] The term "priority" simply refers to the hierarchy of liens in the real estate and the corresponding rights of lenders and other lienholders. This system allows lenders "to reasonably rely on previously recorded trust deeds to provide them with an estimate of what their financial position will be relative to other security interests in the same property."[53]

---

[49]UTAH CODE ANN. § 57-4a-4(1).

[50]*See DiMeo v. Nupetco Associates, LLC,* 2013 UT App 188, ¶ 7, 309 P.3d 251, 253 ("[i]n other words, the pledged property is used as collateral for the obligation and can be foreclosed in the event of default.") (citations omitted).

[51]*See* UTAH CODE ANN. § 57-3-102(1).

[52]*See* UTAH CODE ANN. § 57-4a-2.

[53]*Nature's Sunshine Products, Inc. v. Watson,* 2007 UT App 383, ¶ 13, 174 P.3d 647, 651.

2. Trust Deeds

Deeds of trust or "trust deeds" are covered extensively in Utah statute and constitute the most common form of security instrument used to secure real estate loans (generally referred to as "promissory notes") in Utah.[54] A "trust deed secures the obligations due under a note by transferring a security interest in real property to a trustee to be held until the debt is repaid . . . ",[55] and the trustee has the power to sell the real estate to satisfy the debt.[56] In a typical transaction, the borrower signs a promissory note in favor of the lender and also signs a trust deed under which the borrower is the "trustor" and the lender is the "beneficiary."[57] Title to the real estate then transfers to the trustee named in the trust deed and the trustee has the power sell the property if the borrower defaults on the loan obligation (subject to certain notice and other requirements contained in Utah statutes).[58] The trust deed is then recorded, creating a lien on the real estate and imparting notice to other lenders for purposes of priority.

3. Mortgages and Non-Judicial Foreclosure

In many states, traditional "mortgages" are used for real estate secured transactions.[59] Mortgages are distinguishable from the trust deeds used in Utah because: (a) there are only two parties (the debtor-mortgagor and the lender-mortgagee),[60] distinguished from the three parties under a trust deed (trustor, beneficiary and trustee);[61] and (b) title to the real estate remains with the borrower-mortgagor until foreclosure

---

[54]*See* UTAH CODE ANN. §§ 57-1-19—57-1-44.

[55]*See* note 54, *supra.*

[56]*Capital Assets Fin. Servs. v. Lindsay,* 956 P.2d 1090, 1095 (Utah Ct. App. 1998) *aff'd sub nom. Capital Assets Fin. Servs. v. Maxwell,* 2000 UT 9, 994 P.2d 201.

[57]*See* UTAH CODE ANN. §§ 57-1-19(1), (2).

[58]*See* UTAH CODE ANN. § 57-1-23.

[59]*See* http://title.grabois.com/ (United States map designating "lien theory" and "title theory" states).

[60]*Bybee v. Stuart,* 189 P.2d 118 (Utah 1948).

[61]*See* UTAH CODE ANN. §§ 57-1-19.

occurs,[62] distinguished from a trust deed where title transfers to the trustee.[63]

Another distinction relates to foreclosure of the borrower's interest in the real estate in the event there's a default on the loan. In most cases, states that use mortgages ("lien theory" states) rely on a judicial process to foreclose on the borrower's interest in the real estate, which generally requires court filings to foreclose the mortgage, which can create significant delays depending on the court's backlog.[64] In contrast, trust deeds are generally foreclosed "non-judicially"- because title is transferred to the trustee, the trustee has the power to foreclose and sell the property in the event of a loan default, which doesn't require court supervision.[65] There are, however, restrictions on the qualifications for trustees under real estate trust deeds, and only active members of the Utah state bar, depository institutions, trust corporations and title insurance companies may act as trustees.[66]

D. PURCHASING REAL ESTATE

1. Deciding Who Will Own the Real Estate

If you're purchasing real estate as an investment, one of your first decisions should concern ownership of the real estate. As previously discussed, individual ownership of real estate is generally discouraged because if, for example, someone is injured on the property and obtains a judgment for damages (in excess of any insurance coverage) against the property owner, you'll be individually liable for payment. For that reason, it's advisable to purchase investment property through a business entity, such as a limited liability company, corporation or partnership, which limits individual liability for the business entity's respective shareholders, members or partners (discussed in Chapter 4-13).

---

[62] *See Interstate Land Corp. v. Patterson*, 797 P.2d 1101, 1106 (Utah Ct. App. 1990).

[63] *See* UTAH CODE ANN. §§ 57-1-20, 57-1-23.

[64] *See generally* Brady Dennis, *Foreclosure Backlogs Taking Longer To Process*, THE WASHINGTON POST, June 30, 2011, http://www.washingtonpost.com/business/economy/foreclosure-backlogs-taking-longer-to-process/2011/06/27/AGlYtksH_story.html

[65] *See* UTAH CODE ANN. § 57-1-23.

[66] *See* UTAH CODE ANN. § 57-1-21.

2. Assessing the Risks

As you've seen, in addition to the potential market risks that accompany investments in real estate (such as those intensified during the 2008 financial crisis),[67] there are also other significant risks associated with purchasing real estate, including title risks and potential liability for environmental hazards located on the purchased property.

(a) *Title Risk*. Title risk includes the possibility of previously recorded liens or encumbrances on the property that could affect your right to peaceable possession of the property. As we'll discuss later, in most circumstances title associated risk can be mitigated by obtaining title insurance from a qualified title insurance company, but in some cases certain unrecorded easements or other encumbrances may not be disclosed in a title report.[68] Recorded documents impart constructive notice of their contents to a purchaser, but a purchaser may also be subject to encumbrances when the purchaser (i) has actual knowledge of an encumbrance, or (ii) has actual knowledge of or certain facts or circumstances that would give rise to a duty to inquire further,[69] such as viewing a dirt path running across the property prior to purchase.

(b) *Environmental Risk*. Both Federal and Utah laws impose potentially serious liabilities on real estate owners for environmental contamination,[70] including fines, penalties, civil lawsuits, environmental cleanup and potential restrictions on your use of the property. Therefore, conducting adequate environmental due diligence to uncover potential liabilities before purchasing a property is highly recommended, particularly when you're aware that the property has been used to

---

[67] *See, e.g.*, Paul Beebe, *Lax Regulatory Oversight Factor in Biggest Bank Bust in Utah*, THE SALT LAKE TRIBUNE, June 24, 2012, http://www.sltrib.com/sltrib/money/54297958-79/bank-barnes-loans-million.html.csp (discussing the failure of Barnes Bank, a Utah community bank that was heavily invested in commercial real estate loans and construction land development loans).

[68] *See Arnold Industries, Inc. v. Love*, 2002 UT 133, ¶¶ 28–29, 63 P.3d 721 (holding that purchaser had inquiry notice of an easement even though a title search did not reveal the recorded deed that described the easement because the deed had been improperly indexed).

[69] *See Pioneer Builders Co. of Nevada v. K D A Corp.*, 2012 UT 74, ¶ 24, 292 P.3d 672, 679.

[70] *See, e.g.* Federal Comprehensive Environmental Response, Compensation and Liability Act of 1980 ("**CERCLA**"), 42 U.S.C.A. §§ 9601 *et seq.;* Utah Hazardous Substances Mitigation Act, UTAH CODE ANN. §§ 19-6-301—401.

store hazardous substances (such as purchasing a fuel station with underground petroleum storage tanks). Additionally, conducting proper environmental due diligence before purchasing property can also create defenses to certain environmental liability.[71]

3. Available Professionals

If you've decided to purchase investment real estate, there are a number of real estate professionals who can assist you at various points in the purchase process. The list below identifies some of the key players.

(a) *Attorneys*. Yes, it's a shameless plug for our government sanctioned monopoly industry, but having a competent real estate attorney involved from the beginning of a transaction is vital. The attorney can draft and negotiate the purchase documents, assist in reviewing title and environmental reports, and generally provide counsel on the myriad issues that may arise in a given transaction.

(b) *Title/Escrow Professionals*. As we've discussed, obtaining title insurance to cover any potential title issues is critical. Therefore, engagement of a licensed title company, including a title agent and escrow agent, is also crucial. The title company and its professionals can provide a title report on the property and ultimately provide insurance to insure against title risks. Additionally, title company escrow agents act as neutral third parties to hold purchase funds (subject to escrow instructions).

(c) *Environmental Professionals/Consultants*. Because environmental liabilities can be devastating to a real estate investment, it's a good idea to have an environmental professional on your team to perform environmental assessments to analyze potential risks. There are a number of different certifications for environmental professionals or consultants, but who you choose should generally be based on (i) the specific types of environmental risk that may be involved on the property,

[71] *See* 42 U.S.C.A. §§ 9601(35)(B), 40(B) (describing the "bonafide prospective purchaser" defense to CERCLA liability, where a qualifying owner can avoid liability for pre-existing releases of hazardous substances on real estate).

and (ii) the professional's experience in the specific areas of concern that are identified. For instance, if you're aware that the prospective property has been used for oil or gas production or has housed underground petroleum storage tanks, you'll want to engage a professional with experience in subsurface soil and groundwater investigations.

(d) *Appraisers*. As you probably know, appraisers analyze the current market value of residential and commercial real estate or raw land based on a number of factors. Utah law requires appraisers to obtain and maintain professional licenses,[72] so make sure any appraiser you hire is licensed for the specific type of real estate you're purchasing or selling.

(e) *Professional Engineers and Land Surveyors*. Professional engineers and land surveyors are another form of professional that can be extremely helpful when purchasing real estate. If you're developing property, engineers can assist in planning, design, construction and operation of the project, while surveyors can survey the property to determine boundaries, rights-of-way, easements and other aspects of the property. Similar to appraisers, surveyors are licensed and regulated under Utah law,[73] so make sure any engineer or surveyor you engage is licensed.

4. Getting the Property Under Contract

(a) *Letter of Intent*. If you've identified real estate you'd like to purchase, the next step is moving forward with the purchase by entering into a contract to purchase the property. In most transactions, a preliminary outline of proposed contract terms for the purchase of the property are exchanged between buyer and seller. This preliminary document is known as a "Letter of Intent" or "**LOI**," and should only contain an indication of the parties' intent to enter into a binding purchase agreement at a later time.

---

[72] *See generally* UTAH CODE ANN. §§ 61-2g-101 *et seq*; UTAH ADMIN. R. R162-2g-101 *et seq.*

[73] *See generally* UTAH CODE ANN. §§ 58-22-11 *et seq*; UTAH ADMIN. R. R156-22-101 *et seq.*

LOI's are generally not enforceable as contracts because certain material contract terms are left open for future consideration (such as a final price or closing date).[74] In some cases, however, Utah courts have determined that "agreements to agree" (such as an LOI) contain sufficient material terms to uphold those agreements as contracts,[75] so make sure your LOI doesn't fall into that category.

(b) _Real Property Purchase Agreement Provisions_. We've already discussed some of the contract formation basics, but it's also helpful to review some of the specific provisions you'll likely encounter in a "Real Property Purchase Agreement" ("**RPP**").

i. *Representations and Warranties.* All RPP's contain representations and warranties between buyer and seller. For example, the seller will represent that as of the transaction closing, it will own fee simple title to the property and will have the right to convey that interest through one of the deeds discussed in Section B3. In conjunction with this representation, a title insurance policy will generally be issued to the buyer at closing to insure the buyer against any breach of that representation.

A seller under a RPP may also represent and warrant to the buyer that: (1) it has the authority to execute the RPP; (2) it is in compliance with any agreement that affects the property, and there are no conflicts with any agreements; (3) no eminent domain proceedings are pending; (4) no litigation may affect the sale of the property; (5) there are no mechanic's liens, hazardous materials; (6) the RPP will be a legally binding obligation; and (7) seller is not insolvent and has not filed a bankruptcy petition.

The buyer also makes representations and warranties, including that: (1) it is authorized to enter into the RPP; (2) there are no conflicting

[74]*See Harmon v. Greenwood*, 596 P.2d 636, 639 (Utah 1979) (discussing an LOI and noting that "[s]uch 'agreements to agree' are generally unenforceable because they leave open material terms for future consideration, and the courts cannot create these terms for the parties.") (citations omitted).

[75]*See GeoNan Properties, LLC v. Park-Ro-She, Inc.*, 2011 UT App 309, ¶ 9, 263 P.3d 1169, 1172 (holding that an agreement to enter into a lease contained sufficient lease terms to be enforceable as a lease).

agreements; (3) the RPP will be a legally binding obligation; and (4) buyer is not insolvent and has not filed any bankruptcy petitions.

As either a buyer or seller, you should carefully consider the representations and warranties you're making in a RPP to ensure they're accurate because misrepresentations can create post-transaction litigation (i.e., the representations and warranties aren't just inserted to create more work for lawyers). For instance, depending on the terms of a particular RPP, if a seller represents there are no hazardous materials and that representation later turns out to be inaccurate, buyer can sue seller for the cost of cleanup, property value diminution, and other damages.

ii. *Conditions and Contingencies.* RPP's will also set out buyer and seller's conditions to closing, which simply means the conditions that must take place to form a binding contract. For buyer, conditions to closing may include the accuracy of seller's representations and warranties, that seller has satisfactory title, that seller has complied with obligations under the RPP, and buyer's determination that there are no hazardous substances on the property. Seller's closing may be similar, such as the accuracy of buyer's representations and warranties, authority, and compliance with obligations under the RPP.

iii. *Deadlines.* RPP's also contain deadlines for the transaction, such as the closing date (when the purchase price and title are exchanged) and deadlines for the buyer to conduct due diligence on the property, such as environmental studies surveys and appraisals.

iv. *Default and Remedies.* A RPP will also describe events that will constitute a default by either party under the RPP and the remedies available to the non-defaulting party. For example, seller may be in default if any of its representations and warranties are inaccurate, and the RPP may provide the buyer the right to terminate the RPP, seek other legal remedies or seek "specific performance." Specific performance in an equitable (rather than legal) remedy that allows a buyer to obtain a court order compelling the seller to sell the property to buyer and perform under the RPP. Specific performance is a remedy that is usually only available to a buyer of real estate. The underlying philosophy for this remedy is that because real estate is completely unique, there is usually not a legal remedy that can give buyer the property for which it contracted.

5. Due Diligence

After a RPP is signed by the parties, a buyer will have timelines and deadlines to obtain financing and perform "due diligence" on the property.

(a) *Funding*. Funding for a real estate purchase can take three forms (i) self-financing; (ii) seller financing; and (iii) third party financing, each with their respective benefits and drawbacks.

Self-financing has many benefits; however, from a business perspective it tends to tie up large amounts of capital that could be put to better use elsewhere. Since a large amount of personal capital is invested, greater risk is also created.

In a seller financing scenario, the seller agrees to finance all or a portion of the purchase of the property, generally by receiving a promissory note from the buyer where certain terms (such as the term of the note and interest rate) can be negotiated between the parties. Additionally, seller financing will in many cases require less stringent credit and financial covenants than a third party lender will require. Although seller financing can remedy the personal capital outlays inherent in self-financing, it can also have its own issues depending whether the seller has financed the property from a lender. For instance, if the seller has financed the property via a bank loan, the sale to the buyer and the buyer's subsequent occupation of the property will almost always violate seller's loan document covenants.

Third party financing usually takes the form of a traditional loan from a bank or other financial institution, which can also solve the issue of tied up capital. In many cases, bank financing may be a more difficult process, particularly if the business entity you're using to purchase the property is newly formed. In that case, banks will almost always require personal guaranties from the business entity's principals, which can increase risk to your personal assets if the loan goes into default.

(b) Title Reports. During the due diligence period, you'll work with your attorney and the title company to obtain a title report (or "title commitment") that identifies any encumbrances on the property. Depending on what's uncovered, there may be further negotiations between the parties or significant issues that could kill the deal.

(c) Surveys. In conjunction with the title report, surveys will help to ascertain whether the legal description of the property is correct and whether any unrecorded easements exist on the property, such as consistently used easements through the property[76] or old fence lines that could have created a "boundary by acquiescence."[77]

(d) Zoning. In Utah, almost all developable property is subject to state and municipal zoning regulations. Therefore, you should *always* determine whether the prospective property's current zoning suits your intended business purpose. For example, if you're developing residential homes on raw land, make sure you've complied with all Utah statutes and municipal ordinances relating to the creation of subdivisions. Likewise, if you're purchasing an existing commercial building, conduct research to determine whether the building and its current or proposed uses comply with applicable zoning requirements.

6. Inspections and Evaluations

(a) Appraisals. Depending on the specifics of your RPP, appraisals of the property may be required during the due diligence period. Appraisals help to make sure the price you're paying for the property (or the price at which you're agreeing to sell) represents the property's market value. As previously discussed, make sure you're using

---

[76] *See Pitts v. Roberts,* 562 P.2d 231, 233 (Utah 1977) (determining that a prescriptive easement existed over a portion of a landowner's property).

[77] *See Essential Botanical Farms, LC v. Kay,* 2011 UT 71, 270 P.3d 430 (holding that a landowner's predecessors-in-interest acquiesced in old fence as boundary line with adjoining property, creating a "boundary by acquiescence).

a licensed appraiser who's experienced in valuing the type of real estate you're purchasing or selling.

(b) *Inspections*. Various inspections may be applicable depending on the property you're purchasing. Land surveys may be needed to identify boundaries or unrecorded easements. If you're purchasing property with existing building(s), it's wise to engage property inspectors and/or professional engineers to evaluate various aspects of the structure, including the foundation, roof, and HVAC and plumbing systems.

(c) *Environmental Studies*. At this point, you're probably tired of hearing about environmental issues, but based on the large risk environmental problems can represent, it's almost always a good idea to perform a Phase 1 environmental study (including further studies depending on what the Phase 1 reveals).

(d) *Insurance*. In addition to obtaining a title commitment and associated title insurance, insurance can be purchased for many other potential risks, including environmental risk or risk for breaches of representations and warranties contained in a RPP. If you've identified a specific area of risk associated with the property your purchasing, consult with your attorney and other professionals to determine whether cost effective insurance may be available to mitigate the potential risk.

7. Closing

Assuming nothing has been uncovered during the due diligence period that would allow buyer or seller to terminate the RPP, the purchase of the property will culminate on the closing date established in the RPP. In the simplest terms, at closing the buyer is obligated to transfer the purchase price to the seller and the seller is obligated to transfer title to the property. Although traditionally this was accomplished in a physical meeting (usually at the title company's offices) where documents were signed and money was transferred, in the internet era these transactions are usually performed via email and wire transfers.

E. REAL ESTATE LEASING

Even if you aren't in business to purchase and develop real estate, you'll likely need to enter into a commercial real estate lease as a tenant to facilitate your business operations. Similarly, if you've purchased or developed a commercial property, you may want to lease space in the building(s) to commercial tenants as a landlord. Whether you're on the landlord or tenant side of the transaction, it's good to know some leasing basics so you can effectively negotiate and make an informed decision. To avoid repeating information from different perspectives, we've placed you in the tenant's shoes in many of the hypotheticals below; however, the principles and negotiating points apply equally if you're a landlord.

1. Preliminary Considerations

If you're leasing property for your business, you should first consider the appropriate type of space for the business based on your business goals and requirements. If you're running a retail operation, you don't want to be located in a manufacturing/warehouse area, and vice-versa. Additionally, municipal zoning laws regulate where specific types of businesses may operate, so review those laws prior to committing to a lease. Next, because commercial leases are generally for terms of at least five years, you'll want to make sure that the property you're considering will withstand future expansion during that time period based on your business goals.

2. Negotiating the LOI

Similar to a RPP, lease negotiations generally begin with a LOI. The same principles discussed in section D4(a) apply to lease LOI's, but the terms that are negotiated will be different. Essentially, a lease LOI should describe some or all of the following: (a) tenant and landlord; (b) term of the lease, including any renewal options; (c) premises to be leased, (d) rent commencement date; (e) the amount of rent during the term; (f) any landlord or tenant improvements to the premises; (g) responsibility for utilities and insurance; (h) the cost of additional rent, such as taxes, insurance and common area charges; and (i) the tenant's permitted use, any adjacent incompatible uses, and any exclusive uses.

Although many minor terms and other minutiae can be negotiated during the lease drafting period, the basic terms above should be acceptable to both parties before proceeding to lease negotiation. Specifically, the term, rent, additional rent, rent commencement date and tenant's permitted use in the LOI should be acceptable to both parties. For instance, if the landlord is dead set on a 20 year term and the tenant doesn't want anything longer than a five year term, it's unlikely that the dispute will be resolved during lease negotiation and it likely makes more sense for the parties to go their separte way.

3. Negotiating the Lease and Overview of Certain Lease Terms

In lease negotiations, the respective economic positions of the parties will almost always dictate negotiating leverage. If you're the hottest retailer in town and can demonstrably increase overall shopping center business, you'll be able to command better lease terms with a shopping center landlord than a fledgling retailer, and vice-versa. Therefore, it's always good to understand your respective economic position and establish your priorities at the outset of lease negotiations.

The following provides a brief overview of some lease terms you'll encounter.

(a) *Term*. A lease is simply a contract, and the term of a lease refers to the time period the landlord is obligated to provide the premises and the tenant is obligated to pay rent. Although you should be sure the term is palatable for you and your business before entering into a lease, there are provisions that can be negotiated to alleviate some uncertainty. Renewal options are common and usually give the tenant an "initial term" with options to renew for negotiated future terms. If you're a tenant choosing a lease with renewal options, make sure you understand when the initial term expires and how to accept the renewal option (if it isn't automatic) or decline the renewal option (if it is automatic). Depending on your leverage (particularly in a retail business), a landlord may be amenable to allowing an early termination option if your revenue expectations aren't realized at a certain period in the initial term.

(b) *Rent/Additional Rent*. Rent is obviously the amount you will pay to the landlord monthly to occupy the leased premises, however, leases almost always divide rent into "base rent" and "additional rent." Base rent is the base amount paid monthly during the term of the lease, and additional rent is usually denoted by a specific dollar amount per square foot of the premises. For example, if the leased premises is 5,000 square feet, the lease would provide additional rent at a certain amount ($4.00 per square foot in this hypothetical), resulting in additional rent of $20,000 annually. In many leases, the landlord will estimate additional rent for the first year of the term and then adjust it accordingly for future years. Since additional rent can sometimes be subject to wide variations, it's a good idea to try and negotiate a reasonable cap on additional rent during the lease term if you're a tenant.

Depending on the premises you're leasing, additional rent may include property taxes, casualty and liability insurance paid by the landlord, and common area maintenance ("**CAM**") fees (which cover the costs of the landlord's direct expenses for parking lots, landscaped areas, hallways, elevators, lobbies, etc.). In an office building, shopping cener or other multi-tenant property, CAM costs are usually aggregated and then divided among all tenants on a pro-rata basis based on the square footage of their respective leased premises. When negotiating a lease, always make sure you know exactly what the landlord is including in CAM. If major structural repairs such as roofing or paving are included in CAM, you could be subject to a large CAM bill during the lease term. If the landlord has more leverage and won't budge on certain CAM inclusions, it's always a good idea to inquire whether the landlord has any major upgrades planned during the term of your lease.

(c) *Insurance*. In a typical commercial lease, the landlord will maintain a certain level of liability and casualty insurance covering the property that contains the leased premises. As discussed above, these insurance costs are usually passed on to the tenant in the form of additional rent, but the tenant is also required to maintain liability coverage for the premises in certain coverage amounts. The amount of coverage required can vary depending on a number of factors, such as the tenant's business, the value of the property, etc. Because general liability coverage doesn't usually cover the tenant's personal property, the tenant should always obtain coverage for items such as inventory, equipment and any other personal property not covered by other insurance. In any event, have both your attorney and your insurance agent review the insurance provisions in the lease to make sure they are practical and possible.

(d) *Taxes*. Real property and other taxes paid by the landlord are also estimated and included as a component of additional rent, but similar to CAM, the specific taxes that are included should be reviewed and understood prior to signing a lease.

(e) *Assignment/Subletting*. Leases will always have provisions concerning assignment of the lease or subletting by the tenant, requiring landlord consent. If you're considering subletting during the term of the lease, make sure this portion of the lease is workable. One common area of negotiation is how broadly the term "assignment" is defined: for instance, aside from the tenant physically leasing the premises to a sub tenant, the lease may define assignment as any "change in control" of the tenant business entity. In that case, if there's ever a change in the controlling ownership of your business entity (usually 51% of stock in a corporation or membership units in an LLC), you'll be required to obtain consent to assignment from your landlord.

(f) *Improvements/Maintenance*. It's not common to find premises that fit your business operations perfectly, so some kind of improvement or alteration of the leased premises is usually required prior to commencement of a lease. The question of who will perform and pay for those improvements becomes a negotiating point between landlord and tenant. On the practical side, once you've determined the specific improvements and how they will be paid for, (i) specific plans for the improvements should be attached to the lease as an exhibit to avoid confusion or later disagreement; and (ii) improvement timelines should be specified in the lease.

The lease will also describe the obligations of both parties regarding maintenance of the leased premises.

(g) *Remedies*. A critical portion of the lease will describe the legal and equitable remedies available to landlord and tenant in the event either party defaults on their respective obligations under the lease. In simple terms, a tenant will default by failing to pay rent and a landlord will default by failing to provide the premises or adhering to other landlord obligations under the lease. Pay close attention to the remedies section. Although no one plans to default under a lease, it happens quite often when business expectations aren't met and continuing business operations isn't possible.

4. Keeping your Lease Meaningful

(a) **Lease Summary**. Because commercial leases can quite easily exceed 50 pages of fairly complex material, insist on having a preamble to the lease that is incorporated into the lease and provides a summary critical information such as the lease term, base rent, additional rent, lease commencement date/termination date, contact information for tenant and landlord, and definitions for common capitalized terms or "terms of art" used in the lease. Having a lease summary allows either party to quickly review key terms without having to search through the entire lease or call their attorney and incur additional legal costs.

(b) *Consents, Modifications and Waivers*. Many tenants and landlords get tripped up by failing to obtain consents, modifications, or waivers of certain lease terms in writing. Remember, the statute of frauds applies to estates or interests in real estate, other than leases less than one year,[78] so your lease and any amendments or other agreements between the parties should always be in writing and signed by landlord and tenant.

[78]UTAH CODE ANN. § 25-5-1.

This also reduces miscommunication and misunderstanding, which in turn will reduce the likelihood of future litigation when expectations aren't met.

(c) *Pay Attention to Practical Issues*. In many leases, disagreement or litigation between the parties will be the result of a failure to pay attention to the practical aspects of the tenant's occupancy of the leased premises. If you're a landlord leasing office space to a high tech company that will be running thousands of feet of wire and cable through the building, you'll want to specify the tenant's obligations to remove the wires and cables at the end of the lease term, including repair of any damage they may have caused. On the tenant side, failing to pay attention to the amount of parking could prove disastrous for your business. Although legal issues are also paramount, paying attention to the practical aspects of occupancy can help avoid issues down the road.

F. CONCLUSION

The law is complex and this guide only covers superficial aspects of Utah real estate law, so make sure you contact a real estate attorney before embarking on any transactions.

Chapter 23

Potential Sources of Business Liability

Tort Law for Utah Entrepreneurs

Douglas G. Mortensen[1]

The Nature, Source and Purpose of Tort Law

A Utah entrepreneur may be held civilly liable for harms resulting from a deliberate act, an act of carelessness, the design or manufacture of a defectively dangerous product, or from conducting a business activity which by its nature is ultrahazardous or abnormally dangerous. This is called tort liability.

A tort is a civil wrong, not arising out of contract, which causes harm. Most torts originate in the common law our country inherited from England. Congress and state legislatures sometimes create new torts and often modify existing common law torts.

The purpose of tort law is to prevent harm. When that purpose is not achieved, tort law seeks to shift the burden of harm from an innocent victim to a party who most ought to bear it. This is done through the payment of money damages. The theory of tort law is that the payment of money to an injured party encourages the party responsible for the injury to act in a safer manner to prevent future harm.

Traditionally, torts have been classified into three main categories: **Intentional torts**; **negligence torts**; and **strict liability torts**. Individual torts will be discussed later in this chapter. The prefatory information found on the following pages will provide context and help the reader better understand how tort claims in Utah are handled.

[1]Douglas G. Mortensen is a civil trial attorney who has spent most of his 34 year career representing hurt or aggrieved persons in tort cases. He has served as Chairman of the Utah Supreme Court's Board of Mandatory Continuing Legal Education and on the Third District Court Judicial Nominating Commission. He is a past President and an Honorary Lifetime Member of the Utah Association for Justice (fka The Utah Trial Lawyers Association).

Torts, Crimes, and On-the-Job Injuries.

In a criminal case, the complaining party ("plaintiff") is the government. In a tort case, the plaintiff is a private person or entity. Many torts are also crimes.[2] The government's prosecution of a crime does not preclude the victim of the crime from bringing a civil tort action against the same person.[3] Although a criminal sentence may include a requirement to pay restitution to the victim, such sentence does not preclude the victim from recovering compensation in a civil suit.[4]

When a person in the United States is injured on the job, compensation is paid under Workers Compensation schemes which exist in all states.[5] Neither fault nor damage amount is at issue. The amount of compensation is set by statute.[6] Although an injured worker may pursue claims against third parties responsible for his on-the-job injury[7], he may not sue his employer or a co-worker[8], except under very rare circumstances.[9] Workers compensation awards are modest in amount.[10]

Comparative Fault

In Utah, a claimant who is partially responsible for her own injury may still recover damages for her injury but only if her fault is less than that of the defendant, or if there is more than one defendant, the fault of all defendants combined.[11] The recovery will be reduced by the

[2]False imprisonment, for example, is both a tort and a crime. The tort of conversion has nearly the identical elements of the crime of theft.

[3]O.J. Simpson was accused of murder. While the criminal action was being prosecuted, a civil wrongful death tort action was being pursued simultaneously. A jury found Simpson not guilty in the murder case but a separate jury found him responsible for the wrongful death of the murder victims and awarded the plaintiffs damages accordingly. In *Goldman v. Simpson, (L.A.* Superior Court of California), the jury awarded judgments of $12,500,000.00 to the estates of both victims, $8,500,000.00 to the parents of Ronald Goldman, and punitive damages against Simpson of $25,000,000.00. The disparate results may be due in part to the different burdens of proof applied in criminal and tort cases. See Burdens of Proof, *infra.*

[4]If compensation is awarded in the civil suit, the court may reduce the amount awarded by the amount already received by the victim through restitution imposed in the criminal case. Utah Code Ann. §77-38a-403.

[5]See UCA Section 34A-2-201 et. sec. for Utah's scheme.

[6]For example, if a Utah worker suffers the loss of a hand while working, he would be entitled to compensation in the amount of 66.66% of his average weekly wage for 168 weeks. UCA Section 34A-2-412(4)(a)(ii) .

[7]See UCA Section 34A—106.

[8]See UCA Section 34A-2-105 for Utah's "exclusive remedy" rule.

[9]If an employer fails to provide coverage, the employee *may* sue the employer and recover damages not limited by the scheduled sums. The employee may also recover costs and attorney fees. The employer is barred from asserting any defenses to liability, such as contributory negligence, assumption of risk, or fellow -servant rule. UCA Section 34A-2-207.

[10]See fn. 6, *supra.*

[11]UCA Section 78B-5-518.

percentage of fault attributable to the claimant. A claimant who is 50% or more at fault for his own injury is barred from recovery altogether[12]. Whenever the fault of more than one party is at issue, the trier of fact (the judge unless there is a jury) compares the fault of the respective parties and assesses each party a percentage of that fault – from zero to one hundred, with the total assessment equaling 100%.[13]

BURDENS OF PROOF

A plaintiff in any trial must prove his case. A burden of proof denotes how compelling a plaintiff's evidence must be to prevail. The burden of proof for plaintiffs in most tort claims is "preponderance of the evidence." This phrase means that an alleged fact is "more likely than not" true. Thought of in terms of percentages, this would be 51%. In cases of intentional misrepresentation (fraud) a plaintiff must meet a higher burden of proof: The evidence of fraud must be "clear and convincing."[14] That "clear and convincing standard also applies to claims for punitive damages.[15] This is a burden higher than "more likely than not" but not as high as "beyond a reasonable doubt," the level of proof required in all criminal cases.

DAMAGES: COMPENSATORY AND PUNITIVE

Compensatory Damages

The law allows a tort victim to recover compensatory damages for his loss. Two forms of compensatory damages may be awarded a tort victim: Economic damages and noneconomic damages.[16] Economic

[12]UCA Section 78B-5-817, 818, 819.

[13]This comparison of fault is undertaken in all cases of negligence, assumption of risk, strict liability, breach of express or implied warranty of a product, products liability, and misuse, modification, or abuse of a product. The use of comparative fault in cases involving intentional torts remains an open question in Utah. *Jedriewski v. Smith*, 2005 UT 85.

[14]See MUJI 2d CV118 and CV 1801 and cases there cited. See also *Jardine v. Archibald*, 279 P. 2d 454 (Utah 1955). The "clear and convincing evidence" standard is also applied, by statute, in other types of cases, such as boundary by acquiescence suits. *Essential Botanical Farms, L.C. v. Kay*, 2011 UT 71.

[15]UCA Section 78B-8-201.

[16]These damages have traditionally been labelled "special damages" and "general damages." The writers of Utah's Jury Instructions have recommended that those terms no longer be used, as they are less descriptive and confusing to jurors. The new terms – economic and noneconomic – are intended to be substitutes for the formerly used terms. See, e.g. *Judd ex rel. Montgomery v. Drezga*, 2004 UT 91 and Utah Code ANN. Section 78B -3- 410. See also *MUJI 2d*, CV 2001.

damages include those damages that are quantifiable, such as loss of wages, loss of business profits, loss of future earnings, and past and future medical expenses. Noneconomic damages consist of not readily quantifiable injuries and harms: pain, suffering, loss of enjoyment of life, loss of spousal consortium, etc.

Punitive Damages[17]

In Utah, punitive damages, sometimes referred to as exemplary damages, may be awarded only if compensatory have been awarded. They may not be awarded unless it is established by clear and convincing evidence that

> the acts or omissions of the tortfeasor are the result of willful and malicious or intentionally fraudulent conduct, or conduct that manifests a knowing and reckless indifference toward, and a disregard of, the rights of others.[18]

Because punitive damages are designed to punish as a means of future prevention, the award must be relative to the wealth of the defendant. For example, while an award of $10,000.00 in punitive damages would be significant punishment to a business profiting $50,000.00 per year, it would have no deterrent effect on an NBA franchise. For punitive damages to have their intended effect, the wealth of the defendant must be known. A court in Utah will not allow pretrial discovery into a defendant's financial condition without a preliminary showing that a punitive damage award is reasonably likely and that the request for discovery is not sought for the purpose of harassment.

Having in mind that punitive damages are to deter bad conduct, not to provide a windfall to the injury victim, the Utah legislature has decreed that the punitive damage amount awarded be split between the state and the injured party: The injured party takes the first $50,000 and

[17]Despite the headlines they generate, punitive damages are rarely awarded in Utah and when awarded by a jury are often reduced by the judge presiding over the case. See Emily Gottlieb and Joanne Doroshow, "What you Need to Know about Punitive Damages," Center for Justice and Democracy, Number 4, June/July 2001, pp. 8-9.

[18]UCA Section 78B-8-201.

the balance is divided evenly between the injured party and the state.[19]

The trial court has the discretion to reduce a jury's damage award if it deems it excessive. Appellate courts also have that discretion. A decision of the U.S. Supreme Court in a case appealed from a decision of the Utah Supreme Court indicates punitive damages should rarely exceed a single digit multiple of the compensatory damages awarded in the case.[20]

Deadlines for Filing Tort Actions

A tort lawsuit must be brought within a period of time specified by statute. There are different deadlines for different torts. These deadlines are called statutes of limitations. Entering negotiations or filing a claim with the responsible party's insurer does not constitute filing suit and will not prevent the statute of limitations from running. If one waits too long, one's claims may be time barred by the statute of limitations.

For most tort claims, the statute of limitations begins to run when the cause of action "accrues" which means when all the elements of the tort are present. Some tort claims, however, do not begin to run until the plaintiff discovers or, through the use of reasonable diligence, should have discovered the existence of an actionable claim.[21]

Claims for the following torts are barred if suit is not filed within the time limits specified:

1 year: libel, slander, false imprisonment[22];
2 years: medical malpractice, products liability, wrongful death[23];
3 years: Fraud, trespass, conversion[24];
4 years: negligence claims including those against all nonmedical professionals like lawyers, accountants, architects, et al., and catch-all for all tort claims not specified elsewhere;.[25]

---

[19] *Id.* at Subparagraphs 2 and 3.

[20] *State Farm Mutual Automobile Ins. Co. v. Campbell,* 538 U.S. 408(2003); *Campbell v. State Farm Mutual Automobile Ins. Co.*, 2004 UT 34 (Utah 2004).

[21] Medical negligence suits, UCA Section 78B-3-404; Product liability suits, Section 78B-6-706.

[22] UCA Section 78B-2-302.

[23] UCA Section 78B-2-304; 78B-6-706.

[24] UCA Section 78B-2-305.

[25] UCA Section 78B-2-307.

Statutes of limitations time periods are suspended ("tolled"):

- During the time a defendant is outside the state;[26]
- For one year after the death of a defendant outside the state;[27]
- For one year after the death of a plaintiff:[28]
- During time of war, as to a plaintiff who is an alien subject or citizen of a country at war with the U.S.;[29]
- During the time a plaintiff remains a minor (under the age of 18;)[30]
- During the time a plaintiff is mentally incompetent without a legal guardian;[31]

Jury Verdicts

Tort cases in Utah are decided by judges unless any party to the suit requests a jury. Juries in Utah state court civil trials consist of 8 persons.[32] They need not be unanimous in their findings. Each factual issue in a tort cases is resolved by a three-fourths majority vote. Six jurors must agree on the answer to each question presented. They do not have to be the same six jurors on each question.[33]

INTENTIONAL TORTS

An intentional tort is a wrongful act committed with intent. A person may commit an intentional tort without specifically intending to cause harm. Tort law presumes people intend the normal consequences of their acts. Motive is not required to prove liability. When one does an act intentionally, he may be liable for harm regardless of whether the

[26]UCA Section 78B-2-104.

[27]UCA 78B-2-106.

[28]UCA 78B-2-105.

[29]Id.

[30]Id. UCA 78B-2-108, provided the action accrues while the plaintiff is a minor.

[31]Id. Id., provided the action accrues while the person is disabled.

[32]UCA Section 78B-2-104. But when the amount in controversy is less than $20,000, 4 jurors sit. *Id.* In Federal courts in Utah, however, juries consist of 12 persons and their verdicts must be unanimous.

[33]MUJI 2d CV 139. But see fn. 32 as to jury findings in Utah federal district courts.

person injured was the person at whom the intentional act was directed.[34] Specific intentional torts exist and are commonly divided into discreet categories, such as torts against persons, torts against property, and torts against business interests. Not all intentional acts which cause harm may meet the definition of a particular tort or fit neatly into an existing category of torts. They may nevertheless be actionable if they satisfy the basic purpose of tort law.[35]

Intentional Torts Against a Person

Assault is committed when a person does an intentional act which causes another person apprehension of an imminent harmful or offensive bodily touching.[36]

Battery is committed when the actor actually causes such a contact. Here, however, apprehension is not a factor. A battery can occur even when the victim is unaware of its commission.

False imprisonment occurs when one intentionally confines another person within a boundary against his or her will. Here, the victim must be aware of, and opposed to, the confinement. Store owners have a privilege to detain employees or shoppers suspected of theft provided there is a reasonable basis for the suspicion and the detention is done reasonably.[37]

Intentional infliction of emotional distress occurs when one's intentional actions cause another to suffer emotional distress. In normal daily life, people often suffer emotional distress from the actions of others without the commission of a tort. For this tort to occur, the actor's conduct must be *extreme and outrageous* and the victim's distress must be *severe* and usually accompanied by evidence of physical or psychological injury.

Defenses which a person accused of these torts may assert include self-defense, defense of another, and consent.[38] A person has a privilege

---

[34] *Jeppsen v. Jensen,* 47 Utah 536, 155 Pac. 429, 430-431.

[35] Section 870 of the Restatement (Second) of Torts provides: "one who intentionally causes injury to another is subject to liability to the other for that injury, if the conduct is generally culpable and not justified under the circumstances. This liability may be imposed although the actor's conduct does not come within a traditional category of tort liability."

[36] *Banks v. Shivers,* 20 Utah 2d 25, 26, 432 P. 2d 339,340 (1967).

[37] UCA Section 77-7-12.

[38] A person who accepts an invitation to engage in a fight will be deemed to have consented to any injury he may sustain in that fight unless at any point during the altercation a dangerous weapon is used. See UCA Section 76-5-104.

to use reasonable force – the minimum amount required by the circumstances - to protect himself and his property.[39] While consent generally is a defense to a willful tort, lawful consent may not be given by a minor.[40]

Defamation occurs when one communicates or "publishes" false information about another which injures her reputation. Defamation may be committed through spoken words (slander) or written declarations (libel). Traditionally, declarations are deemed *per se* defamatory if they falsely impute to another the commission of a crime, unchastity, the possession of a loathsome disease, or the poor operation of a trade or business. Unless the person defamed is a public figure, intent to cause harm is not required. If the person about whom the statement is made is a public figure, defamation occurs only if the person making the assertion knows it to be false and publishes it with malice. Truth is an absolute defense to a defamation claim.

The following scenario illustrates these intentional torts:

Jack and Jill are playing a game of squash. While the ball is not in play, Jack raises his racquet above Jill's head as if to strike her. If Jill suffers fright from this intentional act, Jack has committed assault, even if he intended it only as a joke and did not intend to harm her. If Jack actually strikes Jill with his racquet, he has committed battery. If he positions himself in front of the door of the squash court so that Jill cannot leave, though she wants to, he has committed false imprisonment. If he yells at the top of his lungs while chasing Jill around the court: "I am going to kill you Jill for beating me in that game," and Jill is severely distressed by this, he has committed the tort of intentional infliction of emotional distress. If he does none of those things, but Jill tells her friends that he did all of them and falsely tells the police he also raped her on the squash court, Jill has committed defamation.

One may consider remote the likelihood of having occasion to sue or be sued for the commission of any of these common law torts. However, it takes little imagination to see how at least some of these

[39]Utah Code ANN Section 76-2-40 – 407.

[40]*Elkington v. Foust*, 618 P. 2d 37, 40 (1980).

torts may form the basis of claims involving unwanted sexual advances in workplace settings.

Invasion of Privacy occurs when one invades a person's solitude, seclusion, or personal affairs when the person has the right to expect privacy. It may take four forms:

1. Appropriation of a person's identity (name, picture, or likeness) for commercial purposes without permission;
2. Intrusion into a person's seclusion or private affairs (by, for example, rifling through a person's briefcase, eavesdropping by wiretap, scanning a person's bank account, or peeping through a person's window).
3. Putting a person in a false light, such as writing a story attributing to a person ideas not held by the person or actions not taken by the person.
4. Public disclosure of private facts, such as a newspaper's reporting a private citizen's sex life or financial affairs.

Intentional Misrepresentation

Intentional misrepresentation is often known by another word: fraud. A plaintiff claiming ~~that~~ a defendant has defrauded him must prove by clear and convincing evidence that:

1. The defendant made a false statement about an important fact;
2. knowing his statement was false or making it recklessly and without regard for its truth;
3. intending that the plaintiff rely on it;
4. The plaintiff did reasonably rely on it;
5. And suffered damage as a result of doing so.[41]

Silence, when one has a duty to speak, constitutes misrepresentation. Actively concealing an important fact is misrepresentation. If one holds a position of trust over another - such as an attorney, agent, parent or adult

[41]See Model Utah Jury Instruction, Second Edition (MUJI 2d) CV 1801 and cases there cited: *Cardon v. Jean Brown Research,*2014 UT App 35, 327 P. 3d 22;*Yazd v. Woodside Homes Corp.*, 143 P. 3 d283 (Utah 2006).

child - one has an affirmative duty to disclose an important fact. Fraud occurs if the failure to disclose is a substantial factor in causing damages.

A person who lacks fraudulent intent may be held liable for the tort of **negligent misrepresentation** if, being in a better position than the person to whom he makes his representation, he fails to use reasonable care to determine whether the representation is true and the person suffers damage resulting from its being false.

Misuse of Legal Procedure covers three torts: malicious prosecution, wrongful civil proceedings, and abuse of process. These torts occur when one uses the courts with the primary purpose of causing distress, reputational damage, or economic loss to an innocent person.

There are other serious intentional wrongs too often committed in Utah by persons of dubious character against unsuspecting, trusting victims. These intentional wrongs include *affinity fraud, Ponzi schemes,* and misrepresentations in investment solicitation documents. They are covered in Chapter 14 of this text as part of a discussion of state and federal securities law violations.

Intentional Torts Against Property Interests

Trespass to land occurs when one intentionally causes something or someone to enter the land or airspace of another, without permission.

Trespass to chattel occurs when one interferes with the personal property of another. This involves using, but not appropriating, another's property without permission.

Conversion is the civil equivalent of the crime of theft. It occurs when one takes another's property intending to retain possession.

Disparagement of Property is an economically injurious falsehood about another's product or property. **Trade libel** (alleging a product is defective or not what it claims to be) and **slander of title** (casting doubt on a person's legal ownership of property are forms of this tort. Slander of title occurs when one untruthfully and without justification casts doubt on another's ownership of property. An example is the recording of a *lis pendens* (a document indicating the pendency of a law suit concerning the property) when no suit has been filed. Another is a broker filing a lien against a piece of property knowing he had no basis for doing so.

Private Nuisance consists of interference with another's peaceful enjoyment of his own land.

Intentional Torts Against Business Interests

The tort of **injurious falsehood** amounts to defamation against a person's property interest. It must be intentional and malicious. An example is publishing word that another has bad credit when it is not true.

Interference with contractual relations is intentionally causing or conspiring with another to cause a breach of a contract with a third party.[42] The interfering action must be wrongful and malicious and actual damage must result from the interference.[43] This might occur, for example, when the owner of a professional basketball team tries to help an athlete under contract to play baseball for a professional baseball team to escape that contract in order to play basketball for his team.

Interference with prospective economic relations is another tort recognized in Utah. It "protects a party's interest in prospective relationships of economic advantage not yet reduced to a formal contract (and perhaps not expected to be)."[44] In essence, tort liability exists against one who competes for business for an improper purpose or by improper means. Having a predominant intent to harm or destroy a competitor's business rather than build one's own is an improper purpose.[45] Violating a statute, regulation, common law rules, or the established standard of a trade or profession is competing by improper means.[46]

NEGLIGENCE

Negligence is the failure to do what a reasonably prudent person would do in the same or similar circumstances. Its essence is carelessness. A person may be negligent in acting or in failing to act.[47] Entrepreneurs,

---

[42] *Bunnell v. Bills*, 13 Utah 83, 90, 368 P. 2d 597, 601-03 (Utah 1962).

[43] *First Security Bank v. Wright*, 521 P. 2d 563, 567 (Utah 1974); *Soter v. Wasatch Development Corp.*, 21 Utah 2d 224, 226, 443 P. 2d 663, 664 (Utah 1868).

[44] *Leigh Furniture v. Isom*, 657 P.2d 293, 302 (1982).

[45] *Id.*; *Searle v. Johnson*, 646 P. 2d 682, 689 (1982).

[46] *Leigh Furniture v. Isom*, 657 P.2d 293, 302 (1982).

[47] *Dwiggins v. Morgan Jewelers*, 811 P, 2d 182 (Utah 1991); *Mitchell v. Pearson Enterprises*, 697 P. 2d 240 (Utah 1985); *Meese v. BYU*, 639 P. 2d 720 (Utah 1981).

like doctors, accountants, lawyers, architects, engineers, motorists, and all others, have a duty to exercise the level of care reasonably expected of those acting in their respective capacities to avoid injuring others. Negligence occurs when a motorist fails to keep a proper lookout and crashes his car into a car in front of her, when an appraiser fails to discover defects in a home which a reasonably careful appraiser would have discovered, and when an investment advisor or promoter fails to exercise due diligence before recommending an investment.

One scholar has defined negligence as the breach of a duty to behave reasonably which causes foreseeable harm to foreseeable victims.[48] This simple definition embraces the four elements required to prevail on a negligence claim:

1. **A duty owed to the person injured**. People generally owe a duty of care to all persons who could foreseeably be injured by their acting without due care;
2. **A breach of that duty**. This occurs when one acts without reasonable prudence or care;
3. **Causation.** There must be a causal link between the careless conduct and the harm alleged. In the past terms of "causation in fact" and "proximate cause" have been used to indicate when that necessary causal link has been established. Because those terms can be confusing and misleading juries in Utah are now instructed that they may find the causation requirement met if they find that:
    - The person's act or failure to act produced the harm directly or set in motion events that produced the harm in a natural and continuous sequence; and
    - The person's act or failure to act could be foreseen by a reasonable person to produce a harm of the same general nature.[49]
4. **Damages.** Negligent conduct is not "actionable" unless it results in actual harm to a person. For example, a patient who

---

[48]Frank W. Shaw in *Business Law an Introduction,* Second Edition, p. 53.

[49]*MUJI 2d,* CV 209.

learns her surgeon operated on her while under the influence of a narcotic drug will not succeed in a negligence claim unless she can show the surgeon's impairment caused her harm.

Vicarious Liability

Under the doctrine of *respondeat superior,*[50] an employer may be held liable for negligent acts or omissions of an employee occurring within the scope and course of that employee's duties. A person who provide an alcoholic beverage to a person under 21 or to an apparently intoxicated person may be held liable for injuries and damages caused by that person.[51] A parent may be held liable for harm caused by negligent driving of a child, as well as for intentional torts committed by a child.[52]

Proof of Breach of Standard of Care

Generally, expert testimony is required to establish that an investment counselor, a doctor, a lawyer, an engineer, or other professional acted beneath the standard of care expected of persons functioning in that field. However under the doctrine of *res ipsa loquitur* negligence can be established by a showing that the instrumentality of harm was within the exclusive control of the defendant and that what occurred normally doesn't occur in the absence of negligence. A surgeon leaving a pair of forceps inside a patient's body is an example of that.

When a statute, such as a traffic rule, exists which is intended to prevent the type of harm suffered by a negligence claimant, violation of that statute may establish negligence.[53]

Defenses to Negligence

A person accused of negligence may assert that the injured party assumed the risk of injury when choosing to participate in a potentially dangerous activity. The assumption of risk defense requires proof that the risk was fully appreciated and voluntarily incurred.

---

[50] *See e.g. Guss v. Cheryl, Inc.*, 2010 UT App 249, ¶17, 240 P.3d 1142.

[51] UCA section 32A-14a-102.

[52] UCA section 78A-6-1113; 53-3-211.

[53] In some states, it creates only a rebuttable presumption of negligence and in others, like Utah, it is treated merely as a fact from which negligence may be inferred. *See e.g. Paulos v. Covenant Transport, Inc.*, 2004 UT App 35, 86 P.3d 752.

A defendant may also assert that negligence of the plaintiff himself caused or contributed to his injury.[54]

One may defend a claim of negligence by showing he acted in conformity with the standards or procedures commonly followed in his occupation but that will not necessarily save him. The standard is reasonable care whether or not it is followed by the majority of practitioners in a particular field and courts have imposed liability when they find an entire industry is not adhering to a reasonable standard of safety.[55]

STRICT LIABILITY

A person or company who carries on an abnormally dangerous or ultra-hazardous activity may be held strictly liable for harm caused by that activity without regard to fault or issues of the exercise of reasonable care.[56] Strict liability has been applied in cases involving mine blasting, oil extraction, and the storage of toxic waste waters. Applying strict liability is a matter of public policy. A weighing of societal interests is involved. On the one hand, one considers the gravity of harm that might occur from the activity and the likelihood of that harm occurring. One the other hand, one considers the need of the activity in providing products needed in modern society and the burden, expense and feasibility of making the activity completely safe.

PRODUCTS LIABILITY

Injuries sustained in the use of chain saws, crutches, champagne corks, burglar alarms, farm machinery and other consumer products give rise to product liability claims. Typically, the plaintiffs allege negligence and breach of various warranties as a basis for recovery. The stronger claim now is strict liability based on a showing that the product is "defective and unreasonably dangerous" in one or more of three ways:

---

[54]See UCA Sections 78B-5-517-19 and the Comparative Fault section of this chapter, *supra.*

[55]See *Texas & Pac. Ry. V. Beymer,* 189 U.S. 468, 470; *In Re. T.J. Hooper,* 60 F. 2d, 737, 740 (2nd Cir. 1932); *Peterson v. Hanson-Neiderhauser, Inc,* 13 Utah 2d 355, 374 P. 2d 513 at 515-516 (1962). This principle has been applied in modern medical malpractice cases: See *Helling v. Carey,* 519 P.2d 981 (Wash, 1974); *Guilbeau v. St. Paul Fire and Marine Insurance Co.,* 325 So.2d 395 (La. App. 1975)

(1) In the way it was designed; 2. In the way it was manufactured; or 3. In the way its users were (or were not) warned.

A product has a defective design if as a result of its design, it fails to perform as safely as an ordinary user would expect it to perform when used in a manner reasonably foreseeable to the manufacturer.[57] Some courts also require proof that a safer alternative design was available and feasible. [58] So far, no such showing has been required in Utah state courts.

A product has a manufacturing defect when the product departs from its intended design, even if all possible care was exercised.[59]

There is no duty to warn about a danger from a product's foreseeable use which is generally known and recognized. There *is* a duty to warn about a danger from the product's foreseeable use of which the defendant knew or reasonably should have known and which a reasonable user would not expect. If a duty to warn is found, any warning given must be adequate. A warning is adequate if it was designed to reasonably catch the user's attention, was understandable to foreseeable users, fairly indicated the danger from the product's foreseeable use, and was sufficiently conspicuous to match the magnitude of the danger.[60]

Defenses to Product Liability Claims

A product liability claim may be defeated by proof that the claimant misused the product and the misuse was not reasonably foreseeable. A defense of assumption of risk may also be asserted. It would require proof that the claimant knew and fully appreciated the risk of using the defective product and voluntarily assumed that risk, though his doing so was unreasonable. A controversial defense is that the product was subject to and satisfied government regulations and standards. The U.S. Supreme court approved that defense in the case of medical devices which have gone through a "rigorous process" of premarket approval by

---

[56] *Walker Drug Co., Inc v. La Sal Oil Co,* 902 P. 2d 1229, 1233 (Utah 1995)*; Branch v. Western Petroleum,* 657 P. 2d 267, 273 (Utah 1982); Robison v. Robison, 394 P. 2d 87,877 (Utah 1964); Restatement 2d Torts Section 520 (1976); Restatement 3d Torts Section 20.

[57] See MUJI 2d CV1003 and cases there cited.

[58] See, e.g. *Allen v. Minnstar,* 8 F. 3d 1470, 1472 (10th Circuit 1993)

[59] See *Restatement (Third) of Torts: Products Liability*; MUJI 2d CV 1004 and cases there cited.

[60] *House v. Armour,* 886 P. 2d 542 (Ut. App 1994), aff'd 929 P. 2d 340 (Utah 1996).

the FDA[61]. Whether this defense should preclude claims against other products remains the subject of intense debate.

CONCLUSION

Armed with basic knowledge of torts and how they are handled in Utah courts, an entrepreneur should be careful not to commit them and vigilant in guarding against employees and associates committing them.

[61] *Riegel v. Medtronic, Inc.*, 552 U.S. 312, 128 S.Ct.999, 169 L. Ed. 2d 892 (2008)

Chapter 24

Potential Sources of Business Liability

Unfair Trade Practices

Andrew Deiss[1]
Billie Siddoway
Diana Bradley

Unfair trade practices are governed by both state and federal law, and broadly encompass antitrust practices, patent, trademark, copyright laws, as well as consumer protection and non-competition regulations. What follows is a broad overview of the area of law as it applies to Utah and is intended only to provide a business-person with a general understanding of the subject matter. The applicable law is complicated and may subject a person or entity to both civil and criminal liability. Accordingly, a business-person should not rely on the information contained in this chapter; it is critical that a business person consult an attorney before embarking on any activity that may invoke concerns over unfair trade practices.

Unfair trade practices involving consumer protection is discussed in section E of this chapter, and intellectual property issues are also discussed this book. This section focuses more specifically on the regulation of antitrust activities by the State of Utah and the federal government. Utah's antitrust and unfair trade practice laws including the Utah Antitrust Act,[2] the Unfair Practices Act,[3] and the Unfair Competition Act,[4] largely mirror federal antitrust laws, namely the

[1]Andrew Deiss and Diana Bradley are attorneys with Deiss Law PC located in Salt Lake City, Utah. Billie Siddoway is an attorney with Siddoway Law Office, PLLC in Driggs, Idaho. They litigate cases involving unfair trade practices.

[2]Utah Code Ann. §§ 76-10-3101 to -3118.

[3]Utah Code Ann. §§ 13-5-1 to -18.

[4]Utah Code Ann. §§ 13-5a-1-1 to -103.

Sherman Antitrust Act[5], the Clayton Act,[6] and the Robinson-Patman Act.[7] Unfair trade practices are additionally regulated by the Utah Truth in Advertising Act,[8] the Federal Trade Commission Act,[9] several industry specific regulations targeting fair trade practices in the film, gas products, and auto sales industries, and the common law.

Antitrust laws intend to advance free competition in the marketplace by prohibiting certain anti-competitive practices. Generally, antitrust laws seek to prevent acts that suppress or restrict competition especially where such acts inflate prices, restrict production, or control markets in a way that is detrimental to consumers. Both state and federal antitrust laws generally prohibit collusion among market participants attempting to control prices or eliminate competitors. For example, federal and state antitrust laws aim to eliminate horizontal and vertical price fixing arrangements, market allocation, bid rigging, group boycotts, covenants not to compete, exclusion or expulsion from membership in trade associations, resale price maintenance, and tying arrangements that adversely affect market competition. Engaging in these activities may be a violation of state and federal regulations and can subject individuals and businesses to both criminal penalty and civil liability.

PROHIBITED ACTIVITIES

General restraints of trade

Both the Utah Antitrust Act and the Sherman Act generally prohibit individuals and businesses from entering into contracts, combinations, or conspiracies in restraint of trade[10]—agreements to act where collusive parties intend to adversely affect the free market. Utah's Antitrust Act is

---

[5]15 U.S.C. §§ 1–7.

[6]15 U.S.C. §§ 12–27.

[7]15 U.S.C. §§ 13-13b, -21a. *See also Belliston v. Texaco, Inc.*, 521 P.2d 379, 380 (Utah 1974) (the pleading and proof requirements for a Robinson–Patman Act violation are substantively so similar to the requirements of the price discrimination prohibitions of the Utah Unfair Practices Act that a determination of the federal claim would be res judicata on the state claim.); *All Weather Exteriors Distrib., Inc. v. California Wholesale Material Supply, Inc.*, No. 2:06-CV-346 TS, 2007 WL 445281, at *5 (D. Utah Feb. 6, 2007)

[8]UTAH CODE ANN. §§ 13-11a-1 to -6.

[9]15 U.S.C. §§ 44–58.

[10]*See* UTAH CODE ANN. §§ 76-10-3101 to -3118, 15 U.S.C. §§1–7.

nearly identical to the Sherman Act and interpretation of the act is often guided by interpretation of the Sherman Act.[11] Activities in violation of the Sherman Act likely subject individuals and entities to liability under the Utah Antitrust Act.[12]

The Sherman Act prohibits restraints of trade in *interstate* commerce only. Interstate commerce, however, is often interpreted broadly; for example supplying goods to retailers or dealers in different states, the communication of news between states, and the transportation of films between states are considered "interstate" commerce.[13] Where the business activities in question affect interstate commerce may also satisfy the interstate commerce requirement and be actionable under the Sherman Act. In contrast, the Utah Antitrust Act does not impose an interstate commerce requirement; rather, it prohibits unfair trade practices affecting commerce occurring within Utah. Plaintiffs who seek relief under the Utah Antitrust Act must be a citizen or resident of the State of Utah.[14]

Agreements in restraint of trade do not need to be formal or written to violate the Sherman Act or the Utah Antitrust Act. Rather, circumstantial evidence from which a jury may infer an agreement existed may be enough to impose liability.[15]

Not all restraints of trade are unreasonable; likewise, not all are illegal.[16] Rather, restraints of trade are sometimes lawful if they are connected to a legitimate business purpose and are economically efficient. Courts are fairly lenient when examining potential antitrust violations

---

[11] *Flying J Inc. v. TA Operating Corp.*, No. 1:06-CV-30-TC, 2008 WL 4923041, at *8 (D. Utah Nov. 14, 2008). *See also Diaz v. Farley*, 15 F. Supp. 2d 1138, 1150 (D. Utah 1998) *aff'd*, 215 F.3d 1175 (10th Cir. 2000)

[12] *See, e.g., Hinds Cnty., Miss. v. Wachovia Bank N.A.*, 953 F. Supp. 2d 495, 498 (S.D.N.Y. 2013) ("Therefore, since this Court has concluded that UHC has sufficiently alleged a § 1 [Sherman Act] claim against Transamerica, its claims under the Utah Antitrust Act and the Utah Unfair Practices Act also survive Transamerica's motion to dismiss.").

[13] 54 Am. Jur. 2d Monopolies and Restraints of Trade § 10

[14] Utah's antitrust law therefore appears to require that a person suing under the antitrust statute be a "citizen" or "resident," Utah Code § 76–10–3109(1)(a)' . . . this Court holds that Utah's citizenship requirement is properly analyzed as defining the scope of plaintiffs' right to bring antitrust claims (a substantive right granted by the state) and is not merely a procedural provision relating to the litigants' management of claims. *In re Nexium (Esomeprazole) Antitrust Litig.*, 968 F. Supp. 2d 367, 410 (D. Mass. 2013).

[15] *Norfolk Monument Co. v. Woodlawn Mem'l Gardens, Inc.*, 394 U.S. 700, 704 (1969). *See also Lochead v. Alacano*, 657 F. Supp. 406, 417 (D. Utah 1988). ("[B]ehavior may imply an agreement to conspire where no formal agreement has been shown.")

[16] *See, e.g., U.S. v. Columbia Steel Co.*, 334 U.S. 495 (1948).

by employing what is called the "rule of reason test," which subjects an entity to liability only upon a showing of both an unreasonable restraint of trade and an actual adverse impact on competition.[17] However, some acts in restraint of trade are considered *per se* violations wherein proof of the act alone (without proof of an actual adverse economic effect) will subject an entity to liability. Price fixing, group boycotts, division of markets, and tying arrangements are typically considered *per se* antitrust violations.[18] Importantly, because interpretations of Utah's Antitrust Act are guided by federal court interpretations of federal antitrust laws, an act that would be considered a *per se* violation of the Sherman Act will likely be considered a per se violation of the Utah Antitrust Act.[19]

Horizontal Price Fixing

Antirust laws prohibit competitors from making agreements to raise, stabilize, set or otherwise affect prices. Acts of horizontal price fixing are usually considered *per se* antitrust violations—proof of an act of horizontal price fixing will subject an entity to liability, proof of an actual adverse market effect is not required to impose liability. For example, in *Arizona v. Maricopa County Medical Society*, an agreement between doctors in Maricopa County, Arizona (as part of a medical trade group) to set the maximum fees those doctors would seek from insurance plans for medical services provided to policyholders was found to be a *per se* violation of the Sherman Act.[20] The court found the price restraint tended to provide the same economic rewards to all of the medical

---

[17]*See, e.g., Brixen & Christopher Architects, P.C. v. State*, 2001 UT App 210, 29 P.3d 650.

[18]*Northern Pac. Ry. Co. v. US*, 356 U.S. 1, 5 (1958) ("[T]here are certain agreements or practices which because of their pernicious effect on competition and lack of any redeeming virtue are conclusively presumed to be unreasonable and therefore illegal without elaborate inquiry as to the precise harm they have caused or the business excuse for their use. This principle of per se unreasonableness not only makes the type of restraints which are proscribed by the Sherman Act more certain to the benefit of everyone concerned, but it also avoids the necessity for an incredibly complicated and prolonged economic investigation into the entire history of the industry involved, as well as related industries, in an effort to determine at large whether a particular restraint has been unreasonable—an inquiry so often wholly fruitless when undertaken. Among the practices which the courts have heretofore deemed to be unlawful in and of themselves are price fixing, *United States v. Socony-Vacuum Oil Co.*, 310 U.S. 150, 210, 60 S.Ct. 811, 838, 84 L.Ed. 1129; division of markets, *United States v. Addyston Pipe & Steel Co.*, 6 Cir., 85 F. 271, 46 L.R.A. 122, affirmed 175 U.S. 211, 20 S.Ct. 96, 44 L.Ed. 136; group boycotts, *Fashion Originators' Guild of America v. Federal Trade Comm.*, 312 U.S. 457, 668, 61 S.Ct. 703, 85 L.Ed. 949; and tying arrangements, *International Salt Co. v. United States*, 332 U.S. 392, 68 S.Ct. 12, 92 L.Ed. 20." *N. Pac. Ry. Co. v. United States*, 356 U.S. 1, 5 (1958).").

[19]UTAH CODE ANN. § 76-10-3118 ("The Legislature intends that the courts, in construing this act, will be guided by interpretations given by the federal courts to comparable federal antitrust statutes and by other state courts to comparable state antitrust statutes.").

[20]457 US 332 (1982).

practitioners in the trade group "regardless of their skill, experience, training, or willingness to employ innovative and difficult procedures in individual cases."[21] Because such restraints could discourage market entry, experimentation, and entrepreneurial development, the Court held the agreement was a *per se* violation and did not require evidence of an adverse economic effect.[22]

Not only can entities be subject to liability for entering into agreements with competitors to set prices, agreements to set credit terms,[23] discounts, and freight prices, or entering into purchase agreements intended to limit the supply of a commodity can subject entities to liability as well.

Vertical Price Fixing

Vertical price fixing arrangements involve agreements among manufacturers and distributors rather than direct market competitors. Typically a vertical price fixing agreement is one between a manufacturer and a group of distributors to terminate the distributorship of a particular distributor. Vertical price fixing arrangements will violate state and federal law if manufacturers and distributors are shown to have a meeting of the minds or a common scheme between them, and are generally held to a rule of reason standard (a plaintiff must prove actual adverse economic impact to bring a successful Sherman Act or Utah Antitrust Act claim).[24]

Agreements between a manufacturer and distributor that give a distributor the exclusive right to sell a manufacturer's product within a given geographic area (so called exclusive distributorship arrangements) and agreements where a distributor agrees to resell the product of a single manufacturer (so called exclusive dealing arrangements) may be considered vertical price fixing arrangements that are prohibited by the Clayton Act, and in Utah may be enforced under the Utah Antitrust Act.[25]

---

[21] *Id.* at 332.

[22] *Id.*

[23] *See, e.g., Catalano, Inc. v. Target Sales, Inc.*, 446 U.S. 643 (1980)

[24] *Leegin Creative Leather Products, Inc. v. PSKS, Inc.*, 551 U.S. 877 (2007)

[25] *See Brixen & Christopher Architects, P.C. v. State*, 2001 UT App 210, 29 P.3d 650. *See also* Utah Code Ann. § 76-10-914.

Bid Rigging

Bid rigging schemes, where competitors engaged in a bidding process for a contract will agree in advance which among them will submit the winning bid, can violate both state and federal law. Bid rigging is typically viewed as being *per se* unlawful.[26]

Horizontal bid rigging schemes include: bid suppression, where competitors agree to withdraw a bid or refrain from bidding on a particular contract; courtesy bidding, where competitors agree to submit bids with inflated prices or unfavorable terms to create the appearance of competition and hide the existence of the inflated price of the seemingly reasonable bid; and bid rotation, where competitors submit bids but take turns as to which competitor will submit the lowest bid.

Vertical bid rigging schemes can also violate state and federal law. For example, collusion among manufactures and distributors to include only a particular manufacturers product in their bids in return for bonus payments may violate state and federal law.[27]

Group Boycotts

Antitrust laws frequently prohibit business entities from excluding their competitors from dealing in their products. Group boycotts can take on different forms. A group of distributors may not pressure a supplier to refrain from selling its products to other distributors outside of the group. Similarly, trade associations or trade groups may not intentionally exclude or expel an entity from membership with the intent of chilling that entity's ability to participate in a given market.

For example, in *Klor's Inc. v. Broadway-Hale Stores, Inc.*, the U.S. Supreme Court found that a group of retailers, manufacturers, and distributors dealing in home appliances violated the Sherman Act when they agreed to refuse to sell to the plaintiff or to sell to the plaintiff only when conditioned on unfavorable terms at discriminatory prices.[28] The court found the conspiracy was a *per se* violation of the Sherman Act and the violation would stand even if the defendants could show their

---

[26] *Brixen*, 2001 UT App 210 *citing State Oil Co. v. Kahn*, 522 U.S. 3, 10 (1997) and Utah Code Ann. § 76-10-920 (1)(a) (1999) renumbered as Utah Code Ann. § 76-10-3112.

[27] *Brixen*, 2001 UT App 210, ¶¶ 38-39, 29 P.3d 650.

[28] 359 U.S. 207 (1959).

actions were reasonable under the circumstances.[29] Further, the violation was not defendable despite the fact that only one small business with little economic power had been affected.[30]

Under the Utah Antitrust Act, courts tend to focus on the intent of the conspirators in addition to the form of the boycott to determine if certain acts constitute a violation.[31] For example, conspirators who engage in bribery schemes with the intent of affecting a market may be in violation of the Utah Antitrust Act.[32]

Group boycott violations can subject entities to both criminal and civil penalties.[33]

Group boycotts are often deemed *per se* illegal, however not all types of group boycotts are *per se* illegal.[34] *Per se* violations generally involve a business (or businesses) with dominant market position that makes a concerted effort to cutoff a competitor's access to supplies, facilities, or markets.[35] Vertical group boycotts are not *per se* illegal and typically require evidence of actual adverse market affects to be actionable in court.[36]

Market Allocation

Agreements among competitors to divide customers or territories are commonly considered *per se* violations of Sherman act and the Utah Antitrust Act. These agreements may violate antitrust laws because they effectively give each competitor a monopoly in their defined (agreed upon) region of the market. For example, in *Palmer v. BRG of Georgia, Inc.*, the U.S. Supreme Court found a market allocation agreement

---

[29] *Id.*

[30] *Id. See also Radiant Burners, Inc. v. Peoples Gas Light & Coke Co.*, 364 U.S. 656 (1961) (Sherman act violation even where victim was single individual and defendants actions would have minimal economic impact)

[31] *State v. Thompson*, 751 P.2d 805, 813 (Utah Ct. App. 1988), *rev'd on other grounds*, 810 P.2d 415 (Utah 1991)

[32] *Id.*

[33] UTAH CODE ANN. § 76-10-920

[34] *See Northwest Wholesale Stationers, Inc. v. Pacific Stationery & Printing Co.*, 472 U.S. 284, 290, 293–94 (1985).

[35] *Flying J Inc. v. TA Operating Corp.*, No. 1:06-CV-30-TC, 2008 WL 4923041, at *8 (D. Utah Nov. 14, 2008).

[36] *Id. See also, Diaz v. Farley*, 215 F.3d 1175, 1185 (10th Cir. 2000); and *Coffey v. Healthtrust, Inc.*, 955 F.2d 1388, 1392 (Court Year)

between companies wherein one company agreed to withdraw from the Georgia market in exchange for the other company withdrawing from the remainder of the U.S. market violated the Sherman Act.[37]

Tying Arrangements

Tying arrangements exists where an entity requires that another entity or an individual purchase one product in return for a contract involving another (desired) product.[38] Some tying arrangements do not require the purchase of the tied product, but rather require the purchaser to refrain from purchasing the tied product from a different supplier. Tying arrangements deny free access to the market for the tied product and are often considered *per se* illegal if they substantially affect the market of the tied product and the seller has strong economic power.[39] However, the Supreme Court has noted the "Court's strong disapproval of tying arrangements has substantially diminished. Rather than relying on assumptions, in its more recent opinions the Court has required a showing of market power in the tying product."[40] Thus, in *Illinois Tool Works*, the Court determined that no violation could exist unless the plaintiff could show the defendant had market power in the tying product..[41]

Most tying arrangements involving the sale of commodities are further prohibited by the Clayton Act; violations of the Clayton Act may not require proof of an adverse impact to impose liability.[42]

Utah does not currently have a code provision that is directly comparable to Section 3 of the Clayton Act.[43] However, the Utah Attorney General has prosecuted tying arrangements under Utah' Antitrust Act. In addition, the Utah Motor Vehicle code prohibits tying arrangements in automobile financing.[44]

---

[37]498 U.S. 46 (1990)

[38]*See* ROBERT EMERSON, BUSINESS LAW 520 (5th ed. 2009).

[39]*N. Pac. Ry. Co. v. United States*, 356 U.S. 1, 5-6, (1958).

[40]*Illinois Tool Works Inc. v. Indep. Ink, Inc.*, 547 U.S. 28, 28 (2006).

[41]*Id.* (arguing that proof of market power is necessary "because a patent does not necessarily confer market power upon the patentee.").

[42]15 U.S.C. § 14 (2012).

[43]ABA SECTION OF ANTITRUST LAW, STATE ANTITRUST PRACTICE AND STATUTES 48-11 (Harvey I. Saferstein et al. eds., 4th ed. 2009)

[44]*Id.* (citing UTAH CODE ANN. §§ 41-4-1 to -6).

Monopolization or attempts to monopolize

Both the Utah Antitrust Act and Section 2 of the Sherman Act prohibit monopolies, attempts to monopolize, and conspiracies to monopolize.[45] A monopoly obtained through patented products, business skill or luck does not usually violate antitrust law.[46] However, monopolistic mergers that substantially lessen competition or create a monopoly in either a product or geographic market can violate state and federal antitrust laws.[47] While horizontal mergers are unlawful if they substantially lessen competition, vertical mergers and conglomerates may not raise the same issues and do not likely violate antitrust law.[48]

To determine if a given defendant has monopoly power, courts examine defendant's market share, but may also consider barriers to entry, market conditions and econometric data.[49]

Attempted monopolization may violate state and federal antitrust laws where an entity has both the intent and power to monopolize a market. For example, in *Aspen Skiing Co. v. Aspen Highlands Skiing Corp.*, the Court found the decision of an owner of three ski resorts in Aspen, Colorado, to discontinue its participation with (the only) independent ski resort in Aspen in an interchangeable "all-Aspen" lift ticket, violated the Sherman Act as an attempt to monopolize because the jury concluded the owner of the three ski resorts had no *legitimate* business reason to discontinue its participation in the "all-Aspen" pass.[50] The court held that although a business entity with monopoly power does not have a duty to engage in joint programs with competitors, the right is not unqualified; liability may be imposed where evidence of the effects on consumers the business entities involved supports a conclusion that the business entity had no legitimate reason to refuse to deal with another entity.[51] In considering attempts at monopolization courts also

---

[45]*See* 15 U.S.C. § 2 (2012) and Utah Code Ann. § 76-10-914(2).

[46]EMERSON, *supra* note 37, at 521.

[47]*See* 15 U.S.C. § 2; Utah Code Ann. 76-10-914(2); and EMERSON, *supra* note 37, at 523.

[48]EMERSON, *supra* note 37, at 523.

[49]*Id.* at 524–25.

[50]472 U.S. 585, 602 (1985) (Business are free to exercise their discretion as to which parties is chooses to deal with, however this discretion is limited to situations where the entity acts "*[i]n the absence of any purpose to create or maintain a monopoly.*").

[51]*Id.* at 586.

consider impacts on consumers, and the extent to which unnecessarily restrictive acts impair competition.[52]

Interlocking directorships

An interlocking directorship exists where an individual serves on the board of directors or as a high level officer of two or more competing companies. The Clayton Act generally prohibits interlocking directorships where each of the two companies is worth at least $10-million.[53]

Price Discrimination

Sellers are generally prohibited from charging different prices to different buyers for commodities of similar quality and grade if the sales occur close in time and the effect of the discriminatory sales substantially lessens competition, or tends to create a monopoly. Price discrimination practices can violate both the Robinson-Patman Act and the Utah Unfair Practices Act.[54]

Utah's Unfair Competition Act

Utah's Unfair Competition Act prohibits companies from intentionally engaging in unfair, unlawful, or fraudulent business practices that harm the value of intellectual property and that constitute: patent, trademark, or trade name infringement, malicious cyber activity, a software license violation, or predatory hiring practices.[55] A person or entity harmed by a violation of the Act may bring a private cause of action so long as the alleged violation of the act is reasonably related to the purpose of the act (to prevent unfair competition).[56] To support a successful claim under Utah's Unfair Competition Act, a plaintiff should allege facts supporting material diminution in value.[57] When alleging

---

[52]*Id.*

[53]15 U.S.C. §19.

[54]ABA SECTION OF ANTITRUST LAW, *supra* note 42, at 38-13.

[55]UTAH CODE ANN. §§ 13-5a-101 to -103.

[56]*See digEcor, Inc. v. e.Digital Corp*, No. 2:06-CV-437 CW, 2009 WL 928679, at *4 (D. Utah Apr. 2, 2009); and *Ecosure Pest Control, Inc. v. Eclipse Mktg., Inc.*, No. 2:09-CV-1108, 2010 WL 3363071, at *4 (D. Utah Aug. 23, 2010).

[57]*See Rock Media Club, LLC v. Mentchoukov*, 2012 WL119505, at *4 (D. Utah 2012) (claim under Utah Unfair Competition Act dismissed for failure to allege facts support claim of material diminution in value).

trademark infringement, a successful claim should show that the alleged violation constitutes "intentional business acts or practices" which the court usually analyzes based on standards of "commercial use" under the Lanham Act.[58]

Unfair Competition under Utah Common Law

Not all unfair competition disputes are governed by statute alone. Judge-made law—common law—can also play a role. Under Utah common law, "unfair competition includes—but is not limited to—passing off, palming off, imitating, and causing or likely causing confusion or deception."[59] Unfair competition consists of a person or entity attempting to pass off the goods of one party as the goods of another. It is not usually not necessary for a plaintiff to demonstrate actual confusion between the products to impose liability, rather establishing a likelihood of confusion may be enough to impose liability.[60]

Industry specific trade regulations in Utah

In addition to the general unfair trade practices regulated by federal and Utah law discussed above, Utah has enacted several industry specific acts aimed at addressing unfair business practices in specific industries. These acts regulate trade practices in the gasoline products and motor fuels,[61] music and film,[62] automobile franchise,[63] health spa,[64] health insurance,[65] consumer sales,[66] telephone solicitation,[67] secondary

---

[58]"Utah law governing unfair competition, infringement of a patent, trademark, or trade name requires 'intentional business acts or practices,' similar to the requirements of the Lanham Act." *Utah Lighthouse Ministry, Inc. v. Discovery Computing, Inc.*, 506 F.Supp.2d 889, 902 (D. Utah 2007).

[59]*Overstock.com v. SmartBargains, Inc.*, 2008 UT 55, ¶13, 192 P.3d 858, *citing Allen's Prods. Co. v. Glover*, 414 P.2d 93 (Utah 1966); *Budget Sys., Inc. v. Budget Loan and Fin. Plan*, 361 P.2d 512 (Utah 1961); *Hi–Land Dairyman's Ass'n. v. Cloverleaf Dairy*, 151 P.2d 710 (1944); *Beard v. Bd. of Educ.*, 16 P.2d 900 (Utah 1932); *Rocky Mountain Bell Tel. Co. v. Utah Indep. Tel. Co.*, 88 P. 26 (Utah 1906).

[60]*Id.*

[61]UTAH CODE ANN. §§ 13-12-1 to -8; and §§ 13-16-1 to -13.

[62]UTAH CODE ANN. §§ 13-10-1 to 13-10b-401; and §§ 13-13-1 to -7.

[63]UTAH CODE ANN. §§ 13-14-101 to -308.

[64]UTAH CODE ANN. §§ 13-23-1 to -7.

[65]UTAH CODE ANN. §§ 13-5b-103.

[66]UTAH CODE ANN. §§ 13-11-1 to -23.

[67]UTAH CODE ANN. §§ 13-25-101 to -111.

market,[68] debt management,[69] consumer credit,[70] and automobile financing[71] industries.

Liability for engaging in unfair trade practices

Both individuals and entities can be criminally penalized or civilly liable for violating state and/or federal antitrust laws. Antitrust violations can be investigated and (if necessary) prosecuted by federal or state agencies. In Utah, antitrust and consumer protection violations are enforced by the Division of Consumer Protection within Utah's Department of Commerce.[72] In addition, the Utah Attorney General's office actively investigates and prosecutes state and federal anti-trust violations.[73] Both the Utah Antitrust Act, and the Unfair Practices Act, empower the attorney general's office with the ability to prosecute trade violations.[74]

The Utah Unfair Practices Act provides that any person or the State of Utah may maintain an action to enjoin unfair trade practice violations. A plaintiff does not have to allege or prove actual damages to bring a claim under the Utah Unfair Practices Act. However where a plaintiff sustains and can prove actual damages, the Act allows for recovery of three times the amount of actual damages sustained and court costs. An individual or entity that knowingly violates the Utah Unfair Practices Act can result in misdemeanor charges for each violation and a fine of up to $5,000 and/or 12 months imprisonment.[75]

The Utah Unfair Competition Act also provides for a private cause of action for persons who are injured by unfair competition. Plaintiffs may recover actual damages, costs, attorney's fees, and in some cases, punitive damages.[76]

---

[68]UTAH CODE ANN. §§ 13-32-101 to -107, and §§ 13-32a-101 to -117.

[69]UTAH CODE ANN. §§ 13-42-101 to -141.

[70]UTAH CODE ANN. §§ 13-45-101 to -401.

[71]UTAH CODE ANN. §§ 41-4-1 to -6.

[72]UTAH CODE ANN. §13-2-1 (2).

[73]*Antitrust,* OFFICE OF THE ATTORNEY GENERAL, http://attorneygeneral.utah.gov/protecting-utah/from-fraud/antitrust/ (last visited November 8, 2014).

[74]UTAH CODE ANN. §§ 13-5-2.5 (5), 76-1-3105.

[75]UTAH CODE ANN. §13-5-14.

[76]UTAH CODE ANN. §13-5a-103.

The Utah Antitrust Act provides that the Attorney General may bring an action for injunctive relief, damages, and/or civil penalty against any individual who violates the Act.[77] Individuals may be charged with a civil penalty of up to $100,000 for each violation of the act; entities may be charge with a civil penalty of up to $500,000 for each violation of the Act.[78] The Utah Antitrust Act also provides for a private right of action for residents injured by or threatened with injury by violation of the Act, and allows for injunctive relief and damages, recovery of three times the amount of actual damages incurred as a result of the violation, costs, and attorney's fees.[79] Finally, anyone who violates the Act by engaging in price fixing, bid rigging, dividing markets, or group boycotts may be guilty of a third degree felony and may be subject to a fine of up to $100,000 for individuals, or $500,000 for entities.[80]

Both state attorneys general and the US attorney general may prosecute antitrust violations.[81] Penalties for Sherman and Clayton Act violations can be very severe, imposing liabilities for up to $1 million for individuals, and $100 million for business entities.[82] In addition, Sherman Act violations can subject individuals to criminal penalties with up to ten years in prison.[83] Individuals injured by antitrust violations may have private causes of action for injunctive relief, costs, attorney's fees, and three times the actual damages incurred as a result of the violation.[84]

Conclusion

When dealing with other business entities, businesses operating in Utah should be careful to avoid engaging in agreements with the intent of unfairly affecting inter and intra state markets. These agreements can include agreements to divide market or agreements designed to hinder another entity's ability to enter the market. Such agreements may subject businesses to both civil and criminal penalties.

---

[77]Utah Code Ann. § 76-10-3108.

[78]*Id.*

[79]Utah Code Ann. § 76-10-3109,

[80]Utah Code Ann. § 76-10-3112

[81]15 U.S.C. §§ 15(a), 15(f).

[82]15 U.S.C. §1

[83]*Id.*

[84]15 U.S.C. §15

CHAPTER 25

BUSINESS INSURANCE

PROPERTY INSURANCE

GARY JOHNSON[1]

Part of every business plan should be the management of risk, which comes in many forms. A commercial enterprise can self insure, i.e., set aside a certain amount of its revenue to provide for any losses that occur from its operations. On the other hand, a business can utilize the insurance industry to protect it from potential losses. Property insurance is designed to help businesses manage a certain kind of risk: damage to the business' own property – in whatever form – which may result in property damage or business interruption.

In an insurance contract in which the insurer promises to protect the insured from harm suffered directly to the insured's person or property, there are only two parties to such an agreement: the insured, who is the first-party, and the insurer, who is the second-party. Such "first-party" insurance is commonly referred to as "property insurance." We use the term "first-party" to refer to an insurance agreement where the insurer agrees to pay claims submitted to it by the insured for losses suffered by the insured. In contrast, a "third-party" situation is one where the insurer contracts to defend the insured against claims made by third-parties against the insured and to pay any resulting liability up to a specified dollar amount. We will discuss third-party liability insurance in the next section below. "Third-party" insurance is commonly referred to as "casualty insurance."

[1]Gary L. Johnson is a shareholder at the Salt Lake City, Utah law firm of Richards Brandt Miller Nelson. His practice is devoted primarily to insurance law and products liability. Mr. Johnson is a Fellow of the American College of Coverage and Extracontractual Counsel, a member of the International Association of Defense Counsel and he is a member of the Defense Research Institute.

Commercial Property Coverage:

Many insurers provide first-party property insurance in standardized insurance policies. The Insurance Services Office (ISO) is a common source of policy forms for "Commercial Property Coverage" issued by most standard insurers. Commercial Property Coverage provides coverage to a policy holder for "direct physical loss or damage" to covered property, at an insured location (usually listed on the Declarations page or in a schedule of properties), that arises from a "covered cause of loss," which is a term usually defined in your insurance policy.

Generally, under first-party property coverage, the insured must establish a direct physical loss to covered property proximately caused by a peril insured against during the policy term. Most standard homeowners and commercial business property policies limit recovery to physical damages.

The standard building and personal property coverage form issued by insurers typically describes the property protected in the policy as the buildings listed, business personal property and the personal property of others. The term "building" is usually not defined in the policy. Check your policy to make sure that "fixtures" are listed in both the building property section and in the business personal property section of the policy.

An additional area of covered property under your policy should be "personal property of others" that is in the care, custody or control of you or your business. The ISO property coverage form extends this grant of coverage to property of others not just to property located in a covered building, but also to personal property within 100 feet of the described premises.

Any commercial property policy you obtain should specify the type of property that is covered and what types of property will not be covered. The typical commercial property policy should cover most types of property commonly used by or owned by commercial businesses. (*Always review the terms of your commercial property coverage with your insurance agent so that you understand what is and what is not covered in your business operations. For example, some property policies do not cover damage to foundations of buildings if the foundations are below the surface of the ground if there is no basement. There is no substitute for asking your agent for clarification.*)

You need to be aware that under most standard commercial property policies, certain types of business property have limited coverage. Often, electronic data, valuable papers and records, and fine arts (statuary, porcelains and china) as well as jewelry, watches and precious stones, will have restrictive coverage.

As noted above, your property insurance will indemnify you for a "covered cause of loss." Most commercial property policies are available with either a basic cause of loss form or a broad cause of loss form. As with all things, the scope of your coverage is dependent upon how much you are willing to pay in your premium. Your basic cause of loss form should include such perils as fire, lightning, explosion, windstorm or hail, smoke, vandalism, sprinkler leakage or sinkhole collapse. Sometimes you may see limited coverage extended for fungus, wet rot, dry rot and bacteria.

In insurance, however, what is more important than what is covered is what is not covered. Often, property policies will exclude all coverage for flood damage and most other types of water damage. Another exclusion seen on almost all commercial property policies is damage from earth movement/earthquake. You may be able to obtain an endorsement adding earth movement coverage, which will vary in cost depending upon your location.

Almost every property coverage policy contains what is called the "Vacancy Clause" in one form or another. This vacancy clause provides that there is no coverage for certain enumerated risks if the building where the loss or damage occurs has been vacant for some specific period of time (60 days in the ISO Commercial Property form). (*If you know that a building you own or lease is going to be vacant for any substantial length of time, talk to your insurance agent. There are endorsements you can buy for a policy that will provide some measure of coverage for your unoccupied building.*)

Another common exclusion in business property policies is for damage to your premises resulting from an interruption in utility service that originates away from your business premises. For example, if the utility substation that provides power to your business is hit by lightning, the damage caused to your operations by the interruption in power is usually not covered by the standard business policy. Many of these standard exclusions can be addressed through endorsements which provide some type of coverage for the claim.

One of the most important forms of property coverage you may want to obtain is "business income and extra expense coverage." From the standpoint of insurers, the term "business income" usually means the net profit or loss before income taxes that would have been earned or incurred by you had there been no loss, plus the continuing normal operating expenses that you incur when running your business.

Basically, business interruption coverage provides that the insurance company will pay the actual loss of business income that you sustain due to the necessary suspension of your operations during the "period of restoration." The suspension must be caused by direct physical loss of or damage to property at premises which are described in the Declarations of the insurance policy and for which a "Business Income Limit of Insurance" is shown in those Declarations. The loss or damage must also be caused by or result from a "covered cause of loss."

In other words, a commercial property insurer will pay for your loss of business income that results from the stoppage or slowdown of your business operations during the time needed to repair or replace the damaged property. (*The importance of providing adequate business records relating to your operations cannot be overemphasized. It is good business practice to keep good records, and it will be invaluable to you in proving your business interruption claim.*)

The term "period of restoration" is often defined in commercial property policies to begin 72 hours after the time of the direct damage loss and the period of restoration ends when the property is (or should have been, given the exercise of due diligence) repaired or replaced, or when you have resumed operations at a new permanent location. The time that the period of restoration starts can be varied with an endorsement.

It is important for you to understand what insurers mean when they say the "necessary suspension" of your business operations. This term is defined in the standard business policy to mean either a slowdown or cessation of your business activities. In other words, you do not have to be completely put out of business in order to have coverage for business interruption.

Commercial Inland Marine Insurance:

First-party property coverage for businesses comes in a variety of forms. As noted above, the standard – and most common – form of property coverage addresses coverage for the buildings, business personal property and potential income loss a business may sustain. Businesses, however, often have property risks involved in the transportation of goods or relating to a business property that is not kept at the premises and is not a building or what is defined as business personal property. One type of insurance that addresses this exposure to a business is called "Commercial Inland Marine" insurance. Historically, most transportation of products and goods in the United States were handled over waterways (by ships moving in the ocean city to city, or by barges on rivers or canals).

As the United States expanded, and products and goods began to move over railroads, and then motor vehicles and aircraft, insurance companies took the older marine forms of coverage and applied them to inland transportation. Although there are many different categories of commercial inland marine policies, the basic types of coverage available to businesses are for domestic goods in transit; bailee's customers; movable equipment and unusual property; property of certain dealers; and instrumentalities of communication and transportation.

Inland marine insurers provide coverage for your property shipped domestically by rail, tractor/trailer, aircraft, or even while in the possession of the United States Postal Service.

A "bailment" exists when merchandise is left to be held in trust for a specific purpose and returned when that purpose has ended. The "bailor" is the owner of the goods or merchandise, and the "bailee" is the one in possession of the merchandise. Most commercial general liability insurance policies (which we will discuss in the next section below) exclude the exposure your business will have when it holds in bailment goods or merchandise of another under what is called the "care, custody, and control" exclusion. A form of inland marine coverage, however, provides that necessary protection.

Certain types of mobile equipment may constantly be moving from location to location and subject to transportation exposures that are not covered by standard commercial business policies. Certain kinds of property that is not considered to be "equipment," like cattle or expensive artwork your business may own, are eligible for endorsements called "floaters." Again, these are risks that may not be covered under the standard commercial policy, but which you should be able to cover under inland marine coverage.

Certain specialty businesses, e.g., jewelers, high-end special equipment sellers, retailers who specialize in the sale of fur stoles or fur coats, etc., may find that their inventory is not adequately covered by the standard commercial property policy. These types of specialty dealers can find coverage under inland marine policies.

There are reasons to purchase Commercial Inland Marine coverage even when your Commercial Property form might provide some protection. Inland Marine coverage forms are generally broader in scope of coverage for this particular type of coverage. You can purchase Inland Marine coverage in an "all risks" form, which will probably contain fewer exclusions than the standard property policy. Any business that imports or exports products should talk to its insurance agent about Inland Marine coverage. (*A variation on the two types of polices we have discussed above is the "Commercial Output Policy." This policy combines in a single policy features from both Commercial Property forms and Inland Marine coverage. If your business involves the manufacturing and transportation of products, talk to your agent about whether a COP policy will work for you.*)

Commercial Crime Insurance:

Another type of property coverage which every business should consider is commercial crime insurance. In your standard Commercial Property form, employee dishonesty is almost always an excluded cause of loss. For many years, a substantial percentage of small business bankruptcies were caused by some form of crime. Some insurers treat the type of business differently, making distinctions between retail operations and financial institutions.

Although Commercial Property forms cover the theft of some property, most crime insurance policies address some combination of "money," "securities," or "property other than money and securities." Money is often defined to mean currency, coins and bank notes in current use and having a face value, as well as traveler's checks, registered checks and money orders held for sale to the public. "Securities" are often described as negotiable and non-negotiable instruments or contracts representing either money or other property.

Crime policies usually address two distinct types of risk: (i) business organizations other than financial institutions, and (ii) financial institutions. The former type of coverage is usually provided on a commercial crime coverage form. The latter type of coverage is usually provided on some sort of fidelity bond or financial institution coverage form. (*Your insurance agent should be able to tell you whether the ISO commercial crime forms, the Surety Association of America crime protection forms or the American Association of Insurance Services commercial crime program best suits your business's needs.*)

As with all insurance, crime policies contain exclusions. Certain types of property are excluded from coverage. Always be sure to review your policy to read the definitions of "money," "securities," and "property other than money and securities," so that you understand what property is included and what property is excluded from your crime coverage.

Some of the areas often covered under crime policies are employee dishonesty, forgery and alteration, theft, robbery, and computer fraud. The last mentioned is not the least important. Some commercial crime policies exclude coverage for theft performed with a computer. If your policy form excludes computer fraud, talk to your agent about a computer fraud coverage form or endorsement. (*Remember, crime coverage, including computer fraud coverage, does not typically insure against loss from theft of your trade secrets or other confidential business information you may have. Also, generally computer fraud coverage does not extend to damage from the introduction of a computer virus unless you have purchased a separate endorsement for that risk. Again, talk to your agent.*)

How the loss occurs is often crucial to invoking crime coverage. Crime policies generally look at losses caused by either employees or "anyone but an employee." Employees are usually defined broadly under crime policies. Almost always, losses caused by two categories of persons are always excluded from crime policies. Usually this will include the named insured and any partners of the named insured whether acting alone or in collusion with other persons.

CHAPTER 26
BUSINESS INSURANCE
CASUALTY INSURANCE

GARY JOHNSON[1]

For better or for worse, litigation has become the number one dispute resolution mechanism in the United States. There are a variety of ways to manage the risk that comes when someone claims that your business has harmed them in some fashion.

One mechanism businesses can use to address litigation risk is "self-insurance." This solution requires the business to set aside a certain amount of its revenue to provide for any losses that occur, i.e., losses that could usually be covered under a general liability insurance policy. Revenues that would normally be used for premium payments are added to a segregated fund that is used to pay incurred damages to third parties. This is a solution centered on the business retaining the risk rather than having an insurer take that risk for the business in exchange for a premium payment.

For most small businesses, self-insurance is not a practical solution from an administrative standpoint. It is much easier to purchase liability insurance. When we talk about purchasing liability insurance, we are talking about a contractual arrangement under which the insurer agrees to defend and indemnify the insured against loss or damage arising from injuries to third parties. Under this arrangement, insurance is purchased in order to transfer the risk of harm to others to a professional risk bearer by means of the underwriting process.

[1]Gary L. Johnson is a shareholder at the Salt Lake City, Utah law firm of Richards Brandt Miller Nelson. His practice is devoted primarily to insurance law and products liability. Mr. Johnson is a Fellow of the American College of Coverage and Extracontractual Counsel, a member of the International Association of Defense Counsel and he is a member of the Defense Research Institute.

Commercial General Liability Coverage:

One of the most common ways that businesses protect themselves from third-party claims is through the purchase of a policy based on the Insurance Service Office's (ISO) Commercial General Liability coverage form (CGL form).

The current version of the CGL form provides coverage for a business for its "premises/operations" and its "products/completed operations" activities. There is a distinction in these extensions of coverage that you need to understand.

For example, liability insurance protection for a manufacturer for the process of producing or manufacturing goods is generally termed "premises liability" while liability protection coverage for the manufacturer once the goods are finished and moved away from the manufacturing premises is generally referred to as products liability coverage. Similarly, a business that performs a service on the premises of others, such as a general contractor, can obtain coverage while his work is in progress in the form of operations liability coverage insurance and, after the work is completed, by completed operations liability coverage.

The premises liability portion of a CGL policy provides a manufacturer with the same type of coverage that an operations liability portion of a CGL policy provides the service business. The CGL form melds both types of coverages together as "premises/operations" coverage.

Likewise, products liability coverage for a manufacturer equates to completed operations coverage for the service business. That type of coverage, "products/completed operations," is also built into the contemporary CGL form. The insured can delete products/completed operations coverage by endorsement, and thereby lower its premium.

We need to be clear that premises/operations coverage and products/completed operations coverage are not separate or distinct types of coverage, rather they are the same type of coverage for bodily injury and property damages, just for a different time period. In other words, by building in premises/operations coverage and products/completed operations coverage into one policy, the ISO has enlarged the timeframe in which an event may occur that damages a third-party and still be covered by the same liability policy.

In the contemporary ISO CGL form, coverage for claims against your business for bodily injury or property damage is contained in what is called "Coverage A" (bodily injury and property damage), and includes premises/operations and products/completed operations hazards caused by an occurrence. The term "occurrence" is a defined term in the CGL form that requires that the incident giving rise to the claim be accidental in nature.

One of the primary purposes of CGL coverage is to protect businesses from third-party claims for bodily injury or property damage resulting from accidents. A typical CGL policy broadly defines the damages to which it applies and then specifically lists exclusions to the broad grants of coverage. Some of the typical exclusions found in Coverage A of the CGL form are for intentional acts, harm to your own employees (that is why you should have Workers Compensation insurance), the threatened or actual dispersal or release of pollutants from your premises, property damage to property in the care, custody or control of the business and property damage (with some notable exceptions) to the business's own work. (*There are numerous exclusions in Coverage A, Coverage B and Coverage C which you need to carefully review to understand what is not covered under your CGL form.*)

Personal Injury and Advertising Injury:

The contemporary CGL form contains two additional coverage grants: Coverage B (personal and advertising injury) and Coverage C (medical payments). The event giving rise to coverage under personal and advertising injury is an "offense" committed during the policy period. Coverage B does not require bodily injury or property damage as a predicate to invoke its application. "Personal and advertising injury" is a defined term that includes false arrest, malicious prosecution, wrongful eviction, libel, slander, invasion of privacy and – if done in the named insured's advertisement – infringement of copyright, trade dress, or slogan, and misappropriation of another's advertising ideas. (*Note that the current CGL form specifically excludes coverage for personal and advertising injury arising out of the infringement of copyright, patent, trademark, trade secret or other intellectual property rights, except that the exclusion does not apply to infringement, in the business's "advertisement," of copyright, trade dress or slogan.*)

The types of offenses listed in the CGL form as necessary predicates to invoke coverage for personal and advertising injury are, generally speaking, behavioral predicates involving intentionality to complete them. This does not mean that traditional insurance requirements, such as moral hazard and the fortuity requirement with respect to harm caused by these intentional acts, are not still necessary.

The scope of Coverage B is constrained by a number of specific exclusions implicating moral hazard. For example, there is an exclusion that bars coverage for personal and advertising injury that is caused by or at the direction of the insured with the knowledge that the act would violate the rights of another and would inflict "personal and advertising injury." While the offenses that define personal and advertising injury will occur as a result of deliberate acts, the harm caused by the offenses cannot be intended and still invoke the benefits of Coverage B.

Medical Payments Coverage:

Coverage C (medical payments) requires an insurer to pay medical expenses for bodily injury caused by an accident on the insured's premises, or related areas, or because of the insured's operations, all regardless of fault if the expenses are incurred and reported within one year of the accident. This coverage is like no-fault premises liability insurance. This coverage is intended to pay for injuries sustained by members of the general public while on your business premises or exposed to your business operations. The fundamental distinction between Coverage C and Coverage A and Coverage B is that while both of those grants of coverage are fault based, Coverage C pays without regard to the fault of the insured. Modern business practices, however, may call for additional protections, separate and apart from the traditional CGL form.

Cyber Coverage: A prime example of a newly emerging risk that all businesses need to be aware of is the problem of incurring liability for data breach and privacy violations. Unfortunately, attacks by criminal data hackers is becoming more and more prevalent.

To protect against this type of harm, a business can obtain different forms of cyber and privacy insurance coverage. Available from some insurers is privacy notification and crisis management expense coverage. This coverage form will pay the costs to determine the cause of the data breach and secure the site to prevent further intrusions, notify customers that their personally identifiable information has been compromised, set up a call center for them, monitor their credit, and hire a public relations firm to assist your business in dealing with the crisis.

A separate type of coverage you may want to consider is regulatory defense and penalties coverage. This form of insurance protection pays the expenses required to deal with the multitude of state and federal regulators who become involved when a breach occurs and also covers the fines and penalties leveled by these agencies (one of the few forms of insurance that provides such coverage). Lastly, you may want to consider information and privacy liability coverage, which pays the costs (e.g., settlements or judgments and defense costs) that your business incurs when it is held liable for the unauthorized disclosure of its customer's personally identifiable information.

These types of liability coverage may sometimes be made available by different insurance companies under a variety of names: privacy and network security insurance, security and privacy protection insurance, information security and privacy insurance. You will need to review the proposed coverages carefully to make sure that the Insuring Agreements provide to your business the type of coverage you really want. You may want to check with your commercial property insurer to see if they sell special endorsements you can add to your commercial property coverage which may provide you with the same or similar types of insurance coverage.

Business Auto Coverage: A common risk exposure many businesses face arises from any operation in which that business utilizes its own fleet of motor vehicles. If this is an exposure you face, your business will want to obtain commercial automobile insurance, or what is known as "business auto coverage" (BAC).

The BAC policy usually consists of declarations, common policy conditions, the business auto coverage form and any endorsements that will add or expand your coverage. There will usually be a section in the policy which is labeled "Covered Autos" and calls for the entry of one or more numerical symbols for each type of coverage to be provided. These symbol entries indicate the types of coverage obtained by the insured. Each type of coverage will have a limit of liability and, where applicable, deductibles applicable to each coverage.

Depending upon the size of your fleet, the types of autos or trucks used, and other conditions, your business should be able to tailor the type of BAC it obtains. One of the first categories you need to consider is the type or class of covered auto you want to insure. Is it just automobiles or trucks that your company owns? Is it autos and/or trucks that you lease or rent? Does your business operate mobile equipment, such as bulldozers or front loaders? Do you want to extend coverage to vehicles your business does not own but which your employees may be using from time to time? These are all issues you need to discuss with your insurance broker to make sure you obtain the correct protection for your business operations.

Garage Coverage: If your business is involved in the repair of motor vehicles, equipping motor vehicles with accessories, or the garaging of motor vehicles, the exposure of such a business to third parties can involve risks that are sometimes covered by CGL forms and sometimes covered by BAC forms, but may be excluded by both forms.

In such a situation, your insurance broker will recommend that your business obtain what is called garage and truckers insurance. The garage liability policy was developed for auto-related businesses to provide three basic coverages: (1) liability insurance, a general and auto liability coverage in a single insuring agreement; (2) physical damage insurance, coverage for damage to those covered autos specified in the policy; and (3) garage keepers insurance, which provides coverage when the insured business is legally responsible for damage to non-owned vehicles, such as those belonging to customers.

Directors and Officers Coverage: Finally, it is important to remember that not just the business, but corporate officers as well, face third-party liability claims in the operation of the business. To manage the risk of the liability of directors and officers, insurance can be purchased separate and apart from corporate indemnification agreements. Most standard directors and officers liability policies ("D&O policies") provide two grants of coverage. The first provides coverage to past, present and future directors and officers of the corporation and the second grant of coverage is for the parent corporation and, depending on the wording, insured subsidiaries for amounts paid by the corporation to indemnify a director or officer for loss.

Almost all D&O policies are "claims made" policies. Claims made policies are insurance policies under which coverage is invoked only for a claim first made during the policy period against a director or officer. This is different from the "occurrence" type of policy discussed above.

Most D&O policies now specifically define the types of wrongful acts for which they provide coverage. Historically, D&O policies provided coverage for any breach of duty, neglect, error, misstatement, omission or other act done by directors and officers alleged by a claimant as a result of their actions as directors and officers.

As noted, some insurers have very specific definitions of what they consider to be a wrongful act. Some policies only provide coverage for negligent acts or errors. It will be very important to carefully review the Insuring Agreement so that you understand the scope of coverage that is being made available to corporate management and to the company under the D&O policy you purchase.

There are a number of well-established consequences of corporate behavior for which D&O coverage is not available. Specifically, most D&O policies do not provide coverage for the return of financial gain or benefits that are improperly received by the company and/or its officers. Usually, bodily injury and property damage (which is covered under your CGL form) will be excluded from a D&O policy. Any judgment that is enforced against the company or its officers as a result of active and deliberate dishonesty is not covered under the policy. Also, unless you get a special endorsement, your D&O policy will not cover liability for the company or its officers arising out of any violation of the Employee Retirement Income Security Act of 1974. To protect the business against ERISA liability claims, a separate policy is usually required.

Professional Liability Coverage: If your business provides professional services, you will need a professional malpractice policy (what is commonly referred to as an "errors and omissions" policy). Almost all professional malpractice policies: policies for healthcare providers, design professionals, attorneys, accountants or others, are presented to their purchasers in the format of a "claims made" policy, as opposed to the "occurrence policy" discussed with reference to CGL policies (although CGL policies can also come in a claims made format).

A claims made policy protects against claims made during the term of the policy irrespective of when the act giving rise to the claim occurred. Because transmittal of the notice of claim to the insurer during the policy period triggers coverage under the policy, it is considered to be an important aspect of the claims made policy. In other words, failure to comply with the reporting requirements of a claims made policy has been held by many courts to bar coverage. Although a harsh consequence, the reporting requirements in claims made policies are enforceable.

Malpractice policies often provide coverage for an insured's "wrongful act," which is often defined in the insurance contract as any breach of duty, neglect, error, misstatement, or omission in the furnishing of professional services. Please read the policy terms carefully. Malpractice policies often include provisions which reduce the available policy limits by the amount expended on defense of the claim.

REFERENCES:

Robert B. Holtom, UNDERWRITING PRINCIPLES AND PRACTICES (3D ED. 1987)

International Risk Management Institute, COMMERCIAL LIABILITY INSURANCE, Volumes 1-3 (2013)

International Risk Management Institute, COMMERCIAL PROPERTY INSURANCE, Volumes 1-3 (2012)

Gary L. Johnson, THE PRACTICAL ART: ON THE ARCHEOLOGY AND ARCHITECTURE OF LIABILITY INSURANCE CONTRACTS, 78 Defense Counsel Journal 133 (2011)

Gary L. Johnson, The CONTOURS OF PROPERTY COVERAGE: SOME REFLECTIONS ON THE VACANCY CLAUSE, 21 Coverage No. 5 (2011)

Richard D. Turner, Steven Hom, II, Peter R. Kensicki, MULTIPLE-LINES INSURANCE PRODUCTION, Volumes 1 and 2 (2d Ed. 1986)

Chapter 27
Creditor's Rights
Piercing the Corporate Veil

T. Jake Hinkins[1]

Many entrepreneurs are so focused on getting their business up and going that they do not spend a lot of time thinking about potential liability – they should. Organized or incorporated entities that limit an owner's liability, which include corporations, limited liability partnerships and limited liability companies organized under Utah laws, are generally considered separate from their individual owners. Legally, they are separate entities. "The purpose of such separation is to insulate the stockholders from the liabilities of the corporation, thus limiting their liability to only the amount that the stockholders voluntarily put at risk." *Salt Lake City Corp. v. James Constructors, Inc.*, 761 P.2d 42, 46 (Utah Ct.App.1988). While the company and its owners are legally separate entities, there are situations where the entity and the individual owners are considered one in the same. It is the goal of this section to help you, as an entrepreneur, avoid situations where your established entity is disregarded and you are held personally liable.

One of the primary purposes of establishing a corporation or limited liability entity is to remove or at least limit the liability of shareholders (in the case of a corporation), members (in the case of a limited liability company) or limited partners (in the case of a limited liability partnership). The idea of "piercing the corporate veil" allows creditors of the entity to strip the owners of the limited liability

[1]T. Jake Hinkins practices civil litigation and is the founding member of Anderson Hinkins LLC and its predecessor Hinkins Law, LLC. Jake is a graduate of the University of Nebraska College of Law, Southern Utah University and Snow College. Jake enjoys spending time with his beautiful wife and kids when he is not practicing law.

protections they sought if the creditor shows that the shareholders in question have utilized the corporation or limited liability entity in a manner that shows that there is a unity of interest between the entity and its owner(s) and the owner(s) have used the entity in a manner that either perpetuates fraud or promotes some form of injustice.

The case of *Jones & Trevor Marketing, Inc. v. Lowry*, 284 P.3d 630 (Utah 2012) provides guidance on how one can go behind the effectual "veil" created by incorporating or establishing a limited liability entity to hold individual owners personally liable. In the case of such owners, this case provides guidance on how to avoid the pitfalls that will lead to such liability. *Lowry* is a contract-dispute case wherein one of the parties became insolvent, and the plaintiff tried to pierce the corporate veil of the insolvent company to enable the plaintiff to attach liability to the individual shareholders of the insolvent company. In Utah, the courts will generally follow a two-part test to determine whether the established entity should be disregarded and the individual owners held personally liable.

The Utah Supreme Court established a two-prong method for determining eligibility requirements in order to disregard a stockholder's limited liability in *Norman v. Murray First Thrift & Loan Co.*, 596 P.2d 1028 (Utah 1979). The Court stated that:

> "There must be a concurrence of two circumstances: (1) there must be such unity of interest and ownership that the separate personalities of the corporation and the individual no longer exist, viz., the corporation is in fact the alter ego of one or few individuals; and (2) the observance of the corporate form would sanction a fraud, promote injustice, or an inequitable result would follow."

The *Lowry* court explained in slightly more detail the two-part test of the *alter-ego doctrine* that must be satisfied before a creditor can pierce the corporate veil. The two separate portions of the test have been described as the (1) formalities and (2) fairness requirements. The formalities portion of the test refers to the formalities established by state statute governing the entity (whether it is an LLC, partnership or corporation. An entrepreneur should become familiar with the appropriate statutes or seek the advice of legal counsel to ensure that the appropriate formalities are followed from the creation of the entity forward. The formalities portion of the test can be as simple as going through the appropriate checklist to make sure the requirements are met, so an entrepreneur needs to be aware of what is on that checklist.

The court in *Lowry* addressed the formalities part of the test when it stated "there must be such unity of interest and ownership that the separate personalities of the corporation and the individual no longer exist." This means that the entity and its owner(s) are one in the same and while the name may be different, there is no legitimate difference between the two. They are operating autonomously.

The second part of the test that must be reviewed is whether "the observance of the corporate form would sanction a fraud, promote injustice, or an inequitable result would follow." This means that because the entity and the owner(s) are operating as one, if the court allows the owner(s) to hide behind such a façade then the outcome would either be illegal or unfair. The two-part test associated with the alter ego doctrine is somewhat amorphous and thankfully the courts have provided some additional direction on factors that may be considered in determining whether one can pierce the corporate veil or alternatively whether one can avoid having the corporate veil pierced.

The other considerations discussed in the *Lowry* case come from a case entitled *Colman v. Colman*, 743 P.2d 782, 786 (Utah Ct.App.1987). The factors were discussed as useful considerations, so there is not a set formula in determining what weight if any to give the eight factors, but they are useful to provide additional guidance. The factors are as follows:

> (1) undercapitalization of a one-man corporation; (2) failure to observe corporate formalities; (3) nonpayment of dividends; (4) siphoning of corporate funds by the dominant stockholder; (5) nonfunctioning of other officers or directors; (6) absence of corporate records; (7) the use of the corporation as a facade for operations of the dominant stockholder or stockholders; and (8) the use of the corporate entity in promoting injustice or fraud.

The court in *Lowry* was very clear that these factors were useful to consider, but stressed that the analysis is a very fact specific analysis. The analysis must happen in each different case because no one factor is determinative, and none of the eight factors are actually required elements that must be proven to prevail. It is conceivable that in certain circumstances only one of the factors may be met and the court could still allow the creditor to pierce the corporate veil. The determination will rely heavily on the relationship between the owner(s) and the entity.

In *Dockstader v. Walker*, 510 P.2d 526, 528 (Utah 1973), the Utah Supreme Court laid out some concerns to be aware of in situations where an entrepreneur is the sole owner and is operating the business as a shell entity when it stated:

> The doctrine [of corporate disregard] generally applies to situations known as 'one-man corporations,' i.e., where one man owns practically all of the stock either directly or through others who hold it for his use and benefit, and where the stockholder uses the corporation as a shield to protect him from debts or wrongdoings. It cannot be applied to make a stockholder liable for the legitimate debts of a corporation unless he is so closely allied with the corporation through ownership and management as to enable the courts to see clearly that the corporation is but a sham and it is the stockholder who is doing business behind the corporate shield.

Entrepreneurs should be especially cautious in following the appropriate formalities when they will be the sole owner of the company. Because single-member entities or one-man corporations are typically run by that individual as well, the formalities need to be strictly followed because the courts may view the fairness factors more skeptically where the company and the individual have been operating as one in the same.

CHAPTER 28
CREDITOR'S RIGHTS
FRAUDULENT TRANSFERS

T. JAKE HINKINS[1]

Entrepreneurs need to be aware of situations where transfers they make can be undone if those transfers are made fraudulently. If an entrepreneur makes a transfer that harms the rights or the company's creditors, then there is the possibility that a court could come in and ignore the transaction as a void transaction. It will be as if the transaction did not occur, or the court could allow liability to pass to a new entity if the individual sets up a new entity to avoid paying creditors. In both of those situations, the transactions are voidable because improperly trying to escape from company creditors will be viewed as potential fraud and may allow creditors to attach to successor entities.

One factor that is important to consider when looking at transactions is whether the transaction is commercially reasonable. A commercially reasonable transaction is one that appears to be an arms-length transaction that is not unfairly giving preference or favoring one party to the detriment of the other. For example, if a company has creditors and feels that it is in the company's interest to sell a large asset of the company. It may sell the asset and likely avoid allegations of fraud if the asset is sold to a third-party for a fair market price. The reason this is not fraudulent is because the asset was replaced with another asset (in the form of cash) that is still owned by the company. Alternatively, if a company sold its primary asset to one of the owners of the company for something less than market value, then that transaction looks like a fraudulent transfer and is more likely to be challenged by creditors. The creditors in the second-scenario would likely argue that the self-dealing transaction should be voided to allow

[1]T. Jake Hinkins practices civil litigation and is the founding member of Anderson Hinkins LLC and its predecessor Hinkins Law, LLC. Jake is a graduate of the University of Nebraska College of Law, Southern Utah University and Snow College. Jake enjoys spending time with his beautiful wife and kids when he is not practicing law.

the company to retain the value of the asset and thereby provide a greater likelihood of the creditors being paid.

"The law has long held that transfers of property designed to place a debtor's assets beyond the reach of the debtor's creditors are void as to the creditors." *National Loan Investors, L.P. v. Givens*, 952 P.2d 1067, 1069 (Utah 1998). If an entrepreneur attempts to transfer company assets to avoid paying these debts, then there is a high likelihood that such a transfer could be challenged and unwound.

There are also several situations where an entrepreneur should be wary of involvement in transactions where their company could be held liable as a successor. Pursuant to *Macris & Associates v. Neways, Inc.*, successor liability is defined as the moment "where one company sells or otherwise transfers all its assets to another company." In addition, this case specifies that the purchaser of a company will be held liable for prior debts if:

> The purchaser [of the company] expressly or impliedly agrees to assume such debts; the transaction amounts to a *consolidation* or merger of the seller and purchaser; the purchasing corporation is merely a continuation of the selling corporation; or the transaction is entered into [by the seller and purchaser] fraudulently in order to escape liability for such debts.[2]

As outlined in the above example, successor liability occurs when a new owner/purchaser of a corporate entity takes on the previous debts of the entity he/she purchased. Successor liability applies to those who dissolve previous companies as a means of either avoiding liability for debts or, for those who see fit to expand at the expense of a prior entity. Why is this significant? Often, when a purchaser wishes to avoid payment on debts, he/she is involved with a fraudulent conveyance or transfer.

[2]*Macris & Assocs., Inc. v. Neways, Inc.*, 1999 UT App 230, ¶15, 986 P.2d (748) (citation omitted).

Utah follows the Restatement (Third) of Torts § 12, which allows for successor liability in four cases:

> (1) where the successor agrees to assume the liability of the predecessor; (2) where the transaction was a fraudulent conveyance designed to escape liability for the debts or liabilities of the predecessor; (3) where the transaction is a consolidation or merger with the predecessor; or (4) where the transaction results in the successor becoming a continuation of the predecessor.

See Herrod v. Metal Power Prods. (Utah 2008); see also *Macris & Assocs., Inc. v. Neways, Inc.*, 1999 UT App 230, ¶ 15, 986 P.2d 748, 752, *aff'd*, 2000 UT 93, 16 P.3d 1214. We will briefly analyze each of these situations to assist the entrepreneur in avaoiding situations of potentially significant liability. In the first situation, the case suggests that the successor entity would have to actually agree to assume the debt. If you do not intend to accept liability, then do not expressly agree to assume the liability and do not impliedly assume the liability. Careful drafting of asset purchase agreements can be key to avoiding liability.

It can often be important to have an understanding of who you are doing business with, and that is the idea behind the second situation described above. If the entity with whom you enter into a transaction is entering into the transaction to avoid liability on prior debts or liabilities, then the transaction will need to be analyzed as we previously discussed to determine whether it meets the indicia of a fraudulent conveyance. If it appears fraudulent, then the transaction could be voided or the successor entity may be liable to the prior creditors.

The third successor liability situation arises where there is a merger or consolidation. If the original entity will continue to exist, then you have to understand that everything that entity brings with it, the good and the bad, will come with it. Even if the merged company has a new name, the new entity does not escape liability if liability previously existed in the prior entity.

The fourth situation involving successor liability is likely the most legally and factually complex of the four situations. In situations where there was a prior debt or other liability that existed in a given entity, if the owners of that entity leave and start a new entity doing the same or similar business, then the law provides a way for the creditors of the prior entity to go after the new entity as a "successor" to the previous entity.

The takeaway for fraudulent conveyance and successor liability situations is (1) to properly protect yourself and understand the ramifications of the contracts into which you enter; (2) if a legitimate debt is incurred, then properly address the debt and do not try to simply avoid the liability by shifting or transferring assets; and (3) recognize that where legitimate debt or liability has been incurred, trying to start a new business, either through a new establishment, merger, or consolidation, where the business is doing the same thing may not protect you from previously incurred liability.

CHAPTER 29
BANKRUPTCY
PERSONAL

TED CUNDICK[1]

Claims Against the Company

A conscientious business owner should be informed about the consequences of an inability or failure to repay creditors. Most businesses will struggle at one time or another to stay current on their payments to creditors or deal with other cash flow issues. Knowing one's rights and responsibilities in this situation can minimize the stress of an undoubtedly stressful situation.

Some creditors are in a better legal position to ensure they are repaid than other creditors. Creditors who have obtained a security interest in the assets of the company (or in the assets of the company's owners) have legal rights in those assets. The most common kind of security interest is a purchase money lien. A company, needing funding to purchase the equipment that it will use to manufacture its product, goes to a bank and obtains a loan. The bank wisely insists that before it will make the loan, the business must provide some collateral, usually including the very equipment that will be purchased with the loan proceeds. The bank requires the borrower to sign both a note (the document that reflects the business's obligation to repay money) and a security agreement (the document that gives the bank rights with respect to the collateral). If the business owns real property, the bank will often take a security interest in the real property as well (in the form of a deed of trust or mortgage on the property). Having obtained a security interest, the bank is in a better position to ensure that the business repays the loan.

---

[1]Ted Cundick is a shareholder at Prince, Yeates & Geldzahler, and an adjunct professor at the J. Reuben Clark Law School at Brigham Young University, teaching debtors' & creditors' rights and business reorganizations. He graduated with high honors in 2003 from the Marshall-Wythe Law School at the College of William and Mary, and clerked for the Honorable Bill Parker of the United States Bankruptcy Court for the Eastern District of Texas.

Security agreements, collateral pledges, deeds of trust, and mortgages are all forms of consensual liens—that is, they reflect security interests created with the consent of the borrower. Creditors can also obtain security interests without the borrower's consent, if a statute provides a mechanism for doing so. Liens arising by statute are generally known as statutory liens. In Utah, a judgment recorded in the real property records of a county creates a judgment lien on the real property located in the county and owned by the judgment debtor. U.C.A. § 38-5-1. Utah statutes also allow for contractors to obtain statutory construction and preconstruction liens. U.C.A. § 38-1a-101 et seq. Federal tax liens often arise under statute, particularly for the non-payment of trust fund taxes like payroll taxes. More obscure statutory liens also exist, for repairmen, storage companies, providers of livestock feed, shipping companies, and attorneys (who can obtain a statutory lien on the recovery in a lawsuit). *See generally* U.C.A. § 38-2 et seq. Courts can also impose equitable liens, which require a showing of "a debt or duty owed by one party to another and a *res* to which the obligation may be fastened." *Telluride Global Dev., LLC v. Bullock (In re Telluride Global Dev., LLC)*, 380 B.R. 585, 595–96 (B.A.P. 10th Cir. 2007).

No discussion of security interests would be complete without some mention of the Uniform Commercial Code. Virtually every state has enacted some form of this model law, including Article 9a, dealing with secured transactions, which Utah has enacted at U.C.A. § 70A-9a. The statutes found in this chapter of the Utah Code explain in detail the things creditors must do to create, perfect (that is, make enforceable against others), and enforce security interests. Basically, once a security interest is created, it is enforceable as between the creditor and debtor (the security interest is at that point said to have "attached" to the collateral). U.C.A. § 70A-9a-203. But in order to make the security interest enforceable against all the world, a creditor must give notice of his security interest in the proper place and proper way (a creditor must "perfect" his security interest). U.C.A. § 70A-9a-301. Failure to follow the most minute details of the Uniform Commercial Code can render a security interest invalid against third parties without notice. *See Rushton v. Standard Indus. (In re C. W. Mining Co.)*, 2009 Bankr. LEXIS 2372, *44 (Bankr. D. Utah 2009) (avoiding a security interest where financing statements listed the debtor as "CW Mining Company" instead of its registered organizational name, "C.W. Mining Company"). The Debtor's registered organization name is "C. W. Mining Company" (periods after the letters and spaces between). The Financing Statements each list the Debtor's name as "CW Mining Company" (no periods included). The Financing Statements failed to properly list the Debtor's registered organization name. Debtors should be aware that once a creditor has attached and perfected his security interest, his security interest extends not only to the collateral pledged, but also to the identifiable proceeds of that collateral. U.C.A. § 70A-9a-315. Also, a security interest generally[2] follows the collateral when it is sold, meaning buyers should take care to ensure that outstanding security interests are extinguished when buying used goods. *Id.*

For example, consider an excavating company, Digger Co., which owns a backhoe. When Digger Co. purchased its backhoe, it borrowed the funds to do so from Big Bank, and gave Big Bank a security interest in the backhoe. Big Bank perfected its security interest. Eventually, Digger Co. decided that it had too many backhoes, and decided to trade the backhoe with Unvigilant Digging, Inc., in exchange for a skid loader. Unvigilant Digging, Inc. delivers the skid loader to Digger Co., and takes possession of the backhoe. Digger Co. stops making payments to Big Bank, and puts the skid loader to work. When Big Bank starts trying to figure out how to collect the balance of its loan, it might pursue Unvigilant Digging, Inc., because its security interest continues in the backhoe. Big Bank might also assert its security interest in the skid loader, which constitutes the proceeds of the backhoe in the hands of Digger Co.

Generally, when a business is struggling to pay its debts, it has already encumbered all its assets with liens. Secured creditors seeking repayment in these circumstances generally proceed first against their collateral, then compete with unsecured creditors in the chase to find unencumbered assets, including unencumbered cash, that could be used to satisfy their claims against the company.

---

[2]The common exception to the general rule involves the sale of inventory in the ordinary course of business. When a consumer buys goods at Kohl's, a security interest in Kohl's inventory does not continue in the goods sold in the ordinary course of business. U.C.A. § 70A-9a-320.

Most creditors, even secured lenders, are far more interested in getting the cash they are owed than recovering their collateral. When a debtor misses a note payment, the creditor will usually begin by begging, pleading, or demanding payment. They may even offer accommodations (like deferral of a few payments) to allow the borrower time to get things in order and resume making regular payments. Only when these efforts fail do they begin to consider more drastic remedies. Eventually, a secured creditor will generally declare the note to be in default, accelerate the balance of the debt (almost all notes include a provision requiring a borrower to immediately repay the full loan balance upon an event of default, like missed payments), and commence collection efforts. Creditors with properly perfected security interests have the right to proceed directly against their collateral—that is, they may take steps to repossess their collateral without judicial involvement, so long as they do not breach the peace. If a secured creditor cannot retake possession of his collateral without breaching the peace, he must seek assistance of a court. A writ of replevin, issued by a court, instructs the sheriff to take possession from the debtor of goods in which the creditor has a special property interest (for example, pledged collateral). Utah R. Civ. P. 64 and 64B.

Unsecured creditors have fewer remedies available to them. Typically, they must first reduce their claims to judgment, by proving up their claims in court. If the amount owed is less than $10,000.00, a creditor may proceed by filing an affidavit in small claims court. If the amount in controversy exceeds $10,000.00, a creditor may proceed in county district court. Ultimately, assuming a debtor has no defenses to a creditor's claims, and the creditor presents sufficient evidence to prove the bona fides of his claim, the court will enter a judgment in favor of the creditor. A judgment liquidates the amount of the debt and memorializes the debt in a way that will allow creditors to seek repayment using judicial processes. A judgment will often not ensure ultimate repayment, however, because most debtors do not have sufficient unencumbered assets to simply satisfy a judgment. Instead, obtaining a judgment usually marks the beginning of collection efforts, which may or may not yield recoveries sufficient to justify the expense of pursuit.

Judgment in hand, a creditor may ask a court to issue various writs to take possession of assets to satisfy the judgment. Utah R. Civ. P. 64.

A writ of attachment allows a judgment creditor to seize property in the possession of the judgment debtor to satisfy the judgment. Utah R. Civ. P. 64C. A writ of execution is available to seize property in the possession or under the control of a debtor, and sell that property to satisfy the judgment. Utah R. Civ. P. 64E. A writ of garnishment is available to seize property owned by or owed to the debtor while the property is in the hands of a third party, in satisfaction of a judgment. Utah R. Civ. P. 64D. In rare circumstances, usually involving a debtor attempting to avoid a creditor's collection efforts, a creditor may succeed in obtaining a writ prior to the entry of a judgment (a "prejudgment writ"). Prejudgment writs are available only upon a showing of a substantial likelihood of success in the underlying claim, among other required proof. Utah R. Civ. P. 64A.

Claims Against the Owners or Managers of the Company

Often, entrepreneurs are asked to personally guarantee company debts. Contractual guarantees are by far the most common way that individuals can be held liable for company debts. In Utah, there are two types of guarantees, guarantees of payment and guarantees of collection. A guarantee of payment requires the guarantor to pay the obligations of the borrower, even if the creditor has not made demand upon the borrower. A guarantee of collection requires only that the guarantor pay the borrower's obligations *after* the lender has made demand upon the entity that is principally liable for the debt. *See Strevell-Patterson Co. v. Francis*, 646 P.2d 741, 743 (Utah 1982). Guarantees are subject to the statute of frauds—that is, they must generally be documented in a signed writing to be enforceable. U.C.A. § 25-5-4(1)(b).

Because guarantees are so ubiquitous in the context of small business commercial lending, discussion of the rules in the absence of personal guarantees is relatively unimportant. However, trade creditors often fail to obtain contractual guarantees, and tort victims have no opportunity to contract for a business owner's personal liability for company debts. Therefore, there are circumstances when the general rules of owner liability for company debts are not overridden by the contractual guarantees so often given by business owners.

Owners of properly-formed businesses are generally not personally liable for claims owed by the company. U.C.A. § 48-3-304. This limited liability is a fundamental advantage of corporate organization as discussed more fully in this book. *See generally Jones & Trevor Mktg. Inc. v. Lowry*, 2012 UT 39 (Utah 2012) ("Ordinarily, a corporation is regarded as a legal entity, separate and apart from its stockholders. The purpose of such separation is to insulate the stockholders from the liabilities of the corporation, thus limiting their liability to only the amount that the stockholders voluntarily put at risk."(internal citations omitted)). The protection afforded to the owners of a properly-formed business is often referred to as the corporate veil. Despite the general protection afforded by the corporate veil, there are theories of liability that can be employed against business owners to seek to hold them personally liable for company debts.

Piercing the corporate veil (or invoking the alter ego doctrine) refers to the action of a court to abandon the protections afforded to most company owners. "If a party can prove its alter ego theory, then that party may 'pierce the corporate veil' and obtain a judgment against the individual shareholders even when the original cause of action arose from a dispute with the corporate entity." *Jones & Trevor Mktg.*, 2012 UT 39 at ¶ 13. As the Utah Court of Appeals has stated:

> To disregard the corporate entity under the equitable alter ego doctrine, two circumstances must be shown: (1) Such a unity of interest and ownership that the separate personalities of the corporation and the individual no longer exist, but the corporation is, instead, the alter ego of one or a few individuals; and (2) if observed, the corporate form would sanction a fraud, promote injustice, or result in an inequality. ... Certain factors which are deemed significant, although not conclusive, in determining whether this test has been met include: (1) undercapitalization of a one-man corporation; (2) failure to observe corporate formalities; (3) nonpayment of dividends; (4) siphoning of corporate funds by the dominant stockholder; (5) nonfunctioning of other officers or directors; (6) absence of corporate records; (7) the use of the corporation as a façade for operations of the dominant stockholder or stockholders; and (8) the use of the corporate entity in promoting injustice

or fraud. ... The rationale used by courts in permitting the corporate veil to be pierced is that if a principal shareholder or owner conducts his private and corporate business on an interchangeable or joint basis as if they were one, he is without standing to complain when an injured party does the same.

Colman v. Colman, 743 P.2d 782, 786 (Utah App. 1987). The list of factors to be considered in *Colman* is not exclusive, and other authorities have noted up to twenty relevant factors that may be considered in determining whether to pierce the corporate veil. *See* 114 Am. Jur. 3d. *Proof of Facts* 403, § 10 (2010). Whatever the factors, the key for individuals seeking to avoid personal liability for their business's debts is to honor the corporate form: organize properly (with the advice of counsel); capitalize the company with adequate working capital; hold corporate board and shareholder meetings; keep minutes at those meetings; pay fair salaries to owners working as management; pay dividends to all shareholders; and honor all distinctions between the corporation and its owners. By doing so, business owners give Courts a reason to honor the corporate veil. Veil piercing is a fairly extreme remedy that courts do not take lightly, *Jones & Trevor Mktg.*, 2012 UT 39 at ¶ 15, but if corporate formalities are ignored in ways that strike courts as unfair, owners are at risk.

Aside from veil piercing, owners, officers and managers of companies should be aware that their personal conduct can lead to personal liability if they participate in tortious conduct of the business. Tortious conduct is conduct involving a breach of a duty owed to an aggrieved individual. Even though "an officer or director of a corporation is not personally liable for torts of the corporation or of its other officers and agents merely by virtue of holding corporate office, [one] can [] incur personal liability by participating in the wrongful conduct. ... [B]oth limited liability members and corporate officers should be treated in a similar manner when they engage in tortious conduct." *d'Elia v. Rice Dev. Inc.*, 2006 UT App 416

> at ¶¶ 38 and 43. Corporate officers or members face personal liability when they participate in a corporation's tortious acts.

Owners, officers and directors may also face personal liability for receiving improper distributions from the company. U.C.A. § 48-3-406. A company may not make distributions to owners if such distributions would render the company unable to pay its debts as they come due, or otherwise render the company insolvent. U.C.A. § 48-3-405. Officers and directors may also be held personally liable for allowing or authorizing improper company distributions. U.C.A. § 48-3-406.

Fraudulent Transfers

Another common way principals of a company can become personally liable to creditors of the company is by receiving a fraudulent transfer. Suppose a small excavating company realizes that it is drowning in debt. The owner-operator of the company doesn't want to lose a particular backhoe, which is owned free and clear of any liens or other encumbrances. Rather than allow creditors to get a judgment against the company and execute on the backhoe, the owner-operator decides to transfer the backhoe to himself personally (or to a family member) so that executing creditors of the company cannot seize the backhoe. The company sells the backhoe, worth $20,000, to the owner-operator for $1,500. Obviously, this transaction is not fair to the business's creditors, who had access to equipment worth $20,000 to satisfy their claims, but now have access to only $1,500 in cash. State law will not allow this inequitable transaction to stand.

Utah, like the vast majority of states, has enacted the Uniform Fraudulent Transfer Act. U.C.A. § 25-6-1. The Uniform Fraudulent Transfer Act gives creditors harmed by a transfer such as the one described in the previous paragraph a cause of action against the person or entity that received the transfer from the business. There are two basic types of fraudulent transfers: actually fraudulent transfers, requiring a showing that the transferor intended to defraud his creditors; and the far-more-common constructively fraudulent transfer, requiring a showing of certain inequitable circumstances justifying recovery, regardless of the transferor's actual intent.

To avoid a transfer that was made with actual intent to hinder, delay, or defraud creditors, a creditor must either prove the intent of the transferor (who is unlikely to admit his intent), or prove that there are sufficient indicia of fraud to convince the court of the transferor's intent. The Uniform Fraudulent Transfer Act provides a non-exclusive list of certain indicia of fraud (often called the "badges of fraud"), including whether:

a. the transfer or obligation was to an insider;
b. the debtor retained possession or control of the property transferred after the transfer;
c. the transfer or obligation was disclosed or concealed;
d. before the transfer was made or obligation was incurred, the debtor had been sued or threatened with suit;
e. the transfer was of substantially all the debtor's assets;
f. the debtor absconded;
g. the debtor removed or concealed assets;
h. the value of the consideration received by the debtor was reasonably equivalent to the value of the asset transferred or the amount of the obligation incurred;
i. the debtor was insolvent or became insolvent shortly after the transfer was made or the obligation was incurred;
j. the transfer occurred shortly before or shortly after a substantial debt was incurred; and
k. the debtor transferred the essential assets of the business to a lienor who transferred the assets to an insider of the debtor.

U.C.A. §25-6-5(2). When a sufficient showing of some or all of these elements is made, a court should determine that the transfer was made with actual intent to defraud creditors, and the transfer may be "avoided," or undone. Alternatively, the court may allow the complaining creditor to seize the transferred asset (or other assets of the transferee) to satisfy the claim against the company. U.C.A. § 25-6-8. Note that it is the fraudulent intent of the transferor, and not the intent of the transferee, that determines whether the creditor may recover. However, if a transferee has taken in good faith and paid reasonably equivalent value, the transfer may not be avoidable. U.C.A. § 25-6-9.

As stated above, it is far more common that a creditor seeking to avoid a fraudulent transfer will present evidence that the transfer was "constructively fraudulent" rather than actually fraudulent. To prove a constructively fraudulent transfer, a plaintiff must prove that the transfer was made in exchange for less than "reasonably equivalent value" and at a time that the debtor was insolvent (or that the debtor became insolvent as a result of the transfer). U.C.A. §§ 25-6-5 and 25-6-6. Much of the litigation in this area centers on what constitutes reasonably equivalent value. In the example above, $1,500 is obviously not reasonably equivalent value for a backhoe worth $20,000, but what if the owner had paid $15,000 for the company's backhoe? $17,500? Judge Clark of the United States Bankruptcy Court for the District of Utah examined this question in *In re Richardson*, 23 B.R. 434 (Bankr. D. Utah 1982). He rejected use of any fixed percentage as a cutoff for reasonably equivalent value, finding that "[i]n some cases, no less than 100 percent of fair market value may be a reasonable price."

A few other points about fraudulent transfers bear mentioning. Note that if a company is not insolvent, and does not become insolvent by transferring away an asset, then the transfer is not avoidable regardless of the value of the asset transferred. So in the excavating example above, if the company is doing well financially and can afford to dispose of a $20,000 backhoe in exchange for only $1,500 (without putting its creditors in jeopardy), it is free to do so. Transfers are more likely to be avoided if made to an insider. Also, the ways to measure insolvency vary depending on whether the creditor seeking to avoid the transfer only became a creditor after the transfer, or was a preexisting creditor at the time of the transfer. The intricacies of this distinction are beyond the scope of this book, but can be understood by examining U.C.A. §§ 25-6-5 and 25-6-6. Finally, the explanations above deal with the transfer of a backhoe, but the transfer of a lien on backhoe for less than reasonably equivalent value would be no different. Indeed, the term transfer is defined broadly to include "every mode, direct or indirect, absolute or conditional, or voluntary or involuntary, of disposing of or partying with an asset or an interest in an asset..." U.C.A. § 25-6-2(12).

CHAPTER 30
BANKRUPTCY
COMMERCIAL

TED CUNDICK[1]

Introduction

Unfortunately, some businesses eventually fail, and others come so close to failing that they need to be restructured in bankruptcy in order to survive. There are several different types of bankruptcy cases, but this book will address only the three most common: chapter 7, chapter 11, and chapter 13. A chapter 7 bankruptcy is often called a liquidation, because the basic premise of the case is that the business or individual filing chapter 7 anticipates the liquidation of essentially all its assets, leaving either an inoperable (and usually defunct) business, or an individual ready to have a fresh start freed from her pre-bankruptcy debts. A chapter 11 bankruptcy is often called a reorganization, because the basic premise of the case is the restructuring of a business's assets and liabilities in order to emerge from bankruptcy leaner, meaner, and better equipped to handle the company's modified debt burden going forward. Chapter 11 debtors strike a new deal with their pre-bankruptcy creditors, hoping to repay a portion of their old debt over time. Chapter 11 proceedings are also occasionally used to liquidate businesses, particularly where there is some ongoing business to wind down before an eventual liquidation. Finally, a chapter 13 bankruptcy is often called a wage-earner's bankruptcy, because only individuals with regular income are eligible to file chapter 7. 11 U.S.C. § 109(e). Chapter 13 case mechanics are mostly beyond the scope of this book, but some understanding is important for businesses dealing with consumer debtors who file chapter 13. Businesses are not eligible to be chapter 13

[1]Ted Cundick is a shareholder at Prince, Yeates & Geldzahler, and an adjunct professor at the J. Reuben Clark Law School at Brigham Young University, teaching debtors' & creditors' rights and business reorganizations. He graduated with high honors in 2003 from the Marshall-Wythe Law School at the College of William and Mary, and clerked for the Honorable Bill Parker of the United States Bankruptcy Court for the Eastern District of Texas.

debtors, nor are individuals with personal debts exceeding certain limits (currently $1,149,525 in secured debts and $383,175 in unsecured debts as of 2015). 11 U.S.C. § 109(e). Occasionally, an individual will file a chapter 11 petition for eligibility reasons or in order to take advantage of more robust provisions for creditor treatment available in chapter 11.

Bankruptcy is a matter of federal law, and bankruptcy cases are filed in a federal bankruptcy court. U.S. Constitution, Art. I, Section 8, Clause 4 ("The Congress shall have Power to ... establish ... uniform Laws on the subject of Bankruptcies throughout the United States."). Although federal law provides the framework for a bankruptcy case, the bankruptcy code incorporates state law for many substantive questions. The vast majority of bankruptcy cases are commenced with the filing of a voluntary petition by the debtor itself, though there is a procedure for a certain minimum number of creditors to join together to file an involuntary bankruptcy case. 11 U.S.C. § 303. A debtor may oppose an involuntary petition, but it often will instead allow the case to proceed, and convert it to chapter 11 in order to try to rehabilitate the business.

The Bankruptcy Estate

The commencement of a bankruptcy case creates an estate, which is a separate legal entity from the debtor. 11 U.S.C. § 541. At the filing of the petition, all interests of the Debtor in property become assets of the bankruptcy estate. *Id.* In a chapter 7 case, a trustee is appointed to oversee liquidation of the estate's assets; in a chapter 11 case, the management of the debtor, at least initially, remains in control of the estate, and manages the assets for the benefit of creditors. In this role the debtor's management is known as the debtor-in-possession. Management can control (to some extent) the bankruptcy process as debtor-in-possession, but often creditors grow restless and seek appointment of a chapter 11 trustee (or conversion of the case to chapter 7). If management has engaged in unethical behavior, fraud, or gross mismanagement, the appointment of a trustee is highly likely. 11 U.S.C. § 1104. Creditors often successfully assert gross mismanagement; their first piece of evidence is the fact that a bankruptcy filing was necessary.

Creditors evaluating their likely recoveries from a bankruptcy estate should be mindful that individual debtors are allowed certain exemptions under state law (incorporated by federal law, see 11 U.S.C. § 522), which allow an individual debtor to retain some assets from the bankruptcy estate. In Utah, the exemptions are modest: $30,000 (or $60,000 for a couple) in a homestead; $3,000 in a motor vehicle, qualified retirement accounts, unemployment and disability benefits, basic home furnishings, a year's supply of provisions, and de minimus amounts for animals, books, musical instruments, and tools of the trade. U.C.A. § 78B-5-505 and 506.

Automatic Stay

Usually a creditor's first exposure to a bankruptcy case involves the automatic stay. Under any chapter, the filing of a bankruptcy petition generally stays all collection efforts, giving the debtor a breathing spell during which essentially no creditors can improve their position vis à vis one another. The automatic stay arises automatically (surprise!) with the filing of a bankruptcy petition, and stays the commencement or continuation of litigation that could have commenced pre-petition; the enforcement of any prepetition judgment; all acts to take possession of the debtor's property or property of the bankruptcy estate; all acts to create, perfect, or enforce a lien on the Debtor's property; all acts to collect prepetition debts from the debtor; and the setoff of mutual debts owing to the debtor. 11 U.S.C. § 362(a). In other words, any legal thing a creditor could do to improve his position in his collection efforts is automatically stayed for a period lasting anywhere from approximately 90 days to several years, or until a creditor obtains permission (known as "relief from stay") from the bankruptcy court to proceed.

All business owners should have a basic understanding of the consequences of the automatic stay, because acts taken in violation of the automatic stay are void. *Franklin Sav. Ass'n v. Office of Thrift Supervision*, 31 F.3d 1020, 1022 (10th Cir. 1994). This means that if somebody engages in any kind of transaction involving assets of the estate, they are at risk that the transaction may be undone (and they may find themselves on the short end of attempts to be made whole). For instance, a bank agreeing to refinance a mortgage with a bankrupt debtor, by proceeding without considering and seeking relief from the automatic stay, could lose its security interest in the home, and find that it has become an unsecured creditor. *See Hopkins v. Suntrust Mortg., Inc.*, 441 B.R. 656, 667 (Bankr. D. Idaho 2010). Furthermore, individuals injured by a willful violation of the automatic stay are entitled to damages, including punitive damages. 11 U.S.C. § 362(k).

If a creditor desires relief from the automatic stay, he may proceed to ask the bankruptcy court to modify or lift the automatic stay. This relief is most often sought by secured creditors, who have rights in the collateral that has become property of the bankruptcy estate. One way to obtain relief is to show that there is cause for relief from stay. 11 U.S.C. § 362(d)(1). The most common type of cause justifying relief from stay is that a secured creditor's interest in the collateral is not "adequately protected," meaning that the creditor faces a risk that during the pendency of the automatic stay, his collateral may depreciate or become insufficient (perhaps due to the ongoing accrual of interest) to ensure that the creditor can preserve his secured status as it existed on the petition date. Alternatively, a secured creditor can obtain relief from stay by showing that there is no equity in the property that could benefit the estate, and the collateral is not necessary for an effective reorganization. 11 U.S.C. § 362(d)(2).

Oftentimes, creditors who are oversecured by a significant margin cannot obtain relief from stay, and must instead essentially wait for the bankruptcy process to play out. In a complex chapter 11 case, that may take many months, and even years. But the oversecured creditor has few options other than to wait, enjoy the ongoing accrual of interest, and monitor its collateral while the debtor figures out how to restructure and resume payments.

Bankruptcy Schedules, the Meeting of Creditors, and Debtors Examinations

The fresh start obtained by a debtor in bankruptcy is offered in exchange for a debtor's willingness to "open his cloaks" and allow his creditors a full and complete view of his financial condition. This unfettered look at the debtor's finances is accomplished in three ways. First, the debtor is required to file statements and schedules that list his assets, identify his creditors, set forth his budget, and disclose his recent relevant transactions. Fed. R. Bankr. P. 1007. These schedules are typically filed with the bankruptcy petition, but may also be filed within the two weeks following the filing of the petition. Soon thereafter, the case trustee or the United States Trustee will convene a meeting of creditors. 11 U.S.C. § 341. Creditors are welcome to attend this meeting, where the debtor is placed under oath (outside the presence of the bankruptcy judge), and the trustee and creditors are given an opportunity to ask a few questions and learn the basics about the debtor's financial condition. If further investigation is required, a debtor's examination can be used to explore in more depth all issues surrounding the debtor-creditor relationship and the debtor's financial condition. Fed. R. Bankr. P. 2004. Creditors should be mindful of the opportunity to use these three tools to better understand the opportunities for recovery in a particular case. Debtors should be mindful that there are significant consequences for making a false statement in connection with a bankruptcy case. 18 U.S.C. §§ 152 and 157 (noting that bankruptcy fraud carries a penalty of up to five years in federal prison).

The Bankruptcy Discharge

Individuals file bankruptcy in the hopes of discharging at least a portion of their debt. A bankruptcy discharge allows a bankruptcy debtor to extinguish his personal liability on a debt (note that the debt itself is not extinguished, only the debtor's liability on the debt; third parties liable with the debtor continue to be liable for the debt). The rules about how and when a bankruptcy discharge is entered vary greatly between chapter 7, 11, and 13 cases.

In chapter 7 cases, only individual chapter 7 debtors are eligible to obtain a discharge. 11 U.S.C. § 727(a)(1). Businesses that file chapter 7 do not obtain a discharge because the assets are liquidated and the business becomes defunct. The chapter 7 discharge is typically entered about 100 days after the case is filed. Several circumstances can minimize the effect of the bankruptcy discharge, either by excepting certain debts from the discharge, 11 U.S.C. § 523; or by denying a debtor's discharge entirely, 11 U.S.C. § 727. A great deal of the litigation in bankruptcy court is brought to determine whether a particular debt should be excepted from discharge, and whether a debtor has engaged in conduct that precludes entry of a discharge all together.

Congress has determined that certain debts should not be dischargeable in bankruptcy. Principal among these are most tax obligations, most domestic support obligations, debts incurred by fraud, debts arising from willful and malicious injury, debts arising from defalcations while acting in a fiduciary capacity, and student loan debts (except in extreme circumstances). 11 U.S.C. § 523. However, in order to establish that a particular debt is of a kind to be excepted from discharge, there is often a very short fuse (60 days from the first date set for the meeting of creditors) for filing a complaint on such question. Fed. R. Bankr. P. 4007.

Congress has also determined that certain behavior should disqualify a debtor from obtaining a bankruptcy discharge. Grounds for denial of a chapter 7 discharge include: concealing assets with intent to hinder, delay, or defraud creditors; failing to maintain adequate books and records; failing to explain a loss or deficiency of assets; making a false oath or account in connection with a bankruptcy case; failing to wait six to eight years after one's most recent bankruptcy discharge; and refusing to obey any lawful order of the court. Again, the time for objecting to discharge is short, running 60 days from the first date set for the meeting of creditors. Fed. R. Bankr. P. 4004.

In a chapter 11 case, a debtor must propose and confirm a plan of reorganization in order to discharge its prepetition debts. Effectively, the debtor proposes a new contract with its creditors, and if it is able to garner enough support for the new contract, it discharges its old debt in exchange for a promise to perform under the plan (the new contract). There are many requirements for confirmation of a chapter 11 plan, the most important of which are: the "best interests of creditors" test, which requires that the plan deliver to creditors at least as much as they would have received in a chapter 7 liquidation; and the "absolute priority rule," which requires that no interest-holders receive anything of value (including interest in the reorganized debtor or the exclusive opportunity to invest in the reorganized debtor) under the plan unless senior creditors are paid in full. 11 U.S.C. §§ 1123 and 1129. There are many more confirmation requirements that are beyond the scope of this text. If the court confirms the plan, the effect of confirmation is the discharge of the debtor's prepetition obligations. 11 U.S.C. § 1141.

In a chapter 13 case, the quid pro quo of the debtor's discharge includes the commitment to pay all of one's disposable income over a three to five year period to satisfy the prepetition claims of creditors. Because a debtor cannot "earn" his discharge without making plan payments over time, the chapter 13 discharge of debts does not occur until plan payments are complete. Once all payments required under the plan have been made (and a few other requirements met), the debtor receives her discharge.

Claims

When a debtor files his bankruptcy schedules, he includes a list of all the people or entities to whom he owes money. Notice is then sent to these individuals, either instructing them to file a proof of claim by a certain deadline, or informing them that there is no immediate need to file a claim, because it is unlikely that the estate will recover any assets that could be used to satisfy creditor claims. It is very important that creditors desiring to participate in the bankruptcy timely file a proof of claim with the bankruptcy court, because failure to do so may preclude one's opportunity to share in the assets of the estate or in the plan payments proposed by the debtor. (However, one should note that filing a proof of claim may submit one to the jurisdiction of the court where the bankruptcy case is pending.) A form for filing a proof of claim is available in the forms library on the website of the United States Bankruptcy Court for the District of Utah (www.utb.uscourts.gov). When filing the proof of claim, attach all documents that would help the Court determine the bona fides of the claim.

In some cases, major claims are disallowed because some minor requirement (like the deadline to file claims) is overlooked. A significant exception to the requirement to file a proof of claim arises only in chapter 11 cases, where, if the debtor in its schedules admits that the claim owing to a certain entity is not contingent, disputed, or unliquidated, and if the debtor schedules the claim in the appropriate amount, then the scheduled claim can be deemed allowed.

If proper documentation and exhibits are attached to the proof of claim when filed, the claim may be deemed allowed so long as the trustee does not object. Whenever a claim is based on a written document, redacted copies of the document should be attached to the proof of claim to substantiate the loss.

One of the questions the proof of claim form asks is whether the claim asserted is a secured or unsecured claim. In bankruptcy, secured claims are not as broad as the concept outside of bankruptcy. For instance, suppose a bank has a third position trust deed on a piece of real property worth $500,000, but the first and second mortgage holders are owed $600,000. Outside of bankruptcy, the bank still holds a secured claim, and if the homeowner wants to sell the property, she's going to have to get a release from the bank (which the bank may willingly give once they realize the amounts owed to the 1st and 2nd trust deed holders). In bankruptcy, the bank would not be a secured creditor, because the inquiry is not whether a lien is noted on title (it is), but instead whether there is any equity in the collateral that could be used to repay the claims of the particular creditor. 11 U.S.C. § 506(a).

Secured creditors may determine that it is not in their interest to file a proof of claim. Security interests generally pass through bankruptcy unaffected, so a secured creditor may decide to rely on his lien to protect him from the debtor's default. The creditor's recourse against the collateral survives the bankruptcy, while the creditor's recourse against the debtor is discharged. Of course by choosing not to participate, the secured creditor waives any right to share in whatever funds the trustee is able to recover and distribute to creditors. However, in some circumstances a prudent creditor may determine that the likelihood of any repayment from the estate is a benefit insufficient to outweigh the burden of submitting oneself to jurisdiction in a far-flung locale.

Some claims are also entitled to priority over general unsecured claims. 11 U.S.C. § 507. Common priority claims include:

- the administrative expenses of the bankruptcy professionals (11 U.S.C. §507(a)(2));
- the actual and necessary costs of preserving the bankruptcy estate (see 11 U.S.C. § 503(b));
- domestic support obligations (11 U.S.C. § 507(a)(1));
- wages, salaries, and benefits earned within 180 days of the bankruptcy petition (11 U.S.C. § 507(a)(4) & (5));

- recent taxes (11 U.S.C. § 507(a)(8)); and
- damages arising from injury caused by an intoxicated driver (11 U.S.C. § 507(a)(10)).

Priority claims are entitled to payment in full before general unsecured claims receive any distribution from the bankruptcy estate.

Trustee's Powers

One of the Trustee's jobs in a bankruptcy case is to maximize the assets available for distribution to creditors. The Bankruptcy Code gives the Trustee (or debtor-in-possession) authority to recover some assets transferred prepetition, in order to further the goal of equal distribution among similarly situated creditors.

Trustees often seek to recover preferential payments, or "preferences." 11 U.S.C. § 547. A preference is a payment made to or for the benefit of a creditor, made within 90 days (or one year if the creditors is an insider of the debtor) before the bankruptcy filing, while the debtor was insolvent, for or on account of antecedent debt, that enables the creditor to receive more than is otherwise would have received on account of the debt. 11 U.S.C. § 547(b). Creditors who receive preferential payments have several defenses, including contending that the creditor extended new value to the debtor after the transfer, that the transfer was a contemporaneous exchange, that the transfer was made in the ordinary course, or that the payment was too small to meet certain statutory minimums. 11 U.S.C. § 547(c).

The typical example of an avoidable preference involves a business that is owed $20,000 for goods sold some time ago. The creditor begs and pleads for payment, and finally the struggling debtor makes an $8,000 payment 30 days before filing bankruptcy. The trustee then sues the creditor to recover the preferential payment. Because the debtor was insolvent when the payment was made, the payment was made on account of antecedent debt, within 90 day before the bankruptcy, and enables the creditor to recovery more than he would have otherwise gotten in a chapter 7 bankruptcy, the payment constitutes a preference. The creditor business tries to raise defenses, but none are availing, because this was old debt, the payment was beyond the ordinary course of business, and there was no new credit extended post-payment. The business must return the $8,000 to the Trustee, who then uses the money to pay claims. This often strikes the creditor as remarkably unfair, in light of the fact that even if it had kept the $8,000, it would still be owed an additional $12,000. However, the policy behind the statute is that this creditor, who happened to be able to grab a payment on the eve of bankruptcy, should not be able to jump in front of other creditors who were not so fortunate.

Bankruptcy trustees also make use of additional avoiding powers. Trustees can avoid unperfected liens (security interests not properly recorded in the appropriate state or county offices), 11 U.S.C. § 544, and fraudulent transfers (as addressed in Chapter 30, supra), 11 U.S.C. § 548. All these powers are wielded for the benefit of creditors, allowing the trustee to attempt to maximize the assets available to liquidate and distribute for the benefit of creditors.

Chapter 13 Bankruptcy

While businesses are not eligible to be chapter 13 debtors, a basic understanding of chapter 13 is important for any business that deals with consumers, because such businesses are often creditors in chapter 13 cases. The concept of a chapter 13 case is far different from other chapters. The goal of a chapter 13 debtor is to keep his property and repay his prepetition creditors over time at least the value of what they would have received if the debtor had filed a chapter 7 case. Consumer debtors often choose to file chapter 13 in an effort to save their home from foreclosure, though their efforts are not always successful. A chapter 13 plan sets forth the debtor's ability to make payments over 3-5 years, and the distribution of such payments to various classes of creditors, including secured creditors, priority unsecured creditors, and general unsecured creditors. The chapter 13 trustee's job is much different than that of a chapter 7 trustee; a chapter 13 trustee is mostly a payment administrator and compliance officer, ensuring that a chapter 13 plan complies with the bankruptcy code (and objecting when it doesn't), and that all payments are made and distributed as required under the plan (and asking the court to dismiss the case when they aren't).

Changes to the bankruptcy code made in 2004 force some families out of chapter 7, leaving chapter 13 as their only viable alternative to obtain a discharge. If a debtor's debts are primarily consumer debts, he will be ineligible to file chapter 7 if he earns more than the median income for a similarly-sized family in his state, 11 U.S.C. § 727(b), and has disposable income sufficient to repay a statutorily-set percentage or amount of the claims against him. This test has come to be known as the "means test."

The process for confirming a chapter 13 plan involves proposing a plan that promises to pay all of one's projected net disposable income over time to the trustee. Projected disposable income is determined by filling out forms similar to tax forms, with allowance for certain reasonable expenses. Unlike in a chapter 11 case, creditors do not vote on whether to accept or reject the chapter 13 plan; instead, the court determines whether the plan complies with the requirements of the bankruptcy code. The debtor commences making payments to the trustee within 30 days of the case filing, and continues making monthly payments while the details of the plan are negotiated. If the debtor succeeds in making all payments required under the plan, the debtor receives a discharge upon plan completion. Most debtors fail to make it through their plans, because having committed all their disposable income to the plan, they are ill-equipped to deal with unforeseen circumstances and job loss. While they could petition the court to modify the plan to deal with such circumstances, often the urgency that necessitated the filing is attenuated, and debtors fail to follow through with their plan payments. A completed chapter 13 plan is somewhat rare.

CHAPTER 31
INTELLECTUAL PROPERTY
COPYRIGHTS

JEFF HOLMAN[1]

INTELLECTUAL PROPERTY OVERVIEW

Copyright is a protective right given to authors of creative original works to protect against most forms of unauthorized copying, distribution, and derivation. Generally, copyrights are one type of protection for intellectual property. Intellectual property generally refers to intangible assets that someone claims ownership in by virtue of creating those assets. Additionally, intangible assets may be transferred from the original creator to another person or entity.

Intellectual property rights typically cover four general areas:

1. **PATENTS**
   a. Patents cover inventions of new things.
   b. In the United States there are three types of patents: utility, design, and plant.
   c. Patents are issued only after a thorough examination process administered exclusively by the federal government.
2. **TRADEMARKS**
   a. Trademarks cover words, graphics, logos, and even sounds and colors that are used as branding for specific products or services.

[1]Jeff Holman is a shareholder at Parsons Behle & Latimer. Mr. Holman combines business experience with legal expertise to guide innovators through the innovation process. This strategic framework helps creators, inventors, investors, and organizations Innovate with Confidence®.

b. Trademarks can be federally registered after an examination process with the federal government.

c. Trademarks can also be registered with state governments.

3. COPYRIGHTS

a. Copyrights cover works of authorship recorded in a tangible medium.

b. Copyrights are registered with the federal government, but do not go through an examination process.

4. TRADE SECRETS

a. Trade secrets cover any form of secret information that derives independent economic value for the secret owner.

b. Trade secrets are not examined or registered by government bodies, but are kept confidential.

Independent Copyright Systems

Copyright systems are administered by governments and international organizations to allow inventors to receive exclusive protection for their works of authorship. Different countries and international organizations have their own laws, rules, and procedures to apply for or enforce copyright protection.

In addition to forming their own copyright systems, many countries also participate in international treaties or agreements that specify procedures for protecting the rights of foreign works from other countries. The protection of foreign works often depends on "points of attachment" which show a connection between an eligible work to be protected and member countries participating in a particular treaty. For example, an author's nationality can provide a point of attachment. Similarly, the location where the work is first published can provide a point of attachment. However, some countries offer little or no copyright protection to foreign works. A list of countries and applicable relations maintained by the US with those countries can be reviewed in Circular 38A, *International Copyright Relations of the United States*, available online from the US Copyright Office.

The copyright laws and regulations established and administered by different governing bodies can change over time. Copyright laws, rules, and procedures can change as new laws are passed, new regulations are adopted, or new interpretations are established through the courts. This chapter will focus primarily on the copyright system currently established in the United States, with some additional discussion of the international patent application system.

Original Works of Authorship

The fundamental premise of the U.S. copyright system is to offer authors a mechanism to protect their "original works of authorship" from unauthorized copying and use. Under constitutional and statutory authority, the U.S. government agrees to give certain rights to authors in a number of different artistic categories, including:

- Literary works
- Musical works, including any accompanying words
- Dramatic works, including any accompanying music
- Pantomimes and choreographic works
- Pictorial, graphic, and sculptural works
- Motion pictures and other audiovisual woks
- Sound recordings
- Architectural works

These categories can be interpreted very broadly, for example, to cover computer programs as "literary works" or architectural plans as "pictorial, graphic, and sculptural works." Also, the original works of authorship must be fixed in a tangible form of expression. For example, a performance of a dramatic work must be recorded, lyrics of a musical work must be written or recorded, and sculptural works must be sculpted. The intangible concept of an artistic work by itself cannot be protected under copyright laws.

Ineligible Works

Some categories of material are not eligible for federal copyright protection. Some examples of ineligible works include:

- Works that are not fixed in a tangible form of expression
- Titles, names, short phrases, and slogans
- Familiar symbols or designs
- Mere variations of typographic ornamentation, lettering, or coloring
- Mere listings of ingredients or contents
- Ideas, procedures, methods, systems, processes, concepts, principles, discoveries, or devices
- Works consisting entirely of information that is public property or information

Protection for the Author

Copyright protection rests with the author who creates the work. This protection begins when the author places the work in a fixed or tangible form. Only the author or those deriving their rights through the author can rightfully claim copyright.

Copyright protection can be subdivided into several independent exclusive rights. These exclusive rights include reproduction, distribution, preparation of derivative works, public display, and public performance.

Publication of the work by the author is not required for copyright protection. But if a work is published, copyright protection may require the author to have certain ties to the United States (e.g., be a citizen or resident), require the publication to occur in the United States or a foreign country participating in a treaty or agreement, or require the publication to be by the United Nations or another authorized international organization. For unpublished works, copyright protection is available regardless of the nationality or domicile of the author.

Co-Ownership for Co-Authors

For works created jointly, the co-authors are co-owners of the copyright in the work. For collective works, or collections of individual works that are combined into a single form, the authors of the individual works hold the copyright to their own work, while a separate copyright for the overall arrangement of works (the collective work) is held by the author of the overall arrangement.

Works Made for Hire

In the case of works made for hire by an employee, the employer is considered to be the author. A "work made for hire" is specifically defined in copyright law as:

1. a work prepared by an employee within the scope of his or her employment; or
2. a work specially ordered or commissioned for use as:
   - a contribution to a collective work,
   - a part of a motion picture or other audiovisual work,
   - a translation,
   - a supplementary work,
   - a compilation,
   - an instructional text,
   - a test,
   - answer material for a test, or
   - an atlas,

if the parties expressly agree in a written instrument signed by them that the work shall be considered a work made for hire.

Term of Copyright Protection

The term of protection available for copyright depends on when the work was originally created and whether the work was published.

For works originally created on or after January 1, 1978, the term of protection runs for the life of the author plus an additional 70 years after the author's death. For co-authored works, the term is measured by the last surviving author plus 70 years. For works made for hire, the term is 95 years from publication or 120 years from creation, whichever is shorter. Anonymous and pseudonymous works have the same term as works made for hire.

For works originally created before January 1, 1978, the term depends on the publication status of the work. If unpublished by January 1, 1978, the term is the same as for works originally created on or after that date (see above), with some additional minimum terms depending on whether the work was later published after that date but before December 31, 2002. If published or registered before January 1, 1978, the term varies depending on automatic renewal periods, but currently grants up to 95 years of protection.

Congress holds the power to alter the term of copyright protection available under federal statute, and has changed the term multiple times over the years. Many speculate that changes in the statutory copyright term are driven by the pending expiration of rights held by prominent entertainment industry conglomerates.

For more information on the duration of copyright, see Circular 15A, *Duration of Copyright* published by the US Copyright Office.

Fair Use

Although federal statutes grant exclusive rights to copyright owners, there is also a federal statute that allows "fair use" of a copyrighted work without permission from the author or owner. The statute generally states that uses of a copyrighted work for purposes such as criticism, comment, news reporting, teaching (including multiple copies for classroom use), scholarship, or research are not considered infringement of the copyrighted work. For specific cases, the statute establishes a set of factors that might be considered by the courts. These factors include:

1. the purpose and character of the use, including whether such use is of a commercial nature or is for nonprofit educational purposes;
2. the nature of the copyrighted work;
3. the amount and substantiality of the portion used in relation to the copyrighted work as a whole; and
4. the effect of the use upon the potential market for or value of the copyrighted work.

The following explanations describe examples of each of the above factors that tend to favor a finding of fair use (instead of infringement):

1. noncommercial, nonprofit, and transformative uses;
2. the original work is published and less creative (or more factual);
3. use of smaller portions, unless it's the 'heart' of the original work; and
4. limited commercial harm to the market of the original work.

The US Copyright Office is prohibited from offering legal advice about specific fair use situations, but has compiled a list of cases that discuss fair use situations in different jurisdictions. That list can be browsed or searched at http://copyright.gov/fair-use/fair-index.html.

Copyright vs. Possession of a Work

The ownership of a copyright is distinct from the ownership of the work itself. Mere ownership of a book, manuscript, painting, software program, digital music file, electronic recording, or other copy of a work does not give the owner of the work the copyright to the work. This allows an author to transfer the ownership rights of the work to another person to possess the actual work, without transferring the copyright to the new possessor.

Transfer of Copyright

A copyright is a personal property right. While its existence derives from federal statutes, the ownership of a copyright is subject to state laws and regulations that govern person property rights. In general, a copyright can be transferred between people or other legal entities through sale, gift, inheritance, or other typical forms of ownership transfer.

A copyright owner may transfer some or all of his or her copyright. To transfer rights on an exclusive basis, the transfer must be in writing and signed by the owner of the rights conveyed (or an authorized agent) in order to be valid. No written agreement is required to transfer rights on a non-exclusive basis. In instances where written contracts are used, the transfer of copyright ownership can be recorded with the US

Copyright Office. As with other recordations, recording a copyright transfer provides legal notice of the new ownership to third parties who might express an interest in the copyright.

Under certain circumstances, it is possible to terminate a grant of rights after 35 years. For older copyrights, other termination rights or timeframes might apply.

Copyright Registration

An author or owner of copyright has a certain level of protection available without obtaining federal copyright registration. However, federal copyright registration is a relatively simple legal formality that is accompanied by several advantages. These advantages include:

- establishing a public record of the copyright claim
- accessing federal courts to bring an infringement suit
- establishing prima facie evidence in court of the validity of the copyright and facts stated in the certificate (if filed within five years of publication of the original work)
- making it possible to assess statutory damages and attorney's fees (if filed within three months of publication or prior to an infringement of the work)
- reserving the right to record the registration with the U.S. Customs Service for protection against the importation of infringing copies

Registration Procedures

Compared with patents and trademarks, the copyright registration process is very simple. U.S. copyright registration requires submission of an application form, a filing fee, and a copy of the work to be deposited with the Copyright Office. The fee is nonrefundable, and the deposit is nonreturnable. Also, the type and form of deposit will depend on the type of work for which registration is requested.

The application may be submitted by the author, a person or organization with ownership of all the rights under the copyright, or the owner of an exclusive right (one of many subdivided and transferrable rights of the overall rights). Additionally, a duly authorized agent of the preceding people or entities can act on behalf of the person or entity.

The application can be filed in either paper or electronic form. Several advantages are given to the electronic form, including a lower filing fee, faster processing time, email confirmation of the submitted application, online payment, online status tracking, and electronic submission of certain types of deposits. However, some specific types of applications must be filed in paper form.

After the application is filed, the author will receive a certificate of registration if the work can be registered. The effective date of registration is assigned as the date on which the Copyright Office received all of the required submissions—the application, fee, and deposit. Otherwise, if the work cannot be registered, the Copyright Office will send a rejection letter or contact the author via letter, telephone call, or email to request further information.

Preregistration

For certain categories of works that historically are subject to prerelease infringement, it is also possible to preregister a work. Preregistration is not a substitute for registration, but allows an infringement action to be brought before the authorized commercial distribution of a work and full registration of the work. In other words, preregistration makes it possible to enter the federal courts before actual registration is completed. This makes it possible once the full registration is complete to receive statutory damages and attorneys' fees in a related infringement action. In order to qualify for preregistration, the work must be unpublished, in the process of being prepared for commercial distribution, and a type of work with a history of infringement prior to authorized commercial distribution (e.g., motion pictures, sound recordings, literary works, computer programs, etc.).

Copyright Enforcement

Copyright law creates a federal cause of action for copyright infringement, or the unauthorized copying of an original work of authorship. There are some basic requirements to consider before taking action against a potential infringer.

The infringement action must be brought in federal court by a party who has standing. In order to have standing the party must be the legal owner or exclusive licensee of at least one exclusive right of a copyright. Authors typically have standing to sue an infringer, unless the author has transferred his or her right to another person or entity. Once an author transfers the exclusive rights, the new owner has the right to sue for infringement based on the exclusive rights the new owner holds. When there are co-authors, it is possible under certain circumstances for either co-author to sue for infringement without obtaining permission from the other co-author.

The infringement action must be based on a valid and registered copyright. Although registration is not required to obtain copyright protection generally, registration is a prerequisite for filing an infringement suit in federal court.

Also, the infringer must be notified of the infringing use. The use of the symbol '©' or other copyright information on a copy of the work can serve as the required notice. Otherwise, the owner may notify the infringer in another manner.

The infringing action requires proof of copying of the original work and infringement of an exclusive right, such as reproduction, distribution, preparation of derivative works, public display, or public performance. Copying can be shown by evidence of direct copying. Alternatively, copying can be shown through circumstantial evidence showing the infringer had access to the original work and the infringing work is substantially similar to the original work.

Defenses to Infringement

If liability is found, the strict liability nature of copyright infringement does not give consideration to whether or not the copying was unintentional or inadvertent. However, there are a number of other possible defenses that can be relied on to justify the otherwise infringing action. These defenses include expiration of the statute of limitations (typically three years), fair use, first sale, grant of a license, DMCA safe harbors, and more. The first sale defense refers to an owner's right to use his or her own copy of a work, including reselling it or gifting it to another person, without infringing the rights of the copyright owner.

The DMCA safe harbor defense relates to claims against online copyright infringement and establishes specific procedures for providing notice and requesting that an internet service provider take down an infringing use.

Additional Resources

In addition to the information provided in this chapter, the US Copyright Office maintains several useful factsheets and circulars that discuss basic copyright procedures as well as more specific copyright situations. For example, these resources discuss such issues as copyright registration of specific types of works, compulsory licenses, and obtaining permission to use a copyright. The factsheets and circulars can be viewed at http://copyright.gov/circs/.

CHAPTER 32

INTELLECTUAL PROPERTY

TRADEMARKS

CODY WINCHESTER[1]

A. What Are Trademarks?

A trademark is a word, name, symbol, or device that indicates the source of a product.[2] Trademarks provide an answer to the question, "Who makes this?" Perhaps the easiest way to appreciate the importance of trademarks is to imagine a world without them. Imagine purchasing running shoes in a shop where the shoes have no labels or packaging. In the past, I have been pleased with the quality and design of Nike shoes. Not seeing the word NIKE or the SWOOSH design, I must carefully inspect the shoes I want to buy and personally assess the design and quality of the shoes without relying on my past experiences with shoes made by Nike and other manufacturers. Obviously, making a purchasing decision in that world is going to take a lot longer and be much riskier than making a purchasing decision in our world. Trademarks are important because they promote efficient consumer decision making, and the trademark laws are designed to protect the "source-identifying" function of trademarks.

Trademarks commonly consist of words (GOOGLE, COCA-COLA, XEROX), known as word marks, or designs (Mercedes-Benz's TRI-STAR, McDonald's GOLDEN ARCHES), known as design marks

[1]Cody Z. Winchester, of Phillips Ryther & Winchester, is a graduate of Yale Law School and counsels clients with trademarks that rank among the top 100 global brands as identified by Interbrand/Business Week's annual survey on a daily basis. Daniel P. Lyman, 2016 J.D. candidate, Brigham Young University, J. Reuben Clark Law School, provided research assistance.

[2]"Service mark" refers to a trademark applied to services rather than to tangible products or goods. The legal protections available for trademarks and service marks are very similar. For simplicity, this chapter refers only to trademarks.

or logos. Design marks often incorporate or consist of words or letters in stylized script (COCA-COLA displayed in cursive, Spenserian script; FORD displayed in cursive script, inside a blue oval). The source of goods may also be indicated by distinctive packaging (Coca-Cola's contour bottle),[3] product design (Volkswagen's New Beetle auto), service uniform (Playboy's Bunny uniform), color (brown used for shipping by UPS or robin's egg blue used for bags and boxes by Tiffany & Co.), and even, although very rarely, sound (NBC's chimes).

B. Selecting a Trademark.

In the U.S., trademark rights are initially established through use, with federal registration providing certain advantages.[4] So-called "common law" trademark rights are acquired automatically upon use of a trademark in commerce. The first one to use a trademark has the right to prevent subsequent use of the same or confusingly similar trademark in the geographic areas where the trademark has been used in connection with the same types of goods or services. A catchy or memorable trademark is obviously important for marketing and advertising. Equally important is avoiding the burden and expense of starting over with a new trademark after discovering the trademark you originally adopted is already being used by someone else.

The trademark laws are designed to ensure that words are not removed from the English language when they are selected as trademarks. For instance, you may not adopt the mark NEW CARS FOR SALE and then prevent all other auto dealers from using your mark. Regardless of their use as trademarks, words remain available for use by all to convey their primary, or dictionary, meanings. In practice, this means that the less obvious the connection between the mark and the goods the mark is used to sell, the greater the scope of protection the mark will be

---

[3]A product's image or packaging is known as its "trade dress." *See, e.g., Int'l Jensen, Inc. v. Metrosound U.S.A., Inc.*, 4 F.3d 819, 822 (9th Cir. 1993). When trade dress is distinctive, non-functional, and serves to indicate the source of goods, trade dress functions as a trademark and is entitled to the same protections. *See, e.g., Two Pesos, Inc. v. Taco Cabana, Inc.*, 505 U.S. 763, 765 n.1 (1992).

[4]Although not required, registration confers important advantages, discussed in more detail in Section D, including providing constructive notice of use to the public, a legal presumption that the registrant owns and is entitled to use the trademark, a basis for seeking registrations in foreign countries, and increased availability of remedies related to imported infringing goods.

afforded from use by others of the same mark or a similar mark. For this purpose, marks are divided into five categories, ranging from strongest to weakest. The stronger the mark, the greater the scope of protection. The strongest marks are those invented for the sole purpose of functioning as trademarks. Examples of such "fanciful" marks include ZYNGA, KINKOS, CLOROX, KODAK, and EXXON. Fanciful marks are not English words. Next are "arbitrary" marks. These marks may be English words, but, as the term "arbitrary" suggests, have no connection to the goods they are being used to sell—APPLE for computers and ARM & HAMMER for baking soda. "Suggestive" marks *suggest* a quality or feature while requiring the consumer to use imagination and perception to identify the goods—7 ELEVEN (suggestive of convenient hours) for convenience stores or MUSCLE MILK (suggestive of muscle-building nourishment) for protein shakes. "Descriptive" marks describe goods or their functions and are afforded narrower protection—HOLIDAY INN and BED BATH & BEYOND.[5]

Marks categorized as "descriptive" will not be protected unless they are proven to have "secondary meaning" distinct from the mark's primary or dictionary meaning. The concept of secondary meaning recognizes that words with a primary or dictionary meaning "may by long use with a particular product, come to be known by the public as specifically designating that product."[6] Once the trademark owner can demonstrate public awareness of a descriptive trademark, the trademark will be considered distinctive and can be registered with the United States Patent and Trademark Office (USPTO). Although entitled to broader protection, an arbitrary mark may be undesirable because of the advertising that will be necessary before the public equates the mark with your goods. While weak marks will be entitled to less protection at the outset, many weak marks achieve secondary meaning—CHAP STICK, VISION CENTER, WHOLE FOODS, and 1-800-CONTACTS.

---

[5]The line between suggestive and descriptive marks is hazy. "Whether consumers could guess what the product is from consideration of the mark alone is not the test." *In re Am. Greetings Corp.*, 226 U.S.P.Q. 365 (T.T.A.B. 1985).

[6]*Volkswagenwerk AG v. Rickard,* 492 F.2d 474, 477 (5th Cir. 1974); *see also Filipino Yellow Pages, Inc. v. Asian Journal Publ'ns, Inc.*, 198 F.3d 1143, 1151 (9th Cir. 1999) ("Secondary meaning can be established in many ways, including (but not limited to) direct consumer testimony; survey evidence; exclusivity, manner, and length of use of a mark; amount and manner of advertising; amount of sales and number of customers; established place in the market; and proof of intentional

A generic mark refers to the common, dictionary name for the class of goods the mark is used to describe and is not entitled to any trademark protection—NEW CARS used to sell new cars or SUSHI used to sell the Japanese food consisting of bite-sized pieces of rice served with fish or vegetables. If, however, SUSHI was used as a brand to identify goods such as apparel or computer software, the mark would not be generic. In that case, SUSHI would not be used to denominate the class of food known as sushi, but would instead be used to distinguish SUSHI brand apparel or computer software from other brands of apparel or computer software.

C. Avoiding Liability for Trademark Infringement.

Having selected a mark for your product, you must next investigate whether your use of the mark infringes the rights of any prior user. Trademark infringement occurs when use of a mark is likely to cause consumers to be confused about who makes the product bearing the mark.[7] When simultaneous use of similar marks is likely to cause consumer confusion regarding who makes a product bearing the mark, the first one to use the trademark may require the "junior" user to "cease and desist" use of the mark. A use is also infringing if consumers are likely to be confused as to whether the junior user is licensed or endorsed by the senior user.[8]

The trademark laws aim to protect consumers. If use of similar marks by different merchants renders consumers unable to quickly and accurately identify the goods each merchant puts out, market efficiency will suffer. When I seek to buy Nike running shoes because I have known Nike to supply high-quality products and accidentally buy lesser-quality shoes from another merchant because the shoes bear a SWOOSH design that is similar to Nike's, my expectations will be frustrated. At the same time, Nike will not reap the benefit of its high standards and the production of high-quality running shoes will suffer.

---

[7]Infringement of registered, federal trademarks is governed by the Lanham Act. *See* 15 U.S.C. 1117. The Lanham Act's unfair competition provision, 15 U.S.C. 1125, provides protection to unregistered trademarks.

[8]*Id.*

A trademark does not have to be identical to be infringing. Even if you do not believe your company is infringing another's trademark, you may still be held liable for infringement by a court. Subjective good faith is not a defense. The test for trademark infringement is whether simultaneous use of the marks is likely to cause consumer confusion regarding the source of the two parties' products. Whether a use is likely to cause confusion depends on factors such as the strength of the senior trademark, the similarity between the marks at issue, whether there is overlap in the geographic areas in which the parties' goods are sold, and the similarity between the parties' goods.[9] When the goods of two merchants are different and the senior merchant has no intention of expanding into the junior merchant's field of use, identical marks may be used without the risk of consumer confusion. DELTA is used for faucets and for airlines without causing consumer confusion.[10]

Determining whether someone else is using the mark you have selected is an inexact science. The USPTO maintains a searchable database containing the records of active and inactive trademark registrations and applications, known as the Trademark Electronic Search System or TESS, located at *uspto.gov.* Although searching TESS is a critical first step, TESS does not include trademarks registered under state law. Each state maintains a database of trademarks registered in the state. As registration is not required to establish rights in a trademark, checking these databases will not eliminate the possibility that someone else is already using the mark. Search the Internet, trade publications, and newspapers. Attorneys and trademark search firms perform professional trademark searches. If you discover an existing use of the same or similar mark and do not want to select a different mark, you should consult a trademark lawyer to assess the risk.

---

[9]The factors included in the test vary by judicial circuit. *See, e.g., 1-800 Contacts, Inc. v. Lens.com, Inc.*, 722 F.3d 1229, 1239 (10th Cir. 2013) (identifying six factors); *Tana v. Dantanna's*, 611 F.3d 767, 774–75 (11th Cir. 2010) (identifying seven factors); *Brookfield Commc'ns, Inc. v. West Coast Entm't Corp.*, 174 F.3d 1036, 1053–54 (9th Cir. 1999) (recognizing additional factors of likelihood of expansion of product lines and degree of care expected to be exercised by consumers).

[10]The Federal Trademark Dilution Act, 15 U.S.C. § 1125(c), protects famous trademarks from dilution regardless of whether the parties' goods are competing or whether consumers would view the parties' goods as coming from the same source. Dilution refers to weakening in the power of a famous mark to identify goods. Even if, for example, a consumer would not assume that COCA COLA laundry soap was made by The Coca-Cola Company, the power of COCA COLA as a distinguishing brand would be destroyed if the trademark laws allowed use of The Coca-Cola Company's trademark on goods and services manufactured by others.

D. Benefits of Federal Registration.

Federal registration has important advantages. Perhaps most importantly, federal registration serves as *prima facie* evidence of the registrant's exclusive right to use the registered mark in commerce.[11] The registrant is deemed to have nationwide priority of use, without regard to the geographic areas in which the mark has actually been used.[12] A business selling goods in Colorado and Utah that obtains a federal registration will have priority over a business that later uses the same mark in Georgia, even though the senior user has never used the trademark there. Moreover, experienced investors will insist on protections for the intellectual property assets of any business before providing funding.

E. Requirements for Federal Registration.

To be eligible for federal registration, you must have used your mark in interstate commerce. Generally, this means that you have sold goods or provided services to a buyer in another state, U.S. territory, or country. Although no particular magnitude of sales is required, sales that are staged simply for the purpose of satisfying this requirement will not be sufficient. You should document and preserve evidence both of the date you first used your mark and the date you first used your mark in interstate commerce. If you have not yet used your mark in interstate commerce but have a *bona fide* intent to do so, you may seek registration on an "intent-to-use" (ITU) basis. A bona fide intent to use the mark is more than an idea and less than market ready. For example, having a business plan, creating sample products, or performing other initial business activities may reflect a *bona fide* intent to use the mark. In that case, as discussed below, you will be permitted to submit proof of use (together with an additional fee) up to 24 months later. If you will not

[11] 15 U.S.C. §1115(a). Even when the plaintiff has a federally registered trademark, a defendant may have rights to use the mark in the areas in which it had established trademark rights prior to the plaintiff's application for registration. 15 U.S.C. §1115(b)(5); *see also Safeway Stores, Inc. v. Safeway Quality Foods, Inc.*, 433 F.2d 99, 104 (7th Cir. 1970) (holding defendant's use of mark prior to plaintiff's federal registration constituted defense to trademark infringement claim for geographic areas where "such continuous prior use is proved").

[12] *See supra* note 3. Other advantages include the availability of statutory damages under the Lanham Act and the fact that certain rights become incontestable after five years of use. *Park 'N Fly, Inc. v. Dollar Park and Fly, Inc.*, 469 U.S. 189, 197 (1985); *Gruner + Jahr USA Pub. v. Meredith Corp.*, 991 F.2d 1072, 1077 (2d Cir. 1993); *ITT Corp. v. Xylem Group, LLC*, 963 F. Supp.2d 1309, 1318 (N.D. Ga. 2013).

sell goods or services across state lines, your mark will not be eligible for federal registration and you should consider state registration.[13]

You must also answer "no" to each of the following questions:

- Is the mark the generic name of the product itself?
- Does the mark merely describe the product itself?
- Is the mark the same or similar to an existing mark used on similar or related goods or service?
- Is the mark a prohibited or reserved name?[14]

You may submit an application to the USPTO by mail or online at *uspto.gov.* While applications are frequently submitted by trademark counsel, representation by a lawyer is not required. The filing fee is lowest for an application that is submitted online, a so-called "TEAS PLUS application." You will need the applicant's name, address, phone number, email address, and means of electronic payment. The applicant is the person or entity who will own the registration. If the mark belongs to a corporate entity, that entity should be the applicant. If the mark is a design trademark, you will need an electronic version of the design to upload. If you are filing an ITU application, the drawing must show the mark as you intend to use it.

Second, you will need to identify the industry classes in which the mark is used. A worldwide standard has developed for categorizing goods and services by type within one of 45 classes, ranging from International Classification 001 (Chemicals) to 045 (Personal & Social Services). The classifications are used by the USPTO and the courts in determining whether use of similar marks is likely to cause confusion. As of the time of this writing in 2015, the filing fee is currently $325 per class. Overlap between classes is entirely possible, and you do not have to seek registration in every class in which you are using the mark.[15]

---

[13]State registration may deter a junior user, but, compared to a plaintiff with rights established by common law, typically provides no benefits.

[14]15 U.S.C. §1052(a)-(c) identifies prohibited and reserved names.

[15]An online guide to the classification system is available on the USTPO's website: *http://www.uspto.gov/trademarks/notices/international.jsp.*

Third, for each class selected, you will need to provide a "specimen of use," or real-world example of how the mark is actually used, in a format acceptable to the USPTO, such as .pdf or .jpeg. For marks used in connection with goods, an image or picture of the mark as used on the product or packaging suffices. For marks used in connection with services, an image of a sign, brochure, or business card showing the mark used in connection with the services usually suffices. A specimen of use is not required for an ITU application.

Fourth, for each class selected, you will need to identify the goods or services in connection with which the mark is used. Preparing the description of goods and services is typically the most difficult aspect of preparing the application and must be done correctly the first time. In this regard, "close" is not "good enough." Acceptable descriptions are listed in the U.S. Acceptable Identification of Goods and Services Manual or "ID Manual," available on the USPTO's website at *http://tess2.uspto.gov/netahtml/tidm.html.* If the ID Manual contains a description that accurately reflects your goods and services, use it verbatim. If the ID Manual does not contain a description that accurately reflects your goods and services, you will not be able to file a TEAS PLUS application.[16] You will need to submit a TEAS application and pay a slightly higher filing fee. In that case, you will use the "free form text option" to enter a description that, in your own words, accurately identifies your goods or services.

Fifth, you will need to supply the date of first use anywhere and the date of first use in interstate commerce. The date of first use anywhere is the date on which the goods were first sold or transported or the services were first provided under the mark even if that use was only local. The date of first use in commerce is the date on which the goods were first sold or transported or the services were first provided under the mark between more than one state or U.S. territory, or in commerce between the U.S. and another country. The date of first use anywhere must be the same as or earlier than the date of first use in commerce. If you are filing an ITU application, you must include a sworn declaration stating the owner's intent to use the mark. You will file a Statement of Use

[16]You may ask the USPTO to add your desired description to the ID Manual by sending an email to tmidsuggest@uspto.gov.

when the mark is used in interstate commerce. There is an additional fee (presently $100) to file a Statement of Use.

Unlike copyrights and patents, trademark rights can last indefinitely as long as the owner continues to use the mark to identify its goods. The term of a federal trademark is 10 years, with 10-year renewal terms. However, between the fifth and sixth year after the date of registration, the registrant must file a "Section 8 Declaration of Continued Use," swearing that the mark is still in use. The registration is cancelled if the Section 8 Declaration is not filed, and the USPTO does not remind the trademark owner of this deadline.

Use of the ® design is reserved for federal trademarks registered with the USPTO. The ™ symbol may be used on any mark that you wish to designate as a trademark.

F. International Registration under the Madrid System.

Trademark rights are territorial and you will need to seek protection in each country where your goods are sold. You may obtain foreign protection by filing in each country directly or by filing an international application under the Madrid Protocol. The Madrid Protocol, to which the U.S. is a signatory, is an international trademark filing treaty that enables trademark holders to file a single trademark application and extend it to member countries as desired, at any time.[17] The application is based on a U.S. application or registration filed with the USPTO. The USPTO certifies the application and forwards it to the World Intellectual Property Organization (WIPO). If minimum filing requirements are met, an International Registration is issued by WIPO and the application is forwarded to the national trademark offices in the countries you have designated for examination based on their national requirements. Individual national trademark offices that approve the mark will then grant protection equivalent to a national trademark registration. The costs of applications for international registration vary depending upon the identity and number of countries designated and the number of classes claimed. As many countries require use of the

[17]Current members are listed here: *wipo.int/export/sites/www/treaties/en/documents/pdf/madrid_marks.pdf.*

mark within a limited period of time following registration, a staggered filing program, where registration is first sought in the countries where goods will be introduced or the mark will be licensed, often makes sense. Keep in mind that in many countries, trademark rights are acquired upon filing, not upon use as they are in the U.S. Consider applying for trademark rights in the countries where you plan to sell before an opportunist realizes that your brand is valuable and files an application that predates your own.

CHAPTER 33
INTELLECTUAL PROPERTY
PATENTS

JEFF HOLMAN[1]

Intellectual Property Overview

Patents are evidence of rights given to inventors to protect their inventions. Generally, patents are one type of protection for intellectual property. Intellectual property generally refers to intangible assets that someone claims ownership in by virtue of creating those assets. Additionally, intangible assets may be transferred from the original creator to another person or entity.

Intellectual property rights typically cover four general areas:

1. **PATENTS**
   a. Patents cover inventions of new things.
   b. In the United States there are three types of patents: utility, design, and plant.
   c. Patents are issued only after a thorough examination process administered exclusively by the federal government.
2. **TRADEMARKS**
   a. Trademarks cover words, graphics, logos, and even sounds and colors that are used as branding for specific products or services.
   b. Trademarks can be federally registered after an examination process with the federal government.
   c. Trademarks can also be registered with state governments.

---

[1]Jeff Holman is a shareholder at Parsons Behle & Latimer. Mr. Holman combines business experience with legal expertise to guide innovators through the innovation process. This strategic framework helps creators, inventors, investors, and organizations Innovate with Confidence®.

3. **COPYRIGHTS**
    a. Copyrights cover works of authorship recorded in a tangible medium.
    b. Copyrights are registered with the federal government, but do not go through an examination process.
4. **TRADE SECRETS**
    a. Trade secrets cover any form of secret information that derives independent economic value for the secret owner.
    b. Trade secrets are not examined or registered by government bodies, but are kept confidential.

Independent Patent Systems

Patent systems are administered by governments and international organizations to allow inventors to receive exclusive protection for their new and useful inventions. Different countries and international organizations have their own laws, rules, and procedures to apply for a patent or to use or enforce a granted patent.

In addition to forming their own patent systems, many countries also participate in international treaties or agreements that specify procedures for recognizing patent rights from other countries. These joint programs are typically administered by a separate international organization, which specifies the procedures for complying with a set of common rules that all participating countries have agreed to recognize. This type of international cooperation makes it possible for an inventor from one country to apply for patent rights in many other countries, in addition to their own country.

The patent systems established and administered by different governing bodies can change over time. Patent laws, rules, and procedures can change as new laws are passed, new regulations are adopted, or new interpretations are established through the courts. This chapter will focus primarily on the patent system currently established in the United States, with some additional discussion of the international patent application system.

An Agreement with the Government

The fundamental premise of the U.S. patent system is to offer inventors an incentive for publicly disclosing their new and useful inventions. Under constitutional and statutory authority, the U.S. government agrees to give certain rights to inventors in exchange for disclosure of the inventor's invention.

The rights granted to the inventor are relatively broad, but are limited to a specific term or time period. The inventor agrees that the invention will become publicly available at the end of the patent term. In other words, the inventor agrees to dedicate the invention and the inventor's knowledge specifically disclosed in the patent to the public when the life of the patent ends.

Basic Terminology

PATENT or PATENT APPLICATION—For accuracy, it is critical to distinguish between a "patent" and a "patent application." The term "patent" refers to an issued document that has been granted by the governing body (the U.S. government). This gives the patent owner rights that can be enforced against unauthorized infringers of the patented invention.

In contrast, the term "patent application" refers to the documents that are filed with the government body, but have not yet been issued as a granted patent. Thus, patent applications are in the examination stage, or are waiting to be examined, whereas an issued patent has successfully passed the examination stage.

A patent application gives the applicant "patent pending" status, but is not enforceable against infringers. Only an issued patent can be enforced against infringers.

PROVISIONAL PATENT APPLICATION—A "provisional patent application" is a specific type of patent application that also provides "patent pending" status. Provisional patent applications are discussed in more detail below. In brief, provisional patent applications are never examined, so they can never result in a granted patent. Consequently, there is no such thing as a "provisional patent."

PRIOR ART—Prior art refers to certain categories of publicly available information that can be used to show that an invention is not new and/or useful. The most common forms of prior art referenced during examination include other issued patents and public patent applications. However, there are many other types of prior art such as books, academic papers, company technical documents, website documentation, and so forth. Prior art is also used often in litigation to try to show that a granted patent should not have been granted because the invention was not new and/or useful over the prior art that was already available to the public.

INFRINGEMENT—Patent infringement refers to the unauthorized activities that make use of patent owner's rights granted in an issued patent. The issue of infringement focuses on what rights are held by a patent owner, and whether or not someone else is performing activities that use those rights without permission from the patent owner. In many ways, patent infringement is independent of whether or not an invention is patentable.

A Negative Right

Patents grant a "negative right" to the patent owner, making it possible for the patent owner to exclude others from making, using, selling, offering to sell, or importing copies of the invention or discovery. In this way, a patent owner may stop an infringer from practicing the invention. In contrast, patents do not grant to the patent owner a right to make or use the patented invention, because other existing patent rights may be infringed by making or using an invention or discovery. So it is possible for a patent owner to infringe another patent owner's existing patent rights by making or using his or her own invention.

Patent Laws and Regulations

The U.S. Constitution grants to Congress the power "to promote the progress of science and useful arts, by securing for limited times to authors and inventors the exclusive right to their respective writings and discoveries." This is the constitutional basis used to pass federal laws ("patent laws") that govern how patents are granted and enforced.

The patent laws give the executive branch of the federal government the latitude to adopt additional regulations ("patent rules") that govern specific procedures for examining patent applications and granting patents.

These patent laws and rules are used by the U.S. Patent and Trademark Office (USPTO) to manage the patent process for all inventions seeking U.S. patent protection. Similarly, U.S. courts use the patent laws to settle patent disputes.

Individual states do not have patent systems or authority to grant or govern patents. All patents are governed by the federal laws and regulations. However, contractual agreements tangential to patent rights (transferring ownership or licensing rights) are governed by individual state laws.

As noted above, different countries and international organizations have their own laws, rules, and procedures to apply for a patent and to enforce a granted patent. Attorneys or other patent practitioners in each country can assist inventors and applicants through the specific processes in their respective countries.

Types of Patents

In the U.S. there are three different types of patents: Utility, Design, and Plant. Each type of patent has its own filing requirements, examination procedures, term of protection, and criteria for enforcement against infringers.

Utility Patents

A utility patent recognizes an invention or discovery for a new and useful process, machine, article of manufacture, or composition of matter. These categories are often referred to by other names, including methods of use, business methods, methods of manufacture, apparatuses, devices, systems, and other names. The invention or discovery may be entirely new or may be an improvement on an existing method, device, system, or chemical composition.

Utility patents are the most common type of U.S. patent. They are usually valid for 20 years from the time that the patent application was originally filed. Maintenance fees are required at certain times throughout the 20 years in order to keep the patent in force. As with other patent rights, utility patents are only enforceable after the patent goes through the examination process and is granted.

Design Patents

A design patent recognizes a new, original, and ornamental design for an article of manufacture. This type of patent focuses on the ornamental design, instead of the physical structure or functionality.

A design patent is typically valid for 14 or 15 years from the time the patent application was originally filed. There are no maintenance fees to maintain a design patent in force once it is issued. A design patent protects against other ornamental designs that are confusingly similar.

Some products are suitable for protection using both design patents and utility patents. For example, the ornamental design aspects of a product (the shape, icons, graphical or industrial form, etc.) can be protected by a design patent, while utility patents might protect the structural and functional features of the product, how the product is made, and how the product is used.

Design patent protection can also coordinate with the protection offered by copyrights. Like design patents, copyrights protect the works of art or authorship, which are often ornamental in nature. Unlike design patents which can be infringed by confusingly similar designs, copyright protection requires evidence that an infringer copied the work from the original artist or author. There is no requirement to show copying for design patent infringement.

Similarly, design patent protection can apply to designs that are also used as trademarks or trade dress. In particular, the use of a particular new design which qualifies for protection under a design patent can be applied as a brand identifier for specific products or services. Once applied to market or brand the specific products or services, the same design protected by a design patent can also qualify for protection as a trademark or trade dress. The legal tests for infringement of design patents and trademarks are also similar, as both are based on a determination whether there is a likelihood of confusion between conflicting designs.

Plant Patents

A plant patent recognizes distinct and new asexually reproduced varieties of plants. Some aspects of such plants, and the methods of making them, can also be protected by utility patents. Plant patents provide protection for 20 years from the date of filing of the patent application. Given the special nature of this type of patent, and it's relatively limited use, this chapter will not focus on the additional details of obtaining or enforcing plant patents.

The Lifecycle of a Patent

The patent lifecycle can be roughly divided into two stages: 1) obtaining the patent, and 2) enforcing the patent. The typical costs and legal services required for each of these stages can be quite different from one another.

OBTAINING A PATENT

The process of obtaining a patent begins when an inventor determines that he or she has invented something new that is worthy of protection against potential copiers or infringers. The inventor can then submit an application to the governing body (the U.S. Patent and Trademark Office in the United States). The application must meet very particular requirements for both form and substance.

In addition to many formatting rules, the basic contents of a U.S. patent application must include a description of the invention and at least one claim. The description must provide enough detail to teach another person skilled in similar technology how to make and use the invention. And if the invention is conducive to illustrations, then illustrations can be provided and referenced in the description.

The claims establish the legal boundaries of the invention the applicant seeks to protect. Claims can be submitted in various forms, as long as they meet the specific formatting requirements. Also, claims can be directed to different aspects of a single invention. For example, some claims may be directed to a device, while other claims may be directed to methods for making and/or using the device.

Each claim defines an invention, which can impact the type of person or organization who might be expected to infringe that claim. For example, a claim to a device might be infringed by someone who makes the device, someone who sells the device, someone who imports the device, and so forth. In contract, a claim directed to how the device is made might only be infringed by others who make the device (e.g., manufacturers), but not by people who merely use the device without making it. Similarly, a claim directed to how a device is used might only be infringed by others who use the device (e.g., consumers and end users), but not be people who make the device solely for sale to the consumers or end users. In this way, different types of claims can be drafted with different groups of potential infringers in mind.

Once a patent application is drafted and submitted to the patent office, the patent application will eventually be assigned to an examiner. The examiner will review the patent application to make sure it complies with all the formal requirements. The examiner will also search for documentation of "prior art" that might teach some or all of the aspects of the invention claimed in the patent application.

Any reasons why the examiner thinks the claimed invention is not patentable will be issued in an office action. The applicant has the right to respond to the issues raised by the examiner in a response to the office action. For each response, there is usually a fixed response period, although in some cases extensions of time can be obtained through the payment of additional fees. Communications can go back and forth between the examiner and the applicant many times before either the examiner determines the invention is patentable and issues a notice of allowance. Alternatively, the examiner ultimately may maintain that the claimed invention is not patentable. When this happens, the applicant has a couple different options. First, the applicant may stop pursuing the patent application. Second, the applicant may pay additional fees to request further consideration by the examiner. Third, the applicant may pay additional fees and submit documents to initiate an appeal of the examiner's position. This appeal is administrative within the patent office, not within a court of law (although further proceedings could be brought in a court of law).

Once patent claims are determined to be allowable, the applicant will receive a notice of allowance and a statement of the issue fees due. After payment of the issue fees, the patent typically will issue within the next few months. Later, at certain times during the life of the patent, the patent owner will be required to make maintenance fee payments if the patent owner wants to continue the term of the patent. Those fees can be paid at each interval to keep the patent in force through the full term of the patent. However, if those fees are not paid then the patent expires earlier than the full term of the patent.

ENFORCING A PATENT

Once a patent is issued, the patent owner has the right to enforce the patent against infringers. Notably, the burden to enforce a patent is one the patent owner. The U.S. patent office does not monitor for potential infringers of any patents.

A typical infringement scenario includes identifying a potential infringer, performing an analysis of the accused product or method relative to the relevant claims of the issued patent, and then taking some action to notify the accused infringer of the issued patent. This notification can be performed in many ways—the two most common ways are by either sending a cease-and-desist letter or filing a patent infringement suit in federal court.

Cease-and-desist letters usually inform a potential infringer of the patent owner's rights in an issued patent. There are many potential risks that can be raised when a cease-and-desist letter is issued to a potential infringer. One of the most prevalent risks is the possibility that the potential infringer might use the letter as the basis to file a separate suit to have the federal court declare the issued patent invalid. The disadvantage to the patent owner in this situation is that the potential infringer can select the location where the suit will be brought, which likely will be chosen to be inconvenient and/or expensive for the patent owner and, if possible, might be a jurisdiction where courts are historically less favorable toward patent rights.

Instead of contacting a potential infringer through a cease-and-desist letter, some patent owners prefer to initiate a patent infringement suit first and let the suit itself serve as notice to the potential infringer. This allows the patent owner to control more of the choices as to where and when the suit will occur. It also may indicate a higher level of commitment by the patent owner.

Patent negotiations and law suits proceed in many aspects similarly to other negotiations and law suits. Readers may refer to other sections for more detailed information about specific negotiation and/or litigation techniques.

Ultimately, the patent owner will be advocating for validity of the patent claims and infringement by the accused infringer in order to stop and collect damages for the infringing activities and/or establish a licensing arrangement to collect royalties in exchange for authorization to allow the accused infringer to practice the patented claims.

On the other hand, the accused infringer will be advocating for non-infringement of the patented claims. In some situations, the accused infringer will also be advocating for invalidity of some or all of the issued patent claims. For any claims that are found to be invalid, the accused infringer will not be liable for infringement.

Regardless of the initial outcome of the patent infringement litigation, one party or the other (or both) may request that the case be reviewed by an appellate court, which may review parts of the case for proper application of the law and, in some cases, may review whether or not the basic facts of the case were dealt with justly.

Different Fee Schedules

The U.S. Patent and Trademark Office has established a normal fee schedule for most services they provide. The Office has also set up two other payment schedules, often with lower fees, for applicants who qualify as a "small business entity" or a "micro entity" within the established rules.

In general, the criteria to qualify as a small business entity are set by the Small Business Administration and, at the time of this writing, recognize business with less than 500 employees and less than certain annual revenues as small business entities. Qualifying applicants pay about half of the normal fees for some of the services.

Other applicants who have a limited number of prior patent or patent applications, and who make less than a specified amount of income (e.g., three times the poverty level for an individual), and who meet other criteria specified by the Office, can qualify for further reductions in fees as a micro entity. The fees for micro entities are often about half of what a small business entity would pay. Some higher education institutions and other organization can also qualify for micro entity status with the Office.

CHAPTER 34

INTELLECTUAL PROPERTY

TRADE SECRETS

ANDREW DEISS[1]
BILLIE SIDDOWAY
DIANA BRADLEY

Trade secrets are distinct from other types of intellectual property in that their value is derived from their non-disclosure. Unlike patent and copyright protections, which require some disclosure or publication in return for temporary protection, a trade secret is protected only so long as the holder of the trade secret maintains the secrecy of the information. Various factors effect the decision to seek patent or copyright protection versus maintaining a trade secret, including patentability and economic viability.

What is a Trade Secret?

Trade secrets can consist of nearly any kind of intangible property that derives its value from its confidentiality. For example, formulas, processes, complications, patterns, programs, techniques, client lists, business methods, pricing information, and source code can all be considered trade secrets when entities make efforts to keep them confidential. Under Utah law, trade secrets are defined by a three-part test; to be protectable an alleged trade secret must consist of:

1. "information, including a formula, pattern, compilation, program, device, method, technique, or process," that

[1]Andrew Deiss and Diana Bradley are an attorneys with Deiss Law PC located in Salt Lake City, Utah. Billie Siddoway is an attorney with Siddoway Law Office, PLLC in Driggs, Idaho. They litigate cases involving trade secrets.

2. "derives independent economic value . . . from not being known to, and not being readily ascertainable by proper means by, other persons who can obtain economic value from its disclosure"; and
3. "is the subject of efforts are reasonable under the circumstances to maintain its secrecy."[2]

To be considered a trade secret, the process, formula, technique, etc. cannot be generally known or readily ascertainable. When determining whether something constitutes a trade secret, courts consider the relevant experience and knowledge of the specific defendants. For example, in *CDC Restoration & Construction, LC v. Tradesmen Contractors, LLC* the court found that pricing information did not qualify as a trade secret in light of the sophistication of the defendants because the defendants could reasonably know the pricing information.[3]

A combination of "generally known elements or steps can qualify as a trade secret, if it represents a valuable contribution attributable to the independent efforts of the one claiming to have conceived it."[4] The determination of whether the product, design, vision, compilation, etc. constitutes a trade secret is fact-based inquiry, where a court will consider: "(1) the extent to which the information is known outside of the business; (2) the extent to which it is known by employees and others involved in its business; (3) the extent of measures taken by the business to guard the secrecy of its information; (4) the value of the information to the business and its competitors; (5) the amount of effort or money expended by the business in developing the information; (6) the ease or difficulty with which the information could be properly acquired or duplicated by others."[5] For example, in *USA Power*, the Utah Supreme Court remanded the case to determine whether the Plaintiff's development plans for a power plant constituted a trade secret.[6] Although each piece of the development plans (taken individually) was known

---

[2]Utah Code Ann. § 13-24-2 (4).

[3]2012 UT App 60, 274 P.3d 317

[4]*Microbiological* Research *Corp. v. Muna,* 625 P.2d 690, 696 (Utah 1991) (internal quotation marks omitted).

[5]*USA Power, LLC v. PacifiCorp*, 2010 UT 31, ¶45, 235 P.3d 749 (citing Restatement of Torts § 757 cmt. b (1939)).

[6]*Id.*

and ascertainable, the Plaintiff argued the vision of plant when analyzed together constituted a trade secret.[7]

Customer lists (like other compilations) can be considered trade secrets. However, to be considered a trade secret, the evidence much show that great expense and effort was used to obtain the information in the customer list—over and above the normal practice of product sales and development.[8] For example, in *Ikon Office Solution, Inc. v. American Office Products, Inc.*, an employer alleged that a former employee had misappropriated a customer list and contact information in violation of the Uniform Trade Secrets Act; the court stated that although a customer list can be a trade secret where the employer has expended considerable time and money, the customer list at issue was not a trade secret because "a person with a rudimentary knowledge of the industry" could quickly identify the key consumers in the area.[9] The court further held the information included in the list was not a trade secret because it was information that the employee had in his head from years of personally cultivating the accounts.[10]

Maintaining Confidentiality

Companies must make reasonable efforts to maintain the confidentiality of their trade secrets.[11] To do so, companies may: require employees, independent contractors and other business associates to sign non-disclosure agreements; restrict access to the trade secret to only those individuals to whom disclosure is necessary; mark information as proprietary and confidential; monitor access to confidential information; and pursue instances of misappropriation through litigation.

---

[7] *Id. See also Brigham Young Univ. v. Pfizer, Inc.*, Case No. 2:06-CV-890 TS, 861 F.Supp.2dv 1320 (D. Utah Mar. 20, 2012) (finding the elements of Plaintiff's research project to find a drug that functioned through a specific pathway could be combined into a compilation trade secret)

[8] *See In re R&R Assoc. of Pinellas County, Inc.*, 119 B.R. 302, 304 (Bankr. M.D. Fla. 1990) (holding the customer list at issue was not a trade secret because there was "no evidence that the list is the product of great expense or effort on the Debtor's part").

[9] 178 F. Supp. 2d 1154, 1168 (D. Or. 2001).

[10] *Id. See also* 652 P.2d at 700 ("where the customers are not known in the trade or are discoverable only by extraordinary efforts courts have not hesitated to protect customer lists and files as trade secrets. This is especially so where the customers' patronage had been secured by years of effort and advertising effected by the expenditure of substantial time and money).

[11] *See Medspring Group, Inc. v. Feng*, 368 F.Supp.2d 1270, 1278 (D. Utah 2005).""1 F.2d 1012.. eans of obtaining another'ant construction i s an iess. For ex secret claim wher it hadislcousre""1 F.2d 1012.. eans of obtaining another'ant construction i s an iess. For ex secret claim wher it hadislcousre of the alleged

Former employees "may not use confidential information obtained during the course of his or her employment to compete after termination with his or her former employer."[12] Written contracts or formal employment contracts are not required in order to create this duty, rather this duty "is grounded on 'basic principles of equity' . . . and upon an implied contract, growing out of the nature of the employer-employee relation."[13] An employee's duty to abstain from using the confidential information entrusted to her during her course of employment "does not necessarily turn on the existence of a legally enforceable contract."[14] Although requiring employees to sign a non-disclosure agreement is not always necessary to maintain an action for misappropriation of trade secrets, such practices help to ensure that companies satisfy the third prong of the test for trade secrets—utilizing reasonable efforts to maintain the security of the trade secret.[15]

When disclosure of a trade secret is made to a non-employee without requiring that individual sign a non-disclosure agreement, courts are likely to find that no trade secret exits. For example, in *Medspring* the court found the Plaintiff would not likely be successful on the merits of its misappropriation of trade secret claim where it had disclosed the alleged trade secret to both an employee and the employee's boyfriend who was not subject to a non-disclosure agreement.[16]

Misappropriation

The Utah Uniform Trade Secrets Act defines "misappropriation" as:

---

[12] *Envirotech Corp. V. Callachan* 872 P.2d 487, 496–97 (Ut. Ct. App. 1994).

(*citing Muna,* 625 P.2d at 697 "upon termination, employee may use "general knowledge, experience, memory and skill, however gained, provided he does not use, disclose, or impinge upon any of the secret processes or business secrets of his former employer.").

[13] *Id.* (citing *Eastern Marble Products Corp. v. Roman Marble, Inc.,* 372 Mass. 835, 364 N.E.2d 799, 803 (1977)).

[14] *Id.*

[15] *Hammerton, Inc. v. Heisterman,* No. 2:06-CV-00806 TS, 2008 WL 2004327, at *8 (D. Utah May 9, 2008) ("the presence of an express confidentiality or non-disclosure agreement is not necessarily required for a trade secret owner's efforts to be "reasonable under the circumstances."). *See also Water & Energy Systems Technology, Inc. v. Keil,* 1999 UT 16, ¶ 9, 974 P.2d 821 (to establish a claim for misappropriation of trade secrets the Plaintiff was required to show "(1) the existence of a trade secret, (2) communications of the trade secret to [the Defendant] under an express *or implied agreement* limiting disclosure of the secret, and (3) [the defendant's] use of the secret that injure[d] [the Plaintiff]) (emphasis added).

[16] 368 F.Supp.2d at 1278.

a) acquisition of a trade secret of another by a person who knows or has reason to know that the trade secret was acquired by improper means; or

b) disclosure or use of a trade secret of another without express or implied consent by a person who:

(i) used improper means to acquire knowledge of the trade secret; or

(ii) at the time of disclosure or use, knew or had reason to know that his knowledge of the trade secret was:

A. derived from or through a person who had utilized improper means to acquire it;

B. acquired under circumstances giving rise to a duty to maintain its secrecy or limit its use; or

C. derived from or through a person who owed a duty to the person seeking relief to maintain its secrecy or limit its use; or

(iii) before a material change of his position, knew or had reason to know that it was a trade secret and that knowledge of it had been acquired by accident or mistake.[17]

Thus, a trade secret may be misappropriated when it is acquired through theft, bribery, misrepresentation, or breach of a duty to maintain secrecy. Juries may infer misappropriation of a trade secret from circumstantial evidence.[18] For example, where the same individual assisted in creating bids for competing companies, it is a reasonable inference that the individual knew exact numbers used in the first bid and used that proprietary knowledge in assisting the second company to develop its bid.

---

[17] UTAH CODE ANN. § 13–24–2(2).

[18] *USA Power, LLC v. PacifiCorp*, 2010 UT 31, ¶ 50, 235 P.3d 749, 761 ("[A] jury can infer misappropriation under the Utah Trade Secrets Act if presented with circumstantial evidence that shows access to information similar to the trade secret at issue.").

While misappropriation of a trade secret through improper means is actionable,[19] discovery of a trade secret through reverse engineering or independent research is not actionable.[20] In one extreme example, a competitor attempted to acquire knowledge of the chemical process used in a proprietary method for producing methanol by taking aerial photographs of a chemical plant during construction. There the court held that such constituted misappropriation and the competitor's attempts "[t]o obtain knowledge of a process without spending the time and money to discover it independently is improper unless the holder voluntarily discloses it or fails to take reasonable precautions to ensure its secrecy."

Litigating Misappropriation of Trade Secrets—Preemption

The Utah Trade Secrets Act expressly preempts conflicting state remedies that are based on the misappropriation of trade secrets.[21] However, contractual remedies (whether based on the misappropriation of a trade secret or not) are not preempted.[22] Utah courts have stated that the purpose of the Utah Trade Secrets Act "is to preserve a single tort action under state law for misappropriation of a trade secret."[23] Guided by this principle, the court in *CDD Restoration* held "the UTSA preempts claims based on the unauthorized use of information, irrespective of whether that information meets the statutory definition of a trade secret."[24] Thus, "a claim is preempted to the extent that it is based on factual allegations supporting a misappropriation of trade secrets or otherwise confidential information."[25] A non-trade secret claim is preempted if proof of that claim "would also simultaneously establish a claim for misappropriation of trade secrets" irrespective of the "surplus elements of proof" necessary

---

[19]*See, e.g., Envirotech Corp. v. Callahan* 872 P.2d 487, 496 (Ut. Ct. App 1994) (finding misappropriation of a trade secret where the defendant "improperly obtained [the plaintiff's] drawings and then either redrew or copied the drawings).

[20]*See Keamnee Oil Co. v. Bicron Corp.*, 416 U.S. 470 (1974) (no protection against discovery by fair and honest means such as independent invention, accidental disclosure, or reverse engineering).

[21]Utah Code Ann. § 13-24-8(1). ("this chapter displaces conflicting tort, restitutionary, and other law of this state providing civil remedies for misappropriation of a trade secret").

[22]Utah Code Ann. § 13-24-8(2).

[23]*CDC Restoration & Const., LC v. Tradesman Contractors*, LLC 2012 UT App 60 ¶ 41, 274 P.3d 317 (quoting *Mortgage Specialists, Inc. v. Davey*, 904 A.2d 652, 663 (N.H. 2006)

[24]*Id.* ¶ 45.

[25]*Id.* ¶ 48.

to establish that claim.[26] However, a claim that is based on wrongful conduct independent of the misappropriation of a trade secret is not preempted. [27] For example, in *CDC Restoration* the court found the plaintiff's breach of fiduciary duty claim was preempted where the claim was based entirely on the defendant's alleged misappropriation and use of confidential information.[28] A claim for intentional interference based on the alleged use of trade secrets is preempted by the Utah Uniform Trade Secrets Act. *CDC Restoration & Const., L.C. v. Tradesman Contractors, LLC*, 2012 UT App. 60, 274 P.3d 317. *See also Mona Vie, LLC v. FVA Ventures, Inc.*, Docket No. 2:12-cv-152, 2012 WL 1952496 (D. Utah, May 30, 2012) (holding that the Utah Uniform Trade Secrets Act preempts a claim for intentional interference based on the alleged use of confidential information).

Liability for Misappropriation of Trade Secrets

An entity or individual may be entitled to both injunctive relief and monetary damages when seeking redress for violation of a trade secret. Injunctive relief is available to enjoin actual or threatened misappropriation.[29] Monetary damages can be measured by the actual loss caused by misappropriation, the unjust enrichment to the defendant, or a reasonable royalty—the "price that would be set by a willing buyer and a willing seller" for a license in the trade secret, a measure of damages that seeks to recreate "an actual market transaction ... [in] which both parties gain from the transaction."[30] Exemplary damages—up to twice the amount awarded for general damages—may be available if willful and malicious misappropriation exists.[31]

Finally, Utah courts may award attorney's fees to a prevailing party where a claim of misappropriation is made in bad faith, where a

---

[26] *Id.*

[27] *Id.*

[28] *Id.* ¶ 52. *See also Brigham Young Univ. v. Pfizer, Inc.*, No. 2:06-CV-890 TS, 2012 WL 994305, at *1 (D. Utah Mar. 22, 2012) (finding Plaintiff's claims for unjust enrichment, fraud, and negligent misrepresentation were preempted because all were premised on the contention that the defendant wrongfully used and obtained confidential information.

[29] UTAH CODE ANN. § 13-24-3.

[30] *Storagecraft Tech. Corp. v. Kirby*, 744 F.3d 1183, 1185 (10th Cir. 2014) (citing Restatement (Third) of Unfair Competition § 45 cmt. g (1995)); *See also* Utah Code Ann. § 13-24-4.

[31] UTAH CODE ANN.§ 13-24-4.

motion to terminate an injunction is made or resisted in bad faith, or where willful and malicious misappropriation exists.[32] In extreme cases, misappropriation of a trade secret may also subject an individual or entity to criminal sanctions.[33]

[32]UTAH CODE ANN.§ 13-24-5.

[33]Misappropriation of trade secrets may be actionable as theft or wrongful appropriation (which carries with it a penalty ranging from a class C misdemeanor to a third degree felony). *See* UTAH CODE ANN. § 76-6-404.5.

CHAPTER 35

INTELLECTUAL PROPERTY

ANTICYBERSQUATTING: PROTECTING YOUR BRAND

JOSHUA GREEN[1]

We live in a digital world. Long gone are the days when your business only needed to be listed in the Yellow Pages. The advent of the internet opened up drastic changes to how businesses market their goods and services and revealed seemingly endless possibilities for business owners to reach potential customers. The internet has truly globalized economies and expanded the reach of every business. A business's website is now a central part of its marketing strategy and a critical aspect of building its brand.

For trademark owners, however, the internet is a vast sea of problems for protecting their brand. For every legitimate website properly offering its goods to the public there are at least two others that peddle counterfeit products under the trademarks or brand of another. The internet also has made it easier for some to do business by profiting off another's trademarks or brand by claiming or implying affiliation with the trademark or brand owner even though their goods are clearly inferior. Pirates are continually thinking up new ways to profit from the extent trademark and brand owners go to build their reputation by diverting their customers.

Cybersquatting is the practice of registering names, especially well-known company, brand names and trademarks, as Internet domains, in the hope of reselling them at a profit. The Cybersquatter essentially holds

[1]Joshua Green practices primarily in the areas of business transactional and business litigation, with an emphasis on intellectual property issues. In 2015, he started his own practice, the Green Legal Group, P.C., with offices in Salt Lake City and Orem.

a domain containing one's trademark hostage and often offers to sell it to the owner for an exorbitant price. Before business owners became more savvy regarding the internet's marketing potential, cybersquatting became a really big problem with some of the biggest brand names falling victim to a new type of piracy.[2] However, cybersquatting is not a problem of the past, but continues to cause problems for trademark holders.

When dealing with a potential cybersquatter, business owners have a couple of possible solutions at their disposal. Business owners may bring a claim under the Anticybersquatting Consumer Protection Act (ACPA) or they may take advantage of the remedies under the Uniform Domain-Name Dispute-Resolution Policy (UDRP). While the ACPA is a statute under federal law, the UDRP is governed by the Internet Corporation for Assigned Names and Numbers (ICANN).[3] Although both the ACPA and the UDRP help business owners achieve similar results, each are fairly different in how they go about doing it.[4]

I. Using the ACPA to Protect Your Business

To combat the growing dilemma cybersquatters presented to business owners, Congress enacted the Anticybersquatting Consumer Protection Act (ACPA), an addition to the unfair competition provisions in the Lanham Act, in 1999.[5] The ACPA creates a mechanism for cybersquatting victims to stop the cybersquatters.[6] A business owner must bring a claim under the ACPA, generally in federal court, and allege that the cybersquatter (i) is acting with bad faith intent to profit from the business owner's company name or trademarks and (ii) has trafficked

---

[2]*See Nike, Inc. v. Circle Group Internet, Inc.*, 318 F. Supp.2d 688 (N.D. Il. 2004) (where the domain justdoit.net was at issue); *Virtual Works, Inc. v. Volkswagen of America, Inc., et. al*, 238 F.3d 264 (4th Cir. 2001) (where the domain WV.net was at issue because it incorporated Volkswagen's VW trademark); *People for the Ethical Treatment of Animals v. Doughney*, 263 F.3d 359 (4th Cir. 2001) (where the domain peta.org was at issue); *Cable News Network L.P., L.L.L.P. v. CNNEWS. COM*, 177 F. Supp.2d 506 (E.D. VA 2001) (where plaintiff alleged cnnews.com infringed it's CNN trademark); *Ford Motor Company v. Ford Financial Solutions*, 103 F. Supp.2d 1126 (N.D. IA 2000) (where the domain fordfinancialsolutions.com was at issue); *see also*, Clare Nullis, *'Cybersquatter' at juliaroberts.com must getout.now, U.N. court rules*, THE SEATTLE TIMES, June 3, 2000, *available at http://community.seattletimes.nwsource.com/archive/?date=20000603&slug office=4024616.*

[3]*Compare* 15 U.S.C. § 1125(d) (1999) *with* Uniform Domain-Name Dispute-Resolution Policy, October 24, 1999, available at https://www.icann.org/resources/pages/help/dndr/udrp-en.

[4]*Id.*

[5]*See* 15 U.S.C. § 1125(d) (1999).

[6]15 U.S.C. § 1125(a)(1)(C).

in or registered a domain name that is (a) identical or confusingly similar to a distinctive mark or (b) identical or confusingly similar to or dilutive of a famous mark.[7]

In determining the bad faith of the cybersquatter, the court will consider a number of statutory factors:

(I) the trademark or other intellectual property rights of the person, if any, in the domain name;

(II) the extent to which the domain name consists of the legal name of the person or a name that is otherwise commonly used to identify that person;

(III) the person's prior use, if any, of the domain name in connection with the bona fide offering of any goods or services;

(IV) the person's bona fide noncommercial or fair use of the mark in a site accessible under the domain name;

(V) the person's intent to divert consumers from the mark owner's online location to a site accessible under the domain name that could harm the goodwill represented by the mark, either for commercial gain or with the intent to tarnish or disparage the mark, by creating a likelihood of confusion as to the source, sponsorship, affiliation, or endorsement of the site;

(VI) the person's offer to transfer, sell, or otherwise assign the domain name to the mark owner or any third party for financial gain without having used, or having an intent to use, the domain name in the bona fide offering of any goods or services, or the person's prior conduct indicating a pattern of such conduct;

(VII) the person's provision of material and misleading false contact information when applying for the registration of the domain name, the person's intentional failure to maintain accurate contact information, or the person's prior conduct indicating a pattern of such conduct;

(VIII) the person's registration or acquisition of multiple domain names which the person knows are identical or confusingly

[7] 15 U.S.C. § 1125(a)(1)(A).

similar to marks of others that are distinctive at the time of registration of such domain names, or dilutive of famous marks of others that are famous at the time of registration of such domain names, without regard to the goods or services of the parties; and

(IX) the extent to which the mark incorporated in the person's domain name registration is or is not distinctive and famous within the meaning of subsection (c).[8]

These nine factors play a critical role in litigation as cases under the ACPA often hinge on the defendant's bad faith. Thus, a business owner could prove that the allegedly infringing domain name is identical or confusingly similar to its trademarks, but if they cannot show the domainer's bad faith, the whole claim collapses. The business owner may still have other claims under the Lanham Act which are not so contingent on bad faith, like trademark infringement or common law unfair competition, but the ACPA hinges on a finding that the domainer acted in bad faith.[9]

However, even if the business owner can successfully demonstrate the cybersquatter's bad faith, they will still need to demonstrate that his or her trademark(s) are distinctive or famous and that defendant's domain name is identical or confusingly similar those marks.[10] When it comes to determining the distinctiveness or fame of a mark or trade name, the business owner must show that the mark is recognized by the general public to describe their goods or services.[11] Fame will be determined by how widely the mark is recognized by the consuming public, which will be based on a detailed factual analysis.[12] The greater the distinctiveness or fame of a particular mark, the higher the court's level of scrutiny and broader measure of relief.

Whether a domain will be considered confusingly similar is usually based on a multi-factor analysis, which looks at many aspects of the

---

[8]15 U.S.C. § 1125(d)(1)(B)(i)(A)(I)-(IX).

[9]*Id.*

[10]15 U.S.C. § 1125(d)(1)(A)(ii); *see also, City of Carlsbad v. Shah,* 850 F. Supp.2d 1087, 1104 (S. D. Cal. 2012).

[11]*See Dudley v. Healthsource Chiropractic, et al.*, 585 F. Supp.2d 433, 438 (W.D.N.Y. 2008).

[12]*Harris Research, Inc. v. Lyndon et al.*, 505 F. Supp.2d 1161, 1165 (D. Utah 2007).

marks/domains, the goods marketed under each, the channels of trade, class of customers, etc. However, similarity is often not an issue as the domainer usually incorporates the business owner's mark.[13] If a business owner can successfully show that a domainer is acting in bad faith in registering domain names that are confusingly similar to its distinctive or famous trademarks, then the court could order the forfeiture, cancellation or transfer of the domain name to the business owner as applicable.[14] To the extent that the cybersquatter's actions have damaged the business owner, he or she may be entitled to damages for any other violation under the Lanham Act, such as for trademark infringement.[15] Perhaps one of the most famous cases dealing with cybersquatting was *Verizon California, Inc. v. Navigation Catalyst Systems, Inc., et al.*, which by most accounts was the first case where a plaintiff bringing claims under the ACPA won in court.[16] What made this case so unique was that the defendant in that case, Navigation Catalyst, had an automated system for temporarily registering domain names under the five day Add Grace Period implemented by ICANN, often registering domain names that often had nothing to do with anyone's trademarks.[17] Verizon filed suit because the defendants had registered more than 128 domains which all included variations (including misspellings) of the word Verizon and other Verizon trademarks.[18] The primary concern was that the defendant was taking common misspellings of, and in some cases even wholly incorporating, Verizon trademarks and using them in their domain names.[19] Not surprisingly, the court found that each of the domain names were confusingly similar.[20]

---

[13] *See Lahoti v. Vericheck, Inc.*, 636 F.3d 501 (9th Cir. 2011) (where the Vericheck mark was challenging the vericheck.com domain); *DSPT Internationa, Inc. v. Nahum*, 624 F.3d 1213 (9th Cir. 2010) (where the mark "EQ" was being infringed by www.eq-italy.com).

[14] 15 U.S.C. § 1125(d)(1)(C).

[15] 15 U.S.C. § 1125(a).

[16] *See* Eric Goldman, *Domainer Loses Cybersquatting Lawsuit-Verizon v. Navigation Catalyst*, TECHNOLOGY & MARKETING LAW BLOG, August 1, 2008, available at http://blog.ericgoldman.org/archives/2008/08/domainer_loses_1.htm.

[17] *Id.*

[18] *Verizon California, Inc. v. Navigation Catalyst Systems, Inc., et al.*, 568 F. Supp.2d 1088, 1095 (C.D. Cal. 2008).

[19] *See id.* (where Defendant had registered verizno.net, verisonnetwork.com, verisonwirelessplans.com, and vzstore.com).

[20] *Id.*

However, the primary fight was over whether the defendants acted in bad faith.[21] The defendants argued "that their registration of a few 'scarcely recognizable' domain names" did not merit a finding of bad faith.[22] Verizon maintained, and the court agreed, that defendant's actions banked on the "likelihood that a particular domain name might be typed in accidentally by someone trying to type one of [Verizon's] marks or domain names."[23] The court also considered all of the factors of bad faith outlined in the statute and found that defendants had the requisite bad faith. A careful analysis of all of the factors demonstrated overwhelming evidence of the defendant's bad faith.[24] As a result, the court imposed an injunction against defendants from using the infringing domain names and any name that is identical or similar to "VERIZON, VERIZON WIRELESS, FIOS, VERIZON FIOS, VZ, VZACCESS, VZEMAIL, VZGLOBAL, VZVOICE, and VZW."[25]

Filing a claim under the ACPA has its limitations. Despite Verizon's success in 2008, it is one of the few success stories in ACPA litigation.[26] Since litigation in federal court can be prohibitively expensive,[27] as with most litigation, it is often only available to companies or businesses that can afford it. Many, if not most, small businesses can simply not bare the arduous and labor-intensive costs associated with preparing for a ACPA case. Litigation also has no guarantees, which means that a business owner could spend thousands, if not tens of thousands of dollars and still be in the same position he or she was before filing the lawsuit. Many are not willing or unable to take that risk.

Another drawback ACPA claims is the timeframe. Often, lawsuits drag on for months or in some cases, years. Unfortunately, claimants in federal court are at the mercy of the court's, and to some extent, the

---

[21] *Id.* at 1094-95.

[22] *Id.* at 1095.

[23] *Id.*

[24] *Id.* at 1096-97.

[25] *Id.* at 1097-98.

[26] *See supra* note 11.

[27] *See Litigation Cost Survey of Major Companies*, 2010 Conference on Civil Litigation, Duke Law School, May 10-11, 2010, available at http://www.uscourts.gov/ uscourts/RulesAndPolicies/rules/Duke%20Materials/Library/Litigation%20 Cost%20Survey%20of%20Major%20Companies.pdf (outlining the exponential increase in litigation costs since 2000).

opposing party's schedule. This may mean a significant lag in getting the infringing domain taken down.

II. Using the UDRP: Possibly a More Cost-Effective Choice

A practical alternative to the ACPA is the ICANN sponsored UDRP, which is an international set of rules and regulations governing the process by which domain names are cancelled.[28] "Under the policy, most types of trademark-based domain-name disputes must be resolved by agreement, court action, or arbitration before a registrar will cancel, suspend, or transfer a domain name."[29] However, in cybersquatting cases, there are expedited procedures a trademark holder can initiate by filing a complaint with one of ICANN's approved dispute-resolution service providers.[30]

Regardless of whether a trademark owner uses the ACPA or the UDRP, he or she will need to work through ICANN to cancel a registration. However, the UDRP requires domain owners to submit to a mandatory administrative proceeding before one of their approved arbiters.[31] Business owners must file a complaint with the approved service provider of their choice and allege that:

> (a) domain name is identical or confusingly similar to a trademark or service mark in which the complainant has rights;" (b) that the domain was registered in bad faith; and
>
> (b) [the domain owner] has no rights or legitimate interests in respect of the domain name; and
>
> (c) [the] domain name has been registered and is being used in bad faith.[32]

---

[28] *See generally*, Uniform Domain-Name Dispute-Resolution Policy, https://www.icann.org/resources/pages/udrp-2012-02-25-en?routing_type=path.

[29] *Id.*

[30] *Id.*

[31] *Id.*

[32] UDRP, Domain Name Dispute Resolution 4(a)(i)-(iii).

The elements, although worded slightly differently, are almost identical with the ACPA.[33] The UDRP adopts a four-factor test for determining the registrant's bad faith in lieu of the ACPA's nine factors, which arguably makes it easier for trademark owners to demonstrate bad faith.[34]

Although the cost of the arbitration must be born by the party making the complaint,[35] the streamlined approach of the UDRP to resolving domain disputes helps keep the costs down. The average cost for a UDRP arbiter is between $1,300.00 - $5,000.00,[36] which is likely to be much cheaper than litigating an ACPA claim in federal court. Claims made under UDRP are also much faster.[37] In general, baring special circumstances, the arbiter's decision should be made within a couple of months from the date the complaint was filed.[38] Even with special circumstances, a decision within 90 days is called for under the rules.[39]

Yet, one of the drawbacks to going through UDRP is that a trademark owner's only remedy is cancellation or transfer of the infringing domain name.[40] Thus, if the trademark owner is otherwise harmed and wants to recover damages for the infringement, they will have to take their claim to federal court under the Lanham Act.[41] However, if a trademark owner is successful in getting the domain cancelled under the UDRP prior to bringing a claim in federal court,[42] it could give them a lot of leverage if they are looking for damages, which may prompt a settlement.

---

[33] *Compare id.* at 4(a)(i)-(iii) *with* 15 U.S.C. 1125(d).

[34] *See supra* Note 31 at 4(b)(i)-(iv).

[35] *See id.* at 4(g).

[36] *See* National Arbitration Forum, *Fees*, http://domains.adrforum.com/main.aspx?itemID=264&hideBar=False&navID=217&news=26.

[37] *See* UDRP Rules 3-5, 15, https://www.icann.org/resources/pages/rules-be-2012-02-25-en.

[38] *Id.*

[39] *Id.*

[40] *See supra* Note 31 at 4(i).

[41] *Id.*

[42] *See id.* at 4(k).

III. Conclusion

Overall, both the ACPA and the UDRP can be effective tools to stopping a potential cybersquatter. While the ACPA is more dynamic in the remedies it affords (along with the rest of the Lanham Act claims that usually come with a ACPA claim), it carries with it the burden of litigation costs. The UDRP is very streamlined and can be a cost-efficient tool to stop cybersquatters quickly, but is limited in the scope of its remedies. In some instances, it may make most sense to employ both the ACPA and the UDRP. In any case, trademark owners are not helpless against cybersquatters and the damage they can do to one's business and brand. In the end, it is important to remember that there are always options for

CHAPTER 36
INTELLECTUAL PROPERTY LICENSING

BRENT BURNINGHAM[1]

LICENSING FOR PROFIT

From driver's licenses to hunting licenses and business licenses, we are all familiar with what a license is. A license is a right to do something that would otherwise be prohibited, given by someone in authority to authorize the activity. In the realm of entrepreneurship and intellectual property, licensing is a key concept to understand because it opens up tremendous business opportunities. Intellectual property ("IP") has long been recognized as adding value to a business, in the form of patents to protect products, trademarks to create brand recognition, and copyright to protect creative works and works of authorship. However, licensing is a way to extend and elevate the value of intellectual property from protection to direct revenue generation.

Licensing also offers flexibility and alternatives to the fundamental question of whether to build or buy what you need in your business, whether it is technology, sales force, branding, etc. Licensing makes business less about who owns an asset and more about who controls an asset and in whose hands the intellectual property can be best put to use. Licensing is about leverage – getting better results with what you already have or can obtain access to. It is a key ingredient to effective collaborative business models, and some not so collaborative models.

---

[1]Brent M. Burningham, J.D., M.B.A., is a registered patent attorney and entrepreneur. He was previously a senior tax associate in the Boston office of PricewaterhouseCoopers LP, serving high tech start-ups and large, multi-national public companies before spending several years as general counsel to multiple private manufacturing and natural health product companies. In private law practice, he brings a multi-disciplinary perspective to his clients in intellectual property, transactional, tax and litigation matters.

Using licensing in your business model, you can change your thinking from viewing intellectual property and its enforcement as a necessary business expense, to thinking of intellectual property as an important aspect of your business development and revenue generating plans. Further, licensing is not limited to patents. It can be applied to nearly any intellectual property.[2]

Owners of intellectual property – whether patent, trademark, trade dress, copyright, trade secret[3], possess rights incident to ownership. In the case of patent, for example, ownership entails the right to exclude others from making, selling or using the patented invention. Some individuals misinterpret the patent owner's right to exclude others from doing something as an absolute right of the owner to do or make the patented thing themselves. In some instances, however, those rights are not absolute, but are subject to the rights of other owners of patented technology as well.

Many law students are introduced to this concept with the following classic example of the three-legged chair.

The Patented Three-Legged Chair

Consider Inventor A has invented and patented a three-legged chair. The patented scope of the invention is a seating platform supported by three legs. Thus, Inventor A has a right to exclude others from making, using and selling a chair having three legs[4]. As a practical matter, Inventor A can use his right to exclude others to give himself a market advantage as the only person able to commercialize the three-legged chair for the life of the patent.

Now consider that Inventor B finds the three-legged chair to be too unstable, but when the platform is supported by a fourth leg, the chair is much more stable. Imagine that Inventor B applies for a patent and is successful in patenting the invention of the four-legged chair as a seating platform supported by four legs. When it comes to commercializing the

---

[2]Licensing trade secrets is highly discouraged considering a license is generally temporary in nature and, being a contract, is subject to possible breach and loss of the secrecy through which a trade secret has value.

[3]See chapters of this work for additional treatment of patents, trademarks and trade dress, copyrights and trade secrets.

[4]Those familiar with patents understand that the wording of the claims is critical to defining the scope of patent protection. Discussion of claims drafting is beyond the scope of this discussion.

four-legged chair, is Inventor B unfettered in his right to commercialize the four-legged chair even while Inventor A's patent for a three-legged chair is in effect? What about a third inventor, Inventor C, whose patented invention is the student desk which is a four-legged chair with integrated writing surface?

The short answer to both questions is "No" – both the four-legged chair and the student writing desk infringe the three-legged chair patent, because the four-legged chair in both instances has three legs. The fact that it also has a fourth leg, which is in and of itself a patentable improvement, does not diminish the fact that it has three legs and infringes the patent for a three-legged chair. Further, Inventor C infringes both Inventor B and Inventor A if he proceeds to manufacture student desks, even though his chair with integrated writing platform is itself a patented improvement. For the life of the three-legged chair patent, Inventor A has a right to preclude others from making, selling or using any chair having three or more legs, because all inherently have three legs. Inventor B, and others interested in dealing in chairs having three or more legs have a duty to respect the rights of Inventor A for as long as the patent for the three-legged chair is in effect. Inventor C must respect the rights of multiple prior patent owners in pursuit of his own business surrounding student desks.

Setting the Scene for The License

In the example above, Inventor A has created a situation with licensing potential as the owner of three-legged chair technology. Inventor B may go merrily on his way making and selling four-legged chairs without regard to Inventor A's patent.[5] However, such action would infringe the rights of Inventor A. Inventor B's manufacture and selling of four-legged chairs is subject to the risk that Inventor A may enforce his patent by suing Inventor B for infringement damages. Worse yet, all of Inventor B's distributors may be subject to similar risk for selling, and his end customers may be subject to risk for using, the infringing chairs.

[5]While patent infringement is against the law, like other business decisions, it is sometimes deliberately engaged in when seen as advantageous from a cost-benefit standpoint. However, penalties for so-called willful infringements are higher than those for unintentional infringement. Patent invalidity searches and freedom to operate searches and opinions are often obtained for guidance, and to avoid potential finding of willful infringement when conducting business in close proximity to protected technologies.

Everyone in the chain of commerce of the infringing product has become a potential target for an infringement suit by Inventor A. Inventor A has been given the authority, by statute, to enforce its patent. It follows then that Inventor A has the authority to grant licenses to those whom he permits to deal in three-legged chairs, and others whose products, like the four-legged chair or student desk, would otherwise infringe on his rights. Thus the license could be freely negotiated between the inventors or their assignees, for the benefit of both patent owners.

Patent rights are typically assigned to a company; usually the employer of the inventor or the sponsor of the research. For the ensuing discussion, Inventors A, B and C, will be substituted with Company A, B and C. Under this construct, Company A is effectively the gatekeeper to the market for three-legged chairs and all chairs dependent on this patented technology. Company A can use the patented technology and make three-legged chairs and exclude all other infringing product manufacture and sale. But, interestingly, Company A can't make, use or sell four-legged chairs or student desks without infringing others, because those patented technologies are owned by Company B and Company C, respectively.

Voluntary Licensing

In the chair example, Company B would be wise to have researched the market and been aware of the patent rights of Company A.[6] Once those pre-existing rights were identified, Company B could approach Company A for a license to use its patent. This function is often the domain of a licensing executive in the technology office or business development arm of the business or organization. For entrepreneurs, it is just another of your many hats.

Often the patent owner/licensor is interested in licensing the patent to the licensee because the licensee has an interest in, and ability to expand the licensor's reach to new markets. In a licensing transaction, the licensor grants the license for the licensee to use the licensor's technology in exchange for a royalty paid by the licensee. The net result is that the

[6]Patent searches are often recommended to determine patentability, patent validity/invalidity and freedom to operate. They can be ordered through your patent attorney or directly through a number of commercial search services, however, interpretation of search results is best performed by a patent attorney and is often delivered in the form of a written opinion.

gross revenue from the licensee will be less that would have been realized from the sale of the actual goods, but without the licensor incurring the costs and allocating the resources typically required to produce such sales.

For example, the licensor doesn't need to build new sales force, engage in new marketing, buy tooling, carry inventory or incur other typical costs of sales to enjoy the benefits of the increased market and revenue. The royalty itself becomes the revenue source, one without a direct cost of goods sold and without most indirect costs. Consequently, a licensing transaction can be very profitable. It is sometimes considered easy money with the effort of receiving the royalty often jokingly considered to be that of picking up the check from the mail. But there is a great deal more to it, not the least of which is the creation of the underlying subject matter of the license.

Compulsory Licensing

Assume that Company B did not approach Company A for a license to the three-legged chair technology it would have been infringing Company A's patent by making or selling the four-legged chair. In the case where a patent or other intellectual property has been infringed, the owner of the infringed property can demand the infringer take a license to avoid further infringement. These interactions often start with the patent owner sending a demand letter advising the infringer of the infringement and demanding that the infringement stop or that the infringer take a license to continue operating in the protected space. In response, the infringer may agree to a lump sum settlement for past infringement together with an ongoing royalty to be paid by the infringer/licensee under the terms of a new license agreement.

In the event no settlement can be reached, the patent owner can file suit to obtain a judicial remedy. In some cases, patent owners skip the demand letter and jump right to suit, using the suit as additional leverage to force the license either through settlement of the suit, or ultimately by obtaining a favorable judgment through the courts. Patent litigation is often high-stakes, bet-the-company litigation where a negative result can put a company out of business. Sometimes, it is only a licensing deal that can save the infringing company from closing its doors entirely.

Anatomy of a License

In practical terms, licenses are just special purpose contracts, so standard contract principles apply. Common provisions include identification of the parties, the purposes and term of the contract. Definitions of key terms or terms of art in the industry that are critical to understanding the deal should also be included.

Special subject matter for licenses includes key provisions defining what the scope of the license is, often referred to as the license grant. It may also address what is expressly not granted, whether by reservation of rights by the licensor or license restrictions. It may identify what is included to be delivered to the licensee as part of the license, or items that may be required to be purchased by the licensee. Whether or not the license is exclusive or includes the right by the licensee to sublicense are also included here. Licensees may also be granted "most favored" status meaning they will always get the most favorable licensing deal available to any of the licensor's licensees.

Because technology is improved over time, and frequently in response to market demand which may be in closer communication with the licensee than the licensor, it is important to address what is to become of improvements made by either the licensee or the licensor. This includes such issues as whether improvements will be included in the license, which party will secure patents, which party will pay related costs, and which party will be the assignee of the patented improvement.

The status of the licensed subject matter is also very important. The parties will generally make representations and give one another warranties related to the deal. In the case of the licensor, representations and warranties may include that the licensed patent is valid and that the deal being executed is not in violation of any other deal the licensor has. A licensee, on the other hand, may represent and warrant that it is authorized to enter the transaction. Both parties may want to define what the consequence should be in the event a representation fails, such as by a licensed patent being subsequently challenged or invalidated, or in the event the license is breached or terminates while any litigation or other issue is pending.

Because many patent licenses are compulsory licenses arising from infringement situations, many licenses will address issues related to the resolved infringement, such as forgiveness for payment. They will also frequently address what each party's duties are with respect to infringement by others, considering such infringement may affect the market and the value of the license. These provisions may assign which party is responsible to file suit against infringers or, conversely, to defend suits brought by others alleging infringement by the subject patent or licensed products.

Equally important is the consideration to be paid for the license. Licenses may be royalty free or royalty bearing. Royalty bearing licenses may be paid with royalties stated as a percent of sales or profits, fixed amounts, per unit amounts or other combinations. Royalties may also be triggered by the completion of milestones reached by either party. Further, the licensee may be subject to minimum royalties, even if milestones aren't met, and and such minimum royalties may be credited against earned royalties.

In connection with payment, currency must be designated. In the event of international transactions there may be issues of currency exchange. In addition, royalties may be paid in equity as opposed to currency. Equity deals open up a whole range of issues such as what company's equity is to be used, licensee or a new company, valuation of the stock and class of stock to be used as consideration.

A number of training, reporting and auditing matters are also important to be addressed.[7] These may include the type and frequency of licensee inspections, if any; and technical support that may be provided to train and enable the licensee. The nature and frequency of licensee reporting is also important to address.

Lastly, the license will also include typical boilerplate provisions concerning interpretation, integration of any preceding oral arrangements, choice of law, dispute resolution, notice, assignment, and signatures. Consistent with other business contracts, the parties to the license agreement have latitude to make the best agreement they can mutually agree upon. Of course, as with other agreements, there could be a significant disparity in the bargaining power of one of the parties over the other, especially in the case of the compulsory license.

[7]Sample licensing checklists are readily available via the internet. Such examples are good starting points; however, you should adapt them to your own business needs and style. For a customized list, or consultation regarding issues unique to your transactions, seek the advice of competent intellectual property counsel.

The License Grant

In an effort to give some additional substance to the lists above, some additional detail is provided here. The grant both identifies and defines the scope of what is being licensed. For instance, licenses can be so complete as to be almost an entire conveyance of the intellectual property being licensed. Licenses can be granted that are perpetual in duration, cover the entire world, and every market channel, without an obligation to pay royalty, and include all liability and obligations of maintaining and enforcing the licensed intellectual property falling on the licensee. On the other hand, the license can grant less than all of the rights on any one or more of a multitude of aspects. An example would be narrow license for a specific use, in a small market, for a limited period of time and requiring reasonable royalties.

Territory

A license can be granted to a defined territory. Territories can be actual geographic territories, or they can be defined as markets, or combinations of the two. A licensee could be granted rights to market only in a certain territory defined as a certain continent, in certain countries, or states within a country. Alternatively, a license could be granted only for the licensee to sell in a certain marketing channel, such as through specific named big-box retailers, or through an online storefront. Obviously care must be taken to ensure that the rights granted to multiple licensees are consistent and avoid conflict. For instance, you wouldn't want to grant rights to one licensee in a geographic territory, and to another according to market channel, where the territory granted to the first and the channel granted to the second may overlap.

Some technologies may have application in different industries. If so, it may make sense to grant a license to one licensee limited to the industry where it has a strong market presence, but grant another license to a second licensee strong in another industry. Basically, the goal should be to put the license in the hands of the party best capable of being successful in commercializing your intellectual property, and defining the scope of the license to coincide with the licensee's strength.

Term or Duration

As a company grows and evolves, so does its licensing needs. Licensors and licensees may grow along with one another, and be a substantial reason for one another's mutual success, but that is not always the case. The licensee you have at sales of $1 million, may not be the licensee you want when your target is sales of $100 million. Consequently, you may want to have a way out of the license in three to five years. At the same time, licensees may be reluctant to deal with you if your time horizon is so short that they may not recoup their investment over the term of a short license. These things should be taken into account when negotiating the duration, and possible renewal, of the license agreement.

Performance

Typically, you enter a license agreement to obtain a commercial advantage you couldn't achieve yourself, or don't want to allocate resources to. Even so, a nonperforming licensee is no better than having no licensee at all, and it can be worse. Therefore, it is common to require the licensee to meet certain performance standards as a condition to maintaining or renewing a license. These are generally measured with the same criteria the royalties are calculated on, namely sales volume or pieces sold, etc. In a startup without sales history, it may not be unusual to have the licensee commit to a certain level of investment in the development or marketing of the technology, in the form of dollars budgeted and spent on the project in lieu of sales benchmarks, at least until sales becomes, or should have become a reliable measure.

Performance may also relate to the quality of the product or service delivered by the licensee. Especially in the case of trademark licensing, which denotes that the goods or services provided originate from the licensor, you want to include the performance criteria or product specification subject to the license, and include a right to inspect or audit the goods and services for compliance with the specification, as well as auditing the correct use of the mark.

The Royalty

The royalty component of the license is often stated as a royalty rate, usually a percentage of sales. It may be based on gross sales or net sales, or some other meaningful measure. Gross sales is often a preferred sales measure because net sales or profits are often subject to differences in accounting methods and may be manipulated to reduce reported amounts. Alternatively, royalties could be stated as a piece rate. Royalties may include fixed, lump-sum payments as well as variable payments.

With regard to establishing an appropriate royalty rate, valuation of the intellectual property is important. There are a variety of valuation methods, including cost, market value and income approaches. While these are useful in establishing boundaries, in practice you will get whatever you can negotiate. Further, different industries, or different levels in the chain of commerce, tend to have different typical royalty rates. If you research your industry, you will become familiar with royalty rates commonly paid for certain types of licenses in your space, but always keep in mind, no two deals are exactly alike. Be willing to be flexible to get the licensee or the deal you want. At the same time, if you intend to grant many similar licenses, standardization will help you keep track of them better from a compliance perspective.

As your business grows, there may be times you need strong data to back up your royalty rates. For this purpose, there are data aggregators whose businesses revolve around the collection and sale of royalty data. In large commercial transactions, it is not uncommon for parties to pay tens of thousands of dollars to such companies to obtain reliable and well documented royalty information to support their decision making and negotiations in such transactions.[8]

In some cases, you may not want to charge a royalty at all. This is particularly true where the license is one concerning a trademark and the purpose is to promote the broad recognition of the mark. Allowing the mark to be freely used encourages its use by the licensee, under your supervision, and allows the licensee's efforts to augment your own efforts at building brand strength and good will. In this regard it is important

[8]Reliable royalty rate information is also essential when conducting and defending intercompany transactions involving "transfer pricing" among members of an affiliated group where such transfers require arm's length treatment and are subject to tax authority scrutiny.

to document that trademarks obtained will be obtained in the licensor's name and that the good will associated with them belongs to the licensor on termination of the license. Otherwise you may encounter disputes when switching trademark licensees at some time in the future.[9]

Licensing Examples

Following are examples of both low piece-rate, and high piece-rate royalties. The first is a royalty for a license on a proprietary yet common electrical connector used ubiquitously in computing devices. The royalty may be an initial lump sum amount to have access to the technology, of perhaps $10,000, followed by a small amount per connector used in a device, on the order of cents per connector. In a market where millions of devices are sold, and assuming 10 such connectors per device, even a $0.05 royalty per connector could result in millions of dollars in revenue during the life of the license.

The second example is that of a an airfoil design that when incorporated into a commercial aircraft results in fuel efficiency saving the airline millions of dollars in annual fuel economy. Such an item may command a royalty of tens of thousands of dollars per installation, not necessarily because the item is inherently that expensive to produce, but due to its economic benefit, it is that valuable to the licensee or its customer.

Compliance

Obtaining and measuring compliance with a license is always important. This is especially true in the case of compulsory licenses where the licensee was not interested in licensing in the first place, having previously decided it was better to go around you than through you to employ your technology or intellectual property. Therefore, including provisions to assist in obtaining compliance is important. The administrative burden of ensuring compliance is also one of the costs of licensing.

Obtaining compliance with a license is best when you have done a good job of selecting a readily available revenue or profit metric as

---

[9]This is especially in cross border transactions where you may authorize the licensee to obtain the local trademark on your behalf as part of the license due to their familiarity with local law and language.

the license base. The license agreement should require that the metric be reported on a periodic basis. This could be monthly, quarterly or annually. This typically corresponds to the period for which royalties are paid, however it doesn't always need to be so. It is possible to have the license be an agreed flat, or rolling average monthly rate which is an estimate, with a periodic reconciliation to actual on a less frequent basis.

Regardless of the royalty structure, the periodic reporting is intended as a way for the licensor to review the number and determine whether the payment of royalties is consistent with the numbers being reported. There can be discrepancies even between what is reported and paid, and what should have been reported and paid. While these discrepancies may result from unscrupulous licensees, they may also result from human error in data entry, poorly selected metrics, or poor implementation of the selected measurement in the management information system or reporting tool. For this reason, it is important to have a provision that enables the licensor to audit the licensee periodically, either directly, or more commonly through its agents – a CPA or consulting firm retained by the licensor specifically for that purpose. To avoid the overuse of the audit right and the intrusion and interruption it imposes on the licensee, such audit rights should be limited in frequency, commonly no more than once annually. It is often common to limit how far back such an audit can go, to avoid reauditing the same period multiple times, but to ensure you can audit all time periods once unless waived.

Licensing as a Business Development Tool

In the chair example, there were several licensing opportunities. Without licensing, and without infringing, the only active business would be that for three-legged chairs. By engaging in licensing, the licensor of the three-legged chair could increase its revenue by licensing both Company B and Company C to market their own four-legged products under the license. Company A could go a step further by licensing Companies B and C, or other third parties, to produce three-legged chairs as well, increasing the number of sources for its own patented invention in the process. Company A could go further still by obtaining licenses from Companies B and C , so-called cross-licenses, so that Company A could enter the markets for four-legged chairs and student desks to augment its own product line.

If Company A prefers to deal with fewer people, Company A could license Company B to not only use the three-legged chair technology but to license it to others in a sublicense, in exchange for a higher royalty. That way, Company B could license to Company C a package with both the three-legged chair and four-legged chair technology. The royalty to Company A need not be at a higher stated rate, it could be higher in the sense that it is charged on a larger base of both the Company B sales and Company C sales, channeled and reported through Company B. Thus the possible business combinations and relationships between licensors and licensee can be endless depending on the structures and technology combinations desired.

Intellectual Property as the Business

The value of intellectual property has become widely demonstrated, not just as a component of a viable business, but as the basis of the business. Entire companies have been established for the sole purpose of acquiring, maintaining and enforcing intellectual property rights. It is the business model of so-called "Patent Trolls" to acquire patents, monitor the market for potential infringers, and pursue such infringers to obtain infringement damages and compulsory licenses.

More commonly, however, intellectual property development, acquisition and monetization occurs in the course of ordinary business, springing up around things the entrepreneur or business is already doing or intending to do. Consequently, most intellectual property is developed internally for use in the business, but that doesn't have to be the case.

Identifying Licensing Opportunities

Many entrepreneurial minded individuals or existing businesses may find that a diligent search of existing intellectual property could help them find a match in something they would like to pursue commercially. This is true of venture capital groups as well. It is growing increasingly common for venture capital to be channeled into special purpose funds the sole purpose of which is to search out and identify suitable candidates for acquisition, and further development.[10] In similar fashion, inbound licensing candidates can often be found using similar methods.

In the licensing space, licensing target candidates are often found among the surplus in portfolios of companies that have existing IP but ultimately opted not to pursue the related project for one reason or another. This is particularly true of large organizations that have high required returns on investment or pursue only projects having a certain minimum potential market size. Smaller organizations with lower ROI requirements or smaller target market requirements may be willing and able to profitably take on such projects. In these scenarios, both the large organizations as licensor and the smaller organization or individual licensee win. The large organization can outbound license its small projects and recoup costs and gain revenue from what would otherwise be an abandoned project, and the small organization licensee can inbound license a project that may already have substantial research and development and proof of concept behind it, and supply the needed manpower and marketing resources to see it through.

Bankruptcy estates may also be good sources of existing intellectual property that could be revived and used successfully by new management or repurposed in new markets.[11] University technology transfer offices are also good sources of existing intellectual property that may be suitable for commercialization outside the university setting. These scenarios may be more suited to outright acquisition, but licensing opportunities are also possible.

Franchising is an example of elaborate application of licensing principles. In a franchise agreement, the franchisee licenses from the franchisor the entire business model, generally including all the patents, trademarks, and other intellectual property, and further including related infrastructure resources and support, but usually limited to a finite geographical territory.[12]

---

[10]For an introduction to search funds see "A Primer on Search Funds", Stanford Graduate School of Business, September 16, 2013, http://www.gsb.stanford.edu/ces/resources/search_fund_primer.html.

[11]Saab automobile company was purchased out of bankruptcy to become a new electric vehicle manufacturer, National Electric Vehicle Sweden AB. Stoll, John D. (2 December 2013). "Saab Automobile Is Poised to Resume Production". *Gasgoo Automotive News*. Retrieved 4 March 2015.

[12]While licensing in its barest form is unregulated, states vary on what degree of licensing entails a regulated business opportunity or franchise arrangement. Regulation in this area is generally related to the fact franchises are promoted like securities as investments for entrepreneurs rather than as business to business transactions. Franchising is addressed further in this work.

Academic Resources

The research university setting provides another interesting licensing option. Not only do university technology transfer offices maintain portfolios of university developed intellectual property for outbound licensing, they are frequently in a position to assist inventors and companies in developing outside intellectual property. A university may be able to take on a project either on a contract basis for hire, under a collaboration agreement as a university project when aligned with existing university sponsored research, or in conjunction with federally funded research grants. However, the potential downside of these collaborations can be that the resulting improvements in the intellectual property are encumbered by obligations to the government or the university. Nevertheless, they can be good options under the right circumstances with both parties benefitting, and having opportunities to commercially exploit the results, typically through cross-licensing arrangements.

Conclusion

Licensing can be a powerful addition to a business plan. Licensing from others, granting licenses to others, or both, can add to your market reach and market penetration and increase your product offering. Licensing offers a way to increase revenue with low direct costs, leveraging the resources of others. Opportunities to license are highly available, if you know where to find them, and readily implemented through typical contracting principals. Taking time to identify your own intellectual property, and that of others operating in your markets, will surely reveal licensing options. Don't let them go to waste. Turn unused or underutilized intellectual property assets into profits through licensing.

Additional Resources

Additional information on licensing can be found through the following organizations, to name just a few:

- The Licensing Executive Society ("LES"), at www.lesusacanada.org;
- The Intellectual Property Owners Association ("IPO"), at www.ipo.org;
- Association of University Technology Managers ("AUTM"), at www.autm.net;

- The World Intellectual Property Organization ("WIPO"), at www.wipo.int;
- The International Trademark Association ("INTA"), at www.inta.org; and
- The Copyright Clearance Center ("CCC"), at www.copyright.com.

CHAPTER 37

HUMAN RESOURCES

EMPLOYEES OR INDEPENDENT CONTRACTORS

NANCI SNOW BOCKELIE[1]

Introduction

Nearly every employer has felt the urge to fire its employees and re-hire them as independent contractors or consultants.[2] Employers want to avoid the costs and hassles of doing payroll. They want to avoid having to withhold and pay employee income taxes, Medicare, FICA, and federal and state unemployment taxes. A business without employees does not have to buy workers' compensation insurance or worry about immigration issues and I-9 forms. Independent contractors do not earn vacation, sick leave, holiday pay, health insurance, bonuses or retirement plans. By reclassifying even some of its workers, a business may reduce the number of state, local and federal regulations with which it must comply. A worker may agree to the classification to get a larger paycheck without tax deductions, the ability to claim business deductions, and scheduling freedom.

Misclassification of workers can lead to costly litigation by a governmental agency or a disgruntled worker, or create due diligence issues for a transactional client. However the issue arises, the client will need advice on what law applies, who gets to decide the proper treatment as employee or independent contractor, and what risks and penalties the

---

[1]Nanci Snow Bockelie received her law degree from the University of Utah College of Law in 1985, *Order of the Coif.* She practiced in New York City and Newport News, Virginia before returning to Utah. Since 1999 she has operated the Bockelie Law Office, PLLC, in Salt Lake City, providing transactional legal assistance to small business owners.

[2]As used in this Chapter, the term "independent contractor" includes all workers who do not receive a W-2 from their employer, whether called freelancers, consultants, temporary workers, 1099 employees, contract employees or something else.

worker or employer will face for a misclassification.

This chapter presents an overview of these legal issues and provides the tools to answer clients' questions. It lays out the laws and tests most commonly used, and shows the application of these rules in real life. This Chapter does not address every law applicable to employee classification issues, or all possible consequences. For example, whether a person's earnings come as an employee or independent contractor can have repercussions under bankruptcy and copyright laws, which are beyond the scope of this chapter. Many cases have addressed the legal issues involved in employee classification, some arriving at inexplicably inconsistent results. The law remains highly factually based. The practitioner must remain aware of these complexities and be prepared to provide individual analysis to any client with questions involving employee classifications.

Background

In some areas, the law is neutral. In the realm of employee classification, however, the law has a bias towards finding such a relationship. Keeping this bias in mind when advising clients can help the lawyer thread through the morass of case law statutes and regulations that might apply to a client's situation. The law favors finding an employee-employer relationship for two main reasons: to protect workers, and to protect federal and state coffers.

Employee protection laws include minimum wage and overtime laws, laws governing child labor, equal opportunity laws, worker's compensation and unemployment insurance programs, and occupational health and safety rules. Most of these protections do not apply to independent contractors. Thus, finding an employee-employer relationship allows agencies to maximize the protection these laws offer. The less altruistic reason – protecting governmental sources of income – exists because trust taxes, such as Medicare and Social Security taxes, account for as much as 35% of all federal revenues.[3] The employer-employee relationship provides a mechanism for timely collection of

---

[3]See, e.g., Tax Policy Center, *Tax Topics, Payroll Taxes,* http://www.taxpolicycenter.org/taxtopics/Payroll-Taxes.cfm and the Center on Budget and Political Priorities, "Policy Basics: Where Do Federal Tax Revenues Come From?" http://www.cbpp.org/cms/?fa=view&id=3822 (accessed 9/20/2014)

these taxes and enlarges the pool of responsible people from whom the government can collect the taxes.[4]

The development of employee protection laws has a long and sometimes violent history. The struggle of workers to wrest concessions from management goes back to colonial times in America. More than 100 years before Congress enacted the Fair Labor Standards Act (FLSA) in 1938, young women mill workers in Massachusetts went on strike to protest reduced wages.[5] These hard-won laws serve valuable public purposes, and represent a compromise between the pull of labor groups and the push back of management and ownership. President Franklin D. Roosevelt stated that the FLSA would "give a policy backbone to his belief that goods that were not produced under 'rudimentary standards of decency' should not be 'allowed to pollute the channels of interstate trade.'"[6]

Of course, not everyone agrees that classifying more workers as employees benefits those workers. Allowing broad treatment of workers as independent contractors can benefit the worker and the economy as a whole. Some of these benefits include workforce flexibility, avoidance of fixed costs and other economic barriers to efficient contracting, and the satisfaction workers can achieve by being "their own boss."[7] The course through the competing interests of workers, employers and government will depend on the identity and needs of the client.

The ABC's of Regulation

The pull of workers for legal protections and the push-back of employers seeking to limit the burden of regulation has created a confusing mosaic of agencies, laws and regulations. A lawyer analyzing employment status must consider an alphabet soup of regulation. Federal agencies include the Social Security Administration (SSA), the Internal

---

[4]*See, e.g.*, 26 USCS § 6671 and 26 USCS § 6672 (employer's officers and those with check signing authority personally liable for trust taxes)

[5]AFL-CIO, Labor History Timeline at http://www.aflcio.org/About/Our-History/Labor-History-Timeline; see also Zinn, Howard, *A People's History of the United States*, Harper Collins (2003 ed.) at 115.

[6]Cowie, Jefferson, "The Future of Fair Labor," The New York Times, June 24, 2013 (http://www.nytimes.com/2013/06/25/opinion/the-future-of-fair-labor.html (accessed 9/20/14)

[7]Eisenach, Jeffrey A., "The Role of Independent Contractors in the U.S. Economy" (Navigant Economics LLC, December 2010), available at http://www.aei.org/files/2012/08/22/-the-role-of-independent-contractors-in-the-us-economy_123302207143.pdf

Revenue Service (IRS), the federal Department of Labor (DOL), the Equal Employment Opportunity Commission (EEOC) and even the Occupational Safety and Health Administration (OSHA). State agencies may include departments of labor (the Labor Commission in Utah), tax and revenue (the Tax Commission in Utah), and unemployment (in Utah, the Workforce Services or WFS).

Federal laws apply when a federal agency seeks to collect federal taxes or enforce a federal law or right. State laws apply when a state agency seeks to enforce its own statutory or common law worker protections. An agency's purpose affects the standards it applies. As a result, a person can be an employee for wage and overtime purposes, but not under IRS tests; for worker's compensation purposes but not for FLSA; or for *respondeat superior* purposes but not for employee taxes. The lawyer will need to know the type of work, the location of the business, and which agency is making the inquiry to accurately advise the client.

Categories of Employees and Independent Contractors

Employees receive regular paychecks, from which the employer withholds the proper amount of income, Social Security and Medicare taxes. In addition, the employer pays the employer portion of Social Security and Medicare taxes, and pays federal and state unemployment tax. At the end of the year, the employer gives each employee a W-2 form detailing the employee's earnings and the amounts withheld by the employer. An independent contractor, on the other hand, gets a 1099 at year end, showing the gross amount earned. The independent contractor must pay its own taxes. Employees are covered by worker's compensation insurance, minimum wage and overtime laws; an independent contractor cannot rely on wage and overtime protections, and will not be able to collect unemployment or worker's compensation insurance if terminated or injured.

Initially, these distinctions make employee classification seem fairly straight forward; a worker is either an employee or an independent contractor. The simplicity fades in actual practice, however. The complex history of the reasons behind employee classification laws – that push and pull of competing interests – has lead to not just two classifications of workers, but four:

- *Common law employees,* those workers the common law traditionally recognizes as employees, who do not fall into any other category;
- *Statutory employees,* workers defined by statute as employees, even though they might otherwise be an independent contractor (corporate officers, 26 USCS § 3121 (d)(1); certain food and beverage delivery drivers, fulltime life insurance agents, piece goods workers who work at home and return finished good to the employer, and full time travelling salespeople selling at wholesale, 26 USCS § 3121(d)(3));
- *Statutory non-employees,* defined by statute as not employees, even though they may work for just one employer and share other characteristics of an employee (certain direct sellers, real estate agents 26 USCS § 3508; and certain domestic companions, 26 USCS § 3506);
- *Independent contractors,* workers who have their own business or profession and offer their services to the public.

In addition to these categories of workers, employee leasing continues to expand as a means of avoiding the hassles of being an employer, and raises its own issues, addressed below.

Classifying Workers – The IRS Tests

The IRS collects employment taxes. It provides both general guidelines and specific tests to determine whether a worker should be classified as an employee or independent contractor. The broad principals of classification are:

- If the business controls the methods and details of the work, an employer-employee relationship likely exists. The amount of control actually exercised by the employer does not matter, "it is sufficient if the employer has the right to do so."
- Workers who "follow an independent trade, business, or profession, in which they offer their services to the public, generally are not employees."

- The description of the job and the intent of the parties does not matter. If an employer-employee relationship exists, the parties cannot change that relationship by agreement or terminology.[8]

In addition to reiterating those general standards, the IRS's Revenue Ruling 87-41 also set out twenty detailed factors to assist the practitioner in classifying a worker as an employee or an independent contractor under the common law rules. *See Sidebar, "IRS Twenty Factor Test."*

On its website, the IRS organizes the twenty factors into three groups: Behavioral Control, Financial Control, and Type of Relationship.[9] The behavioral control factors involve the business' right to control how the worker does the job; the financial control factors address issues such as timing and method of payment, provision of tools and resources, the opportunity for profit or loss, and whether the business reimburses expenses. Relationship factors include whether a contract exists, when and on what grounds each party can end the relationship, how long the relationship may last, and what benefits the business provides to the worker.

Employees under FLSA

The Fair Labor Standards Act requires the payment of minimum wage and overtime for most workers in the U.S. It covers enterprises with annual sales exceeding $500,000. It also covers employees in enterprises of any size, if they (or their employer) engage in interstate commerce. Since most employees use some aspect of interstate commerce (the U.S. Mail, a telephone, email, a credit card terminal, for example), the latter test greatly extends the reach of the act.

FLSA contains numerous exemptions to its broad coverage, however. Some exclusions depend on the type of work (for example, certain domestic service workers and computer service workers; certain amusement park workers) and some depend on the location of the work performed, such as outside salespersons who "customarily work away

---

[8]These basic guidelines are set out in IRS Revenue Ruling 87-41, available at https://www.michigan.gov/documents/wca/wca_irs_revenue_ruling_87-41_390318_7.pdf.

[9]http://www.irs.gov/Businesses/Small-Businesses-&-Self-Employed/Independent-Contractor-Self-Employed-or-Employee

from the employers place of business." The exemption for executive, administrative and professional employees requires a minimum salary level, as well as specific job responsibilities.[10] Many of the exemptions lack any apparent rational basis, and seem driven more by lobbyists than any distinction among types of jobs.

The standards for classifying workers under FLSA overlap, but do not mirror, the IRS standards. The DOL applies a six prong test to determine a worker's proper classification under FLSA:

1. Whether the work an integral part of the employer's business.
2. Whether the worker's managerial skills affect his or her opportunity for profit or loss.
3. The relative investments in facilities and equipment by the worker and employer.
4. The worker's skill and initiative.
5. The permanency of the relationship.
6. The nature and amount of control exercised by the employer.[11]

The DOL cautions that "an agreement stating that [the worker] is an independent contractor is not controlling" because the reality of the working relationship, not its label, determines the appropriate classification.[12]

State Law Issues

States also have worker classification laws. As employers seek to minimize their overhead by classifying workers as independent contractors, states have become more interested in enforcing these laws. Between 2007 and 2014, 24 states, including Utah, enacted laws directed at reducing employee misclassification.[13] The federal government has supported this push with grants to help states identify

---

[10]*See* 29 U.S.C. § 213 and regulations such as 29 CFR 541.400 (computer related occupations); 29 CFR 541.502 (outside salespeople); and 29 CFR 541.100 (executive/managerial exemption).

[11]See http://www.dol.gov/whd/regs/compliance/whdfs13.pdf

[12]*Id.*

[13]See "Independent Contractor Compliance and Misclassification Legal Blog" http://independentcontractorcompliance.com/legal-resources/state-ic-laws-and-selected-bills/

misclassified workers. In 2013, the federal Department of Labor budget included $10,000,000 in grants to states, and $4,000,000 for its own internal investigators to recover unpaid employment taxes.[14] This recent governmental focus on worker-classification makes it more important than ever for lawyers to have the tools and knowledge to give clients accurate information on this subject. *See Sidebar, Recent Changes in State Laws* for a discussion of some recent state law changes.

Utah

In Utah, the Department of Workforce Services (WFS) and the Labor Commission are the primary agencies concerned with employee classification. The Labor Commission makes initial determinations about coverage under workers' compensation laws, and WFS oversees the unemployment claims. The Labor Commission and WFS each apply slightly different tests for when a worker is an employee; those tests also differ slightly from the tests applied by the IRS or DOL.

Workers' Compensation Factors

Worker's Compensation laws have a very broad reach and are intended to be liberally applied. *Olsen v. Samuel McIntyre Inv. Co.*, 956 P.2d 257, 260 (Utah 1998). The Utah statute defining an independent contractor for workers' compensation purposes focuses almost entirely on control. To be an independent contractor not covered by workers' compensation insurance, the worker must remain independent of the employer "in all that pertains to the execution of the work." Utah Code Ann. § 34A-2-103(2)(b)(i).

Broad coverage under workers' compensation insurance benefits both workers and employers. The employee gets automatic coverage, without the need to prove damages, but in exchange, gives up the right to greater damages through a lawsuit.[15] Payment of workers' compensation premiums insulates the employer and other responsible parties from all litigation involving injured workers. In fact, the Workers' Compensation

[14]U.S. Department of Labor, *FY 2013 Department Of Labor Budget In Brief* at 3 & 24, http://www.dol.gov/dol/budget/2013/PDF/FY2013BIB.pdf (accessed 9/20/2014)

[15]Utah Code Ann. § 34A-2-105(1) provides "The right to recover compensation pursuant to this chapter for injuries sustained by an employee, whether resulting in death or not, is *the exclusive remedy against the employer* and … any officer, agent, or employee of the employer … and all other civil liability whatsoever, at common law or otherwise. …" (Emph. added).

Act lays out steps an employer can take to bring contractors and others not ordinarily considered employees into the umbrella of its workers' compensation coverage as "employees." Utah Code Ann. § 34A-2-103 (7)(f)(ii) and (iii).

Case law in Utah has long recognized this breadth of coverage. In *Murray v. Wasatch Grading Co.*, 73 Utah 430 (Utah 1928), the state hired the defendant to build a highway near railroad tracks belonging to the Denver & Rio Grande railroad. The railroad asked plaintiff, its employee, to assist the defendant. Plaintiff was injured while doing so. The court found that the plaintiff was employee of defendant highway construction company for workers' compensation, because his work was subject to its control. *Id. at* 441. *See also Utah Home Fire Ins. Co. v. Manning*, 1999 UT 77, P12, P18 (Utah 1999) (subcontractor with independent business who was hired by general contractor was employee of general contractor for workers' compensation purposes because general contractor had the right to control the work performed by subcontractor).

Employee Classification for Unemployment Purposes

Unlike most other classification schemes, Utah's unemployment act focuses on the independence of the worker's business. The law presumes an employee-employer relationship unless the employer can show that "the individual is customarily engaged in an independently established trade, occupation, profession or business." Only after that test is met will the courts look at the employer's control over the "means of performance" of the work. Utah Code Ann. § 35A-4-204(3)(a) and (b). A showing that a worker has an independent business, raises "a rebuttable presumption that the employer did not have the right of or exercise direction or control over the service." Utah Admin. Code R994-204-303 (1)(c).[16]

Recent Utah case law reflects this focus. In *Petro-Hunt, LLC v. Dep't of Workforce Servs.*, 2008 UT App 391, the court never reached the issue of control, as the evidence did not show that the worker had an independently established business. 2008 Utah App. at P22 &

[16]This Utah focus on the business of the worker has evolved over time. In the *See Sidebar: Utah Factors* for a discussion of the changes Utah's laws governing the determination of employment and the fifteen factor test the state uses today.

P31. Similarly, although the worker in *BMS Ltd. 1999, Inc. v. Dep't of Workforce Servs.*, 2014 UT App 111 (Utah Ct. App. 2014) had signed an "independent contractor's agreement" with BMS, the court found the worker to be an employee. The worker "had not owned a delivery business prior to his relationship with [BMS], did not have a separate place of business or a business license, had not advertised his delivery services, and had not intended to establish an independent business." 2014 Utah Ct. App. at P14. *BMS* thus identifies for the practitioner several ways a worker can meet the independence test, by organizing as a separate business, obtaining a business license, using business cards, or advertising its general availability to other businesses. While none of these acts by itself can guarantee the outcome, each makes a finding that the worker is an employee more difficult in a review by WFS.

ENFORCEMENT ISSUES

Statutes of Limitation

The applicable statute of limitations in employee classification issues depends on who is bringing the action and whether the employer acted willfully. The limitations periods set out in Table 1 provide guidance; some statutes have detailed provisions that can vary or add requirements to the time periods. Note also that some periods do not begin to run until "the taxpayer file[s] the required return, or the Tax Commission file[s] on the taxpayer's behalf in order to administratively determine the amount of tax due." *Gay Hill Field Serv. v. Bd. of Review*, 750 P.2d 606, 609-610 (Utah Ct. App. 1988). The practitioner should always research the applicable statute of limitations, whether advising a client who wants to avoid litigation, or representing an actual or potential plaintiff or defendant.

Agency, Authority	*Limitations Period*	*Applies to*
FLSA -- 29 USCS § 255	2 years	Employee claims against employer for unpaid minimum wages, unpaid overtime compensation
IRS -- 26 USCS § 6501 (a)	3 years	Time for IRS to assess withholding taxes
IRS -- 26 USCS § 6501 (c)(1)	None	Failure to file return or willful attempt to evade tax, with or without false return
IRS -- 26 USCS § 6502 (a)	10 years	Time after assessment of tax for IRS to levy or bring action
Utah Tax Commission -- Utah Code Ann. § 59-1-1410 (1)	3 years	Time for Tax Commission to assess withholding taxes
Utah Tax Commission -- Utah Code Ann. § 59-1-1410 (3)	None	Failure to file return, or willful attempt to evade tax, with or without false return
Utah Workforce Services -- Utah Code Ann. § 35A-4-305 (1)(g); Utah Code Ann. § 78B-2-305 (4)	3 years	Time for WFS to file action to collect contributions, interest, penalties, and assessed costs
Individual/ Workers' Comp. -- Utah Code Ann. § 34A-2-417	6 years	Filing of claim for reimbursement of medical expenses
Individual -- Utah Code Ann. § 78B-2-305; Utah Code Ann. § 78B-2-307; Utah Code Ann. § 78B-2-309	3, 4 or 6 years	Time period depends on cause of action, whether tort claim, unwritten contract or written contract

Penalties and Fines

Regardless of how the issue arises, the employer will bear the brunt of the penalties and costs of misclassification. Some of the fines and penalties an employer can face are detailed in Table 2. The lawyer should ensure that owners and officers of separately organized entities understand the possibility of personal liability and the possibility of criminal penalties for some willful behavior.

Statute or Regulation	*Amount of Fine/Penalty*	*Notes*
Failure to file withholding return, 26 USCS § 3509(b)	5% of the tax due for each month the tax remains unpaid, up to a maximum of 25%	Potentially liable parties for IRS fines include owners, officers and anyone authorized to sign payroll
Failure to deposit (pay) withholding taxes, 26 USCS § 3509(a)	0.5% per month up 25%	Reduced by amount of any failure to pay penalty
26 USCS § 6601	Interest on unpaid taxes	Accrues on all unpaid amounts due
Failure to deposit Trust taxes, 26 USCS § 3509	2% of the tax due for each month the tax remains unpaid, up to a maximum of 15%	
Willful evasion, 26 USCS § 3509, 26 USCS § 7201, 26 USCS § 7202, 26 USCS § 7203	Criminal penalties, range from maximum of $10,000 up to $500,000 for a corporation, plus prison	For willful evasion of taxes or willful failure to pay or file return
Penalties, 26 USCS § 6656, 26 USCS § 6672	Penalty equal to 100 % of the unpaid tax	Against any responsible individuals
Wage and overtime violations, 29 USCS § 216(a)	Fine up to $10,000 plus prison up to 6 months	For willful violations
Wage and overtime violations, 29 USCS § 216(b)	Unpaid wage or overtime + equal amount as penalty plus attorneys fees and costs	Employee may recover from employer
Retaliation, 29 USCS § 216(c)	Legal and Equitable remedies plus attorneys fees and costs	For retaliating against employee who complains or takes action
Utah Labor Commission, Utah Code Ann. § 34A-2-209	Class B Misdemeanor for failure to obtain workers' compensation insurance	Applies to employer and officers
Utah WFS – failure to pay Utah Code Ann. § 35A-4-305	Payment of unpaid contributions plus interest at 1% per month	Plus a 5% penalty if not paid within 10 days of written demand
Utah WFS – failure to file Utah Code Ann. § 35A-4-305	5% of the contribution due if 15 or fewer days late, additional 5% if later, up to 25% maximum, with $25 minimum per filing	WFS can "determine" the wages paid, and determination becomes final if employer does not contest within 10 days

A New Wrinkle: Leased, Occasional, and Temporary Employees

Employers often turn to temporary workers, leased employees and other types of "contingent" employees to increase their bottom line. Using third party sources for workers to fill staffing needs allows employers to avoid the headache and overhead of an internal payroll. Employers may also seek to avoid federal regulations that only apply to businesses of a certain size.[17] Unfortunately for the employers, off-payroll workers may remain employees, depending on the amount of control and whether the worker has a bona fide independent business.

[17]For example, the American with Disabilities Act (ADA) applies only to employers with more than 15 employees, 42 USCS § 12111(5)(A); the Family Medical Leave Act (FMLA) applies only to employers with 50 or more employees, 29 CFR 825.104, and the Age Discrimination in Employment Act (ADEA) applies only to employers with more than 20 employees, 29 USCS § 630(b).

It does not matter that the temporary or occasional worker agrees to the classification, or works for the employer for only a short time, as the Microsoft case covered in the Sidebar below demonstrates. It also may not matter that the business hires the worker through a temporary agency or employee leasing service. Regulations at both the federal and state levels sometimes treat such employees as joint employees of both the end-user and the leasing agency.[18] A determination that an off-payroll worker is an employee can allow such workers to participate in benefits offered to other employees and affect the employer's liability under the FMLA, AEDA, ADA and other federal acts.

The Costs of Misclassification

The alphabet soup of regulation can leave employers uncertain about their choices for classifying workers. Even an employer who acts in good faith can wind up on the wrong side of an employee classification dispute. The costs can escalate quickly, as a complaint by a single worker put the entire workforce at issue. *See, e.g., McGuire v. Department of Employment Sec.*, 768 P.2d 985 (Utah Ct. App. 1989). McGuire, a quadriplegic, hired a series of nurses to provide him care, treating each as an independent contractor. One of the nurses filed for unemployment benefits. A resulting audit led to a determination that McGuire had misclassified all six nurses he had hired. 768 P.2d at 986-987. The costs of making a misclassification escalates with the size of the business involved and the number of affected workers, as demonstrated by recent cases involving Microsoft and FedEx Ground Systems, discussed in the Sidebars following the chaper.

Complications for the practitioner

Along with the alphabet soup of regulations, practitioners dealing with employee classification issues must also contend with sometimes conflicting case law. Two Utah cases, *Tasters, Ltd. v. Department of Employment Sec.*, 863 P.2d 12 (Utah Ct. App. 1993) and *New Sleep v.*

---

[18] *See, e.g.,* 29 CFR 791.2 and 29 CFR 825.106 (joint employment under the FLSA); Utah Code Ann. § 34A-2-103 (making the client of a professional employer organization the employer of a covered employee under workers' compensation); Utah Admin. Code R994-202-102 and -103 (distinguishing between employees working for a "temporary help company" and "professional employer organization').

Department of Employment Sec., 703 P.2d 289 (Utah 1985) demonstrate these complications. Both cases dealt with worker classification for unemployment insurance purposes. *New Sleep* involved waterbed installers, and *Tasters* involved product demonstrators in stores. The *New* Sleep court found the installers, mostly college students, to be empoyees, because none had an independently organized business. 703 P.2d at 291-292. In *Tasters*, the Utah Supreme Court found the workers to be independent contractors, reversing the Court of Appeals and the Department of Employment Security's finding that the workers were employees. The *Taster's* Court made no finding that the workers had an independently established business. *See* 863 P.2d at 24-25.

New Sleep was decided under the old A-B test; *Tasters* under the IRS 20 factor test. That difference does not fully explain the divergent outcomes of these two cases, however. As the Court of Appeals noted in the first appeal, "In amending the statute … the legislature did not change the test's emphasis on 'control and direction,' or on 'independent establishment in business' . . . but merely attempted to clarify its application." *Tasters, Ltd. v. Department of Employment Sec.*, 1991 Utah App. LEXIS 80 at *11 & n.3, 163 Utah Adv. Rep. 64 (Utah Ct. App. 1991). Mostly, the Court seemed upset with the way the Department of Employment Security reached its determination. *See, e.g. Id.* at 20 and 21 (discussion of areas where the board exceeded its discretion).

The treatment of "name bands" playing short term gigs in hotels and clubs provides another set of difficult to reconcile cases. Utah has long held that all the band members are employees of the establishment, not the booking agent or band leader. *See, e.g., Utah Hotel Co. v. Industrial Comm'n*, 151 P.2d 467 (Utah 1944), *Black Bull, Inc. v. Industrial Comm'n, Dep't of Employment Sec.*, 547 P.2d 1334 (Utah 1976), *Bigfoot's, Inc. v. Board of Review*, 710 P.2d 180 (Utah 1985). The court in *Black Bull* justified this result by noting the difficulty of collecting unemployment insurance premiums from "some transient music makers who no doubt have vanished with the four winds into the fogs of the seven seas." 151 P.2d at 1336. The Utah cases stand in stark contrast to a U.S. Supreme Court case, *Bartels v. Birmingham*, 332 U.S. 126 (U.S.1947) also involving the employment status of name bands. The Supreme Court came down on the other side of the issue, finding that the band leader was an independent contractor, and the employer of the band members.[19] Although *Bartels*, a Social Security case, involved a different sets of rules, the underlying tests all rely on issues of control and independence. The practitioner must remain aware of these divergent outcomes in advising clients.

Conclusions

The law of employee classifications remains in flux, as employees strive to reduce their overhead and administrative burdens, and governmental agencies attempt to maximize tax revenues and employee protections. The practitioner must consider the many legal complexities surrounding this area of the law. Those complexities include the multiple agencies charged with enforcement, the goals of those agencies, and the conflicting interests of employers and workers. In addition, outcomes are highly factually dependent. Understanding the legal issues and the client's factual situation will allow the practitioner to provide clients with competent legal advice in this area.

[19]Although an old case, Bartels remains good law., and courts continue to cite it for the principal that under FLSA, "'employees are those who as a matter of economic reality are dependent upon the business to which they render service.'" Thompson v. Blesssed Home, Inc., 2014 U.S. Dist. LEXIS 68417 (E.D.N.C. May 16, 2014), *quoting Bartels* at 130.

SIDEBAR 1
IRS Twenty Factor Test

The twenty factors set out in Revenue Ruling 87-41 address almost every aspect of the relationship between a worker and employer. The IRS developed the factors from prior cases and rulings, to help agents, courts and others determine whether a worker should be classified as an employee or an independent contractor. The factors provide guidelines only, and the relative importance of the factors will vary with the circumstances. The twenty factors are paraphrased as follows:

1. Instructions: Can the business instruct the worker about when, where and how to complete the work? If so, the worker is ordinarily an employee.
2. Training: Training generally indicates an employee-employer relationship.
3. Integration in the workforce: higher integration generally shows an employee-employer relationship.
4. Services Rendered Personally: A requirement that the worker must complete the services personally indicates control over the methods, a hallmark of an employer-employee relationship.
5. Hiring, Supervising and Paying Assistants: The ability of a worker to hire assistants, and supervise and pay those assistants, likely makes the worker an independent contractor.
6. Continuing Relationship: A continuing relationship typically evidences an employee-employer relationship.
7. Set Hours of Work: This indicates control and an employee-employer relationship.
8. Full Time Required: This also indicates an employee-employer relationship.
9. Doing Work on Employer's Premises: Another hallmark of control and therefore an employee-employer relationship.
10. Order or Sequence Set: This also indicates control and an employee-employer relationship.

11. Oral or Written Reports: This factor indicates "a degree of control."
12. Payment By Hour, Week or Month: Payment by time period worked, rather than by result, generally supports the finding of an employee-employer relationship.
13. Payment of Business And or Traveling Expenses: An independent contractor typically pays its own expenses, while an employer will reimburse its employees for on the job expenses.
14. Furnishing of Tools And Materials: An independent contractor typically furnishes its own tools and materials.
15. Significant Investment: The greater the investment in the work by the worker, the higher the likelihood that the worker is an independent contractor.
16. Realization of Profit or Loss: the right to realize a profit or loss generally demonstrates that the worker is an independent contractor.
17. Working For More Than One Firm At A Time: An independent contractor may perform services for many people at the same time, while an employee typically works for only one employer.
18. Making Service Available To General Public: An independent contractor holds himself out as available to the general public.
19. Right To Discharge: The greater right the business has to terminate the employee, the more likelihood that the worker is an employee.
20. Right To Terminate: A worker who has the right to unilaterally end the relationship is more likely an independent contractor.

The Revenue Ruling warns users to apply "[s]pecial scrutiny . . . in applying the twenty factors to assure that formalistic aspects of an arrangement designed to achieve a particular status do not obscure the substance of the arrangement."

SIDEBAR 2
Recent Changes to State Laws Concerning Independent Contractors

Many incentives exist for companies to classify workers as independent contractors instead of employees. The harms from misclassification include lost tax revenues, harm to workers from lost benefits and economic disadvantage to competitors who classify their workers as employees. *Craig v. FedEx Ground Package Sys.*, 686 F.3d 423, 430-431 (7th Cir. Ind. 2012). Between 2007 and 21014, twenty-four states, including Utah, enacted or updated legislation designed to reduce the misclassification of employees as independent contractors.

The Utah statutory changes of interest include a 2008 amendment that broadened the definition of those who commit workers' compensation fraud to include people who "intentionally, knowingly, or recklessly * * * misclassify an employee as one of the following so as to avoid the obligation to obtain insurance coverage as mandated by this chapter or Chapter 3: * * * (A) an independent contractor." Utah Code Ann. § 34A-2-110 (2)(a) and(b)(iii)(A). In addition, in 2011 the legislature created a "Worker Classification Coordinated Enforcement Council," intended to "coordinate regulatory and law enforcement efforts related to misclassification." Utah Code Ann. §§ 34-47-201 and 34-47-202(1). The Council has members from the Labor Commission, Workforce Services, the Department of Commerce, the Utah Tax Commission and a non-voting member from the Utah Attorney General's office. Utah Code Ann. §34-17-201.

Other states enacting statues designed to limit employee mischaracterization include:

- Arizona: Act Defining "Indications of Control" (H.B.2150) (enacted 3/29/12)
- California: Independent Contractor Willful Misclassification Law (S.B.459) (enacted 10/9/11)
- Colorado: Misclassification of Employees as Independent Contractors Law for Purposes of the Colorado Employment Security Act (H.B. 09-1310) (enacted 6/09)

- Connecticut: Act Concerning Employee Misclassification (S.B. 454) (eff. 7/1/08); and Act Implementing the Recommendations of the Joint Enforcement Commission on Employee Misclassification (H.B. 5204) (enacted May 5, 2010)
- Delaware: Workplace Fraud Act (Title 19, Section 3501 et seq.) (enacted 7/31/09)
- Florida: Act Defining the Term "Independent Contractor" (H.B. 311) (enacted 5/4/11)
- Illinois: Employee Classification Act (820 ILCS 185) (eff. 1/1/08)
- Indiana: Independent Contractor Information Sharing Law (S.B. 0478) (eff. 7/1/09)
- Kansas: Misclassification of Employees to Avoid Tax Withholding, Contributions and Reporting Requirements (H.B. 2135) (enacted May 12, 2011)
- Louisiana: Act Providing Graduated Penalties for Misclassification (S.B. 472) (eff. 8/1/12)
- Massachusetts: Independent Contractor Misclassification Law (enacted 1990, as amended 1992, 1993, 1998, 2004)
- Maryland: Workplace Fraud Act of 2009 (S.B. 909) (enacted May 7, 2009) and Amendments to Workplace Fraud Act (S.B. 272) (enacted 5/2/12)
- Maine: Act to Ensure that Construction Workers are Protected by Workers' Compensation (LD 1456, HP1008) (eff. 1/1/10), Independent Contractor Status of Truckers and Couriers (LD 1099, SP 332) (eff. 5/31/11), Uniform Definition of Independent Contractor for Unemployment Purposes (LD1420, HP437) (eff. 6/10/11)
- Minnesota: Act Clarifying Definition of Independent Contractor and Creating Pilot Project for Construction Contractors (S.F. 1653) (enacted 5/14/12); Independent Contractor Law (MN Stat. 181.723) (eff. 7/1/08)

- Nebraska: Employee Classification Act (for Construction and Delivery Services) (LB 563) (eff. 7/15/10)
- New Hampshire: Act Relative to the Definition of Employee (S.B. 92) (eff. 1/1/08)
- New Jersey: Construction Industry Independent Contractor Act (N.J.S.A. 34:20-1 et seq.) (enacted 7/13/07)
- New York: Construction Industry Fair Play Act (S 5847C) (A 8237A-2010) (enacted 8/27/10), Commercial Goods Transportation Industry Fair Play Act (A 8451-2013) (eff. 4/10/14)
- Pennsylvania: Construction Workplace Misclassification Act (H 400) (enacted 10/13/10; eff. 2/10/11)
- Rhode Island: Suspected Misclassification Information Sharing Law (H 7564) (enacted 6/25/12; eff. 6/25/12)
- Vermont: Act Related to Misclassification of Employees to Lower Premiums for Workers' Compensation and Unemployment Compensation (H. 647) (eff. 7/1/10)
- Washington: Determination of Independent Contractor Status Law (H.B. 1701) (eff. 6/12/08)
- Wisconsin: Worker Classification Compliance Law (S.B. 672) (eff. 1/1/11)

Source: http://independentcontractorcompliance.com/legal-resources/state-ic-laws-and-selected-bills/

SIDEBAR 3
Development of Utah Statutory Rules and Analysis Factors

Employment classification under Utah Workers' Compensation law has long focused on control. In the main opinion in *Stover Bedding Co. v. Industrial Comm'n*, 99 Utah 423 (Utah 1940) the court found the worker was an independent contractor because the evidence showed "that there was no control or right of control over the details of his work as a salesman." *Id.* at 427. While the court also mentioned "nature of the business or occupation; which party furnishes the instrumentalities and tools; the place of work; the time of employment; the method of payment; and the intent of the parties to the contract," it never addressed the existence of an independent business. Justice Wolfe, in a dissent, reviewed the historical development of the law and argued for the adoption of a test that focused more whether "the so-called independent contractor really is engaged in an independent calling." *Id.* at 429. Neither the Utah legislature nor courts have taken his suggestion. *See, e.g., Bennett v. Industrial Comm'n*, 726 P.2d 427, 429 (Utah 1986) ("it will almost always follow that if the evidence shows that an "employer" retains the right to control the work of the claimant, the claimant is the employer's employee for workmen's compensation purposes"); *Mallory v. Brigham Young Univ.*, 2014 UT 27 at P20-P22, 332 P.3d 922 (Utah 2014) (right to control is sufficient to finding a applying master-servant relationship for workers' compensation purposes).

The law used to determine a worker's status for unemployment purposes has not remained so static. Initially, Utah used a two part ("A-B") test: to be an independent contractor, the worker must be "free from control or direction over the performance of those services" and be "customarily engaged in an independently established trade, occupation, profession, or business of the same nature as that involved in the contract of service." In 1981 Utah moved to a three part test, often referred to as the "ABC Test," still used by many states.[1] The three-part ABC test requires finding that the worker is (A) free of control "both under his contract of hire and in fact;" (B) the service the worker provides is

---

[1] *See* discussion of some of these laws at http://www.nelp.org/page/-/Justice/2011/2011IndependentContractorReformUpdate.pdf?nocdn=1

"outside the usual course of the business . . . or is performed outside of all the places of business of the enterprise" and (C) the individual is customarily engaged in an independent business.[2] In 1986, Utah went back to a two-part test, retaining the A and C prongs of the ABC test.[3]

In 1989 1996 Utah adopted the IRS's 20 part test. *Tasters, Ltd. v. Department of Employment Sec.*, 163 Utah Adv. Rep. 64 (Utah Ct. App. 1991). It continued to use variations on this test, *see, e.g.*, 1991 Ut. HB 26, Ch. 174 (setting out one version of the 20 part test) until 1996, when it enacted the current test.

Currently Utah uses a two part test that requires an initial finding that the worker has an independently established business or trade. Utah Code Ann. § 35A-4-204(3)(a). Only after that finding is made does the inquiry move to control issues. Utah Code Ann. § 35A-4-204(3)(a) and (b). Regulations enacted under the Code set out a fifteen point test divided into these two areas of inquiry. Utah Admin. Code R994-204-303. The factors are:

I. Factors for determining whether the worker has an independently established business:

    1. Separate Place of Business. A separate place of business favors classification as an independent contractor.
    2. Tools and Equipment. A worker who has a substantial investment in the tools needed to do the job will more likely be classified as an independent contractor.
    3. Other Clients. If the worker provides similar services to other clients, the likelihood exists that the worker is an independent contractor.
    4. Profit or Loss. An independent contractor can realize a gain or loss from the operation of his or her independent business.

[2] *Tasters, Ltd. v. Department of Employment Sec.*, 163 Utah Adv. Rep. 64 (Utah Ct. App. 1991) at 27, n17

[3] Allen v. Industrial Comm'n, 732 P.2d 508 (Utah 1987) at n6.

5. Advertising. An independent contractor may advertise or otherwise let the public know his or her availability to perform services.
6. Licenses. A worker who has obtained a business license and other licenses needed to carry on his or her business is most likely an independent contractor.
7. Business Records and Taxes. The worker's business records and tax records should match the reality of the business relationship with the employer.

If the employer meets the burden of proving the worker has an independently established business, a rebuttable presumption exists that the employer did not have a right to control the methods or details of the work. That presumption can be overcome, however.

II. Factors to measure control and direction:

1. Instructions. The need to follow instructions from the employer on the methods of completing the work is a key hallmark of an employee.
2. Training. The more training the employer supplies to the worker, the more it looks like an employer-employee relationship.
3. Pace or Sequence. A requirement to complete the work at a particular pace or in a particular sequence indicates an employer-employee relationship.
4. Work on Employer's Premises. Requiring work to be performed at the employer's place of business indicates an ability to supervise the work, another hallmark of an employer-employee relationship.
5. Personal Services. An employee generally must complete all assigned work, and cannot hire assistants or third parties to perform the work.
6. Continuous Relationship. "A continuous relationship does not exist where the worker is contracted to complete

specifically identified projects, even though the services relationship may extend over a significant period of time."

7. Set hours of work. Having set works to complete the work shows an employer-employee relationship.
8. Method of Payment. Payment by the hour, day, week or month indicates an employer-employee relationship, "unless it is just a convenient way of paying . . . a fixed price agreed upon as the cost of a job."

These fifteen factors "are intended only as aids in the analysis of the facts of each case. The degree of importance of each factor varies depending on the service and the factual context in which it is performed." Utah Admin Code. R. 994-204-303. The practitioner should be careful to note the version of the rule in effect at the time of any court decision.

SIDEBAR 4
The High Cost of Misclassification

In the 1980s Microsoft hired a number of workers on a "temporary basis." It classified these workers as independent contractors and paid them out of its accounts payable account instead of through its payroll department. The workers were otherwise "fully integrated" into Microsoft's workforce, and some worked for Microsoft for years. *Vizcaino v. Microsoft Corp.*, 97 F.3d 1187, 1190 (9th Cir. 1996), aff'd *en banc Vizcaino v. Microsoft* Corp., 120 F.3d 1006 (9th Cir. 1997); cert denied, *Microsoft Corp. v. Vizcaino*, 522 U.S. 1098 (U.S.S. Ct. 1998). When Microsoft hired the temporary workers, it told them that they were not eligible for any benefits. *Id.* The IRS audited Microsoft in 1989 and 1990. It determined that Microsoft should have classified the temporary workers as employees. Microsoft agreed to the reclassification and paid the back taxes and other penalties. 97 F.3d at 1191.

The story does not end there, however. Microsoft hired some of the "temporary" workers as regular employees, and offered the others the choice of being terminated or continuing to work for Microsoft through a temporary agency that would provide payroll services. *Id.* A group of the former temporary workers then sought to participate in Microsoft's employee stock option plan and other employee benefits. At this, Microsoft balked, and class action litigation ensued. In the litigation, Microsoft argued that the workers had agreed to forego all participation in employee benefits when they signed their independent contractor agreements. Microsoft convinced the lower court, but the appellate court disagreed. *Id.* at 1197. As common law employees, the workers were entitled under ERISA to participate in the employee stock option plan not only during the time they were misclassified by Microsoft, but also after they become employed through the temporary agency. *Id.*

Microsoft then sought a rehearing *en banc*. The Ninth Circuit affirmed the appellate ruling *en banc*. *Vizcaino v. Microsoft Corp.*, 120 F.3d 1006 (9th Cir. 1997). Following that decision, Microsoft reached a settlement in which it agreed to pay the plaintiff class nearly $97 million, including just over $27,000 in attorney's fees, *Vizcaino v. Microsoft Corp.*, 142 F. Supp. 2d 1299 (W.D. Wash. 2001), aff'd *Vizcaino v. Microsoft Corp.*, 290 F.3d 1043 (9th Cir. 2002), cert denied, Vizcaino v. Waite, 2002 U.S. LEXIS 8338 (U.S. S. Ct. 2002). This case and the FedEx cases discussed above demonstrate the high cost of misclassifying workers.

SIDEBAR 5
FedEx Ground Cases – Determining the Right to Control

FedEx Ground trucks deliver packages and overnight letters to businesses. The trucks sport the FedEx logo and drivers wear a FedEx uniform. Yet FedEx long treated these drivers as independent contractors. Each driver signed an "Operating Agreement" stating on page one that "Both FedEx Ground and Contractor intend that Contractor will provide these services ***strictly as an independent contractor***, and not as an employee of FedEx Ground for any purpose."

In the early 2000s, drivers for FedEx Ground Systems across the country began filing class action lawsuits against FedEx, alleging that FedEx wrongly classified them as independent contractors. Many of the separate class actions (including a Utah case) were consolidated into one multidistrict litigation in the Northern District of Indiana (the MDL court). In December 2010, the MDL court granted full or partial summary judgment in favor of FedEx and against the drivers in nearly all the cases. In re FedEx Ground Package Sys., 758 F. Supp. 2d 638 (N.D. Ind. 2010).

The MDL found that Operating Agreement language persuasive "because the intent expressed was so clear." 758 F. Supp. 2d at 658. The Court also cited to provisions in the Operating Agreement that gave the drivers "entrepreneurial opportunities." Id. at 658-659. These opportunities included the right to hire helpers or replacement drivers, their responsibility for acquiring and keeping their vehicles in good repair, and their ability to "sell" their routes to another driver.

The decision by the MDL Court in 2010 made it appear that the FedEx drivers would remain independent contractors across the country. The tide has now turned, as several appellate courts have recently found the drivers to be employees. In August 2014, the Ninth Circuit court reversed the MDL court's summary judgment in two remanded cases, *Slayman v. FedEx Ground Package Sys.*, 2014 U.S. App. LEXIS 16623 (9th Cir. August 27, 2014), based on Oregon law, and *Alexander v. FedEx Ground Package Sys.*, 2014 U.S. App. LEXIS 16585 (9th Cir. August 27, 2014), decided under California law. In both *Slayman* and *Alexander*, the Ninth Circuit found the drivers to be employees as a matter of law. The Ninth Circuit wasted no time in going beyond the words of the Operating Agreement; immediately after its opening sentence in *Alexander,* the Ninth Circuit Court said:

> The drivers must wear FedEx uniforms, drive FedEx-approved vehicles, and groom themselves according to FedEx's appearance standards. FedEx tells its drivers what packages to deliver, on what days, and at what times. Although drivers may operate multiple delivery routes and hire third parties to help perform their work, they may do so only with FedEx's consent.

2014 U.S. App. LEXIS 16585, *2-*3. Nor did the "entrepreneurial opportunities" on which the MDL court relied convince the Ninth Circuit. A driver seeking to hire a helper, or expand his routes could do so only with FedEx approval. *Alexander*, 2014 U.S. App. LEXIS 16585 at *30; *see also Slayman,* 2014 U.S. App. LEXIS 16623 at *25. Because the actual text of the Operating Agreement gave FedEx significant right to control the manner and methods the drivers used to complete their work, the court ruled that the drivers must be classified as employees. *See* 2014 App. LEXIS 16585 at *16-17; 2014 App. LEXIS 16623 at *20-21.

Another of the remanded cases, *Craig v. FedEx Ground Package Sys.*, 686 F.3d 423 (7th Cir. Ind. 2012), involved Kansas law. When the driver appealed after remand, the Seventh Circuit determined that it could not determine the drivers' employment status under Kansas law, and certified the question to the Kansas Supreme Court. *Id.* at 431-32.

The Kansas Supreme Court issued its ruling on October 3, 2014. *Craig v. FedEx Ground Package Sys.*, Case No. No. 108.526 (Kan. 2014). That court noted that although the question appears simple – is the driver an employee or independent contractor – the answer "defies such simplicity." After agreeing with the Seventh Circuit that the case was a close one, the Kansas Court said "the company carefully structured its drivers' operating agreements so that it could label the drivers as independent contractors in order to gain a competitive advantage.... This is a close case by design, not happenstance." The Kansas Court concluded that the drivers were employees, saying FedEx "established an employment relationship with its delivery drivers but dressed that relationship in independent contractor clothing." *Id.*

In addition to these three cases, other courts have reached similar results recently.[1] *Alexander* alone directly affects nearly 2,300 FedEx Ground drivers in California. As the Seventh Circuit noted in *Craig*, these decisions will likely directly affect thousands more drivers at FedEx as well as many other workers in other industries. 686 F.3d at 430-431. According to one commentator, these decisions will cost FedEx hundreds of millions of dollars, in addition to the costs of litigation. "FedEx avoided health care, workers' compensation, paid sick leave and vacation, retirement and more. FedEx made drivers pay for their uniquely FedEx branded trucks, FedEx branded uniforms, and FedEx scanners. Plus, fuel, insurance, tires, oil changes, maintenance, even workers' compensation coverage." FedEx will also have to assume these costs going forward, and will have to pay these drivers a competitive wage (including overtime pay), and pay all penalties assessed against it by governmental agencies.[2]

[1] *See, e.g., Wells v. FedEx Ground Package Sys., 979 F. Supp. 2d 1006 (E.D. Mo. 2013)*; *Gray v. FedEx Ground Package Sys.*, 2014 U.S. Dist. LEXIS 123906 (E.D. Mo. Sept. 5, 2014) (allowing plaintiff driver who prevailed in *Wells* to pursue a fraud claim against FedEx for damages resulting from FedEx's failure to allow him to participate in its employee benefit plans); *Scovil v. FedEx Ground Package Sys.*, 2014 U.S. Dist. LEXIS 33361 (D. Me. Mar. 14, 2014) (settlement before trial with driver class receiving approximately $5.8 million). In *Schwann v. FedEx Ground Package Sys.*, 2014 U.S. Dist. LEXIS 15533 (D. Mass. Feb. 7, 2014) the court certified the question of employee status to Massachusetts Supreme Judicial Court. It has not yet written a decision on the certified question.

[2] Wood, Robert W. , Forbes On-line *"FedEx Misclassified Drivers As Independent Contractors, Rules Ninth Circuit"*, August 27, 2014 http://www.forbes.com/sites/robertwood/2014/08/27/fedex-misclassified-drivers-as-independent-contractors-rules-ninth-circuit/, accessed 9/25/2014. *See also Gray v. FedEx Ground Package sys.*, 2014 U.S. Dist. 123902, awarding 24 plaintiff drivers nearly $30,000 in court costs alone, not including any attorneys fees.

CHAPTER 38

HUMAN RESOURCES

NONCOMPETITION AND NONSOLICITATION AGREEMENTS

ANDREW DIES AND BILLIE SIDDOWAY[1]

Restrictive Covenants

Noncompetition, nonsolicitation and nondisclosure agreements are examples of restrictive covenants. Restrictive covenants can be part of the sale of a business or part of an employment or contractor relationship.

Used in the sale of business, a restrictive covenant may limit a seller's right to open or operate a new competing business in the same market. This restriction protects the buyer's expectation in the continued performance of the business purchased.

In the employment context, restrictive covenants may bar an employee from working for a competitor, soliciting customers, soliciting coworkers, or disclosing confidential information during employment or after termination. Such restrictions allow the employer to share relationships and confidential information while safeguarding against the risk that the employee will abscond with them.

Restrictive covenants may be referred to as non-compete, non-solicit, non-dealing, non-poaching, anti-piracy, non-recruitment, non-hire, anti-raiding, or confidentiality provisions. Whatever the name, the validity of these covenants is analyzed in the same way.[2]

---

[1]Andrew Deiss is an attorney with Deiss Law PC. Billie Siddoway is an attorney with Siddoway Law Office, PLLC in Driggs, Idaho. They represent clients seeking to enforce or invalidate restrictive covenants.

[2]Restrictive covenants—including agreements "that the employee will not compete with the employer, disclose private information, or solicit the employer's customers"—are all subject to the same test of enforceability. *TruGreen Companies, L.L.C. v. Mower Brothers, Inc.*, 2008 UT 81, ¶ 11, 199 P.3d 929. *See also System Concepts, Inc. v. Dixon*, 669 P.2d 421, 425–26 (Utah 1983).

Validity of Restrictive Covenants

As a public policy matter, the State of Utah supports competition and free access to employment.[3] Restrictive covenants are generally disfavored under Utah law.[4] This means that a restrictive covenant must be written and signed—they will almost never be implied.[5] The restriction must be "necessary for the protection of the business" and impose no greater restraint than "reasonably necessary to secure such protection" to be enforceable.[6]

In 1951, the Utah Supreme Court imposed a four-part test to analyze the validity of a restrictive covenant. Under the *Rose Park* test, a restrictive covenant is valid only if it is:

> [1] supported by consideration,
>
> [2] negotiated in good faith,
>
> [3] necessary to protect confidential information or goodwill, and
>
> [4] reasonably limited in time and geographic area.[7]

Although this test arose in the analysis of a covenant negotiated in the sale of a business, [8] it is also applied to restrictive covenants arising in the employment context.[9]

First Requirement: Consideration

Consideration is something of value given in exchange for a promise or performance. It is necessary to give some form of consideration to validate a restrictive covenant. However, it is not necessary to provide separate consideration. For example, in the context of the sale of a

---

[3]*See, e.g.*, Utah Code § 76-10-3115 (authorizing the attorney general to advocate the policy of competition); Utah Const. Art. XII Sec. 19 ("Each person in Utah is free to obtain and enjoy employment whenever possible, and any person, or corporation, their agent, servant or employee thereof, may not maliciously interfering or hindering in any way, with any person from obtaining, or enjoying employment or , or their agent, servant, or employee may not maliciously interfere with any person from obtaining employment or enjoying employment already obtained from any other person or corporation.")

[4]*St. Benedict's Dev. Co. v. St. Benedict's Hosp.*, 811 P.2d 194, 198 (Utah 1991) (holding that restrictive covenants are not favored by the law and will generally not be implied).

[5]Some employers incorporate restrictive covenants in employee handbooks and ask employees to sign an acknowledgment of receipt of the handbook, rather than sign the covenant. The Utah courts do not appear to have addressed the validity of this practice. However, the best business practice would be to sign a written agreement containing the restrictive covenant.

[6]*St. Benedict's*, 81 P.2d at 198 (Utah 1991) (*quoting Allen v. Rose Park Pharmacy*, 237 P.2d 823, 826 (Utah 1951)).

[7]*TruGreen*, 208 UT 81, ¶ 11 (citing *Rose Park Pharmacy*, 237 P.2d at 828).

[8]*Rose Park Pharmacy*, 237 P.2d at 826.

[9]*See, e.g., Robbins v. Finlay*, 645 P.2d 623, 627 (Utah 1982).

business, consideration for a restrictive covenant can be part of the payment given for the business. In the context of an employment relationship, consideration may be an offer of employment or continued employment.[10]

It is not enough to promise to provide something of value. Consideration must actually be delivered. For example, if a separate payment is offered for the restrictive covenant, and then the payment is not provided, the covenant is invalid. Similarly, if consideration is tied into the payment for a company or an offer of employment, and the payment or employment is not provided, the covenant is invalid.[11]

In some states, an employer must provide separate consideration to an existing employee in order to validate a restrictive covenant. However, this is not the case in Utah. Even if a Utah employer does not present a restrictive covenant to an at-will employee until well after the employee has started working, the promise of continued employment is sufficient consideration to validate the covenant.

Second Requirement: Good Faith Negotiation

Since the adoption of the *Rose Park* test, Utah courts have repeatedly restated that restrictive covenants are enforceable only if negotiated in good faith. However, the appellate courts have not identified many examples of bad faith. Examples of bad faith may include the following:

- Promising payment in exchange for signing the covenant, and then refusing to pay.[12]
- Offering employment with the intent of employing an employee only long enough to bind the employee to a covenant not to compete.[13]

Third Requirement: Legitimate Business Interest

In Utah, restrictive covenants are only valid if used to protect a legitimate business interest. Utah courts recognize three such interests:

---

[10] *See System Concepts*, 669 P.2d at 426 (recognizing continued employment as consideration).

[11] Restatement (Third) of Employment Law § 8.06, *ill.* 15 (T.D. No. 4, 2011).

[12] *Hopkins v. Hales*, 2008 UT App. 95, ¶ 6, 182 P.3d 402.

[13] *Rose Park Pharmacy*, 237 P.3d at 826 (Utah 1951) (citing *Wark v. Ervin Press Corp.*, 48 F.2d 152, 156 (7th Cir. 1931)).

(1) confidential information, (2) goodwill, and (3) an investment in education or training of an employee.[14]

Most confidential information is subject to the Utah Uniform Trade Secrets Act, Utah Code § 13-24-1, *et seq.*, and discussed more fully in the Trade Secret section of this text.

Goodwill is defined as "a business's reputation, patronage, and other intangible assets that are considered when appraising the business."[15] A company's customer base is the goodwill component most likely to be subject to a restrictive covenant.[16] A covenant may be necessary where an employee will "likely draw away customers from his former employer if he were permitted to compete nearby."[17]

If a covenant is used to protect goodwill, then an employer seeking injunctive relief must show that the employee is "special, unique or extraordinary."[18] In one example, the Utah Supreme Court found that an employee was "special and unique in comparison to other employees" where she provided managerial and marketing services beyond the roles of other "employees with sales related positions."[19] In contrast, a salesman did not meet this heightened standard where there was nothing to indicate that he "had any greater effect on plaintiff's goodwill, or other legally protectable interest, than the competition of any other salesman employed by a competitor of plaintiff."[20] Because his covenant served no purpose other than to restrict him from competing with a former employer, the covenant was void.[21]

The "special, unique or extraordinary" standard prevents employers from excluding employees with a "common calling," such as salesman, from working in their field. To address this concern, Utah courts hold that "general knowledge and expertise" as well as the "efficiency and skills

---

[14] *See, e.g., System Concepts*, 669 P.2d at 426.

[15] *PC Crane Serv., LLC v. McQueen Masonry, Inc.*, 2012 UT App 61 ¶ 2, 273 P.3d 396 (*quoting Black's Law Dictionary* 763 (9th ed. 2009)).

[16] *See PC Crane*, 2012 UT App. 61, ¶ 2.

[17] *Kasco Servs. Corp*. v. Benson, 831 P.2d 86, 88 (internal citations omitted).

[18] *Id.*

[19] *System Concepts*, 669 P.2d at 426, n. 11 ("Defendant's special and unique services included management of sales activities and customer referral on a national level, extensive personal promotions in advertising media, products development and design consultation, development of sales methods and general promotion of products.").

[20] *Robbins*, 645 P.2d at 628.

[21] *Id.* at 627.

which an employee develops through his work belong to [the employee] and not to his former employer."[22]

A restrictive covenant that does not protect a legitimate interest, but that exists to restrict competition is not enforceable. [23] Restrictive employment covenants must be "carefully drawn to protect only the legitimate interests of the employer."[24] Employers should avoid overreaching, as it can be construed as restricting competition rather than protecting legitimate interests. If confidential information is adequately protected by a non-solicitation agreement, then an additional non-compete may be overreaching.[25] For example, if an employer could protect goodwill by barring an employee from contacting the employer's fifteen customers for two years, then an additional covenant barring the employee from working in the industry for two years may be unenforceable.[26]

Fourth Requirement: Reasonableness

Finally, to be enforceable the restrictions that a covenant imposes must be reasonable. "The reasonableness of a covenant depends upon several factors, including its geographical extent; the duration of the limitation; the nature of the employee's duties; and the nature of the interest which the employer seeks to protect such as trade secrets, the goodwill of his business, or an extraordinary investment in the training or education of the employee."[27] The most frequently cited limits on reasonableness in Utah case law are time and geographic scope.

Courts analyze these factors on a case-by-case basis, taking into account the particular facts and circumstances of each situation.[28] These factors should be considered together. For example, a more limited geographic scope might suggest a longer time period is permissible.

Utah courts have approved a broad range of time restrictions in restrictive covenants. Reasonable time limits may be more generous in

---

[22] *Id.* at 628 (*quoting Hallmark Personnel of Texas, Inc. v. Franks*, 562 S.W.2d 933,936 (Tex. Ct. App. 1978)).

[23] *Robbins*, 645 P.2d at 627.

[24] *Id.*

[25] *See generally Robbins*, 645 P.2d 623.

[26] *Id.*

[27] *Id.* at 627.

[28] *System Concepts*, 669 P.2d at 427.

the context of a sale of a business. For example, the Utah Supreme Court has approved a twenty-five year non-compete arising from the sale of a business.[29] Periods of seven and five years have also been upheld.[30] However, in the employment context, restrictions are typically limited to one or two years.[31]

A geographic restriction is reasonable if it is limited to the area where a business "has been and is seeking its market."[32] If a company's market is nationwide, some limitation other than a geographic restriction may be more appropriate. For example, in one case where a company had just 2,500 potential clients in the United States, an activity-based restriction was deemed more appropriate than a geographic restriction.[33] There is no hard line test for validating the geographic restriction in a restrictive covenant; however, courts are more likely to void an agreement on the basis that it lacks a geographic restriction where the customer base at issue is local.[34] Activity-based restrictions rather than geographic restrictions may be more appropriate for companies engaged in internet-based commerce.

Litigation Arising from an Employment Relationship

Lawsuits involving restrictive employment covenants typically arise in one of two circumstances: (1) an employee seeks to invalidate a covenant, or (2) an employer seeks to enforce a covenant.

Employees may ask the court to declare that a covenant to which they have agreed is invalid.[35] Utah courts are authorized to issue a declaration of invalidity even before any wrongdoing may have been committed.[36] This procedure allows an employee to determine whether the covenant is enforceable before accepting a position with a competitor

---

[29] *Valley Mortuary v. Fairbanks*, 225 P.2d 739 (Utah 1950).

[30] *Electrical Distributors, Inc. v. SFR, Inc.*, 166 F.3d 1074,1085 (10th Cir. 1999) (seven year restriction); *Rudd v. Parks*, 588 P.2d 709 (Utah 1978) (five year restriction); *Rose Park Pharmacy*, 237 P.2d 823 (five year restriction).

[31] *See, e.g., System Concepts*, 669 P.2d at 426 (upholding a two-year non-compete); *Kasco Servs.*, 831 P.2d at 88–89 (Utah 1992) (recognizing an eighteen-month restriction). *Compare, e.g., Tahitian Noni Int'l v. Dean*, Docket No. 2:09-CV-51, 2009 WL 197525 (D. Utah Jan. 26, 2009) (holding that a three-year non-compete was unreasonable where it would effectively destroy the defendant's career in the industry of his choice).

[32] *System Concepts*, 669 P.2d at 427.

[33] *Id.* at 426–27.

[34] *Id.* at 427.

[35] Declaratory Judgment Act, UTAH CODE ANN. §§ 78B-6-401 *et seq.*

[36] *Kapetanov v. Small Claims Ct. of Ogden*, 659 P.2d 1049, 1051 (Utah 1983).

or taking some other action that may violate the express language of the covenant.

If an employee has violated a covenant, an employer may file an action against the employee to enforce the agreement. In some circumstances, the employer may also sue a new employer in a tort or conspiracy action related to the employee's conduct.

Prior to litigating a restrictive employment covenant, there are number of concerns that the employee or employer should consider. These include but are not limited to the following:

1. The party seeking to enforce the covenant generally has the burden of proving that the covenant is valid and enforceable.[37]
2. Because restrictive employment covenants are disfavored, they may be strictly construed against the employer.[38]
3. The covenant may be governed by the law of a state other than Utah, and may require that any lawsuit be brought in another state. This may be the case if the covenant contains a choice of law provision selecting the law of another state or if one of the parties or business entities resides in another state with an interest in the outcome.[39]
4. In some states, courts are authorized by statute to edit the covenant to make its restrictions reasonable and enforceable.[40] The question of whether to authorize this power (called "blue penciling") has not yet been decided in Utah. However, courts in other states have explained why blue penciling should not be employed.[41] Notably, if a covenant may be edited rather than voided, employers have no incentive to impose reasonable restrictions in the first instance.[42]

[37] *See System Concepts*, 669 P.2d at 425–26.

[38] *See St. Benedict's*, 811 P.2d at 198 (holding that restrictive covenants are not favored by the law).

[39] *See, e.g., Innerlight Inc. v. Matrix Group LLC*, 2009 UT 31, ¶¶ 14–16, 214 P.3d 854.

[40] *See, e.g.,* Idaho Code 44-2703.

[41] *See, e.g., Moore v. Curtis 1000, Inc.*, 640 F.2d 920, 923 (8th Cir. 1981) (internal citations omitted) ("Employers covenant for more than is necessary, hope that their employees will thereby be deterred from competing, and rely on the courts to rewrite the agreements so as to make them enforceable if their employees do compete").

[42] *Id.*

5. Employers face a significant risk if a form covenant is invalidated. Under principles of *res judicata*, if one employee is successful in defeating a covenant, it could effectively invalidate form covenants used with other employees.[43] The employer would thus be required to have all employees sign a new, less restrictive covenant, and former employees would not be bound by the overly restrictive covenant. On the other hand, if an employer succeeded in enforcing a covenant against one employee, that decision would not be binding on other employees, who may assert different arguments or defenses.
6. In extraordinary cases, where a party uses the litigation processes wrongfully to stymie competition, damages may be available. For example, if an employer brings a bad faith claim to prevent an employee from working for a competitor, and the employee ultimately wins the lawsuit, the employee may bring a subsequent action against the employer for abuse of process or wrongful use of civil proceedings.[44] Such cases are not common, but do occur.

Litigation Arising from the Sale of a Business

Lawsuits challenging a restrictive covenant negotiated in the sale of a business are similar to litigating employment covenants. As discussed above, the *Rose Park* test for validity applies to both employment covenants and sale of business covenants. However, reasonable time restrictions may be substantially longer when the covenant arises in the sale of a business context.[45]

---

[43]Issue preclusion (also called collateral estoppel) prevents a party from re-litigating an issue that has already been before the court. "A party seeking to invoke collateral estoppel must establish that: (1) the issue decided in the prior adjudication is identical to the one presented in the instant action; (2) the party against whom issue preclusion is asserted was a party, or in privity with a party, to the prior adjudication; (3) the issue in the first action was completely, fully, and fairly litigated; and (4) the first suit resulted in a final judgment on the merits." *Buckner v. Kennard*, 2004 UT 78 ¶¶ 13, 99 P.3d 842.

[44]A wrongful use of civil proceedings claim requires "(1) the actor initiating the prior proceeding acted without probable cause, and primarily for a purpose other than that of securing the proper adjudication of the claim; and (2) except when they are ex parte, the prior proceedings terminated in favor of the person against whom they [were] brought." *Anderson Dev. Co. v. Tobias*, 2005 Utah 36 ¶ 64, 116 P.3d 323 (internal quotation marks omitted). "[T]o establish a claim for abuse of process, a claimant must demonstrate [f]irst, an ulterior purpose; [and] second, an act in the use of the process not proper in the regular prosecution of the proceedings." *Id.* ¶ 65 (internal quotation marks omitted).

[45]*See* footnotes 29–31, *supra*.

Litigation Remedies

A remedy is the award granted by the court in litigation. In cases involving restrictive covenants, there are a number of remedy options, including: declaratory judgment, injunctive relief, and monetary damages.

A declaratory judgment, discussed above, consists of a declaration from the court that the covenant is, or is not, valid. A declaratory judgment has the advantage of seeking a court ruling before assuming the risk of breach and accompanying damages.

Injunctive relief is the power of the court to ban conduct that would violate the covenant. A temporary restraining order is an emergency order, often granted at the outset of a case on little or no advance notice, barring conduct for a period of up to 14 days.[46] Preliminary injunctive relief is issued at the outset of the action to prevent certain conduct while the case is pending.[47] Permanent injunctive relief is granted at the conclusion of a case, ordering a party to take certain action, or refrain from taking a particular action, for a time certain.

Monetary relief takes the form of a judgment for the payment of money. Monetary relief may consist of actual damages, liquidated damages and litigation expenses.

Actual damages are measured by the claimant's lost profits, which are the profits that the claimant would have earned but for the breach of the covenant.[48]

Liquidated damage is an amount specified in the covenant or contract (*e.g.* the covenant may specify that if the employee breaches the non-solicitation provision, the employer will be entitled to liquidated damages of $5,000 per breach). To be enforced, a liquidated damages amount must represent a fair and reasonable estimate of the amount necessary to compensate the injured party.[49] Liquidated damages that are grossly disproportionate to an estimated injury or that are designed to penalize the breaching party will not be enforced. A claimant cannot

---

[46]Utah Rule of Civil Procedure 65A(b).

[47]Utah Rule of Civil Procedure 65A(a).

[48]*See TruGreen Companies,* 2008 UT 81 ¶ 18.

[49]*Robbins,* 645 P.2d at 625-26.

recover liquidated damages and actual damages, but may be able to plead both in the alternative and elect a remedy as the litigation progresses.

Attorneys' fees and costs of suit can be significant in restrictive covenant litigation. The prevailing party may be entitled to reimbursement of attorneys' fees if provided in the contract. Costs of suit, which are typically a small percentage of litigation expenses, are generally awarded to the prevailing party as a matter of course.[50]

Attorney Exception

In Utah, attorneys are generally exempt from restrictive covenants. The professional rules governing lawyers bar any employment agreement or settlement agreement that restricts lawyers from practicing law.[51] Utah has not yet recognized a statutory or regulatory exemption for any other profession or industry, although strong policy reasons for exemptions may exist, such as in the case of medical professionals.

Drafting Considerations for Employers

While it is a common practice to use a uniform restrictive covenant for all employees, the better business practice is to customize restrictive covenants for each employee—especially for each key employee. To the extent a restrictive covenant is designed to protect confidential information, the protected information should be identified with as much particularity as possible, identifying how the employee subject to the covenant will have access to that information. For covenants designed to protect goodwill, restrictions to customer relationships should be limited to those that the employee will develop and maintain in the course of his or her employment. Applying these limitations will provide the best opportunity for the employee to understand and abide by the restrictions, and it will increase the likelihood that a Utah court will uphold the validity of the covenant.

[50]Utah R. Civ. Procedure 54(d).

[51]Utah R. Prof'l Conduct 5.6.

CHAPTER 39

HUMAN RESOURCES

POLICY AND PROCEDURE MANUALS

DENNIS GLADWELL[1]

Executive Summary: Almost all top tier business concerns develop HR policies and procedures. These can be excellent tools to welcome employees, to ensure a relatively consistent application of company policies, create a desired culture, and provide answers to commonly asked employee questions. If poorly written, however, policies can entangle an employer in a network of promises or representations the company cannot keep. The CEO should recognize that few employees read a Policy and Procedures Manual. Reading is reserved for HR managers and plaintiff attorneys. The HR community consistently makes the mistake of mixing a "Handbook", which should be limited to introducing an employee to the company and answering common questions, with "policies and procedures".

Discussion. The terms - "Handbook, HR Manual, Company Guidelines, Policies and Procedures" have no statutory or legal definition and invariably are mixed together in one binding. The more sophisticated the Human Resource Department, the more likely the Guidelines, Policies and particularly the Manual will be overly cumbersome, too detailed, full of representations the company cannot keep, and be full of legalisms HR managers occasionally do not understand.

[1]Dennis Gladwell graduated from the University of Utah College of Law, 2ND in his class, Editor in Chief of the Law Review and Order of the Coif. He practiced for 30 years at Gibson Dunn & Crutcher in Los Angeles where he was a Partner in the Labor and Employment Law department. He is an adjunct Law Professor at the S.Q. Quinney College of Law.

A best practice would be to create a handbook that is given to the employee upon hiring, and serves the same purpose as a road map, or a "Welcome to BYU" flyer.

A. The Handbook

An introduction that: (1) welcomes the employee and (2) tells the employee briefly about the company, its products, the names of the management team, how long the company has been in business, its web site and telephone number. The official welcome page is signed by the President or CEO.

A" Let's Get Started" -section.

1. When do employees get paid.
2. How to open a direct deposit into your checking account.
3. Where is the first aid station. Where is the HR department.
4. Where is the cafeteria - and what are its hours.
5. How do I get a sticker for the employee parking lot.
6. Who do I contact if I am sick.
7. A map of the "campus" if there is more than one building - if not, a diagram of the building .
8. Company or department Dress Code
9. Holidays
10. And so on . . .

B. Policies and Procedures

A second binding would contain policies and procedures available to each employee but they do not need to be published and passed out. All supervisors would have a set at their desk to guide him/her, and multiple copies would be available at HR. Best practice would be to place each policy on line, not only to save publication costs and to provide ready access to all employees, but to allow HR to update, modify, and delete policies as the need arises without having to re-distribute paper copies.

Below listed are core topics that a Company should include:

1. Attendance policy.
2. Sick leave and vacation policy.
3. Open door policy.
4. Non discrimination policy.
5. Sexual Harassment Reporting Policy.
6. Protecting Intellectual property.
7. Policy prohibiting weapons on company property.
8. Non solicitation policy (prohibiting employees or guests from trying to sell goods or services on company premises).
9. Benefits Section.
10. Disciplinary policy.
11. And so on . . .

C. Policies to draft with care.

1. Vacation accrual: A significant percentage of employees like to "bank" sick leave or vacation days and trade them in for cash down the road. This undercuts the purpose of vacation and sick leave - to refresh employees and to ensure they stay home when sick. The answer is to stop the accrual after 2x the yearly accrual. For example.

"Each employee receives ten days of vacation a year. Some years an employee may not be able to take all of the vacation he has accrued. An employee may carry over unused vacation days up to a maximum of 20 days. At that point no new vacation days will accrue until after one or more banked vacation days are used".

2. At Will Clause. Wrongful termination actions based on policies and procedures can be eliminated in Utah by including this or a similar statement in the Handbook and policy binder.

"No policy, no procedure, and no statement made by a manager will constitute a binding contract or agreement between the employee and the company. An employee remains at will throughout his employment.

An agreement is only binding on the Company if it is spelled out in a document and signed by senior management."

D. Policies and statements to avoid.

1. Lay off principle. You need to develop a layoff policy based on the needs of the company with respect to a "particular layoff." In other words, do not commit yourself today to something that might not work five years later.

2. Rose-colored descriptions of the company's treatment of employees. " We are the best, we treat all employees with the utmost integrity, you are our greatest asset and so on". Plaintiff lawyers seize on these implied promises. Second, the person reading these statements is already an employee. He will only value actions, not statements.

CHAPTER 40
HUMAN RESOURCES

AMERICANS WITH DISABILITIES ACT

DAVID CASTLEBERRY[1]

GENERAL SUMMARY

Title I of the Americans with Disabilities Act (ADA) prohibits discrimination against applicants and employees on the basis of disability when the employee or applicant is qualified to perform the job with or without a reasonable accommodation. Failure to comply with the requirements of the ADA exposes the employer to both civil and criminal liability in the form of civil penalties, imprisonment, payment of lost wages, compensatory and punitive damages, as well as compelled hiring, reinstatement or promotion of affected employees.

The ADA was amended in 2008 with the Americans with Disabilities Act Amendments Act or ADAAA. Before the ADAAA was passed, many claims against employers failed because the individual was not considered as disabled under the law. Now, the ADAAA provides that the definition of disability should be construed broadly, which greatly increases the number of individuals who may now be considered as disabled under the law.

The ADA applies to all employers engaged in an industry affecting commerce who have at least 15 employees each working day for 20 or more weeks in the current or preceding calendar year. 42 U.S.C. § 12111(5). The ADA protects individuals with a physical or mental

[1]David Castleberry is a partner with Manning Curtis Bradshaw & Bednar LLC. Mr. Castleberry represents clients in federal and state court and before administrative agencies on issues dealing with state and federal employment law claims. He also provides counsel to clients with respect to issues relating to employment law.

impairment that substantially limits one or more major life activity, who have a record of such an impairment, or who are regarded as having such an impairment, whether or not the impairment limits or is perceived to limit a major life activity, and who, with or without reasonable accommodation, can perform the essential functions of the job. 42 U.S.C. § 12102(2), 12111(8); 29 C.F.R. § 1630.2. An individual who has an impairment that is episodic or in remission is covered if the impairment would substantially limit a major life activity when active. 42 U.S.C. § 12102(4)(D). The ADA does not preempt any state laws establishing equal or higher protections of the rights of disabled persons. 42 U.S.C. § 12201(b).

Prohibited Conduct

Generally, the ADA prohibits employers from discriminating against an applicant or an employee in regard to job application procedures, hiring, advancement, discharge, compensation, job training, and other terms, conditions and privileges of employment on the basis of: (1) a physical or mental disability that substantially limits the individual's major life activities; (2) a record of such a disability; or (3) being regarded as having such a disability, whether or not the disability limits or is perceived to limit a major life activity. 42 U.S.C. § 12112(a), 12102(2); 29 C.F.R. § 1630.2(g), 1630.4. An employer may not discriminate against an individual because such individual has opposed any act or practice made unlawful by the ADA. Neither may an employer coerce, intimidate, threaten, or interfere with any individual in the exercise or enjoyment of any right granted or protected by the ADA. 42 U.S.C. § 12203; 29 C.F.R. § 1630.12.

Medical Examinations and Inquiries

An employer may not conduct a medical examination or make inquiries of a job applicant as to whether such applicant is an individual with a disability or as to the nature or severity of such disability. 42 U.S.C. § 12112(d)(2). An employer may, however, make pre-employment inquiries into the ability of an applicant to perform job related functions. 42 U.S.C. § 12112(d)(2); 29 C.F.R. § 1630.13, .14(a).

An employer may require a medical examination after an offer of employment has been made to a job applicant and prior to the commencement of the employment duties of the applicant, and may condition an offer of employment on the results of such examination, if all entering employees are subjected to such an examination and the medical file created is separately maintained and treated as confidential. Post offer, employment entrance medical examinations and inquiries do not have to be job related and consistent with business necessity unless criteria are used to screen out persons with disabilities. 42 U.S.C. § 12112(d)(3); 29 C.F.R. § 1630.14(b).

Medical examinations and inquiries of existing employees must be job related and consistent with business necessity. This does not prohibit an employer from making inquiries into the ability of an employee to perform job-related functions. 42 U.S.C. § 12112(d)(4); 29 C.F.R. § 1630.14(c).

Mandated Conduct

An employer is required to make reasonable accommodations for qualified individuals with a disability during employment or when necessary to allow a job applicant to perform the essential job functions of the position. 42 U.S.C. § 12112(b)(5); 29 C.F.R. § 1630.9. "Reasonable accommodation" may include:

- Making existing facilities used by employees readily accessible to and usable by individuals with disabilities,
- Job restructuring, part time or modified work schedules,
- Reassignment to a vacant position, acquisition or modification of equipment or devices, appropriate adjustment or modifications of examinations,
- Training materials or policies,
- The provision of qualified readers or interpreters, and other similar accommodations for individuals with disabilities, and
- Making the workplace and interview location readily accessible.

Notice

The covered employer must keep posted, in a prominent and conspicuous place, a notice explaining the ADA. 42 U.S.C. § 12115; 29 C.F.R. § 1601.30.

Reporting/Record Keeping

The ADA imposes certain record keeping obligations on covered employers. 42 U.S.C. § 12117; 42 U.S.C. § 2000e 8(c); 29 C.F.R. § 1602. Employers of 100 or more employees, unless exempted, must submit a yearly report (Standard Form 100). The employer must keep a copy of the most recent annual report. 29 C.F.R. § 1602.7 et seq. Employers who require medical examinations must keep those records separate from other records. 42 U.S.C. § 12112(d)(3).

Records made for the purpose of an employment action (e.g., hiring, firing, promotion) must be kept for at least one year from the making of the record or the employment action, whichever is later. Records made for the purpose of termination must be kept for one year after the termination. When an employment action is challenged under the ADA all relevant records must be kept until the final disposition of the complaint. 29 C.F.R. § 1602.14.

Exceptions

An employer may enforce a requirement that an individual not pose a direct threat to the health or safety of other individuals in the work place. A "direct threat" means "a significant risk to the health or safety of others that cannot be eliminated by reasonable accommodation." 42 U.S.C. § 12111(3), 12113(b); 29 C.F.R. § 1630.15(b).

Illegal drug use is not a disability; however, an employer cannot discriminate against an applicant or an employee who has used, but no longer uses, illegal drugs. Prohibition of drug use at the workplace and administration of drug testing is not prohibited by the ADA. 42 U.S.C. § 12114; 29 C.F.R. § 1630.3(a), 1630.16(b).

CHAPTER 41

HUMAN RESOURCES

DISCRIMINATION BASED ON RELIGION

DENNIS GLADWELL[1]

Executive Summary: This statute, like the ADA, has two legal components: a discrimination prohibition and an accommodation obligation. Its accommodation obligation is far less demanding than accommodation under the ADA. It usually involves working around an employee's Sabbath or religious holiday observance request. Unique to this statute, discrimination claims frequently are made by one employee against other employees. For example: playing religious music, preaching to fellow employees, offering prayers or badgering other employees to participate in bible study. More difficult issues arise with religious head dress and beards.

Discussion. Title VII defines discrimination on account of "religion" to include all aspects of religious observance and practice, as well as "belief". 42 US.C. section 2000e (j). It explicitly requires "reasonable accommodation of an employee's religious observance and practice." The hallmark case for years has been *Trans World Airlines, Inc.* v. *Hardison*, 423 U.S. 63, 53 L.Ed. 2d 113 (1977). It involved an employee's request to refrain from working on Sunday and the impact of the request on a seniority clause in the union contract. The Court established a "*de minimus*" cost standard as the litmus test with which to measure the accommodation obligation an employer bears. Unlike the ADA, which might require a ramp or elevator to be installed, or other significant financial investments in equipment in order to ensure that an

[1]Dennis Gladwell graduated from the University of Utah College of Law, 2ND in his class, Editor in Chief of the Law Review and Order of the Coif. He practiced for 30 years at Gibson Dunn & Crutcher in Los Angeles where he was a Partner in the Labor and Employment Law department. He is an adjunct Law Professor at the S.Q. Quinney College of Law.

employee, with a disability, can perform the work, the accommodation obligation under this statute is quite minimal. Usually this involves working around an employee's Sunday worship requests, and allowing observance of religious holidays such as Christmas, Easter, Ramadan, and similar sacred dates.

Dress or grooming practices of eastern religions fall under the umbrella of accommodation. Jewish yarmulke, Muslim headscarf, uncut facial hair of Sikhs, Rastafarin dreadlocks are examples. On the other hand, the company has wide latitude in establishing dress standards, particularly when the employee deals with the public, or there is a health or safety issue. See, *EEOC v. United Parcel Serv.*, 94 F.3d 314 (7th Cir. 1996). A company's grooming standard for a counter sales person can be more vigorously enforced than dress standards for a fork lift operator in the yard. See, *Coulter v. Costco Wholesale Corp.*, 390 F.3d 126 (1st Cir. 2004) (employer may require employees to cover facial piercing). Medical providers have almost *carte blanche* to establish any dress, hair, or cleanliness standard. The same applies to cooks and food servers in restaurants.

Requests for accommodation should trigger an interactive process between the employee and his supervisor. If there is only *de minimus* impact on the employer, the requested accommodation should be granted. Examples of accommodation include flexible scheduling, voluntary shift substitutions, job reassignments, modification of responsibilities, rotating Sunday shifts, allowing religious garb to be worn underneath a required company attire.

Sample Statement of Company Policy. "The Company prohibits treating an employee differently because of her/his religious beliefs. Additionally, the Company prohibits employees from making unwelcome solicitations to discuss religious topics, forming bible study groups at work, and making derogatory comments about the religious beliefs of others."

To this latter point, frequently religious discrimination claims are filed against the company <u>and</u> a fellow employee for obnoxious or boorish religious solicitations or preaching. See, e.g *Peterson Hewlett Packard Co.*, 358 F. 3d 599 (9th Cir. 2004) (employee lawfully terminated for refusing to remove prominent postings of Bible passages condemning homosexuality). Courts have prohibited employees from evangelizing while working; upheld discharging an employee for claiming other employees were immoral or ungodly; have condoned ordering employees to turn off loud Christian music; prohibited employees from wearing a graphic anti-abortion pin in the workplace; prohibited employees from greeting customers with "god bless you" and "praise the lord". In *Shapolia v. Los Alamos Nat'l Lab* 992 F.2d 1033(10th Cir. 1993) the court held that an employee stated a claim of discrimination by alleging that he was terminated for not being a Mormon.

CHAPTER 42

HUMAN RESOURCES

PRIVACY IN THE WORKPLACE

DAVID CASTLEBERRY[1]

The Tension in the Law between Employee Privacy Violations and Negligent Hiring

Social media allows an employer to gain an extraordinary amount of information about a job applicant or a current employee, and employers are using this information to make decisions. *See* Note, Negligent Hiring and the Information Age: How State Legislatures Can Save Employers From Inevitable Liability, 53 Wm. & Mary L. Rev. 1397 (2012). "One 2010 study commissioned by Microsoft found that 78 percent of recruiting and human resources personnel used search engines to evaluate potential employees, and 63 percent visit social networking sites as part of the screening process." *Id.* "The same study found that 70 percent of [those making hiring decisions] had rejected candidates in light of the information that they gleaned from Internet searches." *Id.*

While the Internet and social media provide useful information to employers about job applicants and about current employees, it is a double-edged sword. The Internet and social media also reveal protected characteristics about applicants or employees that the employer might never have known about before the Internet. Further, the Internet Employment Privacy Act, effective May 2014, places limits on an employer's ability to request personal information from job applicants. *See* U.C.A. § 34-48-101 et seq. The Act prohibits employers from

[1]David Castleberry is a partner with Manning Curtis Bradshaw & Bednar LLC. Mr. Castleberry represents clients in federal and state court and before administrative agencies on issues dealing with state and federal employment law claims. He also provides counsel to clients with respect to issues relating to employment law.

requesting a prospective or current employee's username and password for any personal Internet account. U.C.A. § 34-48-201(1). The Act is largely aimed at employers seeking access to social media accounts of applicants and employees. If an employer engages in such conduct and takes any adverse action, including failure to hire, the aggrieved person can bring suit and receive up to $500 in damages. U.C.A. § 34-48-301(2).

On the other hand, if social medial would have revealed that an applicant has violent tendencies or history but the employer failed to uncover this information as part of its pre-screening process, the employer may be liable for negligent hiring. Utah law allows an employee or even a third party to sue an employer for negligent employment. To prevail on a claim for negligent employment, the employee must prove that the employer's "negligence in hiring, supervising, or retaining its employees proximately caused her harm." *Retherford v. AT & T Communications of Mountain States, Inc.*, 844 P.2d 949, 967 (Utah 1992). While an employer may be held liable for its employee's actions if the employee acted within the course and scope of his employment while committing the negligent act, an employer may be held directly liable for its own actions or inactions based on the tort of negligent employment. *Birkner v. Salt Lake Cnty.*, 771 P.2d 1053, 1059 (Utah 1989) (affirming the entry of judgment against the employer for negligent supervision despite concluding that the company was not vicariously liable for the employee's sexual battery). *See generally J.H. v. West Valley City*, 840 P.2d 115, 124 (Utah 1992) ("Regardless of whether an employer may be held liable [for its employee's actions], an employer may be directly liable for its acts or omissions . . . ."). Because of potential liability, an employer has incentive to learn as much as possible about potential employees and current employees.

An employer should try to learn as much as possible about applicants and its current employees for legitimate business reasons to avoid a claim for negligent hiring, training, or supervision. At the same time, the employer must ensure that each employment decision it makes is based on legitimate, nondiscriminatory, and non-retaliatory reasons. Further, an employer should ensure that its Internet and social media searches are tied as closely as possible to legitimate business concerns.

Finally, to avoid liability, an employer should be aware of possible claims based on Utah privacy torts, criminal history background check requirements, and drug and alcohol testing requirements.

Utah Privacy Torts

Because of the tsunami of information available online about individuals, an employer should be well-versed with privacy torts and state and federal statutes regarding the employment relationship. While not an exhaustive list, below are some of the issues of which employers should be aware. Utah recognizes three privacy torts that may arise in the employment context: (1) intrusion upon seclusion; (2) public disclosure of private facts; and (3) false light publicity. *Stein v. Marriott Ownership Records, Inc.*, 944 P.2d 374, 377 (Utah App. 1997); *Cox v. Hatch*, 761 P.2d 556, 563 (Utah 1988). An intrusion upon seclusion claim arises when the employer commits "an intentional, substantial intrusion, physically or otherwise, upon the [employee's] solitude or seclusion . . . that would be highly offensive to the reasonable person." *Turner v. General Adjustment Bureau, Inc.*, 832 P.2d 62, 67 (Utah App. 1992) *overruled on other grounds by Campbell v. State Farm Mut. Auto Ins. Co.*, 65 P.3d 1134, 1165 (Utah 2001). When making a threshold determination of offensiveness, a court may consider such factors as the degree of intrusion, the context, the conduct and circumstances surrounding the intrusion, as well as the intruder's motives and objectives, the setting into which he intrudes, and the expectations of the individual whose privacy was invaded. *Stein*, 944 P.2d at 377. An employee must have a reasonable expectation of privacy with respect to the area of intrusion. Courts have held that guessing an employee's email password may be highly offensive. *Fisher v. Mt. Olive Lutheran Church*, 207 F.Supp.2d 914, 920, 928 (W.D. Wis. 2002). Thus, employers should not circumvent passwords or other restrictions to learn more about an employee or applicant. *See* Note, Negligent Hiring and the Information Age: How State Legislatures Can Save Employers From Inevitable Liability, 53 Wm. & Mary L. Rev. 1397 (2012).

An employer can be liable for the tort of public disclosure of private facts if the employer publicizes – in a way that would be highly offensive and objectionable to a reasonable person of ordinary sensibilities –

matters concerning an employee's private life. *See Shattuck-Owen v. Snowbird Corp.*, 2000 UT 94 ¶ 11, 16 P.3d 555. Employers may share information about employees with co-workers or management as long as the information is shared only with individuals who have a legitimate interest in the information. The employee's freedom to divulge information about employees diminishes as the private and sensitive nature of the information increases. For example, if an employee is sexually assaulted at work, the employer should be careful to share information to others only as necessary to conduct an investigation into the assault. *Id.* Otherwise, the employer may face liability for public disclosure of private facts.

Employer liability can also arise if the employer publicizes a matter that places the employee before the public in a false light, if the false light would be highly offensive to a reasonable person and the employer knew or disregarded whether the publicized matter was false. *See Watkins v. Gen. Refractories Co.*, 805 F.Supp. 911, 918 (D. Utah 1992). False light claims differ from unreasonable publicity claims in that the private information disseminated by the employer must be false or misleading instead of private. A claim for defamation may arise under similar facts. *Cox*, 761 P.2d at 558-559.

Because of these common-law-invasion-of-privacy torts, employers should be careful when monitoring voice mail, email, or an employee's computer network. Common law invasion of privacy claims may arise when an employee has a reasonable expectation of privacy with respect to communications or information that is monitored by the employer. Because personal, sometimes confidential, communications typically find their way into communication systems provided for business use, it is necessary to have a clear policy statement published and distributed to employees that advises that the employer's communication systems are intended for business-related purposes and that they are monitored for business reasons. Incidental and occasional use of the employer's communication systems may be permitted, but employees should be advised that such communications will be treated no differently from other messages and that the employer's confidentiality and business interests require it to reserve the right to access and, when appropriate, disclose all communications created or sent within its communications systems. Also, any covert surveillance of employees should be undertaken with great caution and only after consulting with legal counsel. Therefore, employees should use the employer's communication systems with the understanding that all messages and communications may be available for review by any authorized employer representative and that such communication systems should not be used for personal communications that the employee considers confidential. If the employer advises its employees that their computer activities on the office system are monitored, employees most likely have no reasonable expectation of privacy in records accessed using the employer's server.

Criminal History

Decisions from the Equal Employment Opportunity Commission (EEOC) restrict the use of criminal history information in the employment context because of the disparate impact such considerations have against minorities. For example, courts have found that since an arrest is not conclusive of any wrongdoing and since minorities have historically been targeted for arrests in a disproportionate manner, arrests should not be considered absent a strong showing of "business necessity." *See Gregory v. Litton Sytsems, Inc.*, 316 F.Supp. 401 (C.D. Cal. 1970), *modified on other grounds*, 472 F.2d 631 (9th Cir. 1971). Further, the "business necessity" required to use arrest records is demanding, and is almost never satisfied.

While employers may more freely use information about a criminal conviction in employment decisions about an arrest, the EEOC has explained that a criminal conviction may not serve as an automatic bar to employment. To satisfy Title VII, a conviction-based disqualification must still be justified by "business necessity." This standard is more lenient in the context of convictions when compared to arrests. In the conviction context, EEOC decisions require the following factors to be considered in determining "business necessity": "(1) the nature and gravity of the offense, (2) the time that has passed since the conviction and/or the completion of the sentence; and (3) the nature of the job held or sought." EEOC Policy Statement on the Issue of Conviction Records under Title VII of the Civil Rights Act of 1964, as amended, 42 U.S.C. § 2000e et seq. (1982) (2/4/87).

Drug and Alcohol Testing

Utah's drug and alcohol testing statute permits an employer to collect samples from and test prospective and current employees for the presence of drugs or alcohol. Utah Code Ann. § 34-38-1 et seq. Testing must conform to requirements in the statute. For example, the testing must be conducted according to a written policy, and may require testing to determine employee impairment, as part of investigations into workplace accidents or theft, to maintain safety, or for productivity or quality concerns. Employers following the procedures required by statute are protected from certain forms of civil liability when disciplinary action is taken against an employee based upon negative test results.

CHAPTER 43

HUMAN RESOURCES

EQUAL PAY ACT

DENNIS GLADWELL[1]

Executive Summary: The 1963 Equal Pay Act, 29 U.S.C. section 206(d) is the only statute that spells out the precise discrimination formula : unequal pay for work requiring the same skill, effort and responsibility. The Equal Pay Act frequently is over-looked by Title VII plaintiff attorneys in favor of the more straight forward theory of proof under the broader category of sex discrimination. Four statutory defenses are available: Unequal pay based on seniority, a merit system, quantity or quality of work or upon any factor other than sex.

Discussion. The Equal Pay Act actually is part of the Fair Labor Standards Act (the Federal Wage and Hour Law), although it is administered by the EEOC. Because it is part of the FLSA, an employee does not need to file a claim of discrimination, and can proceed directly to court.

The statute reads in pertinent part: "No employer shall discriminate between employees on the basis of sex by paying wages at a rate less than the rate at which it pays employees of the opposite sex for equal work on jobs which require *equal skill, effort* and *responsibility*, and which are performed under *similar working conditions*. There are four defenses or exceptions: Unequal pay due to (1) a seniority system, (2) a merit system, and (3) a system that measures quantity or quality of production, or (4) a differential based on any factor other than sex. 29 U.S.C. section 206 (d). To comply with this Act, an employer may not reduce the hourly rate of an employee.

[1]Dennis Gladwell graduated from the University of Utah College of Law, 2ND in his class, Editor in Chief of the Law Review and Order of the Coif. He practiced for 30 years at Gibson Dunn & Crutcher in Los Angeles where he was a Partner in the Labor and Employment Law department. He is an adjunct Law Professor at the S.Q. Quinney College of Law.

The language of the Act has fostered understandable litigation over the phrase "similar working conditions". For example: is there a difference between a night shift and day shifts, between weekend work and work on Monday through Friday, or between jobs that require heavy lifting (which are usually filled by men) and the more routine tasks on a retail store the floor: lifting, sorting and supplying (predominately filled by women). Costco's, Macy's and Lowes' floor work are examples. The phrase "equal skill, effort and responsibility" has been construed to mean "substantially equal" . As a general rule, Courts have demanded a clear showing that the jobs in question are in fact equal before penalties or accommodations are imposed. *Beck-Wilson v. Principi*, 441 F.3d 353 (6th cir. 20006).

Although culturally there is a general disparity between the wages of men and women, when viewed simplistically as two groups, equal pay violations have been more difficult to prove when the equal pay algorithm is applied. See, generally, *The Pay Gap, the Glass Ceiling, and Pay Bias: Moving Forward Fifty Years after the Equal Pay Act,* ABA Journal of Labor and Employment Law, Vol. 29, Number 3, 2014. Since 1963, from postal workers to fast food servers, from nurses to physicians, from school teachers to bus operators, men and women generally have been paid substantially equally for the same work. Much of the immediate post 1963 litigation, for 15 years, centered on vestiges of clear discriminatory practices dating from the 1930's. The professions, nursing, physicians, attorneys, accountants, are examples of employment where wage disparities seldom exist as between the sexes.

The more realistic concern for the 21st Century employer is the difference in pay and advancement opportunities for women in higher level management positions - the glass ceiling. Even in this setting the employer will see a Title VII action far sooner than an equal pay claim. No separate policy statement is needed.

CHAPTER 44

HUMAN RESOURCES

FAMILY AND MEDICAL LEAVE ACT

DAVID CASTLEBERRY[1]

GENERAL SUMMARY

Federal law governs an employee's ability to take job-protected leave. Utah does not have statutes that govern this situation. The federal Family and Medical Leave Act (FMLA) imposes an obligation on affected employers to provide eligible employees with up to 12 work weeks of unpaid leave per year. Leave can be used in connection with the birth, adoption, or foster placement of the employee's child; the employee's care for a seriously ill spouse, child, or parent; or the serious illness of the employee. Failure to comply with the requirements of the FMLA exposes the employer to liability in the form of fines, payment of lost wages and benefits, as well as compelled reinstatement and/or promotion of affected employees.

Coverage

FMLA applies to any employer engaged in commerce or in any industry or activity affecting commerce, who employs at least fifty employees during twenty or more workweeks in the current or preceding calendar year. Public agencies are covered employers without regard to the number of employees employed. 29 U.S.C. § 2611(4); 29 C.F.R. § 825.104-108.

[1]David Castleberry is a partner with Manning Curtis Bradshaw & Bednar LLC. Mr. Castleberry represents clients in federal and state court and before administrative agencies on issues dealing with state and federal employment law claims. He also provides counsel to clients with respect to issues relating to employment law.

To be eligible for FMLA leave an employee must: (1) have been employed by the employer for at least 12 months; (2) have worked at least 1,250 hours during the 12 month period preceding the taking of leave; and (3) work at a worksite where 50 or more people are employed by the employer either at that worksite or within 75 miles of that worksite. 29 U.S.C. § 2611(2); 29 C.F.R. § 825.110-11.

FMLA does not supersede any laws or collective bargaining agreements that provide more generous family or medical leave rights. Nor does the FMLA modify any anti-discrimination laws. 29 U.S.C. § 2651; 29 C.F.R. § 825.700-02.

An employee is entitled to 12 weeks of leave. 29 U.S.C. § 2612(a)(1); 29 C.F.R. § 825.112-114. The leave may be unpaid. 29 U.S.C. § 2612(c); 29 C.F.R. § 825.207. An employer may require certification by a health care provider regarding the health condition. An employee who has taken leave for their own serious health condition may be required to obtain certification of their fitness to return to work. 29 U.S.C. § 2613(a); 2614(c)(3); 29 C.F.R. § 825.305 .308, 312.

Following FMLA leave, an employee is entitled to return from leave to the position of employment the employee left or to an equivalent position. 29 U.S.C. § 2614(a); 29 C.F.R. § 825.214-215. Group health benefits shall be maintained throughout the employee's leave as they would have been maintained had the employee continued in employment. If the employee fails to return from leave the employer can usually recover premiums paid during the employee's leave. 29 U.S.C. § 2614(c); 29 C.F.R. § 825.209-13.

Notice

Each employer must post in a conspicuous place, where notices to employees and applicants are customarily posted, a summarization of the requirements of the FMLA. 29 U.S.C. § 2619; 29 C.F.R. § 825.300. An employer must provide in its employee handbook a written explanation of the FMLA. If the employer does not have a written handbook the employer must provide the employee requesting FMLA leave written guidance and specific notice concerning the employee's rights and obligations under the FMLA and the consequences of failing to meet those obligations. 29 C.F.R. § 825.300.

Record Keeping

Employers must maintain for three years: basic payroll and identifying employee data; dates and hours of FMLA leave taken; copies of employee notices of leave; documents describing employee benefits and policies regarding leave; payments of employee benefits; records of disputes regarding FMLA leave; and medical certifications. 29 C.F.R. § 825.500.

No Interference/Retaliation

An employer must not interfere with, restrain or deny the exercise of rights provided under the FMLA. Nor may an employer retaliate or discriminate against an employee for asserting rights under the FMLA or opposing any practices made unlawful by the FMLA. 29 U.S.C. § 2615.

CHAPTER 45

HUMAN RESOURCES

AGE DISCRIMINATION IN EMPLOYMENT ACT

DAVID CASTLEBERRY[1]

The Age Discrimination in Employment Act (ADEA) prohibits age discrimination against persons 40 years of age and older in hiring job applicants and with respect to compensation, terms, conditions or privileges of employment. Failure to comply with the requirements of the ADEA exposes the employer to both civil and criminal liability in the form of civil penalties, imprisonment, payment of lost wages, and liquidated damages, as well as compelled hiring, reinstatement or promotion of affected employees.

Application

ADEA applies to all employers engaged in an industry affecting commerce who have 20 or more employees each day of at least 20 weeks in the current or preceding calendar year. 29 U.S.C. § 630(b). The ADEA protects any current, prospective or former employee over age 40 with the exception of certain governmental employees. 29 U.S.C. § 630(f). ADEA does not preempt laws that meet the standards of the Act. 29 C.F.R. § 1625.10(g). Laws that do not meet the standards of the ADEA are superseded. 29 C.F.R. § 1625.6(c). The commencement of an action under the ADEA supersedes any parallel action under state law. 29 U.S.C. § 633.

Prohibited Conduct

ADEA prohibits employers from refusing to hire, discharging or

[1]David Castleberry is a partner with Manning Curtis Bradshaw & Bednar LLC. Mr. Castleberry represents clients in federal and state court and before administrative agencies on issues dealing with state and federal employment law claims. He also provides counsel to clients with respect to issues relating to employment law.

otherwise discriminating against individuals 40 years of age or older with respect to compensation, terms, conditions or privileges of employment. 29 U.S.C. § 623(a). Employers should not publish any advertisement relating to employment that indicates any preference, limitation, specification or discrimination based on age. 29 U.S.C. § 623(e). The ADEA generally prohibits involuntary retirement. 29 U.S.C. § 623(f)(2); 29 C.F.R. § 1625.9. However, the ADEA does not prohibit the compulsory retirement of certain high level employees at the age of 65 employed for the prior two years in a bona fide executive or high policymaking position and entitled to an immediate annual retirement benefit of at least $44,000.00. 29 U.S.C. § 631(c); 29 C.F.R. § 1625.12. Employment applications requesting an age or birth date are closely scrutinized and should be avoided. 29 C.F.R. § 1625.5. Generally, an employer cannot establish a pension plan that reduces benefits on the basis of age. 29 U.S.C. § 623(i). However, a pension plan can have minimum age requirements for retirement benefits. 29 U.S.C. § 623(i).

Mandated Conduct

The employer must keep posted, in a prominent and conspicuous place, a notice explaining the ADEA. 29 U.S.C. § 627; 29 C.F.R. § 1627.10.

Employers must maintain payroll records which contain the name, address, birth date, occupation, rate of pay, and weekly compensation for three years, 29 C.F.R. § 1627.3(a), employers who make the following records must maintain them for one year: job applications; resumes; records of promotion, demotion, and transfer; job postings; test results; physical examinations; and written descriptions of benefit plans and seniority and merit systems, 29 C.F.R. § 1627.3(b). If an action is brought against an employer for violation of the ADEA, the employer must keep all required records until the final disposition of the action. 29 C.F.R. § 1627.3(b)(3).

Waivers of rights under the ADEA must be "knowing and voluntary." Among other requirements, any waiver of rights under the ADEA requires that a twenty-one day consideration period and a seven day revocation period be allowed to the releasing employee. A 45 day consideration period is required if the waiver is related to an exit incentive program. 29 U.S.C. § 626(f).

CHAPTER 46

HUMAN RESOURCES

WORKING ADJUSTMENT AND RETRAINING NOTIFICATION ACT (WARN)

DAVID CASTLEBERRY[1]

GENERAL SUMMARY

The Worker Adjustment and Retraining Notification Act (WARN) requires employers to provide 60 days' notice to employees prior to the temporary or permanent shutdown of a worksite or prior to a mass layoff. Failure to warn employees exposes the employer to liability in the form of civil penalties and payment of lost wages and benefits.

Coverage

WARN applies to all employers who employ at least 100 full-time employees or 100 or more employees, including part time employees, who work at least 4,000 hours per week, exclusive of overtime. 29 U.S.C. § 2101(a)(1); 20 C.F.R. § 639.3(a). WARN protects employees who may suffer an employment loss as a consequence of a worksite closing or a mass layoff. 29 U.S.C. § 2101(a)(5). Employee rights under WARN are in addition to any laws or contractual rights or remedies of employees. 29 U.S.C. § 2105. Additionally, notice given in good faith

---

[1]David Castleberry is a partner with Manning Curtis Bradshaw & Bednar LLC. Mr. Castleberry represents clients in federal and state court and before administrative agencies on issues dealing with state and federal employment law claims. He also provides counsel to clients with respect to issues relating to employment law.

compliance with WARN does not violate the National Labor Relations Act or the Railway Labor Act. 29 U.S.C. § 2108.

Mandated Conduct

WARN generally requires employers to give 60 days' written notice prior to a plant closing or mass layoff to the following: (1) each affected employee; (2) employee representatives; (3) the state dislocated worker unit; and (4) the chief elected officer of the local government in the area affected by the closing or layoff. 29 U.S.C. § 2102; 20 C.F.R. § 639.5, 639.6. Notice requirements are detailed in 20 C.F.R. § 639.7. "Plant Closing" and "Mass Layoff" are defined in statute. Notice is not required if closings or layoffs are the result of relocation or consolidation of the employer's business if the employer offers to transfer the employee with no more than a six month break in employment and the transfer is within reasonable commuting distance or the employee accepts the transfer without regard to the commuting distance. 29 U.S.C. § 2101(b)(2); 20 C.F.R. § 639.3(f)(3), 639.5(b).

CHAPTER 47

HUMAN RESOURCES

CONDUCTING INTERNAL INVESTIGATIONS

CHRISTOPHER B. SNOW[1]

A. INTRODUCTION: WHY INVESTIGATE?

Are investigations worth the business interruption and toll on the human resources of your Company? Absolutely. Workplace investigations are a legal necessity now more than ever. Courts and administrative labor and workforce agencies expect Companies to conduct sophisticated, thorough and timely investigations into alleged employee misconduct, i.e., hostile work environment, sexual harassment, discrimination, and internal complaints of a serious nature. In fact, the EEOC's enforcement guidelines advise employers to set up a "mechanism for a prompt, thorough and impartial investigation in alleged harassment," and that "as soon as management learns about the alleged harassment, it should determine whether a detailed fact finding investigation is necessary." And, importantly, the law rewards Companies who take complaints of discrimination and other misconduct serious enough to investigate.

1. Affirmative Defenses. In *Burlington Industries, Inc. v. Ellerth*, 524 U.S. 742 (1998), and *Faragher v. City of Boca Raton*, 524 U.S. 775 (1998), the Supreme Court established an affirmative defense available to an employer accused of sexual harassment. The affirmative defense is

[1]Christopher B. Snow has practiced employment law for over a decade, exclusively representing Employers in Utah and throughout the United States. He currently chairs Clyde Snow & Sessions Employment Law Practice Group and is a frequent lecturer and trainer on employment law workplace compliance. Mr. Snow has successfully litigated and defended management before the Utah Anti-discrimination Division, the Equal Employment Opportunity Commission, State and Federal Court and in Government Investigations.

available only to employers who prove by a preponderance of the evidence: (1) the employer exercised reasonable care to prevent and promptly correct any harassing behavior, and (2) the plaintiff unreasonably failed to take advantage of any preventive or corrective opportunities provided by the employer or to avoid harm otherwise. When determining whether an employer qualifies for this defense, Court's will look carefully at whether the Company investigated the alleged claims of harassment or discrimination, and then assess the quality and credibility of the workplace investigation. *See, e.g. Silver v. General Motors Corp.,* 225 F.3d 655 (4th Cir. 2000) (finding GM established first prong of *Faragher* affirmative defense because sexual harassment policy was "widely known" and GM promptly investigated the employee's complaint and took remedial action against the harasser.); *Vincent v. Aztec Facility Services, Inc.,* 2007 U.S. Dist. LEXIS 67732 (N.D. Tex. Sept. 12, 2007) (barring employer from establishing affirmative defense because Company did not conduct a vigorous investigation and the investigator conceded she did not follow the Company's standard procedures for investigating a harassment complaint.)

2. **Liquidated Damages.** Under the Age Discrimination in Employment Act ("ADEA"), liquidated damages in the form of doubling an award of back pay damages are available to Plaintiff employees who establish a "willful" violation. The Supreme Court interprets willful to mean a violation in which the employer knew, or showed reckless disregard as to whether its conduct was prohibited by the ADEA. Liquidated damages are also available under the Fair Labor Standards Act ("FLSA") in the form of doubling lost wages. A proper workplace investigation will make it very difficult for employees to prove willful violations under the ADEA or the FLSA.

3. **Punitive Damages.** Title VII allows for punitive damages in discrimination cases. Punitive damages will be assessed when an employer engages in discriminatory practices with "malice or with reckless indifference to the federally protected rights of an aggrieved individual." But, the Supreme Court has stated an employer cannot be liable for punitive damages if the manager's challenged actions "were contrary to

the employer's good faith efforts to comply with Title VII." *Kolstad v. American Dental Ass'n* 527 U.S. 526, 546 (1999). In other words, an employer must "make a good faith effort to educate its employees about these policies and statutory prohibitions" and "make 'good faith efforts to *enforce* an antidiscrimination policy.' " *Cadena v. Pacesetter Corp.*, 224 F.3d 1203, 1210 (10th Cir.2000) (*citing Kolstad,* 527 U.S. at 546).

4. **Preservation of Evidence.** When faced with a discrimination or other workplace complaint, the potential for litigation should be presumed. The Company will be in a better position to defend itself if an internal investigation was immediately commenced after the incident, and timely completed. The investigation will uncover and create evidence that may be valuable in defending your claim. You might also find evidence that incriminates the Company. While your instinct might not be to preserve that evidence, if you fail to do so, the Company could be liable for a spoliation of evidence claim in Court. Spoliation claims deal with the destruction of evidence and courts can enter severe monetary and other sanctions against Company's that are found to have engaged in spoliation. The type of evidence you uncover and be required to preserve may include electronic and/or tangible data, information, documents, objects, text messages, social media postings, witness interviews, email messages, etc.

5. **Insurance Policy Compliance.** Some insurance policies require the insured to investigate and report incidents that have not (yet) risen to the level of an actual "Claim" under the policy. Most employers understand when they are sued to tender the claim to the insurance company immediately. But many employers do not realize the duty to investigate, preserve evidence, and report incidents and occurrences that carry the potential of litigation and the potential of invoking insurance coverage. Failing to properly investigate and report claims that may result in covered litigation may jeopardize your Company's coverage and you will be left to pay defense costs and any damages.

6. **Non-legal Reasons.** Your workforce needs to trust management to consistently enforce its policies and procedures.

Management cannot establish this trust without actively investigating complaints of discrimination and other work place issues that inevitably arise. Moreover, when you establish a consistent pattern of investigating formal and informal claims of misconduct, employees will think twice about violating Company polices because they know such violations will not be ignored. Workplace investigations deter misconduct.

B. INVESTIGATION TRIGGERS

The circumstances that might lead to an investigation are enumerable, but some examples may include:

- Complaints by an employee of specific discrimination or harassment;
- Observation of discrimination, even if the discrimination is not reported;
- Violations of company rules or policies;
- Suspected violation of drug or alcohol abuse;
- Misappropriation of trade secrets or other intellectual property;
- Abuse of social media sites;
- Fraud or other misconduct;
- Release of confidential information (e.g., HIPAA violations);
- Theft, vandalism or other sabotage;

C. PRE-INVESTIGATION PROCESSES.

1. Establishing Investigation Policies and Procedures. Does your Company handbook set forth proper investigation policies and procedures, such as (1) when an investigation should be conducted, (2) who should conduct the investigation, (3) how to conduct the investigation, (4) how and under what circumstances employees may report incidents or request an investigation? Employers should maintain and disclose these policies to managers and employees so there is clear notice that investigations may occur during employment, and so the designated investigators (HR, counsel, other managers) are prepared when legal lighting strikes! Incidents in the workplace develop quickly and require immediate action. There generally is little time for a thorough review of investigation policies and procedures so the proper training should be provided on a regular basis. Importantly, employer's investigation policies should include an electronic communications privacy standard that sets employees' expectations with respect to the monitoring, reviewing and even confiscation of company computers, phones, email accounts, text messages, public social media postings, and voice messages.

2. Selecting the Investigator. Determining who should conduct the investigation is an important part of the initial planning. The investigator should know the basic techniques of investigation and have a thorough understanding of the company's policies and procedures, as well as a solid grasp on the relevant law, with the assistance of counsel. Whenever possible, the investigator should not have close ties to either the complainant or the accused employee. The investigator should also be able to:

- develop a rapport with witnesses;
- employ a variety of techniques to obtain information from witnesses who may be angry, embarrassed, defensive or otherwise reluctant to cooperate;
- effectively interview witnesses regarding uncomfortable or delicate subjects;
- ask appropriate follow-up questions on new information revealed during an interview;
- and judge the credibility of witnesses.
- It is also important to consider the credibility of the investigator because if the matter results in legal action the investigator could be required to testify on behalf of the employer. If the investigator chosen is not an attorney, it is helpful to have counsel available for the investigator to seek guidance and advice.

a. An Investigator from within the Company. Choosing an internal investigator typically lowers the cost of the investigation for the employer, especially if the individual is already an employee. Internal investigators can typically initiate an investigation more quickly than an external investigator because they are likely more familiar with the company's organization, procedures and policies, and goals. An internal investigator is usually already located at or near the site of the complaint and may be familiar with the individuals involved. An internal investigator will also likely give management greater control over the scope of, and the individuals involved in, the investigation.

On the other hand, an internal investigator may appear to lack impartiality and independence. Business may be interrupted because the investigator will often still have to regular duties to attend, making it difficult to quickly and efficiently complete the investigation. Subordinate employees may feel uncomfortable speaking with an investigator if he or she is also a supervisor. Choosing an investigator from human resources may alleviate some of these concerns. A human resources employee may be considered by other employees to be more impartial in part because they are one step removed from of the day-to-day operations and disputes of the workplace. Additionally, those from human resources have often received training on workplace disputes and investigations.

b. An Outside Investigator. External investigators (regular outside counsel, Accountants, or Security Personnel) should be considered particularly where the incident at issue involves serious misconduct that is likely to lead to litigation, or that involves high-level executives. External investigators should also be utilized when a conflict of interest exists between the investigator and the parties involved in the incident at issue.

External investigators have several advantages over in-house counsel. For example, external investigators may be able to more quickly complete the investigation on a project specific basis. External investigators are also likely to have developed and focused investigative skills and a unique grasp of the legal ramifications and information obtained. Moreover, external investigators will likely be perceived as independent and objective and they typically gain a greater respect from interviewees who have to participate in the investigation. An external investigator might be more comfortable asking certain questions as well. And, if necessary, it is typically easier for an external investigator to stand up to management.

Importantly, the use of outside counsel to conduct the investigation invokes the attorney-client privilege and work product doctrine. The witness interviews and other important elements of the investigation will be protected and the results of the investigation private. For the attorney-client privilege and/or work product doctrine to attach, counsel must conduct the investigation for purposes of providing legal advice or in anticipation of litigation.

One deterrent for employers is the additional and sometimes high cost of hiring an outside investigator. But depending on the potential exposure, or the threat of litigation, it may be money well spent.

Rule 3.7, Lawyer as Witness. Rule 3.7 addresses the lawyer-witness issue and provides:(a) A lawyer shall not act as advocate at a trial in which the lawyer is likely to be necessary as a witness unless:(1) The testimony relates to an uncontested issue;(2) The testimony relates to the nature and value of legal services rendered in the case; or(3) Disqualification of the lawyer would work substantial hardship on the client.(b) A lawyer may act as advocate in a trial in which another lawyer in the lawyer's firm is likely to be called as a witness unless precluded from doing so by Rule 1.7 or Rule 1.9.¶5 Rule 3.7 does not automatically require withdrawal.1Rather, Rule 3.7(a) provides that a lawyer may not act as an advocate at trial if she is likely to be a "necessary" witness. Whether or not this lawyer's testimony is necessary is a fact-specific question the lawyer being summoned must resolve. If the testimony is duplicative and obtainable from other sources, her testimony may not be necessary, and the lawyer should not withdraw or should not be subject to disqualification.2 "The naming of a party's attorney does not ipso facto render the named attorney a 'necessary witness' . . . nor does the availability of other competent witnesses for the same testimony automatically render the named attorney 'unnecessary'."

D. ARCHITECTURE OF THE INVESTIGATION.

1. Temporary Remedial Measures. Once a workplace incident occurs that necessitates an investigation, management should immediately and proactively act to ensure that the conduct complained of does not continue to occur during the pendency of the investigation. For example, an employee accused of sexual harassment should be separated from the alleged victim. This might even include leave for the accused until the investigation is complete.

2. Setting the Scope of the Investigation. Not every investigation needs to rise to the level of the Spanish Inquisition. Leading up to the investigation, the investigator should identify the scope and parameters of the investigation, keeping in mind that while the investigation should be thorough, the disruption to the Company's business should be the least amount possible. The investigator should consider and determine:

- What it the subject matter of the investigation?
- What issues must be covered?
- What issues should not be addressed?
- Have the employment policy and procedures at issue been reviewed thoroughly?
- Are there any potential obstacles to proceeding with the investigation?
- What documents should be reviewed and gathered prior to the investigation?
- What electronic information should be included and gathered in the investigation?
- What witnesses should be interviewed?
- When should the investigation be completed?
- Who should be put on leave, if anyone?
- What employees' emails, text messages or electronic media should be reviewed prior to the investigation?

- Does the Company's electronic communications policy allow a Company investigator to review employee emails, text messages and other electronic media?

3. Collecting and Reviewing Evidence. Pursuant to Company policy (including electronic communications policies), the investigator should obtain and review evidence that is related to the investigation. This evidence may include documents, personnel files, written formal and informal complaints, surveillance video, voice mail recordings, text messages, emails, public social media postings, and any other electronic or tangible documents related to the incident. This should typically be completed prior to witness interviews so the investigator has sufficient data to ask appropriate and probing questions during the interviews.

The investigator should maintain a separate investigative file that organizes and preserves all of the relevant evidence, and eventually the investigators findings.

4. General Considerations for Conducting Interviews.

In conducting the interview:

- The investigator should have an additional assistant with him or her who is dedicated to taking copious notes. The interviewer should be focused on the questions and not on the note taking. Also, having an additional person at the interview will provide credibility to the substance of the interview.
- Always start with asking the employee to tell the truth and assure them they will not be retaliated against for participating in the investigation.
- Explain the general purpose of the interview, (there has been a report of sexual harassment against ________, and we wanted to ask you a few questions concerning any knowledge or information you have about the incident).
- Ask broad open ended questions to begin the interview, and narrow the questions as you go.
- Appear impartial and do not take sides during an interview.
- Don't be afraid of silence after you ask a question.

- Follow up with detailed questions on the source of information provided.
- Avoid disclosing the information you received from other witness interviews. The investigator's job is to gather information, and not disseminate it.
- Do not finish the employee's sentences or interrupt the employee's responses.
- Save tough or confrontational questions until the end, but be sure to ask the tough questions to ensure you have all the information the witness has.
- In the event the employee refuses to talk or provide answers to specific questions, the investigator should document the insubordination.

5. The following types of questions should be asked in every investigation:

- Who?
- What?
- When?
- Where?
- How?
- Why did this happen?
- What other employees or individuals might have relevant information?
- What could have been done to avoid the incident?
- What evidence do you have concerning the incident, (notes, emails, text messages, recordings)?
- Who have you told about the incident?

6. Interviewing the Complainant.

- Typically, the complainant is the first to be interviewed.
- The investigator should explain his or her investigatory role to the complainant and acknowledge that the employer takes the complaint seriously and is appreciative of the complainant's willingness to come forward with the complaint.
- It is best if the complaint is received officially in writing. But if the complainant does not wish to give the complaint in writing, the investigator could write the complaint and have the complainant sign it.
- Interviewing the complainant alone is preferred, but often a complainant wishes to speak to the investigator with a companion or confidant in the room. Having someone else in the room may impact the truthfulness or completeness of the complaint and its details. If the employee is non-union, the general rule is to not allow representation or an additional third party attending the interview.

There are many questions that an investigator could ask the complainant, but at the very least he or she wants to ask the basic who, what, where, and when questions.

- Who committed the alleged harassment or misconduct?
- What exactly occurred or was said?
- Where did it occur?
- When did it occur, and how often?
- Did the complainant tell the offender that the conduct was offensive and that it must stop?
- What else did the complainant do to discourage the conduct?
- Is the offensive conduct still occurring?
- Did the complainant report the incident to his or her supervisor or anyone else in management?
- Did the complainant mention the incident to a co-worker or anyone else?

- Did the complainant make a complaint under the EEOC policy?
- Are there witnesses, documents, or other evidence that corroborates the complainant's allegations?
- How did the harassment or misconduct affect the complainant (psychologically, physiologically, and economically)?
- Why does the complainant think this happened?
- Who does the complainant think is to blame?
- What was your working relationship with the accused?
- Does the complainant think this could have been avoided, and how?
- Does the complainant know if the person who harassed him or her harassed anyone else?
- Does the complainant know if anyone has ever complained about harassment by that person?
- How would the complainant like the situation resolved?
- The investigator should not promise anonymity?

7. Interviewing the Accused.

- After interviewing the complainant, the investigator typically should get a response to the allegations from the accused. It may be advisable to interview any available witnesses first, to get a better understanding of what may have occurred, before interviewing the accused.
- The investigator should explain that a claim of inappropriate conduct has been made, and that the employer is attempting to determine whether the allegations have merit before making any personnel decisions. The investigator is simply asking to hear the employee's side of the story with a fair and open mind.
- The accused should be told that all information from the investigation will be handled as discreetly as possible.

- It needs to be clear to the accused that there are policies against any form of retaliation and that it will not be tolerated. Retaliation could result in discipline or even termination, if necessary.

With respect to specific questions for the accused, there is important ground to cover:

- An effective starting point is to ask the accused if he or she is aware of any personnel issues in the workplace. If the employee denies any such knowledge, the investigator should then give the accused a brief description of the allegations against him or her.
- The accused should then be given time to respond to each of the allegations and the investigator should explain to the accused that he or she is expected to cooperate in the investigation and that there will be negative consequences for being untruthful or uncooperative.
- If the accused claims that the allegations are false, ask why the complainant might lie or might have a motive to make false claims.
- If there is a specific policy violated in the complaint, the accused should be asked if he or she is familiar with the policy and if he or she ever received any training about that policy.
- Ask the accused if there are any persons that the investigator should speak to or any relevant evidence or documents that support the accused's position.

8. Interviewing Additional Witnesses.

As mentioned above, the investigator may want to interview one witness, or many, before confronting the accused. This strategy could minimize the risk of any interference by the accused with the investigation, such as tampering with any possible witnesses.

The witnesses are crucial in attempting to substantiate the allegations of misconduct. They can also help determine the severity of the alleged conduct. To be fair and thorough during the investigation, the investigator must interview any witness identified by the complainant as having personal knowledge of the offending conduct. Along the same vein, the investigator must also interview any witness identified by the accused as having relevant information to support his or her position.

When considering if any other employees should be interviewed, the investigator should consider the possibility of disrupting the workplace. The possibility of disruption should be weighed against any benefit that might be gained by involving more people in the investigation process.

9. Concluding the Interview.

Every interview should be concluded by asking the interviewee if he or she has told the investigator everything. This final open-ended question can help prompt more detail or even one last thing that might be critical to a quality investigation. This question can be as simple as, "Is there anything else you would like to tell us?"

After all of the questions have been asked, the investigator should try and recount or rephrase each significant point that has come to light in the interview. This helps to clarify any misunderstandings and fill in pieces that might be missing in the investigator's record. The investigator should remind the interviewee that it is perfectly appropriate to contact the investigator if he or she has any questions or thinks of anything else he or she would like to tell the investigator about the situation.

In closing, the investigator should remind the interviewee to keep the information discussed during the interview confidential. If the accused is the one being interviewed, the investigator should remind him or her, once again, that retaliation will not be tolerated. Lastly, the investigator should remember that it is okay to re-interview anyone if additional information becomes known that is related to anything that was previously provided in one or more of the interviews.

E. FINALIZING THE INVESTIGATION.

1. Memorializing the Interview and Preserving the Investigation.

The investigator should explain at the beginning of the interview that he or she will be taking notes. The notes that the investigator takes should be factual. Appropriate notes about an interviewee's demeanor may also be included if they are relevant to credibility. An investigator should have a note taker present to ensure that as much detail as possible is recorded. Generally, it is advised to avoid transcribing or recording interviews. A word-for-word recording of interviews is not necessary.

Along with keeping records of the interviews, throughout the investigation, an employer should document the steps that it undertook to investigate the employee's complaint. Written and signed statements from each of the interviewees would be included in these documents. Even if an interviewee states that he or she knows nothing about the relevant events, that fact should be recorded and kept in the records.

It is always best to conclude an investigation with a written summary or report. This report should be written from a neutral prospective and should include the allegations, the investigative steps taken, the witnesses, the standard questions asked, the witnesses' response and the investigators conclusions, including any credibility determinations. The investigator should prepare a final written report presuming that the report will be discoverable in subsequent litigation or administrative actions.

Typically, it is best to separate the ultimate decision maker from the fact finder. Once the investigation is complete, the investigator should discuss all of the facts that he or she gathered with the person or group of people that will ultimately be making the decision or will be giving advice about appropriate action. Then, the employer will work on writing his or her final conclusions. Generally, an employer does not want to save any drafts of this document and the employer's final conclusions should be carefully written, should not speculate, and should not unjustifiably criticize the employer or other employees.

2. Remedial Action.

In the event the investigative report leads management to conclude the accused is guilt of the allegations, or has violated Company policies and procedures, management should take prompt remedial action. The disciplinary action must be reasonably calculated to end the harassment. In determining reasonableness, courts, and the Tenth Circuit in particular, will look at (1) whether the conduct stopped, (2) the timeliness of the employer's response to the complaint, and (3) whether the response was proportional to the seriousness and frequency of the harassment or misconduct. The Tenth Circuit has found the following discipline to meet the reasonableness criteria (though each case turns on its own particular facts): prompt investigation of the allegations, proactive solicitation of complaints, scheduling changes and transfers, oral or written warnings to refrain from harassing or other inappropriate conduct, reprimands, and warnings that future misconduct could result in progressive discipline, including suspension and termination. *See Adler v. Wal-Mart Stores Inc.,* 144 F.3d 664 (10th Cir. 1998).

F. OTHER CONSIDERATIONS.

When conducting an investigation, employers should keep a number of other issues in mind.

1. "Weingarten Rights."

In *NLRB v. Weingarten, Inc.*, 420 U.S. 251 (1975), the U.S. Supreme Court held that unionized employees have the right to request that a union representative be present in an interview that the employee reasonably believes will result in disciplinary action. An employer's failure to honor a protected employee's *Weingarten* rights can be found to have interfered with the exercise of the employee's Section 7 rights under the National Labor Relations Act. *Weingarten* does not currently apply to non-union employees, *see Praxair Distrib., Inc.*, 358 N.L.R.B. No. 7 (Feb. 21, 2012), though it has in the past, *see Epilepsy Found. of N.E. Ohio*, 331 N.L.R.B. 92 (2000), and may again in the future.

2. Protected Concerted Activity.

Employers should also be aware that the National Labor Relations Act prohibits interrogations of employees on their protected concerted activities, subject to an exception requiring the employer to give the employee warnings regarding the employee's rights and assurances that no retaliation will occur as a result of the interrogation. *See Johnnie's Poultry Co.*, 146 N.L.R.B. 770 (1964); *Beverly Health & Rehabilitation Servs. v. NLRB*, 297 F.3d 468 (6th Cir. 2002).

INVESTIGATING WRONGFUL EMPLOYEE CONDUCT AUDIT

1. Do you try to eliminate destructive employees in the hiring process? . . . . Y N DK NA

2. Have you had any employment practices claims in the last three years (including, but not limited to, NLRB, Dept. of Labor, EEOC, FLSA, state agencies, mediations, arbitrations, administrative hearings, internal grievances and attorney demands)? . . . . Y N DK NA

   Past practices are good indications of present ones. Many times a company, after facing a claim, will not make the effort to find out what failure in their management system generated the claim in the first place. Unless we *examine our losses*, and address the *variance* in our system, we will continue to be faced with similar failures. As ancient wisdom has it, *"lessons are repeated until they are learned."*

3. Are you currently aware of any possible employment practice claims?. . . . . Y N DK NA

   There is no time like the present time to deal with problems. Many employers make the mistake of *ignoring, burying* or *denying* their risk exposures. Remember, what employees want most is for you to a) acknowledge they have a complaint and b) make an effort to do something about it; so c) they can get back to doing their jobs.

4. Do you take advantage of the HR That Works "hotline"? . . . . Y N DK NA

5. Do you have a policy for responding to inquiries from the press regarding employment practices claims? . . . . Y N DK NA

   Anything you say about an employee claim outside of your lawyer's office, or in the course of settlement, can be and will be used against you. If you do not have a uniform policy for dealing with the media, we strongly suggest that you *get some advice before saying anything.*

6. Do you have a policy for the reporting of illegal or unethical activity? . . . . Y N DK NA

   According to a recent article by the Wall Street Journal approximately 40 percent of employees would not report unethical conduct to upper level management. In a 1998 poll of 2,000 U.S. employees, 41% said they were aware of unethical or illegal behavior going on at the office! There is simply no substitute for educating employees about ethics and then demanding they speak up.

7. Has the CEO, President or owner of your company made it clear to your employees, in writing as well as verbally, that the company will not tolerate any form of harassment or discrimination or unethical conduct? . . . . Y N DK NA

   There is no substitute for sending a strong message from the top that harassment, discrimination, ethical violations, and other bad behavior simply will not be tolerated. We suggest a well-worded message from the president or CEO in the employee handbook, employee newsletter, annual report and other documents.

8. Do you have an Equal Employment Opportunity policy statement that is on your employment application and in your employee handbook? . . . . .Y N DK NA

   Unless you are in a black-hole, you should have an EEOC Statement.

9. Do you have a written policy prohibiting sexual harassment and discrimination? . . . . .Y N DK NA

   Again, if you do not have one of these policies please use ours. It is important that these policies offer an *alternative line of communication* from the traditional supervisor to supervisor routes. Your human resources department or a third party ombudsman is suggested.

10. Do you have a written procedure for conducting an investigation of any sexual harassment or discrimination complaints? . . . . .Y N DK NA

    How you conduct an investigation goes a long way to satisfying employee concerns as well as those of the various agencies. Your investigation procedure should assure a *prompt and through investigation.* Your investigator should engage in *dialogue,* not preconceived beliefs.

11. Do you have a specifically designated employee(s) to handle sexual harassment and discrimination complaints? . . . . .Y N DK NA

    As stated above, who is assigned to handle complaints is a risk management decision. Whether it is HR or another manager, that person should be trained in conflict resolution, dialogue and investigation procedures.

12. Does your investigation procedure include the following:

Factual summary of the compliant? . . . . .Y N DK NA

Identification of persons interviewed? . . . . .Y N DK NA

Statements obtained under penalty of perjury?. .Y N DK NA

Findings issued?. . . . . .Y N DK NA

Communication of findings to those
on a "need to know" basis?. . . . . .Y N DK NA

Follow up and monitoring? . . . . .Y N DK NA

Personnel systems improvement? . . . . .Y N DK NA

The listed items are basic requirements of a sound investigation process. As soon as you have a significant concern we strongly suggest that you call an employment law hotline or your attorney and get some advice. Courts look favorably on *independent investigations conducted by professional investigators, human resources professionals or employment law attorneys.*

13. Do you educate and train your employees on a regular
basis regarding sexual harassment, discrimination
and hostile environment issues? . . . . .Y N DK NA

Showing your employees a 20-minute video once a year won't get it. The issue of dealing with people who are "different than us" whether they are of an opposite sex, race, age or nationality has a significant impact on the ability to work as a team. Productivity figures as well as risk exposure is at stake. We suggest a *continuous learning approach* towards compliance and the ability to communicate and resolve conflict.

14. Have you inspected the workplace for inappropriate posters, calendars, jokes, or other items which could be looked upon as creating a discriminatory or hostile environment? .Y N DK NA

    Pinup calendars, racial jokes and derogatory e-mails are just some examples of conduct that can generate a *"hostile environment claim"*. While we are not necessarily fans of "cleansing the American workplace", you do have to guard against materials that would be deemed offensive or harassing under anyone's reasonable standard.

15. Do you regularly survey your workers regarding their understanding of, or exposure to, discrimination, sexual harassment and disability concerns? . . . . .Y N DK NA

    In 1998 the United States Supreme Court faced three employers arguing they should not be held responsible for conduct they knew nothing about. The reason they knew nothing about it was because of a thing known as the *"culture of silence."* In order to protect against these claims, employers must make sure they have sufficiently educated their employees and then follow that by asking if they have been a victim of, or witness to, any of these violations.

16. Do you conduct any training regarding the issues of sexual harassment? . . . . .Y N DK NA

    Sexual harassment continues to be a significant source of employee claims and non-productivity. When managers and employees are not educated in this area, they tend to make stupid mistakes that escalate into larger claims. The off-hand remark, the racy e-mail, the inappropriate dinner, are all types of actions that can be easily avoided through education.

17. Do you conduct any training regarding the issue of diversity/ discrimination? . . . . .Y N DK NA

    What was just stated about sexual harassment applies here. The issue of *teaching tolerance* not only helps to avoid lawsuits, it also helps to make employees that much more productive. Educating on these issues must be considered a process. Again, please contact your attorney regarding in-house training, computer-based training and video-based training.

18. Do you conduct any training regarding the issue of age discrimination? . . . . .Y N DK NA

    The battle between the ages is heating up in light of today's new technologies. Very simply, Generation X'ers and Baby Boomers are going off in two separate directions. It will be a challenge for your organization to keep these forces in alignment. Not just to avoid compliance issues but for productivity purposes as well.

19. Do you have a uniform enforcement policy for employee discipline? . . . . .Y N DK NA

    The word discipline is derived from a Latin word whose root meaning is "to learn". The first question to ask when addressing employee conduct is "was the employee's conduct self-induced or systemic in nature?" What lesson needs to be learned? According to Dr. W. Edwards Deming, nine out of ten employee failures are systems failures – not because the employee did not want to do a good job. If it is the employee, then you must get them to "own" their problems. The best way to correct behavior is for the employee to learn for himself or herself, under your guidance. If you do it for them they will never learn.

    As ancient wisdom has it, *lessons are repeated until they're learned.* Lastly, the punishment must fit the crime. One of the biggest problems we see facing managers is their uneven distribution of discipline. If particularly severe discipline is involved you may want to make sure that the human resource manager or another supervisor gives their feedback on the situation.

20. Do you use a standard employee warning form? Y N DK NA

21. Do you have a process which requires an employee to "own" their problems? . . . . .Y N DK NA

    Depending on the nature of the offense it may be wise to give them leave without pay to really think about it.

22. Do you have a well-documented personnel file prior to terminating an employee? . . . . .Y N DK NA

    Document, document, document is a phrase you continually hear from employment lawyers. Despite this sage advice, employer after employer finds itself defending a disciplinary action without proper documentation. Again, we suggest that you use the forms discussed above to help with this process.

23. Do you have a standard pre-termination procedure or checklist?. . . . . .Y N DK NA

    Going through a sound employee termination process is just as important as going through a sound hiring process. Anytime there is a lack of uniformity you expose yourself to discrimination and wrongful discharge type claims.

24. Are all terminations independently reviewed and approved? . . . . .Y N DK NA

    A number of lawsuits filed have been a direct result of a knee-jerk termination. Every termination decision should be independently reviewed by a human resource manager or other manager at the company to make sure emotions are not running high and that your termination process is being followed.

25. Have you corrected legal or management deficiencies brought to light by past employment claims?. . . . . .Y N DK NA

    As ancient wisdom has it *"lessons are repeated until learned"*. We have seen many companies repeat the same failures because they failed to correct variances in their personnel systems. For example, it is our estimate that as many as half of all employment law claims are the result of a poor hiring decision. If the variances in your system are not corrected you will be subject to the same risk exposures on a repeated basis.

26. Do you have a written procedure for handling employee claims?. . . . . .Y N DK NA

    Approximately half of all companies have a written procedure for handling employee claims. It is generally found in the employee handbook. If you have a procedure you should stick to it so as to avoid unequal treatment claims. If you don't have a written policy you should at least have one person in charge who will go through a similar process every time.

27. Do you communicate to your employees your right to inspect desks, lockers, vehicles, bags, purses, etc.?. . . . . .Y N DK NA

    The struggle over *privacy versus protection* in the workplace is one that will continue through the next millennium. The first line of protection is not to create an "expectation of privacy" where there should be none. Very simply, there is very little an employee should be doing during the workday that needs to be considered "private". It is important to define for employees what areas are subject to search or inspection. You should communicate in your employee handbook the fact that you have the right to inspect desks, lockers, vehicles on premise, bags, purses, storage areas, etc.

28. Do you have a policy regarding voicemail, e-mail and internet usage which addresses privacy, confidentiality and harassment issues? . . . . .Y N DK NA

    Today's new technologies have created new issues in this continuing debate of privacy versus protection. Of particular concern are voicemail, e-mail and the Internet. For example, statistics indicate that *70% of all pornographic internet usage occurs between the hours of 9 a.m. to 5 p.m.!* This represents a significant exposure (no pun intended) to your company for claims such as sexual harassment. It also means that your employees may not be focused on what they should be.

29. Do you monitor any employee activities, including but not limited to, computer use, e-mail, phone calls, video surveillance etc.?. . . . . .Y N DK NA

    If you monitor employee's activities you should let them know you are doing so. Explain to them what you are doing and why you are doing it. The "why" of it should certainly be a legitimate business objective. Employers who have gotten themselves in trouble in this area either don't inform their employees or monitor for allegedly legitimate reasons that are outweighed by the right to privacy. The classic example is putting video surveillance in a locker area to prevent theft.

THAT'S IT! CONGRATULATIONS! You should have been able to answer all of the above questions with a "yes" or "not applicable". A "don't know" or "no" answer puts you at the risk of employee claims, or even worse, business failure.

CHAPTER 48

HUMAN RESOURCES

WAGES AND HOURS LAW

DAVID CASTLEBERRY[1]

FAIR LABOR STANDARDS ACT

General Summary

The federal Fair Labor Standards Act (FLSA) establishes a minimum wage to be paid to all employees and requires the payment of overtime wages to non-exempt employees for hours worked in excess of 40 hours during a seven day period. The FLSA proscribes the use of oppressive child labor and prohibits employers from discriminating among employees with respect to wages on the basis of gender. Failure to comply with the requirements of the FLSA exposes the employer to both civil and criminal liability in the form of civil penalties, imprisonment, payment of lost wages and additional liquidated damages, as well as compelled hiring, reinstatement or promotion of affected employees.

Requirements

The FLSA requires that employers pay employees a minimum of $7.25 an hour. 29 U.S.C. § 206(a)(1). The FLSA establishes a maximum workweek of forty hours beyond which compensation of one and one half times the employee's "regular rate" must be paid. An employee's right to receive overtime pay cannot be waived; any exceptions are restricted to the statutory exclusions. 29 U.S.C. § 207(a),(e); 29 C.F.R. § 778. For hourly employees the "regular rate" is their hourly rate. For other employees, the regular rate is determined by dividing the employees' total earnings for the workweek by the total number of hours worked. 29

---

[1]David Castleberry is a partner with Manning Curtis Bradshaw & Bednar LLC. Mr. Castleberry represents clients in federal and state court and before administrative agencies on issues dealing with state and federal employment law claims. He also provides counsel to clients with respect to issues relating to employment law.

C.F.R. § 778.109. The FLSA does not limit the number of hours that may be worked by an adult employee, but requires overtime compensation for hours in excess for forty (40) for the workweek. Overtime pay is not required for hours worked in excess of any daily number, nor is it required for work performed on Saturdays, Sundays, or holidays, or for work done at unusual or undesirable times. 29 C.F.R. § 778.102.

Exempt Employees

Minimum wage and maximum hour requirements do not apply to the certain categories of exempt employees. Some of the categories of exempt employees include:

- Executives: Any individual employed in a bona fide executive position. 29 U.S.C. § 213(a)(1).
- Administrators: Any individual employed in a bona fide administrative position. 29 U.S.C. § 213(a)(1).
- Professionals: Any individual employed in a bona fide professional capacity. 29 U.S.C. § 213(a)(1).
- Computer Employees: An employee paid more than $455.00 per week on a salary or fee basis or at a rate of not less than $27.63 per hour is exempt if the employee's primary duty consists of work that requires theoretical and practical application of highly specialized knowledge in computer systems analysis techniques and procedures; documentation, analysis, creation, testing, or modification of computer systems or programs; and the design, documentation, testing, creation, or modification of computer programs related to machine operating systems. Employees in computer manufacturing or repair or employees dependent upon computer applications and systems are not included in this category. 29 U.S.C. § 213(a)(17).
- Outside Sales: Employees that are customarily and regularly engaged away from the employer's place of business and the employee's primary duty is making sales or obtaining orders or contracts for services or for the use of facilities for which consideration will be paid. 29 C.F.R. § 541.500.

- Seasonal Employees: Employees of recreational or amusement establishments, organized camps, religious or nonprofit educational conference centers if they do not operate for more than seven (7) months per year or in other special circumstances. 29 U.S.C. § 213(a)(3).
- Household Help: Persons employed on a casual basis in domestic service, such as baby-sitting or companionship services for individuals unable to care for themselves. 29 U.S.C. § 213(a)(15).

PAYMENT OF WAGES

General Summary

Employers are generally required to ensure that wages are paid on a semi-monthly basis within ten days of the close of each pay period. When employment is terminated, wages must be paid within 24 hours of termination. When an employee resigns, wages earned are due and payable on the next regular payday. Offsets and deductions from paychecks are severely restricted by regulation and, when permissible, must be reflected on the pay stub provided to employees with their paychecks. Failure to comply with the provisions governing payment of wages subjects employers to criminal sanctions, money penalties and civil liability.

Employers must pay wages earned semi-monthly or twice during each calendar month on days designated in advance as regular paydays. U.C.A. § 34-28-3(1). If an employer hires employees on a yearly salary basis, the employer may pay an employee on a monthly basis by paying on or before the seventh of the month following the month for which services were rendered. *Id.* § 34-28-3(1)(d). An employer must pay for services rendered during each semi-monthly period within ten days after the close of each pay period. If the semi-monthly payday falls on Saturday, Sunday or a legal holiday, payment of wages earned during the semi-monthly period must be made on the preceding day. U.C.A. § 34-28-3(1). An employer must notify employees at the time of hiring of the day and place of payment, the rate of pay, and of any change with respect to any of these items prior to the time of change. After employment begins, such notices may be given by posting a notice at a conspicuous place where the notice will be seen as each employee comes or goes to work. U.C.A. § 34-28-4. Any deduction made from the wages paid must be itemized on a statement or detachable check stub provided to the employee with the employee's paycheck. U.C.A. § 34-28-3(4); Utah Admin. Code R610-3-20.

An employee who is involuntarily terminated must receive a final paycheck within 24 hours of the time of separation. U.C.A. § 34-28-5(1). Persons employed as sales agents and paid on a commission basis who have custody of accounts, money, or goods of the employer are not required to be paid within 24 hours of termination if the net amount due such employee can be determined only after an audit or verification of the employee's sales, accounts, funds, or stocks. U.C.A. § 34-28-5(4). An employee who does not have a written contract for a definite period and who resigns employment may be given a final paycheck together with any deposit held by the employer and properly payable to the employee on the next regular payday. U.C.A. § 34-28-5(2). When the amount of wages due an employee is in dispute, the employer must provide written notice to the employee of the amount of wages the employer contends to be due and shall pay that amount without condition within the proper time period. Acceptance of such payment by the employee does not constitute a release as to any remaining wages. U.C.A. § 34-28 6; Utah Admin. Code R610-3-19.

Each employer must keep a true and accurate record of time worked and wages paid each pay period to each employee employed on an hourly basis. Such records must be kept on file for at least one year after being created. U.C.A. § 34-28-10.

CHAPTER 49

IMMIGRATION

IMMIGRATION CONSIDERATIONS

SHADMAN BASHIR[1]

The focus of this chapter is primarily to describe work visas for immigrants. These visas are divided into two main categories, temporary and permanent[2]. Although there is another classification of visas called exchange visas, they are generally also considered as part of the temporary visas. Another more common term for the general classification is immigrant and non-immigrant work visas.

The United States is a country with protected borders. US immigration laws obtain their legality from this situation. Immigration to United States has no parallel in the modern history of the world. United States is a land of Immigrants and opportunities, which means that the opportunities are not only for its citizens, but for all those who want to come here legally and try to fulfill their American dreams. Anyone in the world can come to the United States, provided they receive permission from the United States government. After living here for a required number of years, they can go through the legal immigration process and become a United States citizen and thereby enjoy the same rights and privileges enjoyed by those citizens who were born within the Country[3]. A person who wants to enter the United States needs a visa[4], which is "an official mark or stamp on a passport that allows someone to enter or

[1]Shadman Bashir was born and raised in Pakistan. He received an L.L.M degree in Comparative Law from California Western School of Law, San Diego, California. Currently Visiting Professor of Law and International Relations at Dixie State University, St George, Utah.

[2]http://www.uscis.gov/working-united-states/working-us

[3]http://www.uscis.gov/us-citizenship/citizenship-through-naturalization/continuous-residence-and-physical-presence-requirements-naturalization

[4]http://travel.state.gov/content/visas/english/general/frequently-asked-questions/what-is-a-u-s-visa.html

leave a country usually for a particular reason"[5]. Generally, United States Citizens who were born outside the US and became citizens through a specific immigration process are called Naturalized Citizens[6], because they became citizens, not by birth within the United States, but by becoming citizens through a process of naturalization.

Foreigners can enter United States legally, either as immigrants or nonimmigrants. When they enter as immigrants, generally their rights to live and work are almost similar to those of the United States Citizens and Permanent Residents. On the other hand, when someone enters United States as a non-immigrant, they have very limited rights regarding living and working within the US. Every year, thousands of foreign workers enter United States to work. Some enter the US as permanent workers[7], while others enter as temporary workers[8]. The distinction between the two, to a large extent, is based on the needs and requirements of the employers who sponsor them. There are different kinds of visas available for this purpose. These visas are classified into different categories, which will be discussed below. The main differences between the categories are based on the unique requirements and restrictions associated with each. Therefore, a prospective employer needs to be well aware of certain basic details regarding each visa, preferably with the help of an immigration attorney, in order to know which kind of visa will be more compatible with his needs.

For example, if an employer wants to hire a computer programmer from South Africa, and he needs the computer programmer to work for him for a couple of years, his best option generally would be the "specialty occupation worker"[9] visa, in other words an H1B Visa. To qualify for this visa, the applicant must have an educational degree and/or work experience equivalent to a US bachelor's degree in the field which is related to that specific job for which the applicant is applying; which, in this example would be the field of computer sciences. This visa is usually

[5]http://www.merriam-webster.com/dictionary/visa

[6]http://www.uscis.gov/us-citizenship/citizenship-through-naturalization

[7]http://www.uscis.gov/working-united-states/permanent-workers

[8]http://www.uscis.gov/working-united-states/temporary-workers/temporary-nonimmigrant-workers

[9]http://www.uscis.gov/working-united-states/temporary-workers/h-1b-specialty-occupations-dod-cooperative-research-and-development-project-workers-and-fashion-models

valid for three years, and can be extended only once by the employer for an additional three years. After working for six years, the term of the visa ends and the foreign worker must leave the country. During the employment period, if the foreign worker quits or is dismissed from him his job, he will lose his nonimmigrant legal status because his status is dependent on the terms and conditions of the specific H1B Visa. In other words, if there is no job, then there is no legal nonimmigrant status. However, if another employer files a new H1B for him, and it is approved, then he can legally stay in the US but must work for the new employer with different terms and conditions. There are many visas similar to H1B, which come packaged with similar conditions and restrictions. For certain visas, there is a yearly cap, which means that only a certain number of visas are available during each fiscal year, which starts on October 1st and ends on September 30th. For example, the yearly cap for H1B is 65,000[10]. But there can be an exception, if the applicant has a master's degree, not just the required bachelor's degree, then another 20,000 H1B visas are available, but it must be remembered that H1B is a nonimmigrant visa.

If a US business wants to hire a foreign worker, then they have to be very clear and specific regarding their own wants and needs in order to prove to the Immigration Department the necessity of hiring a foreign worker. If they can't prove this necessity to the Immigration Department, it is likely the visa will not be approved. Businesses usually hire foreign workers when they are growing or when they need someone with a specific skill, which may be hard to find within the existing US labor pool. Some of the most basic questions for a prospective employer before they can start the process of hiring a foreign worker are as follows:

1. What kind of work is required of the foreign worker?
2. What special skills and qualifications are required for that work?
3. Can the employer not find a local worker with the same skills and or experience?

[10]http://www.uscis.gov/working-united-states/temporary-workers/h-1b-specialty-occupations-dod-cooperative-research-and-development-project-workers-and-fashion-models

4. How soon does the employer need the foreign worker to start working?
5. For how long will the foreign worker work for the employer?

There are many options and routes available for an employer who wants to hire a foreign worker. Based on the answers to the above questions, he can decide which route to take, preferably after consulting an immigration attorney. It's very important for a prospective employer of a foreign worker to have a basic understanding of different work visas and the related conditions. Immigration is a very technical and complicated process. Sometimes an employer, while doing research regarding the different immigration options available for hiring and bringing in a foreign worker from outside the US, may seem to think that the process is simple and straight forward. This kind of thinking will usually encourage a business owner to proceed with the immigration process on his own, without hiring an immigration attorney. This can be huge mistake. The result can be the denial of an immigration application, and it may take much more time and money to complete the process, provided that the process is still possible. It can even be a bigger loss, if the business requirements of the employer are such that it needs the foreign worker to start working as soon as possible.

For example, an entrepreneur wants to open a specialty Indian restaurant, needs a highly skilled Indian chef for the restaurant, and decides to take care of the immigration paperwork himself. He may end up in a long and costly process of bringing in the chef. As a worst case scenario, the application may get denied, which means no chef and no restaurant, unless the entrepreneur can find someone locally. In other words, it's back to square one. Another easier option available for the Entrepreneur is to hire an Indian chef from a country with which US may have signed a treaty such as NAFTA (North American Free Trade Agreement), making the movement of skilled workforce easier between the two countries. Canada is a perfect example for this case, but that may not solve the problem, because it may be hard to find a Canadian Chef who is skilled in Indian cooking and is willing to move to the US and accept the salary package offered for that specific job by the entrepreneur.

This means that even the backup plan may fall flat. If the entrepreneur decides to hire someone who is already in the US and is either out of his legal immigration status, or still has his legal immigration status, but no work authorization, the entrepreneur may end up in violation of Federal Immigration Laws. Had the entrepreneur hired an immigration attorney in the first place, most likely, the situation would have been much better for him.

Some of the most common types of nonimmigrant visas are listed below:

H1A	Registered nurses for temporary employment
H1B	Persons in specialty occupations that require a college or advanced degree; artists, entertainers, athletes and fashion models of distinguished merit and ability (may include persons assisting in their performances)
H2A	Temporary or seasonal agricultural workers
H2B	Persons filling temporary jobs that cannot be filled by US citizens or residents
H3	Professional job trainees in an American company or in the US office of a foreign Company
I	Representatives of foreign information media, representatives of a foreign tourist bureau, or film crew members holding professional journalism credentials and intending to work on news or non-commercial documentaries
L	Managers or executives of multinational corporations, transferred to the company's US office, that have a minimum of one year experience with the company

O Persons of sustained national or international acclaim in the sciences, arts, education, business or athletics, coming to the US to work or perform in their field of achievement

P Entertainers and athletes coming for specific competitions or performances, or who are participating in a reciprocal exchange program between the US and their country, this also includes those performing in culturally unique programs

Q Participants in an international cultural exchange program for the purpose of explaining or sharing their country's culture

R Member of a religious denomination having a bona fide nonprofit, religious organization in the United States

TN Professional workers from Canada or Mexico[11]

There are many nonimmigrant visa categories, which allow the visa status holder to apply for an employment authorization document. These visas include, but are not limited to, visas such as F1[13], V1[14] and J2[15]. These kinds of visas are not generally based on employment, but they give permission to work, which means no specific employer and no specific job. As long as the visa holder has an unexpired Employment Authorization card, he can work almost anywhere. There are some restrictions, such as an employment authorization for foreign students in the US. For example, if school is in session and the student is on an F1 student visa, he can only work for 20 hours or less during that time, and If he works more, then he will be in violation of the immigration laws. If an employer wants to hire someone who lives in United States, and is not a US citizen or permanent resident, then before hiring him,

[11]http://www.uscis.gov/working-united-states/temporary-workers/temporary-nonimmigrant-workers

[12]http://www.uscis.gov/green-card/green-card-processes-and-procedures/employment-authorization-document

[13]http://www.ice.gov/sevis/students/

[14]http://www.uscis.gov/family/family-green-card-holders-permanent-residents/v-visa/v-nonimmigrant-visas

[15]http://travel.state.gov/content/visas/english/study-exchange/exchange.html

the employer must check his Employment Authorization card. If the card is valid and unexpired, then the employer can hire him.

Employment Authorization Document or an EAD[16] is the most important proof of permission to work granted by the United States government. The employment authorization document must be checked by the employer before hiring a worker. Generally, an EAD is granted for one year. There are three broad categories of non-nonimmigrant workers who can qualify for this card, and they can apply for it by submitting the form I-765[17], which is available for downloading at the United States Citizenship and Immigration Services official website.

The form is not only used for a new EAD, but is also used to replace a lost EAD, and also to renew an expired EAD.

The three categories of qualifying workers are listed below:

1. A worker may have authorization to work in the United States as a result of his nonimmigrant status.
2. A worker may have authorization to work for a specific employer as a result of his nonimmigrant status.
3. A worker may be in a category which requires him to file for permission to work.[18]

There are approximately 140,000 immigrant visas available every fiscal year for foreign workers and their spouses and children.[19] If an employer wants to hire a foreign worker for a longer period of time, without the restrictions and conditions of a visa such as an H1B, then he can sponsor the foreign worker as a permanent worker, by filing a petition for him with the Immigration Department. In some cases, before an employer can file the petition, he must get the approval of the Labor Department, by obtaining an approved labor certification. This provides verification that the hiring of the foreign worker will not adversely affect the wages and working conditions of similarly employed

---

[16]http://www.uscis.gov/green-card/green-card-processes-and-procedures/employment-authorization-document

[17]http://www.uscis.gov/i-765

[18]http://www.uscis.gov/green-card/green-card-processes-and-procedures/employment-authorization-document

[19]http://www.uscis.gov/working-united-states/permanent-workers

U.S. workers, and that U.S. workers willing to work or qualified to work that specific job, are not readily available.

The Immigrant Visas listed below are classified into five categories, based on their level of preference.

First Preference EB-1:[20] This preference is reserved for persons of extraordinary ability in the sciences, arts, education, business, or athletics; outstanding professors or researchers; and multinational executives and managers.

Second Preference EB-2:[21] This preference is reserved for persons who are members of the professions holding advanced degrees or for persons with exceptional ability in the arts, sciences, or business.

Third Preference EB-3:[22] This preference is reserved for professionals, skilled workers, and other workers.

Fourth Preference EB-4:[23] This preference is reserved for "special immigrants," which includes certain religious workers, employees of U.S. foreign service posts, retired employees of international organizations, alien minors who are wards of courts in the United States, and other classes of aliens.

Fifth Preference EB-5:[24] This preference is reserved for business investors who invest $1 million or $500,000 (if the investment is made in a targeted employment area) in a new commercial enterprise that employs at least 10 full-time U.S. workers.

Immigration is a highly technical and complicated process. It is true that almost all the relevant information is available at the Department of Homeland Security website for Immigration (USCIS.GOV), and the plain language of the relevant laws and procedures, may make the whole process of hiring a foreign worker seem very simple, easy and straight forward. However, it is strongly recommended that the business hire an immigration attorney to take care of this process. Any mistake during

---

[20]http://www.uscis.gov/working-united-states/permanent-workers/employment-based-immigration-first-preference-eb-1

[21]http://www.uscis.gov/working-united-states/permanent-workers/employment-based-immigration-second-preference-eb-2

[22]http://www.uscis.gov/working-united-states/permanent-workers/employment-based-immigration-third-preference-eb-3

[23]http://www.uscis.gov/working-united-states/permanent-workers/employment-based-immigration-fourth-preference-eb-4

[24]http://www.uscis.gov/working-united-states/permanent-workers/employment-based-immigration-fifth-preference-eb-5/eb-5-immigrant-investor

the immigration process can be costly as well as time consuming and frustrating.

A business must have clear answers to some of the questions asked at the beginning of this chapter. If a business is not sure about its wants and needs regarding a foreign worker, they may end up opting for the wrong kind of immigration status for the worker, especially, if they are doing the immigration paperwork without the help of an immigration attorney.

All lawyers are not equal, so it's always better to do some research before hiring a specific attorney. A good attorney may cost a little more than others, but more experience and a better work ethic will be of great help during the immigration process. It does not mean that any attorney who is charging less for the same amount of work will be less competent, but the difference between the attorney fees, may be due to the location and the kind of cases the attorney deals with. It is always a safe bet to do the relevant research and then make the right decisions.

CHAPTER 50

ESTATE PLANNING

ESTATE PLANNING CONSIDERATIONS

DOUG K. FADEL[1]

I. Estate Planning Considerations

Estate planning is the personal exit strategy for a stockholder, partner or member (collectively "business owner") to leave the business following the business owner's incapacity or death. When a business is in its infancy, business owners tend to be focused primarily on forming and building the business and less interested in liquidating or exiting the business. Estate planning is the process of a business owner executing the necessary legal documents to grant third parties the legal authority to act on behalf of the business owner's interest in the company so that the business owner's investment continues to benefit an incapacitated business owner during his or her lifetime and then inures to the benefit of the business owner's heirs following the business owner's death. In short, the legal documents appoint who will be in charge and where the business interest will go when the business owner becomes incapacitated or passes away.

For single owner entities such as sole proprietorships, single shareholder corporations or single member limited liability companies, estate planning documents generally appoint an agent to take over the business for purposes of liquidating the business and either utilizing the proceeds for the incapacitated business owner or distributing the proceeds to the deceased business owner's heirs. For multi-owner entities, estate planning documents appoint an agent to negotiate with the other business owners or with the company to sell an incapacitated or deceased

[1]Douglas K. Fadel is managing partner at The Fadel Law Firm. Doug has been a practicing attorney since 1994. His practice focuses on estate, retirement, and disability planning; charitable giving; business succession planning guardianship and conservatorship; probate; Medicaid planning; and special needs trusts. Doug earned his juris doctorate from the University of Utah Law School in 1993.

business owner's interest to the company or the other business owners or to continue to allow the incapacitated business owner or deceased business owner's heirs to continue to be owners in the business.

The business owner is the one who decides who shall control and who shall enjoy his or her ownership interest in the business following the business owner's incapacity or death. However, it is the business, through its organization documents and buy-sell agreements, which decides whether the incapacitated business owner or the heirs of a deceased business owner will: 1) be allowed to continue as business owners; or 2) be required to sell the deceased business owner's interest to the company or to the other business owners; or 3) be relegated to the role of a mere assignee.[2]

In turn, a business owner must consider competing objectives when entering into business formation documents. First, a business owner should consider which would be better for the business, allowing inactive business owners (an incapacitated owner or a deceased owner's heirs) to remain in the business or requiring the business or remaining business owners to come up with the cash to purchase an incapacitated or deceased owner's interest. Second, a business owner should consider whether he or she would want to continue in the business with an incapacitated or deceased business partner's volatile spouse, irresponsible children or random charitable organizations or come up with the cash necessary to purchase the incapacitated or deceased business partner's interest. Finally, a business owner should make certain that his or her investment in the business ultimately benefits the business owner or his or her heirs.

A. Planning for Incapacity

A well conceived buy-sell agreement should address what should happen if a business owner should become incapacitated. If a business owner is expected to perform the duties of manager or of employee,

---

[2]The formation documents for closely held corporations, limited partnerships and limited liability companies generally include provisions limiting participation in the business to the current owners. The formation documents will also often include provisions for allowing current owners to assign their interests to certain other individuals or entities (family members, other owners of the company, third parties approved by the other owners). By limiting the assignability, the company hopes to prevent the creditors of owners and other undesirable assignees to become substitute owners in the company. The recipients of unauthorized assignments would have no authority to vote, compel distributions, compel liquidations nor compel company redemptions. Instead, the assignee waits in the wings until the company elects to make distributions to owners which would then flow through to the assignee.

a buy-sell agreement may define incapacity broadly to include any condition which renders the business owner unable to perform his or her duties even though the business owner may be mentally competent. For example, if the business is owned by a group of dentists and each dentist is expected to generate revenue for the business, any condition which makes the dentist unable to perform his or her duties may be an "incapacity" which would trigger a sale of the dentist's interest pursuant to the buy-sell agreement. By contrast, if the business owner is merely a passive investor, incapacity would generally be defined as a mental incapacity which renders the business owner unable to participate in a company vote, unable to receive payments, unable to negotiate a sale of the business owner's interest in the company or unable to execute documents.

Generally, in an active business where a business owner performs managerial tasks or where the business owner is also an employee of the business, the inability to manage or work would trigger an obligation for the business owner to sell his or her ownership interest and the company to purchase his or her ownership interest. If the incapacity which triggers the obligation to sell does not involve a corresponding mental incapacity the transactions may be consummated between the company and the business owner. However, if the incapacity includes diminished mental capacity, the company may not be able to deal directly with the business owner but would instead be required to consummate the transactions with the business owner's agent. However, the appointment of an agent to transact business on behalf of the incapacitated business owner is generally accomplished by the business owner's personal estate planning and not by the business, and unfortunately, many business owners fail to engage in comprehensive estate planning. In turn, the business may be in the position of continuing to deal directly with the incapacitated business owner until the business owner's agent can demonstrate that the agent has the legal authority to transact business on behalf of the incapacitated business owner. It should be presumed that the business owner has legal capacity and legal authority to act on his or her own behalf until the company is presented with the legal documents granting an agent to act on behalf of the business owner.

The definition of incapacity which triggers an agent's authority to act is generally defined by the documents creating the agency or by state law. Business formation documents rarely address the appointment of an agent. However, some business formation documents require that an agent must be a member of the incapacitated business owner's family or another one of the business owners in order for the incapacitated business owner to retain his or her ownership interest in the company rather than having to sell his or her interest pursuant to the buy-sell agreement.

When a business owner becomes incapacitated, there are essentially four types of agents which may be able to act on behalf of the incapacitated business owner: 1) a joint owner; 2) a court appointed conservator; 3) a power-of-attorney; 4) a Trustee.

First, if corporate stock, partnership interest or membership interest is owned jointly by two or more business owners, a joint owner would presumably have the legal authority to unilaterally transact business if the other joint owner were to become incapacitated. Closely held business interests are generally not owned jointly. However, a stock certificate or ledger, a partnership agreement or operating agreement could show joint ownership, and presumably either joint owner could act on behalf of the joint ownership interest.

Second, a court appointed conservator would be granted authority to access an incapacitated person's assets. If an incapacitated business owner has done no estate planning or if the incapacitated business owner does not believe that he or she is incapacitated, a court appointed conservator would be required in order to strip the incapacitated business owner of his or her ability to act and to appoint a conservator as agent for the incapacitated business owner.

Third, the holder of a power-of-attorney would be able to transact business on behalf of an incapacitated business owner. A power or attorney is a written document executed by the business owner granting an agent the ability to act on behalf of the business owner.

Finally, if an incapacitated business owner owns his or her business interest in his or her revocable trust or in another business, a successor Trustee or successor officer, general partner or manager would be acting as an agent for the incapacitated business owner. Generally, when a business owner establishes a trust which is intended to own his or her business interest, the creator of the trust ("Grantor") is also the manager of the trust ("Trustee"). When a business owner forms another business which is intended to own his or her business interest, the business owner is also the officer, general partner or manager of ownership entity.

Owner	**Agent**	**Legal Authority**
Joint Owners	None	Either or both joint owner
Individual (no appointed Power of Attorney)	None	Individual
Individual (has appointed Power of Attorney)	Power of Attorney	-Individual -Power of attorney provided individual does not object -Court appointed conservator if one is appointed takes priority over individual and power of attorney
Trust	Trustee	Trustee (original business owner or successor Trustee)
Business	Officer, General Partner	Specified by business Manager
Court Appointed Conservator	Conservator	Conservator

1. Restrictions on Outside Agents

Some closely held businesses prohibit third party outside agents from acting on behalf ofa business owner even when the business owner becomes incapacitated. The rationale is that the business owners have chosen to go into business with each other but have not signed on to being in business with a business owner's randomly selected agents. Such agreements would specify that during any period, temporary or permanent, the business owner is not able to act on his or her own behalf, the business owner would be treated as a mere assignee with no active role in the company. Some organizational documents would allow an agent to act provided the agent is one of the other business owners or perhaps a member of the family. For example, the Smith family owns a company known as the Smith Waterless Laundry Company, formation documents for the company may limit the recognition of a power of attorney holder or Trustee to other owners of the company or to members of the Smith family.

2. Successor Trustees

Generally, when a business owner establishes a revocable living trust which is intended to own his or her business interest, the Grantor (and sometime the Grantor's spouse) is also the Trustee. The trust should provide a convenient mechanism for the successor Trustee to use trust assets for the benefit of the incapacitated Grantor and his or her loved ones. The trust should also provide detailed instructions regarding the manner of care that should be given to the incapacitated Grantor. Within the trust, incapacity is generally defined as a mental incapacity which results in an inability to effectively manage assets. Determination of incapacity should not necessarily require court involvement. Instead, a trust may provide that the physician regularly attending the Grantor, or two or more other physicians would be authorized to determine the Grantor's incapacity. However, a court determination should be available at the Grantor's option if the Grantor disagrees with the physician's determination of the Grantor's incompetence.

If a trust is the owner of a business interest, the incapacity provisions in the company's buy-sell agreement and formation documents should be drafted to address the incapacity of the grantor of the trust and not the incapacity of the owner of the interest (as the trust cannot become incapacitated). For example, the definition of incapacity contained in the operating agreement of a limited liability company might provide that if a Membership Interest is owned by a trust or business, the incapacity of the human being who is the grantor of the trust or the incapacity of the human being who is the officer, general partner or manager of the business shall cause the trust or business member to be deemed incapacitated.

3. Powers of Attorney

A power of attorney is a document which grants an agent the legal authority to act on behalf of the person granting the power of attorney (the "Principal"). In the context of business planning, the power of attorney would grant an agent the ability to act on behalf of a business owner. The document granting the agent the power to act defines the scope and duration of the agent's authority. Some powers of attorney are drafted broadly in scope granting the agent the ability to do any act which the principal could legally do. Other powers of attorney limit the scope of the agent's authority to completing a single act – negotiate a sale, sign a document, manage an asset. Even if the scope of the agency is described broadly, state law may specify that a particular activity must be specifically authorized in the document granting the power of attorney in order for a principal to grant an agent the ability to conduct that particular act. For example, state law may require a specific provision authorizing an agent to change beneficiaries on retirement accounts and life insurance. Similarly, the formation documents of a company could specify that the company will not recognize an agent's authority to act unless the document granting an agent the authority to act on behalf of the principal specifically references acting with respect to the principal's business interest. In addition to defining the scope of the agent's authority, the power of attorney document should specify when the agency begins and ends. Some powers of attorney come into effect upon signing a document and remain in effect until the principal revokes the power or the principal passes away. Other powers of attorney spring into effect upon a triggering event such as the principal's incapacity and remain in effect until the principal regains capacity or passes away.

Under most powers of attorney, incapacity is generally defined as a mental incapacity. Guidelines for determining incapacity are generally prescribed by the document creating the power of attorney. Usually, the document specifically states that a court determination of incompetency should not be required. In order for a power of attorney to be effective:

- The document creating the power must satisfy the formalities required by the state where it will be used.
- Depending on the state where the power is to be used, the document creating the power might need to be less than two or three years old.
- The agent must demonstrate that a trigger event (if any is required) has occurred—that the principal is incapacitated.
- The company needs to agree to recognize the agent's authority to act for the business owner (some states allow suit against those refusing to recognize power of attorney documents).

B. Planning for Death

1. Methods of Transferring Ownership at Death

When someone passes away, there are essentially three ways that assets may pass from the deceased owner to someone else. In general, all three of the methods work. In establishing a comprehensive estate plan, it is important to make certain that one method for transferring assets does not undermine another. The first way to transfer assets is by what are called "nonprobate transfers." The second method for transferring assets at death is through probate. The final way to transfer assets at death is through a revocable living trust.[3] A deceased business owner's interest in the company or proceeds from the purchase of the deceased owner's interest in the company may pass to others by any one of these three methods.

---

[3]Arguably there is a fourth method for transferring assets. Some employers such as the federal government have default provisions for distributing a deceased employee's benefits to the deceased employee's family members if the deceased employee failed to designate a beneficiary for the employee benefits. These default provisions differ from pay-on-death beneficiary designations in that the recipients are described in terms of relationship to the employee (spouse, child, parent, siblings) rather than a specific individual (Lester Smith). While it is not common, there appears to be nothing which prevents a company from including such a default provision it is formation documents for transferring a deceased business owner's interest to family members following the business owner's death.

a) Nonprobate Transfers

Nonprobate Transfers are referred to as "nonprobate transfers" because assets pass from a decedent to someone else without having to go through the court proceeding known as probate. There are essentially two types of nonprobate transfer. The first type of nonprobate transfer is a transfer which occurs following the death of a joint owner who owns the asset as "joint owner with right of survivorship." If a business interest is owned jointly by two or more individuals "with right of survivorship," upon the death of one joint owner, the asset becomes owned by the surviving joint owner(s). What is required to transfer ownership is to provide the company with the deceased owner's death certificate and request that the company update its records to show that the business interest is now owned by the surviving joint owner(s). If the joint owners are married to each other, the joint ownership may be characterized as "community property" or as "tenancy by the entirety" depending on the state where the couple resides or where the company is located. The rules governing community property and tenancy by the entirety may also have a component of right of survivorship. While Utah law would allow joint ownership of business interests, most business interests are not owned jointly with right of survivorship.

The second type of nonprobate transfer occurs upon the death of an asset owner who has designated a pay-on-death beneficiary. A pay-on-death beneficiary designation is generally a contractual arrangement between an asset owner and a financial institution to transfer assets to a named beneficiary following the death of the asset owner. Pay-on-death beneficiary designations are most commonly used to transfer retirement accounts, bank accounts and life insurance proceeds following the owner's death. In turn, if an individual has completed the necessary paperwork to designate a beneficiary to receive the asset following the asset owner's death, upon the death of the asset owner, the financial institution would transfer the assets to the named beneficiaries. What is required to process the transfer is to deliver a death certificate to the financial institution and to complete the paperwork required by the financial institution. The Utah Nonprobate Transfer Act, the Utah Limited Liability Company Act, the Utah Corporation Act and the Utah Limited Partnership Act fail to address whether or not a business interest may be transferred from the deceased business owner to named beneficiaries by pay-on-death beneficiary designation, the concept has been done and has seemed to work. The concept of freely entering into contractual arrangements appearing throughout the code sections governing business would suggest that parties could contractually agree to allow business owners to transfer company ownership at death by pay-on-death beneficiary designation.

b) Probate

Probate is a court proceeding for the purpose of transferring assets from a deceased person to his or her heirs, devisees or creditors following his or her death. A court action is required to transfer assets because it should not be easy for individuals to simply show up and take assets following someone's death. Instead, the court would insure that the right people receive the decedent's assets. If an individual has a Will, a written set of instructions appointing someone to be in charge of the estate (personal representative, executor or administrator) and specifying to whom assets should be distributed, the Will would generally govern the probate process. An individual who passes away with a Will is said to have died "testate." A Will is a document which provides instructions for allocating a decedent's estate assets upon death. However, a Will has no power over assets which do not become part of the decedent's "probate estate." Assets held in joint tenancy with right of survivorship and assets in which the decedent had designated a pay-on-death beneficiary will not become part of the decedent's probate estate. A Will remains an unused document during the Will creator's lifetime. Upon death, for the Will to work, it must be put through an administrative, court supervised procedure called "probate." While probate horror stories persist, probate in Utah is fairly inexpensive and painless.

If an individual does not have a Will, if the Will is not probated within three years of death or if the Will fails to dispose of all of the decedent's assets, state statutes provide default provisions for distributing assets to the decedent's "heirs." An individual who passes away without leaving a Will is said to have died "intestate." The decedent's heirs are relatives whose priority to receive assets is based on the degree of kinship between the decedent and his or her relative. An unrelated person, no matter how important the person is to the decedent, will not be included as an intestate heir. Domestic partners, lifetime companions, foster children / parents, step-children, charities and pets are not intestate heirs. In order to insure that assets will pass to unrelated parties, a decedent must execute a Will, own an asset in joint tenancy with right of survivorship, sign a beneficiary designation form, or create and fund a trust.

In Utah, probate does not have to be an expensive or laborious process. If there is no contest among heirs (family members) or devisees (recipients under the Will), the probate process can be completed informally by submitting pleadings to the court without personally appearing in court. However, if there is a contest, probate can become expensive and time consuming. Furthermore, if the assets which become part of the probate estate (no joint owner with right of survivor, no pay-on-death beneficiary, no trust ownership) consist of personal property (no real estate) with a total value of less than $100,000, assets can be claimed by sworn affidavit in lieu of conducting a probate.

If a business owner owns his or her business interest in his or her individual name with no joint ownership and no pay-on-death beneficiary, the business interest will be part of his or her probate estate. If the business formation documents or buy-sell agreement provide that the business must purchase a deceased business owner's interest or allow the decedent's heirs to continue to own the business interest, the business must determine who has the legal authority to act on behalf of the deceased business owner. There are three documents which might be provided to the business as proof of authority to act on behalf of a deceased business owner. First, if a Will has been duly probated, the court will issue a document known as "Letters Testamentary" evidencing the authority of a personal representative to act on behalf of the deceased business owner's estate. Second, if a probate action has been initiated for a deceased business owner who died intestate (without a Will), the court may appoint an estate administrator and issue "Letters of Administration" granting someone the authority to act on behalf of the intestate estate or the court may sign an order detailing whom should receive the assets of the deceased business owner's estate. Finally, if the total value of the probate estate is less than $100,000 (including the total value of the deceased business owner's business interest), the business may be presented with an Affidavit of Small Estate.

c) Revocable Living Trusts

A revocable living trust is a trust created during the trust creator's ("Grantor's") lifetime where the Grantor retains control over trust property and reserves the right to amend or revoke the trust. Provided the Grantor is not incapacitated, the Grantor is generally the sole beneficiary (the one entitled to enjoyment of trust property) and the sole Trustee (the trust manager). During periods of the Grantor's incapacity, a successor Trustee manages the assets for the benefit of the Grantor and the Grantor's dependents. Upon the Grantor's death, the successor Trustee distributes assets according to the provisions of the Trust. If the trust is fully funded (all assets are titled in the name of the trust or the trust is named as pay on death beneficiary) the trust can usually be administered without court involvement.

Because a revocable living trust is what the internal revenue code would deem a "grantor trust," where the income of the trust is taxed to the grantor, and the trust is treated as a "disregarded entity" for tax purposes, the trust is not required to have a separate tax identification number. The trust identification number is the Grantor's own social security number. Also, because the Grantor is treated as an owner for tax reporting purposes, there is no need to file a fiduciary return for the trust, and all income should be reported on the Grantor's regular 1040 return.

(1) Forming a Trust

Under Utah law, a trust may be established by simply indicating that assets are to be held in a fiduciary capacity. Unlike creating a Will, establishing a trust does not require adhering to formal execution requirements. However, as a practical matter, formal execution procedures are likely to make a trust less vulnerable to later challenge. Even though the drafting and signing procedures remain loose, executing a trust requires that the Grantor have testamentary capacity and that the Grantor understands what he or she is executing. However, the Grantor need not be able to articulate the purpose of every provision contained in the trust. The trust should be signed by the Grantor(s) and the initial Trustee(s). While they need not sign the trust in the presence of a Notary, it is usually a good idea. If a Grantor's capacity to execute a trust is questionable or likely to be challenged, the Grantor may want to sign the trust in the presence of additional witnesses or video tape the signing of the trust.

(2) Who Could Benefit from Establishing a Trust?

Almost everyone could benefit from having a revocable living trust rather than relying on a will, joint tenancy, or pay on death beneficiary designations.

- Trusts provide instructions for managing assets in the event of disability.
- Upon death, fully funded trusts provide a convenient mechanism for paying final expenses, funeral and burial costs, and taxes prior to distribution to beneficiaries.
- Beneficiaries under the trust can be allocated a specific percentage of the estate or a specific dollar amount rather than merely receiving the fluctuating balance of a particular account under joint tenancy or beneficiary designation.
- Trusts can protect assets from the claims of a beneficiary's creditors (but usually not the Grantor's creditors).
- Trusts can provide a life estate for a spouse or partner with the amount not used by the spouse or partner going to the decedent's chosen successor beneficiaries.
- Trusts are generally easier and less expensive to administer than Wills.
- Finally, fully funded trusts usually avoid probate.

(1) Disadvantages to Creating a Trust.

There are a few disadvantages to creating a trust. First, while trusts are generally less expensive to administer than a will, trusts generally cost more to create and fund than a Will. Second, to avoid probating an estate, a trust must be fully funded. Many attorneys who assist clients with establishing trust and online resources which assist consumers with establishing a trust rely on the client/consumer to fund the trust. Most clients/consumers do not follow-through with the funding. Funding can sometimes become burdensome for those who are not familiar with the process.

(4) Trust Provisions.

While trust documents generally contain a fair amount of standard boilerplate instructions, no two Grantors are alike. In fact, family profiles are becoming increasingly more unique, and many trusts need extensive customization. Nevertheless, there are some general guidelines to follow when drafting the trust.

(a) Grantor Remains in Control.

During the Grantor's lifetime, the Grantor should have complete authority to amend or revoke the trust and add or subtract assets. During periods of the Grantor's disability and upon the Grantor's death, the trust should not be subject to amendment or revocation.

(b) Disability Provisions.

The trust should provide a convenient mechanism for the successor Trustee to use trust assets for the benefit of the incapacitated Grantor and his or her loved ones. The trust should also provide detailed instructions regarding the manner of care that should be given to the incapacitated Grantor. The trust should clearly define "incapacity," and the definition of incapacity in the trust may differ from the definition of incapacity which appears in the business formation documents and buy-sell agreements. Incapacity should be defined as a mental incapacity which results in an inability to effectively manage assets.

(c) At Death.

Following the Grantor's death, the trust should provide for the appointment of a Successor Trustee. However, the designated Successor Trustee does not have the legal authority to act on behalf of the trust until it formally accepts its appointment in writing. If a deceased (or incapacitated) business owner owns his or her business interest in his or her trust, the business should be presented with an Affidavit (sworn statement in front of a Notary Public) from the Successor Trustee as evidence that the Successor Trustee has the authority to act on behalf of the trust. Utah law provides that third parties dealing with a Successor Trustee may rely on such Affidavit as proof of authority, and third parties would not have to examine the entire trust document. The Successor Trustee would gather trust assets, pay the final expenses of the deceased Grantor and distribute the Grantor's Trust assets as specified in the trust.

(d) Businesses Owning Business Interests

Some business owner's elect to own business interest in another business ("Business Entity Investor"). The organization documents of the Business Entity Investor would determine who has legal authority to act on behalf of the Business Entity Investor and who owns the Business Entity Investor. If it is important that the Business Entity Investor be owned and controlled by a particular individual, the formation documents and buy-sell agreement should require that particular individual's involvement as a condition for the Business Entity Investor to remain a business owner.

2. Exit Strategies

While leaving a business can be more difficult than forming and building the business, there are essentially four options for exiting a business whether voluntarily, due to incapacity or due to death: 1) close the doors and walk away; 2) sell the entire business; 3) sell the business interest to the business or to the other business partners; or 4) leave the business interest to heirs.

a) Close the Doors

If the sole purpose of the business is to provide employment to the business owner, when the business owner no longer wishes to remain employed or is unable to continue to perform his or her duties, perhaps the simplest approach for exiting a business is to simply close the doors and walk away. If the business has some inherit value separate and distinct from the work that was being performed by the business owner, one of the other options for exiting the business may be more favorable.

b) Sell Business

If a business has some market value separate and distinct from the work performed by the business owner, but there are no other business owners or family members who would make good candidates to continue the business, the best approach for exiting the business may be to sell the business (or its assets including good will) to unrelated third parties. Most active businesses are likely to have a greater value if the business owner is available to assist in transitioning the business to the new owner. However, in the case of the business owner's incapacity or death, the business owner may not be available to transition the business to a new owner. Instead, a timely sale of the active business would produce the greatest purchase price. The longer the doors remain closed and consumers are directed to other businesses, the less attractive the business becomes to would-be purchasers.

c) Redemption

If a business has multiple business owners or key employees who may become business owners and the inherit value of the company is not tied to services performed by an exiting business owner, the most common exit strategy and perhaps the most lucrative exit strategy is selling the business interest to the business, to the other business owners or to key employees. When a business owner structures an exit strategy which relies upon other business owners or key employees to purchase an exiting business owner's interest, the business owner must consider that he or she may be on the selling end of the transaction or on the purchasing end of the transaction. If both sides of the transaction are not equally appealing, the transaction will not occur.

(1) Purchase Price

If the business is to be sold to remaining business owners or key employees, determining the purchase price may become complicated. If the parties are not related to one another, the parties may negotiate at arms-length to agree on a purchase price without having the transaction be deemed by the IRS as a partial gift and a partial sale. If the parties are related to one another, the purchase price should be fair market value in order to avoid having the transaction be deemed a partial gift (subject to gift/estate tax) and a partial sale.

(2) Life Insurance

Many buy-sell agreements rely upon life insurance to effectuate a purchase of a deceased owner's business interest. However, if a purchase price is tied to the random amount of life insurance which may be insuring a business owner, the value of a business owner's interest may be over-valued or under-valued. This can present an unworkable result if the purchase of a business owner's interest is triggered by incapacity and not by death as the proceeds from life insurance would not be available to fund the purchase unless the business owner dies.

(3) Promissory Note

If there is insufficient cash available to purchase an exiting business owner's interest, the business formation documents and/or buy-sell agreement may provide for the purchase to execute a promissory note in exchange for the exiting business owner's interest so that the payments may be made over time.

d) Heirs as Owners

An exiting business owner may elect to leave his or her business interest directly to his or her heirs for the heirs to continue in the business. This arrangement would need to be authorized under the formation documents and buy-sell agreement of the company. Furthermore, there would need to be compatible business objectives between the remaining business owners and the heirs of the exiting business owners. If business owners who remain actively involved in the business wish to reinvest company profits back into the business and the passive investor heirs of the exiting business owners wish to receive distributions, the conflicting objectives may provide an unworkable relationship.

3. Estate Tax (Death Tax)

The federal estate tax was first imposed as a method for raising federal revenue during times of war. Eventually the estate tax became a permanent source of revenue for the federal government. The gift tax became a necessary corollary to the estate tax to prevent taxpayers from circumventing the estate tax by giving away all assets during life. Estate tax is imposed on the estate of a taxpayer following the taxpayer's death. Estate tax is imposed on the decedent's estate and not on the recipients of the assets. However, if the decedent has not otherwise provided a method for paying the estate tax, the size of a recipient's gift may have to be reduced to cover the estate tax. Estate tax liability is calculated as a percentage of the combined value of all assets owned by the taxpayer at the time of death less certain deductions and exemptions.

Gift tax is imposed on a taxpayer when the taxpayer transfers property to another individual during the taxpayer's lifetime. Gift tax is paid by the person making the gift not by the recipient of the gift. A gift is the transfer of ownership of an asset for less than its fair market value. Unless a gratuitous transfer qualifies for one of the exemptions, exclusions, or deductions, gift tax would be imposed.

A comprehensive history of gift and estate tax is beyond the scope of this chapter. In short, a decedent can gift or bequeath an unlimited amount to his or her spouse (provided the spouse is a citizen of the United States) without paying any gift or estate tax. Additionally, the first $5,430,000[4] transferred during lifetime and/or death to a non-spouse is not subject to gift or estate tax. The tax rate imposed on cumulative transfers which exceed the exemption is 40%. If someone passes away without using up his or her entire exemption, his legal spouse can claim the unused exemption. For example, if one spouse passed away in 2015 without using any of his or her $5,430,000 exemption, his or her surviving spouse could claim the deceased spouse's unused exemption so that the surviving spouse would have an exemption of $10,860,000.

---

[4]The gift and estate tax exemption amount beginning in 2011 was $5,000,000. This amount is increasing annually with inflation. The exemption amount for gifts or bequests made in 2015 is $5,430,000.

In turn, most individuals do not need to engage in estate tax planning because most people would not have a taxable estate.

CHAPTER 51

ESTATE PLANNING

ESTATE PLANNING AND BUSINESS FORMATION AND ADMINISTRATION

DOUG K. FADEL[1]

I. Estate Planning Tie-in With Business Formation and Administration

A well conceived business succession plan requires coordinating the Estate Planning documents of each business owner with the organizational documents of the business. Ideally, the concurrent drafting and executing of estate planning documents and business formation documents may result in a coordinated and seamless business succession plan. More often, however, business planning and estate planning are not conducted concurrently and existing documents may need to be amended so that the business formation documents are compatible with the personal estate plan of a business owner. Typically, new business owners invest their time and resources into forming and operating a business. Only after the business has become successful do many business owners focus on personal estate planning.

A. Conflicting Business Objectives

The owners of some businesses may share a single common business objective such as forming a business to employ the business owners, investing in assets to provide business owners with passive income, starting a business with the goal of selling the business or developing a

[1]Douglas K. Fadel is managing partner at The Fadel Law Firm. Doug has been a practicing attorney since 1994. His practice focuses on estate, retirement, and disability planning; charitable giving; business succession planning guardianship and conservatorship; probate; Medicaid planning; and special needs trusts. Doug earned his juris doctorate from the University of Utah Law School in 1993.

business that will someday be run by the business owner's heirs. When the business objectives of the various owners of a single business differ significantly, the incapacity or death of a business owner may result in disputes and ultimately the failure of the business. If every business owner hopes that the other business owners will buy out his or her interest, there may be no purchaser for the business. If more than one business owner thinks his or her own child will someday take over the entire business, there may be dueling heirs vying for control of the business. Unfortunately, even common business objectives sometimes evolve into competing objectives. In general, divergent business objectives are best resolved by the original business owners rather than by the agents of an incapacitated or deceased business owner.

B. Conflicting Interfamilial Business Objectives

It is not uncommon for a business owner to groom one or more of his or her descendants to take over the business. It is uncommon, however, for all of the business owner's descendants to actively operate the business following the business owner's exit from the business. More common is the scenario where one or more children are actively involved in the business and the other children are not. How does a business owner transition the business to one or more children while treating the other children equitably? One approach has been to leave the business to those who are active in the business and leave cash (often proceeds from life insurance) or other assets to the children who are not actively involved in the business. Another approach is to leave the business equally to all of the children but structure the ownership to grant the control of the business to those who are actively involved in the business. Yet another approach is to require those children who are actively involved in the business to buy-out the children who are not involved in the business. Whether or not the children feel like they are treated fairly depends on the ongoing success of the business. If the business thrives in the hands of the children who are actively managing it, those who are not enjoying the profits of the business feel like they are treated unfairly. If the business suffers in the hands of the children, the children who are forced to continue to run the business question the fairness of their siblings being able to retire early and live on the inherited cash while they have to work for every penny they spend. Perhaps there is no ideal solution, but it is important to understand the conflicting objectives in order to establish the best plan under the circumstances.

C. Drafting Formation Documents and Buy-Sell Agreements to be Compatible with Estate Plans

The terminology used throughout the formation documents and buy-sell agreements of a company should be compatible with the identity of the various business owners. A business interest may be owned by one or more individuals, by a trust, by a business entity or by a charitable organization. Using the death of a "business owner" would seem nebulous when the business owner is a trust, entity or organization. Requiring that all officers and managers also be owners of the company may be awkward if the owners are entities and not individuals. Requiring that a shareholder also be a licensed professional makes no sense if all of the shareholders are professional corporations. If a company is intended to be owned solely by doctors, the organizational documents should contemplate that a doctor may own his or her interest in his or her own name, in the name of a revocable living trust, or in the name of a professional corporation or limited liability company. If a company is to be owned by unrelated investors, the organizational documents should contemplate that an investor may be an individual, a trust or an entity.

D. Drafting Organizational Documents

Organizational Documents of a company generally include the filings with the state(s) where the company is organized and/or conducts business and the agreements and resolutions among business owners. For sole proprietorships, organizational documents may include dba registrations. For general partnerships, organizational documents may include partnership agreements, resolutions, delegations of authority and public notices limiting authority. For limited partnerships, organizational documents may include Certificates of Limited Partnership (sometimes referred to as Articles of Limited Partnership by other jurisdictions and older Utah state filings), registration as foreign limited partnership conducting business in the state, limited partnership agreements, resolutions and delegations of authority, and powers of attorney. For limited liability companies, organizational documents may include Certificates of Organization (also referred to as Articles of Organization by other jurisdictions and prior versions of the Utah Limited Liability Company Act), registration as foreign limited liability company conducting business in the state, affidavits of authority, operating agreements, resolutions and delegations of authority, and powers of attorney. For corporations, organizational documents may include Articles of Incorporation, registration as foreign corporation conducting business in the state, bylaws, agreements, resolutions and delegations of authority, and powers of attorney.

In this chapter, discussion of organizational documents may be treated as separate and distinct from buy-sell agreements. However, buy-sell provisions are sometimes contained within a partnership agreement or operating agreement rather than in a separate buy-sell agreement. If there are buy-sell provisions in the partnership agreement or operating agreement, it is important that they do not conflict with the provisions of a separate buy-sell agreement.

1. Documents Filed with the State

The formation document filed with the state of Utah[2] should be drafted or modified to reflect the accurate required information. Often, business owners start a business by filling out an online form provided by the Division of Corporations and Commercial Code, and the company organizers may not yet have determined the ownership or management structure of the business. Furthermore, fledgling businesses often undergo changes in ownership and changes in management as the business gains momentum. The formation documents filed with the state should accurately reflect the current information as evidenced by the company's other organizational documents and the company's business operations. If an individual general partner transfers his or her general partnership interest to a corporation, the Certificate of Limited Partnership should be amended to reflect a change in general partner. If an individual member of a member managed limited liability company transfers his or her membership interest to a trust or company, it would probably make sense

[2]Articles of Incorporation for corporations, Certificates of Limited Partnership for limited partnerships, Certificates of Organization for limited liability companies, and dba registrations for dbas.

for the limited liability company to be a manager managed limited liability company instead of a member managed limited liability company. If the company changes its address, its registered agent or its management team, the state filing should be updated to reflect the changes. The business is put in jeopardy when business owners and/or their agents are able to utilize discordant organizational documents as fuel to challenge the integrity of the business for a business owner's own personal agenda.

2. Agreements Among Owners

Similarly, the agreements among owners[3] should be drafted, modified and updated to accurately reflect the current ownership of the company, management of the company and options available to the company and/or business owners when a business owner exits the company. The documents should contemplate that an owner may be an individual, a trust, an entity or a charity. Common terminology such as "disability," "retirement," "professional licensing," "member of the family," "spouse," "descendant" and "death" are terms which have no meaning when applied to trusts or entities. Additionally, each individual business owner should negotiate provisions which are compatible with his or her own business succession plan. If a business owner wishes to have his or her interest pass to his or her children rather than allowing a business partner to purchase his or her interest, the agreements should facilitate that objective. If a business owner wishes to have his or her business interest purchased by the other business owners following his or her incapacity or death, the agreements should provide options and mechanisms for funding the purchase. If the company is to eventually transition from owners who are all actively running the business to some owners who active participants and other owners who are passive investors, the agreements may need to provide a mechanism for striking a balance between retaining earnings and distributing profits.

E. Evidence of Ownership

All company records should reflect the correct ownership of the various business owners' interest. A company may elect to evidence

[3]Bylaws, Partnership Agreements, Operating Agreements, Joint Venture Agreements, Buy-Sell Agreements, Covenants not to Compete.

ownership by certificates, schedules, exhibits to agreements or other written documents. If a corporation, partnership or limited liability company is the owner of a business interest, the various state filings, agreements, tax returns and other internal company records should reflect such ownership, and the company should make certain that the proper signature block and signatory appears on all documents executed by the owner entity. If a trust is the owner of a business interest, the various state filings, agreements, tax returns and other internal company records should reflect such ownership, and the company should make certain that the Trustee signs in its capacity as Trustee.

If a business owner initially owns his or her business interest in his or her individual name and subsequently forms a trust or company to own the interest, the business owner should execute the necessary assignment of interest to transfer the ownership interest to the trust. If the formation documents of the company do not allow an individual to transfer his or her interest to a trust or business entity, the company may need to amend its formation documents to allow the transfer. The assignment of interest should be approved by the necessary percentage of other owners and by the management of the company. The company should then update its records to reflect the new ownership.

F. Buy-Sell Agreements

As previously mentioned, some partnerships and limited liability companies include buy-sell provisions in the partnership agreement or operating agreement. Some of those same companies also have a separate and distinct buy-sell agreement. Unfortunately, if the organizational documents and the separate buy-sell agreements are not created at the same time and coordinated with one another, the two documents may have conflicting provisions. In turn, the organizational documents and buy-sell agreements should be drafted and/or revised in conjunction with one another to make certain no conflicts exist. The discussion of buy-sell provisions herein would pertain to buy-sell provisions contained within partnership agreements or operating agreements as well as stand-alone buy-sell agreements.

Buy-sell agreements almost always include death as a triggering event. Some agreements also include disability, retirement, refusal to work, lack of performance, termination of employment, failure to maintain licensing as triggering events. Unfortunately, buy-sell agreements are often drafted using boilerplate forms borrowed from other entities, obtained on-line, or provided by life insurance companies and many business owners sign the documents without reading them. In turn, when the buy-sell provisions are activated, the plan may not work the way that the parties had intended.

1. Purchase from Owner

The buy-sell agreement should specify that the business interest is to be purchased from the actual owner of the business interest, whether the owner is an individual, a trust or a business interest. As simplistic as this may appear, some buy-sell agreements specify that payments are to be made to the owner's "spouse" or "family" or "estate." Trusts and business entities don't have spouses, families or estates.

2. Triggering Events

The trigger events should be those the parties intend to include in the document. It does not make sense for "termination of employment" to trigger the owner's obligation to sell and the company's obligation to purchase if any of the owners are not employees at the time the agreement is signed. Furthermore, trusts and business entities do not retire, become incapacitated or pass away. If the buy-sell provision is to be triggered by a human being who is a Grantor or Trustee of a Trust or an owner or manager of a company, the buy-sell agreement should reference the human being in such triggering events.

3. Obtain Tax Advice

The parties should obtain tax advice pertaining to the income tax consequences and the gift and estate tax consequences associated with determining the purchase price and payment terms. While unrelated parties may be able to negotiate a purchase price without associated gift and estate tax consequences, when the purchase/sale is between related parties, a purchase price other than fair market value may result in taxable gifts/bequests between the parties. Furthermore, depending how the transaction is structured, a business owner may be able to structure a sale to reduce the associated income tax.

4. Determining Purchase Price

The purchase price is generally "fair market value." While unrelated parties may negotiate a purchase price which may appear to deviate from fair market value, when related parties exchange assets for less than or greater than fair market value the transaction may be deemed a partial sale and a partial gift. It is presumed that unrelated parties would negotiate at arms-length, and related parties would not. The following are some of the methods business owners often employ to determine purchase price which would not necessarily reflect fair market value:

- Fixing the purchase price at an amount equal to life insurance proceeds;
- Requiring the business owners to select a purchase price annually;
- Using a formula based on prior years' profits and the selling business owner's *pro rata* share;
- Appraising the assets of the company and applying the selling business owner's *pro rata* share;
- Allowing the selling owner and purchasing owner(s) to negotiate the transaction following the triggering event.

By contrast, fair market value is generally the middle ground equal to the highest price a willing and able purchaser will pay for an asset and the lowest price a willing and able seller will accept as payment for the asset. The buy-sell agreement may require one or more appraisals by individuals or companies qualified to render an appraisal, and certainly an appraisal conducted by a qualified appraiser is more likely to withstand scrutiny. Before fair market value can be determined, it is necessary to determine the nature of the asset being valued. If a business owner owns 100% of the business, the appraisal would presumably be the market value of the company. A company's worth may be determined by its earnings, by its good will, by its assets or by a combination of these factors.

However, if the business owner does not own the entire company, the appraisal would value the business owner's actual interest in the company. It is the intangible ownership interest in the company that is valued rather than the assets owned by the company. What would a willing and able purchaser pay for stock, partnership interest or membership interest? If the selling business owner does not own enough interest in the company to control the company, his or her interest in the company may be discounted for lack of marketability and/or lack of control. Why would someone want to purchase an interest in a company if the purchaser cannot compel a distribution from the company, force a liquidation of the company, compel a redemption of the interest, participate in management of the company or otherwise exercise some control? The answer is that for the right price, almost anything can be sold.

> For example, if an appraiser determines the fair market value of 100% of a limited liability company to be $10,000,000. Logic would suggest that a 20% interest in the company would be $2,000,000 ($10,000,000 X .20 = $2,000,000). However, if the organizational documents of the company require a majority, super majority or unanimous vote of membership interest to do any of the following actions, a purchaser is unlikely to pay $2,000,000 for the membership interest:
>
> - Compel distributions from the company to its members;
> - Sell substantially all of the property in liquidation of the company;
> - Admit any substitute or additional members into the company;
> - Amend the operating agreement;
> - Change or reorganize the company into any other legal form;
> - Dissolve and liquidate the company;
> - Redeem, liquidate, purchase or otherwise acquire the membership interest of a member; or
> - Return the capital of a Member.
>
> Instead, the partial ownership interest in the company would be discounted for lack of marketability and lack of control.

When ownership interest in a business is to be gifted or sold to an heir of the business owner, the discounted value may be viewed as favorable if the transaction results in a reduction of gift tax, estate tax or income tax. However, when the ownership interest in a business is to be sold to the other business owners or to the company, the selling business owner may feel undercompensated for his or her interest. In turn, in negotiating the purchase price provisions of a buy-sell agreement, each party should consider whether discounts for lack of marketability or lack of control should be factored into the valuation.

5. Funding the Buy-Sell Agreement

The parties should develop a strategy for funding the buy-sell agreement. The most obvious source of funding for purchasing a decedent's business interest is life insurance. However, the ownership of the policy and the pay-on-death beneficiary of the policy should be structured so that the sale may be consummated utilizing the proceeds of the insurance. If the business or a surviving business owner is expected to purchase a deceased business owner's interest using life insurance proceeds insuring the deceased business owner, the business or the surviving business owner must be paid the insurance proceeds. It is not helpful to effectuate the sale of the business interest if a life insurance policy is owned by the deceased business owner and payable to the deceased business owner's estate, spouse or revocable trust. If the business owner's estate, spouse or trust owns both the business interest and the life insurance proceeds, the purchaser would need to find other assets to purchase the business interest. Additionally, the identity of the owner and pay-on-death beneficiary may have income tax and/or gift and estate tax consequences to consider.

If the buy-sell triggering event is something other than death or if life insurance proceeds would be insufficient to purchase all of the exiting business owner's interest, the purchaser may have to use its own capital, obtain third party loans or offer a promissory note in exchange for the existing business owner's interest. The buy-sell agreement should provide flexibility to allow the purchasers the ability to thrive in the business but also provide full compensation to the exiting business owner.

6. Failure to Purchase Ownership Interest

A buy-sell agreement may allow for or even contemplate that following a triggering event, a business owner or his or her assigns may continue to own interest in the company. The organizational documents may allow the business owner's interest to retain its status as a full-fledge owner or the organizational documents may allow or require the ownership interest to be converted to the interest of a mere "assignee." In negotiating the buy-sell agreement, a business owner should understand that following a triggering event, a trusted business partner may become an adversary. In turn, if a business owner or his or her heirs is unlikely to remain in a controlling position in the company following a triggering event, the business owner may wish to include provisions in the buy-sell agreement to contractually require the company or other business owner to purchase the exiting business owner's interest, and insure that the company or other business owners have a mechanism for purchasing the interest—use of insurance, use of capital, use of company profits. If it is unlikely or unrealistic that the company or other business owners will be able to purchase the interest, the wisest course of action may be to require that the business be sold to third parties. Unfortunately, it is not uncommon for business owners to lack a realistic exit strategy and simply hope for the best. Perhaps the business will someday be fat with cash. Perhaps that key employee will come around. Perhaps one of the next generation will take an interest in the business and take it to new heights.

G. Keep It Current

It is easy to focus on the business of operating the business and disregard the organizational structure of the business. It is not uncommon for organizational documents and buy-sell agreements to become out dated and antiquated. Best practices would require visiting the organizational structure and buy-sell agreements on an annual basis to:

- Update organizational documents and buy-sell agreements to reflect change of owner (existing owners, assignments to trust, assignments to business entities, admitting new owners);

- Update lists of owners, officers and mangers to reflect correct and current: name, address, telephone number, e-mail address and tax identification numbers;
- Make certain the company continues to be registered with the state(s) where the business is organized and/or where the company conducts business;
- Make certain that the company and the company principals remain adequately insured;
- Make certain that those who are expected to purchase the business interest of exiting business owners following a triggering event have the desire and the financial ability to purchase the interest;
- Make certain that address changes are provided to state agencies, county recorders, venders and tax preparers;
- Consult with attorney and/or accountant to determine whether changes state law or changes tax laws warrant revising the organizational documents or business structure; and
- Determine whether a sale of the business should be pursued rather than attempting to transition the business.

CHAPTER 52

ESTATE PLANNING

WHAT EVERY ENTREPRENEUR SHOULD KNOW ABOUT UTAH DIVORCE LAW

DAVID W. READ[1]

Entrepreneurs, or anyone married or thinking of getting married, should be aware of the divorce process and the pitfalls that perforate it. It is no secret the number of divorces in the United States account for approximately fifty percent of marriages; nor is it a secret the staggering impact a divorce can have on a married couple's financial portfolio. This chapter is not comprehensive, but it will address important aspects of the divorce process.

If you find yourself in a divorce action, you will need legal counsel to help navigate the landscape of divorce law and procedure.[2] Disputes between married couples can be complex and nuanced just as it is with a business dispute. Divorces are challenging because emotions are charged, loyalties conflict, and lives and finances are intermingled. Divorces can lead to complex, expensive and heavily litigated breakups that can harm, or even destroy the marital estate and a spouse's business interests. To some extent, proper planning at various stages of a divorce action can help business owners or investor and their attorneys successfully negotiate this difficult transition.

[1]David W. Read is an assistant professor of business law and business ethics in the Goddard School of Business & Economics at Weber State University. He earned a MSc in Political Theory at the London School of Economics and Political Science and a JD at the University of Houston Law Center. His research interests are in business law, business ethics, and employment law. David co-founded the Utah Journal of Family Law, a publication of the Family Law Section of the Utah State Bar Association. He currently serves as an editor of the Utah Journal of Family Law. David lives in Salt Lake City and maintains a divorce litigation practice along the Wasatch front.

[2]However, one can file his or her own divorce paperwork through the Online Court Assistance Program (OCAP), but no divorce attorney would advise one to do his or her own divorce. *See https://www.utcourts.gov/ocap/* (last visited on November 1, 2015).

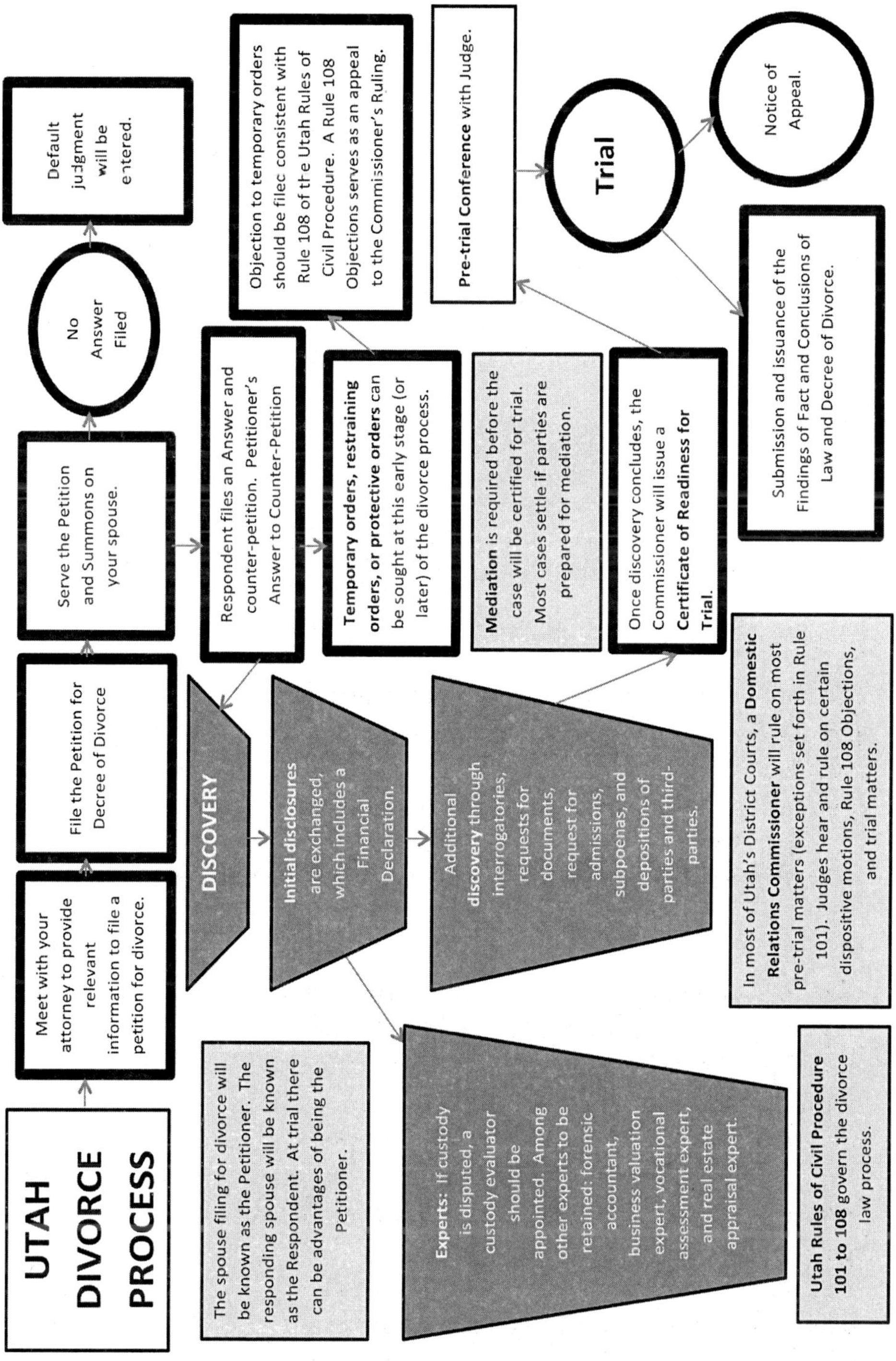
UTAH DIVORCE PROCESS
The spouse filing for divorce will be known as the Petitioner. The responding spouse will be known as the Respondent. At trial there can be advantages of being the Petitioner.
Meet with your attorney to provide relevant information to file a petition for divorce.
File the Petition for Decree of Divorce
Serve the Petition and Summons on your spouse.
No Answer Filed
Default judgment will be entered.
Respondent files an Answer and counter-petition. Petitioner's Answer to Counter-Petition
Temporary orders, restraining orders, or protective orders can be sought at this early stage (or later) of the divorce process.
Objection to temporary orders should be filed consistent with Rule 108 of the Utah Rules of Civil Procedure. A Rule 108 Objections serves as an appeal to the Commissioner's Ruling.
DISCOVERY
Initial disclosures are exchanged, which includes a Financial Declaration.
Additional discovery through interrogatories, requests for documents, request for admissions, subpoenas, and depositions of parties and third-parties.
Experts: If custody is disputed, a custody evaluator should be appointed. Among other experts to be retained: forensic accountant, business valuation expert, vocational assessment expert, and real estate appraisal expert.
Mediation is required before the case will be certified for trial. Most cases settle if parties are prepared for mediation.
Once discovery concludes, the Commissioner will issue a Certificate of Readiness for Trial.
Pre-trial Conference with Judge.
Trial
Notice of Appeal.
Submission and issuance of the Findings of Fact and Conclusions of Law and Decree of Divorce.
In most of Utah's District Courts, a Domestic Relations Commissioner will rule on most pre-trial matters (exceptions set forth in Rule 101). Judges hear and rule on certain dispositive motions, Rule 108 Objections, and trial matters.
Utah Rules of Civil Procedure 101 to 108 govern the divorce law process.

One of the largest, most complex aspects of divorce is the distribution of assets and debts, including those associated with business ownership; a determination of custody and parent-time is also a multi-faceted and costly aspect of divorce. Utah is an equitable distribution state. This means the overriding question in a divorce action is "How does one walk away with a fair portion of the marital estate?"

We live in a society where divorce is common and divorce laws play an important role in all of our lives. Entrepreneurs who understand the basics of divorce laws better understand the inherent risks of marriage and the reality of divorce vis-à-vis their financial portfolio.

UTAH'S DIVORCE PROCESS

When you divorce, you will file a petition (a civil lawsuit) with one of Utah's District Courts. It will cost you $318 for the filing. However, the initial filing is just the beginning of a complex process. In short, the graph on the previous page provides a basic roadmap of the divorce process in Utah.

JURISDICTION: WHERE YOU DIVORCE MATTERS

If you are unable to reach a settlement agreement with your spouse, where you file for divorce makes a big difference. Most states, like Utah, use a set of "equitable distribution" rules to divide the marital estate. They serve more as a guide than a rule. On the other hand, a minority of states apply "community property" rules when they divide a divorcing couple's assets. There are only nine community property states. California and Texas both follow community property rules as do some other western states, such as Utah's neighbors, Nevada and Idaho.

Equitable Distribution States

Equitable distribution rules are loose and vest great discretion in a Court to divide assets between a married couple in a fair and equitable manner, in light of the couple's circumstances. Utah is an equitable distribution state. Judges in equitable distribution states generally consider a number of different factors when they divide a couple's assets. Typically, they consider the ability of each spouse to support him or herself after the divorce. In particular, if a spouse has forgone career opportunities to raise children, that spouse may receive a greater share of the assets. Another example of the power of equitable distribution is the impact of the duration of a marriage. If the couple's marriage only survived a short time, the court may prove reluctant to give one spouse money earned by the other.

Equitable distribution courts will consider the age, general health and vocational training of each spouse when determining an alimony award. Some courts, like Utah, consider the amount of alimony and child support paid by a spouse in deciding if an award of additional marital property is warranted. In short, equitable distribution will not necessarily cut the marital estate in half; it could be more or less than a 50% distribution of debts and assets, unlike community property states.

Community Property States

Fewer states have promulgated "community property" rules when they divide a divorcing couple's estate. In these states, judges simply divide the couple's joint assets in half. Utah is not a community property state. In many ways, this makes for a quick and clean division of marital property. Judges do not attempt to divide assets fairly, so they do not consider the employment prospects, age or health of either party. What judges do is more formulaic wherein the spouses are deemed to equally own all income and assets earned or acquired during the marriage. This means that both the husband and wife are deemed to equally own all money earned by either one of them during the marriage, even if only one spouse is employed. In addition, all property acquired during the marriage with "community" money is deemed to be owned equally by both the wife and husband, regardless of who purchased it. In a community property state, equal ownership also applies to debts. This means both spouses are equally liable for debts. In most cases, this includes unpaid balances on credit cards, home mortgages and car loan balances.

Of course, judges in community property states consider a party's age and employment prospects when they award alimony and child support. In a community property state, a spouse who stayed home and cared for the children may receive generous alimony and child support payments. Some community property states often have strict formulas to determined alimony. Utah does not have an alimony formula, but some advocate persuasively the adoption of alimony guidelines.[3]

Although Utah is an "equitable distribution" state, certain laws and rules govern the divorce process and the grounds for divorce.[4] Most divorces in Utah are resolved on the grounds of "irreconcilable differences" because it is the least expensive route to resolving a divorce.[5]

IDENTIFIYNG AND DIVIDING THE ASSETS AND DEBTS OF THE MARITAL ESTATE

The methods employed by Utah trial courts can be a guide for parties who seek to settle their case. The courts seek to identify the parties' property and then they classify it as marital or separate. The courts will want to value the property to assist them in providing for an equitable distribution of the property. Before classifying the personal property, it must, of course, be identified. After identification and classification of separate or marital property, the fair market value must be determined. In order to establish a value, certain experts may need to be retained (i.e. a real estate appraiser, personal property appraiser, business valuation analyst).

The Utah Court of Appeals spelled out a four-step process for making an equitable distribution of property:[6]

1. Determine whether the property is separate or marital;
2. Determine if there are exceptional circumstances that overcome the presumption that marital property should be divided equally between the parties;
3. Assign a value to each piece of marital property (values are determined by experts);
4. The property will be divided in such a way that the other party will no longer have claim to the property, thus allowing the parties to move on with their lives;

Property is defined as something tangible or intangible to which its owner has legal title. One way to identify property during a divorce

---

[3]Lori W. Nelson and Taryn N. Evans, *Alimony Guidelines – An Idea Whose Time Has Come*, 28 Utah Bar Magazine 4 (2015). A copy of the article can be found online at https://www.utahbar.org/wp-content/uploads/2015/07/2015_edition_4_july_aug.pdf (last visited on November 1, 2015).

[4]Utah Code Ann. Title 30, Sections 1 to 40.

[5]Utah Code Ann. § 30-3-1(h).

[6]*Boyer v. Boyer*, 2011 UT App 141, 259 P.3d 1063.

is through the parties' financial disclosures. Each party identifies their assets and liabilities through a Financial Declaration, which is required by Rule 26.1(c) of the Utah Rules of Civil Procedure. There are number of categories of assets and debts parties acquire during marriage such as the following:

1. **Real Estate:** marital residence, investment properties, land.
2. **Motor Vehicles:** trucks, cars, motorcycles, boats, airplanes.
3. **Household Good:** furniture, jewelry, guns, clothing, refrigerators, washers, dryers, food storage, antique collections.
4. **Other Personal Property:** pets (not subject to a custody dispute).
5. **Bank Accounts:** checking, savings, saving bonds, money market accounts, certificate of deposits.
6. **Investments in Closely-held Businesses:** Limited Liability Companies (LLC), corporations, partnerships, sole proprietorships.
7. **Investment Accounts:** stocks, mutual funds, bonds, options, futures, investments in foreign exchange markets (FOREX), exchange-traded funds (ETF), gold, silver, life insurance.
8. **Retirement Accounts:** 401(k)s, IRAs, other defined benefit or contribution plans, deferred annuities.
9. **Other Assets:** tax refunds, club memberships, intellectual property, frequent flyer miles, online cash accounts (e.g. PayPal), account receivables, music or video libraries (Amazon or iTunes).
10. **Liabilities:** credit cards, lines of credit, mortgages, medical and dental bills, back taxes, account payables, car loans, student loans.

Tips on Uncovering Hidden Assets: If the other party's Financial Declaration is incomplete or vague, their personal property must be identified through other methods such as:

- Interrogatories
- Depositions
- Subpoenas
- Records search
- Interviews of friends and co-workers
- Tax Returns
- Credit card and bank history
- Internet search (social media, Google, other technological devices to track the other party's computer history)

There are a number of methods one can use to identify marital assets. An important method is to review the federal income tax return to determine whether a party's assets show up. The schedules on Form 1040 are an excellent source of information. For example:

- Schedule B: shows interest and ordinary income from dividends
- Schedule C: shows income from sole proprietorships and single member LLCs
- Schedule D: capital gains from sale of investments
- Schedule E: discloses income from rental properties and royalties, reveals ownership in limited partnerships and S Corporations
- Tax refunds that are applied to next year

Keep in mind that not all assets can be located by reviewing the tax returns because assets not generating taxable income will not be on the tax form.

Usually parties do not seek to hide retirement assets, but they can often be overlooked. For example, retirement accounts are not considered when someone changes jobs and forgets to transfer or rollover the firm sponsored account into a separate account. An important reason to have copies of a few years of W2s and/or paystubs is to help identify any withholdings that are/were contributed to firm sponsored retirement accounts.

One place often overlooked is the party's insurance policies. The property insurance policy will list all property that is insured, including the following: Real estate, vehicles, jewelry, and collectibles.

Another method to uncover hidden assets is to review bank, retirement and/or investment account statements to identify unreported assets. Looking for unexplained withdrawals and/or transfers can lead to undisclosed accounts.

Marital v. Separate Property. If a married couple cannot reach a signed, settlement agreement on their own accord, the divorce court will make the final decision on how the parties will divide their property.[7] Property division includes all assets and debts—personal property, real property, and business interests, amongst other assets. Generally, when dividing property in a divorce, the trial court "must identify the property in dispute and determine whether each item is marital or separate property."[8] In Utah, it is well-settled that each party is entitled to all of their separate property and half of the marital property, unless equity demands otherwise.[9]

The difficulty is in discerning between separate and marital property. Utah courts have provided some guidance on the distinction. For example, separate property is all property acquired before marriage (pre-marital property[10]), the appreciation of the pre-marital assets, or property acquired after marriage via gift or inheritance.[11] All other property is deemed marital and it "encompasses all of the assets of every nature possessed by the parties, whenever obtained and from whatever

---

[7] *See generally* Utah Code Ann. § 30-3-5.

[8] *Stonehocker v. Stonehocker,* 2008 UT App 11, ¶15, 176 P.3d 476.

[9] *Burt v. Burt,* 799 P.2d 1166, 1172 (Utah Ct. App. 1990) and *Hall v. Hall,* 858 P.2d 1018, 1022 (Utah Ct. App. 1993).

[10] *Haumont v. Haumont,* 793 P.2d 421, 424-425 (Utah Ct. App. 1990) (The court held that "each party retain the separate property he or she brought into the marriage." However, the court also held that a trial court may reallocate premarital property as part of an equitable property division.).

[11] *Mortensen v. Mortensen,* 760 P.2d 304, 308 (Utah 1988) (holding that "trial courts making 'equitable' property division[s in a divorce should,] generally award property acquired by one spouse by gift or inheritance during the marriage (or property acquired in exchange thereof) to that spouse, together with any appreciation or enhancement of its value, unless (1) the other spouse has by his or her efforts or expense contributed to the enhancement, maintenance, or protection of that property, thereby acquiring an equitable interest in it, . . . or (2) the property has been consumed or its identity lost through commingling or exchanges or where the acquiring spouse has made a gift of an interest therein to the other spouse. An exception to this rule would be where part or all of the gift or inheritance is awarded to the nondonee or nonheir spouse in lieu of alimony as was done in Weaver v. Weaver, supra. The remaining property should be divided equitably between the parties as in other divorce cases, but not necessarily with strict mathematical equality."

source derived."[12] However, separate or pre-marital property may lose its "separate" nature by commingling it with marital property.[13] An example of co-mingling is illustrated in *Bradford v. Bradford* where the husband conveyed his separate interest in a piece of real property to both him and his wife.[14] The act of the husband changing title to the real property effectively extinguished the separate nature of the real property, thus converting into marital property. Like in *Bradford,* if a spouse's real property converts to martial property it will be subject to division if the parties divorce.

The separate character or identity of the inheritance, gift, pre-marital property may be retained if kept in segregated accounts and portfolios. Although titling the property in your own name will help, it may not be sufficient to defend against a commingling claim. Moving a pre-marital investment from one account or medium to another does not alone destroy the separate nature of the segregated account.[15] Commingling issues raise difficult questions. For example, what happens if one spouse brings money into a marriage and that money is used as a down payment on a house? Does the spouse lose the down payment (owned before marriage)? Utah courts, naturally, have held that it depends. In one case, the down payment did not need to be divided equally between the parties because "the appropriate treatment of property brought into a marriage by one party may vary from case to case."[16] In another Utah case, the Court of Appeals upheld the trial court's ruling that the wife's stock was separate property although proceeds from the sale of the stock were occasionally used for family purposes and some of the proceeds were deposited into marital bank accounts.[17]

Property division in Utah's equitable distribution scheme does not require the division of property be equal. In making the distribution,

---

[12]*Dunn v. Dunn*, 802 P.2d 1314, 1317-18 (Utah Ct. App. 1990).

[13]*See Supra* at n. 8.

[14]*Bradford v. Bradford*, 1999 UT App 373, 384 (the husband conveyed his interest in the home to both him and his wife as "joint tenants with full rights of survivorship and not as tenants in common." This language has legal significance in real estate law, but also in a divorce. The language signals that the parties own it as join marital property, which is subject to equal division if the parties divorce.

[15]*Burt v. Burt*, 799 P.2d 1166, 1169 (Utah Ct. App. 1990).

[16]*Newmeyer v. Newmeyer*, 745 P.2d 1276, 1277 (Utah 1987).

[17]*Kimball v. Kimball*, 2009 UT App 233.

Utah courts will consider a number of factors, including "the amount and kind of property to be divided, the source of the property, the parties' health, the parties' standard of living and respective financial conditions, their needs and earning capacities, the duration of the marriage, and the relationship the property has with the amount of alimony awarded."[18]

You must be able to trace the money or asset as being separate property. Communicate clearly with your spouse about what is or is not marital property and the keep the line of ownership clean (tracing it) so as to avoid the claim of commingling. For example, if you receive an inheritance and you don't want the inheritance to take on the nature of marital property (subject to division), you should keep the inheritance titled in your own name. However, Utah courts have long held that property can be distributed regardless of which party's name appears on title.[19] If it is an inheritance in the form of cash, for example, keep it in a segregated bank account in your name only. Always keep in mind that separate property is never out of the divorce court's reach; an equitable distribution court, such as in Utah, may award an interest in your separate property to your spouse in "situations where equity so demands."[20] Pre-marital agreements can assist in demarcating separate from marital property. A pre-marital or "prenuptial" agreement is a valid, enforceable contract and so is a post-nuptial agreement (a signed agreement entered after marriage and before divorce).[21]

Identifying, valuing, classifying, and making an equitable distribution is one of the primary objectives in divorce (more about alimony and child custody issues below). Let's review how a few larger assets are addressed under Utah divorce law.

Real Estate: One of the largest assets or debts arising from a marriage is real property. The easiest way to identify real estate holdings is to conduct a public records search on the County Auditors website. The auditor's office will likely have information on the property

---

[18]*Moon v. Moon*, 790 P.2d 52, 56 (Utah Ct. App. 1990). *See also Naranjo v. Naranjo*, 751 P.2d 1144 (Utah 1988).

[19]*Hoagland v. Hoagland*, 852 P.2d 1025 (1993) (citing *Hogue v. Hogue*, 831 P.2d 120, 122 "here the husband had, prior to his marriage, conveyed to the wife a ranch as a means of protecting the property from husband's creditors. The couple then married and divorced. The trial court awarded husband an undivided one-half interest in the property. On appeal, we held that the court had not abused its discretion in awarding husband a one-half interest in the ranch, in part because the trial court had found that Husband conveyed the property to protect it from creditors."

[20]*Mortensen v. Mortensen*, 760 P.2d 304, 308 (Utah 1988)

[21]*Jacobsen v. Jacobsen*, 2011 UT App 161, 257 P.3d 478 (holding that a signed agreement entered into in anticipation of divorce was enforceable for purposes of property distribution.).

owner and an estimated value of the real property for tax purposes. The estimated value reported is not likely to represent the fair market value of the property. In order to determine the fair market value of the real estate, a real estate appraiser must be retained as an expert.

Retirement Plans: Retirement plans are large marital assets. Retirement and pension plans may include defined benefit plans, defined contribution plans, 401(k) plans, state and federal government retirement or pension plans, private employer benefits, and some military retirement benefits. Retirement and pension plans may be regulated by federal and state law and by plan policies.

A marital portion of the retirement funds are to be divided equally. "A marital portion" is considered to be the funds accrued either 1) from the date of marriage to the date of separation, or 2) from the date of marriage to the date of divorce. As a general rule, anything paid into any type of retirement or pension plan by either party from the date of the marriage to the date of the divorce is marital property.

Spouses may agree between themselves how much of a retirement account each spouse should receive. If the spouses cannot agree to how much each spouse is entitled to, the judge will likely apply the formula from the Utah Supreme Court case of *Woodward v. Woodward*, 656 P.2d 431 (Utah 1982). The courts understand the *Woodward* share to be as follows: multiply one-half of the value of the account by the number of years the parties were married and divide by the number of years the employee has worked. For example, if the account value is $30,000 and the parties were married for 7 years and the husband worked for 12 years, the wife's share would be $8,750:

$30,000	x	1/2	=	$15,000
$15,000	x	7	=	$105,000
$105,000	/	12	=	$8,750

Other factors affect this formula, including the date of separation, or whether one of the spouses has done something unreasonable, such as spending, destroying, or giving away marital property.

If a retirement account is to be split or transferred to the other spouse, then a special order, separate from the divorce decree, called a

Qualified Domestic Relations Order, or QDRO (pronounced *kwădrō*) must be signed by the judge. The person who administers the retirement or pension plan cannot divide an account or pay benefits to a spouse who did not contribute to the plan without a QDRO. Once a QDRO is signed by the judge and approved by the plan administrator, the plan administrator will divide the account or pay the benefits according to the QDRO, rather than the pension plan.

One ought to consider whether or not a loan has been issue from the retirement account before the parties reach a certain agreement on how to divide the retirement funds. If there is a loan, the question is who assumes it.

Social Security. Social Security is often overlooked as a retirement benefit; however, if a couple is married for ten years or longer, when reaching age 62, the lower or nonearning spouse may be eligible to collect derivative Social Security benefits based on the former spouse's earnings records. The derivative benefit is equal to one-half the amount the former spouse is eligible to collect. The non-earning spouse on the verge of the ten-year period may want to consider delaying the divorce until the ten years is met.

To be eligible for Social Security benefits, a person needs to earn 40 Social Security credits. A person can earn up to four credits per year, and become eligible for retirement benefits after working 1 0 years. Retirement benefits are calculated using the highest 35 years of earnings. These earnings are then applied to a formula to arrive at a basic benefit at a full retirement age of 65 or older.

Stock Options. Stock options can constitute a significant portion of the divorcing couple's assets. Their fluctuating value, variation in vesting methods and the tax consequences of their transfer can all affect a divorcing party's portion of the settlement in a drastic way. Your divorce attorney will assist you in identifying and assessing the value of the stock options and use the appropriate formula for their division correctly. Some issues to look for are whether the options are vested or unvested; if not vested, you must determine the vesting date—what happens if the options were awarded during marriage, but vest after the date of separation or divorce? Other questions to consider: What type of stock options are analyzing: incentive stock options or non-qualified stock options? Is the stock restricted? What are the tax consequences of the stock options?

Debts. As it is with assets, so it is with debts. Debts need to be identified, classified as marital or separate, valued, and distributed equitably (not equally) between the parties. Utah Code 30-2-5 spells out how debts are to be handled:

> (1) Neither spouse is personally liable for the separate debts, obligations, or liabilities of the other:
>
> (a) contracted or incurred before marriage;
>
> (b) contracted or incurred during marriage, except family expenses as provided in Section 30-2-9;
>
> (c) contracted or incurred after divorce or an order for separate maintenance under this title, except the spouse is personally liable for that portion of the expenses incurred on behalf of a minor child for reasonable and necessary medical and dental expenses, and other similar necessities as provided in a court order under Section 30-3-5, 30-4-3, or 78B-12-212, or an administrative order under Section 62A-11-326; or
>
> (d) ordered by the court to be paid by the other spouse under Section 30-3-5 or 30-4-3 and not in conflict with Section 15-4-6.5 or 15-4-6.7.
>
> (2) The wages, earnings, property, rents, or other income of one spouse may not be reached by a creditor of the other spouse to satisfy a debt, obligation, or liability of the other spouse, as described under Subsection (1).

Valuing Business Interests in a Utah Divorce

Married couples often acquire business interests during marriage or they bring business interests into the marriage. The business interests must be identified, valued, and divided through some type of equitable payout or offset. This process of valuing the business interests can be the most involved, complicated, and expensive part of a divorce action. A business owner who is divorcing must understand what a business valuation expert will do in a divorce case and the various methods employed to value a business. It is paramount to understand that all businesses are not treated the same under Utah law. A divorce attorney, accountant, and business valuation expert will help divorcing parties understand their own unique circumstances.

Identifying: First of all, if one is not sure if their spouse has acquired a business interest, business ownership interests in a closely-held business may be identified on the party's tax returns. If the business income flows through to the individual tax return, this income can be found on Schedule C or E of the individual's federal tax Form 1040. If the business is a C Corporation, the income does not flow to the individual return; however, the individual return may still identify any interest or dividends received from the C Corporation on Schedule B of their tax return.

Valuing. Here's the deal: the marital portion of the business will be shared equally between the divorcing parties. However, arriving at a value of the marital portion is not a simple, nor is it an inexpensive process. Valuation of a business interests or the business itself is a complicated and nuanced process. There is relatively little case law on this process, but the case law is instructive and useful.

Let's start with a discussion of the question, "What is my business worth?" or "What is my spouse's business worth?" When you ask this question you are really asking to know either the price or the value (i.e. valuation) of the business. Many people use the terms price and value interchangeably. However, the terms are quite different. Basically, a business appraisal, or valuation, may produce a specific value necessary for division of the marital portion of the business in a divorce action (as well as other legal reasons). A price, on the other hand, is what the market might pay for the business. Most buyers and sellers of a business really want an idea of price, but that is not to be confused with what happens in a divorce because there is not typically a buyer or seller in a divorce. With that said, if neither of the parties are retaining ownership of the business, and the parties decide to sell the business, the marketplace will likely determine what the divorcing parties will get, which, in turn, will be divided between the parties.

Choosing the Business Valuation Methods: The fair market value of a business interest must be determined once business interests are identified. A business valuation expert will conduct a business valuation to make this determination. The valuation expert will determine the financial condition of the business interests. Part of this analysis includes a determination of whether any adjustments need to be made to the financial statements. Making adjustments to the financial statements provide a picture of the value of the assets and the financial operating results of the business. Examples of some normalizing adjustments include:

- Recasting the income statement;[22] and
- Recasting the balance sheet.[23]

Once your data is prepared, it is time to choose the business valuation procedures. Since there are a number of well-established methods to determine business value, it is a good idea to use several of them to cross-check your results. All of these analyses have has an associated cost to them, so you will need to work with your divorce attorney and the business valuation expert to determine the best course of action with the divorce budget available to you.

Keep in mind that there are three primary valuation approaches to be considered: asset approach, income approach and market approach. A business valuation expert and divorce attorney can elaborate on these different approaches as you move forward with the business valuation.

The set of methods you choose to determine your business value depends upon a number of factors. Here are some key points to consider:

- The complexity and value of the company's asset base.
- Availability of the comparative business sale data from the market.
- Business earnings history.

---

[22]Investopedia states the following about recasting income statements: "The act of amending and re-releasing a previously released earnings statement, with specified intent. Some of the most typical reasons for recasting earnings are to show the impact of a discontinued business or to separate out earnings-related events that are deemed to be non-recurring or otherwise non-representative of normal business earnings." (last visited on November 1, 2015, http://www.investopedia.com/terms/e/earningsrecast.asp#ixzz3tIYeBrif).

[23]There are number of balance sheet items that may need adjusting; however, the overall purpose of recasting the balance sheet is to make sure the value of assets and liabilities accurately represents the business earning power.

- Availability of reliable business earnings projections into the future.
- Availability of data on the business cost of capital, both debt and equity.

All known business valuation methods fall under one or more of these fundamental approaches. However, business owners should be aware of some problems that can arise when married couples start a business together. One potential problem is the result of how a married couple may assign the ownership and management of the business when the business is first created. It makes a big difference if one spouse owns a controlling interest in the business because they likely have more decision-making power with the business and day-to-day decisions. This power imbalance can be frustrating to the minority-owning spouse as a divorce unfolds. However, this does not mean the non-controlling interest spouse is stripped from an equal share in the business interests.

Alimony. Alimony (also called spousal support) is designed to enable the spouse receiving support to maintain the standard of living during the marriage and to prevent the recipient spouse from becoming a discharge on the State of Utah.[24] There is an enormous body of case law deciphering the multitudinous marriages and how much, how long, and in what nature alimony should be awarded. Unlike some states, Utah does not have a formula (like child support) to determine alimony.[25] Because there is no formula, Utah courts must consider a certain number of factors. Those factors are as follows:

(8)(a) The court shall consider at least the following factors in determining alimony:

(i) the financial condition and needs of the recipient spouse;

(ii) the recipient's earning capacity or ability to produce income;

[24] *See Noble v. Noble*, 761 P.2d 1369, 1372 (Utah 1988).

[25] Some divorce attorneys advocate an alimony formula: Lori W. Nelson and Taryn N. Evans, *Alimony Guidelines – An Idea Whose Time Has Come*, 28 Utah Bar Magazine 4 (2015). A copy of the article can be found online at https://www.utahbar.org/wp-content/uploads/2015/07/2015_edition_4_july_aug.pdf (last visited on November 1, 2015).

(iii) the ability of the payor spouse to provide support;

(iv) the length of the marriage;

(v) whether the recipient spouse has custody of minor children requiring support;

(vi) whether the recipient spouse worked in a business owned or operated by the payor spouse; and

(vii) whether the recipient spouse directly contributed to any increase in the payor spouse's skill by paying for education received by the payor spouse or enabling the payor spouse to attend school during the marriage.

There are a number of other considerations to be analyzed in a spousal support determination.[26] If one is contemplating divorce, or is served divorce papers, it behooves them to seek advice and legal counsel early on in the process about the issue of alimony. Note that alimony is tax-deductible unlike child support.

Custody. Children are expensive, but they are even more expensive after a divorce. A very short overview of how custody works in Utah is essential. The physical custody arrangement is one of the factors in determining child support. In Utah, there are two classifications of custody:[27] legal custody and physical custody. Under each classification of custody, there are sub-classifications: sole and joint.

Legal custody has to do with a parent's rights regarding their minor children's education, decisions, and other significant decisions. Physical custody has to do with the care of the minor children. In order to determine custody, if the parties cannot reach an agreement, the courts look to the best interests of the children.[28] The courts must look to a number of statutory factors in determining what is in the minor children's best interests. In a custody dispute, it is often helpful to have a custody evaluation expert involved. A discussion about the nuances of

[26] *Mortensen v. Mortensen*, 760 P.2d 304, 308 (Utah 1988) (holding that "Any significant disparity in the division of the remaining property should be based on an equitable rationale other than on the sole fact that one spouse is awarded his or her gifts or inheritance. The fact that one spouse has inherited or donated property, particularly if it is income-producing, may properly be considered as eliminating or reducing the need for alimony by that spouse or as a source of income for the payment of child support or alimony (where awarded) by that spouse. Such property might also be utilized to provide housing for minor children or utilized in other extraordinary situations where equity so demands.").

[27] Utah Code 30-3-10.1

[28] *See* Utah Code 30-3-34 for the factors the court will consider: http://www.le.state.ut.us/xcode/Title30/Chapter3/30-3-S34.html?v=C30-3-S34_2015051220150512

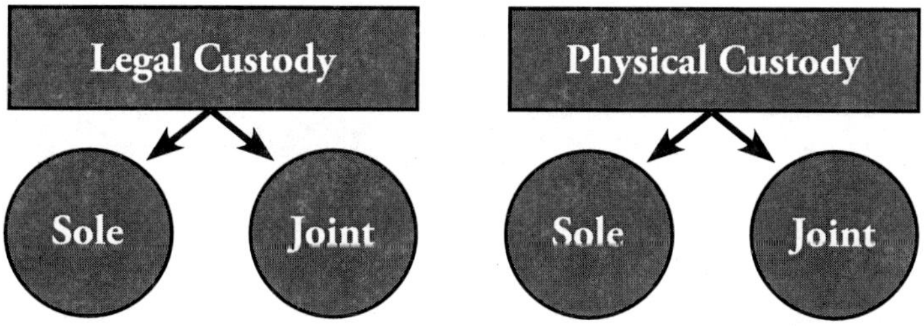

custody battles is more complicated and involved than can be addressed here. However, some advice: 1) consult a seasoned divorce attorney on the issue of custody before (if possible) you decide to divorce; and 2) if you want a shot at sharing custody of your minor children, do not move out of the marital residence. The courts determine physical custody by the number of overnights the children spend in the parent's care. Joint physical custody begins with a minimum of 111 overnights.

Child Support. Child support is determined by a calculation.

Number of children +
Physical custodial arrangement
(if joint custody, the number of overnights
each party has the minor children) +
The gross income of the parties
(usually based on a 40 hour work week[29]) =
The child support amount.[30]

[29] *See* Utah Code 78B-12-203(2) for the determination of gross income for child support purposes, http://www.le.state.ut.us/xcode/Title78B/Chapter12/78B-12-S203.html?v=C78B-12-S203_1800010118000101

[30] The child support calculator can be found here: https://orscsc.dhs.utah.gov/orscscapp-hs/orscscweb/action/public/custodyWorksheet/show

For example, depending on the custodial arrangement, if there are two minor children and parent 1 makes $30,000 each year and parent 2 makes $120,000 each year, the following child support amounts will apply.

Custodial Arrangement	Child Support Award
Sole custody	$1,550 paid to parent 1.
Joint custody with parent 1 having 183 overnights and parent 2 having 182 overnights.	$599 to the parent 1.
Joint custody with parent 1 having 235 overnights and parent 2 having 130 overnights.	$1,446 paid to parent 1.

Domestic Violence and Protective Orders. A final word on domestic violence: do not commit it or your divorce case will suffer a deathblow. Domestic violence is a crime and you will have to retain a criminal defense attorney to defend you. If you do not know of a criminal defense attorney, contact the Utah Association of Criminal Defense attorneys for a referral. If you threaten to harm your spouse, or you actually harm your spouse, a protective order will likely be granted against you. On the other hand, if your spouse threatens or causes harm to you, you should report it to the police immediately and seek a protective order. Domestic violence must be taken seriously. Keep in mind that a number of divorcing parties *seem* to manufacture a domestic violence setting to gain the advantage in a custody dispute. Be on guard for those tactics and do not allow a situation to escalate.